Henry James

FRED KAPLAN

Henry James

THE IMAGINATION OF GENIUS

A BIOGRAPHY

THE JOHNS HOPKINS UNIVERSITY PRESS

BALTIMORE AND LONDON

Originally published in 1992 by William Morrow and Company, Inc.
© 1992 by Fred Kaplan
Printed in the United States of America on acid-free paper

Johns Hopkins Paperbacks edition, 1999
9 8 7 6 5 4 3 2 1

The Johns Hopkins University Press
2715 North Charles Street
Baltimore, Maryland 21218-4363
www.press.jhu.edu

Library of Congress Cataloging-in-Publication Data

Kaplan, Fred, 1937–
   Henry James : the imagination of genius : a biography / Fred Kaplan.
      p.   cm.
   Originally published : New York : Morrow, c1992.
   Includes bibliographical references (p.   ) and index.
   ISBN 0-8018-6271-X (acid-free paper)
   1. James, Henry, 1843–1916.   2. Authors, American—19th century Biography.
   3. Authors, American—20th century Biography.   I. Title.
PS2123.K36   1999
813′.4—dc21
[B]   99-20973
                                                                                         CIP

A catalog record for this book is available from the British Library.

For Rhoda

Contents

Illustrations

HENRY JAMES, 1895
Courtesy of Leon Edel

THE PLAYBILL FOR *GUY DOMVILLE*, 1895
Courtesy of Leon Edel

GEORGE ALEXANDER AND MARION TERRY IN *GUY DOMVILLE*,
ACT III, 1895
Courtesy of Leon Edel

HENRY JAMES, DUNWICH, SUFFOLK, 1897,
PHOTOGRAPH BY LESLIE EMMET
Courtesy of Leon Edel

HENRY JAMES, ROME, 1899, PHOTOGRAPH BY GIUSEPPE PRIMOLI
By permission of the Houghton Library, Harvard University

HENRY JAMES, 1899, AT A GARDEN PARTY GIVEN BY THE CRANES AT
BREDE HOUSE, SUSSEX
Courtesy of the Barrett Collection, University of Virginia Library

HENRY JAMES, 1900, PORTRAIT BY ELLEN "BAY" EMMET
Courtesy of Leon Edel

HENRY JAMES IN THE GARDEN AT LAMB HOUSE, RYE, EAST SUSSEX,
C. 1900
By permission of the Houghton Library, Harvard University

HENRY AND WILLIAM JAMES, RYE, EAST SUSSEX, 1901
By permission of the Houghton Library, Harvard University

MORTON FULLERTON, C. 1900
Courtesy of R.W.B. Lewis

HENRY JAMES AND HOWARD STURGIS AT THE MOUNT, LENOX, MASS.,
1904, PHOTOGRAPH BY EDITH WHARTON
Courtesy of Katherine Sturgis Goodman and Miranda Seymour

HENRY JAMES, EDITH WHARTON, AND TEDDY WHARTON AT THE
MOUNT, LENOX, MASS., 1904

HENRY JAMES (*WITH CIGARETTE*), 1905, PHOTOGRAPH BY KATHERINE
ELIZABETH McCLELLAN
By permission of Smith College Archives, Smith College

HENRY JAMES, 1905, PHOTOGRAPH BY KATHERINE ELIZABETH
McCLELLAN
By permission of Smith College Archives, Smith College

HENRY JAMES, 1905, PHOTOGRAPH BY ALICE BROUGHTON

EDITH WHARTON, 1907
Courtesy of Beinecke Library, Yale University

EDITH WHARTON (*SMOKING*), 1908
Courtesy of Beinecke Library, Yale University

Experience is never limited, and it is never complete; it is an immense sensibility, a kind of huge spider-web of the finest silken threads suspended in the chamber of consciousness, and catching every air-borne particle in its tissue. It is the very atmosphere of the mind; and when the mind is imaginative—much more when it happens to be that of a man of genius—it takes to itself the faintest hints of life, it converts the very pulses of the air into revelations.

HENRY JAMES, "The Art of Fiction," 1884

To live over people's lives is nothing unless we live over their perceptions, live over the growth, the change, the varying intensity of the same—since it was *by* these things they themselves lived.

HENRY JAMES, *William Wetmore Story*, 1903

Mr. James's most successful mask [at a Christmas party] was a fat old lady with side curls—which made us so hilarious that he had to send for a shaving-glass to see himself in. "Why," he propounded, "don't we all wear masks and change them as we do our clothes?"

THEODORA BOSANQUET, *Diary*,
December 25, 1908

Henry James

One

REMEMBERED SCENES

1843-1855

(1)

As the brutal Civil War in America came to an end, a young American, slim, handsome, dark-haired, of medium height, with sharp gray eyes, began to write stories. By the literary standards of his time, he had a plain, direct style. He wrote in the alcove of a yellow-toned sunlit room in Cambridge, Massachusetts, where he pretended to study law. He had not fought in the war. His two younger brothers were soldiers, still engaged in the most massive conflict since Napoleon had made Europe his empire. The twenty-one-year-old Henry James, Jr., preferred to be a writer rather than a soldier. His motives for writing were clear to himself, and they were not unusual: He desired fame and fortune. Whatever the additional enriching complications that were to make him notorious for the complexity of his style and thought, the initial motivation remained constant. Deeply stubborn and persistently willful, he wanted praise and money, the rewards of the recognition of what he believed to be his genius, on terms that he himself wanted to establish. The one battle he thought most worth fighting was that of the imagination for artistic expression. The one empire he most coveted, the land that he wanted for his primary home, was the empire of art.[1]

(2)

On a summer day in 1872, "when the shadows began to lengthen and the light to glow," twenty-nine-year-old Henry James, Jr., now bearded and full-figured, returned to Venice for his second visit. Italy had become the home of his imagination, the place where he could most be himself. The sensual richness of what seemed to him the sweetest place in the world cast its melting warmth on the frozen coldness of his New York and New England childhood and youth. As he entered the city of soft watery wonders, he made his way to the little square at Torcello. Half a dozen young boys played in the delicious silence. They seemed "the handsomest little brats in the world, and each was furnished with a pair of eyes that could only have signified the protest of nature against the meanness of fortune. They were very nearly as naked as savages." One small boy seemed "the most expressively beautiful creature I had ever looked upon. He had a smile to make Correggio sigh in his grave. . . . Verily nature is still at odds with propriety. . . . I shall always remember with infinite tender conjecture, as the years roll by, this little unlettered Eros of the Adriatic strand." It was as if Eros had risen from the Adriatic waters in the immaculate form of a handsome Italian boy.[2]

(3)

In December 1915, an elderly, thick-figured, clean-shaven Henry James lay on his deathbed in his apartment in London. The cannons of war had exploded in his consciousness the previous year with the devastating force of memory and betrayal. The beautiful young men of his English world were being obliterated on the battlefields and in the trenches. The flames exploding from the artillery's percussion flared also with the glow of "the rocket's red glare" of his American childhood. Various fires, some public, some personal, possessed much of the past and the present: the fire of his father's burning leg in a childhood accident; the fire in Newport during the Civil War, when, as a volunteer fireman, he had wrenched his back so badly that the pain became for him a representation of his own need to have a wound; the flames of the night in 1863 when one of his younger brothers had been wounded in the assault on Fort Wagner; the steady, stubborn fire within himself that expressed his ambition for fame and money; the conflagrations in his fiction, especially the burning of the "spoils" of Poynton, anticipating what the fires of war were to destroy fifteen years later; and the small domestic fires at Lamb House, his home in Rye, on the grate of which he had periodically over the years burned stacks of all the personal letters he had received.

Six years of frequent illness had pushed him into nervous and physical collapse. A stroke now partly paralyzed him. He had had a nervous breakdown in early 1910, a year after he had made his final visit to Italy. The death of his brother William in August 1910 had been a painful disaster that had left a gaping hole of disconnection in his life and memory. The man who had prided himself on taking possession of many things was now being taken possession of. As he lay dying in a London winter, his mind wandered into increasing incoherence. He called for his secretary to take dictation. He had writing he wanted to do, significant hallucinations he wanted to express. He would still "discover plenty of fresh worlds to conquer, even if I am to be cheated of the amusement of them." As his secretary took his dictation, he imagined himself Napoleon, with his parents and siblings as the royal family of talent spun off by the brilliance of his own genius. With an imaginary imperial eagle in his hand, he attempted still to extend the empire of art.[3]

(4)

The son of a loving, realistic mother and a talented, impulsive father, Henry James, Jr., was born in Greenwich Village on April 15, 1843. New York was the city of his childhood. Later, vastly transformed, it became one of the sometimes attractive but always fearful cities of his imagination. For him, the city's transformation epitomized the change from the mid-Victorian era of his childhood to the modern world of his adult years. He was to remember it with affection and pleasure. These accelerating changes to New York and to the rest of what he thought of as the civilized world occasioned his regret and sometimes his deep pain. He did not easily take to change, especially when it threatened values and ways of life that he believed had permanent value.

He was born into a Presbyterian family that had been for generations committed to Calvinism and to business. His mother's maternal grandfather, Alexander Robertson, left Reading Parish, near Edinburgh, for New York City in the mid-eighteenth century. His mother's paternal grandfather, Hugh Walsh, emigrated about 1770 from Killingsley, County Down, Ireland, to Philadelphia and then to Newburgh, New York. Her mother, born in 1781, was named Elizabeth, the tenth child of Mary and Alexander Robertson. She married James Walsh, a marriage that produced six children, four sons—the young Henry's maternal uncles—and two daughters: Mary, Henry's mother, born in 1810; and Catherine, his much-loved Aunt Kate. On the paternal side, the record is less defined. His grandmother's parents were John and

Janet Rhea Barber from County Longford. His grandfather's parents, who provided the commonplace James name, were farmers from Bailieborough in County Caven, about fifty miles northwest of Dublin.[4]

The Irish and Scotch ancestry is definitive. There seems not to have been a drop of English blood in the families. Nor of artistic blood. The Robertson and the James families directed themselves to business, particularly to trade and real estate. The emigrations from Scotland and Ireland had been motivated mostly by the economic fluctuations that periodically brought recession and depression to the linen trade and to agriculture. The collapse in the market for Irish linen had sent Alexander Robertson to New York, where he flourished as a merchant, his business and his home in lower Manhattan. Combining patriotism with profits, Hugh Walsh had first prospered through contracts to sell provisions to the Continental Army, and then as a general merchant and shipline owner. But the Robertson and the Walsh fortunes were modest, especially since the patriarchs had eleven and nine children respectively. Mary Robertson Walsh James inherited a minor amount, which had been reduced to even less by the time of her death in 1881. The Barber family seems to have prospered also, Catherine's father "a farmer of great respectability and considerable substance." It was their son–in–law, though, who became such a phenomenon of commercial success that he provided his family with one of the first great American fortunes.[5]

In 1789, the year in which the American Constitution was created, William James emigrated from County Caven, where he had been born in 1770. For the ambitious young businessman, America was a land where Irish antagonism to England made it easy to be a patriot. The revolutionary war forged a national consciousness that he could immediately share. Opportunities readily repaid ingenuity and hard work. William James traveled northward up the Hudson Valley to Albany, where he worked for two years as a merchant's clerk. With his own stake, he became a tobacco merchant on a small scale; then he expanded into produce. By 1800, he had opened two more stores. Then he bought ships to move his produce up and down the river. He devoted himself to business, as high a calling in his own eyes as it was in the eyes of his community, and of his Presbyterian God.

Marrying in 1796, his first wife died within a few months of giving birth, in the spring of 1797, to twin sons. William married again, in 1798, this time to the daughter of a wealthy Irish Catholic landowner. His second wife gave birth to a daughter the next year and died soon afterward. In 1803, he married twenty-one-year-old Catherine Barber. They had ten children—Henry's paternal aunts and uncles, and, of course, his father, born in 1811. Resolutely proceeding with his own manifest destiny, William James became the premier business citizen of Albany, an influence in state politics, a money and power broker to be reckoned with, a successful advocate, beginning about 1815, of the project to build the Erie Canal, and then a heavy investor in land along the canal and in the western states that he expected the canal to be the first step toward opening. In Syracuse, he was the major landowner, his holdings including the valuable salt pits. He owned forty thousand undeveloped acres in Illinois and land in Michigan. At his death in 1832, his estate was probated at a value of about three million dollars, reputedly the second largest private fortune in New York State, by modern standards an immense amount of money at a time when there were no estate and income taxes.[6]

What happened to the money, "the admirable three millions," the loss of which was a "haunting wonder" to Henry James, Jr? His grandfather had had a genius for earning and investing money, but his children had a talent only for dissipating what he left them. Like many nineteenth-century millionaires, William James made children with the same regularity with which he made money. At his death, there were twelve major heirs. Through death and voluntary exclusion, he had no heirs with an interest in business. Neglect and incompetence resulted in the investments not being protected effectively. The heirs all lived on the interest of the inherited capital, and often enough on the capital itself. "The rupture with my grandfather's tradition and attitude was complete," his grandson was to write toward the end of his life, trying to make sense of what had happened to the family money. "We were never in a single case . . . for two generations, guilty of a stroke of business." In a volatile economic world, money that did not grow, shrank.[7]

(5)

The small boy who opened his eyes in April 1843 to the world of his parents' three-story brick home at 21 Washington Place learned throughout his lifetime only some of the special features of his father's early life. He was to discover little to nothing about Henry senior's struggle with his own father, a conflict for money and self-assertion that extended beyond old William James's grave. "Our dear parent," Henry junior wrote in his old age, "we were later quite to feel, could have told us very little, in all probability, under whatever pressure, what had become of anything." On the contrary, the father could have told his children exactly what had happened to the three million, and precisely enough the story of the gradual reduction of his own portion of the inheritance. These matters were not, however, discussed in the James family, and the attenuated distress that Henry junior felt concerning them reflected his partial awareness of his father's pain, and his own vivid distress at the fact that he and his three brothers had to struggle to earn their livings.[8]

Henry senior had a restless, rebellious insistence on contention and self-assertion from an early age. From his father he wanted unquestioning, unqualified love. He both feared him and hated his fear. Ultimate things were involved, since his father on earth identified himself closely with, and was identified in the minds of his children with, the Father in heaven. Theirs was a Presbyterian deity who insisted that merit had to be demonstrated through discipline, obedience, and hard work. Salvation was a gift of grace. Some would be given the gift and others, not. William James soon suspected that Henry senior was not one of the fortunate. He probably also sometimes had in mind the parable of the Prodigal Son and the hope that a small sinner might become a small saint. His son's early sins were ordinary. He was an indifferent student. He was not interested in his father's business. He had a sharp, argumentative tongue. He stole change from his parents to pay for candy. He developed, at ten years of age, a liking for "raw gin and brandy." His sins, he later explained, expressed an irrepressible natural energy, a delight in the things of this world, and a visceral protest against a God whose insistence on the taint of Original Sin put human beings at war with nature and their natural selves. If God were indeed such a son of a bitch, he would defy him.[9]

In 1824, at the age of thirteen, Henry senior's life was radically changed. As part of an outdoor chemistry experiment at Albany Academy, the boys ignited small paper balloons, fueled by burning turpentine, to demonstrate that the balloons would fly if the air inside were heated. Balloon after balloon lofted into the sky in an ascension that was both joyous game and serious lesson. When one of the balloons errantly drifted into a hayloft, the high-spirited Henry senior impulsively pursued it. As he attempted to stamp out the flames, first his trouser legs, and then his flesh caught on fire. His right leg had to be amputated beneath the knee. His mother sat frequently by his bedside. He remembered that in her sleepwalking she would come to his bed and adjust the covers. His silent but deeply pained father signaled his misery. Unfortunately, the stump refused to heal. His confinement went on for three years. "Henry's leg," his sister reported, "is not as well as it was. . . . Instead of progressing it goes back and there is a greater space to heal now than there was before." At the beginning of May 1828, since gangrene seemed likely, "Henry's leg was . . . amputated . . . some distance above the knee. The operation lasted . . . about six minutes, but the most painful part was the securing the arterys, tendons, cords &c. He is now thank God safely through it." Thereafter he stumped through life on a wooden leg.[10]

After a fourth bedridden year, the seventeen-year-old Henry senior reluctantly agreed to attend Union College in nearby Schenectady. As the major financial supporter of the small college, William James expected his son to do honor to the family name and train to become a lawyer. Henry did neither. An energetic cripple, he gambled, drank heavily, spent whatever money came his way, and ran up large bills, using his father's credit as security. The president of the college, who had been the minister of the First Presbyterian Church in Albany where the James family worshiped, tried to help the son of the man to whom Union College owed about seventy-one thousand dollars, secured by mortgages on its land and buildings. One of his father's surrogates warned him that you are "on the edge of ruin . . . that if you do not without delay stop short in the career of folly that you have for a time indulged in . . . you are lost to the world. . . . Convince your father . . . that you repent of the past, and that you determine to act entirely conformable to his advice and wishes. . . . If you do not, you will lose all. . . ." Henry responded by fleeing to Boston, leaving his bills unpaid. "His mind . . . being given to such low pursuit I fear there is no hope for him," his father lamented. With the usual parental pain and surprise, he remarked accurately that his son had been "reared not only by anxiety and prayer but with liberality to profusion."[11]

Forty years later, on "a slippery Boston day," ascending a street that mounted to Beacon Hill, Henry senior pointed out to his namesake the house in which he had roomed for the two or three months that he had hidden in Boston, working as a proofreader for a Unitarian scholar-publisher. "My ambition is awakened," he had written to the one of his tutors at Union with whom he had become intimate. "I have here [in Boston] every advantage, and the least shall not be slighted." The opinion of his elders, though, was that Henry could be saved only by returning home, by learning that economy is a virtue, by taking up business. "He is a bright boy, but has defects of character. . . . Nothing can be done for him till he learns the worth of a father's house." Bright enough to compromise, he returned to Union College in 1830 and soon graduated. After briefly reading law, he found work for about half a year helping to edit an Albany newspaper. He continued to drink heavily. In his old age, as an example of redeemability, he confessed to his youngest, alcoholic son, that in those days he had "rarely [gone] to bed sober."[12]

In December 1832, sixty-two-year-old William James died of a stroke. The shocked family soon learned that he had made a complicated and devastatingly judgmental will. Determined to keep his wealth intact and to protect the future of the family, he had established a trust, under legally binding directives, to sequester most of his wealth for a period of twenty-one years, with the intention of forcing growth through diversified real estate investments. He had determined that his sons would have to prove they were worthy of any inheritance of substance. Each son must "learn some one of the professions, trades or occupations usually pursued in this country and must assiduously practice the same," for the purpose of the will is "to discourage prodigality and vice, and to furnish an incentive to economy and usefulness." The trustees were empowered to adjust the final disposition of the funds after twenty-one years in regard to the degree to which each heir failed to fulfill the conditions of the will by leading "a grossly immoral, idle or dishonorable life." The will provided Henry senior with an annual annuity of only $1,250 and no guarantee of participation in the final division of the estate unless he could demonstrate to the trustees' satisfaction that he had learned a practical profession.

For Henry senior, this was not an expression of the all-encompassing, all-forgiving love that he needed from his father. None of the heirs was entirely happy, though probably only Henry was furious. The widow and minor children had just grievances. To Catherine Barber and her young charges William James bequeathed an annuity of three thousand dollars a year and their Pearl Street home. The sum was insufficient to sustain them adequately, let alone to maintain a life appropriate to the widow of a multimillionaire. She challenged the will on behalf of herself and the minor children. The court soon decided in her favor, though the remainder of the will continued in force. In 1834, Henry senior engaged lawyers and brought suit to break it entirely and force an equitable division of the estate on the grounds that the will violated the state statutes that limited perpetuity.

Partly in search of enlightenment, partly to demonstrate to court and trustees that his father had incorrectly impugned his vocational and moral responsibility, he enrolled the next year in Princeton Theological Seminary, which he attended until 1837, critical of what he thought its Presbyterian narrowness of manner and stingy Calvinistic morals. In July 1835, the Court of Chancery decided partially in Henry's favor. In March 1837, his lawyers were completely successful. The will was broken. A total redivision occured. In July 1843, the final stage in the court-mandated division resulted in stocks, bonds, and mortgages, producing almost $188,000 annually, being divided among the heirs. Henry senior's share provided an income of about $10,000 a year, the sources of which were under his own control. He never added to the capital; family emergencies, general needs, special indulgences, and financial losses gradually reduced it. At the time of his death in 1882, none of his four sons inherited money enough to make any significant difference in their lives.

(6)

With a dead father, a sweet, supportive mother, and about ten thousand dollars a year, Henry senior now felt himself to be his own man. His first venture was a five-month visit to England and Ireland. His James relatives welcomed this "youth gilded an inch thick and shining to effulgence." He came as "the representative of an American connection prodigious in its power to dazzle," the embodiment of "a fairytale from over the sea." Accompanied by a black servant and by his friend and Princeton tutor, Joseph Henry, whose expenses he paid, he later described it to his children as a romp, as a kind of traveling "American circus," enjoying gooseberries in the gardens of their Irish cousins "with a certain beautiful Barbara." He had an eye for feminine beauty, an eagerness for female company. When Henry junior made his first sustained visit to England as an adult, his father shared with him his remembrance of a sense of intoxication so strong, when he had landed in Devonshire forty years before, that he felt he "should fairly expire with delight."[13]

Searching for ideas that would help him with the clash between his natural impulses and his religious inheritance, he discovered, in England, the books of Robert Sandeman, a Christian primitivist from Scotland who advocated a simple relationship between man and God, the supremacy of faith to works, and an ideal Christianity in which the modern, as nearly as possible, approached the condition of the primitive Church. Returning to New York City in September 1837, he wrote a preface for, and then published, at his own expense, an edition of a book by Sandeman. It was the first in a long series of works on religion, most of which were to express his sense of the relationship between God and man, the nature of divinity and of humanity, and the application of his religious ideas to the social and political issues of the day. Sandemanianism soon proved insufficient to his needs. He wanted to read, to write, and to have influence in the world of religious ideas. Lecturing appealed to him. Soon after his return, he began work on a large-scale reinterpretation of the Bible in which Scripture would be revealed to function symbolically rather than literally. The spirit would be seen to justify the Word. The spiritual meaning of the Bible would take precedence over literal interpretation. The current churches would be shown to be narrowing, corrupt, and anti-Christian.

His romanticism expressed his belief that the ways of nature and of the spirit were ultimately one. At the invitation of Hugh Walsh, a classmate at the Princeton seminary, he visited the home of the widowed Mrs. James Walsh at 19 Washington Square. The Walshes were a moderately pious, upper-middle-class Presbyterian family. He and Hugh argued the two unmarried ladies of the house into sympathetic tolerance for their Christian freethinking. Soon Mary Walsh, two years older than her sister Catherine, fell in love with Henry senior. At thirty, much beyond the preferred age for marriage, spinsterhood threatened. "We had a little talk," Henry years later recalled. "I think *she* was on her guard, but I *felt* her *predominance,* wanted her approval, found myself growing diplomatic in order to obtain it. I was conscious of a sort of dread, which I never feel for a man."[14] The ladies soon resigned from Murray Presbyterian Church, where they had been christened. In late July 1840, Mary and Henry were married in a civil ceremony in her mother's home. Eighteen months later, their first child was born, probably named after Henry senior's brother William rather than his father. The next month they moved from the Astor Hotel, where they had been staying, to a newly purchased home at 21 Washington Place, bought for eighteen thousand dollars from his brother John in what may have been a transfer of property to satisfy Henry's back claims against his father's estate.

When Henry junior was six months old, in early autumn 1843, Henry senior decided to sail for Europe with his family. They departed in October 1843, accompanied by "Aunt Kate" and a servant, on the celebrated *Great Western.* Their immediate destination was "some mild English climate" that would be good for his health, since he imagined his chest to be weak. The voyage abroad was also partly an escape. Henry senior had begun his career as a writer and lecturer in New York. He had paid for the publication of his works, and lectured to small audiences. To a new friend, Ralph Waldo Emerson, he complained, "Here I am these thirty-one years in life . . . having patient habits of meditation which never know disgust or weariness, and feeling a force of impulsive love toward all humanity which will not let me rest wholly mute, a force which grows against all resistance that I can muster against it. What shall I do?" Emerson sometimes stayed at the James home on his New York visits, and had introduced his new friend to his Concord friends, including Henry David Thoreau and Margaret Fuller. He bluntly told James that he should, among other things, stay home. "I hate to see good men go out of the country which they keep sweet. . . . It is a great disappointment to lose you now."[15]

At a cottage adjacent to Windsor Park, in May 1844, as his two infant sons played on the green lawns outside, Henry James, Sr., suddenly found himself shaken by uncontrollable fear. At one moment he felt perfectly normal, "sitting at the table after the family had dispersed." The next moment he felt, unexplainably, "a perfectly insane and abject terror." An invisible "damned shape" squatted "within the precincts of the room" and rayed "out from his fetid personality influences fatal to life." After ten seconds, he felt himself "a wreck," at least in the sense of feeling shipwrecked, without rudder or sails. He had looked into the mirror of himself and seen something vicious and corrupt. As the children played happily in the long English twilight, taking their early steps and speaking their first words, he felt absolute self-loathing. Everything he had believed, everything he had attempted, seemed either mistaken or irrelevant. The work he had been engaged in seemed trivial, mistaken. Everything he had done hitherto, he now believed, had been fueled by a pernicious ego.

Relief came slowly, and then with a rush a few months later when he discovered the works of Emanuel Swedenborg, the eighteenth-century Swedish mystic. Swedenborg's books recast Christianity into a Romantic religion of the innately good heart in which the human and the divine had ready interaction and mutual assimilation. Suddenly, Henry senior felt he had a view of the "new heaven and the new earth," a set of images and symbols, and a comprehensive description of human nature. Man's social destiny and his heavenly destiny were the same. His own sinfulness now seemed to him normal and unthreatening, partly because he need not fear punishment, partly because he had assurances that God was love and that God, nature, and man were ultimately in intimate union. Swedenborg was to be his companion through the remainder of his life, "the greatest man intellectually the world has known. Shakespeare is his only parallel, and that is by no means clear to me." The James family returned to New York City in late 1844 or early 1845, significantly changed by what Mary James repeatedly was to call, with good-humored irony, "father's ideas." His lifelong advocacy of Swedenborg, though it brought him some personal peace, helped determine that Henry senior would be a marginal man.[16]

(7)

Henry junior's earliest memory was of wiggling his feet under a flowing robe and seeing, as he was carried across the Rue de Castiglione, the thrust of the 144-foot-high column of Place Vendôme, memorializing Napoleon. The family was visiting Paris, probably in the winter of 1844, before moving to Windsor. Years later a vague recollection surfaced of "a great stately square surrounded with high-roofed houses and having in its center a tall and glorious column." From early on, he had a sense of himself as a voyeur, a keen observer of spaces, and thrusts, and relationships, of being protected by his parents but dependent on his own eyes, feelings, memory. There may have been memories of London, where his father, with introductions from Emerson, met Carlyle, Mill, and Tennyson, of Green Park, and of being walked by his Albany nursemaid. But they were sufficiently attenuated for him to speculate that probably they were secondary, the result of information he had been told later rather than what he himself recalled. It made no difference. Europe, history, art, conquest, spaces filled and spaces to be filled, dominated from his earliest consciousness of himself.[17]

The next memory was of food and summer, of delicious peaches enjoyed in the warm Eden of his Albany grandmother's home. The James family had moved next door, probably in the summer of 1845. Henry senior was fond of Catherine Barber James, "her silk dress, peppermints, lace mittens and gentle smile." While at Windsor, he confessed "to some potent pullings now and then dear Ma in your direction." Having created a nursery for his children, where Harry was teething, though "he is as good as the day is long," Henry senior was frequently overcome by "nursery remembrances" of his own childhood. He was homesick for his mother, for Albany, for America. His son remembered this "infantile Albany as the very air of long summer afternoons," as a place where aunts and uncles formed an extended family, of "a softly-sighing widowed grandmother," whose favorite pastime was to read the "fiction of the day." His grandmother's reading, and then his own, on the veranda, in the garden, in the leather-rich library of the Albany home, remained permanently with him, both as memory and as practice.

After the peaches came ice cream, of which he could never get enough, part of a cherished remembrance that fed the sweet tooth of his associations with his nativity and his native land. He always had a passion for sweets, and for the pleasures of summer weather in a temperate climate. His later distance from Albany never became so great that this early experience did not contribute to the strong loyalty he felt toward his extended family, a warm feeling for aunts and uncles and, especially, cousins. The Albany visits were extended until the family eventually alternated between Albany and New York City, where they still owned, for a short time, their Manhattan home. Mary James, who had returned from England pregnant, gave birth, in July 1845, at 21 Washington Place, to the Jameses' third son, Garth Wilkinson. Soon pregnant again, the next August she gave birth, at their rented home on North Pearl Street, to another son, Robertson, the fourth child in a five-year period. In the autumn, William and Henry attended a kindergarten across the street from their grandmother's house.

Nursery conflicts worked their way through the foursome. As soon as Bob was born, Wilky began to walk and to assert himself, "emphatically the *ruling* spirit in the nursery." William and Henry were partly in and partly out of the nursery, their separateness acknowledged by parents and siblings. Mary and Henry senior settled warmly into their lives as parents, Henry increasingly devoted to studying and advocating Swedenborgian ideas, Mary to supporting her husband in whatever he chose to do. A nursemaid helped with the children. Servants took care of the drudgery. Mary ran the servants and the household, a keen, competent supervisor of domestic economy and harmony. Unlike his own father, Henry senior was always at home. In the morning, he worked at his desk, separated from his children only by his ideas. In the evenings, he read to his wife. They both became Fourierian socialists, envisioning a utopia in which injustice would no longer exist.[18]

Oppression in intimate relationships was particularly detestable to Henry senior. In 1848, he wrote a preface for a tract, which he had translated, by a follower of Fourier. He strongly defended Fourier's idea that marriage should always be an expression of free choice rather than legal obligation. When he somewhat naively plunged into the center of a public controversy about free love, he unexpectedly found himself associated by the public and in the press with advocates of communal sex. He wanted, though, only to reform marriage, not to advocate extra-marital or premarital relations. In an essay on "The Marriage Question," which he published in the *New York Tribune* in 1853, he began a steady retreat from the radical, embarrassing implications of his position into a strong defense of monogamy. The marriage state should be seen, he argued, as the highest state of spiritual relationship, the state that saves men from their natural lust as well as provides the fullest opportunity for a love that transcends the flesh. But the secondary considerations of legal and social sanction were essential.

While the perfect society is a future certainty, "the future is to be secured only on the condition of our rigid fidelity to the law of the present." He still advocated the fullest freedom for everyone, including children, and the desirability of nondirective parents who would let their children flower along the lines of their own choice. But in his argument concerning male-female relationships and parent-child relationships, his generally conservative attitudes constantly qualified his concept of freedom.[19]

As a father he had strong preferences, and communicated them strongly, even if sometimes indirectly. Whereas Mary had the household work, Henry had "ideas," ideas about human perfectibility, about social justice, about marriage, about love, about education. He discussed them with his wife, family, friends, indeed with anyone who would listen. When he met opposition, he argued energetically, sometimes cuttingly. Comparing notes with Emerson about their New York friend, Thoreau remarked to Emerson that James, whom he otherwise admired, is "the most childlike, unconscious and unblushing egotist it has ever been my fortune to encounter in the ranks of manhood." Henry senior advocated freedom, but he desired to persuade people to define freedom in his own terms. "My disposition is so tyrannous," he admitted, "that I can hardly allow another to be comfortable save in my way." From the beginning, he touted the two younger sons for good looks and worldly activities. A proud father, he "thinks [Robertson] better looking than any of his brothers at the same age. I think myself," Mary remarked, "that this may be ascribed rather to an enlargement of Henry's philoprogenitiveness than to any increase in beauty in the family." William and Henry junior were categorized as smart, as studious, and as intellectual.[20]

From the beginning, Henry junior felt a special bond with his mother. As he grew older, if he desired to please anyone, he desired to please her. In the eyes of her second son, she was a constant caring presence whose silence spoke louder than words. Henry senior was, in contrast, a great noisemaker, an actor who could be heard in the back rows. He projected volume(s), arguments, ideas. Mary James was an audience, a more sympathetic other self whom one spoke to even when not speaking aloud. She was dominant, to her children and her husband, "by the mere force of her complete availability." Every time Henry junior thought of childhood, she was there, "at every penetration. We simply lived by her, in proportion as we lived spontaneously." Later, he remembered her sitting in the evening lamplight, her hands at her work, her head tilted toward complete emotional attentiveness. "She lived in ourselves so exclusively, with such a want of use for anything in her consciousness that was not about us, that I think we almost contested her being separate enough to be proud of us—it was too like being proud of ourselves."[21]

(8)

A small boy with bright gray eyes, he kicked ailanthus leaves upward into the air in Washington Square Park, surrounded by the "sense and smell of perpetual autumn." Of average height, dark-haired, and possessing a powerful memory, he constantly, in his remembrance, waded through the leaves of "an Indian summer . . . fascinated by the leaf-kicking process." From an early age, he liked "the joy of lonely walks." He also liked company, though he had a sense of the company of his imagination and the pleasure of sentient observation. He remembered himself (perhaps reading back into his childhood the myth of his adult self) "as somehow always alone in these and like New York *flâneries* and contemplations . . . the so far from showy practice of . . . dawdling and gaping." He wandered the New York City streets, from the Battery to Washington Square, and occasionally beyond.[22]

Henry senior, in the autumn of 1847, had directed the family back from Albany to New York City. He may have had enough of close proximity to his family, or he may have found Albany too provincial. The family resided for almost a year in a rented apartment at 11 Fifth Avenue, around the corner from the children's maternal great-grandparents' newly built house. With his hand clasped by his father's, Henry junior soon was shown a house farther uptown, at the fashionable edge of the city's settled limits, Union Square near Sixth Avenue, at 58 West Fourteenth Street. Henry senior, who had just purchased it, wanted his son's enthusiastic approbation, which he readily got. Union Square "was encased, more smartly" than Washington Square, "in iron rails and further adorned with a fountain." By the summer of 1848, the family had settled into what they expected would be their permanent home; it was baptized in August by the birth of a fifth child, a daughter named Alice. Relatives from Albany frequently stayed with them. Sometime in 1848, his father's brothers, Uncle Gus and Uncle John, appeared in the parlor and announced to Henry senior that the Revolution had occurred in Paris and Louis Philippe had fled to England.[23] For Henry junior, Paris was hardly a memory, and Europe, far away. The family, their few servants, and soon Aunt Kate, filled the house on Fourteenth Street with what seemed all the warmth of which its size was capable. He remembered it as the most settled home of his childhood.

Catherine Walsh had joined the household so soon after the marriage that her presence was strong from the beginning. With uncomplaining good will, she spent much of her life in the family of a sister she loved and a brother-in-law whom she learned to tolerate with bossy affection. Petite, energetic, opinionated, she was a woman of propriety who gladly performed the tasks of unmarried sister and temporary mother. Henry senior enjoyed the doubling of female attentiveness. When, in the autumn of 1852, Aunt Kate began to keep company with a wealthy, retired sea captain and shipowner, a widower named Charles H. Marshall, Henry senior thought it unfortunate. In February 1854, forty-year-old Catherine married her sixty-year-old suitor. The entire James family attended the wedding. Henry senior jokingly denounced the captain "taking away dear good Aunt Kate from us!" She "has always been a most loving and provident husband to Mary, a most considerate and devoted wife to me, and an incomparable father and mother to our children." Though he wished that God would "bless her in her new home, and make it as friendly to her as the old one," his good wishes were touched with regret at the loss of a desirable triangle.[24] Within a short time, Aunt Kate found her husband cheap, mean, and dictatorial. He was not to be tolerated. By 1855, they had separated. Captain Marshall gave back "dear good Aunt Kate" to the James family, where she was to remain, more or less, for the next twenty years.

Each summer the family fled the Manhattan heat. The moves satisfied Henry senior's restlessness and expressed his class expectations. Such migrations were not unusual for the Jameses' neighbors, mostly well-to-do New York families, some of them related to, or themselves in the process of obtaining, fortunes, mostly in real estate. Their children were Henry junior's companions in the streets, at social events, in the schools that he and William were soon to attend, in "the small warm dusky homogeneous New York world of the mid-century."[25] Despite Henry senior's religious nonconformity, the family lived comfortably in an upper-middle-class society, in unprotesting material conformity to the ways of their world. Some of the places in which they summered Henry junior could never afterward locate satisfactorily in his mind. Others were specific, particularly the months spent near Fort Hamilton, in Brooklyn, or those, another year, spent on Staten Island, at a time when everything not lower Manhattan was the country. Summer was for him a series of adventuresome residencies someplace else, usually a boardinghouse or hotel, often near the water, where one lived in strange rooms, where maids and table d'hôtes provided the necessaries, where one met new people, where one got used to the different, the eccentric, and remembered it always. These summer migrations soon became subsumed in the boy's mind with larger voyages, the insistent wrenchings of travel, of residence abroad, that eventually encouraged him to think of himself and his siblings as "hotel children," less tied than most others to some settled place, to some topographical loyalty.

Albany had its attractions, though only sufficient for brief visits, including a trip by William, with Henry in hand, to nearby Union College, where William was convinced he would one day be a student. Henry junior remembered voyages northward from New York City on the newly built Hudson River Railroad, whose construction he and his friends celebrated with frequent treks from Fourteenth Street to the "upper reaches of the city," where there was "a riot of explosion and great shouting and waving of red flags." They imagined their visits "beset with danger." The city inexorably grew, avenues, transport, and housing yardsticking northward: the area between Union Square and Forty-second Street—Murray Hill, Chelsea, the Reservoir—a mixture of farms and newly built homes. Pigs snouted garbage in streets that would one day be the bright-lit center of the world. The first brown-stones began to make what seemed to the elite of mid-nineteenth-century New York their monotonous chocolate extensions east and west from Broadway. To Henry junior, Broadway was "the joy and adventure of one's childhood," stretching, "prodigiously, from Union Square to Barnum's great American Museum by the City Hall." It was the street on which the city pulsated and from which everything radi-ated toward the distant rivers.[26] At one end of it, in the few square miles of lower Manhattan, trade, trading houses, and the stock exchange touched the piers from which wood-masted vessels connected New York with the rest of the world.

(9)

He remembered incidents, places, people, with a tenacious retentiveness to which he later attributed some of his self-formation. Scenes stuck in his mind, details, impressions. Often he was a small, eager-eyed boy walking with his hand in his father's. One August day they took the ferry from Staten Island to the Manhattan studio of Mathew Brady, the photographer, "supreme in that then beautiful art," to sit for a daguerreotype. It was to be a surprise present for Mary James, but Henry senior could not keep its existence a secret. As with the Swe-denborgian message, "the good news in his hand refused under any persuasion to grow stale." Brady photographed father and son. They look out across the generations like characters in a Victorian genera-tional drama of similarity and difference. On another occasion, walking on Fifth Avenue, they met the recently defeated Whig candidate for president, General Winfield Scott, the Mexican War hero, for whom Henry senior had voted.[27]

If Henry junior had an immediate hero, it was his brother William. Less than two years older, William somehow seemed to him superior, partly because of age but also because of energy, sociability, and talent. William seemed stronger and rougher, one of the older boys who already knew how to curse and swear. He also seemed smarter, better able to pick things up immediately. "We were together outside of competition," Henry later chose to believe. "*His* competitions were with others . . . while mine were with nobody, or nobody's with me, which came to the same thing . . . as I neither braved them nor missed them."[28] William spent hours at his drawing board. Henry was quieter, a silent, solitary reader. He preferred to stay alone in his room rather than be active in the back parlor or the dining room. By his tenth birthday in 1853, the brothers were recognized as distinctly different, although they were intimately close. Eight-year-old Wilky joined them sometimes. The family appreciated his congeniality, his pudgy sociability. In contrast, Bob, thirteen months younger than Wilky, seemed impulsive and angry, with a swagger too insecure to be persuasive. Alice, at five, began to search for her place in the family. The personalities of the nursery developed into the personalities of childhood, and the family weighed, sifted, categorized, determined.

Henry senior provided a special problem in regard to vocation. He gave the children, on the surface, nothing to oppose, nothing to rebel against. The Swedenborgian dispensation called for total spiritual freedom, the "only spiritual substance . . . goodness, or human love. . . . So to us in the education of children one gets great help from all this clear knowledge of spiritual laws." The children, though, got no such help. Sunday was no different from any other day in the James household. They could go to any church they desired or to none at all. Henry junior chose the latter, though he yearned for the advantage of not having to make a choice. As to Swedenborg, he protected himself from "father's ideas" by remaining self-sufficiently "incurious." They seemed to him no more than "part of our luggage, requiring proportionate receptacles" for the fifty or so volumes that Henry senior took with him wherever he traveled. So hostile was Henry senior to any institutionalization of religion that he refused to join even the Swedenborgian Church. His son, oddly, could not recall ever having met one of his father's cobelievers. It seemed as if Henry senior reveled in a spiritual exclusiveness so distinct that he practiced a religion of one. "I was troubled all along," his son later admitted, "just by this particular crookedness of our being so extremely religious without having, as it were, anything in the least classified or striking to show for it." When Henry asked his father what he should say about where "we 'went' . . . it was cooler than any criticism . . . to hear our father reply that there was no communion . . . from which we need find ourselves excluded."[29] He would have preferred the social and ritual details of some settled, ordinary institutional affiliation. Why couldn't he go to church, with his family, like everyone else? And, also, why couldn't his father have a job, like everyone else's? What was he to respond when playmates asked him what his father did? To the young boy, it seemed that the family lived outside society.

If Henry senior imposed peculiar burdens in regard to being, he was equally arbitrary and sometimes inconsistent about doing. What were his sons to "do" when they grew up, and how were they, now, to prepare themselves for that? As a model, Henry senior seemed useless, especially in a world in which "business alone was respectable." To your friends, he told his sons, "say I'm a philosopher, say I'm a seeker for truth, say I'm a lover of my kind, say I'm an author of books if you like; or, best of all, just say I'm a student."[30] Though he supported his work as a student by an inheritance insufficient to last beyond his needs, he believed that a vocational orientation for his children would detract from, even subvert, the broad overall opportunity for spontaneous life that the fullest spiritual development demanded. To Henry senior, spiritual development mattered more than anything else, though he complained sometimes of the price that he paid in isolation. A tireless pamphleteer and lecturer between 1845 and 1855, he preached mostly to the curious, to the converted, or to the equally peripheral.

Even school was consented to rather than embraced by Henry senior. With a general indifference to formal education, he sent his two eldest sons to a haphazardly chosen series of schools. In September 1851, William and Henry were enrolled in the Institution Vergnès, near Broadway and Fourth Street, apparently because they would learn languages there, particularly French. Attended mostly by the sons of wealthy Cuban and Mexican planters, it had "a sordidly *black* interior" with a swarm of homesick foreign children and a staff that appeared to be "constantly in a rage." In September 1852, they were transferred to what appeared to them a vastly superior school, on Broadway, run by Richard Pulling Jenks, whom William remembered as sympathetic and congenial. The schoolmasters looked like Cruikshank caricatures. William was encouraged to draw, Henry mainly let alone to read, to absorb what he could in this "small but sincere academy," which he later thought of as "a consistent protest against its big and easy and quite out-distancing rival, the Columbia College School, apparently in those days the favorite of fortune."[31]

In September 1854, they were at a new school, as if continuity were a vice. This time their teachers were the Dickensian "Messrs. Forest and Quackenboss, who carried on business at the northwest corner of Fourteenth Street and Sixth Avenue." It seemed to Henry like a shop, dirty, smoky, and crowded, though it was attended by the sons of many prominent New York families. "It was sociable and gay, it was sordidly spectacular," and everyone seemed, compared to himself, talented in a thousand little ways, especially in "the dreadful blight of arithmetic." But he admired some of the older boys, who dominated the school, and at least "we stamped about, we freely conversed, we ate sticky waffles by the hundred."[32] Sticky waffles were the sweet side of neglect. As Henry junior was to say later, it was "an education like another," as if to dismiss the losses with a stoic shrug and discharge quietly the resentment that he and William afterward felt about the combination of carelessness and irresponsibility that characterized their father's benevolent indifference.

(10)

A warm August breeze helped propel the ferry from Manhattan across the harbor toward "the south Long Island shore." With his hand in his father's, seven-year-old Henry junior was returning from a day's urban holiday to where the family had been spending the summer months of 1850. The night before, a heavy storm with gale-force winds had shattered windows and thrust vessels into the barrier reefs stretching eastward to the tip of Fire Island. Henry junior noticed his father greet an elderly fellow passenger. Within moments, the young boy was introduced to Washington Irving, the famous author and diplomat, a member of Henry senior's small New York world of "our literary men." Whatever Henry senior's low opinion of the worldly Irving, for his son, in remembrance, it was a meeting with "the great man." And Irving's startling news remained fixed in his memory: Returning from Rome, Margaret Fuller, the forty-year-old transcendentalist writer, a friend of Emerson, Hawthorne, and Henry senior, had perished in a shipwreck in "that great August storm that had . . . passed over us" near Fire Island, "in those very waters . . . just outside our big Bay." He was soon, in the presence of his parents, to see a small portrait of Fuller and hear it remarked that it did not "do justice to its original." Fuller was indeed an original in many ways, and her early death was a significant loss. Her attenuated presence in the young boy's memory became part of his ambivalent vision of intellectual women in America.

Irving, Thackeray, Dickens, Shakespeare—from his first reading and theatre-going they became luminous figures in his childhood imagination. He felt most fully himself when he read. Probably he had learned to read at home, under the tutelage of mother and aunt. There may have been the alphabet at the day school in Albany. Grandmother James read all the "fiction of the day," and there were books of all kinds in the James households, in Albany and in New York City. He savored anything he could get his hands on, both in his father's library and in the leather-smelling reading room of his grandmother's Albany home. His father put restrictions on nothing, provided no guidelines. What was available, what appealed to him, Henry could read. Probably there were children's books. If so, he did not attach sufficient importance to them to record their titles or his impressions of them. At Union Square, in 1848, his fingers treasured "steel-plated volumes," the images over which he pondered, the words of which he probably could read. Soon, following William's example, he read Poe's "The Gold Bug" and "The Pit and the Pendulum," and then "Murders in the Rue Morgue," as if ghost stories were of special interest.[33]

At home, he was also read to—in a cultured mid-Victorian family literature provided both individual enlightenment and communal entertainment. One evening in May 1849, he was sent to bed early. Aware that one of his older cousins was about to read aloud the first installment of *David Copperfield,* he pretended to go upstairs. Instead, he hid himself out of sight close-by. Holding his breath, he listened "while the wondrous picture grew, but the tense chord at last snapped under the strain of the Murdstones and I broke into sobs of sympathy that disclosed my subterfuge. I was this time effectively banished." But of course he was totally captured; "the ply then taken was ineffaceable."[34]

For the young boy, Dickens dominated not only in novels but on the stage. An avid theatre-goer at a time when adaptations from novels formed a prominent part of the drama, Henry senior insisted that theatre be a family experience, that from the earliest age his children be exposed to cultural amusement, partly to share his own enthusiasm, partly for the education of the senses and the spirit. For Henry junior, the theatre was an enchantment, wonderful as spectacle, drama, language, and song. He loved the ever-changing gallery of theatre posters that decorated walls and fences, especially at the corner of Ninth Street and Fifth Avenue, "the old rickety bill-board" that "most often blazed with the rich appeal of Mr. Barnum, whose 'lecture room,' attached to the Great American Museum, overflowed into posters of all the theatrical bravery." At the theatres on Broadway and Park Row, he saw adaptations of many Dickens novels, particularly *Nicholas Nickleby,* "with the weeping feminine Smike who was afterwards to become Mrs. Charles Matthews," the wife of the most famous comic actor of the Victorian stage. He saw adaptations of Harriet Beecher Stowe's *Uncle Tom's Cabin,* which he read at its first publication in 1852 and which was immediately staged in New York, "much less a book than a state of vision." At its performance, for the first time he watched the audience response as closely as the stage performers, himself creating performances in his mind out of watching his family watching the drama. The theatre contributed to his growing consciousness.[35]

Listening to the famous Adelina Patti sing, he thrilled at the thunderous applause for "the beautiful pink lady's clear bird-notes." Such acclamation seemed as exhilarating as the performance itself. He sensed, however, the possibility not only of praise but of exposure, even of disapproval, partly to be associated with the audience that his father never had, partly with his own desire for acclamation. On one occasion, which he later referred to as his "great public exposure," he was cajoled onto the stage at a magician's performance. When he could not account for the magician's playing card and handkerchief tricks, he felt humiliated. His friends in the audience snickered. The notion of appearing on the stage both fascinated and frightened him. His preference was for indirect participation somewhere beyond and behind the stage. When he gathered with friends for small juvenile dramatic productions, he preferred to be creator rather than performer. With some skill in drawing, he doodled both for itself and as illustrations for his childish literary works. "I was so often engaged . . . in dramatic, accompanied by pictorial composition—that I must have again and again delightfully lost myself. . . . I didn't at any moment quite know what I was writing about: I am sure I couldn't otherwise have written so much."[36]

Vaudeville performances, circus spectacles, sentimental dramas, art galleries, lamplit slide shows and lectures highlighting the exotic, the spectacular, the educational—Henry senior's libertarianism fearlessly endorsed the widest range of learning experiences, the less organized, the less institutionalized, the better. Though the practice was inclusive, the intellectual and aesthetic discrimination in family discussion was lively, sometimes sharp. With a father who loved to argue and persuade, the children began to develop views and sharp tongues of their own. Young Henry's critical judgment was less voluble than William's, more indirect, and, soon, ironic. What he felt with increasing strength was a love for the theatre. Later, he thought of it as knowledge of the theatre, as if this early intense exposure provided the first strong elements of professional training and an awareness of how plays functioned. The theatre, though, was, for him, not a question of method or technique, but of glamour, and, most of all, of language. One evening his parents returned between acts of a play to fetch only William to join them watching a famous actress perform in Shakespeare's *Henry VIII*. Henry's disappointment was soon replaced by his realization that the most significant performance occurred in his solitary imagination. "I recall it as a vivid vigil in which the poor lonely lamplight became that of the glittering stage, in which I saw wondrous figures and listened to thrilling tones, in which I knew 'Shakespeare acted' as I was never to know him again."[37]

(II)

Suddenly, but not unexpectedly, in June 1855, the James family discovered that it was going to Europe again. The possibility had been on Henry senior's mind as early as four years after their return from England in 1845, and less than two after moving into their house on Fourteenth Street. He had then enumerated various reasons why going abroad was desirable: the cost of enlarging the house to accommodate the growth of the family, the difficulty each year of finding a suitable summer residence, the bad manners that the boys were learning in the city streets, the advantage a European residence would be to their learning French and German, the likelihood that there they would "get a better sensuous education" than in America. He had additional, more personal reasons, particularly his frustration at the lack of recognition for his publications and his "feeling of intense intellectual solitude." Desperately optimistic about the advantages of change, he desired stimulation, partly to escape from the "loud-mouthed imbecility" that he sometimes recognized in his own words. "The thought which is in them," he insisted, "is worthy of all men's rapturous homage." He lived, he believed, in a world in which most people "were too destitute of religion to do me justice as an author." Even Emerson, who expresses himself "much interested in my ideas . . . thinks I am too far ahead. . . . This is because he has no faith in man, at least in progress." Here "man leads a mere limping life."[38] The idea of limping through Europe offered at least the relief of change.

But the trip had been indefinitely postponed. The attractions of New York City held Henry senior for a while, though Europe remained a possibility just beneath the surface of the family consciousness, about which Henry junior felt ambivalent and about which, in later years,

William expressed his own feelings of bitter resentment. Henry junior wanted the advantages of belonging, of being a part of the settled world of these New York years. But Europe held a special place in his distant memories and glittered in his readings and in his imagination as a world of beauty and excitement. There were to be found the achievements of long and settled cultures whose castles and turrets and shining towers he knew from the books he read and the pictures he looked at. With one of his school friends, whose background was Swiss-French and with whom he had discussed collaborating on a work of fiction, he shared an interest in all the wonders of Europe. Still, for the twelve-year-old boy, there were no choices to make. The family awaited Henry senior's decision.

Abruptly, in early spring 1855, Europe became a certainty. By June, arrangements were already made. They would go first to Paris, then to Geneva for a long stay. Henry senior had heard from some casual sources that Swiss schools were excellent. Aunt Kate and a European-born governess, particularly engaged to look after Alice, would accompany them. Henry senior described much and explained nothing to Emerson, who complained that James had jumped "the whole argument, namely, the causes of this astonishing exodus, and dexterously alighted on the interesting episode of [Aunt Kate's] accompanying you." Emerson barely held back his feelings so that his words "should not be too full of patriotic anger and dirges of personal disappointment." His own intense patriotism stirred, Henry senior, watching a golden sunset on the evening of their departure, expressed his hope that "we might be sure of as golden sunniness on the other side. But America evidently is the golden land now, and I feel it deeply as the hour of departure draws nigh."[39] In late June 1855, the family sailed from New York to Liverpool on the S.S. *Atlantic.*

Two

BELONGING

1 8 5 5 – 1 8 6 0

(I)

From Liverpool, in early July 1855, the family immediately went to London. Henry junior suddenly "broke out in chill and fever," diagnosed as malaria. Since the symptoms were intermittent, they could travel, though carefully. For a while he lay in a bed in a London room, "the window open" to the English summer "and the far off hum of a thousand possibilities." Hiring an Italian courier for their European travels, they crossed to Paris. On "a soft summer night," from their hotel balcony, he leaned out into "a fond apprehension of Paris" that included the vivid life of the Rue de la Paix. The next day, the courier took the older boys to the Louvre, where Henry gaped at Géricault's *Raft of the Medusa* with a "splendour and terror of interest," as if the experience had immense implications for his future, perhaps as an image both of shipwreck and of salvation, of the threat of drift and of the excitement of adventure. Soon they were on their way to Geneva, Henry, a temporary invalid, excited by "the romance of travel," with brilliant scenery and sudden startling views, one of which had at its pinnacle "a fresh revelation . . . that [he] recognized with a deep joy . . . as at once a castle and a ruin."[1]

In Geneva, Henry remained mostly in the Old World shadows of his bedroom and his semi-illness. By the time he felt well enough to join William and Wilky at their boarding school, Henry senior had had enough of Swiss schools. A two-month trial had been sufficient. "We had fared across the sea under the glamour of the Swiss school in the abstract, but the Swiss school in the concrete soon turned stale in our hands." In October 1855, they left for Paris, where they quickly overcame the difficulty of finding a hotel with available space large enough for five children, three parents, and a maid. Rents seemed impossibly high. With his father, he visited the international exhibition at the Palais de l'Industrie, and with William, the Louvre again, and then again. They soon crossed to London, where rents were more reasonable, where Henry senior would no longer need a courier to help with languages he did not know, and where there were English friends and English culture. "There's nothing like it after all!" Henry senior exclaimed as the tired, famished family had a cold roast beef supper at their hotel.

Wearing black top hats and black gloves, twelve-year-old Henry and thirteen-year-old William James wandered through gray London streets, staring at the scenery, dawdling at the shop windows, buying paints and brushes for their "eternal drawing."[2] It was the second year of their exile, which the older boy felt were "poor and arid and lamentable years." Henry had been developing, in contrast, a creative passivity, an ability to absorb rather than to resist. A peculiar casual providence in the form of his father had brought him to Europe and demanded little of him other than that he be there. He found his father elusive, self-assertion unnecessary. Let William express the unhappy side of their situation. There was an attraction, even an advantage, to spending most of his time reading, watching, absorbing, without external interference or demands. Henry did have the unpleasant sense of being strikingly noticeable, as if there were something strange about the way they were dressed that elicited curious, unsympathetic stares, attaching themselves "for some reason especially to our feet, which were not abnormally large." He later insisted that he "had no quarrel with our conditions." But he admitted that his own attitude could have been taken "only by a person incorrigible in throwing himself back upon substitutes for lost causes."[3]

London street scenes provided lost causes of their own. He had a "terrified sense," as he and his father, one day the next year, made their way in a cab across London Bridge, of "swarming crowds . . . of figures reminding me of Cruikshank's Artful Dodger and of Bill Sikes and his Nancy, only with the bigger brutality of life." Through the frame of the cab window he saw, as in a picture, "a woman reeling backward as a man felled her to the ground."[4] Schooling continued to be mostly a lost cause. Fortunately, Henry senior soon hired a kind, sensible tutor, a Scotsman named Robert Thompson, though only after being besieged by hundreds of applicants when he naively advertised in the *Times* before asking for letters. Thompson, mild, kind, and shy, would make no harsher injunction than "come now, be getting on!"

Through the spring of 1856, Henry and William continued to wander and to stare, to the museums, to the Royal Academy show, where they saw "the first fresh fruits of the Pre-Raphaelite efflorescence," and to the theatres, where they delighted in Charles Kean in Shakespeare, Alfred Wigan in French melodrama, and Charles Mathews in Sheridan. When the family moved to a rented house in St. John's Wood, Thompson continued to supervise their reading, playing with them in the garden, taking them on excursions to the chief sights of London, the Tower, the Abbey, St. Paul's, Madame Tussaud's, through a city that looked much like the one that years later became James's "permanent headquarters."

In early summer 1856, the family returned to Paris, perhaps because Henry senior wanted them to improve their French. They moved first to a small house on the Champs-Élysées, at a time before the street had been widened, the lower part still residential and crowded with houses that had been there for centuries, "gardens and terraces and hotels of another time." Though apparently they did not meet him, Charles Dickens was their neighbor. For Henry senior, there were "resident compatriots," particularly female friends to whom he delighted in being half avuncular uncle, half romantic friend in a combination of absolute freedom in theory and strict convention in practice. For the family, there were picnics in the suburbs and Bois de Boulogne woodland adventures. A condescending French tutor supervised their lessons, apparently unsympathetic to Henry's translation into English of La Fontaine's *Fables*. A kind, solicitous French governess walked all five James children through the afternoon streets of "her beautiful city" in which glowed, visible to childish eyes, the romance of the Second Empire in the form of "a beautiful young Empress" and "a little Prince Imperial."[5]

Large apartments were rare and rents so high that in August 1856 the family moved into a flat, at a cost of $2,200 a year ($800 more than they were getting for their New York house). It was a flat they had turned down the previous autumn. "This of course we will not be able to do for any length of time," Mary James told her mother-in-law. But "we are enjoying many advantages here that make amends for our losses." They missed New York, they missed America, and they were irritated that the "grossest extortion" was practiced on them "at every turn" by a people "wholly destitute of heart and moral sense." The children found the large Rue d'Angoulême apartment comfortable, though "it's a queer way of living," William wrote to a Fourteenth Street friend, "all huddled up together on one floor. . . . Wilky and Bobby and Alice have commenced learning music and drum on the piano from morning till night. Harry sentimentalises as usual. As we have no companions and cannot play on these nasty narrow French streets, we all have to sally forth every day for a walk." Henry and William frequently walked to the Louvre, particularly by way of the quays of the Left Bank, "with their innumerable old book shops and print shops," and then up the dark, mysterious Rue de Seine, which stretched luxuriously to the Luxembourg Palace. "*Such* a stretch of perspective, *such* an intensity of tone as it offered in those days."[6]

Another effort was made at a school for the older boys, this time with partial success. In early 1857, they were enrolled at the Institution Fezandié, in the Rue Balzac, named after and run by a disciple of Fourier, whose social and educational theories Henry senior had long ago comfortably grafted onto his Christian Swedenborgianism. Progressive education appealed to Henry senior. A coed school "to the liveliest effect," it had some of the flavor of an enlightened experiment, of a step toward a "new heaven and new earth." It was at best "a recreational, or at least a social . . . house . . . quite ridiculous," Henry later remarked, "but . . . wholly harmless. . . . The general enterprise simply proved a fantasy not workable." There were momentary pleasures in Paris. He heard Thackeray, visiting them at their apartment, tease eight-year-old Alice, exclaiming, "Crinoline?—I was suspecting it! So young and so depraved!" Henry took long strolls, when Paris was "bright in the ineffable morning light," with a visiting cousin. While walking one evening in the glare of the gaslight in the Rue de Rivoli, he caught sight of one of his older classmates, "with his high hat a trifle askew and his cigar actively alight . . . in full possession of Paris. There was speed in his step, assurance in his air . . . my first image of what it was exactly to *be* on the way. . . . I went but forth through the Paris night in the hand of my mama; while he had greeted us with a grace that was as a beat of the very wings of freedom!"[7]

In July 1857, they went to Boulogne-sur-Mer, a "sunny, breezy, bustling," fashionable seacoast resort heavily favored by English summer visitors. One afternoon in August, at home alone, he had "strange pains and apprehensions." Outside he could hear the soft sounds of the Boulogne streets. An eerie feeling of something extraordinary happening, something life-changing, came over him. The doctor diagnosed a dangerous typhus infection, "the gravest illness of [his] life," that put him to bed with rashes, fever, headache, and delirium. In the event that he was carrying the lice or mites that transmitted the disease, his head was shaved. "My Harry," his father wrote home, "has been very ill . . . for several days delirious, and he is now extremely weak and low." By mid-September, he seemed "decidedly on the mend and . . . beginning to cost something again in the way of chicken and peaches."

But he "has had a hard time." Inactive for months, when he recovered he felt that a major change had taken place, that his boyhood was over. By the beginning of the new year, William reported that "the only trace of his fever remaining is a scarcity of hair on his head. . . . He has grown taller than I am, and his shoulders are much broader than mine. He is raw-boned in proportion."[8]

In October 1857, returning to Paris from the Boulogne summer to an expensive new apartment on the Rue Montaigne, Henry senior had to face the fact that he had become, suddenly, though he hoped temporarily, much poorer. The stock market crash in New York in September 1857, followed by a general financial collapse, had severely reduced the value of his stocks and bonds. Most of his investments were in railroad stocks, which had been especially hard hit. "Money is *not tight—it is not to be had at all.* There is no money, no confidence & value to anything. A week more of such times and the [banks] will fail." British markets and banks reeled almost simultaneously. The ten-thousand-dollar-a-year credit that he had established with Baring Brothers for their European expenses was jeopardized. "We do not know how long," he wrote to his brother, "we will be able to stay here." To his mother, he wrote requesting that she ask his three brothers to put to his credit with his Boston banker, Samuel Ward, "as large a sum as you can . . . in order that we may escape the worst rigours of the crisis." These commercial disasters signify, he moralized, "the widest *social* disease in the community," particularly among people who had been preaching the Bible but "neglecting it in its *social* application." At first he assumed that they would return home as soon as possible.[9] They went only as far as Boulogne-sur-Mer, where, in the winter, the cost of living was much less than in Paris. The panic soon subsided. Asssets were liquid again. Henry senior decided that they would remain in Europe.

Gradually recovering from typhus, Henry at first stayed mostly at home on the Rue Montaigne and then in the immense house that they rented at the beginning of 1858 on the Rue Neuve Chaussée in Boulogne. The seacoast resort seemed additionally solitary and dreary in the off-season, the major resource being "little English ladies" he met during his regular visits to borrow three-volume English novels from the lending library. In contrast, Henry senior, with his blunt optimism, felt "jovially compassionate towards every dweller in Paris, cut off from the sight of this delicious sea . . . an ocean of sunshine out of doors, making sky and earth & water beautiful." To his sons, the landscape seemed bleaker. William, Wilky, and Bob attended the Collège Communal, which they disliked. The latter two felt particularly neglected, unrewarded, unappreciated, especially at school. William wanted to return home immediately, his mind on questions of vocation and college. "Trade I detest," he wrote to a friend in New York. "I would like to be a doctor, but I fear I could not stand dissections and operations. . . . I am fond of mathematics. . . . I think I would like engineering." Tutored at home for three hours each morning, Henry expressed great fondness for his solitude. He had become a passionate reader, particularly of novels, and a secret writer, though mostly in his imagination. Behind the surface of things, he was convinced, existed obscured or even hidden realities. Illness and personality had made him more fortunate than his brothers during this "long term of thrifty exile from Paris . . . when we had turned our back on the Rue Montaigne and my privilege was to roam on the winter and spring afternoons."[10]

(2)

Years later, he awoke suddenly with what seemed total recall of a powerful dream that he had had sometime before. The setting was the Louvre, the long Gallery of Apollo through which he had first traveled as a child. The shining ceiling and walls had evoked for him in 1855 "not only beauty and art and supreme design, but history and fame and power," the glory of the first Napoleon who had decreed the Louvre into existence and who had made the brilliance of the Second Empire, the Paris that was about to be. In the dream, he was defending himself against an unknown figure on the other side of a door. "The awful agent, creature or presence, whatever he was," was exerting all the pressure he could to push the door open and get at him. What could he do? In a flash he realized he *could* save himself. He needed to turn the tables on his pursuer, his victimizer, himself to become the active agent and to force "the door outward." Immediately, he pushed open the door, and saw that his pursuer, "routed, dismayed, the tables turned . . . by my so surpassing him for straight aggression and dire intention . . . was already a diminished spot" in the distance, fleeing "for *his* life." Suddenly, a great storm broke. A lightning flash revealed that his enemy was fleeing, disappearing down the far end of the Gallery of Apollo.

When the dream actually occurred he never determined. He awakened "in a summer dawn" many years later to its "instantaneous recovery and capture." He recorded the dream in the first volume of his autobiography in 1913. The emotions that created the dream associated with his childhood in Paris probably existed before the first visits to the

Louvre, part of his formative consciousness from the earliest days of his existence, his infancy in the James household and the voyage abroad when he was less than two years old. There is a short distance between the Napoleonic column of the Place Vendôme and the long Gallery of Apollo in Napoleon's Louvre. At the same time, the dream was so vivid in the mind of the elderly writer in 1913 that its design and details have some of the contours of an imaginative creation and some of the emotional power of the needs of an elderly man compensating for the losses of old age with the remembrance of "that immense hallucination." It was "the most appalling yet most admirable nightmare of my life."[11]

Paris excited and attracted him, but he also felt apprehension and self-doubt. He could participate in the glory of the Empire, but he also could be excluded. Family inclusion was insufficient. He needed an outside world of which to be part. Having been snatched away from New York, he had become a family victim as well as beneficiary. In 1856, in Paris, he heard from one of his Fourteenth Street friends that they "were going to try to turn the club into a Theatre And as I was asked w'ether I wanted to belong here is my answer. I would like very much to belong."[12] Distance prevented his fulfilling the wish. The desire, though, spoke to the constant threat of social exclusion and powerlessness. Powerlessness had its attraction. The fullest possible dependency might relieve him of all need to choose. Without choices to make, he could find a passive freedom from responsibility. Henry senior, with Mary and Aunt Kate, made all the choices anyway, despite the father's libertarian rhetoric. Henry junior looked for some space for himself between the rhetoric and the reality, not in defiance but in accommodation. He recognized the advantages of the gilded cage, and of remaining captive to his parents' constricting expression of love. In the cage, he would be taken care of, included in the family and its circle of protection without any restrictions on his feelings and thoughts. That kind of powerlessness protected the inner self. It allowed privacy, which he increasingly cherished. Rebellion would be unseemly, churlish, ungrateful, perhaps even hurtful.

Also, he had an older brother inclined to wave openly the flag of self-assertion, partly because he felt more keenly the problems of vocation and the disadvantages of Henry senior's agenda. From the beginning, William expressed himself more articulately, more assertively, more dramatically. He made family drama. He did his work in public, whether bent over his drawing pad in the parlor or bouncing into the family circle with his latest written or oral effusion. He demanded immediate applause for his achievements. He took up visible space, a dominant presence. Whether or not the family fully believed in William's superiority, for Henry that assumption became an advantage, a small price to pay for additional space for himself, for the benefit of being both coddled and left alone, of being a royal prisoner at the family court in which his elder brother was the Prince Imperial.

If he pursued freedom through the acceptance of limitation, he also pursued it through fantasies of liberation from parental domination. On the one hand, he found attractive the structure imposed by agents beyond his control, with due allowance for the peculiar and contradictory form in which Henry senior provided it. On the other, he dreamed about absolute imaginative freedom, often expressed by fantasies of orphanhood. From early on, he dreamed about being a privileged, romantic orphan of the imagination for whom there were no penalties for absolute freedom. By one stroke of imaginative desire, he could free himself of his father entirely. On the evening in 1849 when, having been ordered to bed, he had hidden himself close-by to listen to the reading of the opening installment of *David Copperfield,* he entered into a number of sacred stories and private scripts. He had listened to Dickens' autobiographical dramatization of his own feeling of being an orphan expressed in David's story of the loss of his parents and the horror of the Murdstones. The cousin who read may have been an orphan, for Henry senior's family offered "such a chronicle of early deaths, arrested careers, broken promises, orphaned children. . . . Part of the charm of our grandmother's house [in Albany] . . . was in its being so much and so sociably a nursuried and playroomed orphanage. . . . Parentally bereft cousins were somehow more thrilling than parentally provided ones."[13]

In the summer of 1854, he had witnessed a dramatic, romantic wail of impending orphanage when he had accompanied his father to the Rhinebeck estate of his uncle. His father had been called in the hope that he could persuade his sister not to return to her husband, who was infectiously ill with tuberculosis. While cries of protest and grief came from the house, the young boy crept off with an older cousin to a viewpoint above the river. Looking down on the Hudson, "I somehow felt," he later remarked, "the great bright harmonies of air and space becoming one with my rather proud assurance and confidence, that of my own connection, for life, for interest, with such sources of light."[14] His aunt, returning to her husband, soon followed him to the grave, leaving four orphaned daughters, one of whom was to become a cherished alternative self and in the fortunes of each of whom he was always interested. In orphanhood, he felt freedom, romance, literature, an alternative world in which the choices were his, the routes of travel to be mapped out, the initiatives in regard to when to start and where to go under his control, free to choose whether to belong or not to belong.

From early on he wanted to belong to the world of art, in the sense in which one can belong to something that has few boundaries, though formal boundaries were to be important to his life and to his art, as an expression of his need for control as well as his need for freedom. As an artist, he would have the opportunity to be as free as possible from external control but at the same time to have a highly developed sense of where to draw the line, of where to begin, of where to end, of what should be included and what should be excluded. As a child, reading and writing were mostly private, solitary. They helped him escape into the inner freedom that substituted for the outer freedom that he did not have, although that freedom was precisely what his father claimed to provide. William and Henry knew better. If there was going to be an empire of art, he was not sure that he wanted it to be, or that it could be, conjunctive with the empire of the James family. But he was sure that he himself wanted to be the emperor.

He was to learn that there were no emperors in America. In the raw provinces of mid-nineteenth-century America, a native artistic culture was still inchoate, literature still mostly imported from abroad. In New York City, no museums existed other than the most minimal galleries, including the precursor of the Metropolitan Museum, to which Henry senior took his children as avidly as he took them to the theatres. There were few representations in America of the glories that had been Greece and Rome, Renaissance Italy and France. When the James family went eastward to Europe, they did not pass en route shiploads of European art on their way to American homes. That was not to happen for almost fifty years. Europe, still, had some of the attraction of an alternate world. But it came to the young boy through the channel of family control of which he needed both to enjoy the benefits and to reject.

That interplay extended into his adult life, particularly in his embrace of Europe, in his commitment to a foreign residency so extensive that he identified strongly with the land of his adoption while successfully resisting becoming absorbed by it. He recognized that Europeans would never accept him as a European and that he would never think of himself as anything else but an American. The plaintive desire of the young boy to belong became eventually a recognition that he always paid a price for whatever belonging he achieved, and that certain types of belonging were incompatible with his needs. He was always to have a country, but from a distance. He was never to belong to the estate of marriage. His dream of "straight aggression and dire intention" expressed his need to free himself from his father's control and ultimately from America's. His otherness would become a crucial element of his art.

(3)

In spring 1858, Henry senior decided to bring his family back to America, to the "tonic skies of the great & free Western Republic." There were rumblings of war in Europe, the English "greatly alarmed at Louis Napoleon's preparations" and "the European sky [seemed] very lowering politically." Probably such prospects did not seriously influence his decision, though they were part of a number of considerations, including homesickness and frustration. Europe seemed even less fertile ground than America for the seeds of Swedenborgianism. To most Europeans, he was simply another well-to-do American with run-of-the-mill eccentric ideas who had published some obscure, unavailable books and who spoke no language other than English. In France, the James family friends were mostly Americans. The English seemed to Henry senior "an intensely vulgar race . . . the abject slaves of routine" who "love all that wear their own livery, but they don't even *see* anyone outside of that boundary." When abroad, America looked better than when he was at home. American virtues had begun to shine in his eyes: democracy, vitality, a country where "the advanced thought belongs of right to the youngest and most vital blood."

His eldest son, though, had a clear sense of what he thought the ruling principle ought to be in regard to the James family: "I think," William remarked, "that as a general thing, Americans had better keep their children at home." The departure from Liverpool in June 1858 came as a relief to all members of the family, though the question of where home was still had to be dealt with. From the children's point of view, any place that was America provided a topographical authentication of their Americanness. Henry senior's Swedenborgianism embraced a spiritualism so universalistic, so immaterial, that it tended to obliterate physical boundaries and specific places. In contrast, his children developed a strong sense of "a local habitation and a name." Where in America would they live? Henry senior arbitrarily decided on Newport, Rhode Island, where, by midsummer 1858, they were settled "very comfortably for the present. . . . The boys . . . are as good as good can be . . . utterly abandoned to the enjoyment of their recovered liberty, boating and fishing and riding to their hearts content."[15]

They had, for the first time, become New Englanders, though of a special, peripheral kind. With any place of residence open to them, including a return to New York, Henry senior had chosen a comparatively out-of-the-way summer resort that had flourished in the Colonial period as a major American city but had since contracted into a smaller, more insular town off the beaten track of commercial and intellectual activity. The winters were mild enough for year-round residence, and Newport continued its century-long tradition as a summer watering place for wealthy southerners. A longtime friend and correspondent of Henry senior's, the wealthy Edmund Tweedy, who had a winter home in Pelham, New York, and a summer home in Newport, undoubtedly advocated its virtues, among them his and his wife Mary's presence. More likely than not, Newport's major advantage was its genteel wealth. No one other than tradespeople or working-class people worked.[16] That Henry senior most of the time stayed home without work of the obvious kind would hardly be noticeable. The ghost of his hardworking, self-made millionaire father would be kept at a distance. His children would not be asked questions to which they could have only awkward answers. In Newport, living on independent even if modest means was hardly exceptional.

Newport also provided a way of having only one foot in America, and Henry senior had made no commitment to stay indefinitely. Egress was by water, regular boats departing from the long pier for Boston and New York City. Probably the safety of Newport also appealed to him; it was a place where his children could be protected from practices and values he opposed and where his own peculiarities would not be readily noticed. His sons, particularly the two eldest, were approaching the dangerous age. On the one hand, he wanted them to have normal experiences. On the other, he defined normality narrowly, or at least conservatively. He wanted them to have lady friends. But he also wanted them to be chaste. He demanded of his children manners, courtesies, and respect that adolescence often, as in his own case, rebels against. He wanted to maintain tight family structure and parental control as long as possible. Newport made that easier than it would have been in New York or Boston. When, in August 1858, William had taken the opportunity of a family trip to Albany to visit Union College, almost certain that "within a few months" he would finally be a student there, he soon discovered that he was "greatly mistaken; for on coming to speak with my Father on the subject, I found much to my surprise that he would not hear of my going to any college whatsoever. He says that Colleges are hot beds of corruption."[17] Henry junior could easily anticipate what the response would be when his time came. Henry senior wanted his two eldest sons under the parental eye.

By mid-October 1858, his sense of control over his family was so challenged that he decided to take all of them off to Europe again as soon as possible. He actually booked passage on the *Persia* for departure in late February 1859. Immediately meeting strong resistance, he backed off. "Our friends make such an outcry, and we ourselves felt so much the danger of over-precipitation, that we concluded at last to postpone the leave taking till Spring at least. Our notion was that the boys could do a great deal better over there than here. Young America male and female is too confoundedly fast, the little people rule the big people so unmistakeably, that we begin to tremble for our well established empire over our posterity, and to foresee all manner of doings to their modest and orderly development." Fortunately, he conceded, they do "treat us with the respect that is due to us as considerate parents, and we hope that we may get through the winter without damage. What we shall finally do in the Spring the Spring must determine."[18] Despite his rhetoric about experience, love, and individual freedom, he feared that his children would be damaged by just those things. He had only agreed to a postponement. If things were not the way he wanted them to be by the spring, *he* would determine what they would do.

For Henry junior, meanwhile, Newport proved delightful, almost a magical moment poised between two unsettling voyages. He had an opportunity to belong, which he took good advantage of with an emotional efficiency that expressed the lessons of compensation and substitution that he had already learned. In the summer of 1858, he reveled in an outdoor paradise of stunning walks and rides through the natural seacoast wilderness of pre–Gilded Age Newport. He soon had companions to accompany him on excursions. Two years younger than himself, Thomas Sargeant Perry was a native of Newport, a grandson of Oliver Hazard Perry, the naval hero of the War of 1812, and a great-grandson of Benjamin Franklin. An avid reader and pursuer of literary culture, he was somewhat awkward, somewhat languid, but immediately endearing. Urged by Duncan Pell, a Newport resident who knew Henry senior, Perry and Pell's son called on the Jameses early in the summer and found three of the sons at home. Invited to return to Pell's house with his new acquaintances, Perry walked with them, "Wilky hanging on my arm, talking to me as if he had found an old friend after long absence." While "the rest of us were chattering," Henry "sat on the window-seat reading . . . with a certain air of remoteness. William was full of merriment and we were soon playing a simple and childish game."[19] Despite his air of remoteness, Henry was eager for companionship, for young men of his own age. The relationship with Perry, for whom he soon invented a string of endearing nicknames, immediately became a loving one, with the unselfconsciousness of adolescent male bonding. For two summers and the year between, Perry became the "superexcellent and all-reading, all-engulfing friend of those days," associated, in a lifelong relationship, with these happy times in Newport.

Another new friend was John La Farge. Eight years older than Henry, the son of wealthy French Catholic émigrés to New York City who had made a fortune in real estate, La Farge was an accomplished young painter, already intensely dedicated to his art. Lean and bespectacled, he had a reputation for wide reading and witty talk. After graduating from a Catholic college in Maryland, he had at first studied law and then, with parental support, had lived abroad as an art student. He had come to Newport to study with a well-known American artist and art teacher, William Morris Hunt. La Farge was an immediate presence, his personal flair expressed through black velvet costumes and white summer elegance that gave the artistic life an imagistic vividness, "quite the most interesting person we knew."[20] His immediate affinity was with William, who hoped to be his equal, his peer, both as a personal friend and as an aspiring artist. But the younger Henry could and did learn from La Farge, who introduced him to what seemed the miracles of Browning and especially Balzac. "The yearningly gullible younger" boy readily gave himself up to the enslaving, sophisticated charm of "the good-natured and amused elder."

Beginning in October 1858, William began to take lessons with Hunt. He happily followed La Farge into Hunt's Church Street studio, located behind the Hilltop residence of Hunt's brother, the architect Richard Hunt, who was increasingly responsible for the design of Newport's new mansions. Impetuous, sometimes saturnine, physically adventuresome, William Hunt had studied the realistic style of Thomas Couture in Paris. He had returned to America, attracted to living near his brother and by other Newport advantages, to practice and spread the new aesthetic principles of French realism at a small art school and artist's colony that he had founded. Following his friend and his brother, Henry spent the late fall afternoons in Hunt's studio watching and participating. Henry senior, though, was not at all enthusiastic about his eldest son's enthusiasm for Hunt. He "is celebrated I am told, but his speech is broken and too exclusive."[21] What he meant was that he did not like the idea of William's attraction to art as a vocation and Hunt's influence on him. Both Hunt and La Farge seemed, to his father, obstacles to William's "modest and orderly development" along the lines of which his father approved. With Swedenborg the engineer-physicist in mind, Henry senior strongly advocated a scientific career for William, apparently fantasying about some grand unification of the visible and the invisible.

What he did not want was to give up control over his sons, whom he felt slipping away. In September 1858, Henry junior and the other James sons had been enrolled in the Berkeley Institute, apparently the preferred school for those Newport families interested in education and career. Now it was Henry's turn to join his older brother in being told no in regard to college. Columbia, Yale, "even Harvard . . . moved him in our interest as little" as had Union College. William particularly wanted to go to Harvard. In the summer of 1859, Henry senior looked into the possibility of finding a house for the family in Cambridge. But apparently he could not find a suitable one. Anyway, he declared, "It would not be the place for us in all respect if we could. . . . I have but one *fixed mind* about anything; which is that whether we stay here or go abroad, and whatever befalls our dear boys in this world, they and you and I are all alike, and are after all, absolute creatures of God, vivified every moment by him."[22] To his dear boys it must have seemed as if they had a more immediate father who held absolute dominion over them.

The threat of Europe, which had never been fully removed, rose again. In September 1859, Henry senior began to feel desperate. I have "grown so discouraged about the education of my children here, and dread so those characteristics of extravagance and insubordination, which appear to be characteristic of American youth, that I have come to the conclusion to retrace my steps to Europe, and keep them there a few years longer. My wife is completely of the same mind, and though we feel on many accounts that we are making personal sacrifices in this step, the advantages to the children are so clear that we cannot conscientiously hesitate. . . . I am quite sure that my main object in life . . . is to do justice to my children." His own father had assuredly felt the same way. As it had been three years before, the justification was better schools, the decision presented totally in terms of parental self-sacrifice. On the same day, William disgustedly remarked that "father took it into his head the other day that it was absolutely necessary for our moral and intellectual welfare to return immediately to Europe. . . . We shall probably stay three years!" He "could hardly have conceived such turpitude on the part of a being endowed with a human heart. . . . We are to be torn from our friends and our fatherland once more." It looked to William as if "the rest of the family" was "delighted." But, as usual, Henry simply took the bad news with less open resistance. He was more committed to the inviolability of his inner life and his reading than interested in making a fuss about his father's fixations and self-deceits. In October 1859, the "night Harry and Willie James were going away to Europe," Tom Perry, "in the depths of boyish despair," went down to the Newport pier to bid his friends good-bye. From New York, on the day of their sailing to Le Havre, Henry wrote to Perry that he felt himself "thinking much more of what I leave behind than what I expect to find. Newport and the Newporters are surrounded with a halo . . . which grows brighter and brighter. . . . Good bye to you and every body and every thing!"[23]

(4)

Ten days later, on a frosty mid-October night, the Jameses arrived in Geneva for another go at the Swiss schools that had proved such a failure three years before. Fourteen-year-old Wilky and thirteen-year-old Bob were again sent to a boarding school outside the city. Eleven-year-old Alice was to be tutored at their apartment in the Hôtel de l'Écu, overlooking the rapidly flowing Rhône. William was enrolled immediately in the Geneva Academy, the forerunner of the university, where his father felt that the "true bent" of William's "genius . . . towards the acquisition of knowledge" would be attended to rather than allowing him "to tumble down into a mere painter" under the influence of Hunt at Newport. "Let us go abroad then we said," he wrote to a friend, "and bring him into contact with books and teachers." Henry, his Latin apparently insufficient for admission to the Gymnasium, was sent to a "dreary Institution, squeezed into a tall, dim, stony-faced and stony-hearted house at the very top of the Cité and directly in the rear of the Cathedral," the Institution Rochette, which existed to prepare aspiring engineers for the polytechnical school. Despite the eternal, almost lampless winter twilight, he did not find it all bad, though it was mostly dismal. The students read German and French literature, the latter under a friendly teacher who "brightened our lesson with memories of his time in Paris." Still, school days were insufferably long, consisting mostly of mathematics, which he "so feared and abhorred . . . that the simplest arithmetical operation . . . always found" and kept him "helpless and blank." From the schoolroom window, the most interesting sight to the stifled, frightened boy was the movement of prisoners in the jail across the street. It seemed to him "that none but the most harmless and meekest men are incarcerated." How he longed to be back in Newport. "It was hard and bitter fruit all and turned to ashes in my mouth."[24]

Parental misperceptions had been pointedly epitomized by Henry senior the year before. "Willy is very devoted to scientific pursuits," he wrote to his mother in Albany, and is "an admirable student . . . much dearer to my heart for his moral worth than for his intellectual. . . . Wilky is more heart than head, having a talent for languages. . . . Bob . . . is very clever and promising, having ten times the go ahead of all the rest." Alice apparently warranted no separate remark. "Harry," though, "is not so fond of study . . . as of reading. He is a devourer of libraries, and an immense writer of novels and dramas. He has considerable talent as a writer, but I am at a loss to know whether he will accomplish much."[25] His son's fascination with fiction made Henry senior uneasy, the gap between Victorian three-deckers and Swedenborg an immense one. He thought of novel writing as a narrowing occupation, and later argued against it as a vocation. He had little confidence that his son would accomplish anything as a writer, though when he did he became the proudest of fathers. To the sixteen-year-old boy at the Institution Rochette it all seemed devastatingly incomprehensible.

Relief came in late April 1860, with spring in the air. Except for his classes in French, German, and Latin, he was relieved of attendance at the Institution Rochette and enrolled, like William, as a special student at the academy, his only obligation to sample classes as he desired. "My dear parents, as if to make up to me," he later rationalized, "for my recent absurd strain to no purpose, allowed me now the happiest freedom, left me to attend such lectures as I preferred."[26] He voluntarily sat through innumerable lectures as if they were dramatic or comedic performances, not quite as good as real theatre but interesting as performance rather than as substance. When he attended a dissection at the medical school, he found it slightly too strong for his stomach but physically powerful, as if it were another literary and theatrical genre, the theatre of sensation. Recalled from the world of mathematical forms to the life of the senses, he had time to read again, particularly Trollope and Thackeray, as well as Dickens and Eliot, the "deeper-toned strokes of the great Victorian clock." *The Cornhill Magazine* was sent by Henry senior, who was frequently away during the winter and spring. Usually, he went to Paris, where he found relief from Geneva winter boredom and was entertained by female friends, particularly three Americans he knew from the family's earlier visit. They illustrated anew for him "the frailty of man's dependence on women." Henry junior also had time to write again. Wilky noticed that "Harry has become an author . . . for he keeps his door locked all day long, and a little while ago I got a peep in his room, and saw some poetical looking manuscripts lying on the table, and himself looking in a most authorlike way. . . . The only difference there is between Willy's [poetic compositions] and Harry's labours is that the former always shows his [to everyone], while the modest little Henry wouldn't let a soul or even a spirit see his."

With William, he journeyed in late April to a meeting in the Vaud, characterized by patriotism, brotherhood, and beer, of the main German-speaking Swiss student organization, which William had joined. They both exalted at their liberation from even the comparative freedom of the Geneva Academy, where William's interest in science, real as intellectual enlightenment rather than as vocational aspiration, did not prevent him from being sick to the stomach at the sight of blood. They did not object to their father's decision in the early spring that they were all, with the exception of Bob, to spend the summer learning German at Bonn, though they might have been puzzled by his declaration to a friend that "[I] am always so little wilful about our movements that I am ready the young ones should settle them. So we may be in Europe a good while yet." Henry senior's recently expressed intention that they spend the following winter at Frankfurt am Main seemed *certain* to keep them "in Europe for a year longer."[27]

The boys' desire for Germany was modest. But William and Henry now had the opportunity for a week's walking tour in the Swiss Alps, their ultimate destination Bonn. From Geneva, at the end of May 1860, they ascended to Chamonix, where Henry hurt his foot slightly; then up the glacier to the Mer de Glace; then to Martigny on muleback and up the great St. Bernard, where they stayed overnight at the famous hospice; then down to the warm medicinal baths at Loèche-les-Bains and on to Interlaken. On the first of June they were in Germany. From Frankfurt, they took the Rhine route to Bonn, where the rest of the family had assembled, except for Bob, who had been allowed to join his boarding-school class on an excursion to Italy. The painting virus had spread in the family. Both Wilky and Bob had begun to draw constantly, and Bob to draw well. Still, as far as Henry senior was concerned, they both were destined for business, neither of them "cut out," he told Edmund Tweedy, "for intellectual labour." At Bonn, Henry and Wilky boarded with the family of a professor at the Gymnasium, William with a younger, more attractive tutor. Henry suffered from closed windows, unattractive smells, and asphyxiation. The struggle with the German language, though, had rewards. He enjoyed the willed intensity of immersing himself in something he wanted to learn; he felt that he "*tasted* German." In later years, the language was to grow distasteful to him, the culture the epitome of dullness and insensitivity. Though William would develop affection and reverence for the language and culture, Henry senior thought German impossible and Bonn insufferably dull. With Mary, Aunt Kate, and Alice established in a boardinghouse, he fled to Paris and London. "Mother does nothing but sit and cry for you," William wrote to him.[28]

Before Henry senior left Germany, a momentous decision had been made. The family would return to America in September. The sentence of another year in Europe had been lifted. Soon after their arrival in Bonn in June, William had confronted his father, challenging him "with a beautiful deference." On the grounds that art failed "to uplift the spirit in the way it most pretends to," Henry senior had frequently argued against painting as a career for his eldest son. "What it seems [William] had been long wanting to say," Henry senior remarked, as if he were for the first time learning that William desired to study painting, is "that he felt the vocation of a painter so strongly that he did not think it worth his while to spend any more time or money on his scientific education! I confess I was greatly startled by the annunciation, and not a little grieved, for I had always counted on a scientific career for Willy, and I hope the day may even yet come when my calculations may be realized." Wilky now came out of the closet. "I have come to the conclusion that 'Art' is my vocation," he pronounced. Bob inexplicably proclaimed that it was now his ambition "to go into a dry goods store when we get home." Henry senior immediately took the high pro-American road. He proclaimed "the superiority of America to these countries after all, and how much better it is that we should have done with them. . . . America is 'the lost Paradise restored' to boys and girls both, and it is only our own paltry cowardice & absurd ducking to old world conventionalities that hinder [other Americans] realizing it as such at once." Henry junior was overjoyed to be returning to Newport again. "One-two-three! Bung gerdee bang bang.....!!! What a noise! Our passages are taken in the Adriatic for the 11th of September!!!!!! We are going immediately to Newport, which is the place in America we all most care to live in."[29]

Later, Henry excluded from his autobiography this second James family European residence, partly because he felt that it would show his father to the world in an unattractive light, partly because he himself could not openly face the larger judgments that the pattern might demand or at least suggest. In the spring of 1858, "we fully expected," William had remarked, "when we got home after our former European stay never to come abroad as a body again." A year or so later, Henry senior had come "to the conclusion that America is not the place to bring up such 'ingenuous' youth as myself and my brothers."[30] The family had been wrenched away from Newport. Now, in the summer of 1860, without the slightest self-consciousness about his change of mind, let alone its rapidity, Henry senior had decided that America was the only place in which to raise children. Europe was awful, impossible, for Americans of all ages, essentially a blind, corrupt continent borne down by the heavy weight of centuries of materialism, class stultification, and moral decadence. The reversals made even his mostly subordinate, deeply loving children uncomfortable. And as much as he was happy at the prospect of returning to Newport, Henry junior's sense of the value, for him then and in the future, of further European experience did not sit well with his father's absolutistic rhetoric.

In fact, at the very moment of departure, he had his fullest, richest experience of European attractions. From Bonn, the three boys traveled by train to Paris, to join the rest of the family. On the way, they stopped at Cologne to see the cathedral again, and then came on via Strasbourg, on a train crowded with elegant French aristocrats and haute bourgeoisie on their September holiday journeys to Homburg and Baden-Baden. From the fifth-floor window of their hotel, looking down on the Palais Royal and "up at the New Louvre," Henry felt "more than ever 'penetrated' with Paris." Below, in the wide plaza, swarms of people moved. At the cab station, drivers snoozed, horses wearily stamped, "whisking their feet and tails." A line of brightly uniformed "little squat, brown men in blue and red" came into view. He now saw Paris, almost for the first time, as if the details and the language to describe them suddenly cohered. Now that departure was imminent, the place he was being forced to leave, despite his eagerness to return home, seemed desirable and romantic. Paris glittered as "a shining wonder and splendour . . . statues of heroes, Napoleon's young generals . . . the shining Second Empire."[31] Tramping through the streets, he took a last long sharp look at the wondrous vistas, the high columns, the Napoleonic glory, the inimitable Louvre.

Three

"GARLANDS AND LIGHTS"

1860–1867

(1)

The golden-tipped cane of his attacker smashed the head of Senator Charles Sumner. Momentarily pinned into his narrow seat on the Senate floor, the large, handsome senator rose and staggered, the blows continuing until he fell in a pool of his own blood. When the news of the assault arrived in Paris in late spring 1856, thirteen-year-old Henry junior heard outraged voices and saw tearful faces at a gathering of family and friends at their Champs-Élysées pavilion. Like the senator from Massachusetts, Henry senior also advocated the immediate abolition of slavery. Northern and Swedenborgian views cohered into a James family commitment to emancipation. It seemed to Henry junior, having recently read *Uncle Tom's Cabin,* "as if war had quite grandly begun, for what was war but fighting, and what but fighting had for its sign great men lying prone in their blood?" The next spring, Sumner, attempting to recover in Europe from the nervous shock that would keep his Senate chair empty for three years, paid a call on Henry senior in Paris. When Henry junior noticed that his head had healed so the wounds were no longer visible, he felt disappointed. There was, though, "greatness enough," he later remembered, "visible, measureable, unmistakable, greatness to fill out any picture." His youngest brother years later recalled accompanying his father to Sumner's couchside at a Paris hotel, his beauty and splendor spiritualized, in the boy's eyes, by high principle and the martyr's crown.[1]

When the James family again sailed to Europe in October 1859, Henry senior defended himself against the imputation that their departure was a sign that he did not love his country sufficiently. "I am a

good patriot," he proclaimed, "but my patriotism is even livelier on
the other side of the water." Three days before the James family landed
at Le Havre, John Brown, financed by six Bostonians, raided Harpers
Ferry—the John Brown whose voice, Robertson James would later say,
along with Charles Sumner's, "is forever calling us to build on the
foundations which they laid." Henry senior could not have known that
in the coming years his family would know John Brown's, that he
would readily but painfully meet intense demands on his patriotism,
and that the James family would suffer various wounds and losses in
the war that was coming.[2]

(2)

In September 1860, the family returned to America, never to travel as
a unit again. The voyage westward on the *Adriatic* had been a "dire
tribulation," the weather difficult, seasickness rampant. In New York,
with his feet on solid ground again, sixteen-year-old Henry junior's
seasickness immediately disappeared. His services "as an able-bodied
and willing young man" greatly in demand, he boasted that he didn't
give a second thought to "heaving a 60 pound trunk" over his head.
His brothers responded to queries about what had motivated their
return with the comment "that we went home to learn to paint. People
stared or laughed when we said it." Henry hoped that they would be
admired for patriotism rather than mocked for queerness. The return,
to a rented house at 13 Kay Street, was a relief and a great pleasure.
Newport had the same attractions that it had had the year before,
including the Tweedys as neighbors. La Farge and Perry were still there.
The lean, muscular Hunt, with wide grizzled beard and eyes that "both
recognized and wondered," welcomed William back to his studio. With
little else to do, Henry followed. He had declined to return to Leverett's
school, and Henry senior refused to permit him to go to college. One
day he found his cousin, Gus Barker, posing naked on a pedestal in the
large studio while the advanced students sketched his "kinsman's perfect
gymnastic figure," an embodiment of "living truth." He was dazzled
both by the beauty of his cousin's body and by William's drawing of
"the happy figure," which he obtained and kept for a long time. Generally, while Hunt busied himself with La Farge and William, Henry sat
in the cool solitude of the small studio taking pleasure in drawing copies
of casts, admiring particularly what he thought to be his "sympathetic
rendering of Michael Angelo's 'Captive' in the Louvre."[3]

His own captivity was less dramatic. In Hunt's studio, he felt "at

the threshold of a world." Occasionally, Hunt gently asked him about
his copying, with "a friendliness of tact, a neglect of conclusion." He
took it to be a human rather than a professional interest, partly because
he could see the difference between William's drawings, not to speak
of La Farge's, and his own. This particular door to the world of art was
not one he could pass through, though he was and remained talented
in drawing. As the autumn passed, the question of "what he should do
with his life became more urgent."[4] Henry senior tolerated, and now
even supported, William's desire to become a painter, though he still
essentially disapproved. When opposed, he had given way. Still unready
to put his shoulder against the door, to transform defense into aggression, Henry junior did not push back hard against his father's forbidding
college. When his arguments made no headway, he took no for no and
looked for compensations and substitutions. Day in, day out, he was
in the studio, enjoying the quiet, enjoying the private space. There were
attractive Newport walks, long conversations with Perry, La Farge,
William, with other friends. He did occasional service as "an abundantly
idle young out-of-doors model," especially for La Farge, who painted
a profile portrait of the dark-haired, warm-faced seventeen-year-old,
with full, sensuous lips, aquiline nose, and strong chin.

One of the delights of Newport was his increasing awareness of his
six orphaned Temple cousins, whose mother's wail of distress he had
heard at his Albany uncle's Rhinebeck estate in the summer of 1854.
They were the children of the marriage of Henry senior's younger
sister, Catherine Margaret, to an army officer, Robert Emmet Temple,
who had had a daughter by his first marriage. In 1848, this daughter,
Mary, had married Henry senior's close friend, the well-to-do Edmund
Tweedy. At the death in 1854 of her father and her stepmother, Mary
Tweedy and her husband became guardians of the orphans. When the
James children returned to Newport, they had the opportunity to get
to know their cousins better: Bob and Will, and the four girls, Kitty,
Minny, Elly, and Henrietta, who, beginning in the spring of 1861,
began to spend holidays at their guardians' Newport home. For Henry,
they became part of his daily consciousness. The four young ladies took
on some of the presence of sisters and some of the glamor of female
mystery. But the one who appealed to him most, Minny, rose beyond
attractiveness, in his feelings and imagination, becoming a "shining
apparition . . . a disengaged and dancing flame of thought." Orphaned
at nine years of age, the seventeen-year-old Minny Temple had a brightness of intellect, imagination, and language. She seemed natural, unre-
hearsed, spontaneous, with a lightness of being that, it did not occur
to Henry, might become unbearable, unsustainable. He admired her

precociousness, her brashness, her independence of spirit, "slim and fair and quick, all straightness and charming tossed head."[5]

For amusement, he also had the daily drama of the family assembled. At holidays, cousins and friends sometimes visited, one of whom, Emerson's son Edward, later reported on the level of real, though often comic, conflict and aggression at the dinner table. " 'The adipose and affectionate Wilky,' as his father called him, would say something and be instantly corrected by the little cock-sparrow Bob, the youngest, but good-naturedly defend his statement, and then Henry (Junior) would emerge from his silence in defense of Wilky. Then Bob would be more impertinently insistent, and Mr. James would advance as moderator, and William, the eldest, join in. The voice of the moderator presently would be drowned by the combatants and he soon came down vigorously in the arena, and when, in the excited argument, the dinner knives might not be absent from eagerly gesticulating hands, dear Mrs. James, more conventional, but bright as well as motherly, would look at me, laughingly reassuring, saying, 'Don't be disturbed, Edward; they won't stab each other. This is usual when the boys come home.' " The father, as moderator who always turned partisan; the mother, as common sense, conventional peacemaker; Alice, unheard from, choosing not to compete, withdrawn from the intellectual and discursive give and take; the voice of the eldest son, strong, patrilineal, but not conclusive; Henry junior, emerging from his silence to defend Wilky, and then, no doubt, returning to his privacy, for "his spirits were never so high as those of the others," Perry recalled, and, "if they had been, he still would have had but little chance in a conflict of wits . . . on account of his slow speech, his halting choice of words and phrases"; Bob, contentious, aggressively self-defensive; both younger sons with knives in the hands that are soon to hold swords.[6]

First they were to hold pens. Within a month of the family's return to Newport in September 1860, their parents brought Wilky and Bob to Concord to enroll them in the newly formed Sanborn School. William, busy at Hunt's studio, seemed to be at the right place to train for a career in painting. Henry, too old for school, prohibited from college, and insufficiently talented as a painter, began to devote more and more of his time to writing. He had confessed to Perry that he had a "secret employment." Soon after returning to Newport, continuing to read Balzac and then introduced to Prosper Mérimée and Alfred de Musset by La Farge, he began translating Musset's play *Lorenzaccio,* to which he added some scenes of his own. He also lovingly translated Mérimée's *La Vénus d'Ille,* "as if it were a classic and old," and sent it to a weekly periodical in New York. Neither acknowledged nor rejected, it simply disappeared. Perceived by Perry to be "constantly writing stories," he imitated Balzac, with partly villanous heroes who were "white lambs by the side of the sophisticated heroines," and "who seemed to have read all Balzac in the cradle and to be positively dripping with lurid crimes." He showed his stories to Perry but not to his family. "They were too keen critics, too sharp-witted," potentially "merciless."[7]

While the two elder sons stayed at home, the two younger were escorted by their parents from one utopian fantasy to another, from Newport isolation to Concord radicalism. His long friendship with Emerson had brought Franklin Sanborn's experimental school to Henry senior's attention. A Harvard graduate, Sanborn, with Emerson's encouragement, had revived the Concord Academy, where Thoreau had taught, as an experiment emphasizing coeducation and social interaction. Louisa May Alcott, Ellery Channing, and Elizabeth Ripley supported and taught at the revived Academy. Three of Emerson's children were students. So too was Hawthorne's son Julian. Frank Sanborn, who actively, vigorously advocated abolition, was, by the late 1850s, more interested in political action and a righteous war than in his school and its educational principles. Six months before Wilky and Bob became his students, he had been arrested, tried, and released from the effort of the Senate to force him to testify about his involvement with Brown's raid on Harpers Ferry. It was widely known that he had been one of its fund-raisers and an active conspirator.

When Henry senior brought his sons to Concord in September 1860, to surrender them to the famous Mr. Sanborn," he did so with the strong sense that "a general conflagration" was inevitable. But, with his usual combination of innocence and imperceptiveness, he at first feared a sexual rather than a military explosion. In principle, he favored coeducation, since it gave to "every one of woman born an equal social recognition." But his conservative beliefs about chastity and marriage caused him some anxiety when, arriving at Concord, he saw the attractive girls with whom his sons would be coeducated. Two were daughters of the recently executed John Brown, one of them "tall, erect, long-haired and freckled. . . . I kissed her (inwardly)," Henry senior confessed, "between the eyes." Julian Hawthorne never forgot that "there were a few distractingly lovely girls" as well as some ordinarily pretty ones, the sight of whom made Henry senior wish that he were young again. His own experience had convinced him that men were born to have and pursue lurid sexual thoughts. No expression of such urges was unnatural. Still, purity was the highest value, and marriage with a pure woman was necessary for salvation, for the opportunity to transcend the urges that the flesh feels for the loving that the soul does.

Strongly responsive to feminine attractions, he both delighted in the excitement of women in the flesh and in the exaltation of women in the spirit. Henry senior's principles quavered when Sanborn took the Jameses into the field behind his house "to show how his girls and boys perform together their worship of Hygeia."[8]

Partly by the accident of age, the two sons who would most have benefited from the social advantages of the Sanborn School were kept at home, and the two who most would have benefited from more vigorous intellectual discipline or direct vocational training were enrolled in a school that provided them with little of the former and none of the latter. In Henry junior's recollections, the Sanborn School was "a frank and high-toned experiment . . . which must have represented [for its students] a free and yet ever so conveniently conditioned taste of the idyllic."[9] For both Wilky and Bob the experiment was to be a brief one. The less than hidden, less than idyllic political agenda of their Sanborn School mentors contributed to the idealistic fervor with which they volunteered to fight in the war that was coming.

At home, seventeen-year-old Henry junior's situation during the fall and winter of 1860–1861 was comfortably uncertain. No demands were being made on him. He sought only to protect himself from his family so that he could continue working at his writing. He did this partly by withdrawal, and also by irony. One evening, when Henry senior and Mary were away, Perry found the "unhappy children" fighting "like cats and dogs . . . Harry . . . trying to obtain solitude in the library, with the rest of the family pounding at the door, and rushing in all the time. . . . I pitied poor Harry, and asked him to come and stay with me." Another visitor remarked that all the boys are "full of intelligence and quickness . . . each one of them having strongly marked individuality . . . & little Alice is a very sweet little girl." But the views from outside reflected the viewers as well as the reality. The woman whom Perry was to marry noticed "the poky banality of the James house ruled by Mrs. James where HJ's father used to limp in and out and never seemed really to 'belong' to his wife or Miss Walsh, large florid stupid seeming ladies, or to his clever but coldly self-absorbed daughter."[10]

On the inside, there was no end of teasing, of domesticated and intelligent aggression, of carefully controlled rivalry and evaluation. Henry junior sometimes joined the sibling rebellion against Henry senior's influence, the muted transformation of resentment into humor. When Henry senior was preparing a new book for publication, William amused everyone "by designing a small cut to be put on the title page, representing a man beating a dead horse." During dinnertime discussions, "it was not unusual for the sons to invoke humorous curses on their parent, one of which was that 'his mashed potatoes might always have lumps in them.' " Henry senior's awareness of the family tensions and rivalries sometimes descended to the level of self-pity. Often, though, it had its own humorous edge that expressed itself in the pithy, graceful style that made some of his theological works more readable than their substance warranted. "I often tell Mary," Henry senior wrote to his brother, "when I come thundering down into the dovecote scattering her and the children's innocent projects of pleasure, perhaps merely because I happen to be indisposed to enjoy myself, that I have no doubt they will all get along much better without me than with me; and I have made the same admission to the juveniles. But they all scoff at the idea: they all seem to think that if I should go, the day of doom would arrive for them. I know vastly better."[11]

Unexpectedly, to Henry senior's delight, in the summer of 1861 William suddenly changed his mind about his vocation and announced that he would not be an artist but a scientist. It was as if he had decided that the ultimate rebellion against his father's wishes and authority resided in totally unexpected conformity with what his father wanted. Henry senior, who believed that "under the fires of science . . . natural religion" would die out and revealed religion "adequately and permanently inaugurated," had all along been urging science. Now it was clear to William that his "vocation was . . . quite positively and before everything for Science, physical Science, strenuous Science."[12] Perhaps, during his months at Hunt's studio, he had become aware of the gap between La Farge's ability and his own. Perhaps he had begun to appreciate the likelihood that he could earn little or no money as an artist, at least for some time, and that he had a better chance at financial independence as a scientist. Money was much on the family mind. Mary James regularly reminded her sons that economy was necessary, that they maintained the comfort of their Newport home and the economic well-being of the family on a small margin. In September 1861, with his father's support, William went up to Cambridge to enroll in Harvard's Lawrence Scientific School, an all-purpose academy for prospective scientists and medical doctors, the only school of higher education he was ever to attend. Perhaps Henry junior was baffled, or at least amused, by his brother's sudden change of direction. More likely than not he was to some extent jealous. He had now an additional discomfort to deal with. Wilky and Bob were at school in Concord. William had something important to do in Cambridge. But he himself, at eighteen years of age, was neither at school nor at work in any visible way. And the war had begun.

(3)

In the soft spring weather of April 1861, Henry junior heard in the distance the firing on Fort Sumter and "Mr. Lincoln's first call for volunteers." His sympathies were with the president and the Union cause. The issue of slavery had transformed the James family from mild supporters of the Democratic party into enthusiastic advocates of Lincoln and the newly formed Republicans. On July 4, Henry senior delivered, at the invitation of the citizens of Newport, a holiday oration in which he proclaimed strong liberal convictions and defended the moral necessity of defeating the "dirty struggles . . . the South . . . is making to give human slavery the sanction of God's appointment."[13] In August, Henry went by boat from Newport to visit the army hospital at Portsmouth Grove, "a vast gathering of invalid and convalescent troops, under canvas and in roughly improvised shanties," perhaps some of the wounded from the Battle of Bull Run. Later, he romanticized the experience, invoking a consanguinity with Whitman's "tender elegiac tone." In the sight of the wounded, the ongoing call for volunteers had to be much on his mind. Without ostensible occupation or specific plans, he had to determine an immediate future in which the question of army service rose to his and other people's minds. He believed in the cause. His health was fine, his physical condition excellent. The previous September he had easily carried sixty-pound suitcases. Friends and acquaintances were volunteering. For many New Englanders, the war sounded with the trumpet of moral necessity and beat with the drum of romantic adventure.

As Lincoln maneuvered, through the spring and summer of 1861, to keep the "wavering border states" in the Union, aggressive abolitionists, including Henry senior, worried that the government had a greater commitment to preserving the Union than to freeing the slaves. From London, Robert Browning wrote to his friend in Rome, the American sculptor William Wetmore Story, that "the *spirit* of all Mr. Lincoln's acts is altogether against slavery in the end; but in apprehension of the result of losing the uncertain States he declared his intention to be quite otherwise." Henry senior saw the issue in his own terms. On the one hand, "you have no idea of the enthusiasm in the North on behalf of the Government." On the other, he did not want either Henry or William to volunteer. "Young boys are running away from college to join the volunteers; affectionate old papas like me are scudding all over the country to apprehend their patriotic offspring, and restore them to the harmless embraces of their mamas." He had had "a firm grasp for these days past upon the coat tails of my Willy & Harry, who both vituperate me beyond measure because I won't let them go. The coats are a very long staunch material, or the tails must have been off two days ago the scamps pull so hard. The Virginia news is reassuring however, and I hope I may sleep to-night without putting their pantaloons under my pillow." He justified his "paternal interference": "First . . . no existing government, nor indeed any now possible government, is worth an honest human life and a clean one like theirs; especially if that government is like ours in danger of bringing back slavery again under our banner: than which consummation I would rather see chaos itself come again. Secondly . . . no young American should put himself in the way of death, until he has realized something of the good of life; until he has found some charming conjugal Elizabeth or other to whisper his devotion to, and assume the task if need be of keeping his memory green."[14]

Like many Northerners, Henry senior hoped, if not expected, that the war would be over in ninety days. Twenty-year-old William at Cambridge had a career to pursue. Wilky and Bob, sixteen and fifteen years old, were confined to the temporarily safe though seditious precincts of the Sanborn School. Only eighteen-year-old Henry junior, his mother's favorite and the "angel" of the house, was especially vulnerable. According to Henry senior, his two elder sons strongly fought against his prohibition. The record is minimal, motivations and struggles unclear. Undoubtedly, Henry and William could have enlisted without their father's permission. As arguments, Henry senior's dissuasions could not have been very persuasive. The reasoning reduced itself to a father's understandable desire that his sons stay out of harm's way. How strenuously Henry and William fought the battle of the home front is unclear. Even if they did pull hard initially, their father's power to restrain them was considerable. The long, strong coattails by which he held them back were ones with which he had provided them, coats that he had fitted them for and purchased over the years of their life together. As usual, Henry looked for substitutions and compensations.

He found a timely one on a windy night in Newport, in late October 1861, six months after the war had begun. Close to eleven o'clock, alarm bells began to clang, indicating a fire at a stable at the corner of Beach and State streets. The strong wind quickly whipped a small blaze into a conflagration. The entire building exploded into flames. Spreading rapidly, the fire engulfed another stable and threatened an adjacent home. Volunteer firemen pulled an engine to the nearby Redwood Reservoir to pump water directly to the fire, but the hoses were not long enough. In the intensity of the blaze, horses screaming and dying, they maneuvered the engine as close to the fire as possible and began to pump water from nearby wells onto the flames. With other volunteers, Henry junior helped work the engine. He was suddenly "jammed into an acute angle between two high fences. . . . The rhythmic play of my arms, in tune with that of several other pairs . . . induced a rural, a rusty, a quasi-extemporised old engine to work and a saving stream to flow." Within these twenty minutes of excited rhythmic pumping, Henry apparently sprained his back.[15]

Three days later, well enough to travel to Boston, he visited William, who had nothing negative to report to the family about Henry's health. For William, Henry's visit had a radiance only slightly dimmed by his brother's inability to fulfill his desire for family gossip, as if he had not been "on speaking terms with anyone for some time past," a reference to Henry's characteristic privateness and quietness. During the next six months, he seems to have performed normally. There is no mention of any curtailment of his usual activities, which included sailing and horseback riding. Probably there were cartons to lift, boxes to transport, when the family moved in June 1862 from Kay Street into a house on Spring Street at the corner of Lee Avenue that Henry senior had purchased "at half its worth," establishing, he boasted, his "financial reputation afresh."[16] The backache, though, did become a presence of sorts during the spring, sufficiently explicit for Henry senior to take his son to Boston for a consultation with a specialist. The complaint apparently had no identifiable organic cause. Later on, he referred to his illness as "an obscure hurt." It was apparently sufficiently obscure to the back specialist, "a great surgeon," for him to make light of it. He found no physical condition to explain what was, for Henry junior, "the less and less bearable affliction." He did not prescribe any of the usual mid-nineteenth-century treatments, which included corsets for support and medicines for pain. He did not prescribe bed rest. Like many backaches, Henry's had no identifiable organic explanation, no muscle rupture or other surgically repairable physical origin. The eminent surgeon, in effect, told the young man to put it out of his mind. The backache would take care of itself. Henry, though, had good reasons for feeling the pain acutely.

His was a useful backache, one that he made good use of in ways that were ultimately healthy. It was a limited, economical response to immediate problems. He had a difficult, elusively oppressive father, whom he loved and from whom he needed to free himself. His father had lost a leg in the flames of a fire, an accident that had transformed Henry senior's life, that had given him both a wound and a spiritual mission. With characteristic efficiency and imagination, Henry junior allowed the fire to be only the secondary cause of his own distinguishing accident, which enabled him both to identify with, and to separate himself from, his father. He, too, had a wound. They were equals, in that sense. As an equal, he could be separate, he could be himself. He had a mother whose loving attention to her angelic Harry could be intensified by his explicit need for additional mothering. At the same time, his condition was an added appeal for forbearance to a mother who worried about the financial situation of the family by a son who at the moment had nothing to contribute, not even the prospect of a vocation. He had an older brother who had finally decided on a vocation, to the delight and satisfaction of both parents, having gone up to the Lowell Institute just two months before the Newport fire. Henry's backache allowed him not to compete with William, not even to feel the pressure of having to perform. If it was "obscure," mysterious, not readily identified in its physical origin, this was hardly a difficulty in a family long used to Henry senior's belief in the invisible world, in the primacy of the emotional and the spiritual.

Having volunteered to put out the Newport fire, he now had reason not to volunteer to fight to put out the fires of sedition. He had done his share, so to speak, to demonstrate both his solidarity with the soldiers and his patriotism. A carefully calibrated injury, one of its effects was to enable him to heighten his consciousness about himself, to create an interesting personal history to substitute for the war experience that apparently he preferred not to engage directly. After the accident, his own activities were not so limited that he could not have served the Union cause more directly, in some active if not battlefield capacity, if he had desired. The backache allowed him to do what he most wanted to do: to spend his time reading and writing, to be "just *literary*."[17]

In the summer of 1862, being "just *literary*" fell short of sufficiency, even if not by much, primarily because there was a civil war in progress. Despite the justification of his backache, he felt awkward, self-conscious, embarrassed. In a world on the move, he felt uncomfortable being stationary. He needed something to do, other than the reading and writing that made no visible impression on anyone. He could better present himself as responsible if he were engaged in some structured activity, the most likely of which, attending college, his father just the year before had adamantly opposed. From Henry's point of view, any school would do. With little sense that his father would consent, he hesitantly asked to be allowed to attend Harvard Law School. To his shock and bewilderment, Henry senior casually said yes, that it "wouldn't be wholly impractical" for him to join William at Cambridge. Why had he emphatically been told no the year before, on grounds that condemned the entire experience, and now yes, without reference to the reasons for the previous denial? Perhaps Henry senior did not notice his inconsistency, or, if he did, had no sense that inconsistency was a vice. Perhaps he distinguished between unnecessary exposure to undergraduate amateurism and the vocational imperatives that law school might attend to. He may have felt that since Henry junior had to do something, law school was the lesser of the available evils, with Harvard having the advantage of William already being in residence. Henry junior accepted the change with tactful reference, much later, to his feeling that "the case might originally have been much better handled."

In September 1862, joining William in his Balzac-like boardinghouse in Cambridge, he enrolled in classes at Dane Hall, his first experience living away from his parents' home, his first venture into modified self-sufficiency. The change represented liberation, and at a small cost. In the same month, Wilky, seventeen years old, having had enough of the Sanborn School, enlisted. It was a natural progression from the Sanborn School to the 44th Massachusetts Regiment. Having been "brought up in the belief that slavery was a monstrous wrong," going to war seemed to Wilky, while at home in Newport during the summer of 1862, "glorious indeed." To his parents, "it seemed a stern duty, a sacrifice worth any cost." In September 1862, his father "accompanied [him] to the recruiting station, witnessed the enrollment, and gave [him], as his willing mite, to the cause he had so much at heart." Unwilling to return to the Sanborn School and eager to join his brother, the underage Bob stayed restlessly at home for the next year. He enlisted in May 1863. Apparently in good health, William pursued his scientific studies. Henry, with occasional complaints about his back, began "the Law School experiment" with the notion that it was an experiment in life, a move forward into wider experience. He soon found himself "a singularly alien member" of an academic society to which he had no intention of making a commitment. It met, though, some of his immediate needs, including his need to think of himself as actively doing something, in romantic and even military terms. He became a metaphoric combatant, "the bristling horde of my Law School comrades fairly produc[ing] the illusion of a mustered army. The Cambridge campus was tented field enough for a conscript starting so compromised."[18]

He also felt himself to be an outsider in Cambridge, a place in which he never felt comfortable. It already belonged to his brother, with whom he would not compete. Clear in his mind that he wanted to be "just *literary*," he felt that, given his special circumstances, this was as comfortable a place for him as any available alternative. At the boardinghouse, he transformed, in his mind, daily exchanges and activities into the detailed observation of a Balzac novel. Attending classes regularly, learning almost nothing of what was being taught, he felt clear in his mind that he was learning something else to a greater degree than he could have if he had been learning it at home in Newport. He did not miss one of the morning lectures at Dane Hall. "On dusky winter afternoons," he attended some of the lectures of James Russell Lowell, the poet and scholar of French and Spanish literature. Longfellow's recent successor as professor of European literature and a central member of the Boston literary world, Lowell was to glow in his memory in the lamplight of "the small, still lecture-room." For him, the lecture hall was a theatre. A member of the observant audience, only once did he find himself, to his great discomfort, a performer. As part of an exercise required of all law students, he had to argue in front of the class one side of a case in a moot court. He quavered and collapsed into silence. It was like the "merciless fall of the curtain on some actor stricken and stammering." He felt his "shame for years much in the image of my having stood forth before an audience with a fiddle and bow and trusted myself to rub these together desperately enough."[19] Just as years before, as a child in New York City, he had suffered before his friends the embarrassment of not being able to perform successfully as a magician's assistant, so, too, he now felt the shame of public failure. Rubbing things together desperately did not seem to produce satisfactory results. Shy, anxious, a moderate stammerer, he increasingly feared public exposure.

(4)

Cannon fire tore into the white officers and black soldiers of the exposed 54th Massachusetts Regiment as it waded through the marshes of Morris Island, South Carolina. As they ascended the slope toward strongly defended Fort Wagner, rifle fire struck them full in the face. A few of those who remained on their feet in the rapid night attack of July 18, 1863, actually reached the crest and rose into dramatically exposed silhouette against the skyline. Completely isolated, the men in front of the fort and on the earthenwork bulwarks were immediately slaughtered or captured. The first to be killed was the commander, Robert Gould Shaw. Reinforcements came so slowly that the attack had already been repulsed before the next wave could move forward. In the unnecessary, disastrous frontal assault, more than fifteen hundred Union soldiers lost their lives. There were almost no Confederate casualties.

Less than two months before, Henry senior had come up from Newport to Boston to watch the proud departure of the 54th, the first well-publicized all-Negro regiment, the pride of the Massachusetts abolitionists. From the front of a friend's house on Park Street, close to where, years later, a monument was to be erected to Shaw and his soldiers, he watched "the march of the 54th out of Boston, its fairest of young commanders at its head, to great reverberations of music, of fluttering banners." The house belonged to the poet and medical doctor Oliver Wendell Holmes, one of William's examiners at the medical school, whose son also had enlisted, though in another regiment. "Dr. Holmes . . . came out of his front door, supporting my dear old father," Wilky later remembered, "who had arrived to say godspeed to his boy."[20] For some unspecified reason, Henry junior "had to be helplessly absent." Probably both William and Henry were in Cambridge, if they had not returned to Newport. William's school year had finished. Henry's school career was over. He had officially withdrawn from Dane Hall. One year of law school had been enough.

Wilky had enlisted in company with his good friend Cabot Russell, and had eagerly transferred to the 54th as soon as it had been formed under the orders of Governor John Andrews. Bob had enlisted that same month in the 45th Massachusetts, an all-white regiment, and soon transferred to the newly formed all-black 55th, which saw heavy service in the Carolinas and in Florida. Bob went "off in good spirits," Henry senior remarked, "and though it cost me a heart-break to part with one so young on a service so hard, I cannot but adore the great Providence which is thus lifting young men out of indolence and vanity, into some free sympathy with His own deathless life." Bob's indolence had been literal—he had restlessly spent the previous year at home until he could credibly lie about his age. Henry senior felt that he had never so "loved the dear boy before, now that he is clad with such an aureole of Divine beauty and innocence."

Close behind Shaw in the charge, serving as one of his adjutants, Garth Wilkinson James had proudly led his men forward under the Massachusetts banner, colors that "had never been surrendered to any foe." A shell suddenly tore into his side. "In the frenzy of excitement it seemed a painless visitation." Exhilarated, determined, he kept advancing with his men to a second barrier. As he was about to cross a ditch, a shell tore into the ball of his right foot. He "stood faltering with the shock," then fell to the ground. Still conscious, he dragged himself backward, away from the danger of capture. Ambulance men fleeing from his own regiment overtook him and paused long enough to raise him to a stretcher and carry him away, at which point he lost consciousness. He awoke at the Union hospital at Port Royal, beside hundreds of other wounded and dying soldiers. Even under friendly care, his chances at Port Royal were poor. The shell fragment remained lodged in his foot. Both wounds became infected.

In late July 1863, the family knew that a battle had taken place, that the assault on Fort Wagner had been murderously unsuccessful, that Wilky had participated. Perhaps he was alive, among the wounded. They had no way of knowing except by going to search for him in the hospital wards in the Carolinas. No family member went. Cabot Russell's father traveled to Port Royal to search for his son. Though he did not find him, he found Wilky, whom he brought on a stretcher by boat back to Newport, merging "the parental ache in the next nearest devotion he could find." En route, emergency surgery had to be performed to remove the shell fragment from his foot. Just inside the door of the James house, the stretcher was set down, the doctors forbidding any further movement. The family watched and waited. William put his small medical skills to service, helping with the nursing, and later drew a sketch of his heavily bandaged, comatose brother. Henry watched, and remembered. Within a month, it became clear that Wilky would live; like his father, he limped for the rest of his life. By late summer, his wounds showed daily improvement, "and if there are no more fragments of bone to come out of his foot, he will probably be up and out of bed in a month or two." Less than a year later, he insisted on returning to his regiment.[21]

From fall 1863 to early spring 1864, Henry junior divided his time between Newport and Cambridge, with at least one visit to New York City. He neither attended school nor had any ostensible employment other than reading and writing. The war went on with muted insistence in the distance. Letters from Wilky and Bob brought home to them vividly the war in the South. Dysentery and sunstroke did not preclude Bob's participation in the Union defeat at Olustee, Florida. He was soon promoted to captain, and then appointed to a staff position because of illness. Drinking heavily, rebellious and self-loathing, he wrote long letters to his father arguing matters of religious faith and moral worth. When he considered leaving the army, Henry senior shamed him out of it. "I conjure you to be a man and force yourself like a man to do your whole duty. . . . It is the crisis of your character." To Henry senior, the army seemed the best place for his two youngest sons, both morally and practically. When they visited home, they were restless and out of place. And, as the war came to an end, the prospects for employment seemed tenuous.[22]

The great national relief was suddenly shocked into pain and tears. On the morning of April 15, 1865, Henry junior's twenty-second birthday, the news "of Lincoln's death by murder" resounded "with a wild cry," rocked "as from a convulsed breast," in the James household. Though he felt ashamed at the unfortunate conjunction between his birthday and that death date, his self-exclusion from the army did not preclude his moral and imaginative identification with the nation and the war. In some ways, it heightened it, raising questions of national identity more forcefully or, at least, more consciously than might have been the case if the matter had been simplified by active service. In his own mind, his Americanness was not in question. What did concern him was the question of what the distinctive qualities of Americanness were. Visiting Wilky at the army training camp at Readville, Massachusetts, he thought "the American soldier in his multitude . . . the most attaching and effecting and withal the most amusing figure of romance conceivable." He extended his own romantic feelings into imagining that he had established, in a visit of three or four hours, tender relationships, listening to the soldiers' troubled tales, offering small gifts of money, anticipating "dear old Walt [Whitman]—even if I hadn't come armed like him with oranges and peppermints." His own innocence extended into a view of Americans as naive, America as a place of moral fervor, if not of moral innocence, of spontaneity, of quick and tender connections. While attending the lectures at Dane Hall, he entertained himself constantly in attempting to determine, in his own mind, the kind and the degree of the Americanness of his professors and classmates. This imaginative attempt "probably more helped to pass the time than all other pursuits together. . . . I was getting furiously American," which meant that he felt increasingly curious about the American world around him as he became increasingly conscious of it, both as a local and a national phenomenon.[23] Such imaginative projections of Americanness attracted him partly because they energized his powers of observation and feeling. They were part of his effort to find a subject matter to write about.

When, in early 1864, the family moved from Newport to Boston, he had the advantage of a larger field of vision. The move was occasioned by Henry senior's decision that Newport's charms were now too limited for his own social and professional needs. Henry senior probably assumed that continued residence in Newport would separate him from his sons. Whatever their vocational activities, they were not likely to be pursued in an out-of-the-way and small city distant from the centers of learning, money, and power. There could not be work for any of his sons in Newport. William probably again urged Cambridge residence for the family. "The society here," he told his mother, "must be pleasanter than elsewhere, not so mercantile," and "the natural beauty of the place as soon as you recede a little from Harvard Square is great."[24] Downtown Boston and the Back Bay initially seemed preferable. Perhaps Henry senior remembered his happy months in Boston as a young man in flight from Union College and his father. There seems to have been no thought of returning to New York. To Henry junior, the move to Ashburton Place suddenly brought him within reach of an intense world of literary and artistic culture, the center of American literary life. Could he be not only a writer in America but an American writer, one who helped to define and expand the possibilities of Americanness and make American literature central to American life? Vaguely formed at first, these questions, over the next half dozen years, became more and more sharply put.

Another death had shaken Henry even more than Lincoln's. Rising from bed late one morning in mid–May 1864, he learned that Nathaniel Hawthorne had died. Half dressed, sitting on the edge of his bed, he began to cry. Recently, during otherwise blank months at Newport, he had "taken in for the first time and at one straight draught the full sweet sense of our one fine romancer's work." Here was an American writer whose works moved him, whose genius was immediately recognizable, whose peculiarities even the more relevant because they seemed to be of the essence of the Americanness James was trying to define. More than anything else, reading Hawthorne's works provided him with a sustained claim that American life could be a substantial subject to write about, for literary genius to exercise itself on, notwithstanding what seemed to him the special evasions inherent in romances of the sort that Hawthorne wrote in comparison to the realistic fictions of his much-admired Balzac. America might, he thought, be too thin, too underpopulated with people and things of depth and interest to make a Balzac possible, though his observations of his own Maison Vaquer had begun to suggest otherwise. But the existence of Hawthorne demonstrated "that an American could be an artist, one of the finest, without going 'outside' about it . . . as if Hawthorne had been one just by being American *enough*."[25] His tears at Hawthorne's death, as he sat on what he later called his "belated bed," expressed the loyalty he felt toward a man he had never met. They also signaled his awareness that he had found a literary father whom he could both love and rebel against. The tears expressed the emotional fullness of his recognition that after Hawthorne came Henry James.

(5)

Having been engaged for some years on his "secret employment," nothing of which he allowed to survive, he began to feel, in the middle years of the Civil War, confident enough to make his work public. Still quite gun-shy with his family, he showed some of what he wrote to Tom Perry. He first began hesitantly seeking a larger audience during his happy days of perfunctory attendance at law school. With access to the undergraduate library, he borrowed and read armfuls of novels, "one of the elemental cravings of mankind. We take to it as to our mother's milk."[26] While a law student, he had a room of his own in a boardinghouse in Winthrop Square, with a small nook from whose windows he could see distant low hills. There he sat, book or pen in hand, holding to his nose, even during the cold winter, "the scented flower of independence." From Winthrop Square, he regularly went to Boston to enjoy the cultural and culinary atmosphere of the Parker Hotel and particularly to indulge his "uncanny appetite for the theatre." Fascinated by a veteran actress named Maggie Mitchell performing at the Howard Athenaeum, he wrote her an appreciative letter, with echoes of Thackeray's Pendennis in love with Miss Fotheringay. She responded with a signed copy of the play. Immediately writing an essay extolling what her artistry meant to him, he sent it to a periodical, enrolling himself "in the bright band of the fondly hoping and fearfully doubting who count the days after the despatch of manuscripts." It neither appeared in print nor survives in manuscript.

The next year, his luck and his courage were considerably better. He had written, late in 1863, a brief story, "A Tragedy of Error," which he mailed to a little-known New York magazine, the *Continental Monthly.* Though American literary journalism was at the verge of major expansion, his choices were as yet limited. There existed neither the equivalent of the French *Revue des Deux Mondes* or the English *Cornhill Magazine,* to both of which the James family subscribed. The latter, edited by Thackeray until his death in 1863, epitomized a literary culture thick with magazine publication possibilities. Restricted mostly to Boston and New York, the American literary world offered few outlets for serious short fiction. The distinguished but somewhat tired *North American Review,* founded in 1815, had had a series of well-known Bostonian editors. The *Atlantic Monthly,* founded in 1857, edited by the poet Oliver Wendell Holmes, had recently been purchased by the Boston publisher Ticknor & Fields. In New York, *Harper's Monthly*

Magazine and *Harper's Weekly* published fiction mainly imported from England, the great names of the English high Victorian novel. Though Henry junior had available tactful introductions to both Boston journals, he made his debut as a writer of fiction in a less well known New York magazine, probably because he had accurately assessed the difficulties of the marketplace and the value of his work. The *Continental Monthly* quietly accepted "A Tragedy of Error." Suddenly, in February 1864, he was a published author.

As the first surviving fiction of the almost twenty-three-year-old writer, the existence of which he never acknowledged after its first anonymous publication, "A Tragedy of Error" is interestingly revealing, even anticipatory. Despite his fascination with Americanness, the story is set in a French seaport, partly influenced in setting and plot by Balzac and George Sand. The European conditions provide the safeguard of distancing. The melodramatic plot, in which a married woman and her lover conspire to murder her crippled husband, provides the opportunity for irony and sensationalism, combining the realistic and the romance traditions. The writing is spare, external, noticeably competent, narrated by a third-person storyteller standing outside both his characters and the plot's sensationalism. The most vigorous character is the impoverished, working-class, hired murderer, who kills the married woman's lover by the cliché of a mistake for which no one is at fault. This little twist of an amoral fate demonstrates that the best-laid plans go awry because dissonance is part of the nature of things. The unhappy wife awaits the return of her lover only to see her long-absent husband "limping toward her with outstretched arms," his loathesomeness embodied in his disability. Whatever voices the young writer listened to in creating the story, the biographically alert reader cannot help but imagine that the limping cripple suggests Henry junior's response to his father. Despite efforts at symbolic murder, it was as if the nightmare figure in the Gallery of Apollo had not yet been fully routed, as if the young man, in the substitution of a fictional wife willing to murder her despised husband, still cannot free himself from the possessive cripple.

In his memory, the period from "the spring of '64 to the autumn of '66 moves as through an apartment hung with garlands and lights." The garlands were the first rewards of his years of "secret experiments," his sudden discovery that he had an audience for both his fiction and his book reviews. He was exhilarated knowing that he need not be anonymous and that he might be paid for his work. He began now to find reason to believe that "fortune had in store some response to [his] deeply reserved but quite unabashed design to becoming as 'literary' as might be." For fiction, he needed subject matter. Immediately after the acceptance of "A Tragedy of Error," he began to write some stories (he called them tales) that drew on the late Civil War and the early post–Civil War environment.[27] For reviews, the subject matter was at hand. His avid reading and his eagerness to express his attitudes and judgments resulted in brief articles for the magazines that would have him. Between 1864 and 1866, he published six of his stories and twenty-nine reviews.

During much of the first half of 1864, he eagerly wrote short stories, excited by the possibility of publication, nervous at the likelihood of rejection by the premier journals. To protect himself, in late March he arranged that the response of "the *Atlantic* people" to the story he was about to send them would go to Perry rather than to himself. He could not "again stand the pressure of avowed authorship (for the present) and their answers could not come here unobserved."[28] Rejection slips that came through the Ashburton Place mail transom carried the danger of a public, or at least a family, spectacle, an opportunity for discussion and teasing, especially by William. But he was also happy, and he joked to Perry about being in literary heaven, writing "with a pen snatched from my angel-wing. It is very pleasant up here but rather lonely, the only other inhabitants being Shakespeare, Goethe, and Charles Lamb. There are no women. Thackeray was up for a few days but was turned out for calling me a snob because I walked arm-in-arm with Shakespeare." Having worked hard on some revisions, eager to meet a self-imposed deadline, he felt that, "on the whole, it is a failure . . . tho' nobody will know this, perhaps, but myself. Do not expect anything; it is a simple story, simply told." When he received a rejection slip, he humorously fantasied that the editors of the *Atlantic* would one day be down on their knees begging him for contributions.

Slightly bewildered, mostly happy, in October 1864 he sat in his room in Ashburton Place holding in his hand twelve dollar bills, the first money he had ever earned as a writer. It had come to him with "fabulous felicity." Earlier in the year, on a bright winter morning, he had hesitantly visited Charles Eliot Norton at his large Shady Hill estate in Cambridge, fifty acres of woodland within a short walk of the college. Probably Norton first knew the Jameses from Newport, where his family kept a luxuriously hospitable summer home. A successful businessman, the son of a famous Harvard biblical scholar, sixteen years older than his visitor, Norton was deeply interested in literature and art. Short, dark-haired, delicate-looking, Norton had both earned and inherited money. He had also a strong social conscience, a rigorous classical training, a dry New England courtliness, a gift for friendship and hospitality, and strong moral principles. The consummate intellec-

tual New Englander of wealth, training, energy, and ambition, he sat
at the center of a small but all-encompassing social and intellectual
world. As a young man, he had traveled to India and Europe. In
England, he initiated friendships with some of the outstanding literary
and cultural figures, and was soon an intimate friend of Carlyle and
Ruskin. Italy, particularly Italian art and Dante, fascinated him. In 1863,
with James Russell Lowell, he had "undertaken . . . the editorship" of
the *North American Review,* under a "tolerably liberal" arrangement
with the publisher, in the hope that they could "put some life into the
old dry bones of the Quarterly." In the library at Shady Hill, "the
winter sunlight [touching] serene bookshelves and arrayed pictures,"
he sat, gracious, interested, and friendly, with the young man whom
he knew as Harry.[29] Since Henry junior was interested in fiction, Norton would be happy to have him review a recent volume of *Essays on
Fiction* by a well-known British economist.

Delighted at the opportunity, James wrote his brief review during
the early summer. He sent it, anxiously, to Norton at the end of July,
and soon found himself for the second time in print, now in the prestigious pages of the October 1864 issue of the *North American Review.*
Norton and Lowell apparently liked the review, despite its being almost
unrelievedly negative, perhaps because it went beyond the author's
banal remarks into intelligent general comment on fiction, stressing
that "just as the habitually busy man is the best novel reader," for "busy
people come fresh to their idleness," so the best novelist is the busiest
man. The anonymous reviewer spoke of himself in an assured and
determined voice: "It is because I create [my characters] by the sweat
of my brow that I venture to look them in the face. My *work* is my
salvation." Eager to earn money, to have reason to come out of the
closet of anonymity, to have acceptance letters come to him directly at
Ashburton Place, he proposed to Norton in August that he do another
review. Before the next year was out he had published, in the *North
American Review,* reviews of a novel by Trollope, a new edition of
Carlyle's translation of Goethe's *Wilhelm Meister's Apprenticeship,* and a
volume of Matthew Arnold's *Essays in Criticism,* and of three popular
female novelists of the sort he vividly remembered his grandmother
reading, including Louisa May Alcott's first novel, *Moods.*

A sustained start, it was immediately intensified by an additional
opportunity, also partly due to Norton's support. He began a long,
happy relationship with a newly formed weekly magazine based in
New York City, *The Nation.* In spring 1865, Henry junior met Edwin
Lawrence Godkin, who had come to Boston from New York to raise
money and commission contributions for his new journal. Twelve years

older than the young writer, the Irish-born Godkin had considerable experience as an editor and journalist in England, had traveled widely, and now practiced law in New York. He had in mind to create a magazine that would strongly advocate the post–Civil War political and social views of the liberal Northeast. An expert on military affairs, he had been a reporter in the Crimean War, had published a book about Hungary, and had written extensively about the South. More than a journalist and less than an artist, Godkin was a man of energy, talent, and vision, with an intense commitment to the transformation of America into a pluralistic society based on democratic principles. Norton quickly agreed to be one of his silent financial partners. For the first issue, Godkin asked both Henry senior and Henry junior to write reviews, beginning for the young man "one of the longest and happiest friendships of my life."[30]

Since *The Nation,* a weekly, published many more reviews than the monthly *North American Review,* Henry James, Jr., now had a reliable outlet for as much reviewing as he wanted to do. His income from the two magazines was soon almost enough to make him independent of his father for everything but room and board. Godkin's "admirably aggressive and ironic editorial humour," whose liberal views the young man shared, entertained James. He himself was to entertain the readers of *The Nation* to the number of more than two hundred brief articles during a twenty-year period while still publishing the occasional long review in the *North American Review.*[31] Beginning in July 1865, *The Nation* published nine of his reviews that year, in 1866 twelve, in 1867 ten, in 1868 sixteen. On the one hand, the sheer volume threatened to make it hackwork. On the other, occasional brilliance, a self-assurance that barely seemed immodest, an impression of authority based on wide reading even beyond what a well-read twenty-three-year-old could have mastered, and an evenness of temperament that frequently rose to the level of graciousness made many of his reviews literary criticism of a high quality. He reviewed mostly modern French literature and modern British and American fiction, though he also reviewed books as disparate as Francis Parkman's history of the Jesuits in North America, a volume of essays on Hippolyte Taine's travels to Rome and Naples, to which, he confessed, "we are unable to follow him," and a book on contemporary French painters. He worked within a tradition of general reviewing in which special expertise was less important than literary taste and intelligence.

Not everyone, of course, agreed with his taste. He himself later revised some of his youthful judgments, particularly of Walt Whitman, whose *Drum-Taps* he reviewed in 1865. "An essentially prosaic mind,"

Whitman seemed to him to labor to lift himself "by a prolonged muscular strain, into poetry." With no possibility of anticipating what would later be the irony of such criticism, he faults him for "an anomalous style" (a writer "must have something very original to say if none of the old vehicles will carry his thoughts") and for his lack of respect for the literary taste and judgment of the "democratic, liberty-loving, American populace. . . . This stern and war-tried people . . . is devoted to refinement." Later, Whitman was to become one of his favorite poets. He was to pretend that this early review never existed. Reviewing Dickens' *Our Mutual Friend,* he eagerly separated himself from the novelist whose power had gripped him in his early reading and playgoing, elevating everything of Dickens' through *David Copperfield,* and condemning everything thereafter as forced and labored. Reviewing Louisa May Alcott's *Moods,* he proclaims that he is "utterly weary of stories about precocious little girls," a subject with which he later became fascinated. But it was not the subject but the "author's ignorance of human nature, and her self-confidence in spite of this ignorance," that appalled him. Feeling, sentiment, the female imagination, the strong attraction of the novel as a literary form expressive of a culture and a readership associated with women, was realized at its best in the novels of George Sand. If her one topic is love, at least "the writer who has amply illustrated the passion of love has, by implication, thrown a great deal of light on the rest of our nature." What was clear to him was that feeling had to be balanced in fiction with careful, realistic observation of human nature. George Eliot epitomized the application of the philosophic mind to the writing of fiction. Balzac the novelist, in comparison to Sand the "romancer," provided the supreme example of the necessary dedication of the novel to realistic observation of morals and manners, of the individual and of social life.

Suddenly, he had an occupation as a literary journalist, not so much a career as an honorable, profitable participation in the world of letters completely compatible with his ambitions as a writer of stories. His own duty as a literary critic, he believed, was to be opposed to his author while at the same time maintaining a sympathetic objectivity and subordination. Literary criticism was a high calling. To comment on literature was to comment on life, even to the extent of revealing the skepticism about Providence inherent in his comment that "what strikes an attentive student of the past is the indifference of events to man's moral worth or worthlessness."[32] To evaluate literature was to pursue moral and artistic discriminations that for him were essential concomitants to creating literature of one's own. From the beginning, he took the risk of expressing himself in public about literature and life, about his artistic and moral principles. It was one way to help earn his way as a writer, and the adventure of forming opinion and shaping taste appealed to him. His was a startlingly secure voice. Despite disclaimers, modesty, and general gentleness, he seemed rarely uncertain of its positions. Part of the drama of self-revelation and self-formation inherent in thinking aloud was to pretend that no thinking aloud was being done, that nothing was in process, that the reviews were the expression of a wise, authoritative voice that had reason to feel strongly in public and to feel certain that its basic principles were undeniably sound. The early reviews are bravura performances, examples of genius skating, often gracefully, sometimes brilliantly, on thin ice without ever falling through.

Just as the war ended, James produced a short story that reflects the special sensibility of the nonparticipant who finds his drama in the "unwritten history" of personality and the life of the feelings. A sharply ironic story that uses the Civil War for its situational background, "The Story of a Year" explores Henry's fascination with the tensions of betrayal, adultery, woundedness, and the feminine consciousness. In the tale, set in an unspecified New England location, an attractive but superficial young woman engages herself to a handsome young lieutenant, whose mother warns him about the character of his fiancée. A strong, practical, intensely possessive woman, "Mrs. Ford, who had been an excellent mother, would have liked to give her son a wife fashioned on her own model." When the news comes that Jack Ford has been seriously wounded, his fiancée, Elizabeth, is easily persuaded by Mrs. Ford that the mother will be more useful than she in finding her son, nursing him, and bringing him back. "Like most weak persons, she was glad to step out of the current of life, now that it had begun to quicken into action." While the mother is away in search of her son and then caring for him, Lizzie returns to the pleasures of social life. She falls in love with Robert Bruce, a sincere, aggressive, successful businessman who desires to marry her. Caught between her moral commitment to the severely wounded Ford and her love for Bruce, Lizzie dreams that she is burying her fiancée. Arriving home, he is carried to the door on a stretcher, accompanied by his mother. Lizzie feels conscience-stricken and angry at Mrs. Ford, whom she has grown to hate, a "long-faced nemesis in black silk." Fatally wounded, Ford releases her from her commitment, and dies. Robert Bruce comes to the Ford home and finds Lizzie outside. When she says that she will give him her hand only in farewell, that she means to be faithful to her old love, he is shocked and pained. As he attempts to come after her, she shrieks at him, "I forbid you to follow me." The narrator concludes, "but for all that, he went in."

What James T. Fields, the owner and editor of the *Atlantic* and the owner of the Boston publishing house Ticknor & Fields, made of young Henry's story is unclear, other than that he agreed to publish it. Perhaps he did not feel quite so fully his complaint of the next years that Henry junior's penchant for ending stories unhappily "had an odd, had even a ridiculous, air on the part of an author with his mother's milk scarce yet dry on his lips." A friend of Henry senior's, Fields was the premier literary entrepreneur of New England, married to a petite, attractive younger woman whose preciousness was balanced by her "sweetness of temper and lightness of tact." Committed to native American as well as English literature, Fields made a major contribution to forging a marketplace for American writers, combining shrewd business sense with tact and culture. With his wife Annie, he collected rare books and art, creating a salon in their Charles Street home that seemed both a museum and a rarefied social and literary emporium. The friend and publisher of Hawthorne and Emerson, the neighbor and intimate companion of Lowell and Holmes, all of whom provided literary energy and cultural seriousness to the politically engaged *Atlantic,* Fields and his wife hosted, in their long, bright, overlooking the river living room, every major British as well as every American writer who came to Boston or lived there already.[33]

What the James family made of Henry's story is also unclear. Its autobiographical resonances probably flickered fully enough in their consciousnesses to allow them to see that he had drawn on shared family experiences. He published two more stories with Civil War settings, both in the *Atlantic,* "Poor Richard," his longest, most sustained story so far, and "A Most Extraordinary Case," both tales of rivalry, thwarted love, battle wounds, and illnesses. Frustrated, self-tormented young men are prevented by disability or by illness from competing for love and glory. In February 1866, he published his second *Atlantic* story, "A Landscape Painter," the first of his many tales about artists. With the cooperation of *The Galaxy,* a new literary monthly based in New York, he contributed to its premier, in June 1866, "A Day of Days," one of the best of these early stories. All of them combined romance and realism, and all of them had some of the flavor of what James himself good-humoredly thought of as hackwork, although some had touches of power, even genius. He tried his hand at another story about an artist, "The Story of a Masterpiece," anticipating a theme he was to develop more effectively in later stories, the artist whose portrait of a woman reveals the woman's character and helps determine the fate of relationships. In the sharply dramatic "The Romance of Certain Old Clothes," he both adapted and transformed Hawthorne into a family romance focusing on an incestuous triangle and into an eerie ghost story. Harriet Beecher Stowe told Mary James that "Harry's short story . . . kept her awake at night. It is capitally done."[34] The story, in which the suppressed rivalry between two men is translated into rivalry between sisters, dramatizes the puritan's revenge against materialism and eroticism. This was a theme that James was to pursue for his entire career. The best of these stories anticipated in theme, tone, psychology, and character artistically more successful fictions that he was to write in the future. For now, these stories, along with reviews, sustained him emotionally and financially. They were his entrée into the cultural and social life of literature.

(6)

Among "the lights" of these happy years immediately after the war were a cousin, Minny Temple, whom he had begun to know better soon after the family's return to Newport in 1860, and a young writer from Ohio, William Dean Howells, who had returned recently from Venice, where he had served as American consul throughout the war years, a post earned by writing, in 1860, a laudatory campaign biography of Lincoln. An aspiring poet of mediocre talents and a gifted prose writer, Howells made good use of his European years. Howells married his Vermont-born sweetheart in 1862, and the couple had their first child in 1864, in Venice, where Howells busied himself writing poetry and travel sketches, observing Venetian life, and learning Italian. He was always eager, though, to return to America, to one of "the great literary centres." "Few men live by making books," he told his father, a caustic, poor, idealistic Ohio journalist of Welsh background, in whose shop his son had begun setting type at the age of nine, "and I must look to some position as editor to assist me in my career." In 1860, he had briefly visited Boston, been introduced to the major literary figures, and been honored by having four of his poems published in the *Atlantic*. Fields, looking beyond Boston to a national literature, to the invigoration of eastern culture with western energy and temperament, remembered Howells warmly. After a few months as assistant editor to Godkin at *The Nation*, Howells happily succumbed to Fields's urging that he come to Boston, where Fields promised him "a not unpleasant life hereabouts" as the assistant editor of the *Atlantic*.[35] Assuming his new duties at the beginning of March 1866, at a salary of fifty dollars a week and with the promise that he could presume succession, he had immediate access to the world of Boston literary society. He met James during the summer of 1866, soon after the latter had moved with his family to Cambridge.

When, in spring 1866, the lease for their Ashburton Place house proved unrenewable, the Jameses looked for another furnished Boston house that they could afford. When nothing turned up, except one at a twenty-five-hundred-dollar-a-year rent and a two-year lease, they took a comfortable year-round house, "as comfortable as a city house," for six months at a thousand dollars, in Swampscott, a nearby summer-resort town, "forty minutes by train northward from Boston." Henry spent most of an extended summer there writing reviews and stories. In the fall, the family found a house at 20 Quincy Street, Cambridge, a residential street adjacent to the Harvard campus, "a good, square house of simple proportions," though only "sparsely furnished," with "the best fence in Cambridge for children to walk on," available on a two-year lease at a rent of two thousand dollars. Henry senior and Mary were to spend the rest of their days there. At first hesitant about "drowning" themselves in Cambridge, they quickly felt at home. They were pleased at "the happy fashion in which the University Circle" and the extended Cambridge society "consciously accepted them," and Henry senior found that the horsecars made Boston readily accessible. "We are getting shaken down in our new house," Henry senior remarked in October, "and like it very much." Soon "all the world" had called upon them and treated them "very cordially." By the next summer, they were well settled. The house and the four servants provided them, Mary James told Bob, "with an amount of material comfort which seldom falls to the lot of sinful mortals."[36]

To Henry junior, Cambridge seemed provincial and starchy, too far from the theatres and Boston cultural activities. Soon he made acquaintances and some friends in Cambridge, especially Howells. Seven years older than James, Howells wrote in the summer of 1866 of how "struck" he was with James's work. They breakfasted together. By the end of 1866, they were good friends. "Young Henry James and I had a famous [talk] last evening," Howells told his father, "two or three hours long, in which we settled the true principles of literary art." Though Howells was not to begin to write fiction for some years, he shared James's belief that "the true principles" of fiction are realistic and psychological. He was clear about James's talent. "He is a very earnest fellow, and I think extremely gifted—gifted enough to do better than any one has yet done toward making us a real American novel."

As a minor power in American literature, who soon became a major one simply by virtue of his position at the *Atlantic,* Howells felt he could help advance his friend's career and promote the literary values they shared. The *Atlantic* already held in reserve "Poor Richard," "a slight romance from my facile pen," James called it, whose publication delay until the next summer, probably because of its length, did not seem to trouble him. At the beginning of 1867, James gave Howells his latest story, "My Friend Bingham," which Howells successfully urged Fields to find room for in the March number.[37] Suddenly he had greater access than ever before to the well-paying *Atlantic.* He had a personal friend, a warm admirer, and an ideological compatriot in an office of power.

Howells soon realized, as James had already, that substantial obstacles to literary success existed for writers who defined their art in high terms that deviated from literary tradition and from the taste of the expanding audience of post–Civil War America, which even the high-brow *Atlantic* had in its focus. When James commented in his review "The Novels of George Eliot" that "the writer makes the reader very much as he makes his characters," he might have had in mind his own challenge. Hostile reviews of "Poor Richard" did not shake Howells' faith in James, though they momentarily shook his faith in his own judgment of the public. He still did not "doubt that James has every element of success in fiction. But I suspect that he must in a very great degree create his audience. In the meantime I rather despise existing readers."[38] For Howells, who was to earn a substantial part of his living as an editor, the lesson anticipated a lifelong struggle. For James, who for some time earned much of his living writing for magazines, the lesson *became* a lifelong struggle to shape an audience large enough to pay him sufficiently to support himself as a writer.

Always welcome at the James house, Howells had the special consanguinity with Henry senior of his own father being an avid Swedenborgian, and he himself a moderate one. One evening, when Henry was not at home, he joined Alice and her parents on the porch of the Quincy Street house. "He sat talking a little while when father," Alice wrote, "asked how a certain Mr. Nichols looked. Mr. H. who was sitting all doubled up in a deep armed-chair looking smaller, if possible, than ever, said 'he is about my size, with white beard, black eyes, etc.' when mother ups and says in her inimitable way, 'Ah, then he is a *small* man.' Mr. Howells for about five minutes was quite invisible, in fact mother was for some time the only person in existence; by degrees we one by one recovered ourselves."[39]

From the start, with Howells taking the lead, there had been a bargain struck between the two young writers, a fraternal commitment to encourage and support one another. It was a bargain not of opportunity but of sympathy, whose natural extension into professional supportiveness need not, and probably could not, be separated from the personal affection that raised friendship to the level of absolute loyalty. In taking the initiative, Howells was less shy than James, more businesslike. The elder of the two, he expressed a respect and admiration for the young writer's work that remained steadfast in its appreciation of the value of the totality of his career even when, later, he clearly preferred what James had written as a younger than what he wrote as an older man. As an editor, Howells had the greater opportunity to be of practical help. From the beginning, James had reservations about Howells' work, and when Howells became a successful novelist James distinguished privately between what he thought good and what he thought weak. Still, he had no difficulty stretching his private judgment on the bed of almost unremitting public praise.

Neither of them had any qualms about reviewing the other's work. When Howells published his *Italian Journeys,* James praised it effusively in the *North American Review.* He singled out virtues that were more truly his own, even comparing Howells positively to Hawthorne. In lauding Howells, he uses for the first time the sobriquet "sentimental traveller" that he later regularly applied to himself. The sentimental traveler "takes things as he finds them and as history has made them; he presses them into the service of no theory . . . he takes them as a man of the world . . . a gentle moralist . . . the man of real literary power and the delicate artist . . . with new memories mingling, for our common delight, with the old memories." Howells' commonplace poems he found "all really classic work." Always a gentle critic of those he knew personally, his reviews of Howells' books combined fraternal love with what must have seemed to both men the highest, most justifiable kind of self-interest. They both needed to earn a living, to make their way in the world. They shared an agenda: to create a body of prose fiction whose values were realistic and psychological, to bring into existence a distinctive American novel. James's work eventually rose to levels that Howells' hardly approached. To his credit, Howells recognized this without a sign of false modesty or envy. As back scratching, it was at a high level. As friendship, it was superb.

So, too, was another friendship, though more diffident, more dangerous. Minny Temple seemed a brilliant presence to her slightly older cousin. Strongly attracted to her, he found her the most distinctive, the most substantial, the most vivid young woman he knew. In a world in which women were predictably conditioned into narrow roles, Minny had managed by sheer force of personality to be exceptional. She had information, opinions, and personal force, a vivacious and intelligent personality. To some she seemed opinionated, selfish, egomaniacal, and certainly unfeminine. To young men, she was mostly outspoken, not hesitating to tell one that he was "the most affected creature" she had ever seen. She had political opinions and expressed them strongly. "Highly disgusted" with Lincoln's efforts to keep the border states in the Union, she had criticized him as "very very weak and I don't like at all the way he looks at slavery."[40] To others, she seemed strongly feminine, with a spontaneity and imagination that pushed beyond the normally accepted boundaries into the indecorous, even the prohibited. To Henry, she was exciting, she was dramatic, she had direct erotic appeal in attractive contrast to his own indirection, to his strategies of substitution and compensation, to his way of dealing with the opposition. Minny attacked life. If she was reckless, it was a recklessness that excited him.

He spent every summer that he could in Newport. It was still his emotional home, partly because Minny was there. He found Newport "insistently romantic, romantic out of all proportion," the summers mellow, long, infinitely extended, even during the war years and the depression that immediately followed. On the Newport streets, there were no wounded or crippled soldiers to be seen. "It is scarcely possible to think we have just finished a long and terrible war. Nobody thinks about it, nobody talks about it." Newport is "all shingle and clapboard," the major entertainment driving up and down the main avenue or swimming or, on Saturday nights, dancing at the Ocean House.[41] Henry junior participated in the Newport social life of happy, privileged young people, despite being fully aware, as one of his sad, stern-faced hostesses, the elder Mary Temple, constantly reminded him, that "Rome was burning."

A young lawyer, John Chipman Gray, and an aspiring lawyer and student at Harvard Law School, Oliver Wendell Holmes, Jr., were part of the social circle. As soldiers, both had seen Rome burning. In the summer of 1865, with Minny Temple as their focus, Henry joined them in the White Mountains of New Hampshire where he and Holmes probably shared the one room in the crowded resort that Minny had been able to locate for them. Henry traveled up from Newport, where he had been "living a delicious life, far away from men women and newspapers, with a sky and sea of cobalt," writing in the mornings, loafing in the afternoons, taking long walks, talking endlessly about literature and art with La Farge, keeping an eye of occasional concern on his troublesome back. On one hot night, after days of blue seas,

yellow sands, and lustrous sunsets, he sat at the base of the porch steps
of the home of friends, hearing "the murmur of stirred shrubberies, the
waft, from wide, glowing windows, of dance-music and song . . . the
general presence, above all, of clustered gossiping groups on wide
verandahs, where laughter was clear and the 'note' of white dresses,
waistcoats, trousers, cool." In New Hampshire, the Temple drama
proceeded. Both Holmes and Gray, who seems to have fallen in love
with Minny, flirted and preened. Gray continued to please her. With
Holmes, she soon became "disenchanted," and Mary James, who disliked the tall, thin, arrogantly handsome war veteran and ambitious
lawyer, gladly reported to Alice that Mary Temple now sees him "with
very different eyes from what she did . . . as others do. . . . She talks
of his thinness and ugliness and pinchedness, as well as his beautiful
eyes—and seems to see his egotism."[42]

During Minny's many visits to Cambridge, she stayed with the
Jameses. Henry senior enjoyed the company of the pretty girl. Alice
disliked having a rival for the attention of the men of the household.
"She is not nearly as interesting as she used to be," Alice reported to
William. "She is so much influenced by the last person she has been
with and taken a fancy to that one never knows where to find her."
Still, she looked "very pretty and her manner is certainly fascinating."
Mrs. James celebrated her visits with dinners and parties for the young
people. Wilky's friend Major Gray was "decidely the rage." Clover
Hooper and her sister Ellen came by.[43] In 1867, to the maternal Mary
James, Minny looked "very thin and not so pretty," perhaps an early
sign of ill health. Minny's social world included a new friend and
admirer, Elizabeth Boott, "delightful, devoted and infinitely under"
Minny's charm, a small, plain-looking, talented young woman who
sang beautifully and who had aspirations to be a painter. Three years
younger than Henry, she had moved in her infancy with her wealthy
widowed father, Francis, an accomplished amateur musician and com-
poser, to Florence. They had recently returned to America after almost
two decades of absence. To Elizabeth Boott, Newport and America
seemed exotic, which disconcerted Henry junior. He insisted on maintaining the Bootts as characters in his own European fantasy, the Americans who had been permanently, irretrievably Europeanized.

With all his women friends, but especially with Minny, his strategy
of attachment was a characteristic one of sweetness, loyalty, sympathy,
and identification. "How could I help talking about you," Minny wrote
to a friend, "to any one so *dear* as Harry," who had traveled from
Cambridge to Newport in the early spring of 1863 expressly to see her.
"Harry is as *lovely* as ever, verily the *goodness* of that boy passeth human

comprehension."[44] Being good was his way of being loved. If it lacked the ready potential for making him Minny Temple's lover, *that* apparently was less important to him than being loved in every other way. Without any evident sense that women were not for him, he made use of strategies of friendship that readily sacrificed the sexual for the emotionally intimate. Minny's emotional aggressiveness made his own shyness effective, a passive forcefulness even. It was something that, combined with his sweetness of temperament, Minny and others saw as goodness. He embodied Mary James's receptivity, her permeating presence. He was at once his mother's "angel" and the angel of the house.

In his relationship with Minny, he initially felt some confusion of feeling, some aspiration for the more traditional male role. Henry senior preached to his sons that "the gratification of the sexual appetite in you cannot be in anywise contrary to [God's] will." They should, though, "avoid all impure intercourse with the other sex." Eventually, he told Bob what he undoubtedly told his other sons—that you will "find someone responsive to your spirit, who will give herself in chaste marriage to you, and your life will take a new start." The conflicted message conveyed the acceptance of a powerful sexuality with the mandate of chastity. There was a heavy burden placed on the feminine ideal, the elevation of the woman into man's moral, emotional, and spiritual salvation. Of the three sons who married, the two younger made difficult, unhappy marriages. William's road to marriage was a long, precarious one, and Minny, attracted to him, felt that William, "the same strange youth as ever, stranger if possible . . . has rather *renounced* me, in the depths of his heart, as a *bad* thing."[45] If she were *bad* in William's eyes, it was because she was impure, though not in the physical sense. Sexual activity was not at issue. Relationship to the feminine ideal and to Victorian propriety was the issue. Like Henry senior, William wanted an angelic Victorian wife. Eventually discovering that he wanted no wife at all, Henry junior was attracted to Minny precisely because he was already angelic and Victorian enough for both of them, and found Minny's witty, aggressive, unpredictable femininity exciting.

Nevertheless, Henry junior shared his father's conservative view of the role and nature of women. When, in 1868, he reviewed a series of essays condemning modern women for their materialism, he criticized the essays for their failure to understand the economic and social reasons for the marriage market. "It is a very dismal truth that the only hope of most women, at the present moment, for a life worth the living, lies in marriage, and marriage with rich men or men likely to become so, and that in their unhappy weakness they often betray an ungraceful anxiety on this point. But to our minds there is nothing comical in the situation, and as a field for satirical novelists it has ceased to be actively worked." With anticipations of Millicent Henning in *The Princess Casamassima,* he identifies the criticism of women as class-based. "The real ground of complaint is the insolence and splendor of women of small means." Still, "it is impossible to discuss and condemn the follies of 'modern women' apart from those of modern men. They are all part and parcel of the follies of modern civilization, which is working itself out through innumerable blunders. Their extravagance is a part of their increased freedom, and their increased freedom a part of the growth of society. . . . We are all of us extravagant, superficial, and luxurious together. . . . Women share in the fault not as women, but as simple human beings. As women, they strike us as still remarkably patient, submissive, sympathetic . . . well-disposed to model themselves on the judgment and wishes of men. They reflect with great clearness the state of the heart and imagination of men. . . . If there is any truth in the volume before us, [men] have a vast deal to answer for."[46] Minny had the wonderful attraction of not having to be answered for. Not in the least materialistic, disdainful of the marriage market, she departed from Henry senior's ideal only in her energy, her independence, her imaginative freedom. For Henry junior, these qualities made her ideal.

Four

"AN ABSOLUTE REMEDY"

1867–1870

(I)

Coming into the bright candle-lit rooms at Shady Hill in late November 1867, suddenly he saw "the master." Annie and James Fields had taken Dickens out to Cambridge for a dinner at the home of the Nortons. There he was, "erect and concrete before us . . . as in a sublimity of mastership," the one author whom it "had been laid upon young persons of our generation to feel . . . down to the souls of our shoes." Twenty-four-year-old Henry James, Jr., "trembled . . . in every limb." The meeting took but a moment. Having vainly tried the previous week to get a ticket to one of Dickens' oversubscribed readings, he was also not a guest at the dinner proper. He had been asked, as a sign of Norton's affection, to drop by afterward for the precious introduction. Henry senior, who was among the elect, found Dickens "unaffectedly genial . . . simple and unpretending."[1] To Henry junior, the meeting was almost a moment of epiphany, what he later recalled as a confrontation with his own future.

Weary, harboring his energy, prematurely old, "on the outer edge of his once magnificent margin," Dickens limited the introduction to a few seconds. They encountered one another in the doorway of a room. The young man found remarkable the intensity of the moment of perception, the "passion that may reside in a single pulse of time." Dickens' entire greeting was in his wordless look. For Henry junior, the one meeting was sufficient, the lesson, for him, an enduring one. With his bright red vest iridescent against the Victorian darkness, Dickens seemed to James to be "shining with august particulars." He glowed with the significance of the fullest, strongest, most persuasive artistic achievement of the world into which Henry junior had been born.

For a young man who wanted to be that kind of presence himself, Dickens' presence provided an overwhelmingly powerful suffusion of emotional energy. It was equivalent to James to looking into the eyes of Shakespeare. But the eyes were guarded, self-protective, the "handsome face . . . of formidable character" like a mask behind which some lesson or reward was hidden. Dickens engaged him "by the barest act . . . of the trained eye . . . a merciless *military* eye . . . an automatic hardness." In that moment, James suddenly had revealed to him, "in the most interesting way in the world, a kind of economy of apprehension," the necessary absolute efficiency of getting the most out of the smallest amount of time and the smallest expenditure of energy. The moment required "an immensity more to understand." But he had a lifetime in which to ponder it. He felt triumphant. "It was as if I had carried off my strange treasure just exactly from under the merciless military eye—placed there on guard of the secret."[2]

How to use that secret effectively to the end of furthering his career as a writer was much on his mind. Dickens represented the European literary artist in his fullest embodiment, the writer successfully acknowledged as the representative of both art and life, as a presence, a personage, a figure of the fullest measure, the artist both practicing his art and standing prominently in the forefront of the social relationships that were an important part of what defined the culture in which he lived. For James, now, both his youthful European experiences and his reading gave more force to the possibility that his ambitions as a writer could be furthered better by more exposure to Europe than by staying at home. The excitement of Dickens was, partly, the excitement of England. For literary New Englanders, he was the urban heart of English literature. With the end of the war, some of the excitement of American life had diminished. Henry junior had a sense of the country catching its breath, a moment of consolidation before renewed expansion.

The contribution he anticipated making was conceived in larger, extranational terms, in the prospect of an Anglo-American literary community rather than strictly an American one. America, he felt, of course needed a literature of its own to enrich the thinness of what had so far been provided. But that would take generations to accomplish, not "during your lifetime or mine perhaps," he wrote to Perry, who was in Paris on a European tour. Perry's letters reawakened his happy memories of Europe and fed his growing restlessness. If there were not innumerable impediments, "I would take ship for Havre . . . train for

Paris. . . . I know not why, I can't lay the ghost, but Paris, vulgarized as it has become, haunts my imagination." At some moments, though, America felt to him absolutely vivid, absolutely present. "We are having October weather in September," he told Perry. "This is *American* weather—worth all the asphaltic breezes of Paris." It seemed to him, in his optimism, "that American writers may yet indicate that a vast intellectual fusion and synthesis of the various National tendencies of the world is the condition of more important achievements than any we have seen"—the new "something of our own" that "we shall find . . . in our moral consciousness, our unprecedented spiritual lightness and vigor." Out of American "fermentation and turmoil" something great would come. "We young Americans are . . . men of the future."[3]

Distinctly American as he imagined this new literature would be, he also saw it as essentially a synthesis of the European inheritance. The American dispensation provided the freedom to pick and choose, to transcend the limitations of narrow European nationalisms, to seek new combinations and unexplored opportunities. Literature need not, should not, be parochial. The best art should combine national characteristics with international (which he conceived as European) experience and sophistication. If he could look closely, critically, at culture, not only his native culture but the cultures that had created America, he could rise to a level of sophistication that would enable him to have the chance to create great works of literary art. For that he needed more of Europe. "I feel," he wrote to Perry, "that my only chance for success as a critic is to let all the breezes of the west blow through me at their will. We are Americans born. . . . I look upon it as a great blessing; and I think that to be an American is an excellent preparation for culture. We have exquisite qualities as a race, and it seems to me that we are ahead of the European races in the fact that . . . we can deal freely with forms of civilization not our own, can pick and choose and assimilate and . . . claim our property wherever we find it." Given the newness and the thinness of American letters, it seemed desirable to define the literature that belonged to America as all the literature written in the English language, not only Irving, Hawthorne, Emerson, and new writers like Whitman, but Dickens, Thackeray, George Eliot, "our vast literature and literary history," which "is to most of us an unexplored field. . . . Deep in the timorous recesses of my being is a vague desire to do for our dear old English letters and writers *something* of what Ste. Beuve and the best French critics have done for theirs."

Increasingly restless, he felt the desire to return to Europe, perhaps for a sustained grand tour. Cambridge bored him, despite some friends of his own age, the intellectual and academic community in which he and his family participated, the advantages of summer afternoons and social evenings at Shady Hill, the relationships with the Nortons, the Fieldses, the Emersons nearby at Concord, and other friends like the Sedgwicks, the Dixwells, the Feltons. But "I can't possibly call at such places," he complained, "more often than two or three times in six months; and they are the best in Cambridge," this "frigid, rigid town." In the early summer of 1868, the Nortons left for a long residence in Europe. Sometimes now the Quincy Street house appeared to him "about as lively as an inner sepulchre." His own writing seemed less exciting than it had before, though he continued to turn things out for the money. He made enough to make him partly independent, as long as he lived at home. But he could not go to Europe unless his father paid the bill. For the moment, Henry senior had other pressing expenses. Alice had become seriously, inexplicably ill. Wilky and Bob had become cotton farmers in a disastrous venture in which large sums of family money were being sunk and lost. Miserably sick, William went to Europe for an extended stay to study and in the hope of regaining his health, feeling both self-disgust and guilt at "fattening on the common purse" and "cheating Harry of his *birthright*."[4]

In the spring of 1866, Henry published a brief short story, "A Day of Days," embodying his own postwar restlessness and European fantasies. An aspiring paleontologist about to leave for a long period of study in Europe attempts to visit a distinguished older scholar in the few hours that remain before his scheduled departure. Having toiled for years in one of the "narrowest, darkest, dirtiest, and busiest streets in New York" to earn enough to make the trip possible, the paleontologist is "a man of strong faculties and a strong will." Although he has had little formal education, he has "read a great many books." When he discovers that the scholar is not at home, he finds himself attracted to his sister, with whom he spends the next hours. They feel drawn to one another, and both sense the possibility of an intimate relationship. When she remarks, in response to his comment that a great change is impending in his life, " 'that is what men say when they are going to be married,' " he answers, " 'I'm going to be divorced, rather. I'm going to Europe . . . for five years if possible.' " The intensity of feeling between them prompts him to tell her that if she will ask him to stay he "will see how it sounds." But she will not, because she cherishes her own freedom, and also because she wants him to speak first. Both are ambivalent about commitment. He holds her hand in his for a moment. Then "he raised her hand to his lips, pressed them to it, dropped it, reached the door and bounded out of the garden gate."

It was a garden gate that the young author wished to pass through

himself. "I write little," he wrote to Perry, and only tales, which I think
it likely I shall continue to manufacture in a hackish manner, for that
which is bread. They *cannot* of necessity be very good; but they *shall
not* be very bad." To become the novelist, to become the critic he
wanted to be, "to enter upon any such career I should hold it invaluable
to spend two or three years on English soil—face to face with the
English landscape, English monuments and English men and women—
At the thought of [this] . . . and of possibly having the health and time
to pursue it, my eyes fill with heavenly tears and my heart throbs with
a divine courage." His aim was not to pursue a permanent residence in
Europe but to deal with immediate problems, to reinvigorate as well
as to develop himself. As to British society and its attractions, "we
never read a good English novel (and much more a bad one) . . .
without drawing a long breath of relief at the thought of all that we are
spared, and without thanking fortune that we are not part and parcel
of that dark, dense British social fabric."[5]

(2)

Though there was much to go to, there was much from which to flee.
The cultural limitations of Cambridge and America in 1868 seemed
substantial. But though he missed the substance of a European literature
and society, the crucial problem for the twenty-five-year-old author
was how to save himself from his debilitating family environment.
Illness had become an overwhelming physical fact and a pervasive emotional metaphor. Between 1861 and 1868, each of the five children of
Henry and Mary James became noticeably ill. Only Mary James remained stolidly, uncomplainingly healthy. Henry senior suffered from
heart palpitations, stomach distress, and severe headaches. White-
bearded, mostly bald, Henry senior, almost fifty-five when the war
ended, looked like an old man, "too old to travel," he felt, "beyond
the horse-car tracks." Aunt Kate and Mary ran the household, the
former constantly in pursuit of more effective medical treatment for
her vague, general ailments, the latter "strong in the back, strong in
the nerves, and strong in the eyes so far, and equal to her day."[6]

Her children's backs were correspondingly weak, their nerves fragile, their eyes blighted. Though she had not "until lately taken in the
painful truth" that William "is an invalid," she had no doubt that
temperament and faith provided the straightness of back and calmness
of nerves that proclaimed the health of body and soul. "I am full of
hope about [William] and try to have no desire about his health any

way; nor about Harry's nor about Alice's, but make sure not to loose the precious lessons of love and wisdom sent us in these trials."[7] Alice was suffering a series of nervous breakdowns. Bob and Wilky became physically ill and emotionally dysfunctional. William was suicidal. A testimony to his inherent strength of constitution and, especially, of mind, Henry was less seriously ill than his siblings.

Leading "a delicious life" at Newport and in New Hampshire during the summer of 1865, he watched his three brothers struggle with problems of vocation and health far more severe than his own. William sailed for Brazil in April 1865 with a scientific expedition led by Professor Louis Agassiz, a Swiss-born Harvard naturalist. A neighbor of the Jameses on Quincy Street, Agassiz opposed Darwin's theories and believed that nature supported traditional views of harmony and Providence in the physical world. In Brazil, William saw little evidence to support either Agassiz's assumptions or Henry senior's belief that God "is spiritually molding us under all the events of our earthly history into conformity with his spirit." Unhappy with the tedium and hard physical fieldwork, he quickly concluded that he was "cut out for a speculative rather than an active life," though there were moments when "only savage inarticulate cries can express the gorgeous loveliness" of the wilderness beauty.[8] In May, he came down with a mild form of smallpox, which blinded him temporarily, the beginning of eye problems that remained with him for the rest of his life. Severely depressed, he wished that he had not come to Brazil.

In early 1866, William returned to Boston, working the next summer as a medical assistant at Massachusetts General Hospital. He soon became certain that he did not want to practice medicine, and Mary James agreed that his health was at issue, for "the next year in the hospital would have been a very wearing one physically to him." The next April, with severe headaches, with a frequently aching back, with weak, pained, sometimes blinded eyes, he fled to Europe. He had persuaded himself and his parents, who paid all his expenses, that in Germany he could perhaps recover his health as well as study science. Having been all that winter "on the continual verge of suicide," he felt that he "had to throw up [his] hospital appointment, and fly from a home wh. had become loathsome." When Mary James learned of the rumor among William's friends that he had fled to Europe and put "the ocean between" himself and his "offending family" because of "some dreadful family rupture," she took open refuge in the explanation of ill health.[9]

For William, ill health clearly was a response, an antidote to expectations that he could not and did not desire to fulfill. Laboratory science repelled him. Sex and marriage both attracted and frightened him. Constantly looking for a young woman who would provide the ideal feminine image to transform his hesitation into action, his illness into health, he struggled with the impact on him of his father's idealization of women and his own strong sexual drives, an aspect of which he directed toward Alice. Brother and sister had developed from an early age the partly incestuous rhetoric of lovers, a confusion of feeling that contained the sexual as well as the fraternal. Also, earning a living seemed difficult if not impossible. The family strained under various burdens, particularly substantial financial support of adult children whose movements toward self-sufficiency were noticeably slow. "The prospective burdens of a wife and family being taken off my shoulders simultaneously with this 'mild yoke' upon the small of my back, relieves me," William confessed, "from imminent *material* anxiety." As with Harry, back pains were a mild yoke compared to that for which the back pains substituted. Paris, Dresden, Berlin, the water cure and baths at Teplitz and Divonne, kept William away, prolonged his prevarication, provided rest but not cure. Feeling guilty, he rationalized and apologized, occasionally balancing on the border between self-loathing and suicide. The advantages of travel were paid for by the rhetoric of illness and despair. As always, emotional problems were constantly in search of illnesses.[10]

While William was in Europe, Wilky and Bob worked in Florida, painfully pursuing another James family fantasy. They hoped to turn their high ideals into profits from a cotton plantation whose laborers were emancipated Negroes. Henry senior invested twenty thousand dollars in the enterprise, and Aunt Kate contributed a smaller sum. The family hoped to provide Wilky and Bob with satisfying employment at a time when there were few jobs available in the Northeast. Also, the experiment was ideologically attractive. To the family, it seemed "worth more than all the charity in the world." Though Wilky at first reported the likelihood of great success, there were innumerable problems, including ongoing disagreements with his major partner, corrupt and incompetent local officials, and the hostility of the native residents to outsiders, especially Northerners who had been officers in the hated Negro regiments. Puzzled at local hostility, Wilky innocently told William that "no sensible man can see anything but perfect madness in a crushed people still trying to fight the infallible logic of history." There was also the difficulty of retraining ex-slaves into the working ethic of a capitalistic enterprise. "You have learned from your late experience," his mother wrote consolingly, "a very grave lesson about the unreliable character of the negro, which must be very disappointing to you, but the sooner you learn to truly know them the better. To find that these people with whom your pecuniary interests are so bound up, and with whom you so desire too to have a human relation, are both dishonest and ungrateful, is a truly painful discovery to make. But need we wonder that wearing the chain, they should have the souls of slaves. Nothing but freedom with education will raise them up, and that will be a slow work, and patience and philanthropy to bear with them, will have much to do with successful cotton growing."[11]

Wilky and his colleagues combined their idealism with absolute ignorance of cotton farming. The combination was disastrous. For a short while the family fantasied about high returns on their money. Wilky proudly sent his parents a sample of the first cotton picked. Mary James soon hoped to furnish the rented Quincy Street house with "the proceeds of our cotton crop, and that will be so much on hand towards furnishing our own house when we shall be rich enough to buy one." Reality set in. By late 1866, expectations were tempered. Mary James consoled Wilky and Bob. "We will be contented whatever the result may be. It was too large a sum of money to invest in so uncertain an enterprise but it looked so inviting and was done for the best." By 1868, expectations had disappeared. Wilky desperately, stubbornly, hung on, unable to cut his losses or to admit failure. "I never appreciated home so much as I do now, and I never knew until this new year what it contained of upright, innocent, unprejudiced, unbiased human nature." Brought up in the idealistic world of his father's abstractions, it came as a bitter disappointment to learn that "white men and negroes alike, whether they came from Massachusetts or South Carolina are all bent upon getting the best of each other. . . . Politically and privately, all men, with but few exceptions down here, are working for but one object, that of cheating every one else in order to add a few dollars to their own possessions."[12]

Away from home, Wilky, and especially Bob, had developed what the family thought of as "pernicious habits." Wilky was a heavy smoker, frequently depressed. Bob alternated between alcoholic binges, sexual adventures, and guilty remorse. Wilky developed back pains. At the end of 1867, he had broken down physically and mentally from worry and overwork, looking "very much altered, very thin and sallow, and his mind evidently shaken." Bob soon became chronically ill, with constant stomach problems, backaches, and a persistent cough. Since he seemed "perfectly wretched at home," the family "fitted him out" for railroad work in Milwaukee, "and bade him God speed."[13] Wilky deluded himself, in 1869, into the expectation that the next crop would be successful. By the end of 1870, even Wilky gave up. Henry senior recovered a small amount of his money through resale of the mortgages. Part of the land was abandoned.

(3)

Unlike her brothers, Alice remained mostly at home, a victim of forces that relieved her of the problem of vocation but left her with the sad problem of how to lead a satisfying life without work or marriage. The challenge was met at heavy cost from early on. The daughter of a doting, self-indulgent father, she would have functioned best as her father's substitute for a wife, especially when no young man came to her and her family's rescue. But he already had two wives. Alice looked to her brothers, at first William, then later Henry, as substitutes for lovers. If circumstances had been different, either of them might have become in a more sustained way the husband substitute that Henry became for a short time years later. William wrote her love poems and drew for her erotically charged drawings in which he expressed his phallic desires. Henry junior sometimes competed with William for her attention. Henry senior preached chastity, purity, and the holiness of women to his children. From an early age, Alice felt that her own spirituality was tainted. Bright, witty, alert, still she could not free herself from a family environment in which her limits had been established by theological and emotional rules, some of which were specifically applicable only to women. She turned her victimization into a kind of career, expressing her anger through untreatable illness.

When the family returned to Newport in 1860, Alice, twelve years old, had behind her some fragmented years of European residence, a jumble of Atlantic crossings, of maids and tutors, of the random cultivation of her intelligence and education, of isolation from peers and loneliness. From the beginning there was never a question of vocation for her, as there was for her brothers. Her parents defined her destiny as a replication of their own patterns or as spinsterhood, like Aunt Kate. In the case of the latter, she would remain at home, a care-daughter to her aging parents. Unlike her brothers, even after the return to Newport, companionship remained a major problem. With an excellent sense of humor, or rather of the ludicrous, she alternated between sarcasm and loneliness, a family trait and a family situation. She did not find it easy to make friends. The laughter of girlish amusement and gossip sometimes enlivened her days. She could be spirited, fun-loving, chatty. But early on she learned to defend herself, with a sharp tongue and "high strung" nerves. Often she turned her irony on herself, looking to a combination of humor and self-punishment to get her through difficulties. With a plain wide face, a high forehead, rigorously straight hair tightly pulled and sometimes braided or bunned, she had sharp, bright gray eyes, like Henry, and a burning desire to participate in her own version of the Swedenborgian absolute spiritual freedom that her father preached.

Between 1865 and 1868, Alice hovered on the shadowy boundary between acceptable expressions of frustration and the possibility of sustained emotional illness. What had been readily explained in a female adolescent as high-strung nerves became sufficiently exacerbated in intensity and frequency to seem a serious affliction. Her episodes of "nerves" expressed themselves sometimes in violent trembling, at other times in rigidity, always in loss of self-control, inability to function, crying, screaming, splitting headaches, and loss of appetite. Years later, referring to these episodes as "violent turns of hysteria," she identified one of the major objects of her anger. "I used to sit immoveable reading in the library with waves of violent inclination invading my muscles taking some one of their myriad forms such as throwing myself out of the window, or knocking off the head of the benignant pater as he sat with his silver locks, writing at the table. . . . The only difference between me and the insane was that I had not only all the horrors and suffering of insanity but the duties of doctor, nurse, and straight-jacket imposed upon me."[14] Severely repressed, burdened with guilt, she felt split into the mentally sick person and the controlling monitor whose duty it is to keep the sickness under control. To relieve herself of the impossible burden, she looked for ways to make her illness someone else's responsibility. She could not envision any other recourse but the sickbed, where nature and God could be blamed instead of the family. The medical diagnosis was overstimulation of the nervous system, particularly too much intellectual and emotional activity. It was a typical Jamesian (and Victorian) diagnosis of overwork as the likely cause of illness even for those who did not, in the usual sense, work at all. Various treatments were available, from the popular water cure to mild forms of electric shock, from European travel to local hospitalization. Over the next twenty-five years, Alice tried them all.

(4)

Henry, unlike Alice, could afford to be only a temporary patient. He had a vocation, a small income, some mobility, and the advantages of being a male. Not to be outdone by William's litany of health problems,

"Harry too seems more unwell even than usual," Mary James reported in spring 1867. "I fear he is feeling the effects of too much mental work the last winter—He has given it all up for the present." His back continued to bother him. He had developed chronic constipation, for which he took pills. Always in search of effective medicines for constipation, stomach problems, eyestrain, and headache, the family sometimes drew on William's expertise and his willingness to experiment. They passed around pill bottles and cures with hypochondriacal alacrity. In March 1867, William seemed "doomed to spend his summer among the wards of the Hospital, Alice will 'go around' a little perhaps among her friends, and Harry will flee away to some cool spot if possible where he can sequestrate himself and take rest."[15]

Henry junior was not well, but he was not ill in a way that prevented him from socializing, traveling, reading, writing. Having used ice packs on his back, he now gave up the treatment as "pernicious." The "effects of the ice packs" had been "wonderful for a week or ten days, and then there was a reaction." He had in mind going to New York to get a corset from Alice's doctor. After a Cambridge visit from two of the Temple sisters in April 1867, he went with them to Newport, probably to see Minny, then again in May, joining a "select party," including Minny, the Bootts, John Chipman Gray—a rival for Minny's attention—and Tom Perry's beautiful sister, who soon was to marry John La Farge. Hot weather in June brought illness and the expectation of summer flight. Though he felt "more unwell even than usual," his illness did not prevent him from spending "a better part of every day in Boston" during a two-week visit from La Farge. To Norton, it seemed less like ill health than "a delicacy of nervous constitution." Toward the end of the year, Henry wrote to William, I "am not so well as I was some time since. That is I am no worse but my health has ceased to improve so steadily, as it did during the summer. It is plain that I shall have a very long row to hoe before I am fit for anything— for either work or play. . . . I may have given you an exaggerated notion of my improvement during the past six months. An important element in my recovery . . . is to strike a happy medium between reading etc and 'social relaxation.' The latter is not to be obtained in Cambridge—or only a ghastly simulacrum of it."[16]

But Henry senior could not afford to spread benefits equally among his children. With the combined expenses of William's trip to Europe, the Florida ventures, and Alice's doctors, Henry was forced to remain in Cambridge. When Minny's brother asked for a loan to help sponsor a Texas venture, the Jameses felt they could not decline. Henry senior found these matters both unspiritual and an embarrassment. He left the enforcement of monetary discipline entirely to his wife, a difficult assignment that she handled well. "It is not possible for us," she warned Wilky and Bob, "to incur any expense that *can be avoided*." From Europe, William regularly stressed in tandem his poor health and his studiousness. When depressed, "thoughts of the pistol and dagger and bowl . . . usurp an unduly large part of my attention." When exhilarated, he thought that he might yet be well. For all his guilt, he extended his year abroad to eighteen months.[17]

Henry's impatience and anger were channeled, characteristically, into his work. Cultivating a calm, confident facade, he had the advantage over William of having been successful with his writing. He had a patient temperament that gained some of its strength from his dedication to literature and his literary ambition. If American literature seemed to him now "at a dreadful pass," he himself could not help but enjoy the "perfect *furore* among the young ladies" in Lenox, Massachusetts—where he spent part of the summer of 1867 visiting the Tweedys—"to see the young author." "Harry," Alice remarked, "with his high calm alabaster brow maintains his usual indifference." William, from Germany, eager to find some share of his brother's glory, enlisted Henry's help in attempting to publish reviews of his own. Henry kept his temper, but resented William's presumption and the competition. Alice took mischievous pleasure in reporting his successes to William, including expressive dinner-table conversation. "H. 'I was coming over the bridge this afternoon and stopped a run-away horse.' You may imagine the shouts of the family at this. AK. 'I hope you did not try to stop him by the bridle.' H. 'Would you prefer to have me take hold of his legs?' A.K. 'But you should not run after horses and stop them.' H. 'Would you rather have me run before them?' You must let your imagination supply the manner of this Harry, a good deal of eyebrow nostril and shoulder affectation."[18]

Their fraternal rivalry was mitigated by their love for one another. Henry had no doubt that his parents loved him as much as they loved William. Part of their competition was simply maneuvering for advantage in an economy of scarcity. William had priority. As the elder and the sicker of the two, he had more immediate need for the elusive European cure. Henry impatiently waited his turn, carefully, shrewdly, and publically adjusting the calibrated dials of patience, illness, work, and family sensitivity. Part of the competition, though, centered on the larger, more complicated mechanism of Henry's sexuality. Between themselves and in the family dynamic, William played the active, masculine role to Henry's passive, feminine role—the devil of the house in comparison to the angel of the house. Henry established presence by patience, cunning, quietness, William by impatience and pyrodynamics. From an early age, Henry defined himself in relation to William's forcefulness, his masculinity. Henry had always found it attractive to take the feminine role in his sexual identity, his social life, and his fiction. In love with Minny Temple, he reversed their gender roles and acted as the passive support for her aggressive independence. Deeply attached to William, his love for his brother expressed itself most fully in his fictional dramas of the love and competition between brothers, particularly in four of the short stories he wrote in 1868.

He had two weapons to bring to bear on the sibling struggle, patience and literature. He dramatized his own uneasy passion for William in "The Romance of Certain Old Clothes." Here brothers are refigured as sisters, each competing for the love of the same man, though neither of them love him other than as an object of their competition. After the early death of the sister who had married the object of their rivalry, her husband marries the surviving sister. Symbolically, through the agency of the single husband, the two sisters sleep with one another. The surviving sister becomes the ghostly victim of her dead sister's revenge when she is killed in her effort to possess and wear her dead sister's beautiful clothes. In "Osborne's Revenge," a story that reflects Henry's desire to free himself from William, "intimate friends" are severed by the suicide of one, who kills himself because he has been spurned by a woman. The remaining friend, heartbroken, pursues the woman, on the basis of a note left by his friend, only to discover that the woman was blameless, his dead friend mad. He himself falls in love with the woman, but is rejected, as was his friend. She had been all along and quite publicly and properly engaged to another man. In "De Grey: A Romance," he raises the problem of what would happen if William were to die. Killing William, as well as loving him, was a complicated matter. The melodramatic story depends on the persistence of a curse on the De Grey family that demands that the first love of the male heir of the house, from generation to generation, shall die. With an idle, unstable father, Paul De Grey, like William, spends his time abroad. On his return, he falls in love, learns of the curse, and then attempts to deactivate it; it is not he but his beloved who dies. The most unusual of the triangulated relationships of these stories, here the third "person" in the triangle is the curse itself. "It's always the survivors of a calamity who are to be pitied," the story concludes, a sentiment that Henry was to repeat throughout his life.

The most explicitly homoerotic of the stories, "A Light Man," was published in 1869. Its manipulative narrator, Max, having just returned from Europe, accepts the invitation of his friend Theodore to visit him for a month at the home of his patron, a wealthy, elderly, eccentric man to whom Theodore is a reader-companion. Having symbolically adopted Theodore, old Mr. Sloan has made him the beneficiary of his will. Unstable, unpredictable, a Henry senior–like philosopher of sorts, Sloan transfers his affection from the reliable, loving Theodore to the manipulative, cynical, debauched Max. Max has only the slightest reluctance to betray his friend. They play a sadomasochistic game in which the stakes are Sloan's fortune and Theodore is the victim. "How I should like to give him," Max says, "for once, a real sensation!" Pitting his wits against Sloan's, Max is homoerotically stirred by the challenge of getting Sloan to change his will and make him the beneficiary. "I shall probably never again have such a sensation as I enjoyed to-night—actually feel a heated human heart throbbing, and turning, and struggling in my grasp; know its pants, its spasms, its convulsions, and its final senseless quiescence." Having destroyed his old will, Sloan dies before he can write a new one, and all the money goes to some distant relative.

In September 1868, his parents' patience having come to an end and money in short supply, William finally came home, probably at about the time "A Light Man" was being written. When the story was published in July 1869, Henry had already been in Europe for five months. It was now his turn, and he would do everything in his power to stay away as long as possible.

(5)

From the wind-blown deck of the S.S. *China,* the almost twenty-six-year-old Henry James watched Liverpool come into view. In late February 1869, he had at last escaped from Cambridge. He had in his pocket a letter of credit sponsored by his father that would allow him to stay abroad for at least a year, having persuaded his parents that travel was the best medicine for his elusive ills, that new, broader scenes would do more for his well-being than a whole Cambridge pharmacopoeia. Before sailing, he had visited Minny Temple for an hour in Pelham, New York, seen John La Farge briefly in Manhattan, and tried unsuccessfully to get proofs of a short dramatic sketch he had written for *The Galaxy.* He spent two days in New York, to have a sense of change as soon as possible, and to see his cousin. At Pelham, where the house was "quiet and spacious," Minny forecast that he would be away for a long time, perhaps indefinitely. As they sat in the parlor, mostly laughing, Minny agreed with him that a European trip would be just the right thing for her also. "It was wholly detestable that I should be voyaging off without her." Her humorous exaggerations, her explosive laughter, extended even more widely "the handsome largeish teeth that made her mouth almost the main fact of her face." She seemed to him "erectly slight . . . transparently fair." When he asked her about her seeming sleeplessness, " 'Sleep,' she said, 'Oh, I don't sleep. *I've given it up.*' " If Europe and especially Italy would benefit his health, what might it not do for hers! She would have the opportunity to take on flesh and color in the Italian sun. How wonderful if they could "romantically meet . . . the next winter in Rome." They both took the possibility seriously.[19]

Disembarking in Liverpool on an "overwhelmingly English morning," he happily put his feet on solid land. At his hotel, where "damp and darksome light washed in from the steep, black, bricky street," a coal fire cracked in the drafty fireplace. The waiter could have been in a Dickens novel, and the rustling of the pages of the *Times* in the pages of Thackeray. His own European memories were dim after the passage of nine years. Now, on his own, he felt almost as if coming for the first time, as if he were visiting the familiar but unfocused past. He immediately wrote to his mother to assure the family of his safe arrival. In the morning, startled to see that he had overslept, he missed the train he had expected to take to Chester for a day's sight-seeing. The rain came down in black torrents. The thought of spending a bleak Sunday in Liverpool oppressed him. After breakfast, he just caught the slow train to London that would have allowed him to enjoy the scenery (the weather got better as the train went southward), except for an overly solicitous, elderly, "middle-class Philistine" who insisted on giving him fatherly advice and detailed descriptions of the scenery. He pretended, as the lesser of two evils, to be tired and closed his eyes for much of the trip.[20] Late in the afternoon, he was in London.

Despite the musty discomfort of his hotel in Trafalgar Square, he felt all the excitement of his great adventure. For the first time, he was clearly, unequivocally, on his own. To compensate, he soon got "abjectly, fatally homesick," a brief moment, which he overcame partly by confessing it, "without stint or shame," to his mother. He reminded her how they used to make fun of Henry senior when he returned prematurely from an aborted trip because he could not stand to be away from his family. "Tomorrow, doubtless, I shall be better . . . but meanwhile, until bedtime, let me be my own dear mother's son . . . with my head on mother's lap and my feet in Alice's." He had no hesitation in elaborating on the fantasy of contact, for him the necessary other side of the coin of his staying at a distance.[21]

After looking at a number of dingy lodgings, he had practical recourse to the beneficent Nortons, who had come to England the previous summer and were spending the winter in a handsome house in Kensington. Enjoying his London literary friends while observing with disapproval the disparity between the poor and the rich, Norton had already made up his mind that "to live here would be intolerable; and I shall come back to the barrenness of America more American than ever." With his wife Susan and accompanied by his unmarried sisters Jane and Grace, Norton and his family extended their protection to their young friend. Henry junior knew almost no one in England. Norton knew almost everyone. Immediately helping him with the lodging problem, he put him in touch with someone who put him in touch with "an old servant of some genteel family . . . who lets out his three floors" on Half Moon Street, off Piccadilly, "to gentlemen." He was immediately comfortable, waited on with "obsequious punctuality," in a centrally located area of London that later he was to live in for many years.[22] His landlord recommended a nearby restaurant that reeked of old Englishness, furnished with narrow benches and dark wood, where he ate regularly. He found at once that England was a country in which a bachelor could be well waited on and cared for, where one had a better chance than in America of being lucky in one's servants. His best luck, at the moment, was in the Nortons.

For the first week, the immense size of London almost paralyzed his ability to observe its details. In comparison, New York was a village. "At any given point London looks huge," he was to write some years later, "even in narrow corners you have a sense of its hugeness. . . . Nowhere else is so much human life gathered together, and nowhere does it press upon you with so many suggestions." It gave him "a vast impression of opulence and prosperity." Though "anything but a cheerful or a charming city," it was still "a very splendid one." For the moment, its heaviness flattened him into an "intellectual depression." But he quickly recovered. Innumerable memories of the London of his childhood and his reading merged inextricably with what he was now seeing, as if he were home again after a long absence. In his lodgings, with a muffin and hot tea every morning, with the Norton hospitality providing him with companionship and introductions, he happily felt as if he had been living in "this murky metropolis for a year rather than for ten days. I feel "domesticated and naturalized," he boasted to Alice, "to quite a disgusting extent."[23]

Handsomely welcomed beyond his expectations, he immediately felt England to be a place in which he would like to stay longer than he had planned. He intended to remain a month in London before going

to Great Malvern, the best-known water-cure spa in Britain, to attend
to his health, the ostensible reason for his being abroad. Then he
was to go to the Continent, to Paris and Italy, where the important
health benefit would come from dramatic changes of scene. Somewhere
buried in his traveler's knapsack he had the fatherly and fraternal injunction, almost the obligation, to visit Germany, to learn the language,
and to study something or other. For the time being, with hardly a sign
of ill health and three thousand miles distant from parental expectations,
he began to enjoy London. With Jane and Grace Norton, he delighted
in being an eager tourist, revisiting the sites of his former London
residence, seeing some London attractions for the first time, the Tower,
the Abbey, the Law Courts the churches—especially St. Paul's—the
City, and even taking a boat ride on "a grey, raw English day" on a
penny Thames steamer, the river dirty, the riverbank hideous. He
walked up to Hampstead to pay a call on one of his father's Swedenborgian acquaintances, who almost walked him "to death over the hills
and dales of Hampstead." One day he went to see "Brighton the famous
. . . simply London-on-the-sea."[24]

Disappointed that the National Gallery had closed temporarily, he
went to look at paintings at the Dulwich Gallery, the Victoria and Albert
Museum (then called the Kensington Museum), the Elgin Marbles at
the British Museum, the gardens and galleries at Hampton Court.
Sometimes he went alone, often with one of his Norton friends,
haunting "the museums and galleries . . . with a sense of duty and
excitement that [he] was never again to know." When the National
Gallery reopened, he became aware one afternoon that a little man,
with an immense head dominating his small body and an extravagant
mane of auburn hair, standing near him and talking "with the greatest
vivacity," was Charles Algernon Swinburne, whom he recognized
from a photograph that he had been sent some months before. To be
admiring Titian, and to be admiring Swinburne, at the same time as
Swinburne was admiring Titian, was bliss to the young author. To his
surprise and pleasure, he received two visits from Leslie Stephen, the
prolific literary journalist, now editor of *The Cornhill Magazine,* whose
wife, Thackeray's daughter Minny, made him and Jane Norton welcome for dinner. The kindly, taciturn Stephen, who had been the guest
of the Jameses in Cambridge in 1868 and had met Henry junior in
passing, introduced him to the newly built underground, "a marvellous
phenomenon—ploughing along in a vast circle thro' the bowels of
London, and giving you egress to the upper earth in magnificent stations." It took them from the Stephen home to the zoo at Regent's
Park, which they were able to enter on Sunday because Stephen was a

member of the Zoological Society. Afterward, they returned to the Stephen home for tea and talk.[25]

Tea and talk, talk and tea, in his one month in London "the invaluable Nortons" helped fill his cup with both. At the beginning of his second week, after dinner they all went by underground to listen to Ruskin lecture on "Greek Myths" at University College. Later in the month, he went one morning, again with the Nortons, to visit Ruskin at his home at Denmark Hill. He enjoyed Ruskin's magnificent collection of paintings and "the sight of a quiet opulent long-established suburban English home." Ruskin was locked away in his study, writing, and would not see the visitors. A few days later, with the Nortons again, he was a dinner guest at Denmark Hill. Ruskin seemed to him a man "scared back by the grim face of reality into the world of unreason and illusion" where "he wanders . . . without a compass and a guide— or any light save the fitful flashes of his beautiful genius." He enjoyed the dinner, the company, and most of all one of Titian's portraits of a Venetian doge, "a work of transcendant beauty and elegance."[26]

The Nortons had him to several dinners, at one of them introducing him to the unmarried Mamie Dickens, "plain-faced, ladylike (in black silk and black lace) and the image of her father." Fulfilling the "ancient piety embodied" in his own "private altar to Dickens," he went to look at one particular street off the Strand, known for its "atmosphere," where "the whole Dickens procession marched up and down, the whole Dickens world looked out of its queer, quite sinister windows—for it was the socially sinister Dickens . . . rather than the socially encouraging and confoundingly comic who still at that moment was most apt to meet me with his reasons. Such a reason was just that look of the inscrutable riverward street, packed to blackness with accumulations of suffered experience."[27] He responded to the poverty, the suffering, that Craven Street presented by reading it in terms of Dickens and his own personal sympathy. Like the Cruikshank drawings from *Oliver Twist* that had frightened him as a child, the reality seemed "sinister," depraved, and threatening. Partly in reaction, perhaps, to his father's idealistic abstractions but comfortable upper-middle-class life, and also as a sense of his own mission, he had not cultivated a reforming bone in his body. Sympathy, yes. Reformation, not likely.

When the Nortons took him to the Bloomsbury home and shop of the socialist poet William Morris, "a manufacturer of stained glass windows, tiles, ecclesiastical and medieval tapestry altar-cloths, and in fine everything quaint, archaic, pre-Raphaelite—and I may add exquisite," he admired the beautiful things, including Mrs. Morris, a notorious Pre-Raphaelite beauty. She had been the painter and poet Dante

Gabriel Rossetti's favorite model and, for some time, his mistress. She appeared a haunting image for the young visitor, "an apparition of fearful and wonderful intensity . . . a tall lean woman in a long dress of some dead purple stuff, guiltless of hoops (or of anything else . . .) with a mass of crisp black hair heaped into great wavy projections on each of her temples, a thin pale face, a pair of strange, sad, deep, dark Swinburnish eyes, with great thick black oblique brows, joined in the middle and tucking themselves away under her hair." Before leaving England for the Continent, he visited, again under Norton's patronage, Rossetti's studio, where he may not have known what to make of Rossetti painting "nothing but Mrs. Morris." Like other "exquisite" things of beauty, she was of more interest to him than Morris' socialism.

"Extremely pleasant and quite different from his wife," Morris was "short, burly and corpulent, very careless and unfinished in his dress," a wonderful talker with "a very loud voice and a nervous restless manner," who also seemed the perfect example of "a delicate sensitive genius . . . served by a perfectly healthy body and temper." Morris' sound health had a special attraction to him, to which he had called indirect attention in a review that he had published in *The Nation* the previous summer, remarking, with his hand on his own pulse, that "to call a man healthy nowadays is almost an insult—invalids learn so many secrets. . . . Mr. Morris is a supremely healthy writer." After dinner, Jane Morris reclined on a couch, holding a handkerchief to her cheek to relieve a toothache while her husband read to his guests a portion of one of the unpublished sections of his long poem, *The Earthly Paradise.*[28] For Morris the socialist, the beautiful things he made and wrote existed to anticipate and hasten a more just, more happy state for humankind. For the young writer, the only paradise was there and then, the social and aesthetic richness of this grand moment.

Without either friends or work, he realized that London would have proved untenable for him, even for this one rainy month, if it had not been for the Nortons, and particularly Grace and Jane, whose company he enjoyed more than Charles's, with whom he did not find himself much "*en rapport.*" They could be on the best of terms without ever being intimate friends. He felt it a relief and pleasure to be turned over to the women of the family. With Jane, he went to visit the Darwins, who had been the Nortons' neighbors in Kent. To his disappointment, a call on George Eliot and George Henry Lewes had to be indefinitely postponed, since the Leweses had gone out of town.

"In the best of health and spirits" throughout March 1869, enjoying London despite what seemed to him constant rain, he nevertheless went to Great Malvern at the end of the month. It was part of the original

plan, and he felt it necessary to be vaguely ill. He still suffered occasionally from constipation and back pain in an unhappy, debilitating, but
always intermittent confusion between the mind and the body. At
Cambridge, William had gotten an immense lift from a subordinate
teaching position at Harvard, offered him by Charles William Eliot, the
president of Harvard, and by his sudden but hard-earned realization
that some illnesses were generated by the mind, that not "all mental
disorder requires to have a physical basis. . . . What a difference between me as I am now and as I was last spring at this time!" It might
not be the case that he was physically tainted, the victim of inherited
bad blood and health. If his mind was the cause, then some exertion of
will, some leap of faith, might make him healthy enough to work and
live normally. Henry junior indeed was working and living normally.
Though he complained that he could not read or study, he had very
little time for either, so busy was he with sight-seeing, with visits, with
gathering impressions and experiences. He wrote only letters, but they
were long ones, "diary and letters all in one," by choice rather than
default, on the premise that this was a time for planting, not for harvest-
ing.[29] Still, this opportunity to travel had been based on the assumption
that he was ill, and illness naturally appeared, though in elusive, recalci-
trant, and intermittent forms insufficient to prevent him at any point
from doing what he wanted to do. He soon devised the useful theory
that constant travel was the best thing for his back and bowels.

At first Malvern seemed charming, the view from the hills "literally
immense . . . the whole of gentle England stretched out" at his feet,
the baths deliciously comfortable, the air fresh and invigorating, his
fellow patients amiable, addicted to reading the newspaper all day and
playing cards all evening. Everything about it seemed better than London except that it was boring. "I go in for genius and fame," he
admitted, "even at breakfast and lunch." At Malvern, the incessant
April rains washed into his spirits more than they did in London. The
hydrotherapy also meant that he had to sit constantly in water. By the
second week he was fantasying about other places. The air had become
"dead & muggy & there is decidedly too much water in one's life."
Ostensibly he had come there to deal with his constipation, the prescribed treatment for which was long hours sitting in a sitz-bath. His
appetite remained substantial, as it had been since he had arrived in
England when, much to his consternation, he had found himself "perpetually ravenous for food." He simply ate too much, the continuation
of a pattern that had begun some years before. Often his stomach felt
uncomfortable. Sometimes it actually hurt from the distention, and he

gained weight. Sensitive about his appearance, he saw the graceful proportions of his youthful figure being pushed, shoved, and expanded from within. "I'm at my old trick," he told Alice, "of growing repulsively fat." But he moved his bowels daily, and his back seemed stable. This was good news to report to the family, though he did not want to put it in a light that might suggest either that he had been cured or that he should stay at Malvern. Wanting both his own way and his parents' approval, he asked William to tell Henry senior that "I haven't a moment of deep satisfaction & enjoyment here (& I have had many) but I have immediately thought of him as being the real author of my pleasure—having placed it in my power to be here at all—& having taught me all my life to think & feel properly, so that my thoughts & feelings are possibly not idle."[30]

Restless, bored, from Malvern he went to Oxford, with an introduction from the ever-helpful Norton to a Christ Church College chemist who took him to convocation, and had him dine at high table in the place of honor. The chemist arranged for James to lunch with Mark Pattison, the rector of Lincoln College, "a dessicated old scholar" with a beautiful young wife whom later rumor discredited as the model for Casaubon in George Eliot's *Middlemarch*. On his way to Oxford, he visited Warwick Castle, Kenilworth, and Stratford, with little pleasure or enthusiasm. From Oxford, he went to Coventry. He was impressed most by the English churches, "the greatest works of art" he had yet seen. He had still seen few old master paintings, the London galleries thin, the American museums almost empty. At Blenheim, he saw two or three Italian Renaissance paintings which pleased him. Anthony Van Dyck's portrait of Charles I on horseback took his breath away, "a thing of infinite beauty." The "incredibly rich and pastoral" Warwickshire countryside, "the land one teeming garden," seemed "too monotonously sweet and smooth," the vast show garden of the rich kept up at the expense of the poor. Oxford itself seemed "incomparable, a realized fantasy of beauty and learning." On a perfect early evening, "in the interminable British twilight, the beauty of the whole place came forth with magical powers." As he walked along the river, through the Christ Church meadow, he saw "hundreds of the mighty lads of England, clad in white flannel and blue, immense, fair-haired, magnificent in their youths, lounging down the stream in their punts or pulling in straining crews and rejoicing in their godlike strength . . . elect among men." He entered the Magadalen College courtyard. As he stood looking up "at its great serene tower," he thought his heart "would crack with the fulness of satisfied desire."

It was for him a high moment of Anglophilia, an innocent, diffuse homoerotic passion made intense by his awareness that this moment would be brief, that his days in England were measured. He knew that he looked very little like these golden lads, and he was growing less like them daily. What he imagined they felt, he had never had the opportunity to feel. But here was the counterimage to the Massachusetts Cambridge whose name must have tasted to him slightly of mockery. Here were the elite of the most powerful, the richest, the handsomest country in the world, of the treasure house of English literature and culture, a society of "mighty lads . . . magnificent in their youth." He was not of them, but he could admire and love them, at their best, and, most important, he could pay his tribute to them, to this representation of cultural achievement. "It is . . . satisfied desire that you feel here," that "gives me a deeper sense of English life than anything yet." For the moment, he needed nothing more than to pay his tribute to this romanticized fantasy. He had no doubt that no place existed for him in Oxford.[31]

For the moment, though, he flirted with staying longer in England, "rent in twain by a simultaneous sense of delight at being in this sweet old England and a horribly fascinating vision of starting off to the sour old Continent."[32] The problem was money, not health, though it was to his advantage to make it seem the latter. His letter of credit from Henry senior's banker in Boston provided money to permit at least a year abroad, perhaps two, if he could stretch the funds. The cheapest approach would have been to settle in a single place for a long time. But to do so would be to buy time at the cost of variety and stimulation. Late in March, he had decided against the boredom of Malvern in favor of three weeks of travel before returning to London. He had almost determined to head for the Continent, partly to escape London summer weather, but mostly because if he were to remain indefinitely in England he might never see the Continent on his own. He wrote to his parents, "putting forth a feeler" about the unlikely possibility of their providing him with more money so that he might remain in England and still be able to go to the Continent afterward.

Returning to London in early May 1869, he finally met George Eliot, the only English novelist "to have powers of thought at all commensurate with [her] powers of imagination." In the four reviews of her works that he had published between 1866 and 1868, he both praised her intellect and her style, which combines "the keenest observation with the ripest reflection," and faulted her for being "deficient in imagination." But even her less successful works seemed to him "the production of a noble intellect, of a moral vision equally broad and deep, and of marvellous ingenuity . . . one of the best of English writers . . . an excellent story-teller—a real novelist, in fact—and she is, finally, an elegant moralist." Because of her sensitivity, Lewes rarely allowed her reviews to reach her. Most likely she had not read what James had written about her. She stood large, impressive, and remarkable. Knowing Minny Temple's "adored George Eliot" he sent her a detailed account of his visit, of his "brief glimpse," in which his "main satisfaction" was that he should be able to tell his cousin about it.[33]

This "fairytale of privilege" he also owed to the Nortons. Jane's company and Charles's introduction got him through the usually impenetrable North Bank gate. Lewes was not at home, away on an emergency to get medical help for one of his sons who, suddenly having become ill, was in pain on a couch in a back room. Agitated, concerned, Eliot came through the door from the room in which she had been with the sick young man. Suddenly James saw her for the first time not only as a great novelist but as a person of everyday life, attending to human cares, dressed in a black silk dress, a "lace mantilla attached to her head and keeping company on either side with the low-falling thickness of her dark hair." Immediately she struck him "as somehow *illustratively* great." She also lived up to her reputation for physical unattractiveness, striking him as "magnificently ugly—deliciously hideous. She has a low forehead, a dull grey eye, a vast pendulous nose, a huge mouth, full of uneven teeth and a chin and jaw-bone. . . . Now in this vast ugliness resides a most powerful beauty which, in a very few minutes, steals forth and charms the mind, so that you end . . . in falling in love with her. Yes behold me literally in love with this great horse-faced bluestocking." Despite being on edge, waiting for Lewes' return with morphine, her expression seemed delightful, her "voice soft and rich as that of a counselling angel." As soon as Lewes returned, "in all *his* ugliness," short, bearded, sharp-nosed, the visitors immediately left. Henry junior offered to go in search of a well-known doctor, to which the Leweses agreed. His cab crawled through heavy traffic, and the best he could do as ministering angel, when the doctor was not at home, was to leave a message for him to go to the Leweses as soon as he could. For all this, the visit was deeply satisfying. He soon sent Minny not only a detailed account but a picture of Lewes also. "To think," she remarked, "that my adored George Eliot should have found, among all the human creatures she knew, the most comfort & sympathy from that one."[34] Both Henry and his cousin gave some thought to the phenomenon.

James was startled to learn from his parents and William that his request for more money had touched a very sore nerve indeed. A proposal that he visit Scotland before going to the Continent had met with his mother's sharp disapproval. "My constant aim," he wrote to his father who had written one of his rare letters, so upset was the Quincy Street household by Harry's query about more money, "is to economise and make my funds minister, not to my enjoyment . . . but to my plain physical improvement." The accusation that he had been "extravagant," that he had wasted money on costly, unnecessary travel, "sickens me to the heart." He brazenly explained to his parents and to William that he had thought this over carefully since arriving. He had a rational plan, the result of "an impression amounting almost to a conviction that if [he] were to travel steadily for a year [he] would be a good part of a well man." His three weeks traveling had cost only twenty-five pounds, not that inaccurate estimate of sixty pounds that he had mentioned in a letter. "I have got quite my £25's worth of flexibility in the back, of experience and insight into my condition." Undue economizing would undermine the benefits to his health. He had never felt better than he had felt at Oxford. "I have had," he boasted to William, "a [bowel] movement every day for a month—& at Oxford *two* daily." It was wiser to spend money traveling than remaining at Malvern. "My salvation is much more to be found in locomotion than in baths. . . . I honestly believe that a year's journeying would be a 'sanitary measure' of the 1st excellence."[35]

Not that the funds for the year were really in jeopardy, though there existed the possibility of the accusation of extravagance. William wrote another, blunter letter, particularly emphasizing that if his health permitted travel, it probably permitted study in Germany. "Your words go to my heart," he responded. "The thing on earth I should most like to do would be to make a bee-line for some agreeable German town & plunge into the speech & the literature of the land. . . . But it's painfully evident that I can do nothing of the kind for many a month to come." Study of any sort was out of the question. He still could not do much reading, feeling "the old familiar seediness owing to having tried it a little more than usual during these last days while confined to the house by the rain." His recent experience had taught him that "movement, & more movement & still movement . . . seems to be the best—the only prescription for my ills. . . . I can't sit & read & between sitting & standing I know of no middle state." Would William please communicate this to their parents and urge them to approve his theory with "their blessing?" What he wanted "is firmly to establish it as theory, even should my practice not diverge very widely from that which I originally contemplated. It will certainly not be extravagant & I shall be at best a very tame traveller." Disappointed that his mother had not understood that he had wanted to go to Scotland "not as a spree but as part of an *absolute remedy,*" they should all understand that he had "no desire to be restless or fanciful or wasteful." Since his eight weeks in England had cost under £200, he still had £867. "Upon this sum I build my adventures. It seems to me a good broad foundation. It will not be likely to diminish as rapidly as it has done in the last three months, owing both to lower prices & greater experiences. . . . I wish simply to feel at liberty to spend my letter of credit rather more rapidly than I at first anticipated. . . . When it is gone, I shall come home a new man; I shall of course not ask for more."

Though such assurances were hardly to be taken seriously, they were a necessary part of a family dialectic. His parents had firmly denied his request that they provide additional money for him to extend his stay abroad. Family finances and obligations did not permit it. Henry had withdrawn the request. But he also had taken the opportunity to provide an elaborate rationale, no matter how logically porous, for why he had come abroad in the first place and for the disposition of the remainder of his time and the family's money. He had "told the long story because I felt a need of opening myself & taking hold of my situation." He had told the story also because he had need to create a structure of words that would minister to "the sacred influence of home," bringing it "into harmony with my idea." Most of all, he wanted "father & mother to write & say that they understand & approve my representations." All this, he recognized, was self-centered, but he counted on the charity of his readers to forgive the egotism of his letter. "I am fighting a very egotistical enemy."[36]

In the middle of the summer, a letter came from his mother to her angel. He had aimed his arrow at the right heart. "Your letter last evening opens the deepest fountain in my soul," she wrote, "and my bosom seemed as if it would burst with its burden of love and tenderness. If you were only here for an hour and we could talk over this subject of expense, I could I know exorcise all these demons of anxiety and conscientiousness that possess you, and leave [you] free as air to enjoy to the full all that surrounds you, and drink in health of body & of mind in following out your own safe and innocent attractions." He would please her most if he would "henceforth throw away prudence and think only of your own comfort and pleasure, for our sakes as well as your own. . . . Italy will be just the place for you; and do not I pray you cramp yourself in any way to hinder your fullest enjoyment of it. . . . Take the fullest liberty and enjoy your tastes and inclinations."[37] He received the letter after his arrival in Italy in August 1869.

(6)

From London in the middle of May 1869 he went to Geneva, staying for a month among the pleasurable and the painful sights of his two previous visits. He came via Paris, where he stopped for only one day to see the annual exhibition of paintings at the Salon. From Geneva in the middle of June, he sailed to the far end of the lake, to stay at a comfortable, beautifully situated hotel "perched aloft on the mountain side, just above the Castle of Chillon." Though the air was fresh and the scenery stunning, it rained for a week. "If Europe does not solve the problem of existence," he wrote to La Farge, "it at least helps the flight of time—or beguiles its duration." The question of money still rankled. He had made his case to his parents again, from Geneva, and now he made it one more time, in answer to their most recent letters, which had again stressed the need for the strictest economy. "My lovely mother, if ever I am restored to you sound and serviceable you will find that you have not cast the pearls of your charity before a senseless beast, but before a creature with a soul to be grateful and a will to act." Germany was out of the question. In order to regain his health he would risk "even the appearance of mere pleasure-seeking. . . . I have trifled so long with my trouble that I feel as if I could afford now to be brutal."[38] Though he still held out to his parents some possibility that he would spend the winter in Paris, he had made up his mind that he would finally make his first visit to Italy. The possibility remained that Minny would spend the winter in Rome.

When the sun came out that next week, he became an intrepid, athletic hiker. He explored the trails around Montreux, ascending a local peak with two Englishmen and a German. They started at midnight, climbing for four hours, partly in the moonlight, in order to be at the freezing summit at sunrise, when the "red ball shot up with its usual splendid suddenness." His hiking and climbing feats thrilled his mother, who wrote that "your legs are all right, blessings upon them! They will be your salvation I have not a doubt." His mother's stolid optimism would not be denied, especially with good news. "So my darling boy, the skies are clearing for us all, and health and strength and happy working days lie before us all. So grant it heaven." If only he would attend to his heart, all would be fine. Perhaps having on her mind that

Lizzie Boott might be in love with William, Mary James expressed her hope that Henry would marry. "You know Father used to say to you, that if you would only fall in love it would be the making of you. Possibly Will's susceptible heart may be coming to the rescue of his back." Henry's eyes were more appreciatively on "four lovely young Englishmen," with whom he took long hikes, "the flower of the earth—I am getting, by the way, absolutely to adore the English."[39]

From Montreux he went to nearby Vevey to visit the Nortons, who lived "in great simplicity & great contentment" in a picturesque old farmhouse. He suspected they might be "utterly buried and lonely" and he might repay in a small way their hospitality to him in London by making a visit he would have preferred to avoid. Finding both Charles and his wife feeling ill, he happily left after four days to resume his hiking. He walked from Gersau to Lucerne across the top of a high ridge, "six of the hottest & grimmest hours" he had ever spent. "I never enjoyed a walk as much as that." Staying now in Lucerne, he climbed a nearby mountain with another "young Englishman," whose casual companionship was totally unselfconscious and pleasurably fraternal. His letters home were bulletins about his pursuit of good health, as if the Alpine cure might replace the water cure. At the end of the first week in August, his physical enthusiasm collapsed. He had had enough exertion, and enough of Switzerland, though he felt a "deep satisfaction at being able to do all this healthy trudging & climbing. It *is*—it *is* a pledge of some future potency."[40]

He went to Lucerne in the vain expectation that Aunt Kate, who was on a European tour with a friend, would meet him there. Dispatching his luggage to Milan, he took the steamer to Flüelen, hoisted his knapsack over his shoulders, and for two days walked "the greater part of the Swiss descent of the St. Gothard," finally crossing to the Rhône Glacier, "a wondrous silent cataract of snow framed clean in the rocks." He started to ascend the Grimsel, but suddenly felt too exhausted to make the effort. Taking the coach to the base of the Simplon Pass, at 4:30 the next morning, feeling absolutely healthy again, he walked, with a hired man to carry his bag, to the summit on a superlatively clear day. After dining at the famous hospice, he began his descent into Italy with "the delight of seeing the north melt slowly into the south." Having come thirty-three miles that day, he spent the night at Isella, on the border. In the morning, he took the coach for six hours down to Baveno on the shore of Lake Maggiore, "down, down—on, on into Italy . . . a rapturous progress thro' a wild luxuriance of corn and vines and olives and figs and mulberries and chestnuts and frescoed villages and clamorous beggars and all the good old Italianisms of history." At warm Baveno, amidst the orange trees, he dipped into a "cold bath in a great marble tank" at "a vast, cool, dim, delicious hotel" from whose terrace stairs he took the early evening on the lake, lying back under a striped awning as he was rowed out to the small islands. They partook of what seemed to him "the most striking feature of Italian scenery," an "odd mingling of tawdriness and splendor."

So keen was he to ritualize and memorialize his first descent into Italy that he made the trip twice. No sooner had he arrived than he returned to Switzerland to walk to Italy again by a different route. From Baveno the next morning, he took the boat to the head of the lake, walked ten miles in torrid heat to where the St. Gotthard and San Bernardino roads converge, then the next day climbed for two days to Splügen and then to Thusis. Utterly exhausted, with constantly aching legs, he decided the next morning to give up going any farther into Switzerland and to return to Italy. From Splügen, he walked eight hours over the pass to Chiavenna, where he happily met "Italian beauty heat and dirt" again. From Chiavenna, he went to Colico on the northern point of Lake Como, and then took the lake steamer down to Cadenabbia on the west side of the lake, where he stayed at the spacious Hôtel Belle-Vue, across from Bellagio and the Villa Serbelloni high on the ridge of the promontory where the two lakes meet. Despite the excessive heat, he delighted in "the swarming shimmering prodigality of the landscape . . . convinced and enchanted before Italy and summer." For a moment, he paused, strolling along the shores of the lake, "past the fantastic, iron gates of idle, pretentious villas," undecided whether to go on into the full force of the "potent southern August" or to go back to Switzerland. Entertaining the "ghosts of [his] egotism," in amazement at his own walking feats, he fantasied about an immense walking tour of England for the next summer. Ambivalent about Italy and how he would respond to it, perhaps concerned that his health might be due for a turn, that it might be best to retreat, he hesitated, as if caught for a brief moment in a mild anxiety attack. He soon decided to go on to Venice.[41]

From Cadenabbia, he had traveled to Como, then to Brescia and Verona, arriving in Venice at the middle of September. Venice was simultaneously enchanting and discomforting. The torrid September heat and the mosquitoes distressed him. So too did his sense of the immense gap between his New England sensibility and the luxuriant, pleasure-appreciating "genius of Italy, or the Spirit of the South—or whatever one may call the confounded thing." Immediately plunging into an aesthetic-touristic frenzy of palaces and paintings, of the grand, the idiosyncratic, and the picturesque, of Tintoretto, Bellini, and Veronese, he found it helpful, like many tourists before him, to compare Venice to the unreality of a dream state. The exceptional quality of the city seemed irreconcilable with daily life; "the Venice of dreams" was "awfully sad too in its inexorable decay." No doubt "steady sight-seeing is *extremely* fatiguing," but in principle, he wrote to La Farge, urging him to come abroad and join him, he had a method. Actually, he whirled from site to site, from day to day. "I wish I were a hereditary possessor of one of these old palazzi," he told La Farge. "I would make it over to you for a year's occupancy." He could imagine a year's residence in a palace with his own gondola, "a thing divine." When he felt weary of the feverish passions of the human stories represented in Tintoretto's biblical paintings, he would sit in the Piazza San Marco or stand between the marble columns in the comfortable coolness of the shade, looking back at the Ducal Palace, taking a restful pleasure in "gazing on this work of art which has so little to do with *persons!*"[42]

But he felt uneasy in Venice. Surrounded by sensuality, he felt distant from, even afraid of, his own sensual nature. It helped him to deal with the anxiety that Venice aroused to compare it to Newport "in atmosphere and color. . . . The other afternoon, on the sands at the Lido, looking out over the dazzling Adriatic," it "was just like looking out to sea from one of the Newport beaches, with Narragansett afar." His impression was reinforced by seeing two Newporters, whom he vaguely knew but who did not recognize him, Katherine De Kay Bronson and her husband. If he could have one painting and if he "weren't a base Anglo-Saxon and a coward slave," he confessed to William, "I should ask nothing better than [Veronese's] *Rape of Europa* in the Doge's Palace where a great rosy blond, gorgeous with brocade and pearls and bouncing with salubrity and a great mellow splendor of sea and sky and nymphs and flowers do their best to demoralize the world." But the salaciousness he experienced in Venice made him uncomfortable. Though he had been born in New York, "it's as if," in the presence of Venice, "I had been born in Boston: I can't for the life of me frankly surrender myself."[43]

Sitting one morning in the Ducal Palace, looking at Veronese and Tintoretto paintings, he felt that no matter how long he sat there he would "only feel more and more my inexorable Yankeehood. As a puling pining Yankee, however, I enjoy things deeply." At other moments he had less of a sense of humor about it, berating himself, after leaving Venice, for having been "cold and insensible," for not having been able to give himself up more to her sensual richness, to have "loved her more." He had learned the lesson of the sophisticated, self-conscious traveler. "Wherever we go we carry with us this heavy burden of our personal consciousness and wherever we stop we open it out over our heads like a great baleful cotton umbrella, to obstruct the prospect and obscure the light of heaven." To his "dearest mammy," this loving "son of sons" made it clear that she need not worry that Italy would seduce him. He moved in the direction of intensifying feeling while, at the same time, intensifying fastidiousness. The same Bostonian sense of moral restraint and emotional control that held him back from fully enjoying Venice also made it impossible for him to take more pleasure in the attractive Italian men he saw and admired.[44] Though he had a conventional eye for beautiful women, he had a personal eye for handsome men.

From Venice, he went, via Padua, Ferrara, Bologna, and Parma, to Florence. At Padua, he admired Giotto's frescoes, "the mastery of dramatic presentation . . . the simplicity—the purity—the grace." Whereas a day in Padua sufficed, a few hours in Ferrara gave him a sense of the distinctiveness of an almost desolate city set in a splendid landscape. His interest was in the Italian past, not the present, and particularly in the great painters of the Renaissance. His pilgrimage to Parma was to see Correggio's paintings. In Florence, the riches of the Uffizi and the Pitti Palace astonished him. So too did Florence, in a more comfortable, perhaps more Bostonian, way than Venice. "If I should ever feel like living a while in Italy I fancy I should choose this place." It did not strike him as a particularly cheerful city. On the contrary, it seemed "rather gloomy than otherwise." But it had physical comforts, great museums, a lovely setting, and a sense of bustling life, without the egregious sensuality and otherworldliness of Venice. "I have never seen a city which took my fancy so fully and speedily." He recalled the poetry of the Brownings when gazing at the vistas. Soon after his arrival, toward the end of the first week of October 1869, he took a long walk to Fiesole, exhilarated by what seemed "a lovely country—all pale olives and dark cypresses—with beautiful views of Florence lying in her circle of hills like—like what?—like a chiselled jewel in a case of violet velvet!"[45]

Such literally purple prose expressed both the sincerity of his feelings and his obligation to provide tourist descriptions to the family at home. His descriptions were occasionally artful and playful, occasionally deeply felt and incisive, sometimes conventionally flat. To some extent, he felt like a latecomer, a revenant to scenes already fully described by former travelers, though sometimes it felt to him entirely fresh, entirely new, his Italy. The long letters, strengthening his connection with home, were expressions of love and homesickness from a mostly dutiful son abroad. Though he was almost always alone, with

neither traveling companions nor any welcoming people at his destina-
tions, his conversational Italian had quickly become adequate. But he
had very few introductions, knew almost no one, and found that Florentine and Italian society in general were totally closed to him. Fellow
American tourists he found impossible companions. "A set of people
less framed to provoke national self-complacency . . . it would be hard
to imagine. There is but one word to use in regard to them—vulgar;
vulgar, vulgar. Their ignorance—their stingy, grudging, defiant attitude towards everything European—their perpetual reference of all
things to some American standard or precedent which exists only in
their own unscrupulous wind-bags—and then our unhappy poverty
of voice, of speech and of physiognomy—these things glare at you
hideously." But he also saw virtues in his countrymen, though not of
the social sort. "We seem a people of *character,* we seem to have energy,
capacity and intellectual stuff in ample measure. What I have pointed
at as our vices are the elements of the modern man with *culture* quite
left out. It's the absolute and incredible lack of *culture* that strikes you
in common travelling Americans."

By contrast, he admired the English abroad. They had manners and
language, a social and a cultural civility, particularly the men. "The
[English] women are at once better and worse than the men. Occasionally they are hard, flat, and greasy and dowdy to downright repulsiveness; but frequently they have a modest, matronly charm which is
the perfection of womanishness." But it was to the men that he was
attracted. "One especially, whom I met at Verona, won my affections
so rapidly that I was really sad at losing him. But he has vanished,
leaving only a delightful impression and not even a name—a man of
about thirty-eight, with a sort of quiet perfection of English virtue
about him." Deeply lonely, with nowhere to turn but homeward in his
letters, he signed one of them, to his mother, "your lone and loving
exile." When Norton arrived in Florence toward the end of the month,
scouting for an apartment for his family, Henry junior happily spent
the day accompanying him on his search. He fantasied how wonderful
it would be if his parents and sister would come and join him in Florence, where they would all live together. "But it's a very silly wish.
You would die of loneliness."[46]

Within a few days of arriving in Florence, he began to complain of
being ill again, recounting a summer- and autumn-long history of
valiant struggle with a sensitive stomach and with constant constipation
that belied the absence of such complaints from his letters of the previous months. He had not ever been well, he claimed, since leaving
England. The beneficial effects of the Malvern residence had disap-

peared immediately on touching European soil. Because his stomach was sensitive to fruit, he felt compelled to eat a good deal of meat, always breakfasting on a beefsteak and having meat and a vegetable for dinner. Having eliminated potatoes and wine, this diet seemed sensible to him, at least the best he could do under the circumstances. "Those old attacks of pain [had] almost completely disappeared," but any small error in his diet extended his constant feeling of "hideous repletion." At Venice, his sufferings "came as near as possible to quite defeating the pleasure of my stay." In addition, he was having trouble urinating. "I may actually say that I *can't get a passage*. My 'little squirt' has ceased to have more than a nominal use. The water either remains altogether or comes out as innocent as it entered. For the past ten days I have become quite demoralized & have been frantically dosing myself with pills. But they too are almost useless & I may take a dozen & hardly hear of them. In fact, I don't pretend to understand how I get on. When I reflect upon the utterly insignificant relation of what I get rid of to what I imbibe, I wonder that flesh & blood can stand it."[47]

At the middle of October 1869, as the Florentine weather turned bitterly cold, he had a crisis. Having taken two laxative pills recommended by an English druggist, he suddenly found himself with a painful "species of abortive diarrohea," which forced him over and over again to the toilet. The only discharge was blood. He had, he told William in the specific detail that he spared his parents, fever, cramps, and headache. When he sent for a doctor, he was visited by an Irishman who gave him an injection. He still did not have a bowel movement. When a heavy dose of sulfuric-acid pills finally resulted in an evacuation, he felt better but still miserable. The doctor warned him about the abuse of medication. "He says, what is doubtless true—that my bowels have been more injured by large injections in the past, than by the abuse of medicine. He examined them (as far as he could) by the insertion of his finger (horrid tale!) and says there is no palpable obstruction." He hoped that the doctor's recommendation about diet and exercise would help "till the dawning of some change." It worried him that his back would again become a problem, since he had become convinced that there was an inextricable "relation between the state of my bowels and my *back*." Misfunction of the former would certainly bring on misfunction of the latter. Still, he could walk and read more than he could before leaving Cambridge. Though he would be reluctant to leave Italy with so much left unseen, he felt that he might do well to return to Malvern within three months rather than the six more he had intended to stay. By the end of the month, he had made up his mind "to leave Italy and fly to

England," the only open question whether he should "push on to Rome for a fortnight or depart straightway."[48]

The next day letters and magazines from home raised his spirits. He took them with him to the theatre and read happily between the acts of a Carlo Goldoni comedy. At Pisa, he spent two "very pleasant days" with the Nortons, the knowledgeable Charles acting as his well-informed cultural guide. He also took a long, enjoyable walk by himself. When he returned to Florence, he felt much better. He walked from Florence to a nearby old monastery, "perched up on top of a hill and turreted with little cells like a feudal castle," which he attacked "and carried by storm. . . . On coming out I swore to myself that while I had life in my body I wouldn't leave a country where adventures of that complexion are the common incident of your daily constitutional: but that I would hurl myself upon Rome and fight it out on this line at the peril of my existence."[49] If his existence was imperiled, though, it was not from any external obstacle or force. His bowels provided him with justification for spending this time abroad. The coinage of illness was the most useful currency in the James family. So too was the rhetoric of self-exhortation, of romantic wilfullness, made even more powerful for Henry senior's sons because of his ostensible deprecation of it. For Henry, this, now, was histrionics on the grand scale, energizing military metaphors to heroicize, as well as to give force to, ordinary activities made difficult by emotional hesitation.

(7)

On a cold rainy night, he took the train from Florence to Rome, arriving twelve hours later in the morning light of the next to the last day of October 1869. Allowing himself only time to wash and breakfast, he rushed out onto the Roman streets, "reeling and moaning in a fever of enjoyment." From the Forum to the Column of Trajan, from the Appian Way to the Colosseum, from the Pantheon to St. Peter's, through glorious piazzas, ruins, and monuments, in the next five hours he "traversed almost the whole of Rome." It was a city that did not yet extend beyond the Aurelian Walls, more a large village than a modern city, within whose underpopulated precincts there lay innumerable open fields and deserted ruins. Rome was still ruled by the Vatican, in its last years before disestablishment under the Republic. Later this Rome seemed to James and others, in the retrospect of years, to have been another time and another world. He felt, for a moment, as if he had been given a second, better life. "At last—for the first time—I live! It beats everything: it leaves the Rome of your fancy—your education— nowhere. It makes Venice—Florence—Oxford—London—seem like little cities of pasteboard." Suddenly here was a reality of vivid stones. "Here I am then," he told William, "in the Eternal City" through which the Tiber hurried along, "as swift and dirty as history." He went to sleep that night with the happy delusion that he was "a wiser man" than when he "last rose—yesterday morning" in Florence.

Catholic Rome interested him without exciting him. He enjoyed, as if it were theatre, the spectacular performance during these months of an ecumenical council, in session to strengthen Vatican response to the unification of Italy. Untouched by any of its spiritual or doctrinal elements, he enjoyed "the season of great performances." St. Peter's itself seemed "a first class sensation," its picturesqueness largely a func- tion of its massive size, and the sense that on its marble floors "you stand at the heart and center of modern ecclesiasticism: you are watching the heart-beats of the church." Unlike the Pantheon, St. Peter's seemed "absurdly vulgar," massive, ostentatious, Catholic self-congratulation coming off badly in comparison with the "simple sublime," the "*delicacy* of grandeur" of the more elegant, aesthetically economical structure. "It makes you profoundly regret that you are not a pagan suckled in the creed outworn that produced it." As if to parodically bless his very first day in Rome, he met, on his way back from St. Peter's, "his Holiness," Pope Pius IX, "in person—driving in prodigious purple state—sitting dim within the shadows of his coach with two uplifted benedictory fingers—like some dusky Hindoo idol in the depths of its shrine." The autocratic complacency of papal authoritarianism offended his American liberalism, "like a leaf out of the Middle-Ages," as if modern history, as if the American and the French revolutions, had not happened. When the pope came to say mass at a church opposite his hotel, he had another glimpse of "the Grand Llama" and his retinue. After you have seen "that flaccid old woman waving his ridiculous fingers over the prostrate multitude and have duly felt the picturesque- ness of the scene—and then turn away sickened by its absolute *obscen- ity*—you may climb the steps of the Capitol and contemplate the equestrian statue of Marcus Aurelius." For every Catholic desecration, there was an overbalancing pagan virtue, for every "poor sexless old Pope enthroned upon his cushions," there was a stoic, manly antidote. One "glance at those imperial legs swinging in their immortal bronze, you cry out that here at least was a *man!*"[50]

Offended by Catholic sexlessness and celibacy, he still went happily to a vesper service at the Church of St. Cecilia, with a new acquaintance,

Mrs. Bessie Ward. She was an American resident of Rome and a friend of the James family, who took him under her wing. He was grateful for the company despite the fact that she never stopped talking. The music and singing seemed "divinely beautiful," mostly because it was "immensely florid and profane in tone. . . . In spite of the crowded and fetid church and the revolt provoked in my mind by the spectacular Catholicism," he "truly enjoyed the performance." The Church was powerful, he felt, and not, for him, an evil force, though often a distasteful and uncongenial one. Its worldly elements interested him, its art fascinated him and gave him pleasure. A recent convert to Catholicism, Mrs. Ward communicated the excitement of her conversion, the possibility that once within the Church "you can be perfectly indifferent to the debased and stultified priests and the grovelling peasantry." He had no doubt that she was sincere, and he saw how Catholicism, in Rome particularly, might have the advantage of providing a sensual door into a spiritual house. But "there is a better Rome than all this," the Rome of ancient ruins, the Rome of the classical past, the Rome of the Colosseum in moonlight "beneath a radiant evening sky," of "the great transfigured statue" of Marcus Aurelius, even of "that divine little protestant Cemetery where Shelley and Keats lie buried." By the end of his stay, he was "sick unto death of priests and churches. Their 'picturesqueness' ends by making you want to go strongly into political economy or the New England school system."[51]

But he was not in the least sick to death of their pictures and statues. Day after day, he spent the mornings at the Vatican museums. Having managed to see Michelangelo's Medicean tomb at Florence, he made sure to see Michelangelo's *Moses* in Rome. Though he would have liked to visit the Sistine Chapel, he felt hesitant to inflict upon himself the crowds of ecclesiastics who met there regularly for the activities of the council. The classical sculpture at the Vatican and the Capitol astounded him. From one of the high windows of the Vatican, he had the voyeuristic thrill of looking into the "secrets of the papal household," even imagining that he had seen "one of the pontifical petticoats hanging out to dry." In the streets, "the human picturesque" seemed "quite as rich as the architectural." Though he was quite lonely, he did now have a few people to talk to. At his studio and salon at the Palazzo Barberini, William Wetmore Story entertained visitors of distinction, among whom was the young writer from his home state. Almost twenty-five years older than James, the son of a distinguished Supreme Court justice, Story had settled permanently in Rome to pursue a career as a sculptor. At the end of November, Aunt Kate arrived, her usual bustling, outspoken but much-loved self, having kept him informed by letter of her progression from Vienna to Venice. She pointed out to him that probably all his health problems were due to his not knowing "that the *skins* of grapes are *very* constipating."[52]

In fact, he had almost no health problems since arriving in Rome, though he feared that the virtue of the sulfuric acid pills was "rapidly waning." At the end of November, he had himself examined by "the chief American physician" in Rome, whom he did not find satisfactory. The doctor could find "no apparent or palpable obstruction or organic disorder." James was peeved "that as far as he can see I have only torpor." His back did not bother him at all. Though he felt he could not study in any sustained way, "little by little, on proportion as my bowels keep open, I am getting back the power of reading with impunity." From William's perspective, Rome seemed "to be fattening [Harry's] very soul." Still, he had made up his mind to leave Rome by the end of December, after two weeks in Naples and then Christmas in Rome. "I have seen it pretty well & despite many pangs, am fairly ready to go. The filth that is so remote from godliness & the dead weight of the moral & political atmosphere count for somewhat on the other scale." Germany was still out of the question. "Here I am at 26 with such a waste of lost time behind me." He needed England and America, the language he read and the literature he wanted to write. Deciding to go directly to England, to have Malvern do whatever it could for him, he would return home in the late spring or the summer, "when I shall have been absent about 20 mos." "This devilish constipation of his," William commented, "seems the only trouble with him now." When the news reached Cambridge, Mary James felt that an ache had been taken off her heart "by Harry's decision to come home. And father confesses to the same feeling very strongly."[53]

In Naples, he was revolted by "the hideous heritage of the past," the generations of poverty and oppression. At the end of December 1869, he took the train to Assisi, "thro' the great romantic country which leads up to Florence," then to Perugia and Florence, where he visited the Nortons. On New Year's Day, 1870, he walked along the cold Arno to a sheltered spot from which "all happy graceful Florence was watching the old year decline into its death-shroud of yellow and pink." Two weeks later, en route to Genoa, he felt the loss of a Florence that he had come to love. "Day by day my fondness ripened into this unhappy passion. I have left my heart there and I shall be but half a man until I go back to claim it." From Genoa, he took the Cornice road along the Italian Riviera to San Remo. "There is something hideous in having at such a place to get back into one's carriage. The color of the Mediterranean there is something unutterable—as blue as one has dreamed the skies of heaven. . . . There, too, the last sweet remnant of the beautiful Italian race looks at you with kindly dark eyed wonder as you take your way to the stupid unlovely North." From San Remo, he traveled to Mentone and Nice, where "Italy quite gives it up and Imperial France reigns supreme—France which I used to love—but somehow love no more. That passion is dead and buried."[54]

He spent ten days in Paris. Though at first Paris seemed stale and alien, he shortly felt comfortable, extolling the delights of his daily rhythm. His mornings he spent at the Louvre, afternoons walking, some evenings at the Théâtre Français, others comfortably before his fire in his hotel room. For the first time, he imagined how delightful it would be to live in Paris. When he crossed to England, London seemed ugly by comparison, the English flat and uninteresting, despite the intense interest of his finally getting to visit Rossetti. He missed Italy, which hovered beyond England and France as a more absolute model of beauty. Distance and time began to filter out almost all but the happy memories. But he was still pleased, especially by the wet, low, fast-moving, brightly changing English sky and the always green and now spring-anticipating landscape at Malvern, where he arrived in early March 1870. He walked eagerly and happily through the Worcestershire hills, alternating between longings for home, considerations of staying abroad longer, and the hope that his assiduous shivering in sitz baths would finally, permanently, relieve him of constipation. His mind was much on those he loved, including Minny Temple.

The possibility that Minny would meet him in Rome had been a brief chimera. "If I were by hook or by crook, to spend next winter, with friends, in Rome, should I see you at all?" she had written to him in June 1869. Her presence there, they both knew, was less likely than his. Her news was mainly about her "repeated illnesses." Concerned about *his* health, his homesickness, and the high cost of traveling, she generously offered to lend him money. "How much money would you like me to send you? I have lots," she cheerfully wrote. She loved his letters, which helped her to travel in her imagination to where her body could not go. Whatever wonderful "princes & princesses" he would meet abroad, she urged him to remember that "none of them love you half so well as I do." Actually, "if you were not my cousin I would write to ask you to marry me & take me with you."[55] But marriage between them seemed out of the question, other than as the indirect expression of Minny's frustration with her illness and her lack of opportunities for marriage, travel, and work. Without serious suitors, her poor health and her independent spirit completed what the Civil War had begun—her bedroom a place only for coughing and sleeplessness.

For Henry, his desire for his cousin was suppressed and discharged partly by his sense of his own ill health. He allowed himself the fantasy that some day, once he was healthy again, their friendship "on my part at least might become more active and masculine." But even if they both had been the marrying kind, ill health and consanguinity together made it unlikely that there ever could be a marriage between them. William, expressing the family fear of perpetuating illness, urged Bob to give up his semisecret engagement to a cousin, Kitty Van Buren, the granddaughter of the former president. Like Bob, Kitty had a long litany of physical ailments, including what William called "the family dorsal infirmity. . . . After all, what results from every marriage is a part of the next generation, and feeling as strongly as I do that the greater part of the whole evil of this wicked world is the result of infirm health, I account it as a true crime against humanity for anyone to run the probable risk of generating unhealthy offspring." In addition, "in the majority of cases, consanguineous unions will be hurtful. . . . To me the conclusion is peremptory and inexplorable; at the price of whatever sacrifice abstain from marriage—in such a case it is nothing but a civic crime."[56] Beyond that, and beyond Henry's sexual ambivalence, he felt financially threatened by the thought of marriage. Having someone else dependent on him seemed incompatible with his ambition to be a professional writer.

In the summer of 1869, Minny's Roman fantasy failed. Some family friends had offered to take her to Europe. "Think, my dear," she wrote to Henry in mid-August, "of the pleasure we would have together in Rome—I am crazy at the mere thought." Since two of her sisters were "doing queer things," one of them marrying a man twice her age, "why should I be behind-hand? . . . I must flee this spot, unless I wish to become the prey of a bald-headed Emmet." Henry agreed that his cousin Elly "deserved a younger man." Feeling weak, despite the summer weather, Minny feared that another New York winter "might go far toward finishing [her] up. . . . I would give anything to have a winter in Italy." Before she could post the letter, she had a severe attack of "pleurisy." Enclosing the week-old letter with a new one, she told her "dearest Harry" that she now saw that it would be impossible for her to travel. "It would never do for me to be ill away from home," dependent on the kindness of even the kindest friends. Disenchanted, she no longer had the heart for a European trip. But she assured him that she felt "much better, now-a-days. Good-bye, dear Harry. 'Words is wanting' to tell you all the affection & sympathy I feel for you. Take care of yourself. Write soon. God bless you."[57]

In the gray mild March weather at Malvern, home was much on

his mind. One night he dreamed of meeting Minny someplace during the summer. Another night he dreamed of great succulent piles of fresh American vegetables to substitute for the "absolutely ludicrous" narrowness of an English diet. He also dreamed of going horseback riding every day for exercise. Almost inexplicably, he fantasied about John La Farge becoming his daily companion among the Malvern scenery, despite his "peculiarities" of character, perhaps because La Farge was his reference point for landscape intensity, but mostly because La Farge represented Newport days and emotions connected with America and Minny. Lonely, without companionship, he denounced, to William, the intellectual narrowness and imaginative dullness of the English. They exasperated him not only because "they can't say more, but that they wouldn't if they could." Still, "they are a great people for all that." He was especially tired of "the plainness and stiffness and tastelessness of the women," particularly revolted by "their dreary deathly want of—what shall I call it?—Clover Hooper has it—intellectual grace—Minny Temple has it—moral spontaneity. They live wholly in the realm of the cut and dried." The beauty, grace, elegance, and cleverness of American women seemed to him one of the great achievements of American culture. Suddenly, the achievement was both memorialized and diminished. On the morning of March 26, he received news from his mother, "news more strong and painful than I can find words to express," that weak, tired Minny, apparently no more ill than she had been for some time, had suddenly, unexpectedly, died.[58]

Five

"CATS AND MONKEYS"

1870–1875

(1)

Holding in his hand the letter from his mother, he was, characteristically, at a loss neither for feelings nor words. He spent the morning "letting the awakened swarm of old recollections and associations flow into [his] mind—almost *enjoying* the exquisite pain they provoke." Minny's death seemed an "absolute remedy," devastating in its unexpectedness. He had not given a moment's thought to the possibility that she would *actually* die. Her last six months, he soon learned, had been months of rapid decline. While he had been living her dream of European travel, she had been aware that she was dying, though never admitting that death was certain. Until the last moment of life, desiring to live, she struggled against the inevitable. Two weeks before her death, a pulmonary specialist had told her "point blank that she had less than two years to live."[1]

Who would wish her to be still alive, he wrote to his mother, if her fate were to repeat the suffering of such a painful death? He preferred to think that nothing could have saved her. In his mind, she rested more securely, less threateningly, as happily dead, the only state compatible with such a high capacity to feel life without any practical capacity to live it. Her personality, as well as her health, seemed to him to have precluded accommodation, her spirits too high, rebellious, and independent, too impatient of imperfection to have adjusted to the grossness of physical existence in an imperfect world. "That she was restless—that she was helpless—that she was unpractical," all things that had been widely said about her, now seemed to him true. "She was at any rate the helpless victim and toy of her own intelligence," her future "a sadly insoluble problem." No one could have saved her, no fantasy of rescue was possible. Even the wish that her life might have been prolonged seemed impossible to him without also feeling "some irresistible mission to reconcile her to a world to which she was essentially hostile." He felt the overflowing sadness of her death, "the sense of how much I knew her and how much I loved her."[2]

But he had had no mission to reconcile her to life. He had committed himself elsewhere. She was now, for him, as she had been less fully and finally before, a vehicle for intensifying feeling, for heightening his responses to life, for the experience of carrying with him always "Minny somehow present, directly or indirectly—and with all that wonderful ethereal brightness of presence which was so peculiarly her own." She was "the very heroine of our common scene. . . . Twenty years hence what a pure eloquent vision she will be."[3] Now she was, suddenly, but also gradually, as he worked it through, a catalyst of the memory and a property of the literary imagination. Her death was a gift both to her and to him, and he dealt with his touches of guilt at this self-serving postmortem by his barely conscious awareness that he was simply making use of what had been given to him. Having proved unsuitable for life, she had now been appropriated for art.

That evening in late March 1870, after a long walk in the Malvern hills, he felt "already strangely familiar with the idea of Minny's death." With novelistic enthusiasm, he wanted to know "all of the small facts and details of her last week . . . any gossip that comes to your head," he told his mother. He had no doubt that "by the time it reaches me it will be very cheerful reading," a welcome addendum to the memories of her that he had been soliciting from his own recollection, partly so that her "rare personality" might "shine out with absolute defiant reality," and also because she and her dying were a resource that he would draw on in later years. "It's almost as if she had passed away— as far as I am concerned—from having served her purpose, that of standing well within the world, inviting me and inviting me onward by all the bright intensity of her example."[4]

He resisted, as best he could, transforming "the hard truth that she is *dead*" into allegorical abstractions, into personal paradigms that expressed his emotional needs rather than confronted a stark reality. "While I sit spinning my sentences she is *dead:* and I suppose it is partly to defend myself from too direct a sense of her death that I indulge in this fruitless attempt to transmute it from a hard fact into a soft idea." So, too, did William resist, exhorting himself, "by that big part of me in the tomb with you," to "realize and believe in the immediacy of death!" Minny, he wrote in his diary, "your death makes me feel the nothingness of all our egotistic fury." Learn, he urged himself, to make use of the lesson of her death: that "tragedy is at the heart of us."[5]

For Henry, the fact faded quickly. The lesson was not that of the acceptance of the tragic nature of life. The fancy absorbed him. It was a novel delight to think of Minny without the concern for her health and well-being that he inevitably felt when she had been alive. "She has gone where there is neither marrying nor giving in marriage! no illusions and no disillusions—no sleepless nights and no ebbing strength. The more I think of her the more perfectly satisfied I am to have her translated from this changing realm of fact to the steady realm of thought. There she may bloom into a beauty more radiant than our dull eyes may avail to contemplate." Like Dickens' sister-in-law Mary Hogarth, who also died at a young age, Minny Temple would have had to be invented if she had not existed. Having existed, she needed to be perpetuated, to be made part of the process of the artist's ongoing imaginative development. "In exchange for you, dearest Minny, we'll all keep your future. Don't fancy that your task is done. Twenty years hence we shall be loving with your love and longing with your eagerness and suffering with your patience."[6] For the aspiring novelist, the ultimate facts were those of personal need, of what would be for him the highest possible level of interaction between personal feeling and the impersonality of artistic form. He was putting into practice the lesson of Dickens' "merciless military eye," that economy of perception that took in everything in the briefest of glances, that maximized experience so that the greatest amount of life and art was gained from the smallest amount of energy and time expended.

Italy was behind him now, England a temporary sanitorium. Staying abroad even into the summer seemed undesirable. Minny's death was a barb to a homesickness intensified by Aunt Kate's arrival in England. Distressed by pains in his side and by lingering constipation, despite innumerable sitz baths, he went up to London and consulted a specialist. He felt relieved by the news that he had an ordinary kidney infection that would not bother him much longer. Whatever his health problems, he had no doubt that he could safely imagine a future for himself. What he could not put out of his mind was that "just as I am beginning life, she has ended it."[7]

But he could not see his way to continuing it in Europe. If he returned to Cambridge, he feared that "it's from the life of home that I shall really miss her." Her associations with Newport, with Cambridge, with New York, would make residence in America even more difficult than it might be otherwise. But he had little choice. His parents were not enthusiastic about his staying abroad longer. He missed his family, especially the companionship of William. That he had survived and even overcome loneliness in the interest of a greater good was a triumph, but it was a triumph at a cost that he could not continuously maintain. Exploring various financial scenarios that might help keep him abroad, he saw that none of them could overcome his parents' increasingly reluctant cooperation. To spend the summer in Europe would be to incur "an expense without a very definite object," William explained to Bob.[8] Still not feeling well, Henry told Grace Norton that he hoped "to mend rapidly at home," though why, then, all that money should have been spent on his European cure might have seemed questionable to the family. Still, consistency was not necessary in these things.

To Henry, it was simply time to go home. All parties to the venture shared the feeling that he had had his turn, that he had been long enough abroad on the family purse. "On the whole I am very well disposed toward going—!" But at the same time "I have no heart to dilate on it. It's a good deal like dying. Farewell, beloved survivors."[9] Unlike Minny, he was only crossing the Atlantic. But the death rhetoric appealed to him, partly for the association with Minny, partly because he would have many more chances at life. On the last day of April 1870, he and Aunt Kate sailed from Liverpool, on the *Scotia,* bound for New York.

(2)

Sitting in the spring breeze on the porch at Shady Hill, the grass jeweled with buttercups, the silver trees sparkling with apple blossoms, he felt the air "heavy with whispering spirits." On the veranda with Lizzie Boott and Clover Hooper, he "immensely enjoy[ed] the fun" of a lunch party. The Norton woods swayed partly with the ghostly presence of their absent owners, whose residence in Italy seemed to him a bittersweet reminder of his own presence in Cambridge. Now that he was in America again, what was he "going to do with it?" He complained mildly about how the May breeze felt like August, how unattractively the Harvard campus was being expanded, how the ten days since his return, after an unusually calm, comfortable voyage, now seemed like ten years. His family appeared well, Alice in noticeably better health, William improving, Bob and Wilky managing satisfactorily, Aunt Kate "wonderfully well," energetic, and "delightfully amiable," his parents in good health.

Happily welcomed back into the arms of the family, he seemed to them sufficiently improved in health to justify the money that had been spent on his time abroad. To William's eyes, his brother had returned noticeably changed for the better, his back no longer a problem. Most of all, "he looks tough and stout, and seems in every way a different being from what he used to be." The twenty-seven-year-old Henry had thickened, as if he were a well-fed athlete having difficulty keeping his weight down, "his figure . . . compact and sturdy," he soon wrote in a disguised self-portrait, "and, on the whole, his best point; although, owing to an incurable personal shyness, he had a good deal of awkwardness of movement. He was fastidiously neat in his person and extremely precise and methodical in his habits, which were of the sort supposed to mark a man for bachelorhood. The desire to get the better of his diffidence had given him a somewhat ponderous formalism of manner."[10] With full lips, bright gray eyes, and dark hair receding rapidly, the energy of his face moved upward to its climax in his large forehead. The differentness, though, was more than physical, though the precise nature of that moreness William could not quite define. Neither could Henry, except insofar as he expressed himself with a new frankness about himself that had some of the characteristics of a personal style and carried himself with a moral and aesthetic self-confidence that he had not had before. He had become wiser, in the sense of having found a place for himself within himself, wherever he might be. It was as if his childishness had matured into confident self possession, as if Minny's death had made his own death, let alone illness, impossible for the time being. His European travels had thrown him back upon himself in a way that made him less dependent on any particular place or people, particularly on America and his family.

Within weeks of his arrival in "our dear detestable common Cambridge," William saw the likely result of Harry's return. It would be a visit, not a residence. "I imagine that he will end, when he becomes 'self-supporting,' by spending most of his time" in Europe. "Certainly with his artistic temperament and literary occupations, I should not blame him for the choice."[11] For the moment, there were few choices to be made other than where to spend the summer and how best to put his pen to use to begin to earn the living that might eventually free him from economic dependence. Twenty Quincy Street, which his parents had just purchased, seemed to him flat, stale, even threatening in its probable reimposition of a routine that would quickly make his European experiences seem far away. He was threatened by idleness, by what to do with his time when he was not writing or reading, by a lack of stimulation in a family environment that he knew too well and in a city whose cultural resources seemed thin.

Soon after he arrived, summer gave him the excuse to leave. Much of July 1870 he spent at Saratoga, much of August in Newport, apparently having easily persuaded Godkin that essay-reports on such well-known summer resorts would be of interest to the readers of *The Nation*. He went to Saratoga with the presumption that it was mostly an "elegant wilderness" and found it, in fact, "the embodiment of the complex machinery of a city of pleasure," bustling with shops, tourists, sidewalks, a "dense, democratic, vulgar" place. From the immense piazza of the Union Hotel, he could observe the nascent phenomenon of the American summer resort created on democratic principles and attracting vacationers of every class from all over the country. It seemed filled with "people who know no one, who have money and finery and possessions, only no friends." The men sat with "their white hats tilted forward, and their chairs tilted back, and their feet tilted up, and their cigars and toothpicks forming various angles with these various lines . . . in their faces a tacit reference to the affairs of a continent," people "of a somewhat narrow and monotonous experience." The beautifully dressed women literally wore on their bodies "the democratisation of elegance." Dressing "for publicity," for everyone rather than for themselves or for one person, they dressed for no one and lived "in a sort of splendid social isolation." Their children, "the little girls especially— lean, pale, formidable," roamed the piazzas and the corridors of the hotels far into the night. During the day, the heat, the dust, the glare, did him far more damage, he felt, than the Saratoga waters did him good.[12]

By the end of the month, with his article ready for Godkin, he was happy to leave for two weeks in Newport.[13] In contrast to Saratoga, Newport had the climate of home, the advantage of long familiarity, of a settled, established community, of refreshing ocean breezes. Having expanded only modestly, Newport essentially remained the Newport of pre–Civil War years, its villas still modest by comparison with what was to come later. New England and New York manners were still restrained by Puritan values and public decorum. "Characteristically democratic and American," Saratoga deserved the greater homage as "the heaven of our aspiration," but Newport offered the daily advantages of "the lowly earth of our residence." Still, he had no desire to live with an uncomfortable ideal. He much preferred a comfortable actuality, and Newport that August was comfortable, despite its associations with Minny Temple, despite, or perhaps because of, its European resonances, its "villas and 'cottages,' the beautiful idle women, the beautiful idle men, the brilliant pleasure-fraught days and evenings."

Whereas Saratoga seemed the vacation place of a society "hard at work," where idleness is "occasional, empirical," Newport represented a society in which no one worked. "Nowhere else in this country . . . does business seem so remote, so vague, and unreal. It is the only place in America in which enjoyment is organised," and "a society that does nothing is decidedly more pictorial, more interesting to the eye of contemplation. . . ." And yet, suddenly, Newport, too, seemed to him characteristically American, simply because "nothing . . . can take place in America without seeming very American." For a moment, enjoying what seemed a month of moonlit nights and long days of happy harmony between the natural beauty of the Newport scenery that he loved and the agreeable, charming homes graced by sophisticated people, he fantasied that here was the perfect solution to an "insoluble problem— to combine an abundance of society with an abundance of solitude." For a short moment of the imagination, it tasted like lotus land, the fruit "more than ever succulent and magical." The happy people of the villas of Newport would be purged of their vulgarity by the beneficent beauty of their situation!

The fantasy had its origins in his remembrances of his happy Newport years, in the association of Newport with Europe, in his optimism about the America that would be, in which eventually at least some Saratogas would become Newports. It also took some of its force from the pain he felt at the news of the Franco-Prussian War, which began that summer, the first news of which he heard in "the great hot glare of vulgarity of the aligned [Saratoga] hotels of the place and period drenching with its crude light the apparent collapse of everything we had supposed most massive." Years later, his memories of the nervously shouted telegraphic bulletins "from the shade of an August verandah" took some of their anxiety from another more massive war from which the threat was greater.[14] But, in 1870, the Franco-Prussian War had force enough to make Americans who loved European culture tremble for the damage it might do. For James, there was only one desideratum: "the single strenuous desire that slaughter should cease."

His sympathies, though, were not with the French, despite his general indifference, if not aversion, to what he had felt to be the unimaginative bourgeois stolidity of German culture. Led by William, the immediate family was "strongly with the Germans," partly an expression of William's respect for German scientific culture and his fondness for a country in which he had lived. But the pro-German sentiment was also fueled by disgust with what seemed French arrogance, French "depravity and folly," especially the heightened rhetoric of French nationalism, the utterances of "barbarians and madmen." Decidedly Anglophile Victorians, the James family thought French culture less morally sound, less trustworthy, more shifty and morally unreliable than German. It was a view shared but given less priority by Henry than by William, but a view with enough truth to help carry the day, especially since it seemed clear to Henry that the French rather than the Germans were at fault in the initiation of the war.

He did, though, prefer French republicanism to Prussian autocracy. Politically he identified with liberalism, with the superiority of democratic institutions in the governance of a modern nation. But "the French Republic . . . has not been as yet so brilliant as to offer a very enticing example to latent Republicanism elsewhere." For Henry, an increasingly keen observer of French politics, the problem was that the French practiced republicanism in ways that damaged republican interests and values. Eager for reform, he had no stomach for revolution. He wanted what appeared so elusive, a stable republic in France. Socialism seemed to him economically unrealistic, and its realization, humanly wasteful. Nothing that the Commune could possibly accomplish would seem to him worth the cost in human life and suffering. Though he was later to become increasingly Francophile, to the extent that he now chose sides, he chose, for the only time in his life, to support the German position. But the choice had within it some of the flavor of a curse on both your vicious houses. He had two high emotional priorities. The first was the advantage Italy and Italian republicanism would gain in the defeat of the French, who had been a major force, in alliance with Austria, in the long occupation of Italy. It was Italy with which he most identified, not those "great pretentious lands . . . fiercely cutting each other's throats." The other was his deep moral outrage at what he felt to be the unnecessary waste of human lives, "this hideous tumult of carnage."[15] The Franco-Prussian War, unlike the Civil War in America, which had had the justification of a moral crusade against an unquestionable iniquity, seemed motivated by pride and greed. It threatened European stability in a way that called into question both the reasons for, and the practical possibility of, the sustained European cultural voyage that he had in mind. As a realist who partly idealized Europe, such wars threatened the very cultural values that made Europe so attractive.

Neither war in Europe nor ambivalence about being back in America kept him from a steady commitment to earn his own living. Though "thoroughly content to have returned" when he did, he was determined to "go abroad again on a better basis." But since he had come home for an indeterminate time, he wanted to make the best of it, to "see all I can of America and *rub it in,* with unfaltering zeal." He did not, though, have substantial plans to travel. The American West meant nothing to him, and it would cost more than he could afford. Bob's settling in Milwaukee seemed to him a wilderness burial in "one of the innermost circles of the Inferno."[16] When, in the next year, Wilky journeyed to California with Emerson and Emerson's wealthy son-in-law, who had arranged the trip in the hope that it would revitalize the prematurely tired Emerson, Henry may have found the thought of California exotic. But he did not find it attractive. His American observation eventually had somewhat of a local quality. American culture was predominately an eastern, and even a northeastern, phenomenon, and his Americanness was absolutely clear to him, ineradicable. He wanted to know as much about his country as possible. "I know that if I ever go abroad again for a long residence, I shall at best be haunted and wracked, whenever I hear an American sound, by the fantasy of thankless ignorance and neglect of my native land," an anticipation of a kind of "sentimental purgatory" that, in fact, he was often to experience.

Social life of a satisfactory sort was available. During the first winter of his return, he attended James Russell Lowell's Harvard lectures on Italian poetry and at the end of the summer of 1870, he spent a few days at Concord as Emerson's guest, "pleasantly, but with slender profit." James saw Howells frequently, and spent time with Arthur Sedgwick, Susan Norton's brother, a burly, blustering, affable young Harvard Law School graduate who sometimes contributed articles to *The Nation*. He also met Henry Adams, who had just been appointed a professor of history at Harvard and had assumed the editorship of the *North American Review*. Adams was a short, slim, elegant, and ironical young historian, the increasingly self-dispossessed son of a distinguished American patriarchal family. He seemed to James "a youth of genius and energy—or at least of talent and energy." From their Cambridge associations, James knew Clover Hooper, Adams' future wife, better than he knew Adams. He was to know them both well, with ambivalence, in future years. Adams and he were to do an elaborate, affectionate, but cool dance together into old age and death.[17]

What he needed, though, was "regular and absorbing work." Early in the summer of 1870, Fields and Howells welcomed him back, and he resumed his profitable relationship with the *Atlantic*. His enthusiasm for Howells as a friend was great, his enthusiasm for Howells as a writer, limited. When some of Howells' travel sketches were collected into a volume the next year, he praised the perfection of their limitations. When Howells' first novel, *Their Wedding Journey*, was being serialized in the *Atlantic* late in 1871, he confided to the Nortons the strength of his reservations, which had much to do with his needs to define himself as a writer and to use Howells' limitations to advance his own dialogue with himself about the difficulty of being a novelist in America. For James, Howells' main weakness was his inability to look beyond "what his fleshly eyes have seen." Howells seemed to him a second- or even a third-rate talent, who would "always be a *writer—small but genuine.*" But the American scene "will yield its secrets only to a really *grasping* imagination. This I think Howells lacks. (Of course *I* don't!)." Still, "thro' thick and thin I continue to enjoy him—or rather thro' thinner and thinner." He feared that an American diet would eventually almost starve Howells into invisibility. His concern for his friend was equally concern for himself.[18]

With Howells soon entirely taking over the *Atlantic* and Adams the editor of the *North American Review,* he had two supporters in positions of literary power. He had every reason to believe that *The Galaxy* would continue to be interested in publishing his stories. During his twenty months in Europe, he apparently wrote very little, though he did keep a notebook, and his long letters to his family, which had been cherished and saved, were available to him to make use of. As soon as he returned, he started to write fiction, what William, with his usual mixture of irony and pride, called "a $150 story." He finished "Travelling Companions" during July at Saratoga and sent it to the *Atlantic,* to be published in two parts in November and December 1870. James never republished the story in his lifetime, but its heavy element of Italian cultural travel reportage, its conventional sentimental rhetoric, and its somewhat arch happy ending probably satisfied both Fields and Howells, who had encouraged the young writer to make the *Atlantic* readers happy. That the main character overcomes his concern that to marry means "to abjure" the opportunities and attractions of Europe "and in the prime of youth and manhood to sink into obscurity and care," probably seemed to all the important readers of the story, including Henry's friends and family, a reasonable and healthy resolution.[19]

Sometime soon after his return that summer, or even perhaps while still abroad, he began to write his first novel-length fiction, to be called *Watch and Ward*. By November 1870, he had put the first three parts of what had been planned as a five-part serial publication into the hands of the *Atlantic,* with the expectation that publication would begin in January 1871. He intended to have the remainder of the short novel ready by then. When Fields proposed postponement "for a couple of months," he protested. Since his main motive for wanting to stick to the original schedule was financial, he "would not regret" the postponement if there would be no delay in his being paid. Fields agreed. Publication was delayed till August, when the first of the five sections appeared.

"The subject is something slight," he told Grace Norton, and "a certain form will be its chief merit." With high seriousness, he had "tried to make a work of art."[20] Despite his intention, the result was quite the contrary. The short novel is slight in form but its subject matter is substantial, serious, and autobiographically revealing.

In fact, his mother might have felt some unwarranted optimism in regard to her hope that Henry would marry since the main character of *Watch and Ward,* Roger Lawrence, is obsessed with marrying. "From an early age his curiosity had chiefly taken the form of a timid but strenuous desire to fathom the depths of matrimony. He had dreamed of this gentle bondage as other men dream of the 'free unhoused condition' of celibacy. He had been born a marrying man, with a conscious desire for progeny." Apparently an advocate of Henry senior's doctrine that "marriage . . . alone emancipates one from the bondage of his organization," Roger, a wealthy, naive, good-hearted man of twenty-six, who has been twice rejected by the same woman, finds himself with the opportunity to help Nora, a young girl who is alone, penniless, and vulnerable.[21] He takes her into his home as his ward. Watching her with loving but voyeuristic intensity, he has her educated and trained into young adulthood with the hope that eventually she will become his wife. The story is structured around two triangles, Roger, Nora, and Nora's cousin George, and Roger, Nora, and Roger's cousin, Hubert Lawrence. George unsuccessfully attempts to manipulate and blackmail Nora and Roger. Hubert, already engaged, exploits Nora's finding him attractive until his erotic manipulativeness is exposed. A small-scale female *Bildungsroman,* the story chronicles Nora's growth from childhood to adulthood, in which her key challenge is to deal with the revelation that Roger all along has intended her for his wife. Shocked by the revelation, angry that he had not trusted her earlier with knowledge of his intentions, frightened by the complications, Nora flees, first to George, then to Hubert. Immediately disillusioned with both of them, she feels herself transformed by a sense of self-sufficiency. "She stood there on the pavement, strangely, almost absurdly, free and light of spirit. . . . She hailed the brightness of the day with a kind of answering joy. She seemed to be in the secret of the universe." When Roger comes into sight, she locates the substance of the secret in her realization that Roger was the only man in the universe "who had a heart." His reward is the marriage for which he has long hoped.

A powerful, raw dramatization, which he later neglected to the point of suppression, *Watch and Ward* introduces vividly some of James's major long-term concerns, particularly female puberty rites (courtship and marriage), the education of a young girl into womanhood, the tension between romantic female naïveté and male realism, the degree to which independence and self-sufficiency are possible for young women in our society, the strength, often destructiveness, of male sexual desires, triangular conflicts between two men and one woman, and the overlap between the father and the lover-husband role. With an explicitness that James never repeated, the novel uses sexual language, borrowed almost parodically from the popular novels of the day. In raising Nora to be his wife, Roger imagines that "the ground might be gently tickled to receive his own sowing; the petals of the young girl's nature, playfully forced apart, would leave the golden heart of the flower but the more accessible to his own vertical rays." When Roger and Hubert are in Roger's living room late at night, Nora comes down from her bedroom. "Her errand was to demand the use of Roger's watch-key, her own having mysteriously vanished. She had begun to take out her pins and had muffled herself for this excursion in a merino dressing-gown of sombre blue. Her hair was gathered for the night into a single massive coil, which had been loosened by the rapidity of her flight along the passage. Roger's key proved a complete misfit, so that she had recourse to Hubert's. It hung on the watch chain which depended from his waistcoat, and some rather intimate fumbling was needed to adjust it to Nora's diminutive timepiece. It worked admirably, and she stood looking at him with a little smile of caution as it creaked on the pivot." Perhaps clumsier than he intended to be, if he had such an intention at all, James never again used sexual imagery in such an obvious way.

Roger Lawrence, though physically similar to James, is an autobiographical antiportrait of his creator, one stage in the process of James trying out in his imagination the role that he had no emotional or sexual desire to fulfill. Strongly fathered and mothered, he did not want to be father nor husband. The problematic female role had a greater appeal to him. Nora is partly an extension of James's self into a female sensibility, her growth and education a mirror of his own. Unlike Nora, though, he had fought himself through to a position in which he could begin to feel self-sufficiency. Fortunately, he did not have to resolve the traditional female conflict in the traditional female way, by the continuation of an old dependency or the embrace of a new one. As a man, he could free himself of his father. If he could earn his living, he could travel where he wanted to, live where he wanted, be free to marry or not as he chose. But the conflict, in James's mind and in the society in general, would never be fully resolved into a happy alliance of female identification with male prerogatives. He was to write and rewrite ever more subtly this dilemma of the modern woman, with which he so

strongly identified. As to *Watch and Ward,* however, he later mostly
pretended that it did not exist.

By late 1871, he felt that "the love of art and letters grows steadily
with my growth" and that there was good reason to be optimistic that
he could support himself as a writer.[22] In March and April, he published
"A Passionate Pilgrim" in the *Atlantic.* In two parts, the story later, in
1875, gave its title to his first volume of collected stories. Well received
by readers and friends, the narrative, told in the first person by a James-
like American visiting in England, relates the story of an American who
desires to reestablish his English rights, embodied in an estate to which
he has a tenuous claim. Despite minor merits, the story is partly a
tourist narrative, partly a clumsy series of coincidences and unexplored
subjectivities. "At Isella," brought out by *The Galaxy* in August is the
undeveloped story of a mysterious woman in flight from her husband.
The story exists only to justify the extensive descriptions of the narrator's trip from Switzerland to Italy, which James drew directly from
travel letters sent to his family. Essentially, he was writing travel accounts disguised as fictions and directed at an American audience, most
of whom had never visited Europe.

Americans also had not visited sights closer to home. In September
1871, James wrote an account of a brief visit to Quebec, in the late fall
an account of a stay at Niagara Falls, both published in *The Nation.*
Quebec at first reminded him of Boulogne-sur-Mer, its foreignness a
welcome incursion of European culture on the American continent.
The sky seemed English, but the yearlong dominance of "the chilly
whites and grays, the steely reflections, the melancholy brightness of a
frigid zone," seemed terrible to him. He wanted a milder climate, a
softer place. Niagara he responded to with delight, the falls from the
Canadian side "as sharp as an emerald," constant movement whose
"outline never varies." He hated the hideous tourist shops and salespeo-
ple. But "you purchase release at last by the fury of your indifference,
and stand there gazing your fill at the most beautiful object in the
world." As much as the beauty of nature interested him, cultural atmosphere interested him more. Nature existed as a stimulus to sensibility,
as a catalyst for feeling and expressing oneself and one's culture.

His most revealing story of 1871, "Master Eustace," narrated
by a naive, romanticizing governess, is an extravagantly sensationalistic
Oedipal story about a widowed mother who has, from his infancy,
spoiled her son. When Eustace, returning to England from America,
discovers that his mother has remarried while he was away, he spurns
her for having betrayed him. He soon discovers that the man his mother
has remarried is his actual father, a discovery that results in his mother's

death, his own impotence, and the lifelong alienation of father and son. "Our imagination is always too timid," the governness concludes. A self-conscious variant on the conventional Oedipus/Hamlet plot, the story pushes against the boundaries of puritanical American propriety in dealing with a powerful sexual theme. The story sensationalizes the less dramatic everyday oedipal conflicts of the James household. Henry senior was very much at home, very much married to the perfect wife and mother. If Henry junior crossed the Atlantic in the same direction as had Eustace, he would be leaving behind what Eustace had returned to.

He continued to play with fictional variants of departure. He wrote a strikingly bad one-act play, *Still Waters,* written for inclusion in a pamphlet being published by a number of Boston ladies to raise money for the French victims of the Franco-Prussian War. It was not his first effort at dramaturgy. He had made innumerable childhood attempts to create stage dramas. In 1869, in the same month that he had departed for England, he had published in *The Galaxy* a brief, stilted, conventional two-person one-act drama, called *Pyramus and Thisbe,* in which two lonely, poor young people, both of them ambitious, join to become a couple when they are threatened by eviction from their apartments. Personal concerns filter through the stilted impersonality of the play in the emphasis on ambition, in the interest in loneliness, in eviction, and in change of residence, in the "I can't live here anywhere" abruptness of the eviction notice. For *Still Waters* he received no payment. Constructed as a triangle set in an American summer resort, probably Newport, the play presents a young man, Horace, who is in love with a young woman, Emma. He reveals to Felix that Emma is in love with Felix. After acting as the bridge bringing the two lovers together, Horace makes plans to leave for Europe. The homoerotic element is strong, particularly in Felix's description of Horace: "You're a passive feminine creature, Horace; you have a fellow-feeling for lovelorn maidens." And Horace's extraordinary response: "Why, at heart, we're all in love with you. Happy man!" The dialogue is awkward, with asides and monologues. The characters have no force, no reality, no real presence. But the autobiographical level of the play is simple and strong: the young Horace/Henry's homoerotic impulse, his identification of himself and his delight in playing the second male in a triangle, the male who loses the woman but in doing so gains the other man.

During part of the dry, warm summer of 1871, he made "a very pleasant life of it" at home "in mid-summer solitude" with Wilky. The rest of the family summered on the southern Maine seacoast, William hoping that daily bathing would improve his health. Henry joined them briefly in August. The Bootts, who spent July near the Jameses in Maine, were to leave the next month for Italy, for "an indefinite period," to reestablish residence in Florence. Henry, at Cambridge, lingered "in a darkened room all the forenoon, reading lightish books in my shirt-sleeves," and writing. On one "warm still Sunday morning," in the empty house the scratching of his pen seemed "the only sound in Nature." In the afternoons, he took long walks in the sparsely populated Waltham and Arlington hills, "full of sylvan seclusion and sweet shady breezy coverts which look down on the great blue plain of Boston and its bluer copes of ocean. I lie there, often, on the grass, with a book in my pocket, thinking hungry eastward thoughts." But there were good things, he realized, at home, such as these empty, unhaunted hills and woods that he could populate in his imagination with any shapes he pleased. Emptiness had its advantages. He often sat late into the evening on the veranda at Quincy Street gossiping with Arthur Sedgwick. "I confess that my best company now-a-days is that of various vague moonshiny dreams of getting to your side of the world with what speed I may," he wrote to Charles Norton at the beginning of 1872. "I carry the desire . . . to a morbid pitch, and I exaggerate the merits of Europe. . . . It's a complex fate, being an American, and one of the responsibilities it entails is fighting against a superstitious valuation of Europe."[23]

No doubt his earnings from his flurry of writing in 1871 had contributed to his musing about another European trip, "that fantastic dream of mine of another visitation of England and Italy." Just as in 1868, he had earned at least a thousand dollars, perhaps closer to fifteen hundred, at a time when the purchasing power of the dollar was eight to ten times what it is today. At the end of January 1872, the prospect of a trip to England and Italy arose in a totally unanticipated way. The James family had decided that a European tour would be beneficial to Alice. Her two oldest brothers had been sent to Europe for their health. Her own health had been variable, mysteriously robust at certain times, inexplicably bad at others. Various medical treatments had been sampled, from silent rest to mild electric shock. Why not try the European cure for Alice, especially since, more or less, it had been credited with stabilizing Henry's health and keeping William sane? She very much wanted to go. Probably Henry supported her desire, though they all worried that such a long sea voyage might weaken her, especially if the weather were bad. Still, though her travel opportunities had been limited, she had always responded favorably, as if there were some therapy for her simply in being away from the family. She seemed strong enough to make it likely that she would survive the voyage without undue harm. Certainly, they all felt, she would benefit from the stimulation of European experiences. Willing to dig deeper into the family pocketbook in the interest of her health, her parents were keenly aware that nothing else had worked. There was an element of gathering desperation playing counterchorus to Henry senior's and Mary James's characteristic optimism.

"I feel like first writing PRIVATE in huge letters," Henry told Elizabeth Boott, "and then, in a 'burst of confidence,' as Dickens says, uttering a certain absurdly vague hope I have of getting to Europe by hook or by crook, in the late summer or early autumn next."[24] The hook was the decision of the family that it made sense for Henry to accompany Alice and Aunt Kate during their six months abroad. Henry senior would provide the money for his son's passage and expenses. Beyond that, Henry hoped to manage mostly on his own. Early in May 1872, in New York, he saw Edwin Godkin and made an arrangement to do a series of travel articles for *The Nation*. He was soon joined by his sister and aunt. It was an excellent arrangement for Henry, a slightly comic, portable family that was a traveling pocketbook as well as a temporary shield against loneliness. During their travels together, Alice was frequently assumed to be his wife, Aunt Kate his mother. He did not mind.

(3)

Again he sailed into Liverpool, this time, in May 1872, with lighter, more lively baggage, two women whom he loved. The voyage had been blessed by clear, calm weather, the *Algeria* had been comfortable, Alice had hardly suffered. She set her feet on English soil feeling only slightly fatigued. The expectation that the ladies would return to America in six months was made certain by Henry's immediately going to the steamship office and booking their passage for October 15, 1872, on the same ship on which they had just arrived. His plan was to stay on longer, though how much longer was an open question. It would depend partly on how much he could earn, partly on how he would manage the inevitable loneliness and social isolation. Alice and Aunt Kate were a responsibility but not a burden. Happy to combine the ministrations of both guide and mother substitute, whose primary mission for these months was to contribute to the success of his sister's therapeutic adventure, he made them comfortable at the Adelphi Hotel, showed them the sights of Liverpool, and then brought them to the small, quiet, ancient village of Chester for restful decompression. Aunt

Kate glowingly reported to her sister that Henry is "always at our door about five or ten minutes before breakfast hour, and if you were to see him invariably folding, in the most precise manner, the shawls and rugs, which are brought in from our drives, and smoothing them down in some quiet corner, with the parasols and umbrellas, tears would flow from your eyes, and you would say, he is my own son indeed. He *forgets nothing,* and his care and consideration for Alice is unceasing."[25]

Since she did not need excessive care, he could enjoy her company, as he always had, and take some pleasure in her pleasure at seeing sights he had previously seen. For himself, "I find I am taking England in the calmest, most prosaic manner—without heart-beats or raptures or literary inspiration of any kind. After a certain hour one can't live on the picturesque and extract essential nutriment from it." Whatever excitement he felt he felt as the contagion of Alice's excitement. If he could have had his own way, he would have gone immediately to London, to a world of people and books, to the daily tasks of pen and paper. Instead, they spent a week in Chester, where they bored themselves one morning listening to a flat, childish sermon by Canon Kingsley, which helped James modulate his fantasy that beautiful surroundings necessarily produce beautiful minds. Next they traveled southward through Derbyshire and then to Oxford. Haddon Hall and Chatsworth left him cold. Lichfield Cathedral, Warwick Castle, Leamington, then Oxford and Blenheim delighted him, Alice enjoying "everything to ravishment," especially "the gentle Warwickshire Country." An excellent traveler, Alice "enjoys, admires, appreciates and observes to the utmost possible extent." Her "exploits have become such a matter of course that A.K. and I have almost ceased to notice them. She simply does everything."[26]

As manager of the traveling party's purse, he kept a close eye on expenses. He did not hestitate to elevate comfort over economy. Henry senior had been generous, out of his own benevolence and pathology— so much did he want his daughter to have the best of what Europe had to offer, so painfully did he feel her absence. He had provided a letter of credit, with the expectation that they would spend about five hundred pounds or twenty-five hundred dollars in six months, twenty-five thousand dollars and more in current currency, much more in actual value because of the low cost of services. As soon as Alice left Quincy Street, he moved into her temporarily vacated room for his afternoon reading, where he felt "alone with my darling" whom "we love . . . consumedly as usual and rejoice in every letter that comes as a love letter."[27]

Leaving Oxford, which seemed to Henry junior "the same old Oxford," cultivated, stunningly beautiful, humanly rich, they toured the Wye Valley, then spent two weeks in London. As they traveled, he wrote travel articles, "Chester" and "Lichfield and Warwick" for July publication in *The Nation,* "North Devon" and "Wells and Salisbury" for August publication. "It takes passionate pilgrims, vague aliens and other disinherited persons," he warned his American readers, "to appreciate the 'points' of this admirable country." On July 1, they crossed to Paris and then went almost immediately to Switzerland in pursuit of fresh, cool air and high mountain scenery. "My daughter a child of France!" Mary James exclaimed good-humoredly. "What has become of that high moral nature . . . that you should so soon have succumbed to this assault upon your senses, so easily have been carried captive by the mere delights of eating and drinking and seeing and dressing. . . . How marvellous my dear child your progress seems to be! what a benign medicine this journey is proving to you." A day in Geneva spurred childhood memories. The Hotel Byron at nearby Villeneuve combined ten days of rest, "collecting our wits after our recent furious wanderings," with the happy recollection of a childhood visit they had made there years before. From Villeneuve, Henry happily told his parents that Alice seemed "like a new—like a rejuvenated creature." She "displayed more gayety, more elasticity, more genuine youthful animal spirits than I have ever seen in her."[28]

Ascending to Grindelwald, where Elizabeth and Francis Boott joined them, they had a reunion for which Henry and the Bootts were eager. As they had in America, the much-traveled but lonely Bootts, now living again in Italy, sought the company of their James family friends. Lizzie was especially in need of the company of Americans of her own age. Apparently, they assumed that they were always welcome, as mostly they were. Henry was delighted to see them, Lizzie particularly. "We shall probably be together as long as we remain here. Lizzie is quite unchanged," he reported to William, "save in her singing, which is very improved. . . . She is now not merely a pleasing, but quite a moving, vocalist. . . . Her painting seems to have remained about the same, & her amiability & sweetness are, if possible, even greater." Francis Boott, though, did not like Grindelwald, "& we on our side, are a little disappointed in the air." The views up "the ice-paned glittering gorge of the lower glacier" were spectacular, but the weather was uncomfortably warm. Alice felt even less enthusiasm, particularly about Lizzie, whose company, after a week, began to chafe. The Bootts would be fine, Henry told his parents, "if we could only have them at discretion; but as attachés of our party they conduce a little to nervous exhaustion. This is especially the case in travelling when it makes some difference in Alice's buoyancy whether she is the centre of a body of three members or of six." Undoubtedly, Alice was in no mood to share her rare opportunity to be the center of a party of three and to be liberated both from female competition and paternal authority.

Leaving Grindelwald together, they traveled to Thusis, where they found the cool air refreshing, the landscape "a feast of color and a perfect oppression of lovely shapes." To Alice, though, the air "seemed over-exciting. . . . It made her nervous—rather acutely so—for the 1st time since we have been abroad." It was explained as "a case of climatic antipathy," which expressed itself as nervous collapse, a withdrawal into exhaustion, headaches, and her bedroom. She preferred "cities, monuments, and the *human picturesque*." Parting from the Bootts, they descended to Zurich, from where Henry ironically wrote to Lizzie, who was at Bern, that they were "at last rid of the 'bracing' air we were so eager three weeks since to get (such is life!)." Speaking for himself in the polite plural, "yearning as we are to see you, we shall probably stop a night at Berne." But no more, for obvious reasons. Also, he had enjoyed Switzerland "about as I expected to—not so much but that I wouldn't be willing at any moment to leave it for a more humanly interesting land." Since Alice quickly recovered, they were soon on their way to Italy. From Cambridge, Henry senior had communicated his tardy concern that they were starting for Italy "too early," into health-draining heat. Actually, the heat hardly bothered them at all. Though the Bootts "hurried their journey to Venice for the mere chance of being with us four or five days," the James trio left just before the Bootts arrived. Despite the mosquitoes in Venice making sleep difficult, they spent two pleasurable weeks in Italy. It seemed "almost like a couple of months—it has been so crowded with sensations surprises and pleasures." Alice loved it. In perfect weather, they took a short trip on Lake Como, stopped at Verona, luxuriated in Venice, visiting St. Mark's, Murano, Torcello, the Lido, having their dinner "most breezily on a platform where bathers and diners were strewn in true Italian promiscuity." They ate "innumerable figs" and had "ices every night at Florian's." He confessed that he "enjoyed Italy not, perhaps, precisely as much as the first time, but so nearly as much as to leave little difference."[29]

As they journeyed northward into Austria and Germany, where he found Munich "a nightmare of pretentious vacuity," returning to Italy was much on his mind. From Austria, he told his parents that his "desire to remain abroad has by this time taken very definite shape." He felt, in fact, "as if my salvation, intellectually and literarily, depended on it." That he felt this way was hardly news in Quincy Street. William had had no doubt that his brother would extend his time abroad. If his parents had any doubt at all, it was wishful thinking. He had rhetorically and psychologically prepared them for his seeing off Alice and Aunt Kate from Liverpool on October 15, and of course they all knew that he had no return ticket. When he shared with them his expectation that his travel letters and stories would pay a substantial portion of his expenses, Henry senior generously agreed to act as his business agent, and also to provide him with sufficient money to make up the difference between his costs and his income, including fifty pounds for new clothes. By the third week in September 1872, they were in Paris, where Alice and Aunt Kate saw the sights and the shops, where there were Bostonians to visit with, including the Tweedys, the Nortons, and the Lowells. "I mean to try my luck at remaining abroad," he repeated to William. "I have little doubt that I shall be able to pull through." Paris seemed glittering, brightly attractive, despite the tension and blood still in the air from the violent suppression of the Commune the previous year. "Even after all its tragedies Paris has a certain graceful natural wholesome gayety which is a blessing of heaven." In early October, they crossed to London, "the same terrible great Babylon as ever. Blood-drenched Paris seemed as a glittering bauble beside it." At Liverpool, he saw Alice and Aunt Kate off on the *Algeria*. Free at last, he immediately returned to Paris, with Italy on his mind.[30]

But he found autumn in Paris too attractive to leave as quickly as he had intended. He had reason to leave, since *The Nation* would not welcome his letters from Paris. They already had a regular Paris correspondent. But he feared that "the dissipations and distractions of Rome" would allow him less time for writing than he had in Paris. He also wanted to "dispatch a few literary wares" before he left, perhaps an article for *The Nation* on the Paris stage, certainly a travel essay on the train trip from Chambéry to Milan that he had taken late in August, speeding through the new Mont Cenis Tunnel. Admiring George Eliot's new novel, *Middlemarch,* for "its rare intellectual power, he immediately wrote a review, which he sent to *The Nation*. Liberated from family responsibility, he now had a stretch of time in front of him in which to work as well as to gather impressions. Where he would find outlets, though, for a substantially increased output was unclear. "Let Harry's wares," his mother remarked, "be ever so good, unless he can find a brisker market for them than the Atlantic Monthly & Nation afford, they will neither add to his reputation nor fill his purse. Why doesn't the Atlantic Monthly publish what he gave them a year ago?"[31]

He himself knew quite well why not. As a writer for magazines, his needs would almost always be subject to the magazine's editorial agenda. His style and sensibility, even in his travel letters, did not have mass appeal. When William criticized the travel letters that had recently appeared in *The Nation* as overrefined, running "a little more to *curliness* than suited the average mind," he responded that he had "a mortal horror of seeming to write thin." Though he did not say so directly, he meant that, among other things, writing "thin" was the inevitable result of the thinness of the American scene from which, for the time being and at great cost, he was doing everything he could to escape. William did not hesitate to offer the advice that "what you should cultivate is directness of style. Delicacy, subtlety and ingenuity will take care of themselves." They now began a lifelong, sometimes civil, sometimes exasperating dialogue on the subject of how Henry wrote. He self-confidently responded that "the multitude . . . has absolutely no taste—none at least that a thinking man is bound to defer to. To write for the few who have is doubtless to lose money. But I am not afraid of starving."[32] Still, he needed income, he needed food. He had an appetite, both physical and emotional.

Delaying his departure from "week to week," he extended his stay in Paris until December 1872. Despite what he felt to be execrably cold, damp weather, on occasional bright days the sun poured "over the opposite house-tops" into his little room in the Hôtel Rastadt. He had sufficient company for his needs, at first the Tweedys; Edmund remained "amiable, apathetic and elderly," Aunt Mary was becoming increasingly eccentric. They left for Italy in the middle of October. The Nortons, who were also in Paris, had been in mourning since he had last seen them. In Dresden, the previous February, Susan Norton, a few days after giving birth to a son, had died. She was, Mary James wrote to Bob, "a most lovely woman, the idol of her husband, and her own family." Before leaving Cambridge in May 1873, he had attended the brief service over Susan's ashes at Mt. Auburn Cemetery. As he had stood at the grave, there was "a momentary relapse into winter. . . . The snow flakes began to fall heavily."[33]

In Paris, in October 1872, he was happy to see the Nortons again, particularly Grace, and dined with them occasionally. Norton sent him to call on James Russell Lowell, who was on a long Paris visit, the same Lowell whose voice he had become familiar with when he had attended his Harvard lectures the previous winter. Lowell was a well-known teacher and writer whose presence had been a part of James's life without their ever actually having met, though they had lived "side by side . . . for so many years in Cambridge." They immediately struck up "a furious intimacy." He assured William, though, that they had not "exactly sworn an eternal friendship. . . . He is very friendly, entertaining

and full of knowledge; but his weak point will always be his *opinions*."
Twenty-seven years older than James, at fifty-six Lowell was an experienced Parisian, a student and Harvard teacher of European cultures,
an essayist and poet of distinction, who combined a strong patriotic
commitment to America with an enlightened internationalism. A Republican almost as interested in politics as in books, he was an amiable,
gracious, companionable widower, delighted to have young Henry as
a frequent companion on his long Paris walks, at his deliberations over
the purchase of old books, and as a regular Sunday guest for dinner in
a restaurant near his hotel. The first of the dinners provided Henry with
"the cheapest entertainment" he had "ever enjoyed," an all-out verbal
battle of high rhetorical flourishes and bodily gestures between four
conservatives and one republican. After that, he could "believe anything
of monarchical blindness and folly. . . . The state of mind exhibited by
the whole thing was incredibly dark and stupid—stupidity expressed
in epigrams. If the discussion was really as typical as it seemed to be,
the sooner France shuts up shop the better." Still, French politics are
"very lively and quite interesting and comprehensible even to politically
stupid me." He had his eye on the almost apocalyptic storms exploding
each day at the Assembly, where "the Republic may even now be
decapitated." One morning he "dwelt in serener air" when he spent a
few hours walking with Emerson through the Louvre. "Even when he
says nothing especial," which was often the case, "his presence has a
sovereign amenity, and he was peculiarly himself this morning."[34]

Usually he spent mornings and evenings in his room, afternoons in
the streets, "walking, strolling . . . prying, staring, lingering at book-
stalls and shop-windows." When the rains continued, almost inces-
santly, the Seine overflowed "like a sort of civilized Mississippi." He
wished, he told Lizzie, "to make the most of my last Parisian days."
He had a horrible nightmare. He was back in Cambridge, "a locality
which I appreciate but just now rank below Paris." For a time, he gave
thought to staying longer in Paris, perhaps giving up Rome altogether
for the present. But that did not seem sensible. It was Rome, he felt,
now or never, despite Lizzie's description of what seemed to him too
many Americans there. When Aunt Mary offered him a room in the
Tweedy apartment in Rome, he politely declined. "It would make one
feel the world was terribly small." Having delayed and delayed, he left
for Italy just after the middle of December 1872, traveling overnight
from Paris to Turin, then going on to Florence, spending "a lovely day
in that lovely place," and arriving in the vast, divine sunshine of Rome
the day before Christmas. Soon he was sitting "at my wide open window through which the sun is pouring and bathing me with warmth

and light."[35] He felt smiled on by the Roman weather. His spirits were high.

January to May 1873 he spent in Rome, where he celebrated his thirtieth birthday on April 15, a "solemn fact—which I have been taking to heart." At the end of his stay, he concluded that he had not worked sufficiently hard, that he had not written enough. But there was, he felt, justification for his unproductiveness. From the beginning, he had decided to accept almost all social invitations and to do all the sight-seeing that he desired. He wanted to seize the day and the place. Later, he could make use of what he had received. He felt himself coming of age, though with an oddly uncomfortable disjunction between his opportunities and his ability to make timely use of them. "Little by little, I trust, my abilities will catch up with my ambitions." His dissatisfaction expressed his modest opinion of what, rather than of how much, he had done. If he fantasied about writing a full-length novel, he still kept working on short pieces; they produced income quickly, and they did not demand an extensive commitment of time and energy. Numbers of his reviews and travel articles were already in press. He continued to send stories to his father to channel to the magazines likely to print them. Payment for accepted pieces went to Henry senior to reimburse him for money laid out. Infrequently Henry junior's earnings exceeded the money his father had advanced him, and served to build up his reserve. His father happily corrected his proofs, since it was impractical for him to do them himself from such a distance."[36]

Disinclined to write more travel articles because he felt his impressions were not as vivid as when he had first visited Rome, he kept a notebook in which he recorded daily impressions and possible material for articles. In January 1873, he did a short appreciative essay on Théophile Gautier, which the *North American Review* published in April and for which he received sixty-five dollars. William thought it "brilliant," Mary James told her distant son, "as good, quite as good, as Gautier himself! So prepare yourself for fame." In midwinter, he wrote an extraordinary short story, "The Madonna of the Future," which the *Atlantic* brought out in March. The story dramatizes questions of artistic initiative, productivity, talent, and self-deceit, and the relationship between art and reality. "The Madonna of the Future" is narrated by an older man who tells at a dinner party a tale set in his youth in Florence, where he had met another young American, Theobald, a painter passionately idealistic about art and disdainful of America, who associates the highest achievement that an artist can attain with the depiction of perfect womanhood embodied in the madonna and child. Having been at work on his masterpiece for twenty years, though no one has seen it, he has become the butt of ridicule. Monomaniacally preoccupied with "the true, the beautiful, and the good," Theobald takes the narrator to see his inspiration, Serafina, his model for the perfect madonna. To the narrator, she has only the remnants of coarse beauty. Aware of Theoabald's delusion, Serafina fears that the narrator will disillusion Theobald, which he does, without malice, only by pointing out the reality—that she is old, that she is no longer a suitable model. When the narrator finally sees the canvas of the twenty-year-in-progress painting, it is absolutely blank. While Theobald, who soon dies of brain fever, had "waited and waited to be worthier to begin his great work of art he [had] wasted his life in preparation." When the narrator passes the shop of another of Serafina's admirers, he sees in the window small, realistic, intertwined, playfully erotic statues of monkeys and cats. "For a week afterwards, when ever I was seized among the ruins of Roman greatness with some peculiarly poignant memory of Theobald's transcendent illusions and deplorable failure, I seemed to hear a fantastic, impertinent murmur, 'Cats and monkey, monkeys and cats; all human life is there!' "[37]

It was a refrain that James had begun himself to hear from the voices of French realism, whose views had gripped him from his first reading of Balzac, and from the inner voices of his own urging an increased commitment to the physical basis of life, to an art that created its structure on the building blocks of human nature and human action. He did not, like Theobald, want to waste his life preparing himself to create great art. Emotional and economic conditions did not permit him the luxury of that self-destructiveness. Also, the notion of an art based on abstractions, intellectual or religious, had the bittersweet touch of Swedenborgian illusions, of a world of angels beyond the flesh and blood that daily life provided and that the novel demanded. Any approach connected with Henry senior's philosophic views would inevitably mean failure. Swedenborgian angels, except as metaphors for the exertion of the will and discipline necessary for artistic creation, were inimical to art. He also needed, at least in principle, to confront the role and function of sexuality in human activity.

Just as Fields had encouraged the young writer to provide happy endings, Howells objected to the sexual message of some of the elements of "The Madonna of the Future," particularly the number of repetitions of the comparison of human beings to cats and monkeys. "With such a standard of propriety," Henry told his father, who, ironically, was negotiating with Howells about the manuscript, "it makes a bad look out ahead for imaginative writing." As a matter of necessity and self-interested accommodation, he supported Henry senior's agreeing to have a few of the earlier repetitions of the phrase omitted. But, though Howells clearly knew the reading public better than he did and his father was "quite right to make all convenient concessions," for "what class of minds is it that such very timorous scruples are thought necessary?" Considerably less prudish than many of their contemporaries, no one in the James family thought such concessions necessary.[38]

His opportunities for a rich social life in Rome during the winter of 1873 had seemed good enough to convince him that he would do well to take advantage of the opportunity even at the cost of his work. It was not a matter of being tempted away from his desk. The shy, slightly stammering, young writer from Cambridge thought it might be in his interest to increase his experience of manners and social life. He feared loneliness, one of the likely penalties of expatriation. He quickly saw, especially in Paris, that European society was family based and insular. But expatriate American society in Paris offered little in variety and interest. What point did being abroad serve if one associated mainly with Americans, often uninteresting ones who did their best to recreate America and insulate themselves from European life? The same conditions more or less applied in Rome. But the American community in Rome seemed more varied, lively, and interesting than the American communities elsewhere in Europe, and it was still Rome, the most dramatic expression of "this rich old Europe," despite the major change that had occurred since his visit in 1869: It was now the capital of a united, harmonious Italy that appealed to both his republicanism and his romantic identification with Italian culture.

At first, he missed "the high civilization" of Paris, the theatres, the cafés, the sense of bright lights and economic well-being. "Sight-seeing barbarians are oppressively numerous," and Rome "doesn't amaze" anymore. But soon he got beyond that. By mid-February 1873, Rome "quietly, profoundly, intensely delights and satisfies," despite its "barbarisms and miseries." He had begun, he wrote home, to "mingle enough in society to give a flavor of magnificence" to his life. Mary James rejoiced to hear of his "little sunny room high up" and "that you are a great favorite generally and much sought after in the American social world of Rome!" To William, it seemed that Harry was "drinking social gayety to the dregs in Rome," an experience, he skeptically added, "not without its profits." He had begun to find interesting people with whom to spend time, most of them Americans. The Tweedys were nothing new but still nice to have available. Within limits, he allowed Aunt Mary, who delighted in her handsome, amenable, cultivated "nephew," to carry him off in her carriage on fashionable drives (and sometimes tedious errands). The Bootts were there, Lizzie working at her painting, "very busy, happy and good." Sometimes she makes you fancy "from her deadly languid passivity . . . that she is acutely miserable. But she is evidently very happy."[39] Soon after he arrived, Boott loyally trudged with him up and down innumerable dark staircases as he unsuccessfully searched for lodgings and then decided that his hotel was bargain enough. When he soon saw less of them than he thought they would like him to, he felt guilty. Later, he spent more time with Lizzie; he felt that she depended upon him, and he did not dislike her company.

Soon a welcome guest at "three weekly receptions," he regularly visited Luther Terry's and William Wetmore Story's studios. A painter from Connecticut, Terry, who had lived in Rome for almost forty years, had married Louisa Crawford, the sister of Samuel Ward and Julia Ward Howe. With her first husband, the sculptor Thomas Crawford, Louisa had had a son, Francis Marion, whom James now met and whose later career as an immensely successful popular novelist he envied. The Terry salon and family attracted him, particularly Francis' sister Annie, whom he thought "the most remarkable person I have seen in Rome," beautiful and gifted, though "as hard as flint." In November 1869, he had visited the wealthy Storys for the first time at their fifty-room Palazzo Barberini apartment, where they lavishly entertained English and American visitors in Rome. James was happy to renew the relationship. He entered the palazzo reception room, which had "a *roof,* not a ceiling," through innumerable dimly lit rooms "besprinkled" with waiting servants. Under the high roof, one evening in March 1873, he met Matthew Arnold, "not as handsome as his photographs—or his poetry," with whom he had the thrill of a few minutes of conversation. The Storys themselves were agreeable without being interesting, Mrs. Story "fair, fat, and fifty," Story "friendly, humorous and clever." As a poet and dramatist, Story seemed tedious and vain, never more so than one night when James was a captive audience to Story reading his recent play to a few friends, "a five-act tragedy on the history of Nero!" As a sculptor, Story seemed to him to have merit but not genius, a corroboration of Clover Adams' caustic remark that Story "spoils nice blocks of white marble with his classic Sybils."[40]

Within a week of arriving in Rome, he met the beautiful, histrionic, and emotionally adventuresome Sarah Butler Wister, and her mother, the famous actress Frances Anne Kemble. Eight years older than James, Mrs. Wister appropriated him for a short time. He was flattered by her aggressive attention, and pleased by her beauty. At moments, she reminded him of Minny Temple. "She is almost beautiful and has the handsomest hair in the world; but she is 'intensely conscious,' and diffident and lacks a certain repose comfortable to her self and others." She "nailed" him immediately for a long walk in the Colonna Gardens and for a dinner the next evening. "A beautiful woman," he told his mother, "who takes you to such a place and talks to you uninterruptedly, learnedly, and even cleverly for two whole hours is not to be disposed of in three lines." Mary James reassured him that "Mrs. Wister is too conscious of her own charms to be very dangerous." He soon agreed, and confessed readily that, despite her beauty, "on the whole I don't at all regret that I am not Dr. Wister." At sixty-four, Sarah Wister's mother, "the terrific" Fanny Kemble, was too old to be dangerous. Still, she was wonderful, her "splendid handsomeness of eye, nostril and mouth . . . the best things in the room. . . . Beside her, Mrs. W. looks like the echo of Mrs. K. the voice." The daughter of the actor Charles Kemble, a brilliant actress and dramatic reader, an excellent writer of wide culture and extensive reading, Fanny Kemble had an intellect, a sarcastic wit, and a gift for pungent language that James immediately admired. He saw Mrs. Wister regularly, praising her as a " 'superior' woman but a beautiful Bore."[41] With Fanny Kemble, he developed an intimate friendship.

He found the women of his social world in Rome more attractive than the men, to some extent because he himself was an attractive young man of accomplishments to whom women responded. To the American circle in Rome, with its single women and eligible daughters, he seemed an eligible bachelor. He seemed so, tentatively, though dubiously, to himself. Inevitably, there were grounds for uncertainty, expectations, confusions. Probably Mrs. Wister had more interest in romantic companionship than in an affair. But other women were interested in a husband, just as Mary James and the James family hoped for a wife for the healthiest son of the household. The marriage mill had been grinding in Cambridge—marriages among friends like Clover Hooper to Henry Adams, Fanny Dixwell to Oliver Wendell Holmes, Tom Perry to Lilla Cabot, and marriages in the family. In November 1872, Bob married Mary Holton in Milwaukee. The family inspected with satisfaction the bride-to-be on a Cambridge visit, and Bob consulted with William about his fear of sexual impotence. Wilky soon became engaged, to be married in November 1873 in Milwaukee, where both brothers had settled, to Caroline Cary, a bride-to-be that the James family would have been happy to wish away. All the Jameses agreed in principle with William's generalization that "marriage is the normal state both for men and women, and the healthiest & best in every way," provided that bride and groom were blessed with good health. When he recommended to Harry that if he stayed in Europe he should definitely "get married," Harry responded, "You may expect to hear of my *matrimonio* by the next steamer. Perhaps the chamber maid here, the large-waisted Anna will have me." But Aunt Kate, writing him on the anniversary of the end of his previous year abroad, with "tender memories" of how solicitous he had been to Alice and to her, pronounced an anticipatory matrimonial blessing on the head of the man she and the other women of the family had no doubt was an asset to their sex. "God bless you dear Harry, and make you an equal comfort for life to some sweet loving worthy woman."[42]

He was a comfort, though only temporarily, to a bevy of young women in Rome, at teas, at parties, on horseback rides. In March 1873, he fulfilled a long-postponed fantasy of healthful recreation by renting a horse by the month. Galloping out onto the *campagna,* he felt exhilarated by the freedom and the beauty of the landscape. His riding companions were Sarah Wister and Mrs. Charles Sumner, born Alice Mason, a beautiful, high-tempered young woman about to be divorced from her senator husband, from whom she had long been estranged. They explored together picturesque country ruins and scenes. Alice Sumner shared rooms with Alice Bartlett, a vivacious, intelligent, unmarried young woman. Both "admirable horsewomen," "both very handsome in the saddle," they took their young friend for delightful rides that were "a physical, intellectual and moral education." Both women rode too hard for James. He rode well, securely. But he preferred a manageable horse, a steady trot. He kept up with them, with some fast rides and voluble conversation. But soon he developed a boil and needed a few weeks off the saddle. Deciding that "for me and my infirmities, they ride at rather a tiring rate," he took slower, less frenetic rides from then on, mostly with Lizzie.[43] He found the company of women attractive and educative. But apparently he did not feel compelled to fall in love.

As the Roman winter ended, he happily anticipated the end of his experiment with Roman social life. The "American colony here are a dark side to a brilliant picture." As he walked the Corso, it seemed to him that every other face belonged not only to an American but to one that he knew. When Emerson and his daughter stopped in Rome on their way back from a restorative trip to Egypt, Emerson "as lovely as ever," he did his duty briefly, lending them his pass to the Vatican museums. When the Adamses passed through on their way back from an extended honeymoon tour of the Near East, he saw them briefly, rather "vulgarly laden," he reported to his father, "with material treasures." The Adamses were "very pleasant, friendly. . . . Mrs. Clover has had her wit clipped a little I think, though perhaps she had expanded in the 'affections.' "[44]

If he were to return to Rome for the next winter, he would, he decided, avoid the American colony. He would be a more solitary, more hardworking expatriate. As the Roman spring came on, he decided he would stay as long as he could, despite the other aspect of Rome that dissatisfied him, the langorous effect of the climate. In Rome's relaxing air he had "slept in these three months more than in [his] whole life" before. The struggle was with his puritan conscience and his ambition. Pleasurable as it was, he found it distressing to fall asleep early in the evening over a book that he wanted to read. In early April 1873, the Tweedys went to Albano, the Bootts left for Naples and then Florence. The Wisters left for London and then America. By May, the barbarians were "thinning out very blessedly." In mid-May, as the hot winds began to blow, he hastily said good-bye to friends and traveled north-ward, first to Perugia, then to Florence, then to Switzerland, with the intention of spending three months there if he found himself comfort-able enough to work. He wanted a quiet life, mostly to write, partly to rest. In Bern, where he settled for three weeks, he felt lonely and depressed. He missed Italy, he missed companionship, he missed home. "What is the meaning of this destiny of desolate exile—this dreary necessity of having month after month to do without friends," he wrote to Howells, "for the sake of this arrogant old Europe which so little befriends us?"[45] Restless, he went to Bad Homburg, a famous water-cure resort just north of Frankfurt, where he thought he might attend to his lingering preoccupation with his bowels and general "seediness," and also write. To his surprise, he spent there ten quiet, productive weeks.

Though he soon discovered that he disliked the famous thermal baths (they seemed to him to drain his strength), he found Bad Hom-burg pleasantly cool, manageable, comfortable. He could quickly estab-lish his usual routine of writing in the mornings, walking in the afternoons, reading in the evenings. "A lovely little place," it was "insidiously reconciling" him to Germany, which he had "been hating ever since [he] came abroad, on the evidence of travelling Germans." Bad Homburg was Germany "with many mitigations," with lovely woods and gardens, "perpetual shade," pleasant coffee houses and read-ing rooms, open-air concerts in the evenings. Company was sparse but sufficient for his contemplative mood, for his desire to make up for comparatively workless Roman days. The Tweedys came at the beginning of August, lodging directly beneath him. He fantasied about long walks with Howells around Fresh Pond, about how much longer to stay on in Europe. "Mother loves you more than all her progeny," Henry senior wrote to him.[46] Undoubtedly, the family wanted him home, for emotional rather than for economic reasons.

He had sent two more travel essays to Howells, "Roman Neighborhoods" and "A Chain of Italian Cities." When Howells advised him to write less laboriously, he replied that he knew he was too "ponderous. But the art of making *substance* light is hard."[47] He needed the income from the travel essays, which he did not especially feel like writing. When Howells felt overloaded with James, he recommended that Henry senior try *The Independent,* a liberal New York weekly which published some of the best-known writers of the day. A new magazine in New York, *Scribner's Monthly,* seemed another possibility, particularly for fiction. Henry junior hesitated. He did not like the aesthetically low-toned company that *Scribner's* kept. But the balance sheet continued mostly in his favor. He could sustain himself in Europe by writing as long as Henry senior was willing to act as his banker, regularly advancing money in anticipation of money owed by his son's publishers or on the basis of the possible later return on a manuscript in progress. The investment was a sound one, probably one of the few good investments Henry senior ever made. To some extent, he enjoyed being actively engaged in his son's affairs. But Henry junior felt some minor discomfort, some small gnawing dissatisfaction. He wanted to do this now entirely on his own.

Before leaving Bad Homburg in late September 1873, he finished and sent off to *The Galaxy* the fruit of ten weeks of writing, a beautifully written long tale, "Madame de Mauves," in which a young American woman who romanticizes Europe and Europeans marries Count Richard de Mauves, the brother of her best friend, against the advice of his own mother. In keeping with the French assumption that a man of position may have both a wife and a mistress, he has affairs. The main character of the story, a young American named Longmore, is introduced to the unhappy Madame de Mauves, falls in love with her, becomes a frequent visitor at her suburban home, rejects the overtures of Madame de Mauves' widowed sister-in-law, discovers the reason for Madame de Mauves' unhappiness, and is encouraged by her husband and her sister-in-law to become her lover. Eager to express his passion, Longmore is guided by concern for Madame de Mauves and by his moral sensibility. She values her principles more than happiness, and asks Longmore to desist. He returns to America, to the shock of Count de Mauves and his sister, whose wishes he would gladly fulfill, despite the moral complications of doing so and despite his detestation of them and the values they represent. Two years later, he learns that Count de Mauves has committed suicide because his wife has spurned him. He had fallen in love with her again. "She was stone, she was ice, she was outraged virtue." When Longmore learns of the suicide, he thinks he will go immediately to Europe. But he has strong second thoughts, and then does not go. "The truth is that in the midst of all his ardent tenderness of his memory of Mme. de Mauves, he has become conscious of a singular feeling, for which awe would be hardly too strong a name." Madame de Mauves had demonstrated a strength of will and moral self-certainty that ultimately have transformed her into an image of ice. The story resonates powerfully with James's first articulation of his guiding principle, "Just live!" It dramatizes the problems and confusions that arise when moral directives, national characteristics, and individual personality impinge upon the full, realized embrace of life. Certainly the best he had done so far as a writer of fiction, the writing mostly sparkles with the crystalline vividness of a phrasing that takes some of its luster from an overall economy of form into which so much is richly encoded. He had written his first mature, fully realized story, a small masterpiece that richly anticipates in its art and in its concerns much of the best that is to come.

(4)

In the mild Florentine sunshine of October 1873, an exuberantly healthy William James embraced the brother he had not seen for a year and a half. He had come to Italy for the winter to regain his health, although to everyone else it seemed satisfactory. Apparently he needed at least one last major interruption of his professional progress before he would give up resisting the career his father had from the beginning desired for him. Having finished his first year as a low-paid instructor of physiology at Harvard, he had taken his own pulse and had diagnosed recuperation abroad as the desirable prescription, the illness at issue a "weakness of nerves." "Considering then the example of Alice's improvement in Europe & how easily life will be there this winter with Harry," he had "procured a substitute in [his] college duties" and sailed in October. He had no difficulty convincing himself that despite the drain on his father's capital, despite his detestation of being dependent again, this was "the wisest course." His teaching position would be held for him until his return. He would repay his siblings for this unexpected drain by debiting it against his eventual share of the estate. Having made up his mind in June, he seemed to his mother "remarkably strong and bright . . . so much so as to have at some times relentings." She thought it, though, better for him to go, though more than any other member of the family she felt that his health might be better attended to by attending to it less.[48]

Life together in Florence and then in Rome proved initially pleasurable for both of them. If Henry felt any ambivalence about having to share his Italian adventure with his older brother, he disguised it. He had intended to spend the autumn and spring in Florence. When William, in May 1873, had raised the possibility of coming, Henry immediately discharged his hesitations about another winter in Rome. "I would willingly and joyfully decide to go back." Also, he would not make the mistakes of overextension he had made before. Another Roman winter would be mild, productive, culturally rich, a sound experience upon which to launch what he felt to be his likely return to America the next summer or autumn. William had it in mind to "try to bring him home . . . in June." They stayed less than a month in Florence. By mid-November "his presence is quite an old story, and we have got pretty well used to one another."[49]

In Rome, where they went at the beginning of December 1873, they could not find rooms together. After a month in the same quarters in Florence, they may have been happy to have more privacy. Henry got back his old rooms. The weather was splendidly mild, "as brilliant and clear and still as our finest Octobers and yet even milder than our mildest autumns." William did not take to Rome. Having been reluctant to leave Florence, where he was comfortable, Henry felt disappointed in what seemed to be William's undervaluing of Rome. When, at the end of December, William came down with a mild attack of malaria, Henry was even more unhappy when the doctor apparently insisted that William leave Rome. Henry followed his brother back of Florence, where, at the beginning of the new year, he felt the irony of Florence seeming "a vulgar little village and life not worth the living away from the Corso and the Pincio." He felt a happy victim of the "cruel fascination" of Rome, and joked to Howells that if he could live there for two or three years he would write such wonderful things that he would "quadruple the circulation of the *Atlantic*. Don't you want to pension me for the purpose?" But he did not stay a victim of his brother or of Florence for long. With his penchant for accommodation, he gradually shook off the "ponderous shadow" of Rome. "Florence is as good as need be, and I am getting reconciled to it." His complaints were "from [his] pen's end simply

and not from [his] heart." With the sun pouring into his room, he
soon reestablished his spirits and his writing routine. Unfortunately,
he came down with "a strange and mysterious visitation . . . an affair
chiefly of the *head,*" which he ascribed to his "chronic indisposition,"
constipation. He assured his mother in the event that she should "cra-
zily murmur" that it had been caused by "overuse or abuse" of his
head, that his use of his "head has never been such as would make a
baby wink." Like "a ministering angel," William helped nurse him
for ten days, and then left to join the Tweedys in Dresden. Clearly he
preferred Germany to Italy. He had decided to sail from Bremen to
New York at the beginning of March, "vigorous and brilliant," in his
brother's eyes "*entirely* the Willy of our younger years again—in looks,
spirits, humor and general capacity." Probably his departure was a relief
to both of them.[50]

Once settled, Henry happily stayed on in Florence through the
winter, "liking Florence, Italy and Europe better every day," he confessed to his parents, "though I suppose it is disagreeable to you to hear
it." He found it a good place to work, the months ahead of him a
precious, dwindling treasure. The family preferred him back. It was
not a question of health, but of varying views of where his best interests
lay, personally, economically, professionally. They felt that if he stayed
abroad, a wife was a necessity. "There is something desolate in his
living here as an alien," William had remarked. "I advise him strongly
to look out for a wife—but he positively refuses to think of such a
thing. I hope however that if he stays abroad, he will." But, with or
without wife, the loneliness that they feared he felt in Europe could be
abated at home, in the arms of the family. His mother wanted "to
throw around [him] the mantle of the family affection, and fold you in
my own tenderest embrace." Either family or marriage they thought a
necessity for his happiness. "Your life must need this succulent, fattening element more than you know yourself. . . . Notwithstanding
the charm and beauty that surrounds you . . . the life of your affections
must need the moisture & sunshine, which only home, or the intercourse of a circle of familiar friends can give. I know only one thing
that would solve that difficulty, and harmonize the discordant elements
in your life. You would make dear Harry according to my estimate,
the most loving and loveable and happiest of husbands. I wish I could
see you in a favorable attitude of heart towards the divine institution of
marriage. In the atmosphere of a happy home of your own you would
thrive in every way, especially if your tent were pitched in Europe; but
even in your own less favored land, it would be a blessing to you." All

she meant, Mary James assured him, is that "I see so much in favor of your staying abroad, and I *feel* so much in favor of your coming home, that I am blindly feeling about for some way of reconciling the difficulty."[51] He felt that he had no choice but to return.

In theory, he felt he could be contented with America. But "when I go back I shall need all my ingenuity to put it into practice." Still, no matter the attractions of Europe, he granted that America was the place to which Americans belonged. Any relationship with Europe had to be comparatively artificial. He felt strongly how much Europe had kept him at arm's length, a permanent outsider. There was an "absurd want of reciprocity between Italy and myself and all my rhapsodies about it." Even in Florence, his society was "limited to waiters and washerwomen." But he had no doubt that for himself and others "who have been happy in Europe even Cambridge, the Brilliant, is not an easy place to live in."[52] The key to the limited happiness one could ever have was to be productively at work in a place that nurtured the sensibility and imagination necessary for writing. Such a place would have people of interest and affection with whom he could have ongoing conversations, enriching relationships. He feared that a daily dialogue with his own family would be repetitive and regressive, that a daily dialogue within the "divine institution of marriage" would be equally repetitive and perhaps sexually discomforting. It certainly would be expensive. Wherever he lived, he needed to be able to support himself by his writing. In Europe, he would need, he estimated, about three thousand dollars a year to live comfortably. At home, in Cambridge, he would need considerably less. But to live indefinitely with his family was now inconceivable.

When William left Florence in January 1874, he felt "rather lonely and disconsolate." Spring loveliness "on mountains & rivers & bridges & balmy days & lovely moonlit nights" at first consoled him, then reconciled him. Soon he felt wildly in love with Florence again. He did not want to leave. At an afternoon tea party at one of the villas on Bellosguardo, with its high, beautiful view of the city, he had the pleasant premonition that he would live there one day.[53] Meanwhile, he lived in town in a sizable corner apartment the front windows of which looked out on the attractive Piazza Santa Maria Novella, within easy walking distance of everything. He wrote travel "gossip" and reviews for *The Nation,* the *Atlantic, The Independent.* He wanted, though, to write a full-length novel; he felt ready to do so now, and the money involved was enticing. Having already made up his mind that he would return to America sometime soon, it made sense for him, in his comfortable apartment, in the spring weather, while he had the leisure, to get started. "Endure my absence yet a little while longer," he told his parents, "and I will return to you primed for immortality!"

The terms on which he would sustain immortality were important. In March 1874, he received a letter from the editor of *Scribner's Monthly* proposing that he write a serial novel for the relatively new magazine. He wrote immediately to Howells, with the sense of having an obligation to the *Atlantic* and a preference for its prestige. He wrote to his parents, primarily because he would need their support, since they would have to wait longer to be repaid the money he would need to borrow from them to keep himself afloat while he wrote. Having in mind a novel in twelve monthly parts, to run from November 1874 to November 1875, he wanted twelve hundred dollars, as if he were being paid for twelve short stories. *Scribner's,* he thought, would pay that. The *Atlantic,* he feared, would not. It also would be easier, at a later date, to persuade *Scribner's* to pay a substantial part of his money on their receipt of the manuscript. The *Atlantic* usually did not pay until publication. By the end of April, the matter was settled. Henry senior agreed to extend the money. Howells readily agreed to pay the twelve hundred dollars. James was delighted with the arrangement. The story is "to be on a theme I have had in my head a long time and once attempted to write something about. . . . The opening chapters take place in America and the people are of our glorious race; but they are soon transplanted to Rome, where things are to go on famously."[54] Anticipating that he would name the novel after its main character, Roderick Hudson, he set to work, as the Florentine spring turned to early summer, on a story that he hoped would be both pleasing and significant. He would dramatize his preoccupation with the nature of the artist, the relationship between life and art, and the dialogue between America and Europe.

As the weather became warmer, he moved his writing table from the room overlooking the piazza into the quieter, cooler back room. "Nothing particular happens to me and my time is passed between sleeping and scribbling (both of which I do very well) lunching and dining, walking and conversing."[55] He had hardly any visitors, and Florence seemed very small. At the beginning of June, the heat became scorching, almost blinding, the city empty. He did not want to confront the narrowness, the discomfort, of travel and hotel life. But the heat soon became so unbearable that he finally decided to leave two weeks before he had intended. From Florence, he went northward to Como, where the air was cool and fresh, then northward again to Baden-Baden rather than to Homburg. One summer there, he felt, had been enough.

Baden-Baden seemed an "enchanted valley," comfortable, beautiful. He thought perhaps he might meet the Russian novelist Ivan Turgenev, who was living there, whose novels he admired, and whom he had been writing about for the *North American Review*. But Turgenev had recently moved. James nonetheless felt that if Baden-Baden had been favorable to Turgenev's literary labors, it would be favorable to his.

Writing in the mornings, taking long solitary walks in the Black Forest in the afternoons, listening to the band and eating ices on the terrace in the evenings, he was deeply absorbed throughout July 1874 in *Roderick Hudson*. America was also on his mind, both as a theme of the novel and as an imminent personal destination. He had decided to sail from Liverpool on August 25, to arrive in Cambridge about September 4. "Be sure . . . to have on hand," he wrote home, "a goodly supply of tomatoes, ice-cream, corn, melons, cranberries." By late July, he confessed to Lizzie Boott that he had become bored with Baden-Baden, where he was spending "the dullest five weeks of [his] life." In early August, he went down the Rhine to Holland, then to England for two weeks, where he saw only the Tweedys, who had taken a country house for the summer. He felt moderately depressed but stoical about his fate. "You will enjoy everything, dear Harry," his mother predicted, "for a while at least, from the fact of being at home, and from the fact of our happiness in seeing you." He sailed from Liverpool to New York toward the end of the month. "I don't return with any great gusto, but simply from the force of circumstances." At Quincy Street, welcoming arms embraced him. Mary James was ecstatic. "Harry has come home to us very much improved in health and looks. When he came in upon us from his voyage in a loose rough English suit, very much burnt and browned by the sea, he looked like a robust young Briton. He seemed well pleased to be at home at least as yet, and I trust he will feel more and more for himself, what I daily feel for him, that it is much better to live near his family and with his own countrymen, than to lead the recluse life he so strongly tended to live abroad."[56]

But he had no intention of being absorbed by family life and by Cambridge and Boston society. He would be sociable but not intimate. The question of marriage was in the air, happily for William, uncomfortably for Henry. "When I get married I shall have a cheerful sociable crowd round me," William wrote. They all attended the marriage of Alice Keyes and Edward Emerson on a warm, moist, green day in late September, "old Mr. Emerson more gaunt and lop sided than ever," Ellen Emerson beautiful in a white dress. William complained that all his friends had "been so high toned of late, T. S. Perry, Ellen Gurney,

John La Farge, Clover Adams &c as to get married in secret." Perry had just married Lilla Cabot, a talented paintress with no family money, whom most of the Jameses thought unfeminine and inelegant. What the Perrys would live on baffled them all, since Perry "lives and writes and does everything like a somnambulist." To William, "Harry [appears] very well indeed and seeming glad to be back."[57] But he was not. It was simply a necessary experiment to see if he could earn his living in America, if he could find some combination of income and expenses that would make America a feasible alternative.

Soon he felt Europe "fading away into a pleasant dream." The presence of friends and the lovely October countryside was diverting. But despite the lovely weather, the familiar society—Howells, William, William's friends Charles Pierce and Oliver Holmes, Edward Emerson, Perry, Longfellow, Lowell, the Nortons, his parents and sister—despite having free room and board at Quincy Street, he had made up his mind that he would spend the late autumn and winter in New York. The decision had been made months before, in Europe. Cambridge and Boston were too provincial, too familiar. He wanted a larger scene, without the potential entanglements of family. With much of *Roderick Hudson* in hand, scheduled to begin publication in January 1875, he would soon no longer need advances from his father. Could he write enough reviews, articles, and stories to support himself through the winter of 1874–1875 in New York? During the spring of 1874, from Europe, he had reviewed Howells, Mérimée, Hugo, Flaubert, and Turgenev. His "Florentine Notes" had appeared from April to July, his "Tuscan Cities" in May, "Siena" in June, "Ravenna" in July, three more short articles on the Splügen, Holland, and Belgium in August and early September. In May and June he had published a two-part story, "Adina," in *Scribner's Monthly,* his first publication there, in August "Professor Fargo" in *The Galaxy.* The *Atlantic* had a two-part story, "Eugene Pickering," on hold for October and November.

Beating the usual journalistic bushes, in Cambridge in the autumn and then in New York during the winter, he had an even fuller, more regular flow of books to review and articles to write. He also brought to completion before leaving Cambridge the long-contemplated projects of publishing a collection of the best of his stories and another volume of his travel essays. In early 1873, Henry senior had urged the Boston publisher James Osgood to publish his son's short stories. Always aggressive on his son's behalf, Henry senior proposed an arrangement very much like those through which all his own books had been published. The author would pay the cost of the creation of the stereotype plates and would receive a 15 percent royalty on all copies sold. Henry senior would advance the cost of the plates. In March 1873, Henry had told his father, "I don't care to do it, just now." He did not value his earlier tales enough to republish them, except with extensive revision. He hoped some soon-to-be-written stories would be more publishable, and, in a year or so, he planned to include them in a volume "of tales on the theme of American adventurers in Europe." Also, publication without profit was of no interest to him. He emphatically wanted to distance himself from his father in this regard. In Cambridge, during the autumn of 1874, he agreed with Osgood on an experiment. They would publish *A Passionate Pilgrim and Other Tales* with the publisher assuming the investment costs and the author getting a 10 percent royalty on all copies after the sale of a thousand. They would publish *Transatlantic Sketches* with James paying the $555.00 cost of the plates and receiving a 15 percent royalty on all copies sold. Both would be editions of fifteen hundred copies to sell at $2.00 a book. When the accounts were done in the autumn of 1875, on the former James was owed $88.20, on the latter he owed almost $360.00.[58]

When he arrived there just after the first of the year, he found New York exciting, bracing. "I feel vastly at home here and really like it," he wrote to Howells in Boston. The city of his childhood had expanded and exploded into post–Civil War wealth and chaos, into "a rattling big luxurious place." He had some friends, mainly the Godkins, near whom, on East Twenty-fifth Street, he took a comfortable two-room apartment. Aunt Kate probably was living in mid-Manhattan with her cousin Helen. When Lizzie Boott visited in February 1875, they lunched at Delmonico's; he took to lunching with her there every Sunday thereafter. Sarah Wister and her mother were not too far away, near Philadelphia, where he visited them soon after arriving in New York. He saw a little of Arthur Sedgwick, dining with him at theatrical chophouses, as if they were "naughty Bohemians! Would that I were either!" Elected a member of the Century Association, probably through Godkin, he had the possibility of some social life there. Essentially a stranger in the city of his childhood, attempting to establish a rhythm, a social life, and a livelihood at the worst season of the year, he soon liked New York "decidedly less." With one or two exceptions, he had few social entrées, the city seemed aesthetically *"hideous,"* the winter weather "harsh and wild. . . . I lead a very quiet life and dwell rather in memories and hopes than in present emotions." By April 1875, he confessed that he liked New York "very well—for a week." He also faced a lot of hard, monotonous work, a winter torrent of reviews and essays to pay his bills.[59] Unfortunately, he found New York expensive, more expensive than Italy, more expensive, he felt, than Paris or London would be at a time when the exchange rates favored Americans living abroad.

By late spring, he had given up on New York. If he stayed, without more money and leisure, he would suffer the disadvantages of drudgery in a harsh climate, with few friends or social opportunities, in a material culture where money determined the fabric of daily life. By early summer, he had decided on Paris, for how long he did not know, but "for a considerable period." London was his first choice, his preference. But Paris had attractions. He felt he knew London well and wanted to know Paris better. French literary culture seemed to him, as a reviewer of Balzac, Flaubert, Sainte-Beuve, and Daudet, among others, more on the interesting edge of art and life than the literary culture of England. Turgenev, whom he still hoped to meet, now lived in Paris. He also had an employment scheme for Paris. From Cambridge, after leaving New York in mid-July, he wrote to John Hay of the *New York Tribune,* the assistant to the publisher Whitelaw Reid. Having recently met and liked Hay, a thirty-seven-year-old lawyer and writer from Ohio who had served as Lincoln's secretary during the war, he proposed that Hay help him to become a regular *Tribune* correspondent in Paris on " 'social' matters . . . manners, habits, people . . . books, pictures, the theatre . . . rural excursions," to feed the insatiable American appetite "for information about all things Parisian." He felt that he could fulfill it in "a more intelligent and cultivated fashion" than others. "I have a dazzling vision of doing very good things."

Since the *Tribune* already had a social correspondent in place, the request could be granted only in the event that "his relations with the paper are destined within the next couple of months to terminate." Hay had probably told him about the likelihood of a vacancy. To Whitelaw Reid, Hay remarked that James "would cost not more than half what Houssaye costs. . . . You pay Houssaye $30 for a not very good letter and me, Heaven knows how much for translating it. For, say, $20 or $25 James will write you a much better letter and sign his name to it." He urged Reid to "engage him. . . . You know his wonderful style and keen observation of life and character," and "his name is . . . far more regarded by cultivated people." Although he saw the advantages, Reid was cynical. If you like, he told Hay, "go ahead and make the bargain." But "I doubt whether it is desirable to pay him more than $20 a letter," and don't make it for "a fixed length of time." The readership of the *Tribune* "loves a change now and then."[60] Having expected more money, James was disappointed. But he accepted, with the hope that the lesser amount would be compensated for by a long run. He was to be disappointed there too.

Saying his good-byes in Cambridge, with a letter of credit in hand from his father, he sailed from New York for Liverpool on October 20, 1875. From the calm waters off Sandy Hook he sent his last letter home from American waters. During the crowded, uncomfortable, sometimes nauseating voyage, tumbling and tossing in "boisterous gales," he "loathed and despised the sea more than ever." He would be slow, he thought, to undertake the return trip, if only on that count. On the last day of October 1875, he was in Liverpool, the next day in London, comfortably relaxing "in the livid light of a London November Sunday" in front of a fireplace in a small, inexpensive suite of rooms at a hotel in Piccadilly. "I should like living here," he remarked to his parents, "if I belonged to a club and were in society." But, he boasted, "I take possession of the old world—I inhale it—I appropriate it!"[61] It was a supreme fiction. The appropriation was to work both ways. He needed to be free of the family of which he could never be free. He needed to work out some way to live and to work independently. He wanted to experiment with the price. At the middle of the month, he moved to Paris and began his work.

Six

"PERMANENT HEADQUARTERS"
1875–1878

(1)

In mild, misty mid-November 1875, from the windows of his quiet apartment on Rue Luxembourg, thirty-two-year-old Henry James looked down at "the same old Paris . . . a great bazaar," a glittering "city of shopfronts" before which he could dawdle. Color, variety, food, wealth, material things, Paris presented its surface brightness, its postwar and post–Second Empire rush into material pleasures and political theatre. It seemed a grand spectacle, a public entertainment. In London, a few weeks before, he had rushed to see Henry Irving and Ellen Terry in *Macbeth,* through which "in a sort of melancholy amazement" at how bad they both were and on what evil days the English stage had fallen. Paris itself was better theatre, one's invitation, one's residence, the cost of the ticket more than reasonable. His two-bedroom furnished apartment, pretty and centrally located, cost twenty-five francs a month, and, for another thirty, the excellent porter did every service conceivable. He would give fifty such Parises "for that great interesting old London; but if one can't be in London," where he would need a private social world to compensate for the absence of public entertainment and where his work would be totally free-lance, "this is next best."[1]

Next best was good enough for the time being. With a five-month lease on his flat, he anticipated the pleasures of work and entertainment, particularly his commissioned articles on Parisian cultural and social life for the *New York Tribune* and his fiction and reviews for American magazines. Determined to keep the *Tribune* tightly on his hook, he sent off, within weeks of arriving, "Paris Revisited," his first attempt at a letter. Writing such letters was a knack which, he admitted to Whitelaw Reid, "will have to come little by little."[2] With little sense of the public to whom such letters were to be addressed, he fumbled for a formula. The difficulty of finding congenial subject matter perplexed him. French politics interested him more than he had anticipated in its ongoing drama of the creation of a quasi-democratic National Assembly and Senate out of the still virulent wreck of Orleanism, Bonapartism, Catholicism, and monarchism. But the *Tribune* already had a political reporter in place. He had to be careful not to step into someone else's territory.

Determined to do a professional job, despite misgivings and frustrations, he wrote about art exhibitions, theatre, Americans in Paris and Europe, the new Paris opera house, Paris views and scenery, visits to Chartres and Versailles, military reviews, French literature, particularly the death of George Sand, and his visits to Rouen and Étretat the next summer: a total of twenty articles in all. He never solved the problems of subject matter and tone. Frustrated, constantly on the defensive about something that was not going quite right, he felt by April 1876 "rather sick" of the Paris letters. "But I shall keep it up." He complained to the *Tribune* that it published his letters "at longer intervals" than agreed to and that the headings it provided offended him. Since he was paid only on publication, he wanted his money more promptly. He also wanted his contributions spared from general journalistic contamination, from the *Tribune*'s "vulgarity and repulsiveness." Probably all this would not have mattered if Reid had thought the letters interesting and appropriate for a newspaper audience. As early as mid-March 1876, querying James about his summer plans, the publisher politely tested the grounds for a separation. He would like to be advised early if James planned to be away from Paris, since "some applications have been made for Parisian correspondence, which we have denied at once, preparing to have the benefit of your letters as long as we can." James assured him that he would continue to write his letters through the summer, even if he left Paris for brief periods. Since he would definitely be in Paris for the next winter, "you may therefore continue to count on me."[3]

In order to pay his bills, it was desirable to keep the *Tribune* connection as long as possible. His letter of credit from his father provided security, but he did not want to have to draw upon it. There had been a constant drain on the family resources because of a financial depression that had begun in 1873 and Henry senior's gifts of substantial sums to Bob and Wilky, both struggling with family responsibilities and business failures. From Cambridge, at the beginning of 1876, when he had

had to draw on his letter of credit to pay his London tailor from whom he had purchased a full wardrobe, it looked, for a moment, as if Henry was "living extravagantly." He also had had to cash two additional drafts against the letter of credit for the expenses he had incurred settling in. When Mary James played the usual role of enforcer, her son defended himself, having "had no idea that father's resources were curtailed." Otherwise he "should have been doubly and triply careful." But he expected that future royalties from *Roderick Hudson,* which would go directly to Henry senior, would repay the three drafts at issue. "Unquestionably, the mere process of life in Paris is a conspiracy against one's purse, but I repeat that all things considered, it is cheaper than home."[4]

Aware that he could not slacken his effort if he were to be self-sufficient, he looked for some middle ground between grinding away at his desk and having the leisure to wander and observe. An intensely focused, energetic writer, he managed his time so that long mornings of work were usually sufficient to maintain the flow of Paris letters, reviews, essays, and fiction that he hoped would free him from the complications of the financial lifeline across the Atlantic. "I scribble along with a great deal of regularity," he assured William, "tho' I imagine I don't seem to you to be very productive." But there was a target, a balance to be maintained. "I don't desire to do more, in quantity, than I am forced to," especially of wearisome reviewing. He needed to have the time to look around, to find the proper, balanced interpenetration of experience with imagination. "What I am doing gains me enough money to live comfortably and I rest content with that," he told William in April 1876. But he did so only on the margin produced by regular, disciplined hard work. In 1875, he had published fifty-one reviews, an obituary of Charles Kingsley, a short article on Ernest Renan, a substantial essay on Balzac, and three Paris letters. Some of it was drudge work, some of it, like the essay on Balzac, which came out in *The Galaxy* in the month he had arrived in Paris, quite brilliant. The latter piece anticipated the two things most on his mind in November 1875: Paris and money. "Money is the most general element of Balzac's novels; other things come and go, but money is always there. . . . Paris became his world, his universe. . . . Never was a great genius more essentially local."[5]

As he worked through much of 1876, he still had the intention of making Paris his permanent home. In a year of assiduous hard work, he published twenty-one reviews, one of them in the formal guise of an extended fictional conversation between readers of George Eliot's *Daniel Deronda;* sixteen essay-letters to the *Tribune;* two inconsequential short stories, "Crawford's Consistency" and "The Ghostly Rental," both of them in the well-paying but less well thought of *Scribner's Monthly;* and, beginning in June 1876, the first of the twelve monthly installments of a new full-length novel, *The American,* about a self-made young American who, despite wealth and self-confidence, finds France essentially closed to him. Christopher Newman cannot take possession of that aspect of France he most desires, its traditional elegance and beauty, embodied in the aristocratic Madame de Cintré. Like *Roderick Hudson,* whose serialization in the *Atlantic* concluded at the end of 1875, it is a story of unfulfilled aspirations, of an American baffled by the closed, exclusive nature of the European society whose fruits and flowers he hopes to enjoy.

Having begun *Roderick Hudson* in Florence in the spring of 1874, he had worked on it in Cambridge during the summer, and completed it in New York in the autumn. He had purposely committed himself to a lengthy apprenticeship, a decade of writing stories, essays, and reviews, to prepare himself for the demands of a full-length novel, for the anticipated competition with the great nineteenth-century novelists whose accomplishments he both admired and envied. Neither *Roderick* nor *The American* was cast in his mind's eye as a major work, as a literary gauntlet thrown down to challenge the great and establish his parity. Both were begun under the impetus of financial pressure. *The American,* begun in Paris at the beginning of December 1875, would contribute substantially to his being self-supporting in Europe. On December 1, 1875, he wrote peremptorily to *The Galaxy* that he took it for granted that it "will be ready to publish, on receipt of them, the opening chapters" of a twelve-part novel, at $150 a part, that he had "got to work upon" sooner than he had expected.[6] Expeditiousness, promptness, were important. It was "a matter of prime necessity to get a novel on the stocks immediately," he explained semi-apologetically to Howells: Of course he preferred the *Atlantic,* but *Roderick* had just ceased publication there, he needed fresh monthly payments as soon as possible, and he hoped to offer Howells another novel for the next year. By March 1876, unhappy with still not having a firm commitment from *The Galaxy* for an initial publication month, he insisted that it meet his terms or that he "must forego the pleasure of having the story appear in the magazine." At Howells' request, James instructed *The Galaxy* to send the portion of the manuscript that it had to Henry senior for transmission to Howells. The fee of $150 an installment was unusually high for the *Atlantic,* but Howells was delighted to accept the novel, with publication to begin in June 1876.

In May 1876, "doing nothing but [his] novel, and [his] letters to the *Tribune,*" he was eager to have the novel off his hands, as if six months or so were sufficient time to have devoted to its composition, about the same time he had taken to write *Roderick.*[7] In both cases, he felt some of the impatience of a patience that had been overtried by a long apprenticeship, of a writer eager to have a professional task done with. He exercised the efficiency and dispatch of a novelist who found himself with narratives that fell beneath his abilities and conditions whose fulfillment did not particularly challenge him. Neither novel pushes the edges of his capability. Both novels are records of his attempt to master the technical requirements of a full-length narrative. In *Roderick,* he chose to write about a failed apprenticeship, an anxiety already much on his mind. The central character is a young New England sculptor whose moral character cannot survive, let alone capitalize, on his talents, his early successes, and the attractions of Rome. Supported in Rome by the wealthy New England aesthete-collector Rowland Mallet, Roderick betrays his mother, his fiancée, his patron, and his art. Drawing on his Roman impressions, on Browning's poems about failed artists, on Romantic archetypes that elevate feeling over performance, on hidden touches of the James family dialectic about art, money, parenting, and brother-sister triangles, James drew most of all on his own struggle for financial independence and artistic achievement in this portrait of a failure he was determined to avoid.

In *The American,* Christopher Newman's failure is not one of moral character but of experience. An American primitive in the best sense, the handsome self-made millionaire, graced with good humor and a good heart, finds himself incapable of perceiving the levels of complication that permeate the aristocratic French family whose widowed daughter he wishes to marry. Whereas Roderick fails because of his weakness, Newman fails because of his virtues. He is neither businessman nor anthropologist enough to comprehend that virtues in one cultural context are failings in another. When his attractions persuade the widowed daughter of the aristocratic, reactionary Bellegarde family to agree to marry him, and his money persuades the family to accept him, he is shocked when the family changes its mind. With a damaging document about the Bellegardes in hand, he has the opportunity to avenge himself. To his shock, Claire declines to defy her family, except to take Carmelite vows of absolute silence and total withdrawal. After a year of keeping the Bellegardes in suspense, Newman decides to burn the damaging document, to forgo his revenge, to turn away from the Europe and the values that the Bellegardes represent, without exposing his enemies. He has at least had the satisfaction of frightening them. "The most unpleasant thing that had ever happened to him had reached its formal conclusion, as it were; he could close the book and put it away." When, as he puts the incriminating letter into the fire, he is told by a confidante that he had probably not frightened the Bellegardes because they had counted on his good nature to prevent his using it, he "instinctively turned to see if the little paper was in fact consumed; but there was nothing left of it." He leaves Paris, never to return.

That there were no French families at all for James in Paris, that there was not the hint of social entrée to the native culture, helped eventually to determine his own departure. Paris on the whole pleased him, in the way a glittering toy or an exotic series of shop windows pleases an adult who has determined to enjoy the retrogressive pleasures of an exotic landscape. The son of a serious father, he could no more live indefinitely among a culture of cream pastries than he could live in a New England without cream pastries at all. The French lacked essential seriousness, lacked an interest in the moral and especially in the psychological. "The longer I live in France," he told William, "the better I like the French personally, but the more convinced I am of their bottomless superficiality."[8] *The American* partly expresses his response to what he perceived as French values, an affirmation of the preferability of American strength to European corruption, of the superiority of the values of the New World in regard to honesty, love, marriage, class relations, the idealization of the commonwealth of talent and virtue rather than the rigid hierarchy of birth. Even if the James family sometimes pretended that they were a country of their own, Henry wanted to assert strongly that the individual was more important than the family, that personal achievement should have priority over social inheritance or structure.

That the Bellegardes can depend on Newman's good nature to escape being punished for their moral corruption embodies a fantasy of forgiveness deeply embedded in James's commitment to his family's view of him as "the angelic Harry." Newman's good nature is so excessive that it suggests a deeply restrained anger. Under the most extraordinary provocations, he has held himself back. Though explained partly as a talent for self-control, it seems, in the latter stages of the novel, a self-restraint without a purpose. A businessman who has fought innumerable battles in the rugged West of free enterprise and semilawlessness, he rises to this level of self-renunciation at the price of realism. To maintain power, power must be exerted. One did not make millions in nineteenth-century America by fantasies of good nature, Christian good deeds, forbearance, or renunciation. The feeling that James has most difficulty with in life and in fiction is anger, and the absence of anger in Newman, or his suppression of whatever anger he feels, reflects a fantasy of his creator's, one on which he was to continue to create many, and more subtle, variations.

The novel also embodies James's attempt to think through the problem of how to combine personal freedom with the grand cultural museum that he felt he had to live in to prosper as an artist. When Howells began to express uneasiness and then dismay at the possibility that there would be no happy ending for the *Atlantic* readers, that Newman and Claire de Cintré would not marry, James expressed his amazement that Howells had ever considered such a marriage possible. "My subject was: an American letting the insolent foreigner go, out of his good nature, after the insolent foreigner had wronged him and *he* had held him in his power. To show the good nature I must show the wrong and the wrong is that the American is cheated out of Mme de Cintré." Their incompatibility had been clear to him from the beginning. If they were to marry, where would they live? Who would be their friends? "We are each the product of circumstances and there are tall stone walls which fatally divide us."[9] A marriage between the disparate cultures was impossible. He himself had no such illusions for the novel or for himself. A marriage meant intimacy, acceptance, deracination. For himself, even if he had desired it, it was impossible in Paris. If it were possible in England, it could be so only within narrow limitations and at great cost. But France could no more be a home for him as a self-conscious exile than it could be for his innocent American.

(2)

Soon after arriving in Paris, he had begun to look around for people with whom to spend time. He delighted in the theatre, but even the Théâtre Français had its limits. How many evenings could one spend at entertainments at which actors did all the talking in a language that prevented him from responding at the highest level of nuance and interpretation, no matter how good his French had become? But Paris itself "suits me to a t. . . . I find the Rue de Luxembourg, leading off to the Boulevard as it does, not so very different from Irving Street [in Cambridge] as you might suppose," he told Lizzie Boott. Still, he regretted that the city had lost much of the picturesqueness of the Paris of his childhood, the narrow, crooked, vivid confusion of unreconstructed, pre–Second Empire Paris. The new boulevards seemed hateful, and he bemoaned "the horrible monotony of the new quarters." But he soon prided himself on being mostly "deaf and blind" to his surroundings, satisfied with the small round of his daily affairs, hardly noticing other things. As to his social life, "I see no one to speak of, & I have next to nothing to relate. . . . That is a thing which comes slowly; though if I hang on long enough I hope I shall end by finding it."[10] Though his hope that he would have relations with middle- and upper-class Parisians was never realized, he did from the beginning have "society" of sorts. Three small Parisian communities were open to him: the affluent community of American expatriates; the tightly knit school of French realist writers who made Flaubert their imposing, attractive center; and a group of Russian expatriates, some of them political, some artistic, including the man whom James thought the greatest living novelist, Ivan Turgenev.

The revolving American circle in Paris was peripatetic and not, as it had been in Rome, artistic. Some small overlap existed between the Roman and Parisian worlds, since Paris was on the most frequently traveled route from America to Rome. Alice Mason, Senator Charles Sumner's ex-wife, "handsomer than ever," whose beauty and cleverness James admired, came to Paris for the winter of 1876. He saw her as often as he could. He became friendly in spring 1876 with Baron Friedrich von Holstein, the German diplomat whose reciprocated attentions to Mrs. Sumner had precipitated the breakup of her marriage. This relationship became, like the American community itself, grist for his fictional mill. He spent time with Alice Bartlett on one of her Paris visits. Soon she was to give up European residence for a Texas marriage. There were also birds of passage, Americans in Paris for a month or for the winter season, particularly his Cambridge acquaintance and William's friend, the philosopher Charles Peirce. An isolated philosopher-logician, Peirce lived most of his life at the intersections of genius, eccentricity, poverty, and neglect. He seemed to James less shrill, less provincial, than James had remembered him, surprisingly sweet, and noticeably well dressed. But "he has too little social talent, too little art of making himself agreeable." James liked him without enjoying his company, and their dinners and conversations in the late winter of 1876 had amusing, sometimes baffling disjunctions that contributed to James's feeling little regret when Peirce left for Berlin early in March. When, in July, Peirce spent three days in Paris on his route westward, James appreciated "his profound 1st class intellect, reflected in his ardent eyes," an appreciation that may have had something to do with Peirce's pronouncing himself "an *extreme* admirer of *R. Hudson*: a conquest which flatters me." That he was "a man of genius reconciled me to much that was intolerable in him."[11]

To assuage his own loneliness, he spent time with the former Eleanor Fearing, Mrs. Charles Strong, whom he had met in Rome in 1869.

She was "a poor sick woman," long estranged from her husband, "with an amiability and natural sweetness unspoiled," so he assured his sister. He also met Edward Lee Childe, a nephew of Robert E. Lee, and his wealthy, aristocratic French wife. The Bootts came to Paris from Cambridge in late spring 1876 for the sake of Lizzie's career as a painter. Eventually, he made one lifelong friend among the permanent expatriates, Henrietta Reubell, the daughter of a French father and an American mother. Four years older than James, she hosted an attractive, cultured salon in an elegant residence on Rue Gabriel. There he found warmth, comfort, and companionship over many years of Paris visits. Reubell combined physical unattractiveness with "something very frank, intelligent and agreeable. . . . If I wanted to marry," he smugly told William, "an ugly Parisian-American, with money and *toute les élégances,* and a very considerable capacity for development if transported into a favoring medium, Miss R would be a very good objective. But I don't."[12] In fact, the American community, as the year went on, seemed as a whole more emphatically narrow, sterile, and provincially isolated than he had at first thought it.

He did have entrée to a small but important part of the French literary community. Within a month of his arrival, he visited Gustave Flaubert. He was sufficiently unknown outside France for James to have to explain to Lizzie that he is a "French novelist." To the curious American writer, who had reviewed Flaubert's *Temptation of Saint Anthony* for *The Nation* in June 1874, there was a happy disjunction between what he felt to be the immorality of Flaubert's works and the man's personal sweetness, the paradox of a man worth knowing whose works it was proper that Lizzie did not read. To James, reading Flaubert and Flaubert's disciples, Émile Zola, Alphonse Daudet, and Edmond de Goncourt, seemed essential, a necessary part of his effort to develop his own sense of the relationship between life and art. His initial response to the work of Flaubert and his circle expressed his moral discomfort with bodily details in fiction, with moral and physical ugliness as the center of artistic vision, as well as his desire to assure his puritanical American audience, particularly the editors who objected to the moral atmosphere of his own fiction, that the depiction of immorality in art could have important moral uses. His problem in regard to these writers was simple: He admired their art but disapproved, for personal and for aesthetic reasons, of their subject matter. "To deny the relevancy of subject-matter and the importance of the moral quality of a work of art" struck him as "ineffably puerile." Such writers "talk of morality . . . being put into and kept out of a work of art, put into and kept out of one's appreciation of the same, as if it were a coloured fluid kept in a big-labelled bottle in some mysterious intellectual closet. It is in reality simply a part of the essential richness of inspiration—it has nothing to do with the artistic process and it has everything to do with the artistic effect. The more a work of art feels it as its source, the richer it is."[13]

Apparently Flaubert knew nothing about the young American writer's 1874 review. Like most of his colleagues, he knew, to James's regret, no English. It seemed to James a sign of the complacent insularity of French culture, just as it seemed to him that the compulsion of French writers to divide themselves into separate and hostile schools was antithetical to the cosmopolitanism he valued. Though never less than ambivalent about these French writers, he soon warmed to Flaubert, twenty-two years his elder, whose "person has raised my estimate of his work. There is something even touchingly simple about him." Their first meeting was a success. Flaubert seemed "a great, stout, handsome, simple, kindly, elderly fellow, rather embarrassed at having a stranger presented to him, and bothering himself over what he can say and do . . . with a serious, sober face, a big moustache, and a mottled red complexion . . . like some weather beaten old military man."[14] James was flattered but cautious. "I suppose I shall see Flaubert again once or twice." He soon went most Sunday afternoons up the five flights of stairs to Flaubert's salon on Faubourg Rue St. Honoré, where he met "the little *coterie* of the young realists in fiction."

With Flaubert, he had one delightful long weekday afternoon alone during which, apropos a discussion of modern French poetry, Flaubert exemplified his preference for Théophile Gautier over Alfred de Musset by reciting from memory one of Gautier's short poems. It was a memorable moment, Flaubert "a powerful, serious, melancholy, manly, deeply corrupted, yet not corrupting, nature. There was something I greatly liked in him, and he was very kind to me. He was head and shoulders above the others." The Sunday afternoon conversations delighted him, partly because they titillated him, partly because his curiosity prompted him to transcend his own cultural limitations, partly because he felt he needed to position himself vis-à-vis a group of strange but undoubtedly serious artists. "They are all charming talkers," he told Howells, though "as editor of the austere *Atlantic* it would startle you to hear some of their projected subjects. The other day [Goncourt] said he had been lately working very well on his novel—he had gotten upon an episode that greatly interested him. . . . *Flaubert:* 'What is it?' *E. de G.:* 'A whore-house *de province.*' "[15]

Over the years he became more generous in his assessment of the French realists, eager to stress the positive, more willing to deemphasize his criticism as merely a matter of personal taste. He was aware that his taste had cultural origins that he could never completely and comfortably defend. Eventually, he came to admire Zola who, unlike Flaubert, was his contemporary. At their first meeting, in December 1876, he seemed "a very common fellow," which, from James's point of view, they all were, with the exception of Flaubert. They used obscenities as if they were socially acceptable. They talked in public of subjects often reserved for privacy or silence. They treated sex in their lives and in their fiction as a physical act without any special moral or ideological significance. The fastidious American had no sense of French bohemian style, of the purposeful commitment to flaunting proprieties, to using the language that best expressed the unsentimental materialism that embodied their view of the realities of life. "I prefer," he told Tom Perry, "an inch of . . . Gustave Droz," a popular French sentimental novelist, "to a mile of Daudet. Why the Flaubert circle don't like him is their own affair. I don't care. I heard Émile Zola characterize his manner sometimes since as *merde à la vanille*. I send you by post Zola's own last—*merde au naturel*. Simply hideous."[16]

The next year he urged Perry to read Zola's *L'Assommoir*, a "remarkable and repulsive novel. . . . It is worth it if your stomach can stand it." When he read and reviewed *Nana* in 1880, he found it not only "unutterably filthy" but "inconceivably and inordinately dull." It was not realism, or even naturalism, that was at fault, he thought, but the unfortunate choice of subject matter, which did a disservice to realism by linking it with boring, ugly substance. Also, Zola's lack of artistry distressed him. "It is not his choice of subject matter that has shocked us; it is the melancholy dryness of his execution, which gives us all the bad taste of a disagreeable dish and none of the nourishment."[17] But his taste, or at least his tolerance, for Zola increased. As the long list of titles in the *Rougon-Macquart* series appeared over the next decades, he came to admire Zola's professionalism, his solidity and seriousness as a novelist weighing against his shapelessness and low subject matter. Despite Zola's pessimism and depiction of "unclean things," James increasingly respected his energy, his productivity, his seriousness as an artist, and his total dedication to his ambitious series. Years later, Zola's admirable conduct in regard to the Dreyfus affair elevated him in James's eyes to heroic stature.

Though his respect for the French realists developed gradually, he had always idealized Ivan Turgenev, whose early novels he had read in French and in German beginning in 1870. The Russian novelist's voluntary exile because of political disaffiliation and his lifelong love for a married French opera singer had made him a semipermanent resident of Paris. He was a cosmopolitan traveler intimately familiar with the fashionable places of Europe but without an authentic home of his own. When James missed meeting Turgenev in Baden-Baden several years earlier, he channeled his disappointment into rereading him "in German & beginning a review" to be published in April 1874 in the *North American Review*. He generalized beyond the minor novel at issue, making broad claims for Turgenev's greatness. Turgenev responded that he found "the praise too great and the blame too weak. I do not attribute this impression to diffidence or modesty; it is perhaps one of the many disguises which self-love enjoys."[18] But the mirror that James held up to the Russian writer's work was mutually reflective, for the young writer thought of himself as a qualified American Turgenev. During the next years, as Europe became preoccupied with the tensions of the Eastern Question, Russian liberals like Turgenev and American republicans like James united in abhorrence of Turkish atrocities and of British-French power politics. James, identifying with Turgenev's horror at what seemed Turkish barbarism, emphasized the similarities between America and Russia. "Russian society, like ours," he wrote to his American audience, "is in process of formation." The fascinating qualities James saw in American women seemed reflected in the women in Turgenev's fiction. "It does not seem to us altogether fanciful to say that Russian young girls [in Turgenev] . . . have to our sense a touch of the faintly acrid perfume of New England temperament—a hint of Puritan angularity."

For James, Turgenev uniquely combined technical brilliance, sensitivity to life, people, and language, psychological acuteness, and moral vision. His strongest reservation was one of temperament, both personal and cultural. Though he found Turgenev's gentle irony attractive, he did not admire his pessimism. "The great question as to a poet or a novelist is, How does he feel about life? What, in the last analysis, is his philosophy? When vigorous writers have reached maturity we are at liberty to look in their works for some expression of a total view of the world they have been so acutely observing." The son of an American Swedenborgian, whose family's democratic ideals had found their practical expression in a great Civil War on behalf of human freedom, could not feel temperamentally consonant with an author who everywhere implies "that there is something essentially ridiculous in human nature, something indefeasibly vain in human effort." Granted that "the fermentation of social change has thrown to the surface in Russia a deluge of hollow pretensions and vicious presumptions, . . . that in this discord of crude ambitions the integrity of character itself is compromised and men and women make, morally, a very ugly appearance," still the young writer held "to the good old belief that the presumption, in life, is in favor of the brighter side, and we deem it, in art, an indispensable condition of our interest in a depressed observer that he should have at least tried his best to be cheerful. . . . Life *is*, in fact, a battle. On this point optimists and pessimists agree. Evil is insolent and strong; beauty enchanting but rare; goodness very apt to be weak; folly very apt to be defiant; wickedness to carry the day; imbeciles to be in great places, people of sense in small, and mankind generally, unhappy. But the world as it stands is no illusion, no phantasm, no evil dream of a night; we wake up to it again for ever and ever; we can neither forget it nor deny it nor dispense with it. We can welcome experience as it comes, and give it what it demands, in exchange for something which it is idle to pause to call much or little so long as it contributes to swell the volume of consciousness."[19]

Eager to meet Turgenev at last he called on him ten days after arriving in Paris, at Turgenev's rooms at the home of his friends the Viardots, "apparently his nearest and dearest." To the young man he seemed to combine wisdom with naïveté, great artistry with personal simplicity, "the wit of the artist and the naivete of the infant . . . an ideal genius." He was in the presence and soon in the affections of the writer he thought the greatest alive. "I took an unprecedented fancy to him. He is a magnificent creature, and much handsomer than his portraits." Impressed with his massive, leonine figure, with his athletic bearing and good looks, with the gentle, kind simplicity of his manner, he wanted Turgenev for a friend, for a mentor, for a companion. At the first meeting, they talked for two hours on all sorts of topics. "We got on very well; I think he liked me, and that if opportunity served we might become intimate." There were competitors, though, particularly the Viardots, who kept Turgenev much to themselves. Initally unaware of the bond between Turgenev and the Viardots, he gradually understood that they were part of the limiting fabric of Turgenev's life. Having fallen in love as a young man with the married Madame Viardot, Turgenev and the Viardots had eventually established a domestic triangle that permitted Turgenev's daughter by an early affair to be reared in their household. Turgenev enjoyed the presence of the woman he loved and a stable domestic environment, and the Viardots, in turn, relied on Turgenev's financial support. To James's jealous eyes, Madame Viardot was a rival with whom he soon saw he could not compete. She was "a most fascinating and interesting woman, as ugly as eyes in the side of her head and an interminable upper lip can make her, and yet also very handsome or, at least in the French sense, *très-belle*." To James's astonishment, Turgenev performed every Sunday evening in their games of charades, though he seemed the "least theatrical of men," and gave priority to Madame Viardot's bidding. "The poor man is a slave—the slave of Mme. Viardot—such is the tale."[20]

From the beginning, he fought to establish as close a friendship as Turgenev and the circumstances would allow. Notorious for canceling appointments at the last minute, made an invalid by his constant gout, struggling with the difficulty of finding time for his own writing, Turgenev still managed to respond to the young man's enthusiasm by introducing him to Flaubert, his closest literary friend in Paris, and by having a half dozen additional short meetings with him by early in the new year. "It is impossible to see much of him," James complained to Lizzie Boott, "as he is pre-empted, chronically, by Mme. Viardot, in whose house he lives, & who jealously keeps watch over him: but I have seen him several times, & I greatly like him." He is, James wrote in a review of *Virgin Soil*, "one of the profoundest of observers and one of the most fascinating of story-tellers," his greatest quality "the union of the deepest reality of substance . . . with the most imaginative, most poetic, touches." Early in the new year, James boasted to Tom Perry, "did I tell you I sometimes see Turgeneff & Gustave Flaubert—excellent old fellows both: I hardly know which personally I prefer." By early February 1876, he felt secure enough in the relationship to tell Howells that he saw "a great deal" of the Russian writer "and am excellent friends with him. He has been very kind to me and has inspired me with an extreme regard." They passed "almost the whole of a rainy afternoon" together, talking about literature and Turgenev's approach to writing fiction. They often went together to Flaubert's Sunday afternoon salon. One night at a Viardot music party, James found that his only consolation for being suffocatingly bored by the "interminable fiddling" was that the artist Gustave Doré, "standing beside me, seemed as bored as myself.—But when Mme. Viardot does sing, it is superb."[21]

Turgenev also introduced him to three of his Russian compatriots in Paris. Nicholas Turgenev was a distant cousin, a political exile at whose companionable dinners he became an occasional guest. The warmth of Nicholas' large family and the attractions of their Russian friends was quite pleasurable to James, who found them "an oasis of purity in the midst of this Parisian Babylon." He met Princess Marie Ourousov, the wealthy wife of a Russian industrialist whose salon attracted many writers, a heavy smoking, unassuming, intelligent woman whom James took a liking to and with whom he hoped, vainly, to have a continuing friendship. Most important, Turgenev introduced James to Paul Joukowsky in April 1876. James briefly fell in love. Gifted with wealth, a distinguished literary father, and a minor talent as an amateur painter, the languid, drifting, handsome Joukowsky, six years younger than James, had attached himself to Turgenev, who thought him "the most naive epicurean" he had ever met. To James he seemed "one of the pure flowers of civilization." Despite his dilettantism and political nihilism, James found him irresistibly attractive. By May, their friendship had been sealed with dinners and long talks. "The person I have seen altogether most, of late," he wrote to Alice, "is my dear young friend Joukowsky, for whom I entertain a most tender affection . . . the most—or one of the most—refined specimens of human nature that I have ever known, a very delicate and interesting mind."[22] Though having decided immediately that Joukowsky was much to his taste, he gradually came to believe that he had mistaken either Joukowsky or his own taste. What had at first seemed his Russian friend's amiable gentleness soon seemed weakness and passivity; what had seemed elevation of spirit and ideas, affectation; what had seemed amiability, superficiality; and what had seemed "extreme purity of life," unmanly perversity. In 1881, while musing in his notebook on his friends of his Paris year, his only remark in regard to Joukowsky was "non ragioniam di lui—ma guarda e passa" ["let us not reason about it—but take note and let it pass"].

Whether there had occurred any one confrontational incident of disaffiliation is unclear. Gradually, he decided that Joukowsky was superficial, inconstant, incapable of loving. From his fascination with Turgenev and James, Joukowsky next went to Wagner, whom he thought "the greatest and wisest of men," eventually attaching himself as a disciple to the Wagner entourage in Naples. James visited him there, after some years of separation, for a few days in April 1880. He seemed "indeed the same impractical and indeed ridiculous mixture of Nihilism and bric à brac as before." But Joukowsky now seemed to carry the taint of immorality. The open homosexual and adulterous atmosphere of the Wagner encampment, its public flaunting of sexual preferences and passions, disgusted James. James's admonition to himself suggests that Joukowsky had deeply offended him, about aspects of the self that he did not feel appropriate for explicit language, about things that were unspeakable both in the personal and public sense.

(3)

As the lovely Paris spring of 1876 filled the parks with foliage, he delayed making summer plans. He thought he might spend the summer "quietly, economically, and industriously—perhaps, if it doesn't prove too hot, at Fontainebleau." Paris seemed "wondrous charming . . . every way very lovely." He kept himself busy at work on *The American,* which Howells and the *Atlantic* readers praised highly, and his *Tribune* letters. Howells urged him to make his novel longer. At the end of May, he went to say good-bye to Flaubert, who was having his last Sunday in Paris. After an hour alone with him, some of the disciples arrived, chatting about Zola having been forced to cease the serial publication of a novel for which he had been handsomely paid because subscribers had protested against its indecency. As James left, he "met poor Zola climbing the stairs, looking very pale and sombre. . . . I saluted him with the flourish natural to a contributer who has just been invited to make his novel last longer yet." Anticipating the arrival of the Bootts in Paris in June, he urged them not to delay so that he would still be there when they came. Lizzie had arranged to study with Thomas Couture, who she soon thought "an admirable teacher." When, in July, Lizzie introduced him to Couture, he thought him "an amusing, but a vulgar little fat & dirty old man" who taught a style that had a "charm-less absence of delineation and detail" that did not improve Lizzie's painting. Alice was not surprised. "Feminine art as long as it only remains a resource is very good but when it is an end it's rather a broken reed. Matrimony," she unhappily speculated, "seems the only successful occupation a woman can undertake."[23]

Hot summer suddenly came on strongly. In mid-July, after spend-ing a delightful afternoon with the Bootts in the villa they had taken in a Paris suburb, he left for Étretat, a beach resort on the Normandy coast which he had selected haphazardly. Étretat turned out to be a delight, so cool that he was actually cold, "in a little hollow between two magnificent cliffs, & before a sea as blue as the Mediterranean." He had the occasional company of the wealthy, elegant Bostonians, the painter Edward Boit and his flirtatious wife, whom their friend John Singer Sargent was to paint splendidly years later. Having met and liked them in Rome in 1873, James took happy advantage of their proximity and their "charming old country house" to see a great deal of them.[24] He met and liked a young English journalist, Theodore Child, whose Jewishness he noted and whose handsomeness he ad-mired. Working in the mornings in his room, he took long walks in the afternoons on the cliffs and in the surrounding countryside. Fasci-nated by the French middle class on holiday, he sat on the pebble beach and watched and read.

Reluctantly, he "left cool & breezy Etretat" to keep his commitment to spend the second half of the summer with the Edward Lee Childes at their château in Montargis in central France. Traveling via Paris, where he stayed overnight at a hotel (he had given up his apartment in order to economize when he had left in July), he suffered a miserably "long & horrible journey . . . including a wait of 7 hours in that red-hot hole of Havre." Unexpectedly, the Château de Varennes and the Childes soon raised his spirits. When he arrived on a hazy early August evening, it looked like a setting for an opera, the castle enchanting, "a little moated 15th century chateau . . . with walls 3 feet thick, turrets & winding staircases & a little green river" around it. "I am in clover," he told his mother, "of the deepest sort, the house being as luxurious and elegant within as it is quaint without." Combining Virginia manners with French elegance, the Childes were gracious hosts. They introduced the young writer to the manner in which privileged, wealthy European landowners lived. One afternoon he accompanied Mrs. Childe as she played "Lady Bountiful" to the peasants, astounded at the claim that "some of [them] . . . are worth sixty and eighty thousand dollars—made franc by franc." The "financial troubles at home," the ongoing depression, made money a sore subject. "The sight of the troubles of the more unfortunate classes must indeed be distressing," he admitted to his mother. "I am glad I don't see them, that I see only this strange, thrifty, grasping, saving, prospering France, where alone the commercial disasters are not felt."[25]

From Montargis, he went south to Biarritz and Bayonne, where he rejoined the Childes who were staying at a luxurious villa owned by friends, the most palatial he had ever visited. He crossed into San Sebastían to sample Spanish atmosphere, particularly a bullfight. He took to it, he felt, "more kindly . . . than virtue, or even decency, allows," the brilliant weather, the mountains, the sky, the empty town, "the cloud-shadowed sea." "If I sometimes shuddered I never yawned." Admiring the handsomeness of the Spanish men, the 'gorgeous' matador," he found it all theatre, though neither moral nor beautiful. He "thought the bull a finer fellow than any of his tormentors, and I thought his tormentors finer fellows than the spectators. . . . How is one to state gracefully that one has taken pleasure in a disgusting thing?"[26] When he returned to Paris at the middle of September, he faced a small disaster of his own. Though he had thought that he had reserved his apartment for reoccupation, the owner had rented it to someone else. His effort to economize by saving on the rent for the summer months had backfired. "Annoyed and disappointed," he soon settled for a less attractive apartment in the same building.

He had another setback to face as well. John Hay, his supporter at the *Tribune,* had left "the turmoil of newspaper life" at the end of 1875. In April 1876, Whitelaw Reid had begun laying the ground for terminating his *Tribune* letters. When in August James unwisely asked for a raise to thirty dollars a letter, Reid told James that if he would write shorter, less frequent, more "newsy" letters, "there would be less occasion for a change in the rate of payment." With a presidential campaign under way, with James's letters "on topics too remote for popular interests, the difficulty," he explained, "has sometimes been not that it was too good, but that it was magazine rather than newspaper work." Hurt, angry, James responded that such a change was out of the question. "If my letters have been 'too good' I am honestly afraid that they are the poorest I can do, especially for the money! I had better, therefore, suspend them altogether." Though he told Reid that he had "enjoyed writing them," actually he had not. Still, if he could have continued to write the letters on his own terms, he would have done so in order to have the regular income. Explaining to his father that Reid had "stopped off my letters to the *Tribune*" without mentioning that his request for additional money had precipitated the termination, he consoled himself and Henry senior by admitting that "I am a little sorry to stop, but much glad. I can use the material more remuneratively elsewhere." At the end of the year, he indirectly solicited Reid. "I sometimes wish there were an occasional pretext for writing to the *Tribune*."[27] Reid did not respond.

When he returned to Paris in September 1876, he felt little enthusiasm for his French life. "It is so comfortable and agreeable that I forget that . . . it isn't (to me) really interesting." Though the restaurants were superb, it seemed rather ignoble to stay for the sake of pleasing his stomach. "Restaurants become a burden even in Paris, and one must either starve or marry. I, for my part, shall starve." He could think of few other reasons for remaining. London was on his mind. "I am unlikely to go there, however, until I go there to remain." He saw less of the Flaubert circle. Turgenev, a prisoner of the Viardots, could not be counted on except for occasional company. James's Russian friends were preoccupied with anticipations of a European-wide conflict. "The air is full of war & the whole continent sniping at England." As well as he now knew French, he felt France would forever treat him as "an eternal outsider." The thought of permanent dependence on "the detestable *American* Paris" frightened and repelled him. Paris "in a hundred ways" now seemed "to weary and displease" him.[28]

From Rome, Lizzie, having decided that she had had enough of Couture and Paris, urged him to live in the tower apartment of the lovely villa she and her father had taken. Attractive as the prospect was, he could not go to Italy now. He had "a bad cold & a headful of neuralgia." The cost would be too great. He had other things on his mind. A few days later, he wrote to William, "I am a thinking seriously of going to England, but *please say nothing about it until I decide.*"[29] Without the *Tribune* employment, he felt he needed to have a novel constantly running as a serial in a magazine. It "has defined itself as a financial necessity for me," he told Howells, though he reassured him that his next short novel would have a great deal of marrying and happy endings galore, and that the next beyond that would be "an *Americana*—the adventures in Europe of a female Newman, who of course equally triumphs over the insolent foreigner." In fact, the triumph of the American heroine of *Portrait of a Lady* was to be even less substantial than Newman's.

Though he told Howells late in October 1876 that Italy was still a possibility, actually he had already made up his mind to move to London, "where I shall thrive more effectually than here." The cost of living would be less in London than in Paris. He would be more at home in the country of his own language. English-American subjects were more promising than French-American subjects. Also, he would have letters of introduction from American Anglophiles to help smooth his path. Perhaps English society would prove more hospitable. London, he felt, would certainly be more interesting than Paris. As the center of the literary and political world, it would offer much for him to observe, probably including the collapse of an empire. "The breaking-up will be a big spectacle—may I be there to see! . . . I suppose you will think me a model of inconstancy," he told William, "if I tell you that I have about decided to remove to London on Dec. 1st." In November he felt bored to death by "an overdose of Wagner" at a music party hosted by Joukowsky that lasted from nine o'clock to two o'clock in the morning. Impatient to be gone, he said good-bye to his friends, the Princess Ourousov, "the lovely Mrs. Mason," Turgenev, Joukowsky. "I have burned my ships behind me—let my apartment. I always meant, sooner or later, to go to London," he told a disappointed Lizzie. "& I am only doing it a little sooner." He wrote a loving letter to his father, who had been seriously ill, explaining his decision to try to "fix myself in London in such a way that it may become my permanent headquarters," though he was "sorry to be going to a shadier rather than a sunnier clime."[30] Climate was not the issue. He needed a place where he felt that his art and his life could prosper.

(4)

As he crossed to England in mid-December 1876, the English Channel uncharacteristically shone like glass. The first thing that struck the

thirty-three-year-old writer as he disembarked on a sleety Sunday evening at Folkestone were "the good looks of the railway porters—their
broad shoulders, their big brown beards, their well-cut features." Not
even the darkness of a wintry London, "livid with sleet and fog," not
even the fact that, as he sat writing in the middle of the day, he could
hardly see his pen, shook his immediate determination that he had made
the right choice. An accidental connection brought him to a small,
second-story, "highly genteel" flat at 3 Bolton Street, off Piccadilly.
Frequently, as he wrote, he stared at "the great smutty blank wall
of Lord Ashburton's house." Fortunately, his own landlady provided
excellent arrangements, "the service perfection," including meals
brought to his rooms by a housemaid and an excellent fireplace at which
he could keep his feet warm. His rooms and London life in general
seemed cheaper than his cost of living in Paris, and the abominable
winter weather mostly seemed an acceptable price to pay as a surcharge
against the other advantages, though "the weather is hideous, the
heavens being perpetually instained with a sort of dirty fog-paste, like
Thames-mud in solution. At 11 a.m. I have to light my candles to
read!" When Lizzie urged him to come to Rome for the winter, he
promised that he would come for a visit the next summer or autumn.
"When I think of the Xmases I have passed in Rome & then look out
into the pea-soup atmosphere of Piccadilly I feel like taking to my bed.
Then I remember how bad my bed is, and stay put. But my rooms
otherwise are very comfortable; & I felicitate myself on my migration.
London interests me."[31]

But the dreariness, the aesthetic drabness of London, pained him. He
was horrified by the amount of public poverty and drunkenness, by the
haunting "vision of a horrible old woman in a smoky bonnet, lying prone
in a puddle of whisky." Three dreary London Sundays brought him to a
lonely Christmas in a city in which he knew almost no one. Yet, "in spite
of fog and isolation, & a very dreary Xmas, I rejoice in all things & feel
that I have in me the making of a very good Londoner." By his fireside,
the exterior darkness added to his feeling cozy and secure, facilitating
his concentration for writing and reading. Outdoors, London fascinated
him, despite all its disadvantages and disabilities, "the fogs, the smoke,
the dirt, the wet, the distances, the ugliness, the brutal size of the place,"
the vastness and demands of the social network. He took long walks
in the rain. The plenitude and variety of life astounded him. London had
everything, expressed everything, offered everything. It was, simply,
the capital of the world, "the right place" for a writer of his ambitions
to be. He took it, he remembered in the retrospect of a few years later,
"as an artist and as a bachelor; as one who has the passion of observation

and whose business is the study of human life. It is the biggest aggrega-
tion of human life—the most complete compendium of the world."
On Christmas Eve he wrote to his mother to tell her that his "spirits
never were higher."[32]

Almost from the moment of his arrival in London, he had not been
totally alone. At first, picking up the thread of associations already
made, he visited with the James Crafts, some Bostonians living in
London, oddly enough, for their health. Happily responding to an
invitation from family friends, the Ashburners, who were living near
London, he spent a somewhat disappointing day with them—their
home was less elegant and interesting than he had hoped. The day
before Christmas, he breakfasted at the Arts Club with Theodore Child,
the young English journalist whom he had met the previous summer
at Étretat. Child's Jewishness did not prevent him from being handsome
and looking "very much like Daniel Deronda." He was to become a
valued friend. Sarah Wister, now in London, eagerly—perhaps a little
too eagerly, he felt—welcomed his visits. He lunched with Leslie Stephen, who was even more inarticulate and gloomy than he had been
before, "an impossible companion, in spite of the moral and intellectual
confidence he inspires." He called on George Smalley, the well-estab-
lished *Tribune* correspondent in London and former Civil War reporter,
whom he had met the previous year in Paris. The talented, energetic
Smalley, liberal and sometimes controversial, knew everyone and entertained regularly. He soon extended frequent invitations to James.
Through a letter of introduction, James dined with Andrew Lang,
whom he found witty but facile, a versatile expert at many things who
was to become best known for his work as a folklorist and a translator
of Homer. Lang soon had him to breakfast at his club to meet John
Addington Symonds, with whom he shared a love for Italy, "a mild,
cultured man, with an Oxford perfume, who invited me to visit him
at Clifton." Symonds' perfume was the aura of a homosexuality that
he was not yet ready to think about.[33]

Having been given a half dozen letters of introduction by Henry
Adams, he gradually made use of several. Sarah Wister added six more.
At the Smalleys, early in the new year, he met a number of minor
London luminaries, one of whom, Lady Pollock, immediately invited
him to lunch. At the end of January 1877, at "a splendid banquet" at
the Smalleys, he met Edward Pierrepont, the American minister to
England, the historian James Anthony Froude, and Robert Browning,
with whom he had a long talk after dinner. He was astounded at the
disparity between the profundity of Browning as a poet and his light,
ordinary gossipiness as a social companion. At another dinner that

month he found himself seated next to Anthony Trollope, "the dullest Briton of them all." Within days, dining at Sir Robert Cunliffe's, one of the people to whom Adams had provided an introduction, he met George Trevelyan, the historian and nephew of Macaulay; F. T. Palgrave, who was to become famous as an anthologist of poetry, and who was a noticeably sharp-tongued, catty deflator of the great; and the sculptor Thomas Woolner. At Cunliffe's, he sat next to Samuel Laurence, the artist who had painted the portrait of Henry senior that hung in the Quincy Street dining room. The family did not think much of it. As a conversational gambit, James told Laurence that he had painted his father's portrait; Laurence smugly responded that "that was what every American told him." As he sat writing to his mother about his sudden social whirl, the postman brought another invitation from Lady Pollock. He soon made a point of deemphasizing his social life; he did not want the Cambridge household to think him extravagant with his time. "One must dine somewhere," he explained, "and I sometimes dine in company; that is all."[34]

Sitting in a comfortable chair "in the beautiful great library of the Athenaeum Club" on an evening in mid-February 1877, he wrote with restrained self-satisfaction to his father that he had additional reason to feel grateful to George Smalley. John Motley, the American historian of Dutch culture and former American minister to Great Britain, had done him the extraordinary service of putting him up for a three-month guest membership. Probably, he speculated, he owed Motley's kindness at least partly to Francis Boott having spoken "to him of me at some former date." He "showed me the ropes, & introduced me to the Duke of Argyll!" Smalley did the equivalent at the Savile, "small and modest" but convenient, both clubs in easy walking distance of Bolton Street. At the large, imposing Athenaeum, an establishment center for the political, literary, and religious elite, the philosopher Herbert Spencer was asleep in a chair across the room. "He always is, whenever I come here." The bishop of York sat close by with his nose in a book. In the dining room, the service was excellent, the food cheap. He delighted in the great drawing room, the stacks of magazines and the deep, restful chairs, in the late afternoon teas when "all the great chairs and lounges and sofas [are] filled with men having . . . tea—lolling back with laps filled with magazines, journals, and fresh Mudie books, while amiable flunkies in knee breeches present them the divinest salvers of tea and buttered toast." Already dreading the impending termination of his guest membership in paradise, he told William that the Athenaeum "is a place it takes sixteen years for a Briton to become a member of!—if things go very smoothly."[35]

An avalanche of invitations came throughout the winter and spring of 1877. Though he reminded himself regularly that they needed to be weighed on the scale of his commitment to his work, he confessed to Henry Adams that he was having "a beautiful time . . . drinking deep of British hospitality." Invitations came because he was a literary personage rapidly increasing in fame, because he was a bachelor who could serve a useful social function, because he had introductions from and connections with the long-standing network of exchange between Boston and London, because his conversation, his presence, his appearance, provided satisfactory value as a guest, because he did everything in his power to be liked, to be wanted, to present himself at his best in a world to which he wanted regular access. His rapid success surprised him slightly, gratified him immensely. At the end of January, he boasted to his mother that "when I think that the Season has not yet begun, and that when it does the social wheels here move just fifty time as fast, I begin to tremble. But I shall do, not overdo; and shall get a great deal of profit and wisdom out of it."[36]

He did not tremble when Lord Houghton, the elderly dean of London literary sociability, friend of Dickens, Tennyson, and Carlyle, a successful politician who had obtained public literary distinction as the author of the first book on Keats and private distinction as the owner of the finest collection of pornography in Britain, invited him to one of his famous literary breakfasts. Liking him immediately, Houghton invited him repeatedly, and also provided him with a permanent invitation to a select late-night talking club, the Cosmopolitan, which met twice a week. At one of the meetings, he talked mostly with Trollope, who had been described to him as "all gobble and glare." At a dinner hosted by the poet and novelist Hamilton Aïdé, he met George Du Maurier and Anne Procter. A London bachelor, twenty years older than James, Aïdé was an apparently ageless world traveler. George du Maurier, the writer and *Punch* cartoonist, seemed "a delightful little fellow." Ten years older than James, with a tall, handsome wife, weak eyes, and great charm, he had been raised and educated in France. The widow of a now-forgotten but once famous Romantic poet, the elderly Anne Procter, "a most shrewd, witty and juvenile old lady," soon seemed to him "the best talker" he had ever met in England. She had known all the great writers of the previous fifty years.[37] Like Fanny Kemble, whom he soon began to visit regularly at her London home, she provided both a link to a cultural past that fascinated him and a partial replacement for the distant Mary James.

Behind the "penitential gloom" of London Sundays, he was discovering, there were Sunday salons, conversational afternoons, literary and social evenings. One Sunday he was taken to Edward Burne-Jones's regular Sunday afternoon open house at his studio and "took a fancy to his work, as well as to that of Walter Crane. . . . Burne-Jones is a more considerable affair than I had at first supposed, & his things (I think) the strongest English painting since Turner . . . a marvellous mixture of Italy & England." He urged Lizzie Boott to come to London to study with Burne-Jones. He would be well worth her discipleship. Visits to galleries were less rewarding, though he went regularly. On the whole, he found British painting uninspired, prosaic, with a few exceptions, just as most of the Englishmen he met were "of the 'useful-information' prosaic sort, and I don't think that in an equal lot of people I ever received such an impression of a want of imagination."[38] In Paris, the previous April, he had gone to the impressionist exhibition. He told his *Tribune* readers that he found the paintings "decidedly interesting." But he associated the impressionist painters with the French realistic writers who demanded the actual in art. "The effect of it was to make me think better than ever of all the good old rules which decree that beauty is beauty and ugliness ugliness. . . . The beautiful to them, is what the supernatural is to the Positivists—a metaphysical notion, which can only get one into a muddle and is to be severely let alone. Let it alone, they say, and it will come at its own pleasure; the painter's proper field is simply the actual, and to give a vivid impression of how a thing happens to look, at a particular moment, is the essence of his mission."

During Easter 1877, he had the chance to catch his breath from the social whirl. Apparently, he not been invited to join the English elite at their Easter country-house visits that turned London "from good Friday to Easter Monday" into the playground of the working classes. He strolled "throughout the vast smoky city, beneath the shifting gloom of the sky, the grimy crowds" wandering "with a kind of weather-proof stolidity. The parks were full of them, the railway stations overflowed, the Thames embankment was covered," all the parks "densely filled with the populace." When he looked, he did see "the hard prose of misery, their clothes a bleak parody of the dress of their betters," especially "the battered and bedraggled bonnets of the women, which look as if their husbands had stamped on them, in hob-nailed boots, as a hint of what may be in store for their wearers." Two thirds of the London street faces showed the signs of alcoholism. Earlier in the year, he had found himself, accidentally, swept up in a mass public funeral for a well-known radical political agitator. Immensely impressed by how properly "the decent poor and the indecent" behaved in their mourning, as the funeral cortege stretched away into the distance he "seemed to be having a sort of panoramic view of the under side, the wrong side of the London world." He still thought the English people the handsomest in Europe, more interesting than any other people even in their ugliness. "American ugliness is on the side of physical poverty and meanness; English on that of redundancy and monstrosity. In America there are few grotesques; in England there are many—and some of them have a high plastic, historic, romantic value."

As if to pay his respects to the literary embodiment of the romantic value of redundancy, he went on Easter Monday, in unceasing rain, to Rochester, where he had his many Dickensian associations revivified. At Chatham he asked himself, thinking of the Dickens novel with which he most identified, "Is this not the place where little Davy Copperfield slept under a cannon on his journey from London to Dover to join his aunt Miss Trotwood?" When he saw a photograph of Gad's Hill in a shop in Rochester, he asked the old woman who kept the shop whether Dickens had often visited the town. " 'Oh, bless you, sir,' " she said, " 'we every one of us knew him to speak to. He was in this very shop on the Tuesday with a party of foreigners—as he was dead in his bed on the Friday. . . . He 'ad on his black velvet suit, and it always made him look so 'andsome. I said to my 'usband, 'I *do* think Charles Dickens looks so nice in that black velvet suit.' But he said he couldn't see as he looked in any way particular.' "[39]

He had other days in the country, especially as the spring came on, a number of them visits to acquaintances who had country houses. It was his first taste of English country-house life. On an overnight visit to Oxford in June 1877, having been invited to be a guest at Oriel College, he "made free of the rooms of an absent undergraduate. I sat in his deep armchairs; I burned his candles and read his books," the partial fulfillment of a long-held fantasy. He spent Derby day at Epsom Downs watching the English entertain themselves with gambling and alcohol. One of the young men next to him at the racetrack was "a mere bag of liquor," having fallen from his coach to the ground, "at once too ponderous and too flaccid to be lifted." In the summer, he wandered through London. Not even the heat deflated his enjoyment, his interest in the customs and the scenes. He went as a guest of the wealthy, amiable Charles Milnes Gaskell, Henry Adams' good friend, to Wenlock Abbey in Shropshire, the country home of Gaskell's parents. In August, he briefly visited Warwickshire, where he thought of

George Eliot; stayed at Kenilworth "with some very amiable people; and visited Stratford, "a very sacred place" where his imagination was alive with the presence of Shakespeare. In August, London emptied as it had at Easter, which allowed him to work without interruption. Enjoying a day at Greenwich, even the polluted river, the black barges, and the dirty steamer seemed symbolic representations of "the wealth and power of the British Empire" and of its decline and impending collapse. The decline seemed to him "a tremendous and even, almost, an inspiring spectacle," he wrote to Grace Norton, "and if the British Empire is once more to shrink up into that plethoric little island, the process will be the greatest drama in history!" He responded both with amazement and optimism at the strange news that Lowell, who had become ambassador to Spain, had nominated him to be his official secretary. If he were appointed, he could have a regular salary and, since a secretary notoriously had little to do, he would have ample time to write. He was also "inflamed at the idea of seeing" Spain. He decided to accept if the post were offered. But to no one's surprise, the State Department declined even to consider sending an inexperienced young secretary to assist an inexperienced ambassador. The next year a dissatisfied, lonely Lowell wrote him from Madrid that "the best society" he had ever seen "was in Cambridge, Mass., take it by & large."[40]

The London social whirl through the spring and the entertainments of the summer of 1877 did not delude him into a false sense of belonging. From Washington, D.C., Adams, who had been partly responsible for his opportunities, reminded him of what he needed only muted reminder, the dangers of permanent expatriation. James pretended that he thought it likely that he would return to America to live, perhaps because he did not yet want to be definitive about this with Adams. "I appreciate your warning as to what the future may lead to, and I know that, when the day comes, as I suppose it must, for snapping the cable [and leaving England], I shall need a very heroic tug." But he had "formed no 'relations' " of any consequence, and made no intimacies. "Heaven knows," he wrote to Adams, "one is an outsider here; but the outsider that one must be in Europe one is here in the least degree." He had learned enough about London to know that of all the possible places in Europe it was the best place for him.[41] In London, he could work. He could play as well, in the special social way in which he defined play. He could observe a world that had interest and variety. He could be with agreeable and sometimes interesting people, some of whom lived on a grand scale, as companions and hosts. Little of this was available to him in America.

(5)

London also felt closer to America than had Paris—out of proportion to the actual distance. It was "a comfort feeling nearer, geographically, my field of operation at home." He felt "very near New York," he told his mother, where *The Galaxy,* the *North American Review,* and particularly *The Nation* published his articles more frequently than the *Atlantic.* Partly he wanted to assure her that she need not fear he would draw further on his letter of credit. Still without an English publisher, *The American* was available for sale in London only once his Boston publisher James Osgood shipped copies from America. He had a tentative agreement with the New York–based *Scribner's Monthly* to publish his next novel in serial parts. In early 1877, he sent the final two parts of *The American* to Howells. Unhappy at the large number of misprints and infelicities, some of which William pointed out to him, he blamed them on his not having been able to correct page proofs and on Howells' carte blanche to make alterations. When *Scribner's* decided that it would not begin publishing his new novel before November 1877, he canceled the arrangement and confidently turned again to Howells. If their timing was to be identical, he preferred the *Atlantic.* Initially, *Scribner's* had seemed amenable to beginning in June. If it was to be November, the requisite year would almost have elapsed between *The American* and the new novel. In February 1877, he pressured Howells with the proposal that the editor and readers might not object to having a short novel in six monthly parts that would begin sooner rather than the longer twelve-month novel that he had offered *Scribner's.* He "should not make use of the subject" he had in mind, which is "essentially not compressible into so small a compass. It is the portrait of the character and recital of the adventures of a woman—a great swell, psychologically; a *grande nature*—accompanied with many developments." He would think of a different subject for "the shorter story," which he hoped could begin publication in January 1878.[42]

Howells agreed. Despite pressures and complications at his end, he wanted James's fiction in the *Atlantic.* With both a personal and professional interest in his friend's success, a sense that their mutual fortunes were inextricably connected, he wanted James at home, in Boston. But until then, he could offer James the literary home of the *Atlantic.* There were aspects of the situation James disliked. He would have preferred that *The American* had been published in six substantial installments of approximately thirty pages each (the *Atlantic* pages were double-columned) rather than in what he thought were twelve insubstantial snippets that forced readers to "wait a month for a twenty minutes' nibble." It put the reader in bad humor, the story into shapeless fragments.[43] From Howells' side of the ocean, the problem seemed tonal and ideological. James's style had a studied elegance that made many *Atlantic* readers uncomfortable and impatient. The nonmarrying conclusion of *The American* had disappointed readers and put Howells on the defensive.

Whereas James had the narrative realism of Balzac and the pyschological realism of Turgenev as models, readers of the *Atlantic* generally neither read nor cared to read his points of reference. Popular romances and standard Victorian novels, particularly those of Dickens and Thackeray, determined the expectations of his audience. While James appreciated optimism and idealism in fiction, "something even better in a novelist" is that "appreciation of actuality which makes even the application of a single coat of rose-colour seem an act of violence." Lizzie Boott and Alice Bartlett in Rome were among the readers disappointed by the unhappy ending of *The American*. He teased them that he enjoyed their anger more than their praise. "Such readers are worth having— readers who really care what one does & who pay one the divine compliment of taking things hard." Still, he felt he had been "rapped about the head" with Lizzie's painting brush and Alice's riding whip. "I will dedicate my next novel to both of you under the emblem of a maulstick and a riding whip intertwined." But he did not agree with their criticism. "What would you have had? Come, now, they couldn't have married, when it came to the point, & I never meant they should, or that the reader should expect it. It was very well for Newman to want it & for Mme de C. to fancy for a few weeks it was possible: but she was *not* in love with him. . . . What then could he have done to recover her? She was irrecoverable. It seemed to me that in putting it into Newman's power to forgive & contemptuously 'let off' the haughty Bellegardes, I was doing quite the most dramatic and inspiring thing."[44]

Still, he had promised the beleaguered Howells that his next *Atlantic* novel would have marriages enough, and in this instance Howells was not to be denied. At the end of March 1877, he outlined for him "the four-number tale" for the next year, "a very joyous little romance. I'm afraid I can't tell you at this moment what it will be; for my dusky fancy contains nothing joyous enough." He confided to Tom Perry that Howells' most recent novel in his series of "comedies" seemed to him "a feeble piece of work for a man of his years—and sex!" He was being asked to perform the aesthetic equivalent of neutering his own

work. Since he saw no alternative, he pursued constructive accommodation. Reluctantly, he had something "joyous" in mind, which he
described in good-humored parodic terms, a story "about a genial,
charming youth of Bohemianish patterns, who comes back from foreign parts into the midst of a mouldering and ascetic old Puritan family
of his kindred (some imaginary locality in New England 1830), and by
his gayety and sweet audacity . . . heals their dyspepsia and dissipates
their troubles. *All* the women fall in love with him (and he with them—
his amatory powers are boundless,) but even for a happy ending he
can't marry them all. But he marries the prettiest."[45] Though he himself
would not marry even the prettiest, he could make a novel to suit the
readers of the *Atlantic* out of the fantasy of going home. In *The Europeans,* he transformed the initial idea into a substantially different, more
qualified, subtle, and certainly less joyous comparison of European
and American culture (though the marriages remained). The central
character, an artist, transcends the limitations of both and commits
himself to James's version of the American virtues.

Soon after he conceived the idea for *The Europeans,* he found a
British publisher. Frederick Macmillan, the nephew and son of the
two cofounders of Macmillan & Co. and now the leading force in
the firm's expansion, had mentioned to George Smalley that he
might be interested in publishing a British edition of *The American.*
With an American wife, social standing, substantial business acumen,
and a level of literacy and literary appreciation higher than publishers
usually attain, Macmillan was on his way to becoming one of the
major figures in late-nineteenth- and early-twentieth-century British
publishing. When Macmillan did not contact him, James took the initiative. Would Macmillan be interested in publishing a volume containing thirteen or fourteen articles on French poets and novelists?
Macmillan responded, despite an unenthusiastic report by his in-house
reader who thought it "honest scribble work and no more," that there
was an audience in Britain for essays about French literature, though
they could expect modest sales at best. It seemed to him a sensible
way of beginning an association with James. In mid-February 1878,
Macmillan brought out an edition of 1,250 copies of *French Poets and
Novelists* and in September a small edition of *The Europeans* a few
weeks ahead of the larger edition that Osgood published in Boston.
When a new story, "Daisy Miller," proved a success in *The Cornhill
Magazine* in summer 1878 and a greater success in a small pamphlet
published by Harper's in New York, Macmillan published, at the be-
ginning of 1879, a small edition of James's tales headed by "Daisy."
The next month the publisher brought out the first British edition of

The American. Macmillan initially hoped that James would make money for them both. When that proved in the long run not to be the case, he valued James for the esteem his name brought to the publishing firm. More generous with James, with whom he developed a personal relationship, than with most other authors, he gradually took on some responsibility for supporting a writer whose earnings never justified the unusual advances and other flexibilities of payment that he extended. *Macmillan's Magazine* soon became James's much-appreciated alternative outlet for the serial publication of his novels and shorter pieces. Macmillan now carefully tested the British market for James's fiction, protecting the firm by small printings, and encouraged James with his professional and social support. They were to stay together for over two decades.[46]

As a writer, James's already substantial productivity increased in the five years immediately following his move to London. From 1876 to 1881, he completed *The American,* which he had started in Paris; wrote four novels, *The Europeans, Confidence, Washington Square,* and *The Portrait of a Lady;* collected and published his essays on French poets and novelists; revised and republished, with some hesitation, *Watch and Ward;* wrote ten stories, including the financially successful "Daisy Miller"; collected old stories and new into three separately published volume-length collections; continued to write reviews, literary essays, and travel essays; and wrote an astounding book-length study of Nathaniel Hawthorne. It was an astonishing half decade of performance, for which he had been preparing himself since the late 1860s.

As early as 1875, with the modest success of *Roderick Hudson,* Mary James had no hesitation in boasting that "Harry is rapidly becoming famous." When *French Poets and Novelists* came out, Henry senior thought the essays "the best things that Harry has ever done, and will contribute largely to his reputation. He is writing a new novel, of the success of which he seems himself to be very sanguine. He says compared with any thing he has yet done "it will be as wine to water." Slowly, but with increasing certainty, what the family believed became an actuality, beginning with the success of the *The American,* punctuated with a strong exclamation point by the notoriety of "Daisy Miller," fully achieved by the *succès d'estime* of *Portrait.* Most important, he believed it himself. By the beginning of 1878, long "weary of writing articles about places, and mere potboilers of all kinds," he was about to "give himself up," he told William, "to 'creative' writing. Then, and not till then, my real career will begin. . . . If I keep along here patiently for a certain time I rather think I shall become a (sufficiently) great man."[47]

(6)

During the summer of 1877, he kept delaying his long-promised visit to Italy. The comparative solitude of London allowed him to work assiduously. Also, he was enjoying his brief country excursions. His enthusiasm for England made him reluctant to leave, as if he were not ready, after nine months, for even a temporary separation, though he regularly assured the Bootts in Italy that his departure was imminent. The cool weather pleased him. Each morning the London newspapers reported on the exciting European Russo-Turkish drama, "the horrible butcheries which during all these summer days are going on on the Danube," and on the ominously poor part that "poor old England" played in the conflict. At the beginning of the second week of September, he finally left London. First he visited with Paul Joukowsky in Paris, "to stay with him—as near him—a while before I go Southward," he apologized and explained to Lizzie. "He is ill, unhappy, impoverished & generally uncomfortable by reason" of something the information about which was excised from his letter. "You must be weary of my procrastinations & apparently faithless assurances."[48] The attraction of Joukowsky was so great that he extended his stay in Paris for more than a month.

Whatever Joukowsky's allurements, Paris added to them its usual glitter, the Théâtre Français, the ongoing French political drama, and his Russian friends, particularly Turgenev, who came in from the country especially to see him. Haunted by Russian tyranny and incompetence, Turgenev feared that the republican government in France would imminently collapse or be overthrown. Theodore Child, the correspondent of *The Daily Telegraph,* was in Paris. So too were Fanny Kemble and Frederick Macmillan. Though the Paris September weather was radiant, the French seemed like "an awfully ugly and bilious little race," though France itself "is in a hundred respects a more civilized country" than England. He had "never seen Paris more Parisian . . . better humoured, more open-windowed, more naturally entertaining."[49] At the theatre, he enjoyed Benoît Constant Coquelin's performances. They had been schoolfellows briefly in Boulogne in 1858, and James had seen him perform in 1869. A brilliant actor, with great range and voice, and a writer about the dramatic arts, Coquelin was to attain his popular apogee in his creation of the title role in *Cyrano de Bergerac* in 1897. James now, in September 1877, saw Coquelin's memorable performance in a forgettable play. It seemed a revelation of the power of the stage.

After the performance, he wandered the Paris streets "about the Place de la Concorde, along the Seine, up the Champs-Élysées . . . under the influence not so much of the piece as of Coquelin's acting of it, which had made the thing so human, so brilliant, so valuable." What he felt so powerfully was the longing for theatrical success, for fame and fortune, the vision of the stammering desk-bound writer transformed by the footlights and the applause. Also, he believed theatrical success meant wealth—that each evening a large number of golden coins made their direct transfer from the besieged box office to the pockets of the well-deserving author. The financial rewards, he imagined, would come more quickly and in greater amounts than could ever come from writing fiction. He could repay his parents, help his siblings, and replenish his paternal grandfather's golden three millions of which so far he had seen little or nothing. If he could, he would have immediately begun writing plays. Coquelin's performance "held up a glowing light to me—seemed to point to my own path."

He responded to William's praise of a play by Howells with the mixture of self-parody and seriousness that usually signaled his strong, sincere feelings. "It has long been my most earnest and definite intention to commence playwriting as soon as I can. This will be soon, and then I shall astound the world! . . . I have thoroughly mastered Dumas, Augier and Sardou . . . and I know all they know and a great deal more besides." If he could "only find some manager or publisher" to subsidize him, he would make a compact with him "and sign with my blood, to reimburse him in thousands." When the Théâtre Français came to London in the fall of 1878, he renewed his acquaintanceship with Coquelin, who talked brilliantly, energetically—the embodiment of the artist. As before, all his "latent ambitions" were stirred. But he felt that his "hands were tied" by other work that he had to do. He had writing commitments and an income from his fiction. "I could do nothing," he recalled years later, "and the feeling passed away in smoke. But it stirred me to the depths."[50]

Finally, in late October 1877, he left Paris (where the weather had turned cold) for Italy. He had been promising the Bootts for two years that he would join them there. "I hunger and thirst for Rome," he told Lizzie. But he had been willing to delay the meal. He had been working well in Paris. Fascinated by the political maneuverings of the republicans and the monarchists, he "noted and detested the alacrity with which the Catholic party had rallied to the reactionary cause." On a short trip to Rheims, listening to "the old gentlemen in the red capes" preach in the magnificent cathedral, he was surprisingly "visited . . . by a kind of revelation of the anti-catholic passion, as it must burn to-day in the

breast of certain radicals." When, in mid-October, the election produced a republican majority, he left for Italy. The republican cause
could now manage without his sympathetic daily concern.[51]

In Paris, the theatre, Joukowsky, and other entertainment had absorbed him. By comparison, the Bootts were dull, and Italy was an
obstacle to work. He found them in their rented Bellosguardo villa high
above Florence, about to move to Rome for the winter. Sitting for
hours in their splendid garden "in the autumn sunshine and staring
stupidly at that never-to-be-enough appreciated view of the little city
and the mountains," he avoided almost everyone he knew except the
Bootts and Alice Bartlett. Daydreaming about renting one of the many
nearby villas, in his imagination he rented three or four, took possession, and stayed. Though he had hoped to be able to work on *The
Europeans,* he made little progress there or during the next six weeks in
Rome. He felt impatient to be back in London or, at least, Paris. Despite
lovely weather, despite the absence of the usual tourist horde, Rome
seemed "comparatively common-place and familiar; tho' this only
proves how thoroughly I had enjoyed it in former years."[52] The problem was that he had come for the sake of the Bootts rather than for
himself. Also, he had a strong need to work, and the best of Rome, its
visual beauty and warm, bright weather, kept tempting him outdoors,
away from his desk.

As he had done in Paris, he kept a notebook of impressions for
travel articles. On his way to Florence, via Turin and Milan, he had
stopped at the Bay of Lerici on a perfect autumn afternoon, hired a
boat, and rowed himself across the gulf toward the desolate villa in
which Shelley had spent the last months of his life. Probably some
vague intimations of what became an element of "The Aspern Papers"
rose and dipped with his oars, disappearing beneath the water for a
decade. After visiting the "little battered terrace of the villa," he climbed
to the old castle that hangs high above Lerici, from whose "vine-
decked platform [he] looked out toward the sunset and the darkening
mountains and, far below, upon the quiet sea, beyond which the pale-
faced tragic villa stared up at the brightening moon." He felt the poetic
reverberations of his self-given sobriquet of "the sentimental traveller"
in its poetic mood. Italy and modern life, though, were conspiring
against that familiar, comfortable role. Italian cities, particularly Milan
and Rome, seemed to be rapidly embracing modern architectural and
urban ugliness. He now had no difficulty seeing that human misery
loitered at every Italian street corner. His first concern was for the
sensibility and the viability of his role as spectator. "A traveller is often
moved to ask himself whether it has been worth while to leave his

home . . . only to encounter new forms of human suffering, only to be reminded that toil and privation, hunger and sorrow and sordid effort, are the portion of the mass of mankind. To travel is, as it were, to go to the play, to attend a spectacle; and there is something heartless in stepping forth into foreign streets to feast on 'character' when character consists simply of the slightly different costume in which labour and want present themselves." But he preferred mostly to keep his tourism on the level of spectatorship, and found, as usual, the obvious, evasive rationalizations. After a while, the unhappy scenes "ceased to bear me company. The reason of this, I think, is because . . . the sum of Italian misery is, on the whole, less than the sum of the Italian knowledge of life. That people should thank you, with a smile of striking sweetness, for the gift of twopence, is a proof, certainly, of extreme and constant destitution; but . . . it also attests an enviable ability not to be depressed by circumstances."

He readily admitted, though, "that this may possibly be great nonsense; that half the time we are acclaiming the fine quality of the Italian smile the creature so constituted for physiognomic radiance may be in a sullen frenzy of impatience and pain." Walking along one day, he came in "sight of a young man who trudged upward with his coat slung over his shoulder . . . in the manner of a cavalier in an opera. . . . He sang as he came; the spectacle, generally, was operatic, and as his vocal flourishes reached my ear I said to myself that in Italy accident was always romantic and that such a figure had been exactly what was wanted to set off the landscape." When the young man overtook him, they began to talk. "He presently acknowledged himself a brooding young radical and communist, filled with hatred of the present Italian government, raging with discontent and crude political passion . . . and declaring that he for his part would willingly lend a hand to chop off the heads of the king and the royal family. He was an unhappy, underfed, unemployed young man, who took a hard, grim view of everything and was operatic only quite in spite of himself. This made it very absurd of me to have looked at him simply as a graceful ornament to the prospect, an harmonious little figure in the middle distance. 'Damn the prospect, damn the middle distance!' would have been all *his* philosophy. Yet for the accident of my having gossiped with him I should have made him do service, in memory, as an example of sensuous optimism!" Impatient with his own "sensuous optimism," he was impatient with Italy. His social conscience was too acute, his political consciousness too keen, perhaps sensitized by his concern for the republican cause in France and by the Eastern Question, to provide him with a holiday from realistic observation. By the time he was ready to leave

Rome, he had become sufficiently the spectator again to feel that his enjoyment of Italy had never before been "more exquisite than during those last few days." Still, he told Perry, "it isn't a place for work: one must take one's holiday and depart."[53]

While in Paris for ten days in early December 1877, he read the proofs that Macmillan had sent him, saw Joukowsky, Henrietta Reubell, and other friends, and began to write again. He crossed to dark, dreary London and was delighted to be home. His pattern of work and recreation reasserted itself with a pleasurable familiarity and a productive rhythm. He sometimes daydreamed about the clear, glittering streets and skies of Paris—an occasional "most ferocious fit of homesickness" for that other city. But London was fruitfully demanding, happily self-sufficient. "I have become ridiculously fond of it & am cocknified beyond redemption."[54] He kept at work on *The Europeans for July to October* 1878 serialization in the *Atlantic* and for autumn publication by Osgood in Boston and Macmillan in London. Excited and gratified that he would finally have a novel appearing under the aegis of a British publisher, he hoped that *Macmillan's Magazine* would publish simultaneously with the *Atlantic,* for the sake of both increased audience and a doubling of his profits.

By April 1878, though, he still did not have the manuscript ready to show. His visit to Italy had cost more than he had expected, and money came in more slowly than he had anticipated. Feeling awkward that he had again drawn on his father's letter of credit, he responded both apologetically and assertively to his mother's assumption that he had borrowed even more than he had. She had forgotten to credit against his debt a draft of three hundred dollars that he had had sent directly from New York to Cambridge. He felt he had been awkward, not inconsiderate or, even worse, exploitative. "The sudden extinction of *The Galaxy,*" absorbed by the *Atlantic,* was affecting his earnings, and he might need two or three "more drafts in the spring," which he hoped to be able to repay quickly. He expected substantial profits soon. If his mother would "have a little patience," she would "be very promptly repayed, not only in coin but in reflected glory: of which latter article I propose to furnish myself with a very considerable amount. It is time I should rend the veil from the ferocious ambition which has always *couvé* [smoldered] beneath a tranquil exterior; which enabled me to support unrecorded physical misery in my younger years; and which is perfectly confident of accomplishing considerable things!"[55]

Early in spring 1878, he began to write "Daisy Miller," a short story about an innocent American girl in Rome, which Leslie Stephen accepted for publication in two parts in the June and July *Cornhill.*

Stephen, who introduced James to his fiancée, the charming, beautiful Julia Duckworth ("who has, by a miracle, consented to become, matrimonially, the receptacle of his ineffable and impossible taciturnity and dreariness"), still seemed like a man in perpetual mourning. One evening, he went with Stephen to observe the House of Commons in session, which he found interesting. He "went on dining out occasionally, but always pretty tamely." With Fanny Kemble, he went to see Henry Irving in a play "in which he is better than in anything else—which doesn't mean he is not pretty bad." In March, he met James McNeill Whistler at the home of Christina Rogerson, whose hospitality James now frequently accepted. A clever, freethinking woman, Rogerson was married to a drunkard from whom she led a separate life, which included in the next years a notorious affair with Charles Dilke, a handsome young aristocrat and influential radical politician. Having commented adversely on Whistler's paintings in a review of "The Picture Season in London," he found Whistler himself interesting enough for him to look again and more thoughtfully at his work. In mid-April, he went to one of Whistler's "somewhat classical" Sunday breakfasts at his "queer little house at Chelsea, on the river (near Carlyle's). . . . He is a queer little Londonized Southerner, and paints abominably. But his breakfasts are easy and pleasant, and he has tomatoes and buckwheat cakes."[56] Gradually, Whistler's paintings transformed themselves in his eyes into representations of feeling and hallucination that transcended the limitations of his earlier, more rigid principles. Mostly his increased appreciation of Whistler's art followed his developing appreciation of Whistler himself, his wit, his eccentricities, and his dedication to his art.

James also needed more space, a larger window, the kind of extended living room that a club provided. He had temporary privileges at the Traveller's, which soon expired. Though he was able to find some amenities at the St. James's, which catered to foreigners and diplomats at a monthly fee, he missed the attractions of the Athenaeum. He was on the list for consideration at the Reform Club, where he was being pushed by friends, particularly the influential Dilke, Christina Rogerson's lover. He felt that if he waited long enough he would be admitted. "But there is no danger of it, I am afraid, this year." To his shock and delight, he was "abruptly informed" in May 1878 that his name was "on the point of coming up for ballot." A few days later he was elected "a regular member, for life." He now had a club of his own, a reputable and a formidable one. This was heady stuff, even for a man who had come more and more to take in stride the opportunities and privileges that were coming his way. Probably the process had been facilitated by his reputation as a distinguished American writer living in London whose permanent residence, oddly, everyone thought to be New York City. For the honor of his native country, he paid the forty-two-pound entrance fee immediately. Ironically, he could do so only by writing another draft against his letter of credit, with the hope that he would be able to repay the money shortly. With "many irons on the fire," he was "bursting with writeableness," he told Henry senior.[57]

From "the big tranquil library" of the Reform Club, filled with a collection of English literature so huge that he felt it would last him a lifetime, he looked "out upon the green gardens of Carlton House Terrace." The whole experience made him "feel strangely and profoundly at home here." Paradoxically, he had no doubt that he was "still completely an outsider here." At best, he felt he might become "a little of an insider (in that limited sense in which an American ever can do so)." Nevertheless, he had fulfilled a lifelong ambition, one that as young men in Cambridge he and Tom Perry had shared, the dream of living gloriously in London. "I have made that fantastic past a daily present & a matter of course that I fear I shall never lapse from."[58] To live in London, though, did not mean to be a Londoner, let alone to be English. He felt himself, on the contrary, to be a cosmopolite, a person of many cities, a cultural anthropologist of art and sensibility. His special abilities and his position as an American gave him, he felt, the opportunity to observe and record in his art a complex culture at the end of an era. He was now ready to begin the work for which he had trained himself.

Seven

"THE SENTIMENTAL TRAVELLER"

1878–1881

(1)

Walking out to his carriage in front of the Surrey cottage of George Eliot at the end of October 1878, he was startled when George Henry Lewes, after all the good-byes had already been said, hastened after him. Stopping him at the door, Lewes held two blue-bound volumes in his raised hand. "Ah those books," he said, "take them away, please, away, away!" As James walked to the carriage to rejoin his friend, Mrs. Richard Greville, whose guest he was at nearby Milford Cottage, he looked at the title and saw, to his shock, that it was his own novel *The American*. He felt stunned, dislocated, the victim of an unintended cosmic joke. Apparently, the book his hostess had proudly loaned to her famous neighbors was being returned unread, as an unwanted intrusion. "Our hosts hadn't so much as connected book with author, or author with visitor, or visitor with anything but his ridding them of an unconsidered trifle. . . . The vivid demonstration of one's failure to penetrate there had been in the sweep of Lewes's gesture, which could scarce have been bettered by his actually wielding a broom."[1]

He did not feel quite entirely swept away, even if Eliot and Lewes had declined to read him, though unaware of whom they were declining. Still, the fear of being held disdainfully between two fastidious fingers and pronounced irrelevant, unsuitable, unwanted, was much on his mind. His situation as an American intending to make London his permanent headquarters had a dark side that even his social successes could not obviate. In November 1877 *Scribner's Monthly* published "Four Meetings," a story that expressed one of his nightmares, the fear of being cut off forever from the European experience. A New England spinster, whose lifelong ambition has been to visit Europe, finally gets as far as Le Havre, only to be forced to return to America when a putative cousin, an artist, exploits her passive innocence and borrows all her money. At home, she soon receives an indefinite, demanding guest, a "countess" who claims to be the widow of the now dead cousin. The coarse "countess," perhaps an ex-prostitute, despises America and Miss Spencer. To preserve or gain some advantage for herself, even the advantage of having her morning coffee served to her, the countess would certainly condemn Miss Spencer to death. "Poor Miss Spencer," the narrator concludes, "had been right in her presentiment that she should still see something of Europe"—the condescending cruelty of those who know how to exploit innocence and weakness.

Just as Lewes held up for removal his unwanted copy of *The American,* James holds up for analysis his American narrators in "Four Meetings" and in "Daisy Miller: A Study." When the narrator of the former, a perceptive American whom long residence in Europe has so refined that excessive politeness and respect for privacy have rendered him morally passive, does nothing at all to help "poor Miss Spencer," he reveals himself to be an accomplice in his countrywoman's exploitation. His noninterference principle substitutes the aesthetic responsibility of an observer for the moral responsibility of a participant. As an American too long in Europe, the narrator of "Daisy Miller," Frederick Winterbourne, finds himself unable to act to help an innocent, vivacious young lady to survive behaving in Europe as she is used to behaving in America. Ostensibly abroad to study, Winterbourne spends his time on superficial flirtations and travels. At its best, the story sets up an effective interplay between the limitations of the shallow narrator and those of the young lady. But the dramatic question of the story is whether or not Daisy deliberately flaunts the moral conventions of the Roman society in which she lives. When Winterbourne, having resisted the common opinion that Daisy and her Italian friend, Giovanelli, are having an affair, sees them at midnight in the Colosseum, he concludes that they are indeed having a sexual relationship. The narrator and the author never let us know, other than by indirection, what Daisy is thinking. Without an effective father or mother, she seems an American innocent on her own in a small-minded European culture. Daisy's recklessness can be understood as youthful American assertiveness. She is the new American woman, a variant of Minny Temple, a combination of the young girl who believes that everyone will love her no matter what she says or does and the rebellious woman determined to tell off the world. Winterbourne's imagination is too shallow, too enervated, for him to evaluate her in terms other than the conventional polarity between innocence and experience, purity and sexuality. Like Christopher Newman, Daisy cannot survive in Europe. Through the literary and cultural tradition that disposes of unfit women by mysterious illnesses, James provides a minor coda to the life of Minny Temple, while positioning himself outside the narrator and the main character. At the end, Daisy is dead, and the ineffective Winterbourne, granting that he was destined to make a mistake because he had "lived too long in foreign parts," resumes his superficial life. James's own survival instinct almost visibly emanates through the energies of the story.

To his surprise, "Daisy Miller," in which he had placed no more commercial hope than in his previous stories, proved an extraordinary popular success. *The Cornhill's* middle-class British audience and "Daisy's" middle-class American readers found it sufficiently sexual to be titillating, sufficiently indirect to be morally acceptable, and sufficiently indeterminative in regard to "did she or didn't she" to provoke lively discussion. "It is having an immense run both here [in Boston] & NY," Mary James happily remarked. Howells was delighted. "Harry James waked up all the women with his Daisy Miller, the intention of which they misconceived, and there has been a vast discussion in which nobody felt very deeply, and everybody talked very loudly. The thing went so far that society almost divided itself into Daisy Millerites and anti-Daisy Millerites." Daisy's only sin, James insisted, is innocence, her naive misunderstanding of European conventions and her assertion of her integrity in her refusal to change her behavior. What everyone else takes as a scandalous flouting of proprieties is, for Daisy, perfectly innocent conduct. For her, there is neither smoke nor fire. Most readers saw both, though Aunt Kate had no doubt that Henry's "very clever" story expressed the desire, which "seems to burn in his bones, to vindicate Americans to the European mind."[2] Most important for James, everyone, so to speak, read the story. Howells hoped that, "in making James so thoroughly known, it would call attention in as wide degree to the beautiful work he had been doing for so long for very few readers and still fewer lovers."

For a moment, "Daisy Miller" seemed a breakthrough. A month before its publication, Macmillan had agreed to publish *The Europeans* in London—James "very glad you undertake the book." For its serial publication in 1878 in the *Atlantic,* he received a thousand dollars. "As regards the profits I am afraid there is not much danger of their being 'enormous' . . . but . . . it will be a beginning of my appearance before the British public as a novelist—as *the* novelist of the future, destined to extract from B.P. [British public] eventually (both for himself & his publisher) a colossal fortune!" The comic hyperbole expressed actual hope. Perhaps his reputation would rise to a level of popularity that would produce substantial profits. In 1875, his income had jumped from the under two thousand dollars that it had never previously exceeded to more than twenty-five hundred dollars, the level at which it remained for the next two years. In 1878, it rose to almost thirty-five hundred dollars, most of that from serial publication of novels and from the publication of short stories and essays in magazines.[3] As for "Daisy Miller" itself, the $220 he had received from The Cornhill represented most of his immediate profit. Though he had hoped to sell the advance sheets to an American magazine for simultaneous publication, he unexpectedly found that he was too late. Since English publication had preceded American, American publishers were free, in the absence of a copyright treaty, to publish "Daisy" without any payment to the author, which they promptly did. When Harper & Bros. in New York asked to publish "Daisy" in "Harper's Half Hour Series," they agreed to a 10 percent royalty. But since the pamphlet sold for twenty cents, James earned only two cents a copy. The two hundred dollars he received from Harper's the next year disappointed him.

Since "Daisy" had been a "great hit," he worked on a companion story, "An International Episode," also for The Cornhill, and sold the American rights "outright, copyright and all," for a small sum to the Harper pamphlet series. Macmillan now agreed to bring out English editions of The American and Roderick Hudson. In the fall, he happily told Lizzie Boott he was "in a very good way of work and of growing fame & profit."[4] His mind dwelt optimistically on his anticipated "Americana—a female counterpart to Newman," for which he had received invitations from both The Cornhill and Macmillan's Magazine.

By the next year, he admitted that in regard to "Daisy" and "An International Episode," "having in advance no prevision of their success I made a very poor bargain." Still, he explained to William, "a man's 1st successes are those, always, by which he makes least. I am not a grasping business-man—on the contrary, and I sometimes—or rather, often—strike myself as gaining woefully less money than fame. My reputation in England seems (considering what it is based on) ludicrously larger than any cash payment that I have yet received for it. The Macmillans are everything that's friendly—caressing—old Macmillan physically *hugs* me; but the delicious ring of the sovereign is conspicuous in our intercourse by its absence." Yet, he assured his family, whose financial situation was much on his mind, "I am sure of the future—that is the grand thing." Also, he rationalized, "It is something to behave like a gentleman even when other people don't," as if he could justify his lost financial opportunities by proclaiming his moral superiority to his publishers. At some level of partial evasion, he seems to have been aware that what was at issue were not standards of gentlemanly conduct but his own practical judgment in an aspect of his professional life to which, dependent on his earnings, he always had given importance. Still, he consoled himself and his family, "I shall have made by the end of this year very much more money than I have ever made before; & next year I shall make as much as that again."[5]

With publishers unwilling to pay advances for book publication and with the sales of his books limited because the work had already been widely available in magazines, he needed to increase as much as possible his earnings from serial publication. At the beginning of 1879, he signed an agreement with Macmillan for publisher and author to split equally all profits, after the deduction of Macmillan's expenses, for a volume of stories, the essays on French literature, *The American,* and *The Europeans.* But he faced two problems in regard to the contract. He had no way of checking the publisher's actual expenses, and the profits reported were likely to be small enough to make no significant difference to him. His plan, though, was to double his main source of income, he told William, by publishing simultaneously in English and American magazines. "I shall be able at once to live very comfortably, to 'put by,' and to make an allowance to each member of the family. This is my dream." Money pressures were pinching, if not bruising, his parents. William earned very little. Both Wilky and Bob, who needed regular assistance to stay afloat, seemed to be drowning. Alice was a total dependent. In October 1878, the depression in America had put his parents' money affairs "in a bad way." Aunt Kate also found herself with a "largely reduced income." When he learned of the new losses at home, he immediately apologized for his sluggishness in settling the last of his debts to them. Within the next year, he became aware that his family's losses were even greater than he had imagined. "My father appears to have lost ½ of his property." By the spring of 1879, he was finally square with his financially pressed parents. "In the future I expect to give you money," he assured them, "not to take it from you!" If he could add the profit that he was certain writing for the stage would provide, he and they would never have to be concerned about money again. "I am morally certain I should succeed, and it would be an open gate to money-making."[6]

Though the gate to England and to fortune was only partly open in 1878, fame was another matter. Wherever in the English-speaking world there were serious middle- and upper-class readers, he was being read, with general acknowledgment that he was among the most talented of the young writers, with few or no rivals in regard to psychological subtlety, social observation, and technical effectiveness. "Harry's recent things," his mother boasted, "seem to be making him famous on both sides of the water. The English papers are full of favourable criticism and flattering predictions." He reassured her about the inextricable link between his genius and his character. "Never was a genius— if genius there is—more healthy, objective, and (I honestly believe) less susceptible of superficial irritations and reactionary impulses. I know what I want." Where there was critical carping, it usually focused on the opposite side of the coin of his virtues, a sometimes perplexing "super-subtlety" in presentation and an unsatisfying emotional aloofness. The success of "Daisy" did, though, encourage him "as regards the faculty of appreciation of the English public; for the thing is sufficiently subtle, yet people appear to have comprehended it."[7] He wanted to expand his audience without diminishing his subtlety.

When, at the end of 1878, he published the first of two installments of "An International Episode" in *The Cornhill,* he was confronted by another kind of threat to his anticipated popularity. In the story, two young upper-class Englishmen, to escape the August heat, sail from New York to Newport to stay with Mrs. Kitty Westgate and her sister Bessie Alden. When Lord Lambeth falls in love with Bessie, his friend Percy Beaumont writes to Lambeth's mother, who immediately recalls her son on the specious claim that his father is seriously ill. Bessie likes but is not in love with Lambeth. Having never visited Europe, when she and her older sister arrive in England in the spring, she is overwhelmed by the beauty of the English countryside. Both sisters, though, dislike British class distinctions and British snobbery. When Lambeth, genuinely in love with her, discovers that Bessie is in England, he pays her extensive attention. The question arises whether or not she would accept him if he offers marriage. No one can imagine that she would not. When Lambeth compels his mother and sister to visit the American sisters, the duchess and her daughter are glacially impolite. Lambeth soon proposes. Bessie then tells her sister that they must leave England now, since she has declined Lambeth's proposal. She has turned him down because it does not suit her to marry him. She likes him very much, but she is not in love with him and recognizes that they are very different. She is serious about the things of this world, about ideas and places and expanding the self. He is complacent, the product of a privilege that does not question itself. She loves and admires English history and literature, but not the English, who take it for granted, and not those English attitudes that she finds morally distasteful. Sensitive, intelligent, and independent, Bessie is another representation of James's idealization of the American woman, again with echoes of Minny Temple. In the evocations of New York and Newport the descriptions resonate with the glow of James's memories. In Lord Lambeth's essential goodness and his physical handsomeness, James continues his idealization of the English male, partly expressing his attraction to male beauty, partly his erotically tinged Anglophilia.

William had sharply criticized *The Europeans* for being overcondensed and underdeveloped, and Henry correctly feared he would have much the same to say about "An International Episode." Whatever the story's limitations, he was astonished, though, when some of his English acquaintances expressed unhappiness with its unflattering portrayal of aspects of English culture. He had naively assumed that since he had satirized Americans in England, the English would not mind, in all fairness, his satirizing the English in America. He had balanced, he felt, American virtues with British virtues; the dragons of the story were unwarranted personal and national pride, snobbishness, and cruelty. At first, he was baffled, then angered. "So long as one serves up Americans for their entertainment it is all right—but hands off the sacred natives! They are really I think, thinner-skinned than we!" Finally, he retreated into accommodation. He liked and needed his British friends too much to wound them. More subtlety, not less, was called for—avoidance and evasion, subtlety's necessary allies. "I shall keep off dangerous ground in the future," he told his mother. He needed his British audience, though a sizable portion of it was represented by the "fly-fishing" Tories and the "very vulgar-minded and superficial" people he met at dinner parties. When, a year after the publication of "An International Episode," the editor of the *North American Review* asked him to contribute an article comparing "English & American manners," he declined. "It would be too invidious & ticklish a theme—especially while I continue to reside in England." For an economically and socially dependent guest-resident already concerned, with good reason, that he wrote beyond the interest and understanding of a broad audience, it could be dangerous to be understood too well.[8]

(2)

On New Year's Eve, 1879, he found himself in the company of one of the least thin-skinned of his English friends, the elderly Monckton Milnes, Lord Houghton, his host at Fryston Hall in Yorkshire. "Full of sociable and friendly instincts, and with a strong streak of humanity and democratic feeling," Houghton came into James's room to ask why he had not come down to afternoon tea. Seating himself, with his usual fidgety eccentricity, in a comfortable armchair for a few minutes of conversation, Houghton fell "into a social slumber." In a few moments, he began "to snore violently." James went back to writing a letter.

His excursions into English social life and his meetings with Victorian literary giants were simultaneously dull and fascinating. Many of his preconceptions needed redefinition. At the end of October 1878, he visited Tennyson at his country home at Aldworth with the ever-reliable, celebrity-conscious Mrs. Greville, a "large, elegant, extremely near-sighted and extremely demonstrative lady," who was "an intimate friend" of the poet's. "With her exquisite good nature and her innocent fatuity," Mrs. Greville expressed her warmth for Tennyson by "*kissing him somewhere—quite en famille*—every quarter of an hour." Tennyson did not seem to mind. When Mrs. Greville referred to one of her French relatives, Mademoiselle Laure de Sade, James's attention was immediately provoked. He had certainly heard of the infamous Marquis. Though his knowledge probably exceeded his reading experience, he would read sexually explicit works without the slightest sense of personal impropriety if the work interested him. When a young writer, W. E. Henley, whom he befriended, asked him if he had read Sacher-Masoch, he responded that he had "never read a word by Sacher-Masoch. But if you recommend S.-M. I will try him."[9] In response to Mrs. Greville's, " 'De Sade?' [Tennyson] at once exclaimed with interest—and with the consequence . . . of my wondering almost to ecstasy . . . to what length he would proceed. He proceeded admirably . . . to the very greatest length imaginable, as was signally promoted by the fact that clearly no one present, with a single exception, recognised the name or the nature of the scandalous, the long ignored, the at last all but unnameable author; least of all the gentle relative of Mademoiselle Laure, who listened with the blankest grace to her friend's enumeration of his titles to infamy, among which that of his most notorious work was pronounced. It was the homeliest, frankest, most domestic passage . . . and most remarkable for leaving none of us save myself, by my impression, in the least embarrassed or bewildered; largely, I think, because of the failure . . . of all measure on the part of auditors and speaker alike of what might be intended or understood, of what, in fine, the latter was talking about."

Later in the afternoon, Tennyson, having proposed that he read one of his poems of their choice, took them upstairs to his study. James, who had heard him read before, requested "Locksley Hall." "I sat at one of the windows that hung over space, noting how the windy, watery autumn day, sometimes sheeting it all with rain, called up the dreary, dreary moorland. . . . I asked myself in fine why . . . I failed to swoon away under the heaviest pressure I had doubtless ever known the romantic situation bring to bear." He felt nothing. The reading bored him. "The author lowered the whole pitch, that of expression, that of interpretation above all; I heard him, in cool surprise, take even more out of his verse than he had put in, and so bring me back to the point I had immediately and privately made, the point that he wasn't Tennysonian."[10]

When he met the novelist George Meredith at a dinner late in 1878, James was in partial agreement with Meredith's definition of what it meant to be English. "He hates the English, whom he speaks of as 'they.' 'Their conversation is dreary, their food is heavy, their women are dull.' " Just as Meredith earned his criticism on the margin of his own Englishness, James felt that because he was "so fond of London" he could "afford to abuse it." His own criticism varied with his moods, often balancing derogation with appreciation. "London is on the whole such a fine thing," he told Grace Norton in 1879, "that it can afford to be abused! It has all sorts of superior qualities, but it has also, and English life, generally, and the English character have, a certain number of great plump flourishing uglinesses and drearinesses."[11] Meredith himself he found a delightful dinner companion, a "decidedly brilliant fellow, full of talk, paradoxes, affectations etc.; but interesting and witty." Though he had reservations about the depth and quality of Meredith's mind, he thought him, over the years, the wittiest Englishman he had ever known, a quality that enlivened his company but also infected his prose. As a novelist, Meredith seemed too linguistically ornamental, too verbally decorative, sacrificing realism on the altar of wit and attenuated indirection. He would much rather have Meredith's company than his books. But since Meredith lived in the country, he had his books, which he read, comparing them unfavorably to Turgenev's.

Occasionally, he felt "woefully tired of [London] people and their talk." Frequently bored, sometimes repelled, "I confess I find people in general very vulgar-minded and superficial—and it is only by a pious fiction, to keep myself going, and keep on the social harness, that I succeed in postulating them as anything else or better." At moments, he thought of liberating himself from "the social harness," never again to challenge the approximately 107 times that he calculated he had already dined out during the London social season of 1879. "If you dine out a good deal in London," he wrote to William, "you forget your dinner the next morning—or rather, if you walk home, as I always do, you forget it by the time you have turned the corner of the street. . . . My impressions evaporate with the fumes of the champagne."[12] He may have been exaggerating to deflate the criticism he suspected his Cambridge family had of the waste of time involved in his social life. He was honest, though, with Grace Norton. "You will simply wonder what can have induced me to perpetrate such a folly, and how I have survived to tell the tale!" He might have added, in his effort to impress his family, the amount of money he saved on food. He had, of course, no easy, single answer to his own questions about his folly. The reasons were many, including his calculation that in order to be less of a stranger in a strange land he needed to "stand ready," as he was soon to write in regard to Hawthorne's years in Europe, "to pay with his person." Standing ready often meant sitting to satiety in dull company at long dinners. Beyond that, he was a shy, socially curious man who felt pleasure at becoming a part of the great London literary and social world. He wanted to be wanted, and he needed company, not particularly of single individuals with demands of intimacy, but of varied numbers, even at the risk of superficiality. And now, once having got onto the social Ferris wheel, he feared that if he got off it might not stop for him again. As a bachelor in a foreign world, without family or long-standing friends, the certainty of dinner company at innumerable dinners seemed more attractive than the possibility of frequent solitary evenings.

Still, even while having regular dinner company, he often felt "lonely & speechless. Everything around me is worldly, stuffy, literal, unspeakably Philistine." The winter of 1879 was particularly cold, gloomy, and unsympathetic, with heavy snowstorms and severe economic depression. An oppressively thick fog enveloped London, forcing chimney smoke "into one's eyes and down one's throat, so that one is half blinded and quite sickened." He told his American readers in *The Nation* that the misery of "hard times" visibly pressed as painfully in England as it did across the Atlantic. Politics dominated dinner-table discussions and newspaper columns, especially questions of the extension of the franchise and the interminable Eastern Question. The Liberal party, which he supported, seemed to him to cut as poor a figure as the Conservative in everything except its principles. He felt that England could not, in the long run, afford to abdicate its international presence as an imperial power, though it was to be praised for its moral judgment in assessing many of the calls to arms as not worth the shedding of blood. Still, he forecast that England would do anything to avoid war "until contemptuous Europe, growing audacious with impunity, shall put upon her some supreme and unendurable affront. Then—too late—she will rise ferociously and plunge clumsily and unpreparedly into war. She will be worsted and laid on her back—and when she is laid on her back will exhibit—in her colossal wealth and pluck—an unprecedented power of resistance. But she will never really recover as a European power." Despite these concerns over the long-term fortunes of his world, he found the day-to-day dominance of political discourse insufferable. London "*is* hideously political," he complained bitterly, "& there don't seem to me to be three people in it who care for questions of art, or form."[13] Though he felt that he had more opportunities for literary and social richness in London and England than in New York and America, at moments he felt hostile to the culture in which he had chosen to live. Worse, he felt isolated.

Often, during the cold winter and spring of 1879, his thoughts went "fluttering their wings toward the Roman housetops." He fantasied that the ideal existence for him would be "5 months of London, 5 of Italy (mainly Rome), a month for Paris" and a month for spontaneous excursions.[14] Beneath and behind his Italian daydreaming, though, were two realities, England and America, the England in which he felt he needed to live in order to practice his art, and the America that was a constant part of his consciousness. By March, weary of the sharp east wind and his perpetual sore throat, he told Lizzie that, if practical matters would permit, he would leave immediately for Rome. Despite the dark weather and the stupefyingly innumerable dinings-out, he kept an intense writing schedule. Beginning in late 1878, his imaginative life had directed itself mostly toward America, perhaps as an expression of his renewed need, after having been abroad for more than four years, to rethink and reexpress why he was living in England, perhaps because he felt American yearnings more strongly than he had for some time, particularly for his family.

In October 1878, he had received an unanticipated request from Macmillan to write a short biographical study of either Washington Irving or Nathaniel Hawthorne for the publisher's "English Men of Letters" series. Having decided that if he were to write such a book, he preferred to write on Hawthorne, he hesitated briefly, and then refused. When pressed, he hesitated again. Then, finally, he accepted, partly because of his "desire to make next year as much money as possible." At the beginning of 1879, he happily signed a contract for an outright sale of the British copyright. Macmillan's usual arrangement for world rights for books in the series was a fee of seventy-five pounds, but, as an American citizen, James owned the American rights, which Harper & Bros. in New York queried Macmillan about. When Macmillan gave him the choice of an additional twenty-five pounds or a royalty arrangement of 10 percent on the American sales, he chose to add the twenty-five pounds to the seventy-five already agreed on.[15] Later, when the book sold well in America, he regretted his decision. Both publishers profited considerably beyond the hundred pounds the author earned on a sale in his lifetime of about twenty thousand copies. He was never again, with a minor exception, to sell outright any of his copyrights. By the time he began the writing in summer 1879, his lack of enthusiasm for the project had declined into regret. At the end of the year, he readily confessed to Grace Norton that he had written it "sadly against my will. I wanted to let him alone."

His reluctance in writing *Hawthorne* derived partly from his sense that it would force on him too direct a confrontation with his feelings about America. There was also the money issue. Hawthorne had struggled to become a writer in an antithetical climate in which it was impossible to earn a living as a writer. Writing a biography of America's first great novelist, who suffered because he could not earn enough from his writing to support himself, he constantly had in mind his own financial disappointments, including the absurdly small sum he was being paid for the current project. Unlike Hawthorne, he had made himself an indefinite, if not a permanent, exile from his native land for the sake of his art, which included sustaining himself so that he could practice his art. As well as it was going, it was not going quite well enough. By the end of 1879, when he confessed his feelings about the Hawthorne book to Grace Norton, he had already decided that there were good, even necessary reasons for a visit "home for several months." He had baldly told Norton a full year before that he was "coming home for a year in 1880. Then we can talk."[16] The decision had resulted from numbers of preoccupations, especially the fantasy of triumphant return that he had begun exploring in *The Europeans*.

In *The Europeans,* Eugenia (Baroness Münster) and her brother, Felix Young, come from Europe to Boston, both of them to gain or repair their fortunes. Sophisticated, worldly, calculating, Eugenia is married to a baron from whom she has separated and who wants her, for reasons of state, to agree to a divorce. Eager for new adventures and capable of growth and change, Felix earns his living (and his sister's) as a society portrait painter. In a raw, wintry Boston, brilliantly invoked in the opening paragraphs through the condescending eyes of the Europeanized Eugenia, they introduce themselves to their cousins, the wealthy, puritanical Wentworths. A buoyant, happy artist, Felix is more American than European in values but more European than American in substance. A partial Jamesian self-portrait, he has puritan morality without a puritan sensibility. Partly American by blood, he returns to the continent of his family's origin to discover that his native charm, energy, optimism, talent, and moral sensibility have found their proper climate. Eugenia who is given the chance to marry Robert Acton, a handsome, wealthy, and distinguished friend of the Wentworths, but alienates him with her European sophistication, which takes the form of deviousness and manipulation. To Acton, the beautiful New England countryside, described with tactile, evocative vividness, is home. To Eugenia, it is exotic and alien. In the end, she returns to Europe, not having allowed herself to feel the pull of America, or even to understand, because she does not want to, what America is about.

In *Hawthorne,* James brought into sharper, more realistic focus what he had played with in totally fictional terms in *The Europeans:* his awareness of the losses to be suffered because of his determination to reside in England and the tragic insufficiency of both his options. His choice *had* been made. It had been, he felt, the only realistic choice for him. In *The Europeans,* Felix Young carries the emotional lightness, almost exhilaration, of James's fantasy of a triumphant return to America. In *Hawthorne,* with the disguising devices of biography rather than fiction, he soberly, sympathetically, indirectly, makes the case for the untenability or, at least, undesirability, of American residence for a writer like himself. The argument was not a new one. He had rehearsed it informally in his letters to Howells. He had heard extensions of it in Henry senior's advocacy of the importance of social responsibility and his disapproval of Emersonian individualism. But now he expressed it with deliberate, almost magisterial cogency, evoking sympathetically the difficult situation of Hawthorne as writer in pre–Civil War America, a situation still applicable to the writer in post–Civil War America. For James, "the best things come, as a general thing, from the talents that are members of a group; every man works better when he has companions working in the same line . . . yielding the stimulus of suggestion, comparison, emulation. Great things of course have been done by solitary workers; but they have usually been done with double the pains they would have cost if they had been produced in more genial circumstances." In America, "the individual counts for more, as it were, and, thanks to the absence of a variety of social types and settled heads under which he may be easily and conveniently pigeon-holed, he is to a certain extent a wonder and a mystery." The result for the writer is glorious isolation, but isolation nevertheless.

In thinking about the unpropitious soil of Hawthorne's youth, he had in mind the limitations of post–Civil War Cambridge and Boston for someone with a desire for world culture and a sustaining literary community. "When we think of what the conditions of intellectual life, of taste, must have been in a small New England town fifty years ago; and when we think of a young man of beautiful genius, with a love of literature and romance, of the picturesque, of style and form and colour, trying to make a career for himself in the midst of them, compassion for the young man becomes our dominant sentiment, and we see the long dry village picture in perhaps almost too hard a light." He would soften but never fully relent or regret his decision to seek a sympathetic community in England. He had done what he believed necessary, though he was later to admit he paid an even greater price than he ever anticipated.

For the writer that James desired to be, both the subject matter and fraternal community would be more readily available in London than in Cambridge or Boston or New York. For "the flower of art blooms only where the soil is deep. . . . It takes a great deal of history to produce a little literature. . . . It needs a complex social machinery to set a writer in motion. American civilization has hitherto had other things to do than to produce flowers, and before giving birth to writers it has wisely occupied itself with providing something for them to write about." Fortunes were being earned. A social and an artistic culture was slowly gathering. But it had not yet reached the critical mass that would satisfy his needs. "History, as yet, has left in the United States but so thin and impalpable a deposit that we very soon touch the hard substratum of nature; and nature herself, in the western world, has the peculiarity of seeming rather crude and immature. The very air looks new and young; the light of the sun seems fresh and innocent."

American energy and innocence were to be cherished. But, for him, they were by themselves insufficient to the challenge of creating literature. "One might enumerate the items of high civilization, as it exists in other countries, which are absent from the texture of American life, until it should become a wonder to know what was left. No State, in the European sense of the word, and indeed barely a specific national name. No sovereign, no court, no personal loyalty, no aristocracy, no church, no clergy, no army, no diplomatic service, no country gentlemen, no palaces, no castles, nor manors, nor old country-houses, nor parsonages, nor thatched cottages nor ivied ruins; no cathedrals, nor abbeys, nor little Norman churches; no great Universities nor public schools—no Oxford, nor Eton, nor Harrow; no literature, no novels, no museums, no pictures, no political life, no sporting class. . . . Some such list as that might be drawn up of the absent things in American life. . . . The natural remark, in the almost lurid light of such an indictment, would be that if these things are left out, everything is left out. The American knows that a good deal remains; what it is that remains— that is his secret, his joke, as one may say." But the special twist of this unusual joke, with its cosmic romanticism, the secret revealed in

Hawthorne's *The Scarlet Letter,* in Melville's *Moby Dick,* and in Emily Dickinson's poems, spoke to a different order of reality and literature than he desired to identify himself with, partly because of who he was, partly because of what he wanted America to be.

(3)

His decision, in late 1878, that he would go home for a visit in 1880 expressed his sense that the emotional vividness of his American world was being diminished by time and distance. Each day the pile of unanswered letters on his desk, many of them from across the Atlantic, seemed to remain constant, no matter how many letters he wrote. Home news arrived with the regularity of transatlantic steamers, always attenuated by the time between the occurrence and his receipt of the letter, sometimes sharply punctuated by news so dramatic that the emotional distancing of the delay made little difference. He had learned to live without his family, a triumph of self-assertion for which he had no doubt that he paid a price, both in expenditure of emotional energy and in the inadequacy of some of his substitutions. A crucial center of his emotional life was at a distance, his most intense relationships conducted by mail. He missed his parents, and William especially. His mother and William wrote regularly, Alice, occasionally. He cherished their letters. Mary James confidently believed that "it will give your heart a happier bound every time you open a letter from home." At Quincy Street, they were always "longing dreadfully" to hear from him.[17] He felt both the burden and the inadequacy of a life by correspondence. Crucial events were occurring without his presence—deaths, marriages, births, and especially the closely, tightly woven fabric of everyday activities and feelings that provide the experiences that give each life its particular texture.

Occasionally, home came to him. Sara Sedgwick, Charles Norton's sister-in-law and Alice's envied friend, came to England in the summer of 1877 for a visit. She soon startled everyone who knew her by the announcement that she was engaged to marry William Darwin, Charles Darwin's eldest son. "If they bite in numbers, bear in mind," Alice urged her, "the lone lorn spinster you have left behind." Her fiancé seemed to James the epitome of a well-meaning, innocuous, English liberal, with as little vitality as his wife, who, the next year, when she visited home, struck everyone at Quincy Street "with her sadness and invalidism." Still, James liked them both enough to visit them regularly at their country home and to maintain a long, companionable relationship. He had a sharp, kind whiff of Boston in the form of Elizabeth Peabody, a James family friend, whom he visited on the Isle of Wight in spring 1878. An elderly, shy, self-abnegating woman of great intelligence, she had been a distinguished educational reformer and feminist of the previous generation, the sister-in-law of Hawthorne and a friend of Emerson, Fuller, and Thoreau. He welcomed a long walk with her, the pleasure of her fresh news from home, and "the native *finesse* and animation of the American female mind."[18] In another instance, he had an American home away from home through the hospitality of Russell Sturgis, an American-born senior partner with Baring Brothers who had made a fortune in banking and permanently resided in England, in a handsome London house and a luxurious country estate. Two of Sturgis' sons were to become his friends, particularly the youngest, British-born son by his third marriage, Howard. It was a hospitality that had every attraction for him except the crucial one of intellectual and aesthetic interest. But he was a great favorite among the Sturgises. Being so warmly welcomed outweighed the occasional dullness. It was like visiting family.

Clover and Henry Adams came to Europe early in summer 1879, making London their headquarters for a European year, planning to spend part of the autumn in Paris and the winter in Spain with Lowell. Delighted to see them, James sat up with them one night till one in the morning, "abusing the Britons," one of the Adamses' favorite pastimes, both a privilege of their Anglophilia and an assertion of their Americanness. The Adamses are "very pleasant, friendly, conversational, critical, ironical." Clover, chattering less than usual, seemed calmer. They both appeared a little deflated and depressed, which James imagined might come from their being Milnes Gaskell's house guests in a large London mansion that he had taken for the season for the purpose of hosting his friends. "Henry A. can never be in the nature of things a very gracious or sympathetic companion . . . but they are both very pleasant & doubtless when they get into lodgings will be more animated."[19] He was right. As the summer progressed, they became "excellent company." But not so excellent that he felt he could forsake his work and accept their strongly urged invitation that he go with them to Spain in the fall.

In spring 1878, he had joyful news from home. William had become engaged to marry Alice Howe Gibbens, a serious, intelligent, attractive young lady from Cambridge about whom, after meeting her the previous year, Henry senior had announced to the family that he had found the woman William would marry. Whether it was "will" or "should," it was one of the few instances of Henry senior being both pragmatically wise and helpfully directive. William quickly agreed. He had, though, to spend much of a year attempting to persuade Miss Gibbens to agree, which, with much reluctance and after considerable delay, she finally did. William, at almost thirty-six years of age, still had sufficient emotional, physical, and financial problems to make any practical woman hesitate. Finally, after one false start, an engagement occurred in May 1878. "She has been brought up so simply and economically she will if I mistake not," Mary James remarked, "make an excellent poor man's wife." Henry had no doubt that "my father & mother consider her perfection, & they tell me she is very beautiful." Aunt Kate spoke for the family, with the exception of Alice, when she exclaimed that "we are all prepared to find the new Alice a great acquisition to the family circle. . . . I doubt not we will all love her very much."[20] His parents thought the marriage would be the necessary final push toward their eldest son's emotional and physical salvation.

In early spring, as the engagement became likely, Alice James became "wretchedly ill again, in her old way." She had a nervous breakdown so extreme in May 1878 that she never fully recovered. Attempting to comfort her, even to the extent of momentarily allying himself against William, Henry complained that it is "inconsiderate of William to have selected such a moment for making merry." Alice, her mother wrote to Bob, "has had a nervous breakdown of a very serious character—an aggravated recurrence of her old troubles." Suicide was much on Alice's mind. In one bout of misery, she requested and received Henry senior's permission to take her own life if living became unbearable. Henry senior, "completely absorbed" in caring for her, had his "secret thoughts" as he sat by her bedside "constantly with the truths of immortal life." On William's wedding day, she stayed in her sickbed, "half the time, indeed more than half," Henry senior told Bob, "on the verge of insanity and suicide." Over the next months, she slowly recovered some stability. But she later marked "that hideous summer of '78" as the time "when I went down to the deep sea, its dark waters closed over me, and I knew neither hope nor peace." As William's marriage day approached, he became increasingly anxious. But, he wrote on his wedding night, "every Dr. I have ever spoken to has said that matrimony ought to be the best possible mode of life, for me. Alice Gibbens is an angel if there ever was one—I take her for her moral more than her intellectual qualities."[21] Like Henry senior, both in practice and in doctrine he believed that one of the purposes of marriage was to provide a good angel to counterbalance his inner demon. Alice Gibbens was to endure until her husband's death the burden as well as the blessing of this idealization. His brother in England immediately responded with his blessing, particularly to Miss Gibbens who, he joked, "will need it most."

The news of the engagement did not surprise Henry. William's need to marry had been hovering between the lines of his letters and of his life, especially in his regular recommendations that Henry marry. "I had long wished to see you married," Henry wrote. "I believe almost as much in matrimony for most other people as I believe in it little for myself—which is saying a good deal." Clear in his own mind that marriage was not for him, he occasionally heard rumors that he was engaged or about to be engaged, either to some attractive spinster or young widow." His own feelings on the subject were clear. In a short story that James published in May 1878, the narrator believes that his friend Sanguinetti is in love with a hairdresser's wife when actually, as a fetishistic collector of "pretty things," it is the effigy in the hairdresser's window, an inanimate object, with which he is in love. A comically trivial admirer and collector, he is a grotesque fictional variation of James's own sexual displacement, a man fixated with "pretty things" that are essentially dead. In another story, "Longstaff's Marriage," marriage tensions and resolutions are dramatized as concomitants to blackmail and death. Reginald Longstaff, a perfect English gentleman, who is ill and thought to be dying, falls in love with a beautiful, chaste American, Diana Belfield. When he proposes marriage to her on his deathbed, she, taking it as blackmail, which it is, declines and returns to America. Reginald recovers, apparently because he is angry that she has refused to marry him. During the next two years, Diana appears to be wasting away. Returning to Europe, she confesses to Reginald that she had fallen totally in love with him after she had declined to marry him, actually in the moments of her refusal. Now that she is dying, on her request he agrees to marry her, though he no longer loves her. Since she is angel enough to spare him the burden of marriage to someone he does not love, she soon dies. It is a story with bitter, harsh edges.[22]

As if these two earlier stories were trial runs, he published, in *Macmillan's* in July 1879, "The Diary of a Man of Fifty," a fully realized, brilliant story about anxiety, sexuality, commitment, and marriage. A retired British army officer, who has returned to Florence, meets a young Englishman, Stanmer, who is in love with the daughter of Countess Salvi by her first marriage. Though the general had been in love with the countess twenty-seven years before, he had abruptly left her when he had decided that she was a flirt. The general and Stanmer soon become intimate friends. Fearing that Stanmer will make the mistake of believing the countess' daughter and will not do what he himself did, that is, leave and reject the relationship, the general, who has had doubts about whether he had read his own situation of twenty-seven years ago accurately, warns him not to allow himself to be deceived. Stanmer unhesitantly rejects the general's reading of the situation and the people. Later, in England, Stanmer assures the general that the marriage has turned out to be a stunning success. He also informs the general that he had been wrong about Bianca's mother. The narrator ends with the thought that perhaps he had been too cautious, that perhaps he had misunderstood the countess, that perhaps he had destroyed the possibility of happiness for both of them through his caution, his jealousy, his self-protectiveness, and his lack of romantic spontaneity. "That's a charming discovery," he remarks ironically, "for a man of my age!"

Whatever the emotional sources of James's own disinclination to marry, these stories both reveal and disguise a pervasive anxiety about marriage. Though bachelorhood was self-assertion, it was also rebellion, more readily enacted from the distance of Europe than in Cambridge. As his parents grew older, he and they had to come to terms with the increasing certainty that he would not have two of the experiences, marriage and parenthood, that for Henry senior and Mary James defined human life. Henry senior had tirelessly advocated that "a man's relations to his wife afford the *only* field for the sentiment of spiritual unity with his kind, that this disorderly world allows."[23] The Jameses extolled parenthood as a sacred mission, the family engagement that bound them all to a shared life. For a while, Mary James felt strongly obligated to encourage Henry to marry. Probably Henry senior at some point gave thought to the likelihood that Henry's refusal expressed a purposeful rejection of what he had preached as a sacred necessity. A candid advocate of the naturalness of sexuality and of redeeming natural lust through marriage to an "angel," Henry senior might have pondered the mystery of his son's de facto commitment to celibacy. Probably the Jameses in Quincy Street assumed that there would be, for Henry, no sexual experience outside marriage. Apparently, Henry junior maintained the same assumption. He committed himself to marital and sexual self-sufficiency, to being the "angel" of his own house. From the beginning, he knew that there would be a price to pay, and that the cost would include his parents' disappointment.

William's marriage and the subject in general worked itself into a short novel, with the oddly ironic title *Confidence,* that he conceived of in early spring 1879. The external impetus was a request from the disparaged *Scribner's,* "that painful periodical," which made "a sudden and advantageous proposal" for a serial novel in six numbers, to begin in August 1879 and to be a third longer than *The Europeans,* for which they would pay the handsome sum of fifteen hundred dollars. With "a good idea" in mind, he made the commitment, eager to earn as much as possible in order to set aside time to devote exclusively to the "big novel" he had given thought to and for which he had done some preliminary outlining. With the usual explanations, he apologized to Howells for not offering it to the *Atlantic.* Though he felt slightly contaminated that it would "appear (alas!) in the dreadful *Scribner's,*" he thought it would "be *very good indeed*—much better than the Europeans which I never thought good." Writing rapidly, he finished at the beginning of June, convinced that it was superior to anything he had done before. By the end of the year, he made a partial tactical retreat under fire from William's criticism that, like *The Europeans,* the tale suffered from the thinness that he had come to Europe to avoid. "I have got (heaven knows!) plenty of gravity within me, & I don't know why I can't put it more into the things I write. It comes from modesty & delicacy . . . or at least from the high state of development of my artistic conscience, which is so greatly attached to *form* that it shrinks from believing that it can supply it properly for *big* subjects, & yet is constantly studying the way to do it; so that at last, I am sure, it will arrive."[24]

The story of two close friends, both financially independent, one an artist, the other a scientist, *Confidence* hinges on the former, Bernard, not being able to see that a woman he has briefly met in Italy, and with whom Gordon has fallen in love at Baden-Baden, actually had fallen in love, at first sight, with him. The perceptive artist does not even envision it as a possibility. It then takes him three years to realize that he is in love with her. Perhaps, as critics have suggested, the two friends embody Henry's view of himself and William, the artist and scientist, the man of imagination and the man of dry and controlled reason. But the ironic power of the novel is that it fails precisely because its major weakness is the one that James is usually so alert to avoid. Bernard is someone who should quickly see the reality, or at least give it imaginative consideration as a possibility. If Bernard is a partial self-portrait, the story is a dramatization of the novelist's ambivalence about himself. Henry's conflict and competition with William reveal themselves as subordinate elements to his expression of anxiety about sexuality and marriage. Bernard's unrealistically sustained stupidity dramatizes not only the author's commitment to abjure marriage and the marriage bed but also to leave unspoken, certainly unexplored, the sexual reasons for the renunciation. The tension between Bernard and Gordon has a homoerotic resonance. The object of their confusion and rivalry is named Angela, not so much a Swedenborgian angel but a representation of the angels of the James household, including "our angelic Harry" himself.

Three thousand miles distant from his family, James took pleasure in the loose-knit, comparatively nondemanding "family" of his social world. In spring 1877, he had met friends of Grace Norton—Sir John Clark, a wealthy retired diplomat twenty years older than himself, and his wife, Lady Clark, "a handsome, charming woman of a certain age . . . a rather satirical invalid" who subscribed to and enjoyed reading the *Atlantic*. He liked them both. On a Sunday in mid-September 1879, from a wind-tossed mountain in Aberdeenshire he looked down at Tillypronie, the Clarks' Scottish estate, "the supremely comfortable house lying deep among the brown and purple moors." It was his first visit to Scotland, whose beauty took his breath away. "The great thing is the color . . . & the wonderful velvety bloom of the hills, which are powdered over with all kinds of broken & filtered lights." On the way up, he had stopped in Edinburgh, whose "grand air" impressed him. He took such a "great fancy" to Scotland, he told Macmillan, that he thought, jokingly, that he might settle in Edinburgh. At Tillypronie, the Clarks "could not be a more tenderly hospitable couple. Sir John caresses me like a brother, and her ladyship supervises me like a mother." They were "very good kind people." "Don't envy me too much," he told Alice. For "a cosmopolitanized American," the British country house sometimes has "an insuperable flatness." But at Tillypronie "you get the conveniences of Mayfair dove-tailed into the last romanticism of nature."[25]

London had become sufficiently oppressive for him to enjoy the change that country visits provided. Country houses, though, tended to be less congenial for working. Laboring at an intense writing schedule, he tried to limit country visits to holiday periods. London dinners, with their mixed blessings, provided helpful sociability and diversion at the end of workdays. He exercised with long London walks. The Reform Club provided rest, reading, inexpensive meals, companionable or solitary leisure, and even the opportunity to be a host at tea or, on rare occasions, dinner. He preferred to be a guest, for practical reasons. Late evenings, he often stopped for drinks and talk at Mrs. Kemble's, a woman "with a deep, rich human nature." At the beginning of 1879, he attended a dinner hosted by the Thackeray and Ritchie families at the Victoria and Albert Museum, where he met Mrs. Brookfield, Mrs. Ritchie's mother, with whom Thackeray had been in love and who was his model for Amelia Sedley in *Vanity Fair*. Her youth seemed reflected in the sweet beauty of her daughter. "I don't wonder that Thackeray put her in a book." When he dined with Leslie Stephen and his "remarkably beautiful" bride just after their honeymoon, he saw the usually morose Stephen happy for the first time. She "has cheered him up amazingly; but I don't see what he has done to merit so grandly fair a creature."[26]

At another dinner he met Walter Pater, already well-known for work on the Renaissance, and found him pale, gray, unattractive, "far from being as beautiful as his own prose." James responded unfavorably to Pater's physical appearance and to a preciousness that hinted at his homosexuality. Another time James had the interesting experience of sitting next to Ruskin's former wife, "a very big, handsome, coarse, vulgar, jolly, easy friendly Scotchwoman, and as unRuskinish a being as one could conceive," now married to the painter John Millais; her marriage to Ruskin had been annulled on the grounds of nonconsummation. When Lowell came to London at the beginning of 1880, this time as ambassador to Great Britain, he and James went to lunch with Tennyson at the poet's Eaton Place townhouse, where Mrs. Tennyson kept an open table for spontaneous visits. Impatient, bewildered, James observed that Lowell did not speak to Tennyson and Tennyson did not speak to Lowell. Late in the lunch, he heard " 'Do you know anything about *Lowell*?' launched on the chance [by Tennyson] across the table and crowned at once by Mrs. Tennyson's anxious quaver, 'Why, my dear, this *is* Mr. Lowell!' "[27]

Though he missed London when away, he was determined, for the sake of his work, to get away when it was necessary, especially during "the dreary British summer." The summer of 1879 seemed particularly rainy and oppressive, "the whole country a perfect bog." He was happy to meet two young writers, both of whom were to become friends, Edmund Gosse and Robert Louis Stevenson. Stevenson seemed "a pleasant fellow, but a shirt-collarless Bohemian and a great deal (in an inoffensive way) of a *poseur*." Less talented, indefatigably careerist, Gosse always kept his shirt collar tightly buttoned. Summer solitude and occasional attractive company did not always outweigh the wearisome dirt and heat. As usual, Italy beckoned. The Bootts were regularly sending him invitations. But he worried that Italy would be too expensive. Also, on his previous visit he had found himself too distracted to work well there. Still, he wanted to go and resisted only by an exercise of willpower and common sense.

In the fall of 1879, he went to Paris instead, for a visit of about three months, just as he was to put the finishing touches on *Hawthorne*. He had in mind a new short novel, and thought perhaps that he might begin the major work that he told Macmillan he would probably call

The Portrait of a Lady. "But upon this I observe the Silence of Death!"
He did not rule out going to Italy if the weather became unpleasant. It
did not. Paris was "transcendently civilized, after the grimy Babylon
by the Thames, but one million times less interesting." He had a comfortable apartment. The "warm, hazy, golden September weather" was
lovely. Spending many pleasant hours with the Adamses, who were in
Paris for three weeks on their way to Spain, they dined at restaurants
together almost every day. James found Adams "very sensible, though
a trifle dry," Clover, a woman with "a touch of genius." He spent time
with Isabella Gardner, whom he had met in London, probably through
the Adamses. She was an assertive, narcissistic, flamboyant American
married to a wealthy Bostonian, Jack Gardner. "I have a happy faith
that we shall Europeanize together again, in the future," he told her. In
October he visited the Childes at the Château de Varennes. He felt sorry
for Childe's "false position in the world—his absence of a country, a
career &c, & his being nothing in France except through his wife." He
enjoyed Theodore Child's company. With Hamilton Aïdé, he went to
the country to visit Turgenev, and the next month Turgenev came in
from the country to have breakfast with him. As for his former French
literary friends, Flaubert no longer held his Sunday salon. He was to
die the next year. Zola's "naturalism is ugly & dirty, but he seems to
me to be *doing something*—which surely (in the imaginative line) no one
in England or the U.S. is, & no one else here."[28]

When, near the end of September 1879, he received his annual
royalty statement from Macmillan, he was appalled. Macmillan had
hinted that sales had been minimal. He had immediately wanted to
know "whether you meant they had been nil." Even if they were
small, that "would not prevent me from accepting them." Macmillan
responded with an advance of fifty pounds, half of the sum he was to
receive on the completion of *Hawthorne.* "As a general thing," James
told Macmillan, he had "a lively aversion to receiving money in anticipation for work not delivered & I think that if you had proposed this
yesterday I should have said *No,* for the present. But I should feel
ungracious in returning the cheque—so I keep it." He felt relieved when
he was able to send the completed *Hawthorne* from Paris in the middle
of September. But he still needed money. "Excuse my appearance of
dunning you," he wrote to Macmillan, but "I shld. take it very kindly if
you would include" with the fifty pounds due for *Hawthorne* "whatever
money is owing me" on the sales of the six books Macmillan had
published. "This sum is apparently very small . . . but such as it is it
will be a convenience to me to have it—& not an inconvenience to you,
I hope, to send it, though I believe your regular way is not to settle

these matters till somewhat later." Macmillan sent the small sum the next month.[29]

Inwardly, James was fuming—angry, humiliated, deeply disappointed. In September and October, he negotiated an agreement with *Macmillan's Magazine* and with the *Atlantic Monthly* for the serial publication of *The Portrait of a Lady*, to run from approximately the middle of 1880 to the middle of 1881. He grieved, he told Macmillan, that his other books "should not do better. It seems to me an anomaly that they don't, as they have been on the whole largely and favorably noticed, & apparently a good deal talked about. I hope better things for the serial." At the same time, he wrote to Chatto & Windus asking them what they would pay him for the book publication of *Confidence*. When they offered better terms than precedent indicated Macmillan would, he gave it to them, hoping that this would "operate as a salubrious irritant to Macmillan, who wants my books very much, but doesn't want to pay for them!" He began the same process with Osgood and Scribner's, but left *Confidence* with Osgood, "a weak proceeding, natural to the son of my father," when the Boston publisher plaintively appealed to his loyalty.[30] Five years later, the unfortunate publisher contributed heavily to the commercial failure of *The Bostonians* by declaring bankruptcy immediately prior to its publication.

(4)

Before returning from Paris to London in mid-December 1879, he had taken a few mental half steps in the direction of the Alps. Each time, he had stepped back, with increasingly self-deprecating apologies to Lizzie Boott. He missed London more than he desired Italy. Unexpectedly, there was an immense early December snowstorm that blocked egress from Paris for a few days. Since he felt obliged to be back in London by the middle of January, it now seemed impractical to go south. "The moment seems ill-chosen for a hasty scamper over the Alps. . . . You can't despise me more than you already do," he told Lizzie. But he assured her that it was only a postponement, that he would come in the spring. Fortunately, London was "not a shade darker & several inches less under water" than Paris. Christmas and the New Year he spent at Fryston Hall and Thorne House, where he felt well enough to go to a ball and dance energetically. In London, he dined out regularly, though he claimed he intended "to cultivate a quiet winter, being, after three years of it, very tired of a promiscuous London life."

London itself "is a wonderful, brutal great Babylon of a place, & if one doesn't like it very much, one must hate it: but fortunately I like it."[31]

When the Adamses returned to London in January 1880, he saw them often in the pretty house that they had taken overlooking St. James's Park, his visits including evening conversations starting at dusk and lasting till the early morning. They talked by a blazing fire, James often "with his hands under his coat-tails," affectionately but pointedly arguing with the Adamses about his decision to live in England. Home-sick for Washington, the Adamses felt appalled and betrayed by their friend's rejection of American residence. "Don't be afraid," he had told his old Cambridge friend Grace Norton, "I shall never stray so far from our common nationality as to lose my way back." But the Adamses expressed their doubts. They tried to argue him out of going to Italy. "It is both unnatural and impossible" that he should leave, they told him, "just after they have arrived." They had been counting on his society. "But you should hear," he told Lizzie Boott, "how bravely I defend myself." Beyond Italy, he had on his mind America, where he was determined to return for a visit in late 1880, to see his family and to refresh his American sensibility. "I hold fast to my design of going home," he told Isabella Gardner. He also held tenaciously to his claim that only "an old civilization" could "set a novelist in motion," that "it is on manners, customs, usages, habits, forms, upon all these things matured and established, that a novelist lives."[32]

His defensiveness was exercised by his failure to protect his copy-right in a short story, "A Bundle of Letters." He had unwittingly lost the American rights when he published it, as a favor, in a Parisian magazine edited by his friend Theodore Child. When he learned, in January 1880, that an enterprising Boston publisher had brought out a pamphlet edition that was "selling like Wildfire," he was furious that he had no grounds for legal redress. "They have been selling in thousands," his mother remarked, "but unfortunately Harry reaps only fame." The commercial success of *Hawthorne* also galled him. It sold well in England, even better in America. Ignoring the fact that he himself had made the choice to accept a flat fee, he blamed Macmillan. George Smalley advised him that the answer to such situations was to have professional representation by a lawyer both in England and America rather than deal directly himself with publishers. "If I had dealt with the Macmillans through 'my solicitor' they would not . . . have befooled me to the point of allowing them to appropriate all the profits" of the American sales. When Macmillan gave him as a present a hand-somely bound edition of Hawthorne's complete works, he did not feel assuaged. "I would much rather have my 'rights,' and no presents. But a truce," he told his father, "to this sordid minuteness in which you will not recognize your would-be-gentlemanly son."[33] When Macmillan urged him to write a short biography of Dickens for the "English Men of Letters" series, for which he would pay ten times what he had paid for *Hawthorne,* James briefly mulled it over. If he were to do it, he decided, he would not do it for Macmillan's series but as an independent book to be hawked to the highest bidder. Since to take that one, he would have to postpone writing *Portrait,* he declined.

What angered him even more than the poor deal he had made for *Hawthorne* was the widespread American critical hostility to the book. To many it seemed as if he had attacked Hawthorne and America rather than provided a sympathetic and balanced evaluation. Some reviewers praised it, including the ever-loyal Howells. Edwin Godkin told the James family that it is "the best thing of the kind that has appeared in this generation; and . . . no [other] American living or dead could have written it." Tom Perry praised it highly. The English reviews were especially good. *Hawthorne* "appears to be a good deal liked here," he told Grace Norton. "But whatever *success* it has ought to come from the U.S.A." In America, though, there was such "a mass of the narrowest, most personal, inane criticism poured out upon him personally" that he almost reeled under the onslaught. The American press is "furious over my poor little Hawthorne. It is a melancholy revelation of angry vanity, vulgarity & ignorance. I thought they would protest a good deal at my calling New England life unfurnished but I didn't expect they would lose their heads at such a rate. We are surely the most-thin-skinned idiots in the world, & I blush for my compatriots." But "let us hope," he told Perry, his venomous critics were "not the real American public. If I thought they were, I would give up the country." With neither financial nor critical rewards, he now thought of the book as "ill-fated."[34]

On "a perfect spring morning" at the end of March 1880, James gazed from his open window overlooking the yellow-green Arno and the Ponte Vecchio. At last he was back in Italy, this time for a well-earned holiday and to begin writing *The Portrait of a Lady*. By the time he arrived in Italy, some of the sting of the reception of *Hawthorne* had drained away. He had with him the completed manuscript of a short novel, which he had told Howells was "a poorish story in three numbers—a tale purely American." It was written during the late fall and winter months for publication in *The Cornhill* from June to November 1880 and in *Harper's Monthly Magazine*.[35] He thought it a minor effort, an expression both of the absence of rich detail in American life and of the pressure to write quickly a brief serial fiction that would yield the largest amount of money at the earliest possible time. In February 1879, Fanny Kemble had told him the story of her selfish brother, who, more than anything, had wanted a rich wife and whose manipulations had resulted in failure. It is in essence the plot of *Washington Square*. In his novel, James makes Catherine Sloper, the daughter of a wealthy doctor who defies her father, the central consciousness. Fascinated, as in *Watch and Ward* and the novel he was now about to write, with the female attempting to make her way from adolescence to maturity in a male-dominated world, James readily finds the center of his novel in the complexities of father-daughter relationships and in psychologically and socially complicated courtship rituals. In *Watch and Ward*, Nora Lambert marries a substitute father. In *The Portrait of a Lady*, Isabel Archer marries a frigidly corpselike expatriate American living in Italy. In *Washington Square*, Catherine Sloper does not marry at all. Having determined to be a spinster himself, James had various ways of dramatizing the complexities of his decision. Set in the pre–Civil War New York of his childhood, *Washington Square* is a vividly psychological autobiographical drama.

Catherine Sloper is a victim of her small talents, of her father's strengths, of her aunt's self-serving recklessness, and of Morris Townsend's merciless, egomaniacal greed. The only man who wants to and can protect her is the father she has to rebel against in order to have the man she wants to marry. A sincere, intelligent, and experienced protector of his daughter, Dr. Sloper cannot protect her when she falls in love with a scoundrel whom she has neither the intelligence, experience, nor instincts to see clearly. In the end, Townsend does Sloper's work for him. When the dowry proves to be less than he had anticipated, he declines to marry her. Catherine brutally learns that her father had been right. Though she still loves Townsend, she accepts that he does not love her. Later, she has two additional opportunities to marry, in one instance to a worthy, appropriate man who genuinely loves her. She declines. Her love for Townsend determines that she will remain a spinster, a role for which she shows talent and in which she has many successes. When, twenty years later, Townsend returns, proposing that they resume their relationship with the likelihood of marriage, she bluntly, absolutely refuses him, returning to her knitting, "for life—as it were."

In spring 1880, from his window overlooking the Arno, in one direction James had a view across the river toward Bellosguardo, which he frequently climbed to visit Lizzie Boott, whose relationship with her father had some of the intensity of Catherine Sloper's with hers. Quiet, passive, and stubbornly persistent, Lizzie seemed always to be a student of painting but never a painter. She had brought back with her from Munich her American-born painting instructor, Frank Duveneck, a talented but unsophisticated thirty-two-year-old midwesterner with whom she had gradually developed a quiet intimacy. James immediately thought highly of his paintings, which seemed "remarkably strong and brilliant." What feelings and directions were at issue between Lizzie and Duveneck were a puzzle and a problem to her father and her friends. The previous November, Henry had ironically remarked to William that "the natural & logical thing now seems . . . for Lizzie to marry Duveneck." His words were unintentionally prophetic, though when he met Duveneck in Florence in April he thought that probably there was no danger that that would happen. Lizzie looked "elderly & plain." She works indefatigably at her painting "under the inspiration of her friend & master the uncouth but vigorous Duveneck, to whom she appears to stand in a sort of double relation of pupil & adoptive mother—or at least adoptive sister. I hope she won't ever become his adoptive anything-else, as, though an excellent fellow, he is terribly earthy & unlicked." Lizzie's spinsterhood seemed to him her natural state, partly because he perceived hers in terms of his own, and also because Duveneck seemed to him inappropriate. Duveneck, he thought, would be an incongruous if not impossible son-in-law for the aging but still elegant, fastidious, and demanding Francis Boott.[36]

In the other direction from his hotel was the Uffizi, to which a number of times he escorted another American spinster, a moderately successful, full-figured, and attractive American writer, forty-year-old Constance Fenimore Woolson. Born in New Hampshire to a business-man father, her mother was a niece of James Fenimore Cooper. She had been raised in Cleveland, had gone to school in New York City, had lived in the South, and had begun publishing stories and sketches in 1875. In 1880, she had her first literary success with the publication of *Rodman the Keeper: Southern Sketches*. A friend of John Hay's and of Howells', who published her stories and encouraged her career, she had moved to Europe in 1879 for what developed into almost fifteen years of expatriation. When she had arrived in London in 1879, she had unsuccessfully attempted to be introduced to James. Apparently she had come to Florence with the hope that she would find him there, this time with a letter of introduction from James's cousin, Minny Temple's sister. She had also come for her health. Chronically depressed, a ten-dency she believed she had inherited from her father, she thought a southern climate would counteract her annual winter darkness. "Every

years were not only those of sensation and sensibility but of psychology and artistic structure, of character and life. He felt ready now to capitalize on a long apprenticeship, on a slow, steady, stubborn accumulation and accretion of art and life.

(5)

America and his anticipated departure for home in October 1880 were much on his mind as he wrote. Within weeks of his return from Florence to London, William provided an ambivalent American embrace. William's first words were "My!—how cramped and inferior England seems! After all, it's poor old Europe, just as it used to be in our dreary boyhood!" The English seemed to him superbly "homogeneous . . . solid, so resolute, so spirited," but "with all the terrible uniformity of their arranged lives." William had vacillated through much of the spring about whether to take his summer months in Europe without his wife and child. Home and health weighed heavily upon him. The eager husband had become a devoted but burdened father and a heavily over-worked teacher. His chronic depression led to eyestrain, backaches, irritability, and intense, highly expressive philosophical angst in regard to free will and the nature of human life. When William arrived in mid-June, he looked to Henry hardly changed, "no older . . . with all his vivacity and brilliancy of mind undimmed." As egomaniacally loquacious as ever, William seemed characteristically thin, quiveringly nervous, with a touch of disability. "I can't get rid of the feeling that he takes himself, and his nerves and his physical condition, too hard and too consciously," Henry wrote to his mother. They spent hours talking about change and life. Henry "learned more from him about home affairs in a half hour's conversation, than in a year of letter-writing."[42]

When William embraced his thirty-seven-year-old brother, he noticed that he had to extend his arms wider than ever before. He had been warned the previous year. "I have certainly become a hopeless, helpless, shameless (and you will add, a *bloated,*) cockney. . . . I am as broad as I was long, as fat as a butter-tub & as red as a British mater familias. On the other hand, as a compensation, I am excellently well!" When he had congratulated William on his marriage, William had congratulated him on his gaining weight. "I rejoice in your rejoicings in my fat," he responded, "and would gladly cut off fifty pounds or so and send them to you as a wedding-gift."[43] Despite his striking success as a conversationalist and guest when he allowed Henry to take him to parties, England seemed socially "oppressive" to William. Henry hosted in William's honor a dinner at the Reform Club. "Harry seems to bestride the British lion," William told his parents, "but it takes a good deal of time to get into that position." The position, though, suited Harry well. "As he grows older . . . he is better suited by a superficial contact with things at a great many points than by a deeper one at a few points. The way he worked at paying visits and going to dinners and parties was surprising to me, especially as he was all the time cursing them for so frustrating his work. It shows the perfect fascination of the whirlpool of a capital when once you are in it. You detest it and yet you can't bear to let go your hold. However it will all suddenly stop on a certain day." Whenever that day would be, it would not mean repatriation. "I think [Harry] is so thoroughly at home in England that he will always prefer to make it his head quarters." They had chosen different countries, different paths. Harry's seemed right for him.

They shared the Bolton Street address for four weeks. "William has been with me for a month," Henry told Tom Perry, "enjoying London quietly & entertaining me much with his conversation." But they had different daily agendas. Henry kept at his writing and his usual social entertainments. William saw a few personal friends and professional colleagues, among them Lowell and Adams. "You never saw," he reported home, "such a pair of patriots . . . and [Adams'] little cockatrice of a wife. I use this term most affectionately for she was delightful." But his mind was much on his elderly parents and his own childhood, particularly on the lives they had led when they had all lived in London and on the different paths he and Henry had chosen. "All the while I was there, in the vicinity of Clarges Street, 1/2 Moon Str. and Green Park Piccadilly, I found myself thinking in a manner unexampled in my previous life of Father and Mother in their youth coming to live there as a blushing bridal pair, with most of us children still unborn, and all the works unwritten; and my heart flowed over with a new kind of sympathy, especially for the beautiful, sylph like and inexperienced mother. Then when I went into St. John's Wood and its monotony, and contrasted the life you led there with that which Harry is now leading in Bolton St., it made me feel how few things you laid claim to, and how entirely at that time your lives were given up to us." As a parent, he felt that he now had eyes to see his own parents for the first time. "I have been almost shedding tears every day in London to think of you, my beloved old Father and Mother, standing in your youth before the great roaring foreign tide, often perplexed in the extreme, and wondering how you might best provide for us. Better late than never. But I wish that this new feeling might enable me to be more of a comfort to you in your old age than I have been of late years, with my afflictions." His afflictions followed him to Amsterdam in the middle of July, then to solitary mountain hiking in Switzerland, where, berating himself for having become enraged at the condition of his eyes and at some English tourists nearby, he felt "a sort of moral revolution" pour through him. "Nature, God and Man all seemed fused together into one Life as they used to 15 or twenty years ago . . . a break up of the old worn out condition and pouring in of new strength."[44] He returned almost immediately to America.

By early July, Henry had decided, instead of departing for America late in the summer, to postpone the voyage for a full year. Though he had already booked passage for the twenty-first of August, 1880, he could cancel without any loss of money. Suddenly, he had felt a strong need to remain in Europe for another year, ostensibly to finish *Portrait*, before making so substantial and emotionally demanding a visit. No, he told Grace Norton, "I am not *afraid* to go home; though it seems to me that I well might be." In Cambridge, Mary James happily fantasied that the month that William had "spent with Harry must have been a period of rare enjoyment to both of them." It was also a trial. After William's departure, Henry immediately went to bed with "one of those wretched sieges of pain in my head," he told his mother, that "I have had so often." Actually, he had had them infrequently in recent years, but illness remained the safest stance from which to bring his parents bad news. Perhaps William's visit had been a reminder of the difficulties and strains of life with his family, of the inevitable diminishment of independence and autonomy that the family required. With his long novel only half completed, he explained to his disappointed mother, he needed to stay abroad to finish it in the best possible circumstances. "If by waiting a while I become able to return with more leisure, fame and money in my hands, and the prospect and desire of remaining at home longer, it will be better for me to do so; and this is very possible." Expressing her aches and pains, part of the "*feeling of growing old*," and having just celebrated her seventieth birthday with all her sons at a distance, Mrs. James quickly, self-protectively accepted her son's reasoning. "Some imperative work . . . obliged him to this decision. He seems to regret it as much as we do, and says that when he comes, he wishes to come with entire leisure to see us *all* and stay as long as he desires."[45]

With an almost audible sigh of relief, Henry returned to his work and his recreation, particularly London people and gossip. In Florence, he had gotten the announcement directly from the bridegroom that John Cross, an American whom he had met many times at London

literary meals, had become engaged to marry George Eliot, twenty-
one years his senior. Lewes had died in 1878, shortly after James's
unhappy departure from the Lewes's country cottage with the unread
volumes of *The American* thrust into his hands. From Florence, in
May 1880, he had sent Cross his congratulatory wishes. In August, he
declined an invitation to visit with "Mrs. Cross née George Eliot & her
junior spouse. Aren't you sorry?" he teased Grace Norton, "so that I
might tell you they were grotesque? I don't think they are, but they are
deemed to be." During the Venetian honeymoon, Cross had plum-
meted from their bedroom window into a dark canal in what was either
a nervous breakdown or a suicide attempt, or both. The next year, after
Eliot's sudden death, Cross told James, who sat "in his poor wife's
empty chair in the beautiful little study they had just made perfect,"
that he had felt like "a cart horse yoked to a racer." James's "private
impression" was "that if she had not died, she would have killed him."[46]

He himself, he told his mother in the fall, was "not just now making
any matrimonial arrangements," though he constantly heard rumors
that he had been " 'very attentive' " to numerous spinsters and widows
and the opinion that he would be " 'so much happier' " if only he
would marry. As if from one spinster to another, he explained to
Grace Norton, "I am unlikely ever to marry. . . . One's attitude toward
marriage is a part . . . of one's general attitude toward life. . . . If I
were to marry I should be guilty in my own eyes of an inconsistency—
I should pretend to think just a little better of life than I really do. . . .
I am not moved to that way, because I think my opinion of life on the
whole good enough. I am attached to it, I am used to it—it doesn't in
any way paralyse or incapacitate me (on the contrary), and it doesn't
involve any particular injustice to any one, least of all to myself. . . . I
am happy enough as it is, and am convinced that if I should go further,
I should fare worse."[47]

In London for most of the summer, fall, and winter of 1880, he
kept hard at work on *Portrait*. He made a few weekend visits—in July
to the Sturgis' lovely country home in Surrey; during the summer some
brief solitary stays at hotels in Dover, Folkestone, and Brighton to
escape the heat; and in November to Mentmore to stay briefly with
new friends, Lord Rosebery, the witty, talented aristocrat and liberal
politician, soon to be foreign secretary and then prime minister, and his
wife, Hannah de Rothschild. Their "huge modern palace" was "filled
with wonderful objects accumulated by the late Sir Nathan Meyer de
Rothschild, Lady R.'s father. . . . Lady R. is large, fat, ugly, good-
natured, sensible and kind; and Lord R. remarkably charming." He
liked them both, and, for the moment, was a little dazzled. One of his

fellow guests, John Bright, the radical politician, seemed lively and honest, a good deal like "a superior New Englander—with a fatter, damper nature, however." For Christmas week he went to Falmouth to stay with the Clarks, "kindly, funny, and harmlessly talkative" as usual, where he felt "woefully homesick for Piccadilly—& appalled by the prospect of being dragged" through a howling storm to visit Land's End. "I prefer the Land's Center—i.e Bolton St."[48] In January 1881, he spent a weekend at another of the Rosebery's houses, this one at Epsom near the Downs. He enjoyed the small, sporting house, the paintings, and Smalley's company, his friend as gossipy and talkative as ever.

But he kept to his own "land's center"—his desk—most of the time, his working energy at high pitch partly because he now regularly turned down dinner and other invitations. Soon he felt he had mostly escaped the turning wheel of London social activity, with occasional exceptions. He held particularly long conversations with Fanny Kemble, who, at one visit after another, warned him that she would probably have died and not be there when he next returned. Her mordant predictions had so far remained unfulfilled. Beginning in midsummer 1880, he had begun to send to Howells portions of the novel in progress. It seemed to him to increase "in merit and interest" as he wrote. He told William that its merits were greater than those in his previous work due to the larger canvas on which he worked, making it "inevitably more human, more sociable. It was the constant effort at *condensation* (which you used always to drum into my head . . . when I was young and you bullied me) that has deprived my former things of these qualities." By the new year, the publication of *Portrait* in the *Atlantic* and in *Macmillan's* was well under way. In February 1881, he noted the death of Carlyle, a significant moment in the passing of the old order. Politics was very much in the air, particularly the Irish Question. He favored Home Rule, which he thought inevitable, but for the sake of the English rather than the Irish. The English, he felt, suffered more from the albatross of Ireland than the Irish from England. If he had nothing else to do, he told Tom Perry, he would "run over to Ireland: which may seem strange to you on the part of one satiated in youth with the Celtic genius. The reason is I should like to see a country in a state of revolution."[49] But he had already made up his mind to go to Italy for the spring. London was having record cold and snow. He wanted a warmer, happier place in which to write.

In mid-February 1881, from the balcony of his hotel room overlooking the Tuileries, the Paris sun seemed as bright as April. Happy to be in Paris again, "which as usual seems splendid and charming," he felt unusually expansive. *Portrait* so far had been an immense critical success. The monthly checks from serial publication made him feel flush. He could afford to travel. Italy was ahead of him, even warmer and more beautiful than Paris. He could count on visiting home next autumn on a note of triumph. Though he could hear the low notes, they did not drown out his own high aria of personal and artistic success. "It is the age of Panama Canals, of Sarah Bernhardt," whose acting he detested, "of Western wheat-raising, of merely material expansion. Art, form, may return, but I doubt that I shall live to see them—I don't believe they are eternal, as the poets say. All the same, I shall try to make them live a little longer!"

In Paris, he had three long visits with Turgenev, who looked noticeably older, and was the guest of honor at a dinner hosted by the Childes. Paris struck him "as having the drawbacks of London without the compensations." After twelve days he went south via Avignon, Marseilles, and an unpleasantly overcrowded Nice, to "warm, quiet, lovely" San Remo where he spent almost two weeks. Then it was on to Genoa for a week, where he visited some friends whose winter houseguest was Jane Morris, "strange, pale, livid, gaunt, silent, and yet in a manner graceful and picturesque," with "wonderful aesthetic hair." He loved being in Italy again. In San Remo, he wrote every day, each morning walking "among the olives, over the hills behind the queer little black, steep town," each night reading into the late hours. From Genoa, in mid-March, he went to Milan, where he spent eight days nursing a sore throat, going to galleries and attending the opera. In late March, he went directly to Venice, the destination that had been in his mind from the start, a city that he had visited briefly twice before but for which he had never felt a special attraction. Unexpectedly, this time, he was enthralled. He had "fallen deeply and desperately in love."[50]

Eight

"NEVER TO RETURN"

1 8 8 1 – 1 8 8 3

(1)

Sitting at his writing table, with a view from his fourth-floor window of "the far-shining lagoon, the pink walls of San Giorgio, the downward curve of the Riva, the distant islands, the movement of the quay, the gondolas in profile," he continued writing *The Portrait of a Lady* and fantasied about taking an apartment of his own to which he would return every year. Each morning, after early coffee at Florian's, he bathed, then had a "real breakfast" before going home to work until late afternoon. Afterward he entertained himself with the colorful street life, the handsome gondoliers ("I have never seen so many good-looking rascals"), the golden vistas, the long late spring days, the anticipation of music on the piazza in the evenings. On a short trip away from Venice, he sat one evening in the square of Vicenza "in a flood of moonlight and amid a host of memories." He "was pleased to find that on the whole" he had not quite lost his sensibility. He seemed to himself "to grow young again."[1]

At the end of April 1881, he went to Rome for two weeks. On a Sunday drive into the *campagna* "the exquisite stillness, the divine horizon," brought back to him "out of the buried past all that ineffable, incomparable impression" of the Rome of his two previous visits. But so eager was he to return to the manuscript on his table at Riva Schiavoni that he hurried back to Venice, stopping only to look at the house of the great Italian poet Giacomo Leopardi, and to spend an evening in Rimini. There he struck up an acquaintance with an Italian officer who, happy to talk to a foreigner, walked with him throughout the city. Relieved to be back in Venice, "this time I have drunk deep," he told

Grace Norton, "and the magic potion has entered into my blood." In Venice, he spent time with a footloose, wealthy American, Herbert Pratt, who had elevated spontaneous, nonpurposeful travel, particularly to the Middle East, into an existential art.[2] Hemmed in by inhibitions and financial necessity, James could only admire and envy Pratt's freedom. He made a note to put him into a novel one day.

Two or three evenings each week he dined at Ca' Alvisi, a small Venetian palace on the Grand Canal owned by a wealthy, infinitely hospitable New Yorker, Katherine de Kay Bronson, who lived there with her daughter Edith. A gossipy, generous, weak woman, with a country home at Asolo and a guest wing at Ca' Alvisi purchased from the overflow of a neighboring palace, Mrs. Bronson entertained visiting Americans and intimate friends, like Robert Browning, with lavish warmth. She held "out her hand," he was to write later, "with endless good-nature, patience, charity, to all decently credited petitioners." Perhaps he had seen her in Newport in the 1860s. She had been a passenger on the same transatlantic ship that had brought him from New York to London in October 1875. The view from the balcony of her Venetian palace, "with your elbows on the broad ledge, a cigarette in your teeth and a little good company beside you," soon became for him one of the never-to-be-forgotten epitomes of Venetian happiness. Being in love with Venice did not mean overlooking her blemishes, particularly the "horrible smell" of the canals in warm weather, the decaying buildings, the tasteless modernizations, the hordes of tourists, Venice as "a vast museum . . . a battered peep-show and bazaar . . . the city of the Doges reduced to earning its living as a curiosity-shop."[3] No writer, he felt, could ever meet the challenge of saying something new about Venice.

As he stayed from March through June 1881, he felt himself in the embrace of "a perpetual love-affair." At the Accademia, he mused again over Veronese's *Rape of Europa,* a painting it was "impossible to look at without aching for envy." Through wet, windy March, from his writing desk overlooking the Riva, he gazed at "a little of everything Venetian." In April, he wandered the city, traveled a little. May and June were sun-filled months. Venice seemed a perfect mistress, available, undemanding, encouraging conversation, self-fulfillment, another puff of cigarette smoke, casual possession, the literary life. It also encouraged autonomy, internal musings, memories. There was no question, of course, of staying. Venice's supreme usefulness was in his absence from it. He could have Venice with him in dark London, in distant America. Always, "when I hear, when I see, the magic name . . . I simply see a narrow canal in the heart of the city—a patch of green water and surface of pink wall. The gondola moves slowly; it gives a great smooth swerve, passes under a bridge, and the gondolier's cry, carried over the quiet water, makes a kind of splash in the stillness."[4]

Waving good-bye from his gondola to Mrs. Bronson, who watched him from her balcony, he left Venice at the beginning of July, going directly to Lake Como and staying overnight once again at Cadenabbia. The heat had become intense. The next day he ascended the Splügen into the exhilarating relief, as the night came on, of "cool pure Alpine air." Ten days later, after a week with Fanny Kemble in the high, brilliantly clear Swiss mountains, he was home again, remembering his stay in Venice as "the semblance of a beautiful dream. . . . If Italy looks lovely . . . from the Grand Canal, you may fancy how it looks . . . from Piccadilly." The view from Piccadilly had complications. Desperately frustrated by their inability to help their daughter, the Jameses had remembered how Alice had been resuscitated, even if only briefly, by her European trip in 1872. "There is a prospect," Henry senior wrote, "of Alice & her friend Miss Loring who is a most capable person, devoted to Alice, going to Europe, which I will sell my Albany property to enable her to do." In late May 1881, Alice, "very much better" but still undertaking the voyage "with great effort," sailed with Katherine Loring. Shortly after Henry returned to London in mid-July, he greeted Alice there. "Weaker in body," though stronger in spirit, cheerfulness, and animation than he had expected, she seemed very glad to see him. "She appears much the better for her journey," he told Grace Norton, "but I find in her the marks of five or six years (since we last met) of ill-health. She is, however, wonderfully bright and interested."[5]

His first impression of Katherine Loring confirmed the reputation that had preceded her. The daughter of a wealthy Boston family, intelligent, responsible, twenty-four-year-old Katherine Loring began, in 1873, a friendship with Alice that soon became the physical and emotional anchor of both their lives. Katherine was the director of an educational program to teach history by correspondence to women at a distance from urban centers. She employed Alice, who for a brief period delighted in her achievements as a teacher. A talented invalid, she had strengths of her own, including a witty tongue, a sharp pen, and a proud resourcefulness. A small, energetic, bespectacled woman, Loring had an independence of mind and manner; a self-confidence and a physical competence that Alice admired. They had vacationed together one summer, to Alice's family's bewilderment, in the Adirondacks, and spent another summer touring northern New England. Katherine astounded Alice. "She is a most wonderful being. She has all the mere brute superiority which distinguishes man from woman combined with all the distinctly feminine virtues. There is nothing she cannot do." Though she thought she had sounded the depths of Katherine's virtues, on the Adirondack trip she found that she "had only stirred the surface. . . . She is a phenomenal being," her virtues including her ability to use a gun. "No one knows what she has been & done for me these trying months I have been through."[6] One of the things Katherine had been doing was to provide, after William's marriage, an intimacy that might allay Alice's fear of loneliness, her sense of having been deserted by William, her fear of being abandoned by her elderly parents. She had no work. She would also soon have no family.

The family was astounded, puzzled, mostly pleased. Probably there was some jealousy. Personal and medical efforts to help Alice had proved mostly failures. Her suicidal breakdown in 1878 had almost broken the family's energy and faith. While they had mixed feelings about being replaced by Katherine, they felt a sense of relief and good fortune. "Miss Loring has been a real saviour to her," William remarked. "I don't really know how Alice cd. have got through this year without her." As the intimacy and dependency became stronger in the next ten years, both Henry and William's wife, Alice Howe James, speculated tactfully about the erotic nature of the special relationship. From the beginning, Henry viewed it as an affair of the heart. "Alice indeed seems so extraordinarily fond of Miss L. that a third person is rather a superfluous appendage." As a woman, Alice "is not made as other women," William's wife remarked. But the difference seemed less important than the advantage to Alice of having Katherine to rely on: It substantially relieved the family of a heavy burden. Henry himself, when he met Katherine in July 1881, proclaimed that the advance notice he had received of her virtues had not been unwarranted. "The blessing that Miss Loring is to her it would be . . . impossible to exaggerate," he wrote to his mother. "She is the most perfect companion she could have found, if she had picked over the whole human family."[7]

With Alice safely in Katherine's hands, he continued writing the final chapters of *Portrait* both in London and on country visits, including two to the Roseberys at Mentmore; one to the Macmillans at Walton-on-Thames, where he found the river delightful; and one to the Sturgises at Leatherhead. Despite the pleasures of summer in England, he missed Venice. "The very sound of the name fills me with ineffable yearnings." But he felt at ease in "these delicious old houses, in the long August days, in the south of England." Alice and Katherine seemed "to prefer the liberty and responsibility of being by themselves." When, at the end of July, Alice had a nervous attack, "the expiring kicks of her malady," Katherine took care of her. "She is certainly worth her weight in gold," Henry assured his parents. Alice's spirits were high. Toward the end of July, he put the two American ladies on a train to Scotland. They wanted no other company. At the end of August, he spent ten days with them in a quiet and empty London, enjoying the pleasure his sister took in the city. Then he himself left for Scotland. Before going north, he again changed his sailing date, this time only by one month, from September 24, 1881, to October 20, because he wanted a vacation before departing. He said good-bye to Alice and Katherine, who were sailing in late September directly to Boston. At Liverpool, Alice "wished she was about stepping on the plank to land her in England, rather than on it to carry her away from its beautiful shores."[8]

Scotland, which had been blissful the previous year, was blissful again, the weather the most perfect he had ever experienced in Britain. During one of his visits, he felt he was in a Waverley novel. He tried to reread *Redgauntlet;* but Sir Walter Scott's weakness as a novelist seemed to him expressive of the infancy of the art. He visited the Clarks at Tillypronie. Toward the end of September, the Roseberys hosted him at their Edinburgh estate, from which he was taken to a grand ball in honor of the coming of age of Lord Hopetoun. One of the guests was Princess Mary, who sat by herself on a large dais. "To her at a given moment was dragged (by Lady H.) poor H.J., & forced to sit by her side for ¾ of an hour, in this gorgeous pillory, listening to her regal conversation & her still more royal silences. . . . It was very ghastly."[9]

At the beginning of October, he returned to London, where he settled a variety of business arrangements. He accepted an advance from Macmillan for his next book—though neither he nor Macmillan seemed to have any idea what that book would be—and arranged the final details for the book publication of *Portrait*. The advance, he told Macmillan, "will add to my sense of greatness in returning to the U.S." He wanted to keep his return date open, in the hope that it would be sooner rather than later. Feeling flush, he had decided to keep his Bolton Street flat so that he would have it to return to in three or four months at best, in six months at the most. *Macmillan's Magazine* and the *Atlantic* had each been paying substantially for serial publication of *Portrait*—the *Atlantic* at the rate of $250 an installment—the checks coming with delightful regularity. For the fourteen installments, he earned $5,080, which contributed by far the largest portion of his income, from all publications, of $4,361 in 1880 and $5,525 in 1881. Part of his sense of triumph may have come from his dim awareness that he had earned each year about half of what his father had been receiving annually for most of his life as unearned income. The sum was also more than twice as much as William earned as a professor at Harvard. From the Reform Club, at the beginning of October 1881, he wrote to Howells, graciously praising his friend's new novel and alerting him to look out for him in Cambridge about the first of November. "You will find me fat and scant o' breath, and very middle-aged, but eminently amenable to kind treatment."[10]

At Liverpool, about to embark, he fulfilled his long-postponed ritual of buying "a sea-chair from that horribly dirty old woman opposite the hotel" and had the thrill of seeing stacks of copies of *Portrait* in all the bookstore windows. It made him feel as if he "had not only started but arrived." Just before getting on the boat, he sent Macmillan a list of people to whom to send complimentary copies and urged the publisher on to sell at least five thousand copies of the English edition. He wanted everyone to read *Portrait*. He did not want his English friends to forget him. In a stiff, bright breeze he sailed into the Atlantic. "I am literary to the last," he boasted to his publisher.[11] The self-definition pleased him. It was always what he had wanted to be.

(2)

When he arrived in Cambridge at the beginning of November 1881, he seemed "the same dear Harry who left us six years ago save that he has become a large, stout, vigorous looking man." Having sailed on a steamer bound from Liverpool to Quebec, he disembarked at a small village on the St. Lawrence River and traveled directly to Boston. It seemed to him appropriate that he had stolen "into the country, as it were, by the back door." At Quincy Street, he was joyfully welcomed at the front door, the prodigal son returned, now a triumphant and famous author. To Aunt Kate, one of his previous companions in hypochondria, the astounding physical change was all to the better, a sure sign that the English climate was congenial to his health, an indication that it was "his clear duty to remain" in England "whilst this salutary effect lasts." The entire family, with the exception of Wilky, gathered in Cambridge to greet him. Having separated from his wife, Bob had returned home, struggling with alcoholism, vocational frustration, and raw, ambivalent feelings about his childhood and his father. Aunt Kate had come up from New York City to see the extraordinary sight of Harry transformed. William, with a wife and another Harry, took as much delight as did his brother when two-year-old Henry James

III regularly prattled to everyone that he was "Uncle Harry's fascinating little nephew." For the first time in six years, he embraced his noticeably older parents and even older-looking Aunt Kate. To his shock, his mother looked "worn and shrunken."[12]

It was a happy homecoming, much less difficult than he had feared, much more pleasurable than he had anticipated. He felt the advantages of his success, and he felt no ambivalence about the fact that this was a visit. He would permit not even the possibility of a family appeal to repatriation. "America seems to me delightful: partly because I have kept my rooms in Bolton Street," to which he intended to return by the middle of May.[13] Also, since a month in Cambridge seemed more than sufficient, he had made arrangements with Godkin to spend December in New York, and with the Adamses to spend the first six weeks of the New Year in what he hoped would be warm Washington sunshine. After that he thought he might go farther south, perhaps even west. "I needed to see again *les miens,* to revive my relations with them, and my sense of the consequences that these relations entail."

Toward the end of November, he sought the privacy of a Boston hotel where he could begin to write, in a notebook that he had purchased in London, an account of what he had been doing for the past six years. He wanted to remember; he wanted to record. He did not want to resign himself to losing the experiences and the impressions "of all that comes, that goes, that I see and feel, and observe." He wanted "to catch and keep something of life." It was not too late to recover all these "lost impressions. . . . They are not lost altogether, they are buried deep in my mind, they have become part of my life, of my nature." He did not intend this to be an American journal, an account of the experiences of this visit, but an act of fragmented autobiographical writing at a time when his schedule prevented sustained writing of any sort. As he sat, pen in hand, in his Boston hotel room, his mind was preoccupied with what had happened, with the autobiographical energy of the analysis of a self that he now felt had essentially been fully formed in the six years of adventure and transformation since he had last been in America. What seemed most salient to him, as he made sporadic notebook entries, was the emotional satisfaction he took in, and the credence he gave to, the overarching claim of his personal mythology: that he had triumphed over adversity, over pain and illness, to fulfill almost unerringly the longings and dreams that he had had during those earlier "untried years." "I wanted to do very much what I have done, and success, if I may say so, now stretches back a tender hand to its younger brother, desire."[14]

What he had wanted was to be "just literary," to fulfill successfully

the apprenticeship that would bring him to and through the gates of
fame and material rewards. "I remember the days, the hours, the books,
the seasons, the winter skies and darkened rooms of summer. I remember the old walks, the old efforts, the old exaltations and depressions."
Most of all, he remembered "the feeling of that younger time" when
he had "sat here scribbling, dreaming, planning, gazing out upon the
world in which my fortune was to seek."[15] He did not and probably
could not ask why his personal mythology—either in anticipation or
in autobiographical reconstruction—did not give equal or even any
priority to other desires. He did not ask himself why, like Pope, having
"dipped his blood in ink," he had found it necessary to forgo wife and
children, sexual intimacy and fatherhood. Unlike Pope, he did not seem
to think of his solitary bachelorhood even as a sacrifice. It seemed to
him a natural response to a family that he both feared and loved and
from whom he had long ago decided that he needed to maintain a
permanent separation. Only by separating himself from others could
he make viable as art the emotions that he had developed in response
to his family.

In *The Portrait of a Lady*, whose transatlantic success sustained him
during his return in November 1881, he dramatized, with more subtlety
and complication than ever before, the inner life of the person he had
become. He projected into fictional characters the conflicts and tenuous
resolutions that had been his since childhood. The central emotional
concerns of the author make the novel alive with partially resolved
tensions—mothers so powerful that their children are best off when
they are absent; fathers who are apparently benign but whose touch is
deathly; conflicts of sexuality so severe that they threaten to be debilitating; allegiances so distorting that life can be sustained only with separation; and, even worse, occasional emptiness, hypocrisy, and the disguise
and repression of vital life. The world of *Portrait,* behind the sophisticated portrayal of mores and personality, is a threatening, often deathly
world of repression and annihilation, where no one is happy, no one is
saved, where not even art can be maintained as a compensation available
to any of the main characters. It is a nightmare novel, disguised as a
novel of manners, a salutary, somewhat didactic fiction of the growth
and development of a young lady from innocence to experience.

The young women at the distressed heart of the novel, Isabel Archer
and Pansy Osmond, are Jamesian self-portraits. Isabel gets precisely
what James did not, an inherited fortune, the freedom to make of her
life, through her imaginative vividness, anything she chooses. In her
marriage to Gilbert Osmond, she chooses a form of death. It is not so
much a mistake of innocence as an expression of inner damage, of an

inability to extend her imagination beyond the superficial, the conventional, and the deadly to define freedom with sufficient boldness and courage. Most of all, it expresses a drive toward self-annihilation. Having become the orphan that Henry, as a child, over and over again wished that he were, Isabel dramatizes the Jamesian paradox that the absence of parents can be as damaging as the presence of parents. With a long-dead mother and a father who has dragged her, as Henry senior had his children, numerous times back and forth across the Atlantic, Isabel too readily becomes a European. She misperceives Gilbert Osmond because the deathliness in him deeply appeals to her own repressed feelings of damage, of lack of a coherent, healthy, assertive self. Isabel is a victim of the James household, of the Swedenborgian confusions, of the angel complex, of Henry senior's unconsciously hypocritical detestation of the will and ego. "You must often *dis*please others," Isabel's friend Henrietta Stackpole urges her. "You must always be ready for that—you must never shrink from it. That doesn't suit you at all—you are too fond of admiration, you like to be thought well of."

She is also, like her creator, a victim of Henry senior's ideas about the impurity of sexuality and the saving grace of marriage. Sexually frozen and fearful, she is repelled by Caspar Goodwood's priapic manliness, unaroused by Lord Warburton's gentlemanly, domestic sexual good manners, and drained by Osmond's passive sexual fastidiousness. She makes the worst of the choices available to her. James probably felt that he had made a better choice than his fictional double—that is, no marriage at all. In the portrait of Pansy, James imaginatively provides a version of himself that precedes Isabel. Pansy is an intelligent, inexperienced child whose femininity is shaped by a cleverly expressive, totally controlling father, until she is an absolutely passive Victorian angel, whose ultimate fulfillment will be in becoming the female partner in a marriage dedicated to the satisfaction of male needs. Osmond, unlike Henry senior, has no interest in marriage, for Pansy or anyone, as the highest vehicle of grace and redemption. For him, it is a social and mercenary arrangement. But the result is no different from what Henry senior advocated. Pansy's fragility resonates with Henry junior's vision of the danger to himself of his father's view of female perfection, of marriage as deathly, of sexuality as stultified, of the good son who identifies himself with the good daughter.

In the depiction of the tubercular Ralph Touchett and his wealthy father, James represents, by counterexample, his lifelong fear that such a relationship can only be achieved at the cost of the permanent illness or the death of the son. Fathers are unreliable, deadly, or both. Unlike Henry senior, Mr. Touchett provides Ralph with great wealth, those fabulous "three millions" from the golden days of the family's patriarch, William James of Albany. Ralph dies anyway, his one effort at projection balked in the failure of his cousin to be an example of imaginative freedom sustained, even made possible, by inherited money. To the extent that James felt himself an observer in regard to sex and marriage, Ralph carries some of the author's concern about distancing. It is purchased at a high price. But James himself felt, unlike Ralph, that there were crucial areas of life in which he was an engaged participant, in which his observation rose to the level of intense emotional involvement. In a small, slightly parodic way, Henrietta Stackpole embodies that aspect of James's view of himself. When she marries an attractive, accommodating Englishman, it is clear to Isabel that Henrietta has not "renounced" her allegiance to America, "but planned an attack," as James had when he had arrived in London at the end of 1875. "She was at last about to grapple in earnest with England." Her assault on England includes marriage to an Englishman, an ironic comment on James's assurance to his family and to Grace Norton that he would not be bringing home with him an English bride. He would not marry an English woman, but he would marry England. In the depiction of Mrs. Touchett, Ralph's caustic, mostly absent mother, James comments on his banishment of his own warmly loving, overly engaged mother to America. In fiction, he could resolve the guilt he may have felt by making her the agent of separation. At the same time, when Ralph is on his deathbed, Mrs. Touchett is there, her maternal commitment strong and irrevocable.

The problem of national allegiance, so much on James's mind, reverberates throughout the novel. "Ah, one doesn't give up one's country," Ralph remarks, "any more than one gives up one's grandmother. It's antecedent to choice." The manipulative, experienced Madame Merle, who takes advantage when advantage is presented to her, nevertheless, as an American herself, gives Isabel realistic advice: "You should live in your own country; whatever it may be you have your natural place there. If we are not good Americans we are certainly poor Europeans. . . . We are mere parasites, crawling over the surface; we haven't our feet in the soil. At least one can know it and not have illusions." Henrietta has no doubt what the more difficult path is. "It's nothing to come to Europe. . . . It is something to stay at home; this is much more important." Still, Isabel distinguishes herself from Henrietta. She "didn't see how Henrietta could give up her country. She herself had relaxed her hold of it, but it had never been her country as it had been Henrietta's." In the end, James's position is Isabel's. It was his country. But it had never been his country as it had been the country of those who had not been dragged back and forth across the ocean. It was not his country in the sense that William had made it his through an aggressive counterreaction to his years of childhood deracination. In the creation of strategies to liberate himself from his family, Henry had not balked at separating himself from his country. It had been part of his youthful self-definition as an artist. Europe was the natural place for him, provided he practiced his art, provided his imaginative life flourished. For Isabel Archer, deracination and marriage to Europe mean death. She has no art to substitute for country. Henrietta remarks, with an irony that, in regard to himself, James may have been conscious of, "it's every one's duty to get married."

Having returned to Cambridge with no intention of staying, he had before him the formidable counterexample of William, who was committed to home, marriage, and fatherhood. William wanted no ambiguities in regard to sex, no conflicts in regard to country. Alice Howe James was to be his emotional and spiritual bedrock, his Swedenborgian angel of redemption. More and more, William was becoming an embodiment of what he thought of as manliness, as the essential, willful self-definition that comes from the American ethos of physical and moral action. William wanted to climb mountains rather than observe them, to wear hiking gear rather than evening dress. For Henry, William remained a dangerous and central force, a brother to be loved and to be neutralized. In the portrait of Gilbert Osmond, caustic touches of Henry's problems with William appear. Osmond is a distorted but revealing depiction of Henry's feelings of repressed erotic attraction to William—the man he himself could never be—and of Henry's nightmare vision of what he might have become if he had been, like William, a better son of his father. Osmond, indeed, may be Henry's revenge on William for his brother's lifetime boasts of manly superiority. Unlike Henry, William played, from childhood on, "with boys who curse and swear." What better civilized revenge than to provide the ultrarefined Osmond with traits that make him look and sound suspiciously like William. Osmond, like William, has close-cropped hair, a short-clipped sharp beard, a thin, angular body, and bright, intelligent eyes. Osmond dominates others by means of an articulate and aggressive sensibility. Like William, Osmond is a talented painter who can never rise to the level of brilliance because he lacks genius. Like William, in his brother's complaint, Osmond "takes himself so seriously," as if his own nervous system was the necessary measure and judge of everything.[16]

As much as Osmond embodies Henry's revenge on William, Osmond also has traits that mirror Henry's. They are qualities that express Henry's sense of the continuum between William and himself and the

nightmare vision that his own sensibility and egomaniacal self-involve-
ment, at its most exaggerated, can be as deadly as Osmond's, if it is cut
off from the life-enhancing powers of artistic genius. In the fragmented,
prismatic autobiographical projections of *Portrait,* those dangerous aspects of himself that the author represents in Osmond threaten to destroy those aspects of himself that he portrays in Isabel. No wonder, at
the end, Isabel has to return to Osmond, for better or worse. Her
marriage is a disaster, a projection of the fear of marriage and erotic
consummation that James felt. Her sexuality is stifled by inner anxieties
and outer circumstances, an effective representation of James's sense of
his own erotic impulses. He would like to press against his body and
lips the hard form and passionate kiss that Caspar Goodwood presses
against Isabel's body and lips, his kiss "like a flash of lightning." What
it illumines, though , is a self-awareness that admits that such fulfillment
is as impossible for him as it is for Isabel. Like his heroine, he needs to
return to his own version of Rome in which there will be no intimacy
but in which there will also not be the likelihood of additional betrayal.
What there will be is a greater possibility for freedom, for creating and
refining the self through inner struggle. Isabel's struggle for survival
has been and continues to be an internal one. Her creator's similar
struggle continues. As much as James fears loss, deprivation, betrayal,
and death, to that degree he struggles to make them serve a heightened
awareness of being alive and creative. On his deathbed, Ralph Touchett
powerfully embodies James's vision of the necessary usefulness of the
deaths of those we love, of the death of Minny Temple, of the deaths
that were to occur, almost as if *Portrait* is prophetic, in the James family
in the next year. "There is nothing makes us feel so much alive," he
says to Isabel, "as to see others die. That's the sensation of life—the
sense that we remain."

(3)

After a month in Cambridge, which included a visit to Newport to see
Mary Tweedy, as well as Cambridge and Boston social calls on the
Gardners and Nortons, he went to New York. He was "depressed,"
he told Grace Norton, by way of apology, "with the way my hours"
in Cambridge "are all expended—though the way is usually pleasant.
I mean that they all go. . . . If it were in London I should understand
it; but in Cambridge it's a mystery; & yet not a romantic one." In New
York, life proved even more relentlessly busy, though also glamorous.
Godkin had arranged a social schedule as intense as the one he had

already rejected in London, with the added disadvantage that he could not even spend his mornings in private. Staying with the Godkins on East Twenty-fifth Street, he had long talks with his good-natured, loud-laughing, conversational friend. Lunches and social calls took up a good part of the day. He saw Aunt Kate, who could not get over what a man her darling Harry had become.[17] He responded to a note from Hawthorne's widow "earnestly requesting me to call on her. I did so—in some trepidation, & found her residing in a gorgeous 'up-town' mansion, in black brocade, & with a footman to wait upon her! She wished me to 'sympathise with her about America,' which, strange to say, under the circumstances, she appears to find unsatisfactory; but to this hour I don't know where she was or what she was 'up to.' " The episode puzzled him. Almost every night, from early to late December 1881, either Godkin hosted a dinner or they dined out.

Anticipating going up to Cambridge to spend Christmas with his parents, he vowed *"never again to return"* to New York, a resolution that expressed his feelings about America as well. Like the country as a whole, New York had dramatically expanded in size, wealth, even cultural density, since he had last been there in 1875. It now seemed "a very brilliant" city, though a fearfully expensive one, which "it takes a great fortune to enjoy," and "nothing under a million (sterling) is called a great fortune." A city of people but not personages, of talk but not conversation, "the sense one gets here of the increase of the various arts of life is—almost oppressive; especially as one is so often reminded of it. The arts of life flourish—but the art of living, simply, isn't among them!" Still, he told Macmillan, "New York is a big place, & is rapidly becoming an interesting one. I am struck, throughout, with the rapid & general increase of the *agreeable* in American life, & the development of material civilization." After material wealth would come artistic and cultural density. But that was, he felt, still at least fifty years off. He did not want to wait around. Homesick for London, "like the German woman of letters mentioned by Heine, who always wrote with one eye fixed on her MS & the other on some man—I too pass my life in a sort of divergent squint. One of my orbs of vision rests (complacently enough) on the scene that surrounds me here: the other constantly wanders away to the shores of Old England; & takes the train for Euston as soon as it arrives."[18]

In Cambridge, over the Christmas holiday, he was reunited with Wilky, whom he had not seen for eleven years, and who seemed "wonderfully unchanged for a man with whom life has not gone easy." After Christmas, he took the train to Washington with a brief stopover in New York and then in Philadelphia, where he stayed a few days with

Sarah Wister. He enjoyed her company just a little less than the pleasant Philadelphia society to which she introduced him. In Washington, the Adamses and their circle delighted him. The weather that had been so far "extraordinarily mild & charmingly bright" was even milder in Washington, where his friends were eager to show him the attractions of their adopted city. What had been widely known among Bostonians and New Yorkers as a malaria-ridden mudhole, with no distinction other than as the place where corrupt politicians gathered a few times a year, had changed dramatically enough for James to glimpse its cultural potential. "Fifty years hence this place will probably be (in addition to being the national capital of a country of a hundred millions of people) one of the most charming winter resorts in the world. . . . If we had a paternal government addicted to spending money in embellishments, it might be done in ten years, but the western congressmen won't vote for such luxuries while they want their own forests cleared & rivers dyked. It has to come gradually, but all that sort of thing, in America, is coming." Best of all, to James, Washington was not a city where commerce dominated. It seemed to him "the place in the world where money—or the absence of it, matters least." The arts and the arts of life would have a greater chance to flourish there than in more commercial cities.[19]

Comfortably housed at the Cosmopolitan Club, with a view of the White House and within a few minutes of the Adams home, he spent the month of January 1882 experiencing Washington. Surprised that he could "go to the Capitol and listen to debates without taking out a license, as in London," the city seemed "genial & amusing," though "materially, too much of a village," with the disadvantage, he remarked, of the black population vastly outnumbering the white. "Socially, conversationally, however, it is very cosmopolitan—much more so than our dear Boston. I see a good many people—but I have not fallen in love nor contracted an eternal friendship." At a dinner hosted by the influential James Blaine, just discharged as secretary of state, he met President Chester Arthur, who was "in deep official mourning." Impressed by what seemed Arthur's gentlemanly manners and cultural aspirations, James's novelistic imagination focused on a White House in mourning. Arthur's wife had recently died; he had ascended to the highest position in the country the previous year after the assassination of his predecessor. "The White House is shrouded in gloom. I can see it from these windows as I write—& there is something dramatic in the vision one can't help having of that solitary individual lifted into a great position by a murder, sitting there in the empty mansion in which he may hear the hovering of the ghosts of Lincoln & Garfield."[20]

He was unimpressed with the manners of another temporary Washingtonian, Oscar Wilde, who, barely beyond his twenty-fifth birthday, had begun his flamboyant lecture tour in America that he hoped would make his name widely known on both sides of the Atlantic. Wilde may have hoped to plant the same kiss on James's lips that he had on Whitman's. James and Wilde had met briefly in England. Wilde thought highly of James as a novelist. Horrified at Wilde's self-promotion, James doubted that there was any self, let alone any works, worth publicizing. The fastidious Clover Adams asked him "*not* to bring his friend Oscar Wilde" to tea. "I must keep out thieves and noodles or else take down my sign and go West." Later in January, after calling on Wilde, James told the Adamses that "he is a 'fatuous cad,' " though he had accepted a dinner invitation for that evening at which Wilde would be present. At dinner, Wilde seemed "repulsive," though James probably exaggerated when he claimed that no one looked at Wilde. If not, they were making a conscious effort not to. Acute observers, like Clover Adams, had a sense of Wilde's sexual message. To James's increasing criticism as well as perplexed jealousy, Wilde was, and would continue to be for decades, on everyone's mind and in everyone's gaze. He found Wilde's conversation pretentious, his presence vulgar, his sexual ambivalence and its association with art threatening to his own sexual identity and to his identity as an artist. In the spring, he proposed an idea for a story the essence of which was a contrast between Wilde and himself, "a contrast between the modern aesthete, who poses for artistic feelings, but is very hollow, and the real artist—who is immensely different."[21]

The reunion with the Adamses provided access to social Washington—partly through the daily afternoon teas that they hosted—and daily companionship that smoothed the wrinkles of potential loneliness. They had last seen one another in London in September 1880, at the end of the Adamses' year abroad. The previous fall in Paris they had dined and gone to the theatre together frequently. Their London companionship had been convivial, though Clover could not understand what about London James "finds so entrancing year after year. . . . For once it is very nice—but for life it seems to me a dreary round." The Adamses had reservations about James as a novelist, acerbically expressed in Clover's comment that "it's not that he 'bites off more than he can chaw' . . . but that he chaws more than he bites off." Though John Hay glowingly reviewed *Portrait* in the *Tribune,* Adams, who told Milnes Gaskell that "some of my friends . . . admire it warmly, and find it deeply interesting," did not particularly like it. James, who made no effort to hide his homesickness "for all the soft embraces of the old world," did not find Adams' Washington life interesting. It seemed to him "revolting in respect to the politics and the intrigues that surround it." Clover doubted that James would ever find Washington or America congenial for a long stay, let alone residence. "I think the real, live, vulgar, quick-paced world in America will fret him and that he prefers a quiet corner with a pen where he can create men and women who say neat things and have refined tastes and are not nasal or eccentric." Anyway, the Adamses knew James had no intention of staying in America later than the middle of May. At moments, James felt "desperately homesick" for London, especially when he received letters like one from Fanny Kemble urging him to "get all the good you can from every influence of your native land & come back to your adopted one of smoke & fog & damp & many friends. . . . I think of you almost as if you belonged to me."[22]

Suddenly his visit to Washington was cut short. Mary James had had a difficult summer and autumn, with a lingering bronchial infection that had tired and aged her. Late in January 1881, she became ill again— "asthma complicated with bronchitis." Bob wrote to Henry that it did not seem life-threatening. But Henry was "filled with grief and horror at the news of poor Mother's illness. . . . I cannot bear to think that she suffers, & would come on to see her if I believed it would help her through." The next day, Bob assured him that the doctor says "she is entirely out of danger but the recovery of her strength will be slow." On a Sunday morning, from his room at the Cosmopolitan Club, Henry wrote to her how painful it was for him to think of her suffering. He had seen her many times ministering to others. If "the devotion of the family" has not "provided you with all possible mitigations . . . you have but to send for me, and I will nurse you night and day." Late that evening, as he was dressing to go to dinner, he received a telegram from home, from William's wife: "Your mother exceedingly ill. Come at once." At 11:00 P.M., he went to the Adamses to share the news and bid them good-bye. He could not get a train until the next day, and it would take him thirty-six hours to reach Cambridge.[23] During a long wait to change trains, he learned from his New York cousins that at 6:45 P.M. on Sunday, Mary James had quietly died.

(4)

On a splendid New England winter day, with the snow "high and deep, but the sky as blue as the south, and the air brilliant and still," Henry and his brothers carried their mother to "her well-earned rest" in the Cambridge Cemetery. In the spring, when the snows would be gone and the earth soft, they were to move her from the temporary vault to a gravesite on the ridge at the distant end of the cemetery, with the Charles River and Soldiers' Field nearby, and a view of Boston in the distance. The burial ground was countrylike, with paths that Henry had walked many times in "long, lonely rambles" as a young man, with only the vaguest sense "that some of us would some day lie there."[24] Henry senior, feeble and limping, with Alice and Aunt Kate, followed the raised coffin and the fraternal pallbearers through the narrow paths cut in the high snow. It was the first time the entire family had been together in fifteen years, and it was to be the last.

After some "wretched hours" in New York, the night train had brought Henry on Tuesday morning to Quincy Street. Bob and William had been in Cambridge at her death, Bob "the only boy at home." When Henry came through the door in the quiet early morning, Mary James's spirit "seemed still to be there—so beautiful, so full of all that we loved in her." Going immediately upstairs to see the corpse, he was shocked by the sight of her absolutely still, exhausted face. He felt his "passionate childlike devotion to her" violated by her nonexistence. Those who had been there when she had died seemed to him "extraordinarily calm—almost happy." Not long before she died, she had apologized to Bob for what he had perceived as slights. "Forgive and forget dear Bob all that has passed and promise to love me more than ever, after this exhibition of my infirmity."[25] On Wednesday morning, a friend "read a simple burial service at the house—some scriptures." On the family's request, the service omitted "any reference to her personally." They did not want their thoughts about her trivialized by someone else's words. Then they carried her body to the cemetery, through the high, bright snow, in the winter sunshine.

None of the survivors wished that she had lived. They all felt relieved that they and she had been spared further pain. Henry senior, looking sublimely tranquil, hid his loneliness but not his determination to be reunited with his wife as soon as possible. He soon made it clear that life without his wife was more unbearable than life with his remaining family. Sharing his father's Swedenborgian convictions, Bob felt that "no one who has any vital belief in God can have any other thought for father than one of thankfulness that his own end is so very near." He seemed an aged revenant who, by some benign neglect or minor cosmic accident, had outlasted his wife. The other children had no such vital belief. Alice immediately took charge of her father. William felt deserted but stoical at the loss of the parent whose favorite son he had not been. Aunt Kate felt that her sister's death had made a great void that would not be filled before her own death came. "It can't be very long before I too shall be 'gathered to my fathers.' " Henry communed with his diary, with his literary soul. The deep pain challenged the ineffability of experience, the consolations of language. "It is impossible for me to say—to begin to say—all that has gone into the grave with her. She was our life, she was the house, she was the keystone of the arch. She held us all together, and without her we are scattered reeds. She was patience, she was wisdom, she was exquisite maternity. . . . She is with us, she is of us—the external stillness is but a form of her love. One can hear her voice in it—one can feel, forever, the inextinguishable vibration of her devotion."[26] He felt the vibrations all around him. It did not seem to any of them, for the moment, that Mary James was gone.

In the still, calm house, the family had decided that grief was inappropriate. Having "spent a long self-forgetting life in the service of her family," Mary James now had "her well earned rest." For Bob, the two weeks that he had spent with his mother before her death had been the two happiest of his life. The two weeks after her death he slept every night in her bed, near his father, the two of them frequently talking late into the night about the wife and the mother they had lost and about Swedenborgian mysteries. Wilky returned almost immediately to Milwaukee, hardly changed in appearance, lovably amiable, deeply sad, the lines of failure etched into his bearing and into his face. He was soon diagnosed as having serious heart illness and, within the year, a fatal case of Bright's disease. In late March, Bob left for the Azores, with money partly supplied by Henry, where he intended to stay for at least three months. Separated from his wife and children, he hoped to establish himself as an artist, though so far his frenetic efforts in Boston had failed. Henry was relieved to see that he need not delay his planned mid-May 1882 departure date. He had feared that he might be needed for an indefinite time. But "Alice, I am happy to say, after many years of ill health has been better for the last few months than for a long time; she is able to look after my father and take care of the house." It seemed a miracle of sorts. By late in the month, Aunt Kate made arrangements to return to New York, "Alice feeling quite competent to going alone. . . . Her mother's death seems to have brought new life to Alice."[27]

A week after his mother's funeral, Henry moved to Boston. "I don't wish to *inhabit* Cambridge," he told Tom Perry, who, with Grace Norton, helped him find two furnished rooms at 102 Mount Vernon Street, "the nearest approach (in Boston) to London lodgings." Insisting that the Quincy Street house be sold immediately, Alice, by the beginning of May, moved herself and her father to a rented house—also on

Mount Vernon Street, close to the bookstores that Henry senior loved. She was also having built a summer house on the ocean at nearby Manchester, close to Katherine Loring's home at Pride's Crossing, on property that she had purchased for four thousand dollars. Katherine supervised the building and furnishing. "My father and Alice are almost happy!" Henry remarked. Aunt Kate had a vision of the self-sacrificing Mary James blissful in heaven. "How must she rejoice that to the dear child to whom she gave material existence, she has by her death given spiritual life."[28]

Life in furnished rooms at 102 Mount Vernon Street had attractions. Tom Perry lived nearby, as did Owen Wister, Sarah Wister's twenty-two-year-old son, whom James liked but considered an example of personality and talent shrinking from grandmother to daughter to grandson. A few doors away, on Louisburg Square, Howells greeted him effusively. "I see him constantly," Howells told John Hay, "and we talk literature perpetually, as we used to do in our walks ten years ago. He is not sensibly changed, and, reflected in him, I find that I am not." Howells had recently resigned as editor of the *Atlantic,* which James greeted as his friend's liberation from fifteen years of unsuitable narrowness. "He has led a life of enforced bondage which I never could have endured for a month." With a shared tendency to gain weight and to "feel hopelessly middle-aged," their long strolls together reminded Howells so strongly of the youths they had been that it seemed for the moment as if they were still young.[29]

Walking regularly out to Cambridge to visit his father and Alice, returning in the early spring darkness, Henry felt it to be a healing time. He also visited Grace Norton frequently. He went to the theatre, to museums, to dinners with his friends. But still, he told Henrietta Reubell, "I am leading at present so very quiet a life that your little whiff of the great Parisian hubbub seems to me the carnival of dissipation." On the basis of encouraging discussions the previous winter with the manager of the Madison Square Theatre in New York, he worked on what he hoped would be a financially successful stage version of "Daisy Miller." He made the thin story heavier and more blatantly theatrical, extending it into a three-act comedy with a great deal of talk and little action. On two consecutive evenings, he read it to Isabella Gardner. In early May, he arranged a private printing in order to solicit responses and, he hoped, commitments. But the same theatre manager now "didn't like the play." James felt bitter at what soon seemed to him "ridiculous negotiations" in which the theatre "proprietors behaved like asses and sharpers combined."[30]

From a distance, when she learned the news of his mother's death,

Constance Woolson tried to console him. "I sympathize with you the more, because I have never been my old self since my Father died, but have always felt desolate and oppressed with care without him; and then when, three years ago, my Mother too was taken, there seemed nothing left to live for. A daughter feels it more than a son, of course, because her life is so limited, bounded by home-love; but the son feels it in his own way."[31] He did feel it in his own self-protective, introverted way, but also with the emotional opportunism of an artist looking to use his experience in his art. Mary James, though, was to make few appearances in his work or private writings, except in the rarest of always reverential allusions to a relationship too deep for words, a life too sacred to be anything but silently remembered.

At the beginning of May 1882, he made departure preparations, including a hectic week of farewells and a visit to Manchester, where he found his sister and his father in a pretty house, "with the sea close to the piazzas, and the smell of bayberries in the air." From his father, the day before he sailed, he got a "distinctly widowed farewell" in the form of a letter apparently intended to stand, if necessary, as a final word. "How loving a farewell it is, I can't say, but only that it is most loving. All my children have been very good and sweet from their infancy, and I have been very proud of you and Willy. But I can't help feeling that you are the one that has cost us the least trouble, and given us always the most delight. Especially do I mind mother's perfect joy in you the last few months of her life, and your perfect sweetness to her. . . . I feel that I have fallen heir to all dear mother's fondness for you, as well as my proper own. . . . Good-bye then again, my precious Harry!" Late at night on the day before sailing, James wrote farewell letters to friends, including one to Clover Adams, whom he praised as "the incarnation of my native land." She suspected this was "a most equivocable compliment coming from him. Am I then vulgar, dreary, and impossible to live with?" The voyage across was "the brightest and fairest, as well as the shortest" he had ever experienced. When he arrived at Bolton Street, he felt revivified, though startled to find Bob staying in his rooms. The Azores venture had proved an unhappy disaster. Bob had arrived in London, "nervous and depressed," on the same day that Henry had sailed from New York. Fortunately, he did not stay long.[32]

Relieved to be back in London, he rapidly returned to the rhythms of his daily routines, his walk, his "depraved habit" of late breakfast at one of his clubs, his morning and afternoon work at his desk, his social evenings. The summer suddenly became "uncomfortable, over-crowded." He repaid a network of favors received by maintaining a one-man London escort service for visiting female friends. "There was a difficult moment when . . . Mrs. Boit, Miss Reubell & Mrs. Wister were all here together." As a famous American writer in London, many aspiring American writers besieged his door with introductions. "I like young Americans to come & see me," he told Grace Norton, "though rather wonder why" they come "when I think of the little I can do for them." Two seasoned American professionals were in London for much of the summer—Howells and Osgood. Howells "& his impediments" James helped move into lodgings in South Kensington. With Osgood, he carried on a bitter comedy of self-deception in regard to "Daisy Miller." In mid-June 1882, soon after returning to London, he read the play to the principal of the St. James's Theatre. Nothing came of it. In the fall, he made one last, unsuccessful effort to have it performed, attempting to persuade an actor to use his influence because there was a wonderful part in it for him. The new editor of the *Atlantic,* Thomas Bailey Aldrich, in his eagerness to keep James as a contributor, offered him an irresistible two hundred pounds for publication. Having had a prior agreement to give it to *The Century Magazine,* with Osgood as middleman, now he told Osgood that he had "been induced to review" his decision and give it to Aldrich, "who appears quite to *yearn* for it." The next year the play was published in book form, in response to which the anonymous reviewer for the *New York Tribune* expressed "some surprise—and regret—that such an accomplished writer and acute critic should not have perceived the full extent of the failure which he has now put permanently on record."[33]

Though he made no great claims for the play, James did not share the reviewer's perception. The fault, he concluded, was in the condition of the modern theatre. "I have learned, very vividly, that if one attempts to work for it one must be prepared for *disgust,* deep and unspeakable disgust. But though I am disgusted, I do not think I am discouraged. The reason of this latter is that I simply can't afford to be. I have determined to take a year—even two years, if need be—more, in experiments, in studies, in attempts." But how could be reconcile this with his occasional "woeful hunger" to write another novel? The answer, he thought, was perhaps to do mainly short pieces. He felt time and opportunity slipping away. As if he could force himself into the focus of Dickens' "merciless military eye," he exhorted himself, sitting at his desk at Bolton Street in the early August heat: "If I can only *concentrate* myself: this is the great lesson of life. I have hours of unspeakable reaction against my smallness of production: my wretched habits of work—or of un-work; my levity, my vagueness of mind, my perpetual failure to focus my attention, to absorb myself, to look things in the face, to invent, to produce, in a word. I shall be 40 years old in April next: it's a horrible fact! I believe however that I have learned how to work. . . . When I am really at work, I'm happy, I feel strong. . . . It is the only thing that makes life endurable. I must make some great efforts during the next few years, however, if I wish not to have been on the whole a failure. I shall have been a failure unless I do something great!"[34] But it was not easy to decide what to do.

Late in July, he went to a dinner hosted by Lowell, mostly attended by Americans, though Browning, John Morley, William Lecky, and Aubrey de Vere also were present. Lowell seemed in especially good spirits, with his ill wife away under her sister's care and his affair of the next few years with George Smalley's wife perhaps already under way. If James disapproved, he did so knowing that the Smalleys had a long-standing agreement that they were each to go their own way in such matters. Probably John Hay, in London with "his big, handsome, vaccine wife," was at Lowell's dinner. Having suffered for the last few years from nervous illnesses and severe depressions, Hay had come abroad for his health, partly in flight from Cleveland and his wealthy father-in-law. "Him too I try to look after a little," James told Grace Norton. Emerging "rather breathless and panting" from the high season, in August James breathed a sigh of relief. "The season, thank God, is over, & I have survived it—to feel sure that I shall never pass another—till the next!" His comparatively quiet late summer was punctuated by William's arrival for a two-day visit on his way to the Continent. After months of quiet debate and inner hesitation, William had decided to spend a sabbatical year abroad by himself, mostly studying in Germany. Because he could not afford to take his wife and child, he rationalized that "she and the babe will thrive better without the travelling." "Hereafter," he told his brother, "I'll stay at home. You'll have to come to America if you want to see the family."[35] The injunction was to prove a failure as prophecy. William continued to come regularly to Europe, and Alice eventually came permanently.

Having returned to England only three months before, Henry still had no hesitation committing himself to a long autumn 1882 visit to France. Baffled in his effort to get "Daisy Miller" performed, without for the time having a focused impulse to write fiction, he had agreed to do a series of travel essays for *Harper's Magazine*—to be "expensively" illustrated—under the general rubric of a little tour through the ancient towns of central France, an area that he had previously hardly visited. "This is a sort of work that I have less & less taste for; but I have undertaken it because it is light & (relatively) easy, & promises to be lucrative." Having earned very little since the serial publication of *Portrait*, he needed money. In mid-September he went to Paris, where he spent two days. He proceeded to join Henrietta Reubell, Fanny Kemble, her daughter Sarah Wister, and Sarah's son Owen in the Loire Valley. Tension between Fanny and her daughter produced at least one potentially explosive incident. "I felt, when it was over, as if I had been holding a lighted bombshell for a given number of minutes, & then had been told I might plunge it in a bucket of water. Miss W.'s is a tragic nature, & so much worn, physically, that I am very sorry for her—as she wishes to do everything & when she finds that she can do but a little sinks back in somber despair."[36]

By early October 1882, he was happy to be on his own, though the weather was mostly bad, the towns dull, the work "dreary." After two weeks of Bourges, Bordeaux, Toulouse, and Carcassonne, he felt lonely and homesick. When *Harper's,* without having seen them, decided after all that it was not interested in the articles, he swallowed his anger and soon made an arrangement with the *Atlantic* to publish *En Province* from July to November 1883 and in February, May, and June 1884. Osgood brought it out in a single volume in September 1884 with a new title, *A Little Tour in France.* From Paris, he told Isabella Gardner that he had had an interesting six weeks. "I have seen more of France than I had ever seen before, and on the whole liked it better." But he was happy to be once again in "the city of vice," though "I am leading the same innocent and unagitated life that I drag about with me everywhere."[37] He had the company of John Hay and Hay's good friend Clarence King, whom James had met in September in London, when King lodged on Bolton Street. Hay was now in Paris, with his wife and three children, where he consulted the neurologist Jean-Martin Charcot. He also hoped that Parisian entertainments would lift his spirits.

A secretive, somewhat tragic figure, Clarence King had become for Hay and Adams the epitome of the cultured adventurer. He was a high-spirited, enthusiastic doer rather than thinker, who had parlayed a scientific education at Yale and great personal courage into a number of sensational achievements as a field geologist in the Far West. Two of the results were a scholarly classic, *Report of the Geological Exploration of the Fortieth Parallel,* and a popular success, *Mountaineering in the Sierra Nevada.* Sexually adventuresome and personally flamboyant, King was fascinated by exotic women. For much of his life, he secretly had a black wife and family in Brooklyn. James, at first, could not make him out, but thought him "a delightful creature." An avid collector, King charmed "all the bric-a-brac out of the shops." He philandered "with Ferdinand Rothschild"—whom he had saved millions by exposing a diamond fraud in which Rothschild was about to be duped, and "who appears unable to live without him." At the Grand Hotel, where James stayed on the floor above King, they all dined lavishly and smoked cigarettes together on the balcony. Constance Woolson was in Paris, and Hay, who hoped to promote a marriage between Woolson and King, arranged a theatre party and told Adams, mistakenly, that Woolson, "that very clever person, to whom men are a vain show," had fallen in love with King "at sight and talks of nothing else." James arrived at the end of October, just as Woolson left. "The rain is descending in customary torrents & the gorgeous fabric of the opera, which I can see from my windows, looms ruefully through a curtain of water." It was, still, a pleasurable two weeks. "The theatres are dull, the restaurants are ruinous, the streets are (for Paris) dirty. . . . The government is shaky & lives but from day-to-day & the air has a certain little odour of dynamite."[38] He rather liked it.

When he returned from Paris in late November 1882, he had two mostly lovely weeks in London. "Yesterday," he wrote to Henrietta Reubell, "the whole place was *en fête,* to see the Queen go in state to the city, to open certain law-Courts. She looked more than ever like a housemaid out of place (in a royal coach,) but a big London turnout is always an imposing sight." William was in Germany, having spent some time in the fall in Switzerland and Italy, then in Vienna and Prague, worrying that he had been nothing "but a source of anxiety" to his wife since they had first met. Still, he was happy to be in Germany, which he preferred to Italy, and "full of pity for the poor creatures," like Henry, "who have to live alone." On December 9, Henry, in London, received a telegram from Alice. "Brain softening. Possibly live months. All insist Wm. shall not come." Henry senior had had enough of living alone. Within three days, Henry made all his arrangements. A letter came from Aunt Kate indicating that Henry senior was "decidedly mending," but there was much in the letter to suggest the contrary. It also contained the startling news that Henry junior had been chosen by his father as sole executor. With a letter from his wife indicating the seriousness of his father's condition, William immediately left Germany for England. He arrived just after Harry had sailed on the twelfth, on "this sad errand across the wintry ocean . . . in the hope of seeing my poor father once again before he passes away."[39]

(5)

This time he was too late even for the funeral. Though the voyage was unusually "quick and prosperous" and the Atlantic cooperated, his family had buried his father the very day he stepped off the ship in New York. His father had died at 3:00 P.M. on Monday the eighteenth. He had been buried on that Thursday morning, on the first day of winter, next to his wife, in the Cambridge Cemetery. Henry had not been expected before the twenty-third or the twenty-fourth. Struggling up-town through heavy traffic, he caught a train that brought him to Boston at eleven that night. At the station, Bob was waiting. At Mount Vernon Street, Alice was in bed, exhausted, on the verge of collapse. The enduring Aunt Kate seemed her usual "perfect" self. "They told me everything—or at least they told me a great deal—before we parted that night," much of which he would already have known except that some of the letters sent to him had arrived after his departure. As always, he avidly sought the details.[40]

After his wife's death, Henry senior had decided to end his life. He starved himself to death. He did it purposefully, gradually, across a full year—a benign form of suicide, the climactic irony of his life, a combination of the ego-centered willfulness that he had denounced but always practiced and of the purposeful Swedenborgian disregard of distinctions between body and soul that he had advocated. He had predicted that he would die before the year was out. He managed the prediction economically, effectively.

After a summer with Alice at Manchester, he had limped back to Mount Vernon Street, noticeably fragile. In November 1882, after a severe attack of nausea and faintness, he took to his bed. He made a point of saying good-bye to many of his friends, though "he won't tolerate what he calls 'sentimentality.' . . . He has distinctly made up his mind," William's wife remarked, "not to live and without diseases, that at 73 is a good reason for going. . . . He spoke lovingly and often of you and Harry. . . . I am sure he would be greatly disturbed if he thought either of you were coming."

Toward the end of November, he had two fainting spells. As they watched him lose consciousness, Alice and Aunt Kate thought that he was at that moment dying. Alice kept her composure but collapsed that night. "The faithful Katherine" stayed with her in her room. When he ate a few mouthfuls of food, the first in about a week, the somber doctor assured them that Henry senior "will recover from this acute attack, but he can predict nothing for the future." The exhausted patient slept a good deal. When awake, he urged repeatedly that Henry and William should remain in Europe. He had no need for their presence. If one of them should come, though, it should be Harry, who, because he had no family and because he had made his life abroad, could come more readily than William.[41]

At the beginning of December 1882, Henry senior's mind began to wander. Alice thought that he might be suffering from "brain softening" or "brain fever." When he was urged to eat to avoid starvation, he refused food. He preferred to die and join "his Mary." "His only distress is that he cannot die," Aunt Kate assured Henry, and "of this he complains bitterly; and if his mind goes entirely we would all desire his release as much as he does. *I* desire it *now* for his sake." When he was urged to eat, he explained that he had no need for food, since he was already dead. He had passed, imperceptibly, he explained, into his spiritual form. To Katherine Loring it seemed irrational, "foolish." To William and Henry it seemed no more than a logical extension of their father's lifelong illogical Swedenborgianism. His pulse continued strong until the middle of December, when it began to fade. Quietly expressing his happiness "in the thought of the immortal life, upon which he says he has already entered," he insisted that "he has passed through death and that it has no sting, and wants to tell every one how delightful it is to die." Now he refused to eat anything. On the seventeenth, "he asked Alice for water, the only thing that had passed his lips for 24 hours. As he took it, he said 'What vile-tasting stuff, and what a vile world!' " The next day, at half past two, he exclaimed, "I am going with great joy. . . . There is my Mary!"—and died. "The grand old face" appeared "grave with [the] majesty of a great triumph . . . as if all expectations, all questions were already answered." The two Alices and Aunt Kate, kneeling, "sat about the bed talking of things he had said, and glad that the desire of his heart was granted." Alice wanted an autopsy done to see if he had died of "brain fever." William, she thought, would like to know. The doctor advised against it.[42]

Alice was now alone. "For you, my dear sister," William wrote to her, "this is the most important change in all your life. In some ways it will be a great nakedness, in others a great freedom." For the moment, she collapsed in nervous prostration. The evening before Harry's arrival, Katherine Loring had surprised Aunt Kate presiding over the flames that had moments before been Henry senior's family papers. When Katherine remonstrated, she said "she thought it better that 'the children' should not see them." Alice was furious. In London, William felt frustrated and victimized, angry that he had been urged by everyone not to return and that he had consented. To have been at the deathbed "would have symbolized the unfathomable relation in which he stood to me . . . and would have been one of those things whereof the moment gives a life-long satisfaction, and is incomparable with another gain." Staying in his brother's London apartment, he had anguished over every letter, every telegram, hesitating until it was too late. He learned of his father's death from an announcement in a London news-paper the day before the funeral. The previous week, he had written to his father, acknowledging that "all my intellectual life I derive from you." When the letter arrived, Henry took it to his father's graveside and read it aloud. "I am sure he heard [me] somewhere out of the depths of the still, bright winter air. He lies extraordinarily close to Mother, and as I stood there and looked at this last expression of so many years of mortal union, it was difficult not to believe that they were united again in some consciousness of my belief." William said his own good-bye. "He and Mother are in the Wintry Ground! Good night, good and dear faithful pair! We will come soon enough."[43]

With a splitting headache, Henry went to bed for most of three days, sleeping in his father's bed. He was Henry junior no longer. Even his assumption of primacy brought anguish and problems about which he had to make decisions quickly. He was the sole executor of a will of which he strongly disapproved. So too did Alice, Bob, Wilky, and William's wife. Aunt Kate, Alice believed, probably correctly, had influenced its terms. With little respect for Wilky, she had fed Henry senior's anxiety that Alice would be insufficiently provided for by an equitable division and had urged that she be made sole heir. Alice had vociferously, implacably objected. Either "she would share with her brothers or break the will." Henry senior and Aunt Kate retreated. When, early in November 1882, Wilky had been diagnosed by a Boston doctor as having a "valvulary enlarged" heart," Aunt Kate reportedly remarked, "Why leave Wilky any money" at all, since "he may die at any moment" and has a rich father-in-law who could be expected to take care of his daughter and grandchildren? "Father insisted that he would put on record what he considered justice to his children."[44] Wilky, he claimed, had already received his patrimony in the family money spent on the Florida plantation experiment and in a recent loan of five thousand dollars.

When he read the terms of the will, Henry was distressed, even shocked. Alice inherited property worth altogether about twenty thou-sand dollars. William, Henry, and Bob inherited the commercial real estate in downtown Syracuse, worth about seventy-five thousand dol-lars, with a rental yield of about five thousand dollars a year before taxes and other expenses, to be divided equally between them. Henry senior had instructed that a deduction be made from Bob's inheritance for the money he had spent to buy Bob a small Wisconsin farm. At the time, the farm had appeared to be a freely offered gift. Also, Henry senior had placed a lifetime limitation on Bob's share of the estate, on the assumption that his family would be cared for by his well-to-do father-in-law. That Wilky inherited nothing at all seemed to Henry heartless, even cruel. Henry senior was doing to Wilky what William senior had done to him. Hurt and furious, Wilky had no doubt that Aunt Kate had been a conspirator in the injustice. That explained "why he should suddenly make a will after refusing 72 years to do so, why he should do so in a way privy to Aunt Kate alone . . . why he should discriminate against the only two of his children whose healths are too much impaired to make a living . . . together with the fact that he broke his own father's will for his own benefit. . . ." He would do, he told Bob, what Henry senior had done to William of Albany. "I shall place the matter very deliberately into the hands of a lawyer for contest, and the certain breaking of the will. . . . I shall utterly and entirely disclaim any liability on account of the Florida enterprise." Henry agreed with Wilky's generally accurate account of the history of the plantation fiasco. "I never in any way gave my note for it to father. The property was purchased in his name, and he gave me a power of attorney to run it for him. I labored with it for six of the best years of my life trying to save it, but never received one dollar of benefit from it. . . . I have in my possession a complete chain of accounts of the whole property, also letter after letter of father's trying to induce me to abandon the whole property & fathering the ill-judged involvement himself. The more I think of this discrimination . . . the more unjust and damnable it seems to me."[45]

Disappointed in his father, Henry immediately set to work to rectify an injustice for which he told his brothers and sister no one need be blamed. The exclusion of Wilky had been an excusable deathbed lapse. He did not want to attempt to establish legal and financial responsibility for the Florida experiment. The first, most determinative ground for redistribution was humanitarian. To Wilky, the will "was a base cowardly act of father's, a dark stab at two of his children to whom he owed every gratitude a father could owe to his flesh & blood; a death stab at the only two . . . who dared fight through the war for the defense of the family and the only two who attempted while very young to earn their own living & have earned it steadily ever since."[46]

The burden of being the eldest son at home weighed heavily on Henry. Immediately after Christmas, he felt despondent. Gradually, his headache lifted. His sister-in-law wrote to her husband that Henry worried about Alice's future "and the extraordinary tie between her and Katherine. Then Aunt Kate came in and he dropped the subject, naturally." He insisted on turning over to Alice for her lifetime his share of the income from the Syracuse real estate, about $1,250 annually, on his conviction that he could continue, as before, to support himself entirely by his writing. Confidently expecting William's assent, he asked the family lawyer to send William "a paper of agreement to a redivision," urging him not to "judge that exclusion of Wilky horribly, as regards Father." For the first two weeks of January 1883, he wrote innumerable letters, reassured his brothers, dealt with lawyers, made arrangements for a trip to Milwaukee, kept William informed. In Milwaukee, the farthest west he had ever been, the mid-January winter scene was dismal, snowy, freezing, "a moving wall of icy air." The sight of the broken-spirited, slowly dying Wilky pained him. In the midst of a rheumatic attack, Wilky was deeply grateful for Henry's "loving, tender, moderate and wise counsels." Bob seemed to be doing better, making another effort with his wife, with some financial help from his father-in-law. On his way back to Boston, he stopped at Syracuse for consultations with the family's business agent in regard to the condition, the value, the salability of the property. In freezing weather, he was driven along "*James St., the 5th Avenue of Syracuse, one of the handsomest American streets I have ever seen—named after our James grandfather!*"[47] As soon as he returned to Boston, where the comparative warmth seemed almost "Italian," he was shocked to find a letter from William expressing strong hostility to the redistribution proposal. His assumptions had been incorrect. He had in no way anticipated William's reaction.

Fretting in London since the middle of December, William felt increasingly impatient, explosively angry. London seemed like a prison. "I must . . . save my life by escaping to Paris. Never did a place seem to agree with me less."[48] But what he most hated was that when this crucial family drama had been enacted, he had been offstage, that by a combination of accident and indecision he had been relegated to the role of distant spectator, that as eldest son he had been deprived of the direct participation that his patrimony warranted, and that Henry, rather than he, had been made executor of their father's estate. With a family to whose present and future support he had to give priority, he would not consent to the redistribution. Henry and Alice had only to think of themselves. Bob and Wilky had wealthy fathers-in-law who would, if necessary, provide for their grandchildren. He himself had no such advantage. Calmly, forcefully, Henry responded that, eventually, he must consent. William retreated. At first he attempted to make secondary conditions, among them that Wilky's share of the inheritance should have a lifetime limitation and revert to the James family. Henry insisted that the money would revert to the James family only if Wilky's children died childless. "I hope you will have since made up your mind to agree," Henry wrote to him, "to a re-division *pure & simple*. I think that if you were here, you would do so. What you say about deducting $5000 (the amount furnished Wilky on the eve of his failure) has something to be said for it, but my strong feeling is now & it is in a high degree Bob's & Alice's, that as things are at present this had better not be insisted upon. . . . So I say, Alice feels, & so does Bob, & I therefore (as it is my own earnest feeling) again express the sincere hope that you will by this time have signified to me your assent to the division *pure & simple* . . . making no difference between us on account of money supplied in the past. I have already given Wilky assurance that this would be the arrangement & I feel as if I could not now take upon myself to undeceive him. . . . If therefore, by the time you get this, you have not assented to the literal redivision, let me—I beseech you—hear from you that you have thought better of it & will do so. This will refresh, revive & rest me more than I can say."

William continued to object, though not as forcefully. "For us absolutely to ignore that element in Father's will" regarding Wilky "would be to cast rather a dishonourable [slur] on him, would it not?" He did not persuade his brother. "The will," Henry responded, "was unfortunate in its wholesale character, and the best way to justify Father is simply to assume that he expected us (as he *did* expect us) to rearrange equally." Reluctantly, by late January 1883, William gave in. Henry received the news with slightly exasperated relief at the end of the first week of February. Their next exchange had a quarrelsome edge. William angrily accused Henry of meddling in his personal affairs by arguing that he ought not to return prematurely. "It *was* rather meddlesome in me," Henry admitted, "to have so much to say about the question of your coming back. . . . To meddle seemed the safest thing. . . . I even persist in meddling, so far as to be glad that you have not yet come. . . . I write this with a clear understanding that you won't answer it, and that you will write to me after this as little and as briefly as possible." Henry volunteered that he would not send William's letters on the redivision to Wilky. "I shall let him suppose that you have simply assented to it."[49] At the end of March, William came home.

With a fortieth birthday immediately ahead of him, it did not take him long to get used to being Henry junior no longer, though the transition included a few slips of the pen and cross-outs. The trials, as well as the honor of being his father's executor, continued through the spring, including painstaking, delicate discussions in regard to Bob's desire to withdraw his portion of the inheritance from the Syracuse real estate. Market conditions had to be assessed. Advice had to be solicited. Steps had to be taken in response to both Bob and Wilky's legal and financial arrangements with their wives. Gathering information, writing careful, detailed letters, he managed it all with an effectiveness that might have made William of Albany proud. Under stress, he shrewdly managed the family business affairs and sustained family harmony. When, having failed in his effort to reconcile with his wife, Bob returned again to Boston, Henry encouraged him in his painting, urging him to take lessons, complimenting him on his work. He worried most about Alice. She had broken down repeatedly since Henry senior's death, and in spring and summer 1883 spent time at the Adams Nervine Asylum in nearby Jamaica Plain, where she had electric shock treatment. Unfortunately, nothing medical helped. Katherine Loring's company did. It seemed to her brother that Alice was doomed, more or less, to permanent invalidism. Where would she live? Who would she live with? Feeling responsible, he proposed at the beginning of February that they "set up a common ménage" in London. She shrewdly declined. "We are really both much too fond of our individual independence," he wrote to Fanny Kemble, "and she has a dread of exchanging the comfortable *known* of Boston for the vast unknown of London." On Mount Vernon Street, he and Alice "make an harmonious" couple. "I feel a good deal as if I were married. . . . I feel strangely settled here for the present, & shall probably remain for the summer—but after that—open thy bosom, London of my soul!"[50]

Despite his Boston and Cambridge friends, Tom Perry, Grace Norton, and Isabella Gardner, among others "these unterminated [winter] weeks of Boston and of East wind" seemed to go on forever, his "chief amusements snowstorms and sacred concerts." Within two weeks of William's return at the end of March 1883, Henry left for New York and Washington. He wanted a change of air and scene. Perhaps there was still some tension between the brothers. In New York, beginning in early April, he stayed ten days with Godkin, who was "more genial than ever, overflowing with every species of hospitality." New York, to his surprise, delighted him, "full of types and figures and curious social idiosyncrasies. . . . I only wish we had someone here, to hold up the mirror. . . . It is altogether an extraordinary growing, swarming, glittering, pushing, chattering, good-natured, cosmopolitan place. . . . I never return to this wonderful city without being entertained and impressed afresh." At one of the many dinners Godkin provided, there were two ladies of special distinction, Pierpont Morgan's wife and Mrs. Fred Jones. The latter's daughter, Edith, later to marry Edward Wharton, was to become one of his intimate friends. At a formal dinner, Godkin had "consented to make a speech & I have promised to remain silent; in other words to plunge a fruit-knife into my short-bosom if I am called on for one." When James left for Washington, he must have known that he had left one month too soon to see the spectacular celebration in late May 1883 to commemorate the opening of the "Eighth Wonder of the World," the newly completed Brooklyn Bridge. In Washington, staying at Wormley's Hotel near the Capitol, he socialized mainly with the Adamses and their friends, including a dinner at which he met Elizabeth Cameron, the beautiful, disaffiliated wife of Senator James Donald Cameron, with whom Adams was to fall in love.[51] With Wilky, who joined him in Washington on his way up from Florida, he returned to Boston, with a stopover of a few days in New York, at the end of April.

But what he needed more than a change of scene was work. Before leaving Boston, at the end of the first week of April he had made a proposal to his Boston publisher, James Osgood. In addition to a volume of new stories, he proposed a novel of about half the length of *Portrait* to be set mainly in Boston. Its themes and characters would dramatize his father's preoccupations. He planned a novel that "relates an episode connected with the so-called 'women's movement,' " in which the characters "are for the most part persons of the radical and reforming class who are especially interested in the emancipation of women, giving her the suffrage, releasing her from bondage, co-educating her with men. They regard this as the great question of the day."[52] Remarkably, he directed the proposal to a Boston publisher whom he had no reason to be especially enthusiastic about rather than to Macmillan, as if he could not for the moment see beyond the American scene and glimpse his larger interests. He may have assumed that an English publisher would not be interested in a novel set in America, though that had not been the case with *Washington Square*. More likely than not, he was unthinkingly propelled to Osgood by the connections and the atmosphere of his father's world. *The Bostonians* was to be, among other things, a tribute to the father whose death he was mourning.

He and Osgood agreed that he would write three stories, one of them to be called "Lady Barberina," which, added to the already published but uncollected "Four Episodes," would form a volume to be finished before he would go ahead with the novel. *The Bostonians* will "be of the length of 150 pages of the *Atlantic*," published in six parts, the first to be available, he hoped, by the beginning of 1884. He desired "$4500 for it." For the three new stories, "$2500 seems to me a fair price. . . . I got $500 from the Century for the *Point of View*. . . . For the *Siege of London* I got $750 from the *Cornhill*. . . . The other day Gilder of the *Century* said in writing to me—'Haven't you got any more short stories in you: short as *Four Meetings* and as good?' I mention this to show that there is a demand for these productions." As to copyright, "I don't suppose to make it over to you *forever!*" But he did give it to Osgood for five years. Without any apparent sense of embarrassment or awkwardness, he wrote to Macmillan that he had sold both books to Osgood "to do what he please with for periodical and serial publication, & otherwise both in England & in this country. . . . When the time shall come for your wishing to include them in the little 'choice' edition, you will have to treat with him—not with me." This was an extraordinary departure from his usual insistence on selling American and British rights separately and selling serial and book publication rights separately.[53] It was a better arrangement for Osgood than for James. When *The Bostonians* exceeded in length the six installments he had originally anticipated, James's loss was substantial. Osgood eventually had financial difficulties immediately prior to publication, and the contract that James had signed proved almost disasterous. The ghost of his father hovered over *The Bostonians* in more ways than one.

In early May 1883 he had, at least, the immediate satisfaction of being back at his writing desk at Mount Vernon Street, working on "Lady Barberina" and thinking about another story, to be called "Impressions of a Cousin." He hoped to have the three new stories he had promised Osgood done before his August departure. He solicited, from Whitelaw Reid at the *Tribune,* copies of his 1875 letters from Paris for inclusion in a book of travel essays. Despite his happiness at being at work once again, he felt burdened with "a multitude of . . . cares"; the amount of writing that he had committed himself to now seemed formidable, and family affairs still weighed him down. Wilky was soon laid up with "a violent and terribly painful attack of rheumatism." Henry gently, assiduously nursed him. Though Alice was somewhat better, she remained at the Adams Nervine Asylum in July; there had been "no miraculous 'cure.' " When Wilky returned to Milwaukee, Henry had the Mount Vernon Street house to himself. "I . . . wear no clothes, take 10 big baths a day, & dine on lemondade and ice." Since the house seemed lonely, he was happy to have Bob join him. In June, he turned down an invitation from Annie Fields for a country visit. "I have covenanted to write two (2) books, & I must sit here & write them. In lovelier circumstances I hate my ink stand."[54]

But he soon got away, first to Mount Desert, Maine, and Bar Harbor, for three days in late July, then to his beloved Newport, "the same Newport with a good deal more added. I don't like the additions," he told Grace Norton. But the air was bright, light, cool. Godkin was there. "Newport is always Newport, & the dead past lives again," he confided to Tom Perry—"just a little"—in the interstices of its modern

excrescences, though "lost, forever . . . to the truly romantic soul."
He took "a lovely walk on the cliffs, cocknified & terribly tame now."
When he dined with "Belmonts, Lorillards, Vanderbilts," he did not
enjoy the company. Before going to Maine, he had escaped the Boston
heat with a few days at Beverly, near the Adamses' summer home.
Clover Adams told Elizabeth Cameron that "he inquired tenderly for
you." By early August 1883, he began to feel a frenzied impatience for
departure "at any cost." He said good-bye to Alice, who had come to
town from Beverly to spend his last few days with him. She seemed
better. At the middle of the month, he went to New York, where he
said good-bye to Godkin and visited Aunt Kate overnight at the Dela-
ware Water Gap. "I can't say good-bye," he wrote to Grace Norton;
"I can only say god bless you."[55] As he sailed out of New York Harbor,
he might have seen the newly completed towers of the highest structure
in the Western Hemisphere, the Brooklyn Bridge, from whose observation platforms the views went on forever. It towered over the next
highest building in New York, Trinity Church, the elegant church
of James's pre–Civil War childhood. When he was next to return,
skyscrapers would dominate the vista and the great towers of the
Brooklyn Bridge could hardly be seen.

Nine

"THE GREAT MONEY-QUESTION"

1883–1888

(1)

Relieved to be at home again on Bolton Street, he had no doubt that London in 1883 was the best place in which to experience his home-lessness. As an American in England, he could out-English the English without being English at all. As an artist, at what seemed to him the center of philistinism in the most anti-intellectual culture imaginable, he felt that he had hardly anyone to talk to about what mattered to him most. But he had no doubt that London was the best place for him to be, precisely because it provided more fullness, more drama, more concentration of life, than anyplace else. Its pulsating ugliness, massive variety, abysmal extremes of wealth and poverty, raw power, and utter impotence seemed emblematic of modern urban culture—it was the one international city that made every other city seem provincial. As a voluntary exile from his native country, he continued to be sensitive to charges of betrayal and deracination. The Rough-Rider-to-be found him a handy target. "What was Roosevelt's allusion to, or attack upon, me, in his speech?" he asked Grace Norton, a year after his return to England. "I have heard nothing, & know nothing of it. I never look at the American papers."[1] The American papers, though, kept a regular, possessive eye on him, and he read them more than he sometimes admitted.

Having returned with no question in his mind that he would stay, he decided that at forty years of age he deserved something more substantial than his rented rooms on Bolton Street. He thought he would like a house or a large flat where he could entertain comfortably, where he could provide for himself amenities that a life in furnished lodgings did not permit. Getting his desk in order, he saw more people he knew in a quiet London September than he would have seen in years of Boston. Visiting the Clarks at Tillypronie at the beginning of October 1883, he felt "reduced to weakness by the most rheumatic and repulsive Scotch weather. . . . I returned from America five weeks ago," he told Henrietta Reubell, "& have shaken down very comfortably into the little hole I have made myself here." His irony expressed his awareness that even big holes like London are little holes for an individual life. But he needed a hole someplace, and this one seemed better than the available alternatives. After looking at a house in St. John's Wood, he decided that it was "too far from the centre of things and it was revealed to me in a dream that I should spend half the time on the roads. . . . Sooner or later, I suppose, I shall take a house, but there is no hurry." With a "sudden sense of being very well off" where he was and with a great deal of work to do, he feared as much as he desired domestic stability. "A conjugal Mrs. H. is not among the articles of furniture that I shall put into it." Within the three months since his return, he complained, twenty people had spoken to him "about renouncing" his "happy state," all except three or four having urged marriage. The three or four had wisely counseled, " 'Don't—don't—for heaven's sake!' and I never shall . . . for I find life quite interesting enough as it is without such complicated and complicating appendages." Anyway, society should appreciate the "useful, beneficent, and civilizing" value of an "unmarried man of a certain age. He keeps up the tone of humanity."[2]

He had no desire to share bed, board, and limited income with a domestic partner. "I shall never marry; I regard that now as an established fact. . . . I am both happy enough and miserable enough, as it is, and don't wish to add to either side of the account." With perhaps a veiled reference to his sexual preference, which, for him, at this time, meant an absence of overt sexual activity, he made it clear that "singleness consorts much better with my whole view of existence," including his "absence of desire to have children." He soon remarked, in response to learning of a painful accident that had befallen the son of a friend, "poor boy—and poor woman! I wouldn't be a mother! That's one of the reasons I have never married—because if I had I should have been." He assured Grace Norton, who worried that he might be depressed and lonely, "No, my dear Grace, you must never worry about me. . . . I am very well, very busy, very much in London, & quite cheerful enough. . . . Don't think of me as troubled, depressed or worried. I am steadily learning not to be at all."[3] He had become an autodidact of the emotions, able to apply his own resources of control and sublimation to his life as well as his art. Such accomplishments had to depend on personal resources, a process of self-teaching, a conciliatory dialogue among various aspects of himself.

Two immediate concerns weighed on his spirits—his depleted bank account and his awareness that Wilky was dying. About the first he could do little except to work as assiduously as possible on short stories and articles. Having contracted to write three stories for *The Century,* he struggled against his tendency to create beginnings that necessitated more length than the stories could bear. Aware that he made his material too thick because of his initial fear that it would be too thin, he rationalized that "as one grows older, and sees and learns more, it becomes harder to squeeze this enlarged matter into brevity of form." Inseparable from the problem of art was the "the great money-question." When, in January 1884, he got his end-of-the-year royalty statement from Macmillan, his heart sank. Though he had expected that only a small amount would be due him, he had not imagined it could be so little as just a bit over two pounds "for a year's sale of some seven or eight books."[4] For the time being, he was living on a diminishing bank account and on small sums from stories and articles, with serial income from the unwritten *Bostonians* still in the future.

Late in 1883, thirty-eight-year-old Wilky died. At the end of September, William had made a quick visit to Milwaukee and reported that "he still has a good deal of strength and flesh, and *may,* poor fellow, last weeks or even months. . . . He is excitable and nervous as he never was before—not as apprehensive of dying, but about every passing thing—and his mind is weak and flighty." In mid-November 1883, to the relief of his weary family, Wilky finally died—"such a slow, laborious, inch-by-inch extinction." Henry felt "great regret at not having seen him more toward the last." But "I can't help being glad I was spared all that closing spectacle. . . . I thank heaven it is over, and that he has become simply a genial, gentle, sociable memory, carrying me back to all sorts of innocent rose-coloured incidents in the far past." In the darkening last months of 1883, he painfully remembered his chubby, happy, sociable younger brother in the days before war and wounds, when the future seemed filled with possibility. He wanted Wilky to be buried in Cambridge, "beside Father and Mother. . . . As I must always worry about something," he told William, "I worry now . . . about his burial-place. It would be a great regret to me if he doesn't lie . . . where we must all lie." He was disappointed in his hope.[5] Wilky was buried in Milwaukee.

Despite a clear, bright early winter in London, he was restless enough soon after New Year's Day 1884 to decide to go to Paris for two weeks. He had not finished as much work as he had intended, though he did not blame social diversions. In fact, he had been having what seemed to him a quiet winter. His most regular diversion was an evening a week with Fanny Kemble. He frequently saw Constance Woolson, who had moved, in October 1883, to London, to a flat in Kensington, at least partly in the hope that James would be a regular companion. He told Howells that they saw one another "at discreet intervals." In January, he attended a large handsome dinner hosted by the Lowells. One evening, he was entertained at a midnight supper at the home of his "hospitable (if not otherwise remunerative) publisher," Frederick Macmillan, in St. John's Wood. Afterward, at two-thirty in the morning, he "walked home though the sleeping town." The problem, he felt, was "simply the native spite of time against those who are growing old. . . . The way it *melts* out of one's fingers is only an item of my constant consciousness of today being already tomorrow and tomorrow next month, while work, and plans and fruits of every kind are halting behind in the unrecoverable regions of yesterday."[6] That he had not yet begun *The Bostonians* worried him. Perhaps he could make better headway in Paris. By juggling, he could manage his expenses. He stayed there through February, most days working in his hotel room till midafternoon; being companionable with Henrietta Reubell and Theodore Child in the evenings; meeting a twenty-eight-year-old, American-born, European-raised painter of great talent, John Singer Sargent; renewing his contacts with the heirs of Flaubert, particularly Alphonse Daudet, the Goncourt brothers, and the puzzling, irrepressible, increasingly formidable Émile Zola.

An absent writer was most on his mind, and deeply missed: the gentle, tall, distinguished, silver-haired Turgenev whom he had last seen in November 1884. "He had been very ill, with strange, intolerable symptoms, but he was better, and he had good hopes." James had visited him at his suburban château at Bougival, on the Seine, near the Viardots. His spirits were up, his conversation as warm and vivid as ever. At the end of a few hours, Turgenev, who had to return to Paris, offered James a seat next to him in his carriage, and they drove together back into the city. "For an hour and a half he constantly talked, and never better. . . . I alighted on the boulevard extérieur, as we were to go in different directions. I bade him good-bye at the carriage window, and never saw him again. There was a kind of fair near by, in the chill November air, beneath the denuded little trees of the Boulevard, and a Punch and Judy show, from which nasal sounds proceeded." The next year Turgenev died. To memorialize his death, James published in the January 1884 *Atlantic* a substantial personal article on his friend's life and art. Turgenev's characteristic sadness now merged into the melancholy James felt, remembering how good Turgenev had been to him, how strong he had seemed in bearing, in spirit, in wisdom, in his art and in his ideals. "He was the most generous, the most tender, the most delightful, of men; his large nature overflowed with the love of justice; but he also was of the stuff of which glories are made." Now, in February 1884, Paris was vivid with memories of Turgenev, with the ghost of his greatly missed presence, on the streets they had strolled together, in the cafés where he had waited vainly for Turgenev to come, where on other days he had sat for hours talking with his distinguished friend. He saw Princess Ourousov again, who provided news of Turgenev's other Russian friends—his fellow exiles in Paris—and who upset him with her report that Madame Viardot now complained that Turgenev had been a drain on her family and had impoverished them.[7] The real impoverishment was his own. He missed Turgenev greatly.

Although he found Paris fascinating, as always, he still unequivocally preferred to live in London. He urged "the gifted Sargent . . . who is a remarkably artistic nature & charming fellow," to come to London, if not permanently, then for a long visit. Still, artistic and intellectual life in Paris had more vivacity, more edge, more unrestrained sharpness and experimental boldness. Sitting in his hotel room on the Rue de la Paix, he read "a great deal of 'naturalism.' The distance from Paris to London is surely not hundreds but hundreds of thousands of miles." After spending an evening with Daudet and a morning with Edmond Goncourt, he felt that "their intellectual vivacity . . . make an English mind seem like a sort of glue-pot." He particularly warmed to Daudet, "who has a remarkable personal charm & is as beautiful as the day." When he visited Zola, he was greeted as an old, esteemed friend. What impressed him most about these writers was their seriousness, their dedication to the novel as a literary form. The novel was for them something to talk about, theorize about, and work at with an energy and commitment that made it clear that absolute values were at stake, that art and life had been totally committed to the effort. He did not find in anyone in England such commitment. That these French writers seemed to him unhealthily pessimistic and that they had no limitations in regard to subject matter had less importance to him than their respect for the seriousness of their art. Though "they are the children of a decadence," he told William, they "represent a great deal of truth."[8] Their energy, boldness, and dedication to the imagination outweighed everything else. They were serious. They were interesting.

James had given Daudet special incentive to act the gracious, engaged host by publishing in *The Century* the previous August a laudatory article on the French novelist. He had no doubt that "the main object of the novel is to represent life. . . . The success of a work of art . . . may be measured by the degree to which it produces a certain illusion; that illusion makes it appear to us for the time that we have lived another life—that we have had a miraculous enlargement of experience." Different as they were as writers, he felt a sense of artistic and aesthetic consanguinity. Though not a naturalist, he had stressed in his notebook, while brooding about his artistic principles in Boston the previous year, that "actuality must be my line at present. I may work it with infinite profit." Zola, though, still remained the test case; he pushed his art to the edge of James's moral limitations. James found much to praise in this "man of genius." Still, James's personality, his background, his values, forced him to hold Zola between his fingertips, at a slight distance, as if the latrinal odors could be sniffed but not fully smelled without a principled swoon or at least a gentlemanly distaste. The distance at which he kept him, though, was smaller than ever before. When Zola succeeded most as artist, James succeeded most as appreciative, even admiring reader. When Zola succeeded least, James's moral objections were strongest. He read Zola's every word, more alert to questions of art than of moral fastidiousness. "What is being done in France affects me in all kinds of different ways," he told Tom Perry. "At times I am tired to death of it. Perfection, dirt, ignorance are all mixed up together. . . . It's a filthy world."[9] But he recognized its value and importance.

Returning to London at the beginning of March 1884, he granted that though he raged in his "hours of irritation & disgust . . . against British density," and though his "glimpse of the intellectual life of some of the men" he had seen in Paris renewed his "sense of the Philistinism of this *milieu* & the degree to which an 'artist' is alone in it," he was contented with his lot. He tried to make himself and London better off by entertaining Sargent so hospitably and showing off London so well that the young painter would decide to join him there. At the end of March, on whirlwind days of "superabundant activity," he took Sargent to the museums, to ten artists' studios, including John Millais' and Frederick Leighton's, and to a dinner at the Reform Club, to which he had invited six guests, among them Burne-Jones. "I have been giving him a push to the best of my ability," he told Grace Norton. He thought Sargent charming, handsome, personally naive but artistically sophisticated, with "a certain *excess* of cleverness: too much chic and not enough naivete." His notorious portrait of Madame Gautreau at the Paris Salon that year James "only half liked. . . . I saw it in his studio in the winter . . . a so-called French beauty (*femme du monde*) half-stripped and covered with paint—blue, green, white, black."[10] Specializing in portraits—a genre James respected—Sargent seemed, however, to have his professional eye too cleverly pitched to the level of remunerative mirror rather than independent artistic vision. Still, James thought some of his portraits of 1884 masterpieces. If only Sargent would paint a real picture.

At Millais' and Leighton's studios, he was "impressed, as usual, with the gorgeous effect of worldly prosperity & success that both of these gentleman present. I suppose it is the demon of envy—but I can't help contrasting the great rewards of the successful painter, here . . . with the so much more modest emoluments of the man of letters."[11] Leighton had risen to a condition to which James aspired. An immensely successful painter whom he personally liked but whose work seemed to him "brilliantly superficial," the urbane, agreeable Leighton dominated the public image of the successful artist. As a human being, he was not available. As an artist, he was everywhere. At his death in 1896, James remarked that "I had never known a man so long & so little. But I much admired him; he was very fine." He was also very rich.

How James could himself be financially successful enough as an artist to practice his art in leisure was much on his mind, though his envy of artists like Leighton did not prevent him from pushing Sargent as hard as he could. He especially praised what he thought a wonderful portrait of Mrs. Henry White, the pretty wife of a young American diplomat, that Sargent had sent to the academy show. Disappointed at the harsh reception of another Sargent painting, he felt left "to the consolations" of his "personal enthusiasm. I have, à propos not only of this, but many other things, the most luxurious moments (private) of *diatribe* against the deep-seated Philistinism, the helpless bourgeois density of the English in matters of artistic taste & perception-production. The whole form of art is so smothered up here in humbugging paraphernalia that the wonder [is] it keeps alive at all. . . . I am sometimes overwhelmed by the hypocrisy & pharisaism of English life." Sargent's art had a future, perhaps limited by its cleverness, but, still, "he is more intelligent about artistic things," he told Lizzie Boott, "than all the painters here rolled together." Pleased that he "had been able to make things pleasant and easy for him" during his three-week visit in March 1884, James continued his efforts, when Sargent returned in June, arranging a visiting membership for him at the Savile Club. "I saw and shall probably see again a great deal of him. . . . I want him to come here to live and work."[12] Sargent had reservations, fears. James helped him overcome them. Two years later, the young painter moved to London.

So too did Alice. When Henry departed from America in August 1883, she knew she would miss his gentle companionship. But she had no desire to leave Boston, where her pain was mitigated by familiar routines, places, and people, including William, whose wife had recently given birth to a second son. "I am sorry that he has chosen the inferior sex," Alice commented, "though I suppose it is less on one's conscience to have brought forth an oppressor . . . than one of the oppressed." Traveling abroad seemed beyond her strength. Leaving Katherine Loring seemed inconceivable. Unhappily, Katherine had other obligations, particularly her chronically ill sister Louisa. As much time as they spent together, Alice and Katherine kept separate residences, and Katherine, a partly separate life. "Boston surpasses itself, you know," Alice reassured herself, "when trouble comes." Trouble had come with Katherine's departure, with her sister and father, for England. The European cure had been prescribed for Louisa's tubercular condition. When, in February 1884, the Lorings sailed, it at first seemed as if their departure operated upon Alice "as a sort of stimulus, as her mother's death did." Aunt Kate hoped that there would "not be a proportionate re-action." Apparently, there was. Continuing her search for medical relief, she made a long stay in spring 1884 with a New York doctor. She hated New York. She was "beginning to sympathize with the lady who died and found Heaven delightful 'only it was *not* Boston.' "[13] Still, she found that "electricity . . . has the starching properties of the longest Puritan descent." She felt at least better enough to risk traveling. In America, she had no chance of seeing Katherine. With Louisa settled for the winter in Bournemouth, seventy-five miles southwest of London, Katherine returned to Boston in September 1884 to assist Alice in packing. Having fantasized for so long about how wonderful it would be to live in England, England now, at a time when she would have preferred to stay in America, became the necessary place to be.

Reassuring himself that Alice's independent spirit would not permit impingement on his own freedom, hoping that six months of Europe would make her a well person, Henry went to Liverpool toward the middle of November 1884, with a nurse he had hired, to meet the arriving Americans. Rising early, he embraced the exhausted Alice at seven-thirty in the morning on shipboard. Weeks before, he had assured Grace Norton that he was not "alarmed by Alice's now impending advent. I *may* be wrong, and it *may* wreck and blight my existence, but it will have to exert itself tremendously to do so." But, as he saw that it was necessary to have her carried off the ship and to their hotel, he was shaken by the extent to which her independent spirit was enclosed in a dependent body. Though Katherine was the first line of support, she could not be with Alice all the time. Behind Katherine, there was only himself. Having left Boston ill, she had become more ill at sea, "& had . . . a rather 'tragic' time." He could count, he felt, to a great extent on "the more-devoted-than-ever Katherine Loring . . . whose mixture of seasickness & self-sacrifice on the ship" Alice described "as heroic." But as much as he tried to be optimistic, the dangers were great. "Alice is not, for the present, really well enough to go to London; not well enough to be in lodgings alone, & can't be with me, as I have no room for her maid—nor does my little establishment contain the resources. . . . Therefore . . . after she has rested two or three days here, I shall take her . . . to Bournemouth, where very good accommodation is promised her at the house . . . where Laura L. is." It was, he told Aunt Kate, "a rather dark picture," for himself as well as for Alice. Liverpool got on his nerves. "At the end of four days in this place I feel completely out of the world."[14] He feared that it was prescient of limitations to come.

Though the Cambridge family did not allow him the distance he struggled so assiduously to maintain, at least Alice represented home in its least virulent form. He had a relationship with her that provided him with compensations that he appreciated. With Wilky dead, William and Henry divided the remaining family caretaking. William had great patience for his youngest brother, and he looked after Bob in Boston; Henry, though he could not yet realize the length and extent of his responsibility, looked after Alice in England. She compensated him with her wit, her intelligence, her conversation, which he came to think of as the best available. He felt the moral impact of her courage under adversity, and took pleasure in fulfilling his fraternal responsibility. He soon had no choice but to admit that his "forecast of the consequences of her coming out here have been completely falsified. . . . She will certainly not return to America for an indefinite period."[15] She was to remain in England for the rest of her life. During the next eight years, with and without Katherine Loring, Henry was to be her practical support and empathetic visitor during her variable illnesses; her occasional improvements; her regular relapses; her crises of nerves; her hopes and disappointments with doctors; her alert, sometimes brilliant, always partisan criticism of the British and her passionate advocacy of Home Rule for the Irish; her seasonal movements between London and the country, particularly Bournemouth at first, then Leamington. When he greeted Alice at Liverpool in November 1884, she was a responsibility he had hoped would be light, perhaps even one that he could escape. Eight years later, he was with her, in London, by her deathbed, as he had been with her and available to her, as she desired, always.

(2)

Struggling with *The Bostonians* in the summer of 1884, he felt "oppressed and depressed by the sense of being behindhand with the novel." In fact, he had not even started it yet. If only he could be free of engagements, he would have the pleasure of being immersed in work again. "Then I shall possess my soul, my faculties, my imagination . . . then I shall feel that life is worth living. . . . A *mighty* will, there is nothing but that! The integrity of one's will, purpose, faith. To wait, when one *must* wait, and act when one can act!"[16] He could not afford to wait much longer. Financial necessity pressed hard, so hard that, despite the lack of progress on the novel at issue, he proposed a new novel to be written immediately after *The Bostonians*. High confidence allowed the new proposal, but it was a confidence and schedule sharply tested by his initial difficulty and then his ongoing misjudgment of the length of *The Bostonians*.

His patience was also tested by the consequences of his responsibility to Alice. From rented rooms near his own on Bolton Street, which she had not left for nine weeks, she finally went, in January 1885, to Bournemouth, where Katherine and a hired nurse had charge of her. Ironically, when Louisa Loring's health improved, Switzerland was prescribed. Katherine could not be in two places at once. What he had feared became a necessity. In April, he moved to Bournemouth, taking rooms near Alice's. "I came down here . . . to remain with her indefinitely." She "is *very* ill & weak, & there can be, for the next 4 months, no question of moving her! Her spine is in a most delicate & critical condition. . . . There is for the present nothing to do but wait from week to week. The next couple of months will probably determine whether she has a *possibility* of recuperation, or whether her future decline is to be rapid, certain & fatal. . . . My situation here will not be very gay, as you can imagine; but it might be much worse, the long days are coming on, & the place has a considerable charm."[17]

The most considerable charm of Bournemouth was Robert Louis Stevenson, seven years younger than James, and already well known for his travel essays and his novel *Treasure Island*. In July 1884, his wife and anxious parents had moved his feeble, tubercular body to a small picturesque house in Bournemouth. Thin, small, dark-haired, dark-mustached, with a brave, witty sense of humor, Stevenson was a writer and a spirit James admired, one of the only writers other than himself who seemed to care about writing. "You will find him a young, unique, dishevelled, undressed, loveable young fellow," he told Owen Wister a few years later. "There is a fresh, youthful complacent Scotch mother, a poor sightless (or almost so) American stepson, & a strange California wife, 15 years older than Louis himself, but almost as interesting. If you like the gulch & the canyon you will like *her*." His prose style seemed to James crystalline, flexible, pure, a seriously conceived and crafted vehicle for literary art. In December 1884, Stevenson wrote an essay-letter to *Longman's Magazine* to add his voice on James's behalf to a brief dialogue on "The Art of Fiction" between James and a minor novelist, Walter Besant, whose pamphlet had prompted James's essay. James was grateful. The two writers had already met briefly in 1879, when James had thought him a pleasant but affected bohemian. Now he felt that Stevenson's style "floats pearls and diamonds." His "native *gaiety*" delighted James. "When I reflect," he told Stevenson, "that it proceeds from a man whom life has laid much of the time on his back . . . I find you a genius indeed." The multigenerational ménage in their house high on the west cliff, overlooking the sea, welcomed James. A comfortable chair that had once been Stevenson's grandfather's they renamed "Henry James's Chair," both to honor and to encourage his frequent visits. "I have a great resource, for the evening," he told William, "in the presence here of Robert Louis Stevenson, who is an old acquaintance of mine, ripening now into a friend. . . . His face, his talk, his nature . . . are delightful, & I go to see him every night. He looks like, & reminds me a little of, Shelley—& Tasso!"[18]

Feeling isolated in a pragmatic culture, he now had someone with whom to discuss the art of the novel. The English think "a novel is a novel, as a pudding is a pudding, and that our only business with it could be to swallow it." But art, he believed, "lives upon discussion, upon experiment, upon curiosity, upon variety of attempt, upon the exchange of views and the comparison of standpoints. . . . The only obligation to which in advance we may hold a novel, without incurring the accusation of being arbitrary, is that it be interesting." For a novel, he argued, is "in its broadest definition . . . a direct impression of life; that, to begin with, constitutes its value, which is greater or less according to the intensity of the impression. But there will be no intensity at all, and therefore no value, unless there is freedom to feel and say." For "the province of art is . . . all experience. That is a sufficient answer to those who maintain that it must not touch the bad things of life, who stick into its divine unconscious bosom little prohibitory inscriptions on the end of sticks, such as we see in public gardens—'It is forbidden to walk on the grass; it is forbidden to touch the flowers; it is forbidden.' " Nothing is forbidden for the writer, though "no good novel will ever proceed from a superficial mind." That seemed to him "an axiom which, for the artist in fiction, will cover all needful moral ground." The reader is free to like or dislike, to read or not to read, as a matter of individual taste. But experience itself "is never limited, and it is never complete; it is an immense sensibility, a kind of huge spider-web of the finest silken threads suspended in the chamber of consciousness and catching every air-borne particle in its tissue. It is the very atmosphere of the mind; and when the mind is imaginative—much more when it happens to be that of a man of genius—it takes to itself the faintest hints of life, it converts the very pulses of the air into revelations."[19]

Though Stevenson's mind was less sinuous, his interest in theory less intense, he nevertheless both practiced and thought about the art of fiction with an imaginative verve and a liberal spaciousness that James admired. With a keen appreciation of the psychological novel, he had, like James, no narrow definition of fiction to promote. James admired his optimism—"an observer who not only loves life but does not shrink from the responsibility of recommending it"—and his breadth. "The incomparable virtue of the form he uses is that it lends itself to views innumerable and diverse, to every variety of illustration." Even Stevenson's fascination with adolescence James found part of his charm; it was an obsession that had as much creative potential as any other. Also, it was aesthetically and psychologically reminiscent of James's own renunciation of certain aspects of adult life. For "the idea of making believe appeals to him much more than the idea of making love. . . . Why should a person marry when he might be swinging a cutlass or looking for a buried treasure? Why should he waste at the nuptial altar precious hours in which he might be polishing periods?" Though James appreciated Stevenson's remark that marriage "is a field of battle and not a bed of roses," he also felt the personal force of his friend's declaration that "to Marry is to domesticate the Recording Angel. Once you have married, there is nothing left for you, not even suicide, but to be good."[20]

His friendship with Stevenson, which began in spring 1885, unfortunately never again had the advantage of their being neighbors, except for a short period the next year. James visited him at Bournemouth occasionally in 1886 and 1887. He was concerned about Stevenson's restlessness and bad health, both of which prompted Stevenson to leave

England forever in the summer of 1887. To James, he later became, somewhat comically, somewhat sadly, "the male Cleopatra or buccaneering Pompadour of the Deep—the wandering Wanton of the Pacific."[21] Though they corresponded until Stevenson's death, it was with a sense, for James, of his friend receding, despite occasional letters, into places as unreal as the South Sea island that became his home.

In May 1885, James had the happy news that Louisa Loring's health had improved so substantially that Katherine felt free to return to Alice in Bournemouth. To her brother, it seemed the beginning of "their living together for the rest of such time as Alice's life may last," a "definite understanding between them. . . . We must accept it with gratitude," he told Aunt Kate, whose offer to come to England to nurse her, Alice had declined. "One may think that her being with A. is not in the long run the best thing for A.; but the latter is *too ill* to make the long run the main thing to think about. There *may* be no 'long run' at all; & if there is, a *long* period with K. will work better than a *short* one. . . . A devotion as perfect & so generous as K.L.'s is a gift of providence so rare & little-to-be-looked for in this hard world that to brush it aside would be almost an act of impiety. Not to take it would be to get something much worse. If you could say to Alice—'K.L. isn't good for you: give her up, on trial, for a couple of years,' & *offer her an equivalent* the case wd. be simplified. But one can't. *I* am no equivalent & can't attempt to be! . . . She will get well, or she won't, but, either way, it is between themselves. I shall devote my whole energies to taking the whole situation less hard in the future than I have done hitherto." If Katherine could stay with Alice with sufficient continuity to make it a completely reliable alternative, he would "assent with a good grace. . . . It is the only thing I can do unless I take Alice completely on my own shoulders—which is obviously impossible, from every point of view." If Aunt Kate were to come, Henry sharply remarked, Alice "would then have *five* people under contribution to take care of her, & she has quite enough now."[22]

Comfortable in Bournemouth, away from the demands of the London season, pleased with Stevenson's company, he remained until July 1885. After a short stay in London, he went to Dover, "a favorite & very convenient resort" where he had stayed the previous summer, "for obscurity & a silence in which I may hear the scratching of my pen." He wanted a change from Bournemouth. London was simply too hot, too sociable. Before leaving London, he visited Mrs. Humphry Ward, with whom he had become friendly. He read her novels with bemusement at the phenomenon that she had become and with a keen but gracious sense of how they might be improved. Mary Ward eagerly

read his criticism, though it had no effect on her practice. As he sat
with her, she later recalled, "the western sun was beating on the drawing-room windows, though the room within was comparatively dark
and cool. The children were languid with the heat, and the youngest,
Janet, then five, stole into the drawing-room and stood looking at Mr.
James. He put out a half-conscious hand to her; she came nearer, while
we talked on. Presently she climbed on his knee. I suppose I made a
maternal protest. He took no notice, and folded his arm around her.
We talked on; and presently the abnormal stillness of Janet recalled her
to me and made me look closely through the dark of the room. She
was fast asleep, her pale little face on the young man's shoulder, her
long hair streaming over his arm."

At Dover, in July 1885, his window open, he sat for long hours at
his writing desk, completing *The Bostonians,* thinking about the new
novel he had agreed to write, watching high white sails racing in the
cool breezes on the channel. With Katherine coming, he thought he
would go to Paris in September. Italy tempted him. But Katherine was
not to be counted on indefinitely. He could not, he felt, go too far.
Money was also a problem. "If I had only myself to consider I should
this year go abroad for a long period—giving up my rooms in London
& leaving myself free to remain 2 years." The previous summer, while
he had struggled to begin writing *The Bostonians,* William, in Cambridge, had also begun to struggle with the subject of "father's ideas."
Both of Henry senior's elder sons had been preoccupied with his intellectual and emotional legacy since his death. They needed to put to rest
the problems that their father's life had imposed on them. For William,
the vehicle was a direct, for Henry an indirect, act of filial piety. With
his family in a Connecticut vacation cottage, William returned to Cambridge in August 1884 "to find quiet and leisure" to compile an anthology of his father's writings, a project that had been much on his mind
since Henry senior's death. "I seemed to sink into an intimacy with
Father, which I had never before enjoyed. I trust he takes cognizance
of it, somewhere." With his father's books on hand, he composed a
long introduction to the anthology to explain or at least make intelligible
Henry senior's ideas. It was, he admitted to his readers, a difficult task.
Years later, Charles Eliot Norton reported a remark of Howells' in
regard to a recently published book by William, which was "brilliant
but not clear." "Like his father," Howells said, "who wrote the Secret
of Swedenborg and kept it." William did not succeed in making his
father's or Swedenborg's secrets any clearer. With a typical Jamesian
response, after finishing the volume, he immediately became ill, collapsing into bed with a high fever. Just as there had been no publisher

willing to support Henry senior's books while he was alive, so, too, the publication of *The Literary Remains of Henry James* had to be paid for privately, appropriately with some of the money from the shrunken Syracuse investments.[23]

When Henry received a large packet of copies in January 1885, sadly, "rather embarrassed," he had to admit that he could not imagine any of the British newspapers consenting to review it. He was even at a loss about whom to send free personal copies, other than five or six names that came to mind. Out of the depths of his disaffiliation from his father's religious ideas, he sympathetically remarked to William that "it must have been very difficult to do." He appreciatively read William's introduction but put off reading the selections, though he had long thought that his father's major saving grace was his brilliance as a writer. His ideas "I can't enter into . . . much myself—I can't be so theological nor grant his extraordinary premises, nor throw myself into conceptions of heavens and hells. . . . But I can enjoy greatly the spirit, the feeling and the manner of the whole thing . . . and feel really that poor Father, struggling so alone all his life, and so destitute of every worldly or literary ambition, was yet a great writer." When he put a copy into Alice's hands, she burst into tears. "How beautiful it is that William should have done it! isn't it, isn't it beautiful? And how good William is, how good, how good!" In America, *The Nation* reviewed it harshly. The Jameses felt Godkin, their father's old friend, had betrayed them. Though almost as hurt as William, Henry explained to his brother that *The Nation* prided itself on separating review assignments from personal considerations, though applying their policy "stupidly & unsocially."[24] Ironically, Henry was severely criticized in America, by, among many others, William, when one of the characters in his own tribute to his father seemed to be a parodic portrait of Elizabeth Peabody.

Beginning with its publication in February 1885, two months after the publication of Henry senior's *Literary Remains,* the thirteen installments of *The Bostonians* gave him more pain than pleasure. The Peabody scandal upset him, but less than Osgood's financial difficulties and the novel's failure. From the beginning, James did not allow himself to confront the likelihood that Henry senior's social ideas would be as uncongenial to modern readers as his religious beliefs. They were difficult to dramatize effectively, especially within the six-installment length that he had initially set for himself. In the end, James wrote a novel more than twice as long as he had intended. He had much more characterization than incident, psychology than action, but also, as he confessed to William, he felt too insecure in his grasp of the social issues and the milieu to write concisely. "All the middle part is too diffuse and insistent—far too describing and explaining and expatiating. The whole thing is too long & dawdling. . . . I had the sense of knowing terribly little about the kind of life I had attempted to describe—and felt a constant pressure to make the picture substantial by thinking it out." From the beginning, he had determined that "the whole thing" should be "as American as possible, and as full of Boston: an attempt to show that I *can* write an American story." He "wished to write a very *American* tale, a tale very characteristic of our social conditions, and I asked myself what was the most salient and peculiar point in our social life. The answer was: the situation of women, the decline of the sentiment of sex, the agitation on their behalf." But it was to be, he told Tom Perry, "a remorseless exploitation of Boston. Look out, in Marlborough St; I am especially hard on the far end."[25]

As he cleared his desk to begin *The Bostonians* in the summer of 1884, he had a sense of having at hand strong materials both for this novel and for the next, *The Princess Casamassima*. *The Bostonians* "is to mark a new era in my career," he boasted to Grace Norton, "and usher in a series of works of superior value to any I have yet produced." In August, having finally escaped the social season, he found himself trying to outstare a seemingly implacable blank page, with a "solemn contract to write 2 novels, of which the date of serial publication . . . stares me in the face, & yet no word of which has yet been put to paper!" At the end of the month, in Dover, he was under way, working, he told Macmillan, "very diligently." With something on paper, his optimism returned. "It is a better subject than I have ever had before, & I think will be much the best thing I have done yet. It is called *The Bostonians*. I shall be much abused for the title but it exactly & literally fits the story, & is much the best, simplest & most dignified I could have chosen." Within a year, the six installments having stretched to thirteen, he was to think of it as "the unhappy *Bostonians,* born under an evil star." Actually, it was born under a peculiarly Jamesian constellation. In the three most effectively presented settings of the novel, James invokes the Back Bay of Boston in winter, the Cambridge of Quincy Street and Harvard Square, and the Manhattan of the year he had lived there in 1874–1875. In the minor characters and the ambiance of the women's movement, he drew upon peripheral members of his parents' Boston world, particularly Elizabeth Peabody, with resonances of the world of the pre–Civil War transcendentalists, of Emerson and Margaret Fuller. For the depiction of the Olive Chancellor–Verena Tarrant relationship, he drew distantly on the emerging commitment between Katherine and Alice, "a study of one of those friendships between women which are so common in New England."[26] As Alice desired and needed Katherine, Olive desires and needs Verena. In the Chancellor-Tarrant relationship, ideology and sexuality combine, particularly for Chancellor, into a possessiveness so great, so emotionally strong, that the social, the ideological, and the sexual become inseparable.

In a novel in which the secondary characters, particularly Mrs. Luna, Miss Birdseye, and Dr. Prance, are more vivid than the major characters, it is not surprising that one of the minor characters, Dr. Prance, carries the weight of James's theme that people, including women, do better for the society and for themselves by a dedicated, disciplined application of useful skills and talents than by immersing themselves in politics. It is a definition of women, with his mother and Aunt Kate as models, as supportive, nurturing, loving; such women are not able to be socially, professionally, or personally independent, except at great cost. But if personal independence is determined by the interaction between personality and social structure, if a woman is not to marry, then the road of Dr. Prance is one of the roads worth taking. In Basil Ransom, "the stiffest of conservatives," he creates a character who, in physical characteristics, differs completely from his father but whose ideas embody Henry senior's views of the proper relationship between men and women. Under the guise of religious idiosyncrasy and social utopianism, Henry senior had advocated a supersacramental view of marriage. The place of women is in the household, their highest function as wives and mothers. Carlyle is Ransom's ideological model. In a deft ironic turn, James makes Ransom a noble southerner, an unreconstructed idealist, who embodies the social, secular extrapolations of Henry senior's religious ideas without himself having any religious or theological ideas at all. In his conflict with Olive for the body and soul of Verena, he is inevitably successful. James had read Mill, Ruskin, and Tennyson on the question of the role of women. He had also read Henry senior. He had experienced the atmosphere and learned the values that his father and mother espoused and embodied. Though he had already established a record, from *Watch and Ward* to *The Portrait of a Lady,* of his fascination with the subject, in *The Bostonians* he dramatizes it not only in personal but also in social terms. Henry senior, if he had been alive, would have warmly approved.

(3)

In early May 1885, having sent *The Century* all but the last of the thirteen installments of *The Bostonians,* he had the harsh shock of discovering, as he glanced through the American news in the London *Times,* that Osgood had declared bankruptcy. He had not yet received any money for the novel. He had had, though, the sense that something was wrong. In mid-April, estimating that the publisher owed him about a thousand dollars, he had complained that his letter of January requesting his semiannual royalty statement in regard to books already published had not been answered. "In heaven's name, then, please send me the yearly statement, without further postponement. . . . I am in pressing need of money." With *The Bostonians,* James had made an unusually disadvantageous arrangement. He had had nothing to gain by giving Osgood total control of American rights for five years. For that advantage, Osgood had not given him a sum of money greater than the total he would have gotten from being paid separately and directly by *The Century* for the serial rights, and by Osgood or any other American publisher for the book rights. Probably less.[27] Though he could not have foreseen that Osgood would declare bankruptcy just at a time when money was due him, still, he had intuitively felt some years before that he had been weak in dealing with Osgood and that the Boston publisher had not been fair, let alone forthcoming, in contractual arrangements. His agreement with Osgood for *The Bostonians* had come soon after his father's death, almost as if a novel that was to pay homage to his father's values should be published by someone who had been, for a long time, part of Henry senior's world. It was an act of confused filial piety for which he now feared that he would have to pay a heavy price.

Almost certain that he had lost "a largeish sum of money," he asked Frederick Macmillan's advice, querying him about his interest in the novel if he should regain control over British and even American rights. At first, it seemed that Osgood's creditors might allow him to continue in business. When they would not, it still seemed, as William argued, that Henry "will probably lose little, if anything, and will be only inconvenienced by delay," since Benjamin Ticknor, Osgood's successor, would most likely take on Osgood's obligations. If so, James wanted to renegotiate the contract and recapture British rights. "My original contract with your former firm," he told Ticknor, "was so insanely unprofitable for me that I must claim this relief now that that firm is broken up." After what seemed to him insufferable delays, Ticknor declined to agree to any change in the contract other than its cancellation, if that was what James wanted. James did. "Ticknor's cancellation," though, "has come, unfortunately, too late to be of the same service to me that it would 3 months ago—though I am still glad of it, as it restores me the copyright of the book. The merit of his cancelling 3 months ago was that it would have enabled me instantly to get a sum of money from Macmillan, of which I was much in need, instead of waiting—an indefinite time—for his, Ticknor's, $4000. Not to get the $4000 after I *have* waited so many weeks is a little provoking, for of course the money Macmillan has given me for the book alone is *not* $4000—the sum Osgood was to give me for the serial *and* the book. It is however considerable enough to be very welcome, & I shall have 15 percent on future sales in the 2 countries, instead of having nothing at all on either, from that source, or from Ticknor."[28]

In August 1885, he concluded an agreement with Macmillan, who was to have British and American rights for an advance of five hundred pounds or twenty-five hundred dollars and a 15 percent royalty to the author on all copies sold. Under the circumstances this was a reasonable resolution to a complicated, self-inflicted muddle. He could console himself with the claim that he had lost fifteen hundred dollars rather than the full four thousand. In fact, he had lost at least, at a conservative estimate, three thousand dollars more between the value of the extra installments, the value of the volume of short stories, and the British rights. Though he could not have been expected to foresee that *The Bostonians* would require thirteen rather than six installments, he had had the experience with *Portrait* of writing a longer book than he had initially intended. His unwise departure from his usual practice had stripped him of his protection. He had, as he admitted, given Osgood the benefit of seven extra installments absolutely free and then, in addition, had lost the money he would have received from the original six if he had had a separate contract with *The Century*.

When William and others congratulated him on his having come off well from what might have been a financial disaster, he irritably revealed his feelings about the whole matter. He resented what he felt to be other people's misapprehension of what he had lost. "What do you mean . . . by saying—'now that I am to lose nothing by Osgood!' I lose every penny . . . for the serial, for which he received a large sum from the *Century*." It put him defensively in mind of the fate of his father's books. *The Bostonians* had been a tribute to his father, and now it seemed to emulate his father's failures. "How can one murmur at one's success not being what one would like when one one thinks of the pathetic, tragic ineffectualness of poor Father's lifelong effort, and the silence and oblivion that seems to have swallowed it up." Not since the Peabody controversy of the first installments had there been any interesting response to the novel, adding critical to financial failure.[29]

He had a further shock when, in September 1885, he learned from Macmillan that Ticknor had agreed to give to the British publisher the

British rights to the novel "out and out forever. . . . I said to myself
'What in the world then becomes of that right reserved to me, of
reacquiring the book at the end of five years?' . . . Osgood had not the
right to dispose of the book indefinitely." The contract, he believed,
had given Osgood a five-year lease. After that, all rights should revert
to him. "My recollection is of Osgood making this point in the last talk
I had with him before I left America, and it is almost equally so of the
contract, which was sent to me in London afterwards. . . . As Ticknor
makes no mention of this—with the paper before his eyes—I can only
conclude that I am the victim of some strange *mis*recollection, or that
the clause in question refers only to the M.S." He *was*, for a moment, the
beneficiary "of some strange *mis*recollection." As soon as he returned to
London and examined the contract, he discovered that he was "only ½
right," which in this case was as good as his not being right at all. The
contract "contains the clause I remembered (the 4th) but it applies only
to the U.S.—& is preceded by another . . . for other countries" in
which he had signed away all foreign rights in perpetuity. "As to this
my memory was by no means clear, as it easily isn't about many
things." In law, Macmillan had British rights forever, though neither
he nor James, who now at least had a royalty interest in the sale of
each copy, benefited from it. The book sold badly. This was a sore
disappointment to a writer who had blessed a fellow author's latest with
the invocation that may "God speed the day when, the proper number
of copies triumphantly sold, the half sovereigns shall flow in with a
delicious monotony. My sordid imagination gloats upon the commercial picture."[30] He had only his imagination on which to fall back.
Macmillan did not even make back his five-hundred-pound advance.

That James felt a "pressing need of money," in early 1885, is not
surprising. His income had dropped almost by half from the approximately seventy-five hundred dollars he had earned each of the previous
two years. To compensate for what should have been only a temporary
decrease, he borrowed a thousand dollars from William, as he had
borrowed liberally from his father under similar circumstances. When
Osgood failed, he could not repay the money as quickly as he had
anticipated. He also postponed a trip to Italy, which he now felt he
could not afford. "The great money-question" was indeed a serious
one; he had grown used to a comfortable standard of living—which he
wanted to elevate by leasing a flat—and he had begun to appreciate the
long-term impact on nerves and stability of the fluctuating income of
a free-lance writer. Each time he had to negotiate a contract he felt
himself at a disadvantage as a writer dealing with businessmen. With
trepidation, he soon began to look for someone to represent him.

Except for *The Bostonians* fiasco, he managed his own affairs reasonably well. Even before he had begun the writing of that novel, he had skillfully arranged with Aldrich at the *Atlantic* for the serial publication in 1886 of his next novel, *The Princess Casamassima,* and with Macmillan, who provided a substantial advance of four hundred pounds against royalties, for book publication in Britain and America. Though he failed to get Aldrich to pay him $500 rather than $250 an installment, he gracefully retreated from a tactful but bold business initiative by blaming his faulty memory for the claim that that was what the *Atlantic* had paid him for *The Portrait of a Lady*. Unfortunately, he could not place the *Princess* with a British magazine—a harbinger of the rapidly changing realities of the publishing trade, which were soon almost to eliminate entirely his heretofore profitable opportunities for serial publication. At the end of 1885, though, he still had reason to believe that he would be able to support himself handsomely with the combined proceeds of stories, articles, serial publication of novels, book publication of novels, and book publication of collections of stories and articles. Though his arrangement with Osgood had turned from a poor contract into a substantial loss, he had little reason to fault either his own enterprise or productivity.

(4)

Actually, his most profitable publications, word by word, page by page, were short stories, for which, between 1883 and 1888, he was being handsomely paid, by both American and British magazines. He was paid again, something modest but real, for their publication in book-length collections. Anticipating that he would need the earnings of a substantial number of short stories to carry him over the fallow period while writing *The Bostonians,* he had agreed to write three stories for Osgood for two thousand dollars, "The Impressions of a Cousin," "Lady Barberina," and "A New England Winter." He was separately paid two thousand dollars for their book publication under the title *Tales of Three Cities* and their magazine publication in *The Century*. The first of these stories he completed before leaving America, the other two soon thereafter as he worked through late 1883 and the first half of 1884 to strengthen his bank balance and clear the decks for working full-time on his novel.

With incredible energy, he wrote an additional five short stories in 1884, at least three of them in the spring—"The Author of Beltraffio," for *The English Illustrated Magazine,* and "Pandora" and "Georgina's

Reasons," for syndicated publication in the extremely well paying Sunday *New York Sun*. That newspaper, he told Tom Perry, "has bribed me with gold"—a payment of fifteen hundred dollars. "It is a case of gold pure & simple; & moreover the reasons against my exposing myself in it do not seem to me serious." In his unsuccessful attempt to get Aldrich to agree to five hundred dollars for each installment of the *Princess,* he shared with him the still *"complete and sacred secret"* that he was being paid *"a prix d'or"* by "the New York Sunday *Sun!"* He did not want, he told Howells, his hostile comments about the huge amounts paid to bad popular novelists like Francis Marion Crawford, the young American novelist whose parents James had known in Rome, "set down to green-eyed jealousy." But such success "sickens and almost paralyses me."[31] It was the kind of remunerative commercialization of which he would have liked to have had more.

The extraordinary "Georgina's Reasons," based on a story told to him in March 1884 by Mrs. Kemble, embodies his sense of the melodramatic, explicit sensationalism that would be necessary to make him a commercial success.[32] A strange, baffling, morally quirky story, it is about a false definition of honor, a faithfulness to a pledge to which there is no rational reason to be faithful anymore, about a man who conspires to allow himself to be a victim and also to victimize the woman who loves him and whom he wants to marry. It is also about a self-serving, danger-enjoying, secretively rebellious woman who has an illicit sexual affair and a bastard son whom she sends into obscurity and probable death. Her motivation remains a mystery. None of the implied explanations account for her behavior. We never learn Georgina's reasons. The story is chilling, almost frightening, partly because the material that James is dealing with is more stark, more sexually frank than usual. A variant on the new American woman, Georgina may be an expression of James's nightmare vision of the dark side of the independent woman whose independence may liberate her into perversity. Before such unleashed, powerful amorality, he may fear that men of honor, who value their pledges, may be helpless and inevitable victims. With the audience of the *Sun* in mind, his initial motivation probably had been to write a sensationalistic story, to take his materials from the world and the worldview of his Parisian friends, to appeal to an audience that demanded rawness, naturalism, libidinal starkness. If so, he overreached himself, both in the sense that the story did not establish demand for him as a popular writer for newspaper audiences and did not succeed with the audience he had already won.

So too was the case with *The Princess Casamassima.* Here was another effort to recharge and reform his image as a writer by undertaking a subject matter that he had not previously tried let alone been associated with. Self-consciously, in a more intense and sustained way than in "Georgina's Reasons," he moved, in *The Princess Casamassima,* into foreign territory. He was experimenting not only with the naturalism of his Parisian friends but with the social and political terrain associated with, on the one hand, Dickens, and, on the other, the contemporary anxieties about anarchism, class struggle, and social revolution. Initially, he felt energized by the challenge, though concerned that he had begun ineffectively. "The subject of the *Princess* is magnificent," he told himself in August 1885, but "I have plunged in rather blindly, and got a good many characters on my hands; but these will fall into their places if I keep cool and think it out. Oh art, art, what difficulties are like thine; but, at the same time, what consolations and encouragements, also, are like thine?" From Dover, in September 1885, he complained to Stevenson that he was exerting himself assiduously, "trying to get ahead of that beastly serial in the *Atlantic,* which I hear panting at my heels." He spent a morning in mid-December at Millbank prison, "collecting notes for a fiction scene. You see I am quite the naturalist," he told Tom Perry.[33]

Despite his French naturalist models, there is more Dickens and Balzac than Zola in the story of the illegitimate child of an aristocrat and a servant who demonstrates inherent aesthetic and moral worth despite being born into a sordid world of poverty and political anarchism. It is a Jamesian version of *Oliver Twist* without a happy ending. If Hyacinth is Oliver, Millicent Henning is Nancy, the anarchist plotters are extensions of Fagin and Bill Sikes, the international intrigue an extension of the thieves' den. With an inherent sense of beauty, Hyacinth Robinson is a variant on the Jamesian imaginative trope of what he himself might have been like if he had been born into poverty. As an apprentice bookbinder, Hyacinth demonstrates innate aesthetic taste so great that his elegant bindings transform utilitarian objects into beautiful things. An idealist who hopes for a better world, the young Hyacinth pledges his total submission to the revolutionary will of a mysterious anarchist organization. Years later, a vastly different Hyacinth, who has come to value, after traveling on the Continent, the highest artistic achievements of the culture he had once pledged to oppose, finds that the time has come for him to fulfill his vow. Rejecting violent political action, he chooses suicide rather than murder. In a world filled with inflammatory rhetoric and violent action, James creates a fictional representation of what for him is the horrible premise that first one must destroy before one can create. "I can't believe in reform that begins with deforming," he told John Clark.[34] Politics seemed a dirty business, callous about the preciousness of the individual, more destructive than protective of culture. War was politics at the next stage. There were signs all around him that the European house of books and culture might come tumbling down.

Unlike Hyacinth, Henry had vowed to do only the work he wanted to do, the work in which he believed. When he asked Macmillan in June 1886, with much of the novel written, for the same amount for the *Princess* as he had received for *The Bostonians,* Macmillan counteroffered with four hundred pounds instead of five hundred for British and American rights at a 15 percent royalty. The publisher almost certainly felt that it would not earn back the advance. James had high hopes. But he did not feel in a position to rebel—he needed the money, the *Atlantic* was already paying him $250 an installment, and he was aware that the poor sales of *The Bostonians,* on which Macmillan had lost money, had decreased his market value. Like the major character of the *Princess,* who is also concerned with beautiful books, the limits of his marketability were becoming unhappily clear. He was disappointed, of course. In September 1886, he sent Macmillan the last corrected page proofs. "As my part of the business seems over," he told him, "I won't conceal from you that it would be rather a convenience to me to receive" the remaining £250 now. Macmillan immediately sent him the money. "I hope the Princess will have a career,—& almost think it probable," he reassured his publisher, "though I am cured of presumption." Actually, he was not cured, at least of residual optimism, which carried him with high but eventually smashed hopes into his next novel and then into a period of almost five years of attempting to solve "the great money-question" by writing a series of commercially successful stage plays. Two years after he had received from Macmillan the balance of what was owed him for the *Princess,* he confessed to Howells that he had "entered upon evil days. . . . I am still staggering a good deal under the mysterious and (to me) inexplicable injury wrought . . . upon my situation by my last two novels . . . from which I expected so much and derived so little."[35]

(5)

For many of the short stories that he wrote in these years he relied on the familiar "international theme." Short stories paid well. The international theme had proved popular. Though he had drawn on it successfully for over ten years, its cultural moment had not yet passed. Anglo-American relationships still seemed central to both cultures, the politics and economics of the shifting balance of power of sufficient interest to American and British readers to provide an audience for emblematic fictions that dramatized concrete representations of the clashes and the marriages between the two cultures. James's daily life breathed the air of Anglo-American social relationships. The material was readily available—even too available. He had his doubts, his hesitancies. "Of course internationalism, etc., may be overdone, threadbare. That is to a certain extent a reason against the subject; but a weak, not a strong one." If he had not had the financial need to write a substantial number of stories in a short time, he might have hesitated even more. But "it is always enough if the *author* sees substance in it," he reassured himself.[36] Such reassurances carried him forward into a short novel, *The Reverberator,* and a series of stories, varying widely in quality, most notably "The Siege of London," published in early 1883; "Lady Barberina" and "Pandora," published in the spring and summer of 1884; and "Two Countries" and "A London Life," published in 1888.

A flat, satiric, third-person narrative, "The Siege of London" dramatizes the dilemma of a well-connected American resident of London who is called on by an American divorcée, whom he rather likes, to assist her in passing as respectable enough by British society to marry an English aristocrat whom she loves and who is in love with her. In the end, all the force of the story is with giving priority to personal judgment and to the triumphant alliance between the two Americans and the young Englishman. Neither culture has a lock on snobbery, on overvaluing structure at the expense of the individual. In James's carefully qualified Anglophilia, the depiction of the son-clutching vulturism of the British matriarch—the mother of the liberal, love-stricken aristocrat—suggests James's identification with the American female in love with the British aristocrat. He is the desirable American bride who has made herself available to be loved by, and to marry, the lord of England. In the acerbic "Lady Barberina," James reverses the pattern, dramatizing the dangers of transatlantic unions as being as much a product of individual personality as of cultural dislocation, by showing a wealthy, arrogant, shortsighted American slowly discovering that the British aristocratic beauty whom he has married almost on his own terms has a provincialism equal to his own. The slight "Pandora," combining the international theme with the "new American woman," derives its minor interest from two distinctive features: the protagonist is a German diplomat and the story is set in Washington, giving James the opportunity to "*do* Washington, so far as I know it, and work in my few notes, and my very lovely memories of last winter. I might even *do* Henry

Adams and his wife."[37] The Adamses appear as the entertainingly snobbish Mr. and Mrs. Bonnycastle, alert to the social nuances of Washington life. Their salon runs by a mysterious mixture of high standards and personal whim, and their treatment of Washington politicans, "the representatives of the people," including the president, with mischievous condescension. "Hang it," Mr. Bonnycastle says, "there is only a month left [to the social season]; let us have some fun—let us invite the President!"

Far from finished with the international theme, James was to draw on it, sometimes more as appearance than as substance, into the late 1880s—his most interesting, sometimes brilliant story on the topic, "Two Countries," published in 1888. At the beginning of the new century, he returned to it, though the theme would be vastly transformed by new personal and cultural considerations. In "Two Countries," later renamed "The Modern Warning," a young American woman of Irish background, against the wishes of her liberal brother who detests British antidemocratic values, marries an aristocratic Englishman, a Conservative member of Parliament, after he has given her the assurance that he will never speak or write against America. The siblings, like Henry and Alice, are intensely, passionately committed to one another, with one willing to accommodate, even to embrace and marry, England, the other passionately pro-American and critical of English life. When her husband goes to America on a fact-finding tour, she goes with him in order to visit her brother and renew her American memories. In the narrator's loving description of New York, which Henry drew from his memories of his 1883 visit, she finds the autumn stunningly lovely. When, later, she reads the page proofs of her husband's book about America, his attempt to alert his countrymen to the dangers of democratization, she is deeply pained. Astonished, he thinks her reaction to his moderately stated views excessive. When she reminds him of her "Irish blood" and that "millions of her Celtic cousins found refuge there from the blessed English dispensation," he consents not to publish the book. Though he behaves like a gentleman, she gradually senses that he has removed himself from her. Reconsidering, she tells him that she no longer opposes his publishing it. Her brother, who has finally consented to visit England and who has not been met at the station by his sister as he had expected, arrives at the house just as his brother-in-law is returning home. They are told that the lady of the house has suddenly become very ill. In a wildly melodramatic denouement, they rush upstairs to discover that she has poisoned herself.

He could not readily let go of the international theme; it had been part of the fabric of his own life for so long. Readily available, it seemed

likely to appeal to magazine editors on both sides of the Atlantic. But
the theme had another, even more pervasive level of importance to him
that inhered in the larger patterns of his concern with his situation as
an American permanently residing in England and his vision of a greater
Anglo-American community. The "great money-question" resonated
beyond his personal financial situation into international economics and
politics, into emerging contractual relationships, sometimes explicit,
often implicit, between the great Empire, at whose dissolution he was
happy to have a ringside seat, and the newly powerful, increasingly
wealthy Republic, whose emerging Empire would, in the next century,
include England. His preoccupation for so long with the international
theme is at least partly an effort by a prescient writer to both comment
upon the complications of, and write scripts for, the marriage between
America and Britain. His vision was intensely Anglocentric; he wanted
an American *and* a British audience. He wanted American *and* British
publication, the *Atlantic* and *The Cornhill*, Osgood and Macmillan. He
held up a cosmopolitan ideal that transcended the limitations of the
nationalism of either country. Deeply committed to the predominance
of the English language, he believed its richness could be maintained
only by a sustained commitment by both countries to a union of Anglo-
American values. An economic and political alliance between America
and Britain seemed to him essential. The commonwealth, so to speak,
needed to be extended, strengthened. "I can't look at the English and
American worlds, or feel about them, anymore, save as a big Anglo-
Saxon total, destined to such an amount of melting together that an
insistence on their differences becomes more and more idle and pedantic
. . . simply chapters of the same general subject. Literature, fiction in
particular, affords a magnificent arm for such taking for granted."[38]
The union of the best values and achievements of both cultures would
form a benign imperium. Eventually, America would be more like
Britain and Britain more like America. He hoped that tradition, culture,
and manners would successfully marry money, energy, and democratic
values.

   Frustrated by the crassness of political events, especially the dominance of political rather than cultural discussion, he reacted with strong
hostility because he felt the problems deeply. If he desired to escape
from politics, it was because he felt pained rather than indifferent.
Politicians often seemed corrupt or stupid. Many social problems
seemed either insoluble or destined to be solved badly. As with his
own professional life, "the great money-question" seemed inevitably
to dominate and determine the larger polity. Two issues particularly
preoccupied him in the 1880s, both of them significant impediments to

Anglo-American harmony, one on a narrow professional level that affected his own small pocketbook, the other a larger, more bitter issue that touched on the James family origins as well as on the viability of Britain as an international power. American unwillingness to become a signatory to the international copyright agreement had been a constant irritant to the English for most of the century. The inflammatory question, dominating English politics in the 1880s, of whether Britain should grant Ireland a degree of self-rule caused even more serious tension in Anglo-American relations. America, a republic of immigrants, strongly supported Home Rule. The Irish of Boston and New York City vigorously asserted their Irish nationalism.

On the copyright issue, James stood squarely with the community of authors on both sides of the Atlantic who felt that money that rightfully was theirs was being stolen from them. On the American side, American publishers were able to keep down what they paid American writers, since they had literature available to them from England for which they had to pay little or nothing. On the British side, authors did not receive their fair share of the profits of their works published in the United States—and sometimes received nothing at all. As an American writer living in London, he felt particularly sensitive to the issue. He had the advantage of being able to copyright his work in both countries and consequently suffered less than did British nationals whose works were pirated. Still, he found himself frequently asked to explain or at least comment on what he felt to be his country's indefensible policy. For a shy man, whose patriotism was never stronger than when America was being criticized, the position was an awkward one that he could explain but not condone, though he fervently wished that he would not have to do either. As the agitation for American participation in international copyright became heated late in the 1880s, he published, in *Scribner's Magazine* in New York, an argument, minimally disguised as a fictional dialogue, that touched on international copyright in a way intended to encourage an American commitment. "It has been our misfortune (in the long run, I mean)," one of the American speakers says, "that years and years ago, when the taking [of pirated English books by the United States] began, it was, intelligently viewed, quite inevitable. We were poor then, and we were hungry and lonely and far away, and we had to have something to read. We helped ourselves to the literature that was nearest. . . . You can treat books as a luxury, and authors with delicacy, only if you've already got a lot; you can't *start* on that basis." But what was sensible for a capital-starved young nation was not in the moral, cultural, or economic interest of a wealthy major power. James felt awkward, embarrassed, pessimistic.

When, in summer 1888, Edmund Gosse urged him to attend a grand banquet hosted by the British Society of Authors for American writers to press for a successful resolution of the copyright issue, he declined. He hated public dinners, particularly the speeches. The timing seemed wrong. He preferred "the quiet work & the quiet forbearance of individuals. . . . I feel strongly that in the present state of Anglo-American relations all international *festive* manifestations, all speechifying & palaver, all effusions & intercompliments, are most short-sighted & dangerous—provocative of inevitable reaction—later-coming irony & acrimony."[39]

He did put himself on record, in a letter to the American Copyright League, applauding the work of the League and expressing his hope that America would soon pass copyright legislation. Privately, he worried about the issue of most importance to him, general Anglo-American relations, and expressed his disgust at cultural piracy. "There appears to be a sort of tangled, wrangled condition of things in the relations (of temper) between England & the U.S. which doesn't indicate a rising barometer. It only makes one wish to heaven that if there are to be squalls *we* may hoist a decenter bit of canvas than our old piratical rag. Either as a flag or as a sail: one is ashamed to arise one's head to look at it."[40] It was a great moral and personal relief to him when, in 1891, America finally joined Britain in becoming a signatory to the international copyright treaty. Two generations of British authors, from Scott to Dickens, who had fought aggressively, tenaciously, and sometimes with embittering frustration for their rightful American royalties, may at last have rested more comfortably in their narrow graves, with a sense that justice had been done and that America had put its national adolescence behind it.

Justice for Ireland was another matter, of volatile concern to many more people. Great economic interests were at stake. Irish wealth, little as it was, was mainly controlled by the British. For James, Irish and Scotch-Irish Presbyterian ancestry did make a claim on his allegiance, especially brought to his attention by Alice's fervent commitment to complete independence for Ireland. He mostly resisted the call. With the children of first generation Irish-Catholic immigrants rising to prominence in Boston and New York, he felt no identification. On the contrary, they were a threat to the Republic of his childhood, to the values and manners of the comparatively homogeneous America that existed, at least in theory, before the major immigrations after the Civil War. James was to feel this concern even more forcefully when, at the beginning of the new century, he was to be confronted with the reality of a multilingual culture in which not even the English language seemed anymore to be a unifying national force. Unlike Alice, he declined to identify with Irish aspirations, even with any broader principle of equity and liberalism. He had only two concerns—that Anglo-American relations not be damaged by the differences of national interest that the issue provoked and that Britain itself not be weakened in its effort to deal with Ireland.

Unfortunately, the "eternal Irish strife" seemed sometimes like a horrid, tasteless melodrama, other times like a tragedy without a catharsis, England "all gashed and gory with it." By the mid 1880s, the elderly Gladstone, prime minister and Liberal party leader, had come to the center of the Home Rule stage. James first met Gladstone at a dinner in 1877 where he "made a great impression on me—greater than any one I have seen here—though 'tis perhaps owing to my naivete, and unfamiliarity with statesmen." In May 1884, James had the opportunity to spend a weekend with the prime minister at one of Lord Rosebery's country homes. Gladstone's weakness in regard to Russia and the Sudan made him seem to James now "an incurable shirker & dodger." The two days with Gladstone were "not so valuable as they sound," he told Grace Norton. "He is a *parson* perverted!"[41] The prime minister's religious monomania, self-righteous moralism, and assumption of infallability on all subjects seemed boorish.

The Irish question would not go away. In the cold winter of 1886, there were "only two subjects of conversation" in London—"Ireland & the weather." Both sometimes froze his blood. He alternated between fascination and revulsion. "If I had nothing else to do I think I should run over to Ireland," he told Perry, "which may seem strange to you on the part of one satiated in youth with Celtic genius. The reason is that I shld. like to see a country in a state of revolution." In April 1886, he stood "on tiptoe," like the rest of England, "for the revelation of poor Gladstone's Home Rule Scheme to parliament 2 days hence. The scramble for place to hear him is prodigious. I am sorry to say I haven't one—but I haven't even tried to get it." Though his expectation that the bill would fail proved correct, he had no doubt that Home Rule would come, with "an Irish parliament for Irish affairs," part of the "irresistible march of things." He himself "was resigned to it," mostly because it seemed to him self-destructive for England to attempt to maintain Irish subordination. Ireland will, he explained to Grace Norton, "injure England less with [Home Rule] than she does without it. . . . She seems to me an example of a country more emancipated from every bond, not only of despotism but of ordinary law, than any so-called civilized country was before—a country revelling in odious forms of irresponsibility & license. And, surely, how can one speak of the Irish as a 'great people'? I see no greatness, nor any kind of superiority in them, & they seem to me an inferior & 3rd rate race, whose virtues are of the cheapest & shallowest order, while their vices are peculiarly cowardly & ferocious. They have been abominably treated in the past—but their wrongs appear, to me, in our time, to have occupied the conscience of England only too much to the exclusion of other things. Don't think me brutal . . . or anglicized, which is the same thing; but I fear that if I too want them righted . . . it is because I think other things are considerably more important."[42]

Economic conditions, which he watched closely and with trepidation, got worse as the decade progressed. In December 1890, he expected the collapse of Baring Brothers, one of the banking pillars of British life, would lead to "weeks of alarm & imminent disaster in the city." The financial world seemed "on the edge of quite universal smash, the biggest financial disaster since finance was invented." The depression that had begun in the early 1870s had extended for almost twenty years. The depreciation of the value of land had been precipitous, a severe decline in the wealth of the once wealthiest people in the world. "Every one is poor & growing poorer," he wrote to William. "There is no visible end in store for that. . . . Old England is in a strange state, & destined to unprecedented transformations. I pray she may survive them but I am not sure." With so many international and economic problems seriously threatening England's place in the world, why, he felt, attempt to maintain an unhappy, draining relationship with Ireland? "I think I am more sorry on the whole for the English than the Irish. The former have utterly departed from the turpitude of their ancestors & want only to do justice & consent to reforms; while it would be vain to pretend that the latter are not a totally impractical people. This government can neither satisfy them, shut them up, nor part with them; the problem seems insoluble." Though he was disappointed when Gladstone's Home Rule bill failed, he felt no regret when the electorate deposed Gladstone and the Liberals in July 1886. "I cannot weep for the downfall of the G[rand].O[ld].M[an]. whose ways seem to me to have become terribly personal & pernicious (he is really a furious demagogue)," and of a political party "whose only idea & only program is simply the eternal repetition of his name & his word. . . . I detest *all* the trickiness & brutality of the political spirit to which this unhappy country is now given over & which has converted it for the last year into a howling bear-garden."[43]

He joked, in March 1890, that his plan to take a much-needed brief vaction in Ireland was on the face of it perverse, since "taking refuge *from* Ireland just now, would seem the more natural course." He was rarely capable of even such tepid humor about the subject. "Here there is nothing," he complained to Grace Norton, "but Ireland, & the animosities & separations it engenders—accursed isle! Literature, art, conversation, society—everything lies dead beneath its black shadow." When Parnell came upon the scene, James found his performance stupendous, the drama revivified in personal terms. Excited by "the Satanic Parnell, who has fought like a thousand tigers & may very well *still* carry all Ireland with him; on which he will now throw himself like a tremendous firebrand," the theatrical image had an especially exciting focus for him in "the thrilling, throbbing Parnell trial," in March 1889, some of the sessions of which he eagerly attended. "If one had been once," he wrote to Norton, "and tasted blood, one was quite hungry to go again and wanted to give up everything and live there. Unfortunately, or rather, fortunately, getting in was supremely difficult." The crucial evidence against Parnell, who had been accused of having actively condoned the Phoenix Park murders in Dublin in 1882, turned out to have been forged. "Parnell has behaved atrociously (I mean, of course, quite outside the O'Shea case, as to which, shabby as it was, the cant is nauseous,) but he has shown extraordinary force, audacity & 'cleverness.' The last week has been a real drama—living, leaping & throbbing, with the acts bounding over from day to day—on a huge national stage."[44]

(6)

After ten years in his dark Bolton Street flat, he moved in March 1886 into a spacious, light-flooded apartment, "like a photographer's studio," looking westward across the roofs and greenery of Kensington. It was in a new, handsomely constructed building from whose heights he had sunlight and breezes. From the ground floor, a finely designed cast-iron and wood electric elevator carried him skyward to his fourth-floor residence. In December 1885, "in the most solemn and irrevocable manner," he had signed a twenty-one-year lease, Frederick Macmillan testifying to his "general respectability & solvency." James told him the latter "depends, after all, very much on you." He was thrilled at the prospect of having his own home, his first ever. "It shines before me as a promised land." The large, unfinished flat needed work and furniture, both of which he supplied. By late January, the apartment was habitable, though he felt that he had "no genius for pots and pans." The furnishing and the arranging "has partly amused & partly exasperated & altogether beggared me; & I have only done enough for incipient living-in. But I can do the rest at a snail's—or a pauper's—pace." The cost of the lease was reasonable, the opportunity to rent the flat for the portion of each year that he hoped to be abroad, financially attractive, though emotionally repelling. Still, he would do so, he told himself, if "it will put money in my purse." The freezing winter weather kept him a little longer at Bolton Street, which seemed even more dingy with the bright new apartment in De Vere Gardens in prospect. He made a tedious, anxious search for live-in servants, which produced in early February 1886 a satisfactory couple. For fifty dollars a month for both, they would look after him and the apartment. He felt an immense sense of unwarranted relief. "I don't have to give an order or worry about anything."[45]

When he took possession of 34 De Vere Gardens in March, he felt like an eagle in his aerial nest. It was a moment of euphoria and fulfillment—the lifelong wanderer with a place of personal rest, the permanent alien with a London home of his own. "I shall enter it for life," he had told Henrietta Reubell, "and I shall be as cossu ["well-off"] & bourgeoise as my means will permit, & have large fat sofas . . . everywhere." Since the apartment was commodious enough for him to have overnight guests, he would be able to offer her "a modest hospitality. . . . I will take you anywhere—everywhere . . . to chaperon you. . . . I am surely enough of an old woman for that." It hardly bothered the "old woman" that there were "some romping little wretches of children overhead" on the one floor between him and the sky. "My new quarters work beautifully and haven't a flaw," he told Aunt Kate. At right angles to the northern end of his "short but broad" cul-de-sac, Kensington Road went westward to old Kensington, associated in his mind with Thackeray, and eastward to Hyde Park Corner and the London maelstrom. His exit to the world always had the sight and the attraction, across Kensington Road, of Kensington Gardens, "that paradise, which," he wrote, as he began his first spring in his new home, "is a wondrous thing to find in the heart of a great city."[46]

But the forty-three-year-old Henry James who greeted the London spring of 1886 across the street from paradise found life a limited paradise indeed. "It is astonishing how one's wayside is strewn with *ends* after one has reached middle life!"[47] When he looked into his bright mirrors, he saw a middle-aged man with an expanding waistline, bright gray eyes, a close-cut dark brown beard, and a receding hairline, anchored on angular eyebrows and the smooth bridge of a full sharp nose. The intensity of the gray of his eyes varied from mellow to riveting, with a glow that made them the compelling focus of his face. When he looked into the mirror, he saw an imposing man whose solid body and distinctive head contributed to his presence. People noticed him. People remembered him. Dressing conservatively, he wore dark jackets and light trousers for traveling, for London walking, for country visits, and dark suits for social dinners, always with a white shirt to set off his brown beard, and an attractive bow tie to provide a colorful counterpoint of red or deep blue to his gray eyes. He dressed properly for all occasions—plaids and checks for country afternoons, a high hat for weddings and funerals. At home, while working at his desk, he wore white shirt and bow tie, and often a jacket. In hot weather, in private, he sometimes worked in his undershirt, so much did he hate the heat. His bourgeois attire had become an external skin, a set of codes and habits that he accepted as the necessary condition of his London life. Like Dickens, Thackeray, and Browning, he never would have imagined that the bourgeois conformity of his dress and daily rituals had anything to do with the distinctiveness of his talent, his intellect, and his art.

The question of self-identity distressed him in its most immediate, explicit form—his sense of the gap between how he looked to himself in his mind and how he looked in the most obviously available mirrors. When he looked in the latter, he saw a corpulent, sensual, middle-aged man emerging and receding and then emerging again from the variable outlines of his image of himself as a lithe, handsome, romantic youth. There is "a dreadful aggressor within myself: the symptoms of a portentous corpulence." It was an enemy within. His response expressed his fear at being possessed rather than taking possession of. The expanding flesh implied the sensuality that he had repressed; it was a reminder of the powerfulness of pleasure, of expansive eroticism. He detested being overweight, as if somehow his appetite had betrayed him. He ate well and frequently. Inevitably, he gained weight and then looked both for ways of reducing and exculpatory excuses when either he did not lose weight or gained it again. Mrs. Kemble shocked him when she told him that with such an "hereditary tendency" as his, "neither exercise, nor diet, nor *grief* avails." But his father had been thin, almost frail. So too were William and Alice. Whatever his nervous sensibility, it did not metabolically feed from the same plate as did his body. He exerted himself with a counterattack of exercise, employing a fencing teacher twice a week for an hour each time. He enjoyed the exercise—"a great boon," he told William.[48] But it made little difference to his waistline.

His vanity played counterpoint with his anxiety. When asked by a lady friend to allow her to commission Sargent to paint his portrait, he declined, "for though I wished him infinitely to do the picture, & should have been proud of the result, I didn't wish the lady, generous & flattering though she was, to have it. This sounds like a very fatuous anecdote, & I tell it because I hope you consider me in a general way a modest man." It was more fatuous and self-revealing than he admitted. He was not a modest man, though he preferred to be considered so. Whoever the lady was, the real issue was that whether painted or photographed, he did not like how he looked. Du Maurier made a drawing of him that seemed "pale and weak," and photographs threatened to rob him of the illusions he preferred to maintain. He settled the matter simply. "I am terribly unphotographable & have fewer accumulations of that sort of property than most people." He would confront the camera occasionally, "however ugly it makes me." But only occasionally, and selectively.[49]

When he looked into the mirror, he also saw a man who had renounced marriage, who had never slept with a woman, and who admired the beauty of men but had no sense that that admiration should ever be expressed physically. He lived in a sexually volatile world, at the intersection of the upper middle class and the aristocracy. Sexual adventures and public scandals were a regular part of his London milieu. By the standards of nineteenth-century Cambridge, late-Victorian London was an adulterous Babylon in which widely known extramarital activities were generally tolerated as long as public decorum was not challenged. The subject fascinated him, partly because it could serve as a vehicle for dramatizing the intersection between social conventions and personal desires. With a keen interest in stories, his ear was always open, his attention keen. He missed little. He often knew the people involved. When, in 1885, the "great Dilke Scandal," as one example among many, fascinated London, he admitted that it had "a certain rather low interest." Two married ladies suddenly found themselves free, one by divorce, one by widowhood. Each publically proclaimed that she was engaged to be married to Charles Dilke, who had been the lover of both, as well as the lover of Christina Rogerson, whose husband had also, "strangely enough," James remarked, just died. Christina "has had every expectation that he was on the point of marrying *her*!" The public waited "to see *which* he *would* marry."

For James and his circle the most noteworthy aspect of the imbroglio was that Dilke "had been strangely, incredibly reckless." He also saw it in the larger terms of "the already very damaged prestige" of the English upper class, whose decadence he found both distasteful and fascinating. He had a sense of the last days of the Empire, like "the depraved Roman world upon which the barbarians came down." So "much of English life is grossly materialistic and wants blood-letting."[50]

His disapproval, though, did not block his interest in knowing about such affairs; adultery was a suppressed but strong erotic phenomenon, a morally and socially charged force that provided him with powerful materials for fiction. He had no doubt about what men and women did in bed together. Information and imagination provided him with a voyeur's version of the experience. That was sufficient to his inclination, his needs, and his vocation.

He also had no doubt about what men did in bed together. Homosexual activities were widespread but muted, private, disguised, mostly out of the public eye. The scandal of the Cleveland Street homosexual brothel was one of the few exceptions, until Wilde, in 1895, to James's regret and pain, miscalculated the application of the rules about public display and the vindictive hostility of British society when the codes were flagrantly challenged. James had had, at least since his Paris days, a dim sense of his own homoeroticism, which his position, his personality, his background, and his culture all gave him every incentive to repress. He knew that aspect of his sexuality indirectly, in his idealizations of the beauty of the male body and of male friendship. He had good reason for doing so, including the Criminal Law Amendment Act of 1885, which made even private, consensual homosexual acts punishable by two years' imprisonment at hard labor. He could speak of having fallen in love, as he did with Joukowsky, as he was to do with numbers of men later in his life. But verbal passion did not imply for him physical action. He had no desire to challenge his inhibitions, let alone society's. When Wilde came to trial in April 1895, he found it "hideously, atrociously dramatic & really interesting. . . . It is the squalid gratuitousness of it all"—a version of Dilke's strange recklessness—"of the mere exposure—that blurs the spectacle. But the *fall* . . . to that sordid prison-cell & this gulf of obscenity over which the ghoulish public hangs & gloats—it is beyond any utterance of irony or any pang of compassion! He was never in the smallest degree interesting to me—but this hideous human history has made him so—in a manner."[51]

Wilde, though, *was* interesting to him, insofar as Wilde represented love between men, but abhorrent insofar as he dramatized a flamboyant caricature of unmanly effeminacy. Wilde degraded James's homoerotic ideal and made public statements whose purpose was controversy, self-advertisement, and social disharmony. James thought Wilde suicidal, providing his own gloss on his brilliant but perverse public career, forcing upon himself public humiliation by his "squalid gratuitousness," a tasteless excess combined with mental and moral madness. When James wrote to Grace Norton, "let us be flexible . . . let us be flexible! and even if we don't reach the sun we shall at least have been up in a balloon," he did not mean the flexibility to flaunt public opinion, though he did mean tolerance and self-tolerance in the private sphere. He sympathized with the struggles of many Victorian men, including his close friend, Edmund Gosse, to come to terms with potentially disruptive, inevitably painful homoerotic feelings. He shared the sudden spasms of desire for beautiful young men, the long periods of feeling empty and unfulfilled, and guessed at the difficulty of balancing lives of heterosexual respectability with an awareness of homosexual desire. For Gosse and others it sometimes seemed as if their secret lives were their real lives. James did not think of himself as homosexual. His interest in male beauty was absorbed into comparatively unthreatening idealizations. He had no conscious sense of living a divided life.

But he could not control the expression of his deepest feelings in his art. Two of his powerful short stories, "The Author of Beltraffio" and "The Pupil," express the homoerotic sensuality that had no other outlet. Though he denied that "The Author of Beltraffio" had anything to do with John Addington Symonds, whom he had met in 1877, the denial was a purposeful evasion, an attempt to distance himself and his story from a homoerotic subtext.[52] James knew almost from his first meeting with Symonds, certainly from later discussions with Gosse, Symonds' good friend, that Symonds had lived for some time a divided life. Symonds had become increasingly outspoken about his inclinations, driven by his Victorian need to rescue homosexuality from sinfulness by associating it with ideal Greek values and by his knowledge that his life was sharply limited by his tubercular condition. Three years older than James, by the early 1880s Symonds had left behind his London friends for a life that alternated between Venice, his Italian base for his seven-volume work, *The Renaissance in Italy,* and Davos in Switzerland, where in wintry isolation he attempted to soothe his disease. Having married young, with three grown daughters and a bewildered, long-suffering wife, he had left the law for literature; he had left heterosexuality for the pains of an emerging sexual identity that he found it difficult to struggle against; and he had left London to benefit his health, to write about Italy, and to pursue his passion for beautiful young men.

James and Symonds shared a passion for Venice. Both appreciated beautiful Italian boys, those handsome gondoliers they both gazed at longingly. Though moderately promiscuous in practice, in theory Symonds' idealization of homoerotic love took monogamy as its model, Victorian values in regard to love and marriage as its standard. His only substitution was of a male "wife" for a female. Unlike Wilde, he had no desire to affront the bourgeoisie, though by the 1880s he spoke freely in private about his sexual preferences; he was searching for an audience for what seemed to him a historically sanctioned, psychologically sound defense. James read, with admiration, *The Renaissance in Italy,* and sent his own essay on Venice to Symonds as soon as it appeared in *The Century* in late 1882. Symonds, who did not particularly like James's fiction, sent, in August 1883, words of high praise for their common subject, which pleased James. He decided to thank Symonds himself, though he waited until early 1884 to express "the good will" he felt toward Symonds for what he had "written about the land of Italy," for which he nourished "an unspeakably tender passion. . . . It seemed to me that the victims of a common passion should sometimes exchange a look."[53]

Though they never met a second time, James kept his eye on Symonds, usually with compassion for his ill health and an interest in his effort to advocate, in privately printed and circulated essays, social acceptance of homosexuality. James's own advocacy was infinitely more discreet, more repressed, not so much an advocacy as a muted, indirect admission of shared emotional resonances. That they were "the victims of a common passion" whose focus was more precise than Venice in general he would neither admit to nor act upon. In 1884, Symonds fell in love with a handsome young gondolier, Angelo Fusato. Just two months before, in London, Gosse had been speaking to James about Symonds, "of his extreme and somewhat hysterical aestheticism, etc: the sad conditions of his life, exiled to Davos by the state of his lungs, the illness of his daughter, etc. Then he said that, to crown his unhappiness, poor S.'s wife was in no sort of sympathy with what he wrote . . . thinking his books immoral, pagan, hyper-aesthetic."[54]

Aware that Symonds' wife's disapproval focused on his homosexuality, that "hyper-aesthetic" was a polite synonym for homoerotic, James immediately grasped the situation as story material. He disguised its homosexual base, and recast it into a fiction he could sell for magazine publication. In "The Author of Beltraffio," Symonds becomes Mark Ambient, a great novelist at the height of his powers, whose wife—who disapproves of the moral content of his fiction, which she describes as pagan and immoral partly because it is insufficiently Christian—refuses to read his novels and attempts to protect their young, indescribably beautiful young son from reading them. The narrator of the story, a young writer who worships Ambient, becomes aware that Mrs. Ambient is attempting to protect the boy from what she feels is the contaminating influence, particularly the physical touch, of his father. The writer contributes to the catastrophe by semi-innocently providing her with fuel to intensify her unbalanced anxiety and antagonism. When the child becomes ill, Mrs. Ambient uses his illness to sequester him and deny Ambient access. The boy dies overnight. Mrs. Ambient is responsible for his death. She has denied him medical help, then refused to give him the prescribed medicine. She has, like Medea, murdered her own child, preferring that he be with his father in heaven than with the father he has on earth. When Gosse wrote to tell James how tragic, how powerful, he felt the story, James admitted in response that he had "divined the innermost cause of J.A.S.'s discomfort." He did not follow, he claimed, Gosse's identification of a particular allusion in the story to Symond's homosexuality, about which he was intensely curious to hear more, "devoured with curiosity as to this further revelation. Even a post-card (in covert words) would relieve the suspense of the perhaps-already-too-indiscreet—H.J."[55] "The Author of Beltraffio" dramatizes James's attraction to, and fear of, the horrible consequences of homoerotic love.

Seven years later, he returned with equal anxiety to the same theme in "The Pupil," in which the problematic relationship between an older man and a young boy has both autoerotic and homoerotic resonances.[56] In the tutor, Pemberton, and the pupil, Morgan Moreen, James draws upon the middle-aged man that he has become and the young boy that he remembered he had been. A poor American who has studied at Oxford and remained permanently in Europe, Pemberton falls in love with the son of an American family living abroad. Their seedy mixture of philistinism and bohemianism is attractive to Pemberton, despite the Moreens' shabby values. What keeps him with the family is his love for the boy. The story refrains from any mention of sexuality. But the mutual admiration and love between Pemberton and Morgan is evident in their companionship and the intimate way they talk to one another. Except for dialogue, we see the world of the Moreen family through Pemberton's mind and consciousness. The interior narrative contributes to an atmosphere and a tone that reinforce the autoerotic element. Morgan's parents exploit Pemberton's love by not paying him. Morgan urges that Pemberton and he leave and live together, but Pemberton discovers that he cannot do that; he promises that he will return at a later time, after he has earned some money. From Venice, having heard that Morgan has become ill with a weak heart, Pemberton joins the Moreens in Paris for the ostensible purpose of tutoring Morgan for his Oxford examinations. The Moreens' financial situation is desperate. Reluctantly, they now agree, at their son's urging, that Morgan can leave with him. They will give their son up. "We've struggled, we've suffered," Mrs. Moreen says, "but you've made him so your own that we've already been through the worst of the sacrifice." Ecstatically happy, Moreen looks up at Pemberton's face in expectation of a moment of mutual joy. To his dismay, he sees instead hesitation, anxiety, and fear. Morgan's already weak heart breaks. Pemberton pays the ultimate penalty for his moment of homosexual panic. " 'He couldn't stand it, with his infirmity,' said Pemberton—'the shock, the whole scene, the violent emotion.' 'But I thought he *wanted* to go to you!' " wailed Mrs. Moreen. 'I *told* you he didn't, my dear,' argued Mr. Moreen."

WILLIAM JAMES OF
ALBANY, C. 1820

"Committed to the
practice and the values
of the balance sheet on
earth and in heaven"

CATHERINE BARBER
JAMES, C. 1850

"Silk dress,
peppermints, lace
mittens and gentle
smile"

HENRY JAMES, SR., C. 1830

"Never guilty of a stroke of business"

HENRY JAMES, SR., AND HENRY JAMES, JR,
PHOTOGRAPH BY MATHEW BRADY

"My main object in life is to do justice to my children."

MARY JAMES, C. 1875

"We simply lived by her, in proportion as we lived spontaneously."

CATHERINE WALSH
(AUNT KATE), C. 1870

"Petite, energetic,
opinionated, sharp-
tongued"

HENRY JAMES, SR., C. 1875

The ultimate "marginal
man"

WILLIAM JAMES, 1887,
SELF–CARICATURE RESEMBLING
HENRY JAMES, SR.

HENRY JAMES, GENEVA, 1859

Geneva "was hard and bitter fruit all and turned to ashes in my mouth."

HENRY JAMES, 1860

"Harry has become an author."

HENRY JAMES, 1860,
PORTRAIT BY JOHN LA FARGE

"An abundantly idle young
out-of-doors model"

HENRY JAMES, 1863–64

"As the brutal Civil War
in America came to an
end, a young American,
slim, handsome, dark-
haired, of medium height,
with sharp gray eyes,
began to write stories."

WILLIAM JAMES AT SIXTEEN

"I would like to be a
doctor, but I fear I could
not stand dissections
and operations."

WILLIAM JAMES, GENEVA,
1859–60

"We are to be torn from
our friends and our
fatherland once more."

WILLIAM JAMES AT TWENTY

"He announced that he
would not be an artist but
a scientist."

ALICE JAMES, JUNE 1870

"Seriously, inexplicably ill
[with] a series of nervous
breakdowns"

GARTH WILKINSON JAMES,
C. 1863 (*STANDING*)

As an officer in the black
54th Massachusetts regiment

ROBERTSON JAMES, C. 1872

"Contentious, aggressively
self-defensive"

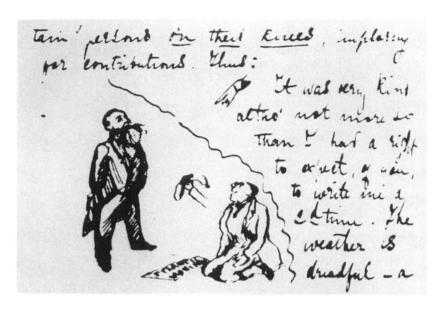

CARTOON BY HENRY JAMES, JR., 1864

Atlantic Monthly editors begging him for contributions

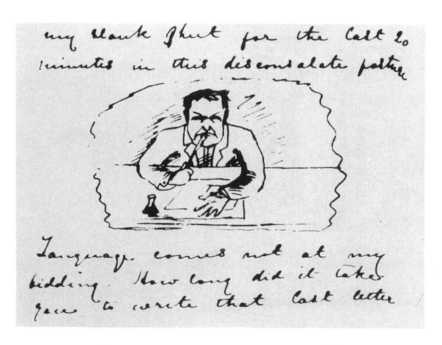

HENRY JAMES, CARTOON SELF-PORTRAIT, 1864

"Language comes not at my bidding."

MINNY TEMPLE, C. 1868

A "shining apparition . . .
a disengaged and dancing
flame of thought"

MINNY TEMPLE, WITH SHORT
HAIR, C. 1868

"Her bedroom a place for
coughing, sleeplessness,
and only the ghosts of men"

PAUL JOUKOWSKY,
C. 1875

"With Joukowsky
he soon swore
'eternal friendship.' "

THE AMERICAN, 1877,
FIRST ENGLISH EDITION

"My subject was:
an American letting
the insolent foreigner
go, out of his good
nature."

ELIZABETH BOOTT, C. 1880

"The quiet, passive, but
stubbornly persistent Lizzie"

34 DE VERE GARDENS, LONDON

ALICE JAMES, C. 1892,
PHOTOGRAPH BY K. P.
LORING

"Some day the rights of
women will be respected,
I suppose."

WILLIAM JAMES, 1887

"Unlike Henry, he aspired
to a style of conversational
lucidity rather than
associational allusiveness."

Yours till death—
Henry James

HENRY JAMES, "YOURS TILL
DEATH," 1890, PHOTOGRAPH
BY ELLIOTT AND FRY

"He is still," William
claimed, "the same dear
innocent old Harry of our
youth. . . . He's really, I
won't say a yankee, but a
native of the James family,
and has no other country."

CONSTANCE FENIMORE
WOOLSON, C. 1890

"Reclusive, shy . . . 'she is
a deaf and *méticuleuse* old
maid—but she is also an
excellent and sympathetic
being.' "

WOOLSON'S GRAVE IN THE
PROTESTANT CEMETERY, ROME

VILLA BRICHIERI, FLORENCE

EDWARD COMPTON AND
ELIZABETH ROBINS IN *THE
AMERICAN*, 1891

"As the curtain came
down, James flung himself
onto Compton. 'In
heaven's name, is it *going*?'
'Going?—*Rather!* You can
hear a pin drop!'"

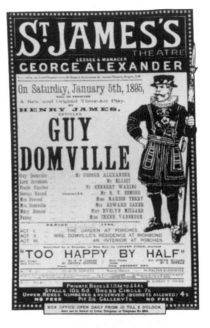

THE PLAYBILL FOR *GUY
DOMVILLE*, 1895

"My poor little play will
be thrown into the arena—
like a little white
Christmas Virgin to the
lions and tigers."

GEORGE ALEXANDER AND MARION TERRY IN *GUY DOMVILLE*, ACT III, 1895

HENRY JAMES, DUNWICH, SUFFOLK, 1897, PHOTOGRAPH BY LESLIE EMMET

"An imposing man whose solid body and distinctive head contributed to his being a presence. People noticed him. People remembered him."

HENRY JAMES, ROME, 1899, PHOTOGRAPH BY GIUSEPPE PRIMOLI

"The city 'breathes almost all its old enchantment on me—& I can scarcely tear myself away. I almost don't mind the 'alterations' & am conscious of nothing but the sweetness.' "

HENRY JAMES, 1900,
PORTRAIT BY ELLEN "BAY"
EMMET

"He thought he looked
a little too much 'the
smooth and anxious
clerical gentleman in the
spotted necktie.' "

HENRY JAMES, 1895

"Photographs appalled
him. He settled the matter
simply. 'I am terribly
unphotographable & have
fewer accumulations of
that sort of property than
most people.' He would
confront the camera
occasionally, 'however
ugly it makes me.' "

HENRY JAMES, 1899, AT A
GARDEN PARTY GIVEN BY
THE CRANES, AT BREDE
HOUSE

"James, who liked Crane,
thought his situation sadly,
tragically impossible and
the sheer anarchic muddle
of his environment
distasteful."

HENRY JAMES IN THE
GARDEN AT LAMB HOUSE,
RYE, EAST SUSSEX, C. 1900

"The charming old red-walled garden with all the pears & plums & figs I can desire growing on the pink South surfaces, & all the old (& new) flowers everywhere"

LAMB HOUSE, RYE, EAST SUSSEX

HENRY AND WILLIAM JAMES, RYE, EAST SUSSEX, 1901

"At Lamb House, James suffered through William's difficult visit and kept assiduously at work."

MORTON FULLERTON, C. 1900

"His enormous sexual energy also flickered in James's direction, partly as a hint of tantalizing secrets that he might share, partly as half-concealed overtures."

HENRY JAMES AND HOWARD
STURGIS AT THE MOUNT,
LENOX, MASS., 1904,
PHOTOGRAPH BY EDITH
WHARTON

"The whole thing here is
really too exquisite to
miss," he wrote to Sturgis,
"& I will keep my arm,
all the while, round you."

HENRY JAMES, EDITH WHARTON, AND TEDDY WHARTON AT THE
MOUNT, LENOX, MASS., 1904

"The air was like champagne, the weather perfect. 'This
exquisite Indian summer day sleeps upon these really
admirable Massachusetts mountains.' " Each drive was
"an adventure on primitive roads that went on and on."

HENRY JAMES (*WITH CIGARETTE*), 1905, PHOTOGRAPH BY KATHERINE ELIZABETH MCCLELLAN

HENRY JAMES, 1905, PHOTOGRAPH BY KATHERINE ELIZABETH MCCLELLAN

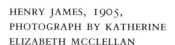

"Why, Howells asked, thinking about 'the folly of nationalities and the stupid hypocrisy of patriotism,' should not James or even he himself 'live forever out of America without self-reproach? The worst is perhaps that he will grow lonelier with age. But one grows lonely with age, anywhere!' "

HENRY JAMES, 1905,
PHOTOGRAPH BY ALICE
BROUGHTON

"To James, sitting for
hours one person to the
right of 'the extraordinary
& rather personally-
fascinating President,' the
conqueror of Cuba was
both personally likable
and culturally ugly."

HENRY, WILLIAM, ALICE, AND MARY MARGARET JAMES,
CAMBRIDGE, MASS., 1904

"He found the Cambridge 'suburban & car-haunting
relation to Boston intolerable,' a tedious inconvenience
for Boston visiting, which included memory-stirring
walks on Beacon Hill in the presence of the ghosts
of Mount Vernon Street."

EDITH WHARTON, 1907

"Too plain-looking to shine in New York social life, too shy to perform in the Boston social milieu, she carried with her a suppressed but restless sense of alienation and desperation."

EDITH WHARTON (*SMOKING*), 1908

"Sometime in spring 1908, Wharton and Fullerton became lovers. 'I am mad about you Dear heart,' she soon told him."

EDITH WHARTON, 1911

"Wharton had the attraction of her comparative youth, her talent, her shyness, her wealth, and her witty sociability."

"HENRY JAMES IN LONDON,"
CARICATURE BY MAX BEERBOHM

"HENRY JAMES AT THE HOTEL
ROOM DOOR," 1904, CARICATURE
BY MAX BEERBOHM

"A NIGHTMARE. MR. HENRY JAMES SUBPOENAED AS PSYCHOLOGICAL EXPERT,
IN A *CAUSE CELEBRE*," CARICATURE BY MAX BEERBOHM

"Cross-examining counsel: 'Come, Sir, I ask you a plain question
and I expect a plain answer!'"

WILLIAM JAMES, 1907,
PHOTOGRAPH BY ALICE BROUGHTON

"I am the more encouraged
to this [resignation],"
William wrote, "by the
fact that my younger and
shallower and vainer
brother is already in the
Academy, and that if
I were there too, the other
families represented might
think the James influence
too rank and strong."

HENRY JAMES AND HENDRIK
ANDERSEN, ROME, 1907

"I feel, my dear boy, my
arm around you. I feel the
pulsation, thereby, as it
were, of your excellent
future and your admirable
endowment."

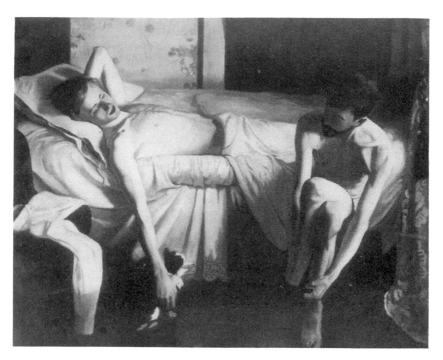

HENDRIK ANDERSEN AND ANDREAS ANDERSEN, PAINTING
BY ANDREAS ANDERSEN

"In Andreas' richly sensuous homoerotic painting, Hendrik,
nude, slender, blond, with deep red lips, reclines in bed, partly
covered with a sheet that rises noticeably over his genitals."

BUST OF COUNT ALBERTO
BEVILACQUA, C. 1899,
SCULPTURE BY HENDRIK
ANDERSEN

"He soon had," he told
Andersen, "struck up a
tremendous intimacy with
dear little Conte Alberto,
and we literally can't live
without each other. He is
the first object that greets
my eyes in the morning,
and the last at night."

HUGH WALPOLE, 1909

"Walpole had become a worshiping acolyte, eager to have as much of his master's company as possible, to elevate him into the supreme deity of high art."

HENDRIK ANDERSEN, C. 1910

"Andersen in Rome seemed at best a warm memory, at worst a baffling, frustrating, infuriating worry, an artist [whose] megalomaniacal sculptures seemed an indication of madness."

HENRY JAMES, HOWARD
STURGIS, AND THE BOITS,
VALLOMBROSA, 1907

"From Rome, in the
middle of June 1907, he
went first to Cernitoio,
near Vallombrosa, outside
Florence . . . where
Howard Sturgis was
staying for the summer
with the Babe."

HENRY JAMES AND
MARY WARD WALKING
IN THE GARDEN AT
STOCKS, HERTFORDSHIRE,
C. 1906

HENRY JAMES AT HIS DESK IN THE GARDEN HOUSE, RYE, EAST SUSSEX,
1906, PHOTOGRAPH BY EDWARD HOLTON JAMES

"Sometimes looking out through the bow windows at the occasional
traffic on West Street, sometimes staring down at the manuscript
or the letters on his table, he sat in the 'little ancient garden house'
that he had 'converted into an excellent work-room or study.' "

HENRY JAMES, 1906,
PHOTOGRAPH BY ALVIN
LANGDON COBURN

"I should warn you," he
wrote to a friend, "I have
cut off every hair of my
beard & am a sight to
behold—most uncanny
& questionable."

HENRY JAMES (*HOLDING
GLASSES*), 1906,
PHOTOGRAPH BY ALVIN
LANGDON COBURN

HENRY JAMES AT LAMB HOUSE, RYE, EAST SUSSEX, 1906,
PHOTOGRAPH BY ALVIN LANGDON COBURN

"It's really an attaching, really in its quiet way, a quite
adorable corner of the wicked earth. And the earth is
so wicked just now. Only Lamb House is mild; only
Lamb House is sane; only Lamb House is true."

WILLIAM JAMES IN THE
GARDEN AT LAMB HOUSE,
RYE, EAST SUSSEX, 1908

HENRY JAMES IN WICKER
CHAIR AT LAMB HOUSE, RYE,
EAST SUSSEX, C. 1907

LAMB HOUSE, RYE, EAST SUSSEX

HENRY JAMES AND ALICE
HOWE JAMES, CAMBRIDGE,
MASS., 1911

"From Nahant, late in
July, he went to 'hot stale'
Cambridge and sadly said
good-bye to Grace
Norton. It seemed to him
probably 'for the last
time.' Alice came down
from Chocorua to be with
him 'at the last.' "

HENRY JAMES, 1912, DRAWING
BY JOHN SINGER SARGENT

"He had three sittings
with Sargent for a charcoal
portrait that Wharton had
commissioned." When she
"found the final version
unattractive, she offered it
to the sitter."

HENRY JAMES, 1912, OIL PAINTING BY JOHN SINGER SARGENT

"James loved the painting. Everything about it seemed wonderful, awesome. He felt 'almost ashamed to admire it too much—& yet can't help being proud of my so limited connection with it.'"

HENRY JAMES, 1913,
PHOTOGRAPH BY HILAIRE
D'AROIS

"He insisted that Sargent
be paid, though he had no
objection to the painter
giving his fee to a young
sculptor, Derwent Wood,
in payment for his creation
of a bust of James, for
which the young artist
took a series of starkly
candid working
photographs."

HENRY JAMES, 1913,
PHOTOGRAPH BY HILAIRE
D'AROIS

Ten

"MISS GRIEF"

1886–1891

(1)

One evening in May 1887, he dressed in a brilliant crimson cape and a splendid black velvet hat and descended from his villa on Bellosguardo into the crowded streets of Florence. The ancient city was celebrating the completion of the ornamental facade of the Duomo, which had taken almost six hundred years to achieve. Resplendent in his Renaissance costume, he danced in a "wonderful tapestried hall" in the Palazzo Vecchio at a grand ball in honor of the king and queen. "I wish you could have seen me," he wrote to Fanny Kemble—"I was lovely!"[1]

No sooner had he moved into 34 De Vere Gardens in early 1886 than he had felt a restless longing for Italy. From across the Alps, invitations came from the Bootts and Constance Fenimore Woolson in Florence, from the Curtises at Palazzo Barbaro and Katherine Bronson at Ca'Alvisi in Venice. His restlessness did not reflect dissatisfaction with De Vere Gardens. "My flat is perfection," he told William, "& ministers, more than I can say, to my health, my spirits & my work." But he had not "crossed the Alps for nearly six years," which seemed to him ages. His fantasy of spending a good part of each year in Italy still flickered. Irked by the constraints that London attractions and routines placed on his reading time, he had reason to exaggerate the amount of work he felt he accomplished away from London. Italian memories and voices called. In February 1886, he was startled with the news from Florence that Lizzie had married Frank Duveneck, an event so long in the making that he had thought it might not happen. Although he was pleased that for Lizzie the marriage was an affirmation of life, he was sad at what he felt the discordances of the match, Lizzie's loss of "independence and freedom," and the difficulties the new situation might create for the elderly Francis Boott. Together, he and Alice sent "a very modest nuptial offering . . . of 2 small pieces of silver" that "would have been more splendid" had he not found himself "terribly pauperized" by furnishing De Vere Gardens. "There may be no Italy for me this spring."[2]

The pauperization was an exaggeration to which he had become increasingly prone as he worried about the unpredictable fluctuations in his income. There were other reasons, though, for postponing a long visit to Italy. He wanted first to finish *The Princess Casamassima,* whose last installment was to appear in the *Atlantic* in October 1886. Some of the income from this he saved for his visit to Italy, and some he set aside to cover what he anticipated would be a lean period of diminished earnings. He had no serial novel in prospect for the next year. Alice's medical prognosis seemed as confused, as bleak, as unsatisfactory as ever. When one doctor diagnosed "gouty diathesis complicated by an abnormally sensitive nervous organization" with "neurosis in her legs . . . brought about by anxiety and strain," and predicted that "her health would improve when she reached menopause," Alice remarked, sardonically, that the latter "seems highly probable as I have had sixteen periods the last year." She had little desire to live that long. It seemed inconceivable to her that she would. For her brother, she was a responsibility that he took on unquestioningly. Without Katherine's presence, his loyalty helped keep him in England. When Katherine, to his delight, returned from the Continent in June 1886 to remain until early July, he helped Alice move to summer quarters in Leamington, the hundred miles' distance from London an expression of Alice's desire not to be a burden to her brother. She soon decided, after Katherine's departure for the Riviera in September, to stay on in Leamington, which appeared to Henry a "depressing solitary little place" but, to Alice, pleasantly quiet and conveniently economical.[3]

Her attempt to assert independence made Italy seem a little closer. So too did the completion, in late September 1886, of the *Princess.* The novel disappointed many of its readers, including William, who continued to be outspoken about his brother's fiction. In the three years since they had last seen one another, William and his wife had become parents twice more, though sorely tested by the death of an infant son. "Poor little mortal," Henry tried to console him, "with his small toddling promenade here below, one wonders whence he came and whither he is gone." He felt most for his sister-in-law. She gave birth the next year to a daughter, Mary Margaret. "These occasions make me indeed feel that I have simplified, though doubtless also (in a sense,) impoverished my life in remaining unmarried." Still living in a rented Cambridge house, William bought, for twenty-five hundred dollars, in the same month that Henry finished the *Princess,* a tract of seventy-five acres with "fine oak and pine woods, a valuable mineral spring, two houses and a barn" on Chocorua Lake near Conway, New Hampshire, five hours by train and carriage from Boston. His career at Harvard had been prospering, his teaching, which he disliked, widely praised. He published widely read papers and gave lectures advocating a psychology within which there were strong elements of realistic pragmatism, physiological materialism, and psychological speculation. "These inhibitions," he wrote Alice, "these split-up selves, all these new facts that are gradually coming to light about our organization, these enlargements of the self in trance, etc., are bringing me to turn for light in the direction of all sorts of despised spiritualistic and unscientific ideas. Father would find in me today a much more receptive listener."[4] Having signed, in 1880, a contract to write a psychology textbook, he felt frustrated at his slow progress on a book that was to take him ten years to complete. Its success was to elevate him from Cambridge to world fame.

William frankly told his brother—who felt exhausted after completing the *Princess,* having written two full-length novels in less than three years and who vowed never again to write a novel "nearly so long"— that he thought his brother's book a failure. Alice, who thought it magnificent, told William off. "I was vehemently indignant for 24 hrs. but now I shrug my shoulders, the Princess being one of those things apart that one rejoices in keeping & having to one's self. It is sad however to have to class one's eldest brother . . . among those whom Flaubert calls the bourgeois, but I have been there before!" Though reviewers, whom Henry did his best to ignore or devalue, were mostly either harsh or indifferent, loyal friends provided praise and support. Edmund Gosse had a genius for slightly unctuous compliments and exercised it regularly, and George du Maurier did not hesitate to tell James how brilliant he thought the *Princess,* how happily surprised he was at his friend's unexpected success in depicting "cockney vulgarity" and "the lower walks of London. . . . No English book that I have read for years either by yourself or any one else has wrapped me up so completely, or held me so intent. . . . Delightful refined & finished as your work has always been, this seems different in mind—much deeper chords are struck & sympathies appealed to."[5] The praise echoed James's own hopes for the book. Its poor sales and reviews disappointed them.

When Lizzie sent him wedding pictures, he responded to her query about why he did not come to join her at Bellosguardo that he was "unprepared with any excuse but the simple allegation that I am an idiot." How lovely it would be to smoke a cigarette with her in the beautiful garden with the best view in the world! He did have other excuses, including a fatigue that he hoped might respond to his spending the summer in his "new-& very conducive-to-quiet-&-work apartment." Finally, the town was quiet after the hectic social season—a springtime of dining out at what seemed mostly dull evening occasions, with only occasional flashes of conversational interest. There had been an inundation of American visitors, which made London seem more and more an American town during the social season and into the summer. He joked that he did not need to return to America to replenish his American experiences. What he called his "widows," whether their husbands were alive or not, came in their usual numbers, including Katherine Bronson, in England for the summer; Isabella Gardner, on her way to Bayreuth; and one of his Washington friends from the Adams circle, Mrs. Henry Cabot Lodge. Mrs. Gardner particularly clung to him. Her eccentric arrogance and deep sadness he found attractive, though she seemed more buoyant than when he had spent time with her in London two years before. Then she had seemed "worn & tired by her travels, but full of strange reminiscences, & in despair at going back to Boston, where she has neither friends, nor lovers, nor entertainment nor resources of any kind left. She was exceedingly nice, while here, & I pity her."[6]

Henry Adams was not one of the visitors, having taken his weary spirit off to Japan, his traveling companion, John La Farge. In January 1886, in Washington, Clover Adams, the most exclusive society hostess in the capital, without any visible anticipation or explanation except the recent death of her much-loved father, had killed herself in her photography studio by drinking potassium cyanide—the same Clover Hooper whom James had known since his Cambridge youth and with whom he had sat happily on the porch in the summer at Shady Hill all those years ago. "Hereditary melancholy" was the convenient, conventional diagnosis. Her Bostonian father had committed suicide, and her sister, Ellen Gurney, whom James admired, was soon to end her life by throwing herself in front of a train. Clover Adams, he wrote to Godkin, has found "the solution of the knottiness of existence. I am more sorry for poor Henry than I can say—too sorry, almost, to think of him."[7]

Two former Parisians had become London friends, one rather elusive, the other clinging. The latter, the novelist Paul Bourget, "an amiable Frenchman," James had met through Sargent in 1884. Bourget was "literary, clever, a gentleman, & an Anglomaniac, but rather affected. I take him next week to spend a day or two at Ferdinand Rothschild's." Eleven years younger than James, the handsome, energetic Bourget had traveled widely. He loved England almost as much as he loved himself. He had the hard-driving ambition of a French man of letters to whom no genre was foreign, and was determined to earn fame and fortune as quickly as possible. In 1885, his novel, *Cruel Enigma,* a seminaturalistic, psychologically steamy depiction of passion and corruption in the French upper classes, became a great popular success. It was the first in a series of successes, which, with his Catholic conservatism, led to his elevation to the Académie française ten years later. Worshipfully admiring James, Bourget spent the summer of 1884 in England. "He is too much of a dilettante," James told Perry, "but he is a very sympathetic & attractive being (aet. about 33) has a most subtle & brilliant little intelligence & is one of the most charming & ingenious talkers I ever met." James liked Bourget, without admiring his work. Their friendship was to be a long one—and James was to excuse what he felt to be Bourget's failings of character and flaws as an artist by blaming French culture rather than Bourget himself. "I have got out of him," he explained to William, "that I know him as if I had made him—his nature, his culture, his race, his type. . . . Your remarks about the putrefaction of the French character are admirable—and oh, how Bourget lights them up!"[8] James provided Bourget with letters of introduction to friends in Italy and in America. He spent time with him in Paris, in the south of France, where Bourget, soon after his marriage in 1890, bought a handsome villa, and in Italy, where in 1893 they spent several enjoyable weeks together. When Bourget dedicated *Cruel Enigma* to him, he was more embarrassed than flattered, the story "so *malpropre*" that he felt compromised in the straitlaced London world.

Sargent, who had left Bourget in James's hands, now spent more time in England than in France. James found Sargent's friendship attractive but his presence "incorrigibly vague & elusive. . . . I have lavished much friendship upon him, & he ought to do the few things I ask him," James complained to Lizzie Boott, "but he is very slippery." He granted, as many people had remarked, that Sargent was spoiled. Still, he got on with Sargent well and liked him immensely. To Sargent he owed the bemusing experience of entertaining at the beginning of July 1885 three French visitors to London, the most noteworthy of them Count Robert de Montesquiou, for whom Sargent had written a letter of introduction. An effeminate, affected, elegantly picturesque homosexual, Montesquiou, who was later to be a source for Proust's Baron de Charlus and whose portrait Sargent painted, was more interested in being introduced to the notorious Whistler than to James. The three

Frenchmen yearned "to see London aestheticism." James found Montesquiou "curious, but slight." At a dinner that he hosted at the Reform Club, James did "proper honour" to Sargent's introduction, entertaining Whistler and the Frenchmen to whom Whistler "desires greatly to show . . . the 'peacock room.' . . . On the whole nothing that relates to Whistler is queerer than anything else."[9] James was scrupulously polite to Montesquiou.

He and Gosse accepted Sargent's invitation to visit Broadway, a pastoral Worcestershire village where Sargent summered with other American expatriate artists, particularly Edwin Abbey and Frank Millet, the latter "a prodigy of Yankee energy and practicality." James found the mildly bohemian atmosphere of the Broadway colony pleasantly attractive. Probably he enjoyed the American voices, the American flavor. He went for brief visits for four consecutive summers. It "does something to keep me 'in touch' . . . with the land of my birth," he told Henrietta Reubell. He found "Sargent . . . quite domesticated there, portraits of ladies, painters' wives . . . & looking very big & brawny & happy. He 'fits in,' beautifully; he would fit in to everything, & isn't critical & fastidious, like you . . . & me!" In the autumn, in Bournemouth, visiting "poor sick Stevenson," he admired "Sargent's little picture of him, shuffling about in his room & pulling his moustache. It is very queer & charming." So too was its painter, so much so that he regretted Sargent's plan to spend the entire summer of 1886 "buried" in Broadway. When James visited, Sargent did "a very pretty *small* pencil drawing" of him, a profile emphasizing his high forehead, sharp nose and intense eyes. His hairline had receded so far back that, joined with the beard in profile, his face seemed divided into half darkness, half light. In late 1887, to James's disappointment, Sargent went to America, "where he set up a studio in New York" and had wealthy "sitters & triumphs & glory," including a portrait of "Mrs. Jack."[10] He seemed always on the move.

James decided that he also needed to move, to leave England for a while. After a difficult few years, he wanted to make an exclamatory break between his years at Bolton Street and the new comfort and creativity that he hoped would be his for the rest of his life at De Vere Gardens. He felt that he had earned a substantial holiday. London had become familiar and convenient, less challenging, more routinized. "I dislike more & more the everlasting social mill of this populous town. It is too dull for a lively place, & too lively for a dull one. Just so, I am too old (in spirit) to go out & yet too young to stay in—& so I get on not without friction." His intention was to spend a few weeks in Florence, where he had friends and happy memories, then a week each in

Rome, Naples, and Venice. His spirits rose in anticipation. "The thought of going to Italy, again, after a long & loathesome divorce, is absolutely rapturous to me." Early in December 1886, he crossed the Alps, traveling first to Milan, where he walked all morning, "drinking in the delicious Italian sun," and then to Pisa, where he had a moment of heartrending nostalgia thinking about the first time he had ever been there. "Do you remember," he asked Grace Norton, "one day when you were all here, your brother, & Jane, & Susan, in 1869—somewhat earlier in the autumn than this. We were all at this hotel & nothing seems to me changed—except everything!"[11] A few days later, in the garden of a Florentine villa, he smoked a cigarette and looked down, with relaxed satisfaction, at what he still thought the most beautiful view in the world. At least *that* had not changed.

(2)

Immediately in view at a neighboring villa was Constance Fenimore Woolson. Their friendship had become a warm one, a relationship built on her adoration of him, their shared profession, and his fondness for a companionable woman he thought both talented and good. Her residence in Chelsea in late 1883 and for much of the next two years had made them frequent companions, though at "discreet intervals."[12] They went to the theatre together. They visited Stonehenge. There was a need for discretion and some distancing, probably because he saw the danger of matrimonial rumors and his position being misunderstood. He valued her intelligence, her dedication to her work, and, most of all, her skills as a listener. Her health, particularly her tendency to find dark days and cold weather depressing, made England difficult for her. She fantasied about warmer climates, particularly Florida and Italy. Leaving London in early 1886, she returned to Florence, the city in which she had first met James.

With Woolson in Italy there was an additional incentive for crossing the Alps again. In May 1886, he asked Francis Boott to look her up at her *pensione* to introduce her to people and liven up her social life. "If Lizzie could take a look at her and attract her to the villa I should be so glad." Reclusive, shy, her isolation and self-reliance probably heightened by her semideafness, Woolson needed to have a hand extended to her. "She is a deaf and *méticuleuse* old maid—but she is also an excellent and sympathetic being." He hoped to join her in Florence in the fall, to visit her after she had settled on Bellosguardo, near the Bootts, in the Villa Brichieri, a fourteen-room house that she had rented cheaply for the next year. As he delayed his departure from London, his impatience grew. He thanked Boott for being attentive to Woolson. "Tell your father I thank him for the kindness which she tells me he has shown her in profusion." With a touch of condescension, he told Lizzie that though he would also be going to Venice and Rome, he would spend enough time in Florence to satisfy both his lady friends. "Our good Fenimore must also be worked in—but I shall be equal even to that. I am only glad you are nice to her—she is a very good woman, with an immense power of devotion (to H.J.!). . . . I don't intend to see *any one* but you & Fenimore."[13]

Woolson's own expectations may have been for greater intimacy between them. At one time, she may have fantasied that marriage was a possibility. If so, her pragmatism and pessimism told her that now, in her early forties, spinsterhood was almost a certainty. Having, like him, to earn her own living, she could bring neither money nor social standing to a marriage. She also had a perceptive awareness of his limitations. His self-absorption and emotional efficiency were unmistakable. Like him, she was compulsively dedicated to her work, one of whose central themes was the tense interplay between the female artist and social conventions. "A man's true earnest love is a great gift," she had written to a friend years before. "The glory of your life has come to you. Everything else is trivial compared to it."[14] She had had to settle for lesser things. Part of her power as an artist lay in the effective projection of the conflict between her needs as a woman and her situation as a writer. Two brilliant stories, "Miss Grief" and "The Street of the Hyacinth"—the first written soon after she had met James in Florence in 1880, the second, two years later—and a third story, "At the Château of Corinne," written in 1887, indirectly track her relationship with him. They express her anger, her disappointment, even her resignation, in a friendship that meant so much to her both in pleasure and pain.

Whether he guessed at his appearances in her stories is unclear. "Miss Grief" presents a fantasy about the ultimate triumph over obscurity of an unrecognized, aging woman writer through the limited, only partly prescient assistance of a minor male writer. In the first-person narration, Woolson presents a narrator who combines elements of James's limited male narrators and elements of James himself. Undoubtedly he read "Miss Grief" and "The Street of the Hyacinth." Perhaps the two writers talked about the stories. But his public criticism of her work, a generous tribute to her talents that he probably wrote in the fall of 1886 while they were together in Florence, focused on an appraisal of her most recent novel, *East Angels,* which he admired. She was an example, he told *Harper's* readers, of the equality, if not the primacy, of women writers in contemporary literature. Her work "breathes a spirit singularly and essentially conservative—the sort of spirit which, but for a special indication pointing the other way, would in advance seem most to oppose itself to the introduction into the feminine lot of new and complicating elements. Miss Woolson evidently thinks that lot sufficiently complicated. . . . It would never occur to her to lend her voice to the plea for further exposure—for a revolution which should place her sex in the thick of the struggle for power." Her strengths are her ability to evoke daily life with evocative details, her compassion for her characters, her sympathetic imaginative powers, "her general attitude of watching life, waiting upon it and trying to catch it in the fact." She had a gift for realism. She had a sometimes too exclusive fascination with the "tender passion," with the female situation and marriage. But insofar as it expressed "the stamp of the author's conservative feeling, the implication that for her the life of a woman is essentially an affair of private relations," he had no objection to make. Between the lines of his public expression of his admiration for her, he implied that here was a woman who suited his values. Henry senior would have approved. She was a writer he could admire without feeling threatened, a woman he could love without loving her as a woman.

(3)

Rather than squeeze into "some small tourist-hole in an insanitary Florentine hotel," he accepted Woolson's invitation to sublease, for the last three weeks of December 1886, the "roomy and rambling" apartment she had rented in the Villa Brichieri on Bellosguardo. It was not convenient for her to leave the nearby villa she was in until the first of the New Year. With a two-year lease on Brichieri, she would have plenty of time to enjoy it. James assured the nervous Bootts that there was no reason to be concerned: The villa would be neither too isolated nor too cold. Probably they were more worried about his relationship with Fenimore, who would be just a five-minute walk away. Happy at the prospect of being neighbors again, he told Francis Boott that he would decline his offer to stack wood in preparation for his arrival. He imagined that Fenimore, "whose devotion—like my appreciation of it is *sans borne*, has stacked me up a pile with her own hands. She is a gallant friend, but I am afraid she has bored you with me. Never mind, you will have your revenge; she will bore *me* with *you*." She had plenty of opportunity to do so. "I see her every day," he told their mutual friend John Hay, "indeed often dine with her."[15]

Although happy to be back in Florence, he disliked the constant rain and the sharp reminders of general poverty and decay. With fires blazing against the December cold, he had in mind work to do. "I am soon to write a *short* novel called 'The Tragic Muse.' I think," he told Grace Norton, "of studying the heroine from you." He began writing an essay on Stevenson for *The Century Magazine* and planned a number of short stories. But the adjustment to Italy took time. His spirits were at first low, his hopes for renewal and energy disappointed. He still imagined that he would remain for six to eight weeks, though he began to entertain the thought of staying longer. When he discovered that Alice, who had moved from Leamington to an apartment near his in Kensington, found her rooms impossibly small, he wrote to her to ask her if she would not do him the favor of occupying his flat while he was away, which would give his two servants something to do and would allow him the possibility of staying away longer, perhaps until the summer? Alice gratefully consented. The "general reluctance" of landlords to rent to invalids limited her choices. "I would gladly give her [my flat], regularly, in winter," he told Aunt Kate, "& spend my winters abroad; but that would end in my never seeing her."[16]

When he moved into a hotel in town at the beginning of January 1887, his room was "flooded with the splendid sunshine" that replaced the December rains. The yellow Arno flowed beneath his window. He was briefly depressed to realize that despite being committed to London, he felt as if a great weight had been lifted from him whenever he was away from it. "The solution, of course, is to be in Italy when one can— not to live, in short, where one *does* live." But that, he knew, was no solution at all. One needed to live where one was, with all one's consciousness alert and active in the present. By the end of the month, he felt more alive again. His fear that his "love of Italy" had become an "extinct volcano" disappeared in an "eruption" of responsiveness. "I find that I am quite capable—to my extreme satisfaction—of enjoying the dear old country as much—*almost*—!!! as I ever did."[17] He found the "*almost*" inevitable. But "almost" was enough.

From the Hôtel du Sud, he had most of Florence within a short walk. January blessedly provided nothing but sunshine, though the weather was cold. He hardly went to look at paintings. "They make me melancholy mad. I only visit Michelangelo, who being mad himself, pushes me back into sanity." He spent mornings at his table, writing the article on Stevenson and an article on London for *The Century*. It is his fullest expression of his awe at a city he found it difficult to live in but impossible to live without—nostalgically evoking "a certain evening . . . the end of a wet, black Sunday, twenty years ago, about the first of March [1869]," from which he dated his adult relationship with "the murky modern Babylon," the "particular spot in the world which communicates the greatest sense of life," the capital of the English language and of the literary life for a writer of English. More ideas for stories occurred to him, which he held in suspension in order to finish the articles, the money for which would help keep him abroad. When the daughter of General George McClellan, visiting in Venice, was surprised that her gossipy account, published in a New York newspaper, of the Venetian social life that she had experienced the previous autumn stirred up angry resentment among her Venetian hosts, he thought it a good idea for a story, "a pendant to *Daisy Miller*." By mid-February, he had "been driving the pen very steadily."[18]

But he had also been driving a social carriage to so many dinners that he felt repelled at the notion that he was being lionized and that he did not decline or at least resist many of the invitations. Though Florentine social life seemed a "thin polyglot world," he found it difficult to say no, a victim of insufficient self-disgust and aesthetic snobbery. "I likewise leave a card on every woman on whose plain face (they are mainly deucedly ugly) my eyes happen involuntarily to have rested." He felt pulled, like a spasmodic puppet, on the strings of habit and social convention, by boring "social importunities," by his habit of saying yes, his insecurity about saying no. He saw friends more than he saw strangers, though even the Bootts sometimes got on his nerves. Francis was his old self grown decrepit, occasionally still eccentric and amusing, but more and more laboring under old age and displacement. He was managing the strangeness of Lizzie being married to Duveneck better than James had anticipated. The miraculous happened—or at least what would have seemed the impossible just a year or so before. Slim, passive, Lizzie at the age of forty gave birth to a son. "Lizzie Duveneck's baby," he wrote to Aunt Kate, "is a little red worm—but Lizzie herself is blooming & evidently most happy. . . . The baby will apparently live & thrive—but Lizzie will plainly be much more of a wife than of a mother. She is much in love with her husband—who will never do much, I think, but who is, all the same, a fine, pleasant polite (though perfectly illiterate) man, whom it is impossible not to like. I shouldn't wonder if L. were to have still a blooming family."[19]

James had two new friends in Florence—the highly regarded American-born doctor William Baldwin who, seven years younger than himself, had become a permanent resident of Florence, a valued, influential member of the American community—and the much younger, intellec-

tually sharp, interestingly argumentative British writer, Violet Paget.
Handsome and energetic, Baldwin was a brilliant diagnostician with an
international reputation both for skill and boldness. Fortunately, at the
moment, James had no need of his professional services, but he enjoyed
his company immensely. Paget was a less companionable personality,
whom he had met for the first time in London in summer 1884. Though
she was not a great writer, he told Perry, she seemed to him "a most
astounding young female, & *Euphorion*," a book of essays on the Renaissance that she had just published, "most fascinating & suggestive, as
well as monstrous clever." A prolific and ambitious writer, the daughter
of a British diplomat who published under the pen name of Vernon
Lee, she made the mistake, in James's eyes, of not only turning to
fiction, where he thought her talents thin, but of dedicating her first
"very radical & atheistic" novel to him. What he liked most about her
Miss Brown was the vicarious pleasure of imagining the profits pouring
in "with a delicious monotony." Though he managed to be civil in
response to the dedication, he resented being associated so publicly
with a novel he disliked and took almost a year to thank her. When she
expressed her pleasure at his forthcoming visit to Florence, he responded
with his usual convoluted, evasive politeness.[20]

In Florence, he found her as "tigrish" as ever, her daily receiving
hour actually three hours. She was often "at home" evenings as well;
her drawing room was one of the most well attended in Florence. Her
social and intellectual life was driven by her angry competition with
her paralyzed half brother, Eugene Lee-Hamilton, a minor poet and
former diplomat—"who is always in her salon, bedridden or rather
sofa-ridden"—and by the constant presence of "a grotesque, deformed,
invalidical *posing* little old mother, and a father in the highest degree
unpleasant, mysterious and sinister, who walks *all* day, all over Florence, hates his stepson, and hasn't sat down to table with his family for
twenty years." Finding Violet and her world more interesting than
repelling, he visited regularly, the reward an intellectual liveliness and
imaginative playfulness that he found nowhere else in Florence. Toward
the middle of January 1887, while he was visiting her salon, he was
introduced to Countess Gamba. Her husband was "a nephew of the
Guiccioli," Byron's Venetian mistress, from whom they had inherited
"a lot of Byron letters of which they are rather illiberal and dangerous
guardians," so Eugene Lee-Hamilton told the attentive James. "The
Countess . . . says the letters . . . are discreditable to Byron; and H.
elicited from her that she had *burned* one of them." That night he jotted
down in his notebook a story that Hamilton told him, prompted by his
remarks about the countess, concerning a "Boston art-critic and Shel-

ley-worshipper. . . . Miss Claremont, Byron's ci-devant mistress (the mother of Allegra) [who] was living, until lately, here in Florence, at a great age, 80 or thereabouts, and with her lived her niece, a younger Miss Claremont—of about 50." The critic "knew they had interesting papers—letters of Shelley's and Byron's—he had known it for a long time and cherished the idea of getting hold of them. To this end he laid the plan of going to lodge with the Misses Claremont—hoping that the old lady in view of her great age would die while he was there, so that he might then put his hand upon the documents. . . . 'I will give you all the letters if you marry me!' "[21]

When James left Florence for Venice in late February, he began the transformation of the two anecdotes into one of his most compelling stories, "The Aspern Papers." Though he had intended to go to Rome at the beginning of February 1887, he had stayed on in Florence. There would be too many people he knew in Rome. Also, he feared that he would be appalled by the widespread "destruction and vulgarization" of the city. Perhaps he lingered for the pleasure of some of his Florentine company. In Venice Katherine Bronson happily provided him with her guest rooms in Palazzo Giustinian-Recanati—the extension to Ca' Alvisi in which Browning often stayed and which Browning's son had just vacated—"a very snug and comfortable little apartment of several rooms, including a private theatre," which may have seemed appropriate for a writer who still dreamed of theatrical success. In early March, Venice was brilliant. "The weather glows—the lagoon twinkles. . . . Venice—even at this crude season—is full of its old magic." Then it began to rain, continuously. "Yesterday there were sinister carts in the Piazza and men who looked like Irishmen shovelling away snow. One was almost sorry to have left Boston." At the middle of March, he became "miserably unwell for two weeks," with a horrible headache, a urinary infection, and what was soon diagnosed as jaundice. It was "the *longest* illness I have had since I was laid up with typhoid fever, so many years ago, at Boulogne." Between his health and the weather, Venice palled. Her "pestilent if romantic emanations" made him ill, he exaggerated, "for a month." As soon as he felt well enough, he decided to return to Florence, preferably to the more quiet Bellosguardo, "to be out of the turmoil" of the city.[22] Probably he missed Woolson and his other Florentine friends.

Other than at occasional moments of useful retrogression, he had been remarkably healthy for over ten years. Having developed sporadic gout, his feet sometimes swelled, and "a bad attack" occasionally got him out of an uninteresting invitation. Sometimes he would have "a savage neuralgic headache." It usually disappeared after a few days, or even more quickly if he refrained from writing and allowed himself bedrest. Occasionally, his back bothered him, but more as a reminder or an excuse than as a realistic problem. One morning, in London in 1882, Gosse found him "stretched on the sofa. . . . His appearance gave me a little shock, for I had not thought of him as an invalid. He hurriedly and rather evasively declared that he was not, but that a muscular weakness of his spine obliged him, as he said, 'to assume the horizontal posture' during some hours of every day in order to bear the almost unbroken routine of evening engagements. . . . This weakness gradually passed away. . . . His manner was grave, extremely courteous, but a little formal and frightened, which seemed strange in a man living in constant communication with the world."[23] Gosse had little sense of the shyness and privateness behind the temporary withdrawal and the elaborate formality. Appearances to the contrary, the world with which he had most communication was the world of his imagination.

After seven weeks in Venice, he returned to Florence in mid-April 1887, to stay until the beginning of June, this time not to the Hôtel du Sud but to Constance Fenimore Woolson's Villa Brichieri. With a servant, whom Woolson had hired, William Baldwin met him at the railroad station and drove him up to Bellosguardo, where Woolson made him comfortable in the apartment directly below hers. She had the first floor of the three-story, fourteen-room villa, he, the ground floor; she had the balcony and he, the garden. Both had a spectacular view. "Now that I am on terra firma—& high as well as firm I am quite as well as my perverse nature ever lets me be," he wrote to a London friend on the day of his arrival. He did not tell her that he was sharing the villa with Fenimore. Keeping their arrangement as secret as possible, he omitted mention of it from his letters, though he did not attempt to conceal it from visitors and local friends. To Alice and William he said no more than that he had "taken some rooms at Bellosguardo." Undoubtedly, he saw Fenimore every day. It was as much of a love affair with a woman as he was ever to have, a daily intimacy that protected daily privacy, that made no physical demands beyond courtesy, no emotional demands beyond friendship.

Baldwin attended to his health, Fenimore and Florence to his spirits. He limited his social life more than he had during his earlier stay. When he walked down into Florence, he strolled through the busy streets without being part of them, he made social calls and attended teas and dinners without the daily proximity that made invitations harder to decline. As he regained his strength, he began to walk most evenings down into Florence for an early dinner, ascending "back again in the balmy night" into the "light pure air." He resumed his visits to the Paget salon. Visitors came, Hamilton Aïdé and Rhoda Broughton; the latter was a prolific popular novelist whom James had met in the mid-1870s and liked "in spite of her roughness." She at first wrote audaciously frank, semi-autobiographical fiction about the problems of young women coming of age, and later satirically sharp, pessimistic novels. He adored living on Bellosguardo, where "the bells of Florence talk to you, at a distance, all day long." Spring blossomed around him, colorfully, exuberantly. Every time he raised his head from his writing table at his "supercelestial" villa, the "most beautiful view on earth" filled his eyes and his spirit.[24] In May, the Duomo *festa* brought pageantry, parades, costumes. Italy seemed glorious again.

Having returned from Venice with images of glittering canals and old palaces brightly fixed in his mind's eye, he began to incorporate the two anecdotes that Lee-Hamilton had told him and the Venetian scenery that had dazzled him into a new story, which he wrote during April and May 1887 at the Villa Brichieri.[25] The two central characters of "The Aspern Papers," the unnamed American narrator and the writer whose letters he desires to possess, were projections of aspects of himself. James sketched a career for the deceased and charismatic writer, Jeffrey Aspern, much like his own. In the relationship between the narrator and Tina Bordereau, who will give Aspern's papers to him as a gift if he will marry her, James touched on one element of his relationship with Constance Woolson, resonating with his lifelong awareness of what he had gained and what he had sacrificed in his decision never to marry. Though the narrator is willing to lie, steal, perhaps even murder, to possess Aspern's papers, he recoils at and rejects the one sure strategy for obtaining what he covets. Marriage, for this narrator, to Tina, or to anyone, is out of the question. He fears marriage more than he loves Aspern. The homoerotic sensibility that allows him to love Aspern recoils from the commitment that he must make if he is to marry Tina. Since his only route to possess Aspern is through a heterosexuality at odds with his nature, he finds, like James, that he cannot quite have either. It is one of James's most narcissistic stories of the problem of divided self-love.

As a schemer, the narrator is an utter failure, insufficiently cunning, ruthless, or bold to carry off his plot successfully. Immature and unsophisticated in his passion for Aspern, he is caught in an infantile fixation that damages his adult life. He makes too much of the Aspern-Bordereau relationship, investing it with a distinctiveness that implies his own emotional retrogression rather than a healthy critical mind or a strong imaginative vision. His scheme from the beginning is seriously flawed, the one alternative of those available to him least likely to succeed. He does not perceive that all such machinations depend on a complicity, silent or otherwise, between the victimizer and the victimized, and that the victimizer must pay a price for his success. The narrator, who wants to be Aspern, can only assume that power through possessing Aspern's papers. The lust for the papers suggests for James the dangers and the attractions of a man desiring to possess another man, of the ultimate union, literary and erotic, between Henry senior and Henry junior, between father and son, between master and disciple.

With a typescript of about half the "Aspern Papers" in hand and the manuscript of the remainder being typed in London, he went again in late May 1887 to Venice, staying for a month, "very happy in this effulgent steam-bath," as a guest of the Curtises in their "magnificent old palace—all marbles and frescoes and portraits of Doges—a delightful habitation for hot weather." A wealthy Bostonian, almost old enough to be James's father, who had been imprisoned briefly for assault after hitting a discourteous fellow passenger on a Boston train, Daniel Curtis had permanently exiled himself, vowing never to return to America. His exile was luxuriously cushioned, from 1881, by Venetian comforts, and then the purchase of the Palazzo Barbaro in 1885. He seemed to have brought Beacon Street to the Grand Canal. His anecdotes, James joked, were "unboreable—or unbearable." Even worse, the Curtises "can't keep their hands off their native land—and their perpetual digs at it fanned (if a dig can fan) my patriotism to a fever."[26] Like her husband, Ariana Curtis was literary without being talented, hospitable without being suffocating. Though he had intended to stay ten days, he stayed a month, working in the cool, vaulted upstairs library, lounging in the unusually spacious garden, developing affection for his obstreperous hosts, becoming even more enamored of Venice than he had been before.

From Florence, James had asked the Curtises to be hospitable to Bourget, who was in Venice, working on a new novel. "You may not (or rather certainly will not . . .) like his novels if you know them—but he is . . . one of the most pleasing minds, to me, of the younger generation of Frenchmen." Late in June, Bourget told him about a beautiful young friend of his who had committed suicide in Rome by jumping "out of the window . . . in her night-dress . . . while in the delirium of fever," which he was to make slight use of in "Two Countries." With Bourget, with the Curtises, with working mornings, sensually quiescent, summer-hot afternoons, and refreshingly cool evenings in large marble rooms or gliding along on the canals, the days passed quickly. He felt he could possess his "soul there; & I adored it

& came near taking a little cheap permanent pied a terre . . . (which was offered me) as an occasional asylum: but didn't—for all sorts of reasons—mainly the fear that if I had a link my love would turn to hate." It was a recurring temptation over the next decade, the fantasy of alternating London with Venice, of a permanent place of his own with a balcony overlooking a canal, where he could watch the gondolas and the handsome gondoliers drift by. But he feared the commitment, both the expense and the routinization. He also feared the sensual relaxation, the emotional complications of a world less restrained by Anglo-Saxon propriety, the fantasies and fantastic images provoked by "the flicker of the canal on [the] gilded roof" of the Palazzo Barbaro.[27]

(4)

He needed to return to London, partly because he had responsibilities there: to his sister, whom he had not seen for seven months; to his apartment, which Alice was about to vacate for a return to Leamington; to his clubs, his friends, and his publisher. He needed to get out of Italy at least to escape the summer heat. Having stayed in Venice two weeks more than he had initially intended, he pursued what he had told Violet Paget, before leaving for Venice, "was his small shy plan of returning" to Florence briefly. He admitted that he "hated good-byes," and did his best to "evade them by subtle arts." After two weeks in Florence, the heat began to become oppressive. He managed to say his hated good-byes to the Bootts and to Woolson. Having promised to stay briefly with Fanny Kemble at Stresa on Lake Maggiore, he went early in July 1887 from Florence to Lugano, where he picked up mail that Woolson had forwarded to him, then to Stresa, where he found his old and aging friend "more & more an extinct volcano—the shadow of her former self." Whenever he was away from London, he worried about her and missed her. He had not seen for eight months the friend whom in London he saw "regularly one night a week," and the changes were noticeable. Also, the heat was unbearable. "I roasted at Stresa," he told Sarah Wister, "in your mother's company. . . . I deplored [her] putting herself at that season into the transalpine oven; but her perversities, as you know, are not less magnificent than her rectitudes." Crossing the Alps in the middle of the month, he went directly, "with only 2 or 3 short stops," to De Vere Gardens. He returned with the high hope that these eight months in Italy had been the first in a series of annual migrations—London from July to March, Italy from April to June.[28]
    Returning to London in July 1887, he rediscovered his comfortable

breezy apartment, which Alice had left "in lovely order." He was pleased to have familiar elbowroom and to enjoy the sunny western windows, with "splendid awnings everywhere." He went almost immediately to Leamington to see Alice, who looked remarkably well "& in all her usual serene not to say brilliant spirits." He made some short country visits, spending a pastoral afternoon with Sarah Wister's sister, a few days with Frank Millet at Broadway, a week in September, "half pleasant, half insupportable," with the Roseberys in the "gilded halls" of Mentmore. He joined Lowell for three days at Whitby, in Yorkshire, experiencing weather so magnificent that he imagined that the long dead summers of his American childhood had come to life again. Lowell seemed as simple, amiable, "expressively kind as ever." No longer ambassador, he had returned to England semipermanently. "He very kindly knocked at my door the morning after my return," James told Grace Norton. With Mrs. Smalley to take care of him, he seemed happy. "I dined with him yesterday," he wrote to Grace Norton, "and she was there—in red velvet—and not her husband. But it is all right and most excellent for both of them."[29]

London entertained him again, dinners with Lowell, Du Maurier, the Smalleys, Mrs. Mason, Mrs. Lodge, late night tête-à-têtes with Fanny Kemble, parties, gossip, anecdotes, relationships, and situations that stirred his sympathy, his values, and his sharply observant novelistic imagination. "My rooms are perfect for quiet work, & quiet work is more & more all I care for. Staying with people is more & more onerous to me." He felt keenly the commercial failure of both *The Bostonians* and the *Princess*. Having fallen on "evil days," he felt impatient that the essays and stories he had written over the past year had not yet been published, as if somehow *The Century* and other magazines were conspiring to publish belatedly. He wanted to reestablish his presence, his desirability, to put out of everyone's minds the recent failures. "I hope during the next ten years to do some things of a certain importance; if I don't, it won't be that I haven't tried or that I am wanting in an extreme ambition. I am able to work better, and more than I have ever been in my life before." His productivity during his Italian months had been, he felt, substantial. He had done essays on Woolson, Stevenson, and London; and four or five stories, including "The Aspern Papers." He felt there was no end to his energy. He wanted to continue to do short pieces—like the brief article on Sargent he was now writing, to which he soon added an article on the Broadway group—to write short stories, to publish novels. He had in mind a brief novel that would highlight the deleterious universality of the journalistic mentality represented by "the odious 'Pall Mall,'" and a longer novel, to be called *The Tragic Muse,* "about half as long (thank God!) as the *Princess,*" which he haltingly began in early autumn 1887. By March 1888, he had agreed that it would be much longer than he had originally planned and be published as a yearlong serial in the *Atlantic.*[30] Financially, it was a sensible decision.

When, in autumn 1887, Katherine Loring left for Boston, with the likelihood of a long absence, he felt the possibility of Italy that next spring slipping away. Katherine's "existence," Alice wrote to Aunt Kate, "must be a mild purgatory. Some day the rights of women will be respected, I suppose." So too was Henry's "a mild purgatory." For him, Katherine's departure meant he must again become "the angel of the house," his sister's nurse. For Alice, Katherine's absence was hell. She "has been wrenched away from me and has now definitely passed from within my horizon for years. . . . I am stranded here until my bones fall asunder, unless some magic transformation takes place in my state." Her health immediately deteriorated. Having just returned from Geneva to Florence, Constance Woolson sent her compassionate sympathy. She also had been ill and depressed, some unspecified "dreary autumn illness" compounded by hard work and loneliness. In October, she indirectly wrote to Alice from Bellosguardo through Katherine, unaware that Katherine had left for America, that she was "grieved to hear that Miss James has been suffering. Tell her that an exclamation burst from me irresistibly, night before last—namely—'I wish she were here this minute!' [Lizzie Boott] was paying me a visit, & we were speaking of Miss James. The broad doors stood wide open; the moonlight outside lighted up my old garden, & the dark, rugged outline of Hawthorne's tower; perfume from a thousand flowers filled the room; & I was so happy to be here that it was almost wickedness! It seemed to me, then, that if Miss James' couch could be drawn across that door, she would enjoy it so much. And *she* would not be wicked. (I hear her exclaiming, 'Yes, I should!')"[31]

By the beginning of the year, Alice's health had improved. The quiet winter at Leamington suited her. "She will probably remain there a long time yet," Henry wrote to Lizzie Boott. . . . "Katherine L. is tied to America by all sorts of complications of illness among her near relatives. I shall not be able to go abroad for any time, more than a fortnight or so—as long as she is beyond the seas. . . . I am also a pere de famille—my little brood increases always—& I have no babies—but have to do it all myself." In the late winter and through the spring of 1888, Alice was "distressingly ill," which put off Italy indefinitely. When, in November 1887, the Bootts went to Paris for the winter, he regretted that he could not take time to join them there. He heard regularly from the Villa Brichieri, happy that Fenimore had "almost recovered." When London became enveloped by wintry fog and darkness, he felt a reawakened sense of the comfort of withdrawal, of London winters as lamplight, cozy fires, and privacy. "One looks within, because there is nothing to look at without & one fishes old fancies out of one's mind & dresses them up as one can." By Christmas, though, it seemed "blacker & more acridly smoky than even my tolerant spirit can stand. . . . I suppose," he told John Clark, that "the ice is on your windows & the snow upon your [Scottish] hills; & a purer mixture than I descry from *my* high casement, on the virtuous housetops of Kensington." One of the minor bright flares was the appearance of Coquelin on the London stage in seven or eight comedies, "including things he doesn't do in Paris. . . . I had really a fete of his three weeks. He came to lunch with me one day . . . & talked for two hours. As it was about his own matters he talked admirably well—but at the bottom of every comedian there is a ferocious sickening vacuity." During Coquelin's six months in London, he saw a good deal of the "insupportable man." London, though, hardly seemed "the capital of pleasure." The Home Rule question fouled the air even further. "How glad I am that I loathe politics and journalism—they justify one's loathing so, from hour to hour, that I shld. be ashamed of myself if I had *ever* liked them."[32] Whatever the outer weather, he was not in high spirits. Work came slowly. The winter wore on.

Suddenly, in March 1888, he had "an unspeakable shock." After a short bout with pneumonia, "dear little quiet, gentle, intelligent laborious" Lizzie Boott unexpectedly died in Paris. "I shall miss her greatly," he mourned, the friend whom he had known for almost twenty-four years, whom he had met in happy, hopeful days all those years ago in Newport. He believed that two of the labors she had died of were marriage and parenthood. His loyalty was to the devastated Francis, who now found himself bound to his son-in-law by a grandson whose mother had left him to the care of two men who had nothing in common but what they had lost. James had never for a moment imagined that Lizzie would die before her father. "It is essentially true that she had undertaken an effort beyond her strength, that she staggered under it and was broken down by it. I was conscious of this as long ago," he claimed to the grieving Francis, "as during those months in Florence when superficially she seemed so happy and hopeful . . . the terrible *specific gravity* of the mass she had proposed to float and carry.—It is no fault of *his*—but simply the stuff he is made of." As with Minny Temple's, he saw Lizzie's death as the only possible solution to her situation, to the impossibility of her carrying the heavy weight of

Duveneck. He consoled himself with an imagined inevitability that made her death somehow seem almost a constructive resolution of disharmonies.

But no rationalization could hold back his tears. He felt "bewildered at the violence of the change," and he imagined that when in the future he looked from Bellosguardo at the rooftops of Florence, he would still feel the violence of Lizzie's sudden departure. "I shall *see* her there, always more than anything else." Unlike Minny, she had not prepared those around her for her death by a lengthy period of illness. The change had taken him by surprise, dislocated his responsiveness. Writing immediately to Duveneck, he offered to come to Paris. But apparently Duveneck had no more need of James than James of him. Lizzie's ashes were taken to Italy for burial "in the dear old Florentine earth—the place where it is best to think of her sleeping, since sleep, forever, she does. That is another complication—of feeling—for I should have liked much to have been able to stand by her grave." But he did not feel he could leave Alice, who was suffering through the spring a series of breakdowns as extreme as she had ever experienced. "The fact that Lizzie has gone," Alice wrote to a mutual friend of their youth, "still eludes one & will ever remain one of the most inscrutable freaks of providence. It has surely been the only violent action of her life." For Henry, such an "inscrutable freak" could best be expressed in the terms that meant most to him. "With what an absence of *style,*" he told Ariana Curtis, "does the world appear to be ruled." In May 1888, as the spring blossomed, Lizzie was buried—"Many people and mountains of flowers. Boott absolutely calm—& Duveneck sobbing." Though he felt strongly the loss of not attending the funeral, letters from Florence—from Woolson, among others—made the scene vivid in his mind. Worried about Francis, he felt "great satisfaction," he told him, in knowing that you are within [Fenimore's] bountiful sphere." A week after Lizzie's death, he went to one of the Rothschild houses for the Easter weekend. The house was full of people. "So life goes on," he told Henrietta Reubell, a fellow mourner who was on the scene in Paris, "even when death, close beside one, punches black holes in it."[33]

After a summer of quiet recuperation and an autumn of work and London companionship, by October 1888 he was eager to get out of London. The summer had been unusually dark and cold, "rank with rheumatism." In early August, as if in imaginative identification with Fenimore, he had "a seizure of deafness, which became very bad." Fortunately, it "proved to be catarrhal & curable. . . . The town is empty," he complained, "but I am not going away. I have no money, but I have a little work." In fact, he had a great deal of work, some short stories recently completed, *The Tragic Muse* just under way. To keep him company at home, he had bought his first dog, a small Scotch terrier, whom he named Tosca and extolled as "the light of my eyes." He had also had enjoyable human companionship—three days in September at Broadway with Sargent, who had returned from America "very big & strong & red & flannelly & lawn tennisy & well, & . . . with him his younger sister [Emily], whom he used . . . as a model for lying on boats. . . . She was jocosely plaintive & they were both charming." He frequently took Sunday walks, especially to Hampstead to visit Du Maurier with a new friend, Jean Jules Jusserand, a French diplomat and scholar, "a little prodigy of literary & diplomatic achievement. . . . He is only 33 & he has written admirably on early English literature & manners & made his way wonderfully in the French foreign office. . . . He is alive to his very small finger tips, ambitious, capable & charming—& if he were a few inches less diminutive I should believe that Europe would hear of him as a diplomatic personage. But he is too short! Up to a certain point, or rather down to it, shortness, I think, constitutes a presumption of greatness—but below that point not." Though the walk up to Hampstead, "which used to be so rural & pretty," had become "all red brick & cockney prose," he enjoyed the aging Du Maurier's company, strolling on the heath with his "pretty daughters . . . & his little dogs. Then we go home & dine with him . . . & walk back to London at 10 o'clock." Du Maurier's great success, *Trilby,* he liked rather than admired. "I love the man & *want* to like what he does—so amateurishly & formlessly, but with such charming good faith & such an infusion of a tender, lovable personality." It made no difference to his friend that Du Maurier's work had grown "weak & monotonous (narrow) with time. . . . He is personally & conversationally the pleasantest creature."[34]

Sick of London, from which he had not been away, except for brief country visits, for fourteen months, he arranged to join Fenimore in Geneva in October 1888. Once he expressed his intention to go abroad, Alice strongly encouraged him, though he did not tell her about his arrangement with Woolson, just as he told Aunt Kate, William, and Grace Norton no more than that he expected "to go abroad for about a month—most of which I shall probably spend in Paris." This was discretion with a clear intention to deceive. Leaving London before the middle of October, he went directly to Geneva, where he and Fenimore stayed at separate hotels—connected by a short boat ride across the narrow lake—his own rooms a portion of the apartment in the Hôtel de l'Écu that he had stayed in with his family as a boy of sixteen in the winter of 1859–1860. "À propos of honey," he told Frederick

Macmillan, whose wife had given him a pot as a departure gift, "this place looks as lovely to me as ever—& the 'little change,' as they say in London, is already doing me good." Having sought out the ghosts of the past, he soon found them congenial. "I am sitting in our old family *salon,*" he wrote to William, "and have sat here most of the time for the last fortnight, in sociable conversation with family ghosts— father and mother and Aunt Kate and our juvenile selves." The weather was stunningly beautiful, filled with autumn colors that reminded him of America. He did "some quiet work," took "some quiet walks," looked "at the admirable blue gush & rush of the Rhône and at the chaîne des Alpes, which has been, every blessed day, fantastically near, clear & fair." He excluded from most of his correspondence that much of this was being done in Fenimore's company. They dined together every evening. He had never before been quite as fond of Geneva. "You share my odd & perverse taste for Geneva," he disingenuously wrote Henrietta, who had hoped that he would be in Paris by then. "I am fond of it—ça me rappelle mes jeunes années" ["it reminds me of my early years"].[35]

If his intention had been to spend only a month abroad, he had already spent three weeks of it in Geneva. At the end of October, he told Ariana Curtis that he was about to leave Geneva for Italy, for two weeks on the Italian Riviera near Genoa, perhaps to conclude with a short stay in Monte Carlo. It was unlikely, alas, that he would go farther south. But he had left London with the claim that he would be away only a month. He had said that he would spend most of it in Paris. Now, instead of going to Paris, he declared for the Italian Riviera and Monte Carlo. His schedule varied with his correspondents. In Geneva through October and beyond, he felt apparently as happy as he had ever felt before. Despite telling Ariana Curtis at the end of October that he was "just bringing to a close a stay of three weeks in this half lovable, half detestable little city," he and Fenimore stayed until mid-November. He felt "cradled into a sort of sentimental good-humour by old, or rather by young, associations. I spent a goodish bit of my early years here, & still feel sociably & affectionately toward certain Genevese things. I came abroad wanting to be quiet & rather *un*sociable—so I dodged Paris & didn't stop till I got here, where I have staid & where my only complications have been to look at the Mont Blanc chain, visible uninterruptedly far . . . & extraordinarily clear & near & fair, hanging over the bright blue lake. . . . The autumn-tints . . . have vied in multi-colouration with those of the jewellers' windows in the Rue du Rhône."[36]

Leaving Geneva for the Riviera and Genoa about the middle of

November 1888, he disarmingly assured a mutual friend that Miss Woolson "is well and flourishing I know." Her address was "Villa Brichieri, *Bellosguardo,* Florence." Whether she went with him to Genoa is unclear. She may have gone directly back to Bellosguardo, as he told Francis Boott, though the route would easily have accommodated their traveling together as far as Genoa. He spent two weeks in Genoa and Monte Carlo, going north to "that terrible Paris," as he joked to the impatient Henrietta, almost at the end of November. By early November, Alice had discovered the truth, which she shared with William and Kate. "Henry is somewhere on the continent flirting with Constance," she told Aunt Kate. To William, at the end of the first week of December 1888, she put it more strongly. "Henry has been galavanting on the continent with a *she*-novelist, when I remonstrated he told me he thought it a 'mild excess.' " Apparently, Alice either knew or assumed that they had traveled together to Genoa and Monte Carlo. A few days after Alice's letter, Fenimore wrote, without mention of Henry, to one of her oldest, dearest American friends. "I am quite scandalously well this winter. Haven't had an ill moment; & am stout as can be. I am so much better—my health so much *firmer*—than it used to be that it is really quite remarkable. I was ill last winter; but that was owing to mental depression."[37] They parted apparently in excellent spirits, with the expectation that they would see one another soon. She would visit London. He hoped to go to Italy the next spring.

(5)

From his high perch above the dark London streets, he looked down, as New Year's Day, 1889, approached, at what appeared a Christmas season almost without joy, a holiday that there seemed few reasons for England to celebrate. The view was Dickensian in the most unhappy way. London "seemed *all* foul fog, sordid mud, vile low black brick, impenetrable English density & irrecoverably brutal & miserable lower classes!" For the first time, he saw, with a distaste and a moral conscience that challenged its attractions, "the vast miseries and meannesses of London." He personalized the discomfort and the ugliness. His body ached with flu, his head was feverish, his pains were sharp. London winter heaviness seemed even to weigh down his imagination. "I miss . . . the relief & refreshment that would come from an occasional skip or jump upward, a flutter of the wings. Nowhere & in nobody & nothing does one find *that* here; & one's own gifts decline & lower their level & standard!" What he had come to London for, London no longer seemed to provide. The freshness of the experience had worn away, "the glamour, the prestige and the mystery." England seemed "frumpy," tattered. He felt the accumulated "simple solid rust" of thirteen years of London life. His imagination could no longer sustain his initial vision. He appreciated the spaciousness, with its three bed-rooms and three sitting rooms, of his De Vere Gardens flat. "It is everything to me." Having "worked *through* a good many superfluities & vanities (not valueless in their hour)," his social commitments were more controlled, his time more at his command.[38] But, from the time of his return to London in late 1888, the balance had changed.

The economic balance had changed strikingly for the better, though he was to discover unhappily that the improvement would be short-lived. He was almost never again to earn as much money as he earned that year. For a moment, though, it seemed as if he could put the commercial failure of his two previous novels behind him. Before leaving for Geneva, he had finished a short novel, *The Reverberator,* which appeared from February to July 1888 in *Macmillan's Magazine.* From Houghton Mifflin in Boston he received twenty-two hundred dollars as half of the advance against the publication in the *Atlantic* of *The Tragic Muse,* which he had begun writing in spring 1888.[39] The *Atlantic* published "The Aspern Papers"; *The Fortnightly Review,* his essay on "Maupassant" and an article on Pierre Loti; *The Century,* his essay on Stevenson, a story, "The Liar," and a review of the works of the Goncourt brothers; *Harper's,* "Two Countries"; *Scribner's,* "A London Life"; *The Universal Review,* a story, "The Lesson of the Master"; *The English Illustrated Magazine,* a story, "The Patagonia"; and, finally, *The Century,* his long essay on "London." It is a dazzling list.

But there was still more. With Macmillan, he negotiated the publi-cation of two volumes of his recent stories, reprocessing them as quickly as possible into additional cash. "The Aspern Papers" made a volume, published with two other stories, in September 1888. "An essential part of the idea, for me, is to have some money," he had bluntly told Macmillan. He proposed another volume, which would contain "A London Life" and three other stories. "My aspiration in regard to these two volumes . . . will not have been fulfilled unless I receive something 'down,' a certain sum in advance, of course I mean, on that 15 percent royalty which I should otherwise have a long time to wait for." To obtain the advance, he gently twisted Macmillan's arm and stretched the literal, though not the emotional, truth. He genuinely felt poor. "I am settling down to write a longish novel (it begins in the *Atlantic* in January next & runs a year) so that for the next few months I shall be engaged on work without immediate return—a strain I am sorry to say that I am not, just now, rich enough easily to stand. I may be asking something so unusual that it is impossible—but without asking I can't know. If it is consistent with your powers to make me such an advance as will ease off the said strain, I shall greatly appreciate the heroics to yours ever."[40]

It was an extraordinary year, in which, his name constantly before the public on both sides of the Atlantic, he pocketed almost nine thousand dollars, and with far less discomfort in the negotiations than had ever been the case before. He had finally put his business interests into the hands of one of the first well-known practitioners of a new profession. In early 1888, on Gosse's recommendation, James hired A.P. Watt to handle his business affairs. Watt had established a reputation as the business representative of numbers of well-known writers, including Rider Haggard, Bret Harte, and Wilkie Collins. "He appeared eager to undertake *me, &* I am promised remarkable good results from it. He is to make one's bargains & take charge of one's productions generally—but especially over here. He takes 10 percent of what he gets for me, but I am advised that his favorable action . . . more than makes up for this—& that even if it didn't the relief & comfort of having him take all the mercenary & selling side off one's mind is well worth the cost. I debated a long time, but the other day he came to see me, & after a talk seemed so much impressed with the fact that I have done much less well for myself than I ought to . . . that I entered into relations with him."

But neither employing a literary agent nor his personal relationship with Macmillan saved James the disappointment of finding that neither Macmillan nor any other publisher was willing to pay for *The Tragic Muse* what he thought the novel was worth. Naturally, he evaluated the market value of his fiction in terms of personal and professional pride, whereas Macmillan evaluated worth in terms of sales. In the past, he had thrown in extra measures of cooperation and money—because of his respect for James as a writer and for personal reasons—but he had lost more money on James's two previous novels than he could comfortably absorb. In March 1890, *The Tragic Muse* having completed its serialization in the *Atlantic,* James solicited an offer. When Macmillan responded with nothing down and two-thirds profit in the future, James articulated a fact that Macmillan knew all too well. "That future is practically remote and I am much more concerned with the present. What I desire is to obtain a sum of money 'down.' " He would try other publishers if necessary. Macmillan then offered a seventy pound advance. "Don't . . . think my pretentions monstrous," James told him, "if I say that in spite of what you tell me of the poor success of my recent books, I still do desire to get a larger sum, and have determined to take what steps I can in this direction. These steps I know will carry me away from you, but it comes over me that that is after all better, even with a due and grateful recognition of the readiness you express to go on with me, unprofitable as I am. . . . Farewell then, my dear Macmillan, with great regret."[41]

Relenting, Macmillan again did the "heroic" thing, which amounted to a lease agreement for which, in return for an immediate payment of £250, the publisher was to have all profits from *The Tragic Muse* for a period of five years. At the end of the period, he was to regain only £80 of the £250 he had paid out. James had been gradually feeling his market value declining, his English audience drifting away. Though he had received the handsome sum of forty-four hundred dollars from the *Atlantic* for the serial rights for *The Tragic Muse,* no English periodical wanted to purchase it. He had the unhappy sense that Macmillan had done all that he reasonably could. The high income he had earned in 1888, he clearly saw, had been the product of extraordinary productivity, particularly the creation and reprocessing of short stories and articles. Articles he wrote primarily to make money to allow him to have sustained free periods in which to write novels. Short stories he deeply believed in. They had integrity, high artistic challenges, and value. But he did not want to write only short fiction, though he tried to rationalize what might be a necessity into a virtue, into a high artistic strategy. After a lunch in May 1889 with Du Maurier, Jusserand, and the famous French literary critic, aesthetician, and philosopher, Hippolyte Taine, he suddenly felt a revived, refreshed interest in the short story. Taine had been talking about Turgenev's short stories with high praise. The conversation did "me a world of good," he told his notebook, "confirming, consecrating, as it were, the wish and dream that have lately grown stronger than ever in me—the desire that the literary heritage, such as it is, poor thing . . . shall consist of a large number of perfect *short* things, 'nouvelles' and tales, illustrative of ever so many things in life—in the life I see and know and feel."[42] The high ambition at least partly reflected the low and declining market for his novels.

As brilliantly as he sometimes managed the challenges of the short story as a form, he constantly felt pressured by the economy it demanded and by the predetermined lengths established by editors— by the necessity to be briefer than his energy and artistic ideas could comfortably adjust to. "I fear," he complained to himself, "that with

all the compression in the world I can't do it in so very short a compass"
as one of his editors demanded. He invoked the inspiration of Maupassant, the writer whom he thought most triumphant in the short story
form. Having met Maupassant through Flaubert in Paris in 1875, he
had renewed his acquaintance with him, particularly in the summer of
1886, when Maupassant had visited England. James entertained him at
dinner, introduced him to Du Maurier and Gosse, and took him to
Waddesdon to visit the Rothschilds. As with the other French realist
writers, James admired Maupassant's artistry but not his morals. The
French writer was celebrated for his love affairs. When Maupassant told
him ribald stories, James never forgot them, particularly the story of a
triangular love relationship between two men and a monkey. In London, in summer 1886, with one of his beautiful mistresses, Blanche
Roosevelt, Maupassant embarrassed James in a restaurant by urging
him to approach an attractive stranger and tell her that Maupassant
wanted to have sex with her. James declined. When Maupassant wanted
James to make the request of a second lady, he declined again. When
Maupassant then wanted him to ask a third lady, James fled.[43] But he
did not flee an appreciation of Maupassant's artistry, nor his brilliance
as a short story writer, which transcended the moral distastefulness of
some of his subjects and which James celebrated in an appreciative essay
in March 1888. To enjoy Maupassant, one needed to accept him on his
own terms, James argued. He was willing to do so. His occasional
hesitation never prevented him from elevating the uniqueness of genius
over commonplace morality. He urged himself to take inspiration from
Maupassant's genius as a writer of short fiction, though with an intensity that expressed his sense of defeat in marketing his own novels and
his discomfort with the limitations of the short story form.

Still, he needed the income from short fiction. In fact, he felt so
strongly the necessity to increase his income that he agreed to write
four articles during 1888–1889, which slowed him in his progress on
The Tragic Muse, and agreed, at the end of 1889, to devote much of the
first three months of 1890 to translating for *Harper's* an unpublished
novel by Alphonse Daudet. "I was bribed with gold—more gold than
the translator (as I suppose) is accustomed to receive." But he also
realized that he sometimes made unwise, even economically unrealistic
decisions. "It was really stupid, and it was needless, to consent," he
reminded himself, in February 1889, in regard to the four essays.[44] It
galled him that he had last worked on *The Tragic Muse* in the autumn of
1888. But without sufficient payment for his work, he felt economically
squeezed. Worse than that, he felt a failure, both personally and professionally humiliated. At a time in his life and career when he had antici-

pated that he would have not only "name and fame" but ample money as well, he felt it was humiliating not so much to ask for more but to be offered less than met his financial and emotional needs.

He had sacrificed much for his art, including, at least in conscious consideration, marriage and fatherhood. He dramatized the sacrifice in a gripping, tightly focused short story, "The Lesson of the Master." Transforming a raw anecdote told him by Theodore Child into a delicately ironic presentation of his own situation, James provides in Henry St. George a version of his own sense of having done too much hackwork over the years, his position as a senior writer whom young writers admiringly consulted, and his fear that his new work might be inferior to his old. The ironic turn is that whereas Henry St. George has been rewarded with affluence, "the angelic Harry" had still to struggle for money. In the young, talented Paul Overt—whose admiration for St. George turns to suspicious resentment when the elder writer marries the woman he himself loves after having advised Overt that marriage is incompatible with a literary career—James neatly, ironically, devastatingly, turns the tables on himself. He delicately exposes the unhappiness of his own situation, in which he feels that he has neither the commercial success of Henry St. George nor the artistic integrity of Paul Overt. Unlike Paul Overt, though, James had unequivocally made it clear that he would not and could not fall in love with a woman in a way that implied a union and a consummation.

In *The Tragic Muse,* which he began to publish in the *Atlantic* in January 1889, a gifted portrait painter, Nick Dormer, modeled partly on Sargent, declines to subordinate his artistic mission to a career in politics, though it means the loss of the woman he genuinely loves and of the immense wealth that he would obtain by marrying her. In contrast to his aesthetic friend Gabriel Nash, Nick, as a portrait painter, envisions art as a representation of, and interaction with, the world of people and things. With touches of Oscar Wilde, who appears in diffused ways in some of the ideas of the novel and in some of the metaphors, Nash wants to make his life a work of art. He wants to live life at the highest level of pure flame, like a Paterean bright light that burns without being consumed or consuming, without a product, without a thing to be called a work of art other than the artist himself. Nick wants to create paintings that can be sold. When he imagines that his portrait of Miriam Rooth as *The Tragic Muse* is fading away into blankness, he is bewildered, perhaps less so than James would have been if he had read Wilde's *The Picture of Dorian Gray,* which began appearing in *Lippincott's Magazine* in July 1890. The latter may have been in part a contrapuntal, slanted response by Wilde to *The Tragic Muse,* whose serial publication was completed in May 1890 and which was published in book form early in June. But Dormer has a Jamesian, not a Wildean, moral and aesthetic problem. In one of his early notes for *The Tragic Muse,* James puts Dormer's dilemma quite clearly. Julia "virtually says to Nick: 'You have great talent—you *may* have a great future. But you have no money, and you can do nothing without that. I have a great fortune and it shall be yours.' . . . She appears soft, seductive—but in it all there lurks her *condition*—her terms. . . . He feels this—feels the *condition.*"[45]

In March 1889, while still in the early stages of writing *The Tragic Muse,* James saw Sargent's "absolutely magnificent portrait of Ellen Terry as Lady Macbeth." It is the kind of painting that Nick Dormer aspires to create. In the painting, Ellen Terry is as "beautiful as an image." On the stage, he thought her "abominable as an actress." But in the riveting portrait, "she is clad in splendid peacock-blue robes, with a cobalt background, like an enamel or a figure in a missal or a mosaic, & with her wondrous green mantle, her iridescent garments, her huge, wild red braids (of dyed horsehair) hanging to her feet, her shining barbaric crown which, with a grand movement of the arms, she is placing on her head—and with, above all, her wondrous pale, fatal, painted, terrible face—half-Medusa, half-Rossetti, with light-coloured eyes & scarlet lips—she is a very distinguished person indeed & a very prodigious image. It is a *noble* picture—very strange, very bold, the result of a wonderfully vivid & direct vision of what he wanted to do & a still more wonderful ability to render it."[46] On the less histrionic stage of *The Tragic Muse,* the young actress Miriam Rooth embodies a contemporary aesthetic version of Lady Macbeth's ambition and dedication.

Having fallen in love with Miriam, the conservative young diplomat Peter Sherringham, for whom the theatre is an ambivalent passion, finds that she will not give up the stage to marry him. She proposes that he give up the diplomatic service to marry her. With touches of an evocation of what the young Fanny Kemble might have been like, perhaps also with Sarah Bernhardt in mind, James portrays in Miriam Rooth an actress of dedication, strength, and immense ambition. In the end, she marries the innocuous, slightly foolish Basil Dashwood, a theatre manager and theatre businessman. She marries him to protect herself from the attention of other men and because he can take care of the business of her career. Unlike Verena Tarrant, her sense of herself— her powers and her ambition—matches her performance talents. If she is ruthless, she must be so to accomplish her artistic ends.

(6)

Frustrated with his commercial failure as a novelist, desperate for money and for public fame, James turned to the theatre. It was only a half turn, prompted by an unsolicited request in December 1888 from a minor actor and producer, Edward Compton, to consider writing a stage version of *The American,* a novel that had been out of his mind and interest for many years. Though he had never met Compton, whose acting company mainly toured the provinces, he had years before met his wife, the former Virginia Bateman, an American actress who frequently performed the female lead in the company's productions. "I remember Mrs. Compton perfectly," he told her husband.[47] Compton's request fell on the fertile ground of past fantasies and present disappointments.

Since his unproduced stage adaptation of *Daisy Miller,* James had believed that there could be no possibility of commercial success for serious, aesthetically ambitious drama. When asked in 1884 to write a stage version of *The Portrait of a Lady,* he had responded that he would consider writing either an original play or an adaptation of a different novel in the near future "on the chance that if you *should* like it, it would open the door to my acquiring a goodish sum of money." In *The Tragic Muse,* Gabriel Nash expresses James's distaste for the "basest concessions" that a playwright who hopes to be produced must make to an audience that demands that the evening's business be limited by the time "between dinner and the suburban train." James took weeks before responding positively to Compton's request. "Much occupied & preoccupied for the moment," he had asked Compton for a few weeks to think it over. It had already been suggested "three or four times (on the last occasion three or four months ago,) & the objections, in every case, appear[ed] to me greater than the inducements." He would give him "a yes or no" shortly.[48] Who had made these suggestions he nowhere says. Perhaps he had in mind to encourage Compton with competition. Whatever hesitation he had was soon overwhelmed by the fantasy of being a wildly applauded author and his hope that now, finally, was his chance to make a great deal of money.

James had long ago developed the habit of feeling poor. His poverty was especially the ache of emptiness, of disappointment. He did not hesitate to express his feelings to close friends. Gosse knew his friend's mind in the late 1880s. "He was disappointed—he made no secret to his friends of his disillusion—in the commercial success of his novels, which was inadequate to his needs, and . . . at no time . . . was [he] really pressed by the want of money. But he thought that he was, and in his anxiety he turned to the theatre as a market in which to earn a fortune." James did not disguise the commercial motive from himself. In late spring 1889, he mused to his notebook about the unexpected turn of events, with little sense that the new venture was to be a painful failure. "I had," he admitted, "practically given up my old, valued, long cherished dream of doing something for the stage, for fame's sake, and art's, and fortune's: overcome by the vulgarity, the brutality, the baseness of the condition of the English-speaking theatre today." But now the prospect had been revived "on a new and very much humbler basis, and especially under the lash of necessity." He decided not to limit his playwriting to a single experimental effort. His approach had a Napoleonic willfulness to it, as if his energies were unlimited, as if creative assertion were tantamount to victory. "I simply *must* try, and try seriously, to produce half a dozen—a dozen, five dozen—plays for the sake of my pocket, my material future. . . . The field is common, but it is wide and free—in a manner—and amusing. . . . Therefore my plan is to try with a settled resolution—that is, with a full resolution to return repeatedly to the charge, overriding, annihilating, despising the boundless discouragements, disgusts, 'écoeurements.' One should *use* such things—grind them to powder."[49]

His approach was technical, his naïveté, immense. Having seen innumerable French farces and comedies, he did not see why he could not adapt or create one for the London popular stage. To attempt to write an intellectually and artistically sophisticated drama would be to insure small audiences and certain failure. He did not aspire to write plays that would be the dramatic equivalents of his fiction. Serious drama would earn him, he imagined, no more money than had serious fiction. He assured himself that theatrical success demanded mainly technical cleverness, literary craftsmanship, and a perceptive evaluation of what London and New York audiences required. If he kept at it, his technical abilities and his craftsmanship would be honed by experience. Success seemed likely. Though he would not always do it happily, he would, he decided, be totally accommodating. He knew, in theory, that writing for the popular stage was a collaborative effort, with scripts subject to constant revision under the pressures of rehearsal and performance. He did, though, from the beginning, underestimate how painfully galling such a process would be, how much he would resent not having full control of what he wrote. His preference was to provide as commercially viable a script as possible before the process of communal revision would begin. For the adaptation of *The American,* Compton would want a happy ending. Christopher Newman, in the stage version, must, James accepted, "get his wife." The battles that he had fought with Howells and other editors for control over his plots, for the baseline of artistic realism, he readily avoided. "Oh, how [the play] must not be too good and how very bad it must be!"[50]

By spring 1890, he had finished adapting *The American,* which he at first called "The Californian," into a four-act play, the second act of which he had sent to Compton three months before. "I have . . . written a big (and awfully good) four-act play," he told Henrietta Reubell in April, "by which I hope to make my fortune." He felt "ravished" by Alice's unreservedly enthusiastic response to her reading of the script. Confined mostly to her sickbed, she embraced the opportunity of vicariously sharing her brother's adventure. Your response, he told her, "makes me feel as if there had been a triumphant premiere and I had received overtures from every managerial quarter and had only to count my gold." He had done, he felt, exactly what was required. "It is all 'art' and an absolute address of means to the end— the end, viz, of meeting *exactly* the immediate, actual, intense British conditions, both subjective and objective, and of acting in (to a minute . . .) two hours and three-quarters." He felt an uneasy combination of intense nervousness and wild optimism. Fortunately, he had someone new to help him arrange and safeguard his gold, a young American businessman, playwright, and novelist, Wolcott Balestier. Recently come to London, Balestier had met James in late 1888, and had soon been employed to replace his agent Alexander Watt, perhaps because he had a special interest in the theatre. To the older man, Balestier seemed a paragon of intelligence and competence, the "perfection of an 'agent.' "[51] Balestier thought the play a likely success, a handsome beginning. So too did another new friend, Florence Bell, the sweetly supportive, intelligent wife of a wealthy Yorkshireman, a writer herself, who adored the theatre.

Most important, Compton liked it enough to begin rehearsals in early November 1890. From Italy, where James spent May through July, he kept one eye on the production plans, the other on the delights of a vacation sponsored by the hospitality of Baldwin in Florence and the Curtises in Venice. Italy was as "delightful . . . thank heaven, as ever. That trick is never played out—that magic always works, & as long as this is the case I think I shall never grow quite old." The warmth, the color, the noise, were revivifying after a winter of London cold and influenza. He was delighted "to find that the taste for [Italy] doesn't leave me in my old age—as some of the tastes of my youth have." He found, though, that he had little taste for the Oberammergau festival, which he attended in June 1890 with the Curtises. The accommodations were uncomfortable, the hours early and long, the crowds immense, the rain incessant, the passion play itself " 'sincere' & tedious." But he loved the Dolomites, "so much more empathetic than the Alps, & all the foreground a universe of glorious blue tumbling rivers & immensities of grass smothered in more kinds of lovely wild flowers than I knew existed upon earth. Above this rise the most splendid individual peaks, not in chains or clusters, but as if cold-shouldering each other (with their collars of snow) each on its own romantic hook." What he loved even more was the beauty, the luxury, the sense of privacy and privilege of the Palazzo Barbaro, which he had to himself for thirty-six hours in July. "I arrived at 6 o'clk. with the intention of simply picking up my clothes & sleeping that night," he told the Curtises. "But the next a.m. it was not in human nature to tear itself away! The day was delicious . . . & your marble halls suffused with the 'tender' note of your absence, were most pleasing & irresistible of all. I strutted about in them with a successful effort of self-deception & tasted for once of the fullness of earthly greatness." Delaying his return to London, he engaged rooms on the cool heights of Vallombrosa, "more than 3000 feet in the air," the furious heat beneath and behind him, "in the most exquisite beautiful spot I have ever seen in my life: mountains & woods & wonderful views—deep romantic shade—all hanging in the cool blue Italian air."[52]

Even in Italy the excitement of the pending production of *The American* played a constant countermelody to his relaxation. In London, imagining that his presence was required at every rehearsal, he kept "dashing off into the country," through November and December, to wherever the Compton group was performing, in preparation for the premiere in Southport, near Liverpool, in early January. The excitement of participating in rehearsals, the communal emotion, the alluring smell of "sawdust and paint," helped him keep his bags packed, his energy flowing. He found himself "visiting all kinds of queer places & passing rheumatic hours on all sorts of draughty stages." He went, with a sense of exhilaration, from the solitude of writing alone to the sociability of working with an acting company that he believed had to revolve around the author. But, ultimately, "it's all for lucre—all for lucre—that gilds the dose."[53] If successful, manager and playwright hoped for a London production in the fall.

While final rehearsals for *The American* continued, he wrote another play, "Mrs. Vibert," later to be renamed *Tenants*. He had finished "(written in a month, working tooth & nail) another drama," he confided to William, "of which I am tomorrow to read," in London, "the

3d (& last) act to the interpreters," two moderately well known actors "who have taken it in hand" in the expectation of a vehicle for themselves, with the encouragement of the actor-manager John Hare, whom James hoped would produce the play. "I have already read them the 1st & 2nd with high success—& the 3d, I know for I am extraordinarily wise about all these matters now—is calculated to please them best." He thought it "pure *movement,* intensely interesting and suspense-producing." The second act he had cut "as effectually and bloodily as the most barbarous dramatic butcher could desire; and have touched and amended the first. My III is, I think, absolutely producible *tel quel*—I learn so fast!" The reading, he was convinced, had been a "high success. . . . My auditors 'rose at' me, gave themselves away and were flushed and effusive." He was not counting on *The American* alone. "I have still other dreams of ultimate lucre, & of a London production of the 2d piece before that of the American, which (unless it is unexpectedly brought to town,) is to be played in England, Scotland & Ireland before it is down, with a cast largely new, here."[54]

By mid-December 1890, while the Parnell drama occupied the national stage, his own stage rehearsals were suspended until the dress rehearsals immediately before the premiere. He breathed more easily but still nervously. He had, he told Ariana Curtis, "polished off the pressing task. . . . I have done so, to a charm (the 'charm' is a manner of speaking,) & now I can take breath." The "imperative . . . dramatic job" that had absorbed him had been the writing of "Mrs. Vibert"— "the composition at high pressure & with extreme rapidity of a *new* play (of which fortunately I had carried the subject & substance in my mind for years,) to meet a special contingency & 'fit' a couple of actors— to whom I have been reading it act by act, with all the success I could have wished." It seemed almost certain that, unlike *The American,* it would be produced first in London, though when was still unclear. Having in mind that Compton would need another play with which to follow up the anticipated London success of *The American,* he devoted much of the second half of December to writing the first act of a third play, "a comedy in three acts," probably an early version of a play later published as *The Album.* He wished to "finish the first [act] *immediately,*" he told Florence Bell. "I did so brilliantly, of course, yesterday." His "of course" suggests some ironic self-deflation, but it released very little pressure from his nervously over-expanded theatrical aspirations. He tried, with limited success, to keep his optimism for *The American* within bounds. "I hope for a success & am presumptuous enough to almost believe in one, inasmuch as, battered, vulgarized, 'cut,' rendered only with humble zeal & without a ray of genius, the poor distracted play, when I see it rehearsed, appears to me to have, in spite of its misfortunes, inherent vitality—to hold up its head and make a fight.''[55]

At Southport for the dress rehearsals, he assessed the play's chances as good, despite the inadequacy of the actors, except Compton himself. He rehearsed to Grace Norton his rationalizations for writing such plays at all. The bottom line was a bottom line: He was trying, in his "old age, & for the most mercenary reasons, to write successful *plays*," having completed two, with a third partly done. He was going to assault repeatedly the citadel until the theatrical walls fell. And why shouldn't they? His plays "are judged by the profession miracles of 'technique!' " and to try "but once or twice is grotesque & trivial." All his theatrical activity, he confided to his Cambridge friend, is ultimately "addressed to the U.S.—which is the dramatic Eldorado. . . . I may even have to go over, to teach my interpreters how to interpret. . . . God speed the sweet necessity.''[56] If London fell, then New York would also. He too would finally have his share of American gold.

(7)

Oscillating between moments of high confidence and hours of sheer terror, he nervously exhorted his friends and family to pray for him, to spend the evening in "fasting, silence & supplication." "You must begin & pray for me *hard*," he commanded Ariana Curtis, "about eight o'clock Saturday [January] the 3rd." There could not be prayers enough. "After 11 o'clock to-night," he told Gosse on the day of the performance, "I *may* be the world's . . . & I may be the under-taker's. . . . I am so nervous that I miswrite & misspell." At the final rehearsal, he listened as if the words had been written by someone else. But the play still seemed to him to have "intrinsic vitality." The five hours until the performance seemed like days. Too nervous to eat dinner, he went to the empty theatre hours early, and onto the stage where he straightened some of the small props and compulsively dusted the mantelpiece. "I *am,* at present," he confided to William, as he waited, "in a state of abject, lonely fear.''[57]

In the wings, during the first act, he hung onto the curtain rod, as if without such support his hollow knees would fall out from under him. As the curtain came down, he flung himself onto Compton. " 'In heaven's name, is it *going*?' 'Going?—Rather!* You can hear a pin drop!' " As he waited in his little cubbyhole behind the curtain in the right wing, he could literally hear the silence and the sound of success. The cavernous Southport theatre suddenly embodied the hushed breath of mutual blessing. The prayers he had asked for were being answered. Between acts, he dashed out to embrace every actor he had the time to put his arms around. It all seemed *"magnificent."* Between the third and fourth acts, Balestier ran to the telegraph office and sent a glowing cable to *The New York Times,* "fifty vivid words" that they hoped would appear on every breakfast table in New York the next day. As the final curtain came down, he gave himself up to the "agreeable sounds" of appreciative applause. Compton had been brilliant. He would end, James assured his sister, by making his portrayal of Christopher Newman "a *celebrated* modern creation."[58] The play had been better than he had imagined it would be. He would make it better still.

With the whole company joining him behind the curtain, he heard a "big universal outbreak . . . for 'author, author, AUTHOR!' " Taking him by the hand, Compton led him alone to the front of the stage for the first ovation of his life. He believed it was the first of many to come. In the highest spirits, he immediately telegraphed to Gosse— "COMPLETE AND DELIGHTFUL SUCCESS UNIVERSAL CONGRATULATION TO WHICH I VENTURE TO ADD YOURS AND YOUR WIFE'S"—and to Alice, who then cabled William—"UNQUALIFIED TRIUMPH MAGNIFICENT SUCCESS UNIVERSAL CONGRATULATIONS GREAT OCCASION FOR AUTHOR GREAT FUTURE FOR PLAY COMPTONS RADIANT AND HIS ACTING ADMIRABLE WRITING HENRY."[59] With applause and congratulations settling sweetly into his ears, he had a celebratory dinner at the hotel with the Comptons, with Balestier and his wife, and with Balestier's friend and partner, William Heinemann, all with glasses of champagne raised high to toast what seemed to him a wildly successful premiere.

But all in all, the performance had been at best a moderate success. William Archer, a young writer, translator, and drama critic—with an interest especially in Ibsen—and a central figure in the burgeoning effort to create a serious modern theatre in London, had a more realistic response. Eager to encourage James, whose fiction he highly respected, eager to discover an English Ibsen, Archer had written to James that he intended to attend the premiere, despite the distance from London. Normally, London theatre critics did not attend provincial performances. London papers, at best, reported the fact of a play in the provinces, sometimes with a quotation or two from local newspaper reviews. James felt anxious about and flattered by Archer's attendance. "I'm afraid you won't find me, to begin with, startlingly unconventional—my notion having been to get well in the saddle *before* I begin to tackle my horse. . . . Look out for prancing and curvetting later. But it's very good of you to look out for anything." Afterward, with the resounding applause of the audience in his ears, he happily responded to

Archer's request that he join him briefly at the hotel. "I think it's a play," Archer remarked, "that would be much more likely to have success in the provinces than in London." He then began, Alice wrote in her diary, "as by divine mission, to enumerate all its defects and flaws. . . . To H, of course, heated from his triumph, these uncalled-for and depressing amenities from an entire stranger seemed highly grotesque, none the less so [that] the young man seemed by nature, divorced from all matters theatrical. In spite of the gloom cast over his spirits, H was able to receive it all with perfect urbanity."[60]

Vistas of gold and triumph seemed to have opened before him. Compton reinforced his great expectations. A "large fortune" awaited both of them. For some time, Compton had yearned to become a London actor and theatrical manager, to have a London theatre of his own. He soon signed a contract to occupy the Opera Comique Theatre, with *The American* the first offering, scheduled for September 1891. In the meantime, he initiated his tour of England, Scotland, and Ireland, performing his repertory of half a dozen or so plays, of which *The American* was given its due once a week for a total of twenty-five performances. To James, the "complete and delightful" success of the play in Southport provoked the regret that he had made the commitment to have Compton take it on tour "all over the place" rather than go directly to London. But the compensation would be that Compton would grow even more into the part. He would also have the chance to make some improvements in the script. Mulling over the chances for a London success, he thought them excellent. If the play had done so well in the limitations of a Southport production, how much better it would do with the advantages of a London theatre and with more professional actresses, especially for the part of Claire de Cintré. "The attention—even the tension—of the [Southport] audience [had been] extremely sensible, the applause irrepressible, the final 'ovation' to the author," he wrote to Ariana Curtis, "who had to come before the curtain, to simper & saulte, everything that notorious literary vanity could desire." Balestier thought the evening had been a success, the most delightful feature of which was that James was now "like a runner ready to run a race. He has the air of one just setting out—a youngster with an oldster's grip and mastery; surely the most enviable of situations."[61]

While Compton traveled, James worked at *his* career. The London papers ignored the play, with the noticeable exception of a friendly, supportive mention by Archer in *The World*. Reviews from the provincial newspapers reached him in the next few months. Pleasantly responsive, their friendliness hardly counted. To James, their tone seemed low, common, not critically serious or even capable. "I have not seen a monosyllabic mention of the Great Fact in the London papers. They seem religiously, superstitiously, banded together to take no notice of what happens in the provinces—the provinces don't exist for them. On the other hand every one seems to know about it." He hoped for much. "Keep tight hold of everything," he told the Comptons, "& we shall all go to glory." When the play was being performed within reach of London, he often attended, sometimes with friends, sometimes to make changes in the script that the Comptons or he or both thought desirable. He insisted that he could show the actors how to do it better. In the middle of January 1891, he spent a day with the company "re-hearsing a 'death-scene' . . . to get it more right, & experimenting with a little new 'business.' Such are our daily duties." Though he was determined to be an all-around theatre man, he could not have made himself popular with the actors. "I show 'em how to do it—& even then they don't know!"[62]

The news of the Opera Comique lease thrilled him "from head to foot." In London, he busied himself at promoting production possibilities for the two other plays he had written. His efforts were unsuccessful. He was disappointed that Compton did not like *Mrs. Jasper* enough to take it on. When he went to Paris in March 1891, he was at work on another play, whose third-act scenario he sent to Virginia Compton, who had wanted to play Mrs. Jasper. The act was "the most difficult [to write] of my long & chequered dramatic career, but I think it is, 'technically,' the best." With John Hare and *Mrs. Vibert,* he started to learn the lesson of slow, gradual disappointment, even heartbreak, that began to plague his theatrical efforts. Hare had agreed, James thought, to act in and produce the play in the spring, then in the autumn or winter of 1891. "The only thing I *do* care to speak of now (and *only* to you)," he told William, "is . . . Mrs. Vibert, which John Hare is to produce at the Garrick. . . . But there are irrepressible delays, produced largely—indeed almost wholly—by the intense difficulties of casting. One tries to write as simple and feasible a thing as possible and still—with the ignoble poverty of the English stage—the people capable of *beginning* to attempt to do it are not findable. There's a career for talent—to act my plays." Whatever the real difficulties, Hare gave up on the play. James kept up his hope for more than two years that Hare or someone else would produce it. Without verbal wit or interesting characters, with a plot that in itself is a tired cliché and has the sad distinction of James avoiding every possibility to make it artistically interesting, the play was never produced.[63]

Soon he was exerting himself to find the right female actress to play

Claire in London. She materialized in Elizabeth Robins, a beautiful, intelligent, and ambitious twenty-five-year-old American, a former medical student at Vassar whose actor husband had committed suicide, supposedly because she had neglected him. She had come to London in 1888, where the publisher William Heinemann had fallen in love with her. As a champion of Ibsen and women's rights, she was an intelligent actress with an agenda—to promote her own career and the modern theatre as embodied in Ibsen's plays. When *Hedda Gabler* had an immense *succès d'estime* in spring 1891, James had less hesitation in praising Elizabeth Robins' brilliant performance than he had in praising the play. She is "the most interesting English-speaking actress (or rather the *only* one,) that I have seen for many a day . . . an American of course." Eager to have Robins for the role of Madame de Cintré, he cultivated her acquaintance. Flattered, she consented. Ibsen, though, puzzled him. He could find no models in English and American dramatic history for his plays. Structurally, formally, their idiosyncrasies irritated and distressed him. Later, he began to appreciate Ibsen's genius.[64]

To a full house of friends, of literary and theatre personalities, drama critics, and an interested public, *The American* had its London premiere in September 1891. Sargent, Du Maurier, George Meredith, Rhoda Broughton, Constance Woolson, the young journalist Frank Harris, the novelist William Norris, the playwright Arthur Pinero, the producer and writer John Augustin Daly, all were in the audience. During the performance, James stayed outside, pacing up and down "the heartless Strand," going through "an ordeal of flame—a *hell* of nervousness and suspense." A modest semifailure, more a social than an artistic success, it was tolerated rather than liked, palatable to some, uninteresting to most. The English critics were gently unenthusiastic, mostly stressing the bald melodrama. The American reviewers were harsher about its melodrama and vulgarity. To many, the play seemed almost a degradation of the novel, which has many weaknesses but an essential integrity, whereas the play seemed all weaknesses without any integrity at all. James was deeply disappointed and stubbornly unrealistic. Perhaps, he thought, revisions could deal with the objections. He admitted that he was "in a rather abnormal state of tension & anxiety. . . . I am learning that the production of a play, in very stiff London conditions, is a complicated & agitating episode—attended with results impossible to foresee & only revealed by palpitating experience. The universal newspaper-press has been on the whole quite awful—& that introduces a potent 'factor' (as *they* say,) of discomfort. But the play, all the same, shows strong signs of life—though, as it's only been a week, it is early to judge. The 1st night *determines* nothing. . . . This thing is now afloat—to sink or swim—& I *think* it will swim." It was difficult, though, for "the poor struggling Stranded one" even to stay afloat.[65] The play paddled in place, despite revisions that he believed improved it considerably, for only seventy performances, until December 1891.

The attendance, in late October 1891, of the Prince of Wales, later Edward VII, gave the play a brief resuscitation. Probably he had been induced to attend by James's new friend, Mary Morton Sands, a stunningly beautiful American who moved at the highest levels of British aristocratic society. Her sister had become Edwin Godkin's second wife in 1884. "I am ashamed to say," Henry wrote to William, "that the P. of W. on Saturday last, gave it a lift by coming and manifesting an intense absorption. It is humiliating to be so beholden—but it isn't all the Prince." Whatever happened now, he wrote to William, he had at least had "an honourable run." He was still not defeated. "Whatever *shall* happen, I am utterly launched in the drama, resolutely & deeply committed to it, & shall go at it tooth & nail. The American has distinctly done me good." He was going to continue to "attack, renewedly & repeatedly the almost impregnable fortress of the theatre. But *you* must come," he told Henrietta Reubell, "on the night the citadel is carried." He was whistling in the dark with ferocious willfulness. "Honour is saved, but I grieve to say nothing else, for the piece made no money and I have not had a *penny* of royalties. (*I tell this to no one.*) On the other hand I am launched & committed, I have had success with the fastidious, and anything else I do will be greatly attended to. Moreover the production of a piece is an education—a technical one. I have had a revelation & I am enlightened."[66] It was to take him three more years to work his way up out of the dark abyss.

Eleven

"THE DARK ABYSS"
1888–1895

(1)

On a moist March day in 1888, sharing a carriage to Kensal Green Cemetery with Robert Browning, he entered a long season of deaths. They dramatized his sense that a great age was passing. His friend Adelaide Procter, a celebrated ancient lady of social and literary distinction, "a kind of window in[to] the past," had died. Having visited her three weeks before her death, she had seemed to him "very pathetic— it was such an image of defeat—almost humiliation." She had had a painful, harassing illness, "a difficult physical extinction." He would miss her greatly, for, though she was "often sad and bitter," she had never been dull, "never common or commonplace." With her great passion for life, her intense social partisanship, he did not see why "when one *minds* as much as that, one shouldn't live for ever." It had been rumored that she had quietly become a Catholic convert so that she could be buried next to her daughter, but he noticed at Kensal Green, with a large number of people attending the funeral, many her old friends, that she was buried at the edge of the Protestant section, "where it touches the Catholic." Someone told him that "she had said almost on her deathbed that the adoration of the Virgin was, for her, an insurmountable stumbling-block and she had not that exalted idea of her sex!" During the long, slow ride to Kensal Green and back, the seventy-six-year-old Browning, who had recently become his neighbor across the street at De Vere Gardens, "was infinitely talkative," their other companion, Alexander Kinglake, a well-known historian, "old, deaf, delicate, distinguished . . . infinitely silent. Mrs. Procter, whose displeasure [Kinglake] had incurred, had not spoken to him for a quarter of a century. She was magnificent."[1]

Late the next year, his neighbor at De Vere Gardens, the chatty, perplexing Browning, whose artistry James thought the most brilliant of any poet of his generation, died in Venice. Having seen Browning often in their overlapping London lives and having liked him a great deal, he felt pleased that it had been "a supremely happy and enviable death," the great poet dying without illness, delay, or pain in his son's Venetian palace, his life culminated "in the fullness of years and honours." When he had been Katherine Bronson's guest at Ca' Alvisi in late winter 1887, James had been honored to work at the same desk at which Browning had written many of his poems. He had probably last seen him in March 1889, before the poet's final trip to Italy, at a dinner to which Browning had been accompanied by his spinster sister. "I talk of Venice with Browning when I meet him," James had written to Ariana Curtis, "& he always tells me the same thing—that the 'dealers' have offered [his son] the eyes of their head for the mere . . . fixtures of his disproportionate palace. . . . I took Miss Browning down, the other day, at a long, dull dinner & Parnell was opposite to us—& he dozed. But Miss Browning didn't!"[2]

His own affection had always been tempered by his puzzlement at the startling difference between Browning the man and Browning the poet, which he transformed into a witty, playful short story, "The Private Life," about a young writer's jealousy of a great older writer who is pursued by a famous actress to write a play with a magnificent part in it for her. The young writer discovers that the public, bluff, banal social lion and the solitary great writer are two distinctly different people, two separate bodies. While one socializes, the other writes. When James had had his first long talk with Browning years before, he seemed "a great gossip and a very 'sympathetic' easy creature." The smooth social lion, though, had a distinctive shagginess, a roughness of voice and manner that expressed itself, for James, in his gruff frankness, even to women. "It is partly what I have always liked him for, that he is exactly the same with everyone & has only *one* sturdy manner & attitude." His reading of his poetry, James remarked, had "all the exhibition of point and authority, the expressive particularisation" that Tennyson did not have. "It came out almost to harshness; but the result was that what he read showed extraordinary life." In Geneva, in October 1888, he had reread most of Browning. "It seems to me that he is on the whole the writer of our times of whom, in the face of the rest of the world, the English tongue may be most proud—for he has touched *every-thing,* & with a breadth! I put him very high—higher than anyone."[3]

He attended Browning's funeral in late December 1889 at Westminster Abbey—solemn but satisfying "national obsequies"—the "magnificent old cathedral . . . in its dim sublime vastness" crowded with celebrities, "the boy-voices of the choir soaring and descending angelic under the high roof." It was the kind of symbolic and ritualistic public occasion that he did not like to miss. He stood, he told the mournful Katherine Bronson, "respectfully" by the grave of "our illustrious old friend," his imagination assessing Browning's distinction and his place in the pantheon of Poet's Corner, which he put into a brief elegiac article, "Browning in Westminster Abbey." He felt a personal and an Anglo-American consanguinity. "His voice sounds loudest, and also clearest, for the things that, as a race, we like best—the fascination of faith, the acceptance of life, the respect for its mysteries, the endurance of its charges, the vitality of the will, the validity of character, the beauty of action, the seriousness, above all, of the great human passion." The master of the dramatic monologue had had much to teach the novelist of relationships, of moral situations and discriminations, of the dramatic rendition of consciousness and human personality. Years later, in his own old age, James was to memorialize Browning again in a lecture to the Royal Society of Literature on the one-hundredth anniversary of Browning's birth, focusing on the novelistic aspects of *The Ring and the Book.* Browning's realism, his fascination with point of view, his intense preoccupation with relationships, particularly between men and women, seemed to James the essence of great fiction. Immediately after the funeral, he joked to Francis Boott, who had disliked Browning, "Would you have left him unburied?"[4]

Though some of the great literary figures of the high-Victorian age lived on into the nineties and into the new century, James, who had been young when they were middle-aged, became an interested spectator, sometimes even a mourner, at the processions of the funerals of the great. When Trollope died in 1882, James marked the event with an evaluative article that criticized him for writing too much and for the limits of his imagination. But, though he had sacrificed "quality to quantity," Trollope still seemed to him "strong, genial, and abundant," a lesser member of the Victorian literary family. Like James, he could never stop writing. Trollope knew better than anyone the English world that he wrote about, and it was a virtue to know something well and write about it intensely, no matter how narrow that world might be.

Though he buried Trollope without a tear, Matthew Arnold's unexpected death in April 1888 shocked him into a few moments of pain, mostly because he had returned Arnold's genial kindness and friendly interest with a familial affection, as if Arnold were a lovable elderly uncle with whom he was never intimate but whose warmth he never doubted. He had met Arnold in Rome in 1873, and saw him occasionally in London. Arnold invariably praised the young novelist's books, beginning with *Roderick Hudson,* which he actually read aloud to his family. "I like him—love him rather," James told Perry, "as I do my old portfolio, my old shoe-horn: with an affection that is proof against anything he may say or do, and proof also against taking him too seriously." Arnold's death was not a heavy personal loss, but it was the loss of an individual whose cosmopolitanism, European sensibility, and sophistication James felt Victorian England would sorely miss. "I went to his funeral," he wrote to a mutual friend, "which might have had a certain beauty," the place very charming and very English, "but was spoiled by dreary weather."[5]

An ambivalent Victorian, he made himself an assessor rather than a personal sympathizer, yet without allowing his long-range cultural views to overwhelm his awareness that these were individual lives. He had little of the hero-worshiper within himself. He had fought too long and too hard to separate himself from his own father to have any need for father substitutes among the literary great. As a young man, he had wept for Hawthorne's passing. But he largely had dry eyes thereafter in regard to impersonal forces. When Dickens died in 1870, he seems to have shed no tears, his homage reserved for the Dickensian dramatizations of *The Princess Casamassima.* Carlyle's death in 1881 seemed only the final event that old age demands, the Carlylean spirit having been embodied in Basil Ransom in *The Bostonians.* The revelations of James Anthony Froude's biography both fascinated and disgusted him—Carlyle "the most disagreeable in character of men of genius of equal magnificence"—though he felt a boundless admiration for Carlyle as a letter writer. He also felt disgust at the moral dust stirred up by Cross's biography of his wife, George Eliot. Her death in 1880, James had remarked, may have been a loss to the culture but had been a lease on life for her husband. The biography, which appeared in 1885, was "full of high decency, earnestness . . . yet what is most alluded to [in the reviews] is the scandalous Bohemian fact that she lived 25 years conjugally with G. H. Lewes without marrying him."[6]

Carrying with him only as much of New England as he could not leave behind, James found British puritanism both salacious and narrow, a combination of titillation and moral hypocrisy. But, he granted, one must take the culture, for better and worse, that is given to one by the accidents of history. "The union Miss Evans formed with [Lewes] was a deliberate step, of which she accepted all the consequences. These consequences were excellent . . . save in an important particular. This particular is the fact that her false position . . . produced upon George Eliot's life a certain effect of sequestration which was not favourable to social freedom of observation. . . . The fault of most of her work is the absence of spontaneity, the excess of reflection; and by her action in 1854 . . . she committed herself to being nothing if not reflective, to cultivating a kind of compensatory earnestness."[7] Becoming more of a Victorian than she otherwise might have been, she compensated for her irregular relationship with an earnestness that raised the moral seriousness of the Victorian puritan revival to the supreme. It was an earnestness that he shared, and yet of which he also disapproved. In life, such moral superconsciousness often overweighted the balloon of flexibility. In art, it was too heavy a burden for a work of art to bear.

If George Eliot thought too much, Queen Victoria, for James the other great woman of the Victorian age, thought not at all. Eliot's greatness as a novelist transcended her gender, but her gender promoted opportunities for women of the sort that her much-admiring Minny Temple had never had and that James had both questioned and promoted. He had reservations about women fulfilling traditionally male vocational roles. Art and artistry most readily left gender behind. Although Henry senior had preached the vocational subordination of women to intensify their spiritual superiority, his son had only a little difficulty in redirecting the unlimited potential of the female back into art and vocation. George Eliot seemed to him a valuable test case. "To her own sex her memory, her example, will remain of the highest value; those of them for whom the 'development' of woman is the hope of the future ought to erect a monument for George Eliot. She helped on the cause more than any one, in proving how few limitations are of necessity implied in the feminine organism." The queen transcended practical considerations only by virtue of her unique position. James saw her as a pathetic prisoner of her rank and a cherished symbol of the dignity of the British Empire. He watched from his London vantage point her approaching death in 1901 as the age that bore her name was ending in an indefensible war in South Africa. "The poor dear old stricken Queen is *rapidly* dying. . . . Blind, used up, utterly sickened and humiliated by the war . . . she is a very pathetic old monarchical figure. . . . I feel as if her death will have consequences in and for this country that no man can foresee. The Prince of Wales is an archvulgarian. . . . The wretched little 'Yorks' are less than nothing; the Queen's magnificent duration had held things magnificently—beneficently—together and prevented all sorts of accidents. Her death, in short, will let loose incalculable forces for possible ill." He watched the funeral procession and the coronation with pleasure in the pageantry and pessimism for the future. "The old Queen's death was a real emotion—quite big & fine; but we have dropped again to Edward." The new king was "fat Edward—E. the Caresser," as he was privately called. "I mourn the safe and motherly old middle-class queen, who held the nation warm under the fold of her big, hideous Scotch-plaid shawl. . . . I felt her death much more than I should have expected; she was a sustaining symbol—and the wild waters are upon us now."[8] He preferred George Eliot in literature and Queen Victoria in life to the ugly chaos, to the vileness and violence, that he anticipated the twentieth century would bring.

(2)

But there were deaths he felt more more personally, whose significance had the ache of private loss rather than the monumentality of the passing of a public age. Lowell returned to England seasonally to spend a portion of his old age as a very public-private figure who confounded his friends with his ability to be happy both with his privacy and with Mrs. Smalley. To James, who warmly greeted his visits, Lowell continued to be "the oddest mixture of the lovable & the annoying, the infinitely clever & the unspeakably simple." As James grew older, Lowell grew younger. Nothing, however, mattered more than that James had become "*very* fond of him" and Lowell was, in return, "inexhaustibly friendly." He enjoyed Lowell's company at London dinners; at the home of a new mutual friend, the popular novelist Lucy Clifford, the widow of the mathematician William Kingdon Clifford; at the home of the Leslie Stephens; and for a number of August visits at Lowell's beloved Whitby summer retreat, with Du Maurier and the Smalleys close by. There, in the last years of the 1880s, he felt the autumnal glow of "the eternally juvenile & most sociable & hospitable Lowell." Lowell's health in the spring of 1890 prevented him from making his annual visit. His "non-arrival," in spring 1891, followed the unhappy news of his being seriously ill. "I seemed to see," James wrote to him, "that you were tied down by pain and weakness, that you were suffering often and suffering much. . . . I have no heart for Whitby on any but *your* terms—the little house in the lane with the view of the Abbey through the loophole in the barn . . . and the religious rite of your coffee-making to usher in the summer's day." A telegram from

Norton was only "rather dryly & meagrely reassuring." Late in the summer, the seventy-two-year-old Lowell died. "It seems as if we measured only now how much we loved him," James wrote to Julia Stephen, who was at St. Ives with her husband and children. "I shall miss him singularly and be long getting rid of the fancy that I shall meet him some day walking across the park."[9]

He remembered how kind, from their first walks together in Paris in 1872, Lowell had been to him. He particularly recalled "his last visit to Whitby," when they had taken a long walk together over "the warm, wide moors" and an excursion by railroad to Rievaulx Abbey. Afterward, they had spent three days together in Devonshire. "I travelled back to London with him, and saw him for the last time at Paddington. He was to sail immediately for America. I went to take leave of him, but I missed him, and a day or two later he was gone." The response to his early 1892 memorial essay on Lowell seemed as vacuous, as darkly empty, as unnoticed as had been the one to his essay on Turgenev. It was as if silence swallowed up even memorials to the dead. "One feels, in this terribly hurrying age and roaring place, as if one were testifying in the desert. In London . . . the waves sweep dreadfully over the dead—they drop out and their names are unuttered." The next summer he spent most of September at Whitby, where, partly as a private memorial gesture, he rented "poor Lowell's little *quartiere*," the very rooms in which he had twice stayed with him.[10]

Young friends died as inevitably as old. In December 1891, Wolcott Balestier suddenly died in Dresden. The thirty-year-old American literary businessman and aspiring author had endeared himself to James by his worshipful flattery, his energetic enthusiasm, and his eagerness to act gratis in the negotiations with Compton. From a wealthy New York Huguenot family, he had come to London from America in 1887 with the intention of an indefinite expatriation like that of the mentor he so much admired. Balestier, who aspired to be a great novelist, soon went into a publishing partnership with the young William Heinemann. James liked him immediately, "the admirably acute and intelligent young Balestier. . . . I think that practically he will soon 'do everything' for me . . . the perfection of an 'agent.' " They saw one another frequently in London. In August 1891, James joined him at the Isle of Wight for almost a week of holiday. "If you will let me," Balestier urged James, " 'assist' at the first performance of the first play of our first dramatist . . . nothing short of legal proceedings to restrain my liberty can prevent my being present."[11]

Balestier genuinely wanted to be useful, to be appreciated. Suddenly, he could neither be useful nor loved. Responding to the shocking news, James immediately left, in early December 1891, with Heine-mann for Dresden. Balestier "had left England ill [with typhoid], 3 weeks previous—& I thought the change of climate & forsaking of high pressure business would work his improvement. But the poison was in him & he has gone—to my very serious loss & sorrow & that of many other people as well." To the "helpless & desolate mother & sister," he felt a moral duty. He followed his young associate to his "dreary Ger-man grave" in a bleak, wintry suburban Dresden cemetery, the two ladies accompanied only by Heinemann and James. He remembered that Susan Norton had died in Dresden. Probably she had been buried in that same suburban cemetery "so many winters ago." He would, he wrote to Grace, look for Susan's grave. Germany itself looked funereal to him, partly, he imagined, because of the season, partly because of the hateful reminders of German militarism, and mostly because of his long-standing sense of German insensitivity. "Everything human is shabby here except Raphael's . . . madonna and the bull-necked mili-tary. I can't do much with the Germans—they are somehow not in my line. One must either really know them or leave them alone. They are ugly & mighty—they have (I think) lots of future, but a most intolerable present." Leaving Germany after a week, he was happy to have this "miserable pious pilgrimage" over with.[12]

To Gosse, who wrote a brief memorial essay, Balestier had seemed overly secretive, not entirely attractive. Much later, Gosse wrote, pri-vately, more harshly, that he "should have detested [Balestier], but that he happened to like me very much. He was a queer, strained, tight little type of strenuous Yankee: not important . . . but curious and original in his common and imitative way!" James complained that the essay was not generous. "To the young, the early dead, the baffled, the defeated, I don't think we can be tender enough." His own brief memo-rial sketch emphasized only praise and loss, the desirability of not judg-ing those who had not lived long enough to provide a record full enough to sustain judgment. "I was greatly attached to him," he readily confessed to William, "for he had rendered me admirable services & was destined to render still more & greater. He was in every way a valuable young life. . . . Many things, many enterprises, interests, visions, originalities perish with him. Oh, the 'ironies of fate,' the ugly tricks, the hideous practical jokes of life!"[13]

Another young friend had been so far distant for so long that his death in December 1894 seemed an additional attenuation rather than a sharply defined departure. Depressed, weighed down by anxieties and losses, he felt "the ghost of poor R.L.S. wave its great dusky wings between me and all occupations." He had already twice before lost

Stevenson, the first time when Stevenson, in 1887, had left Bournemouth for American and South Pacific travels, the second when, in 1890, settling in Samoa, Stevenson had determined never to return, even for a visit. His physical health was barely tenable in the tropics; at best he could imagine returning to England to die. James argued with him "passionately on the question of Samoa and expatriation." But he had to assent to the strength of his friend's claim that he enjoyed health only in the tropics. "I am sorry about seven or eight people in England," Stevenson wrote to him, "and one or two in the States. And outside of that, I simply prefer Samoa." It seemed a "tragic statement" of "permanent secession." James could be equally honest. "I miss you shockingly—for, my dear fellow, there is no one—literally no one." Worst of all, "I can't go with you even in my imagination, and you are for the time absolutely as if you were dead to me—I mean to my imagination of course—not to my affection or my prayers."[14]

It seemed, in April 1890, that Stevenson would make that one last visit to England. But he postponed the tentative date of arrival from June to September, then indefinitely. James doubted he would ever see Stevenson again. Stevenson no more wanted, regardless of health, the Europe to which James had committed himself than James could ever imagine himself visiting, let alone living, in the Samoa that Stevenson had come to love. It soon became clear that Stevenson's flight had become permanent. Stevenson had gone where James's imagination could not follow, except for the sudden access of identification catalyzed by some "beautiful strange things" that Stevenson sent him. They seemed to convey "a sort of dim rumble as of the Pacific surf. My heart beats over them—my imagination throbs—my eyes fill. I have covered a blank wall of my bedroom with an acre of painted cloth and feel as if I lived in a Samoan tent—and I have placed the sad sepia-drawing," a portrait of Stevenson, "just where, fifty times a day, it most transports and reminds me."[15]

James was never to travel outside America and Europe; Stevenson was never to leave Samoa. The dismal rumor came after the middle of December 1894. "The miserable news of Lewis Stevenson's apparent death" agitated him immensely, he wrote to William. "I say 'apparent' because it as yet lacks confirmation . . . just enough to give one a flicker of hope which one's pessimism quickly contradicts. . . . Meanwhile it's all a torment." As usual, he transformed death into a blessing for the departed. "His death, if it be real, seems to me . . . the greatest happiness for him. He thought so, entirely—intensely—himself." The next week, the news was confirmed. "He has gone in time not to be old," he wrote to Mrs. Stevenson.[16]

The deaths of two elderly people came with the emotional force of maternal evocations. A year older than his own mother, Fanny Kemble had for more than twenty years provided him with the opportunity to feel and observe the gradual decline of a woman who accepted him into her home and life as if he had been her own, an unacknowledged child of her American days and marriage. Unlike Mary James, she was a performer, an ironically witty, aggressively acerbic woman who had transformed a successful acting career into a brilliant personality. She could do everything, and do it with a force that made her offstage presence as much a performance as her onstage achievements. Self-taught, widely read, a graceful, thoughtful writer, a brilliant storyteller, she worshiped Shakespeare, whose works she read through annually until her last years. "He was indeed her utterance, the language she spoke when she spoke most from herself." She enjoyed her sharp tongue, and despised Victorian vulgarities and hypocrisies. Having known the great writers and actors of the late-Romantic and early-Victorian world, she was a living connection between the past and a diminished present. Her aunt had been the celebrated actress Sarah Siddons, her father the theatrical star and entrepreneur Charles Kemble. She had "sat to Sir Thomas Lawrence for her portrait . . . breakfasted with Sir Walter Scott . . . sung with Tom Moore . . . listened to Edmund Kean." In her remembrances "she reanimated the old drawing-rooms, relighted the old lamps, retuned the old pianos."[17]

Most of all, she seemed to James someone who had "abundantly lived." Her marriage had failed. As a mother, she so far exceeded the talents and energies of her daughters that whatever their successes, she overwhelmed them with the gap between where they had come from and what they themselves had achieved. She regretted her daughters' problems, but did not allow them to slacken her energies. In James's eyes, Sarah Wister was "enough like her mother to accentuate an immense unlikeness. All the tragedy & none of the comedy—much of the force but none of the volume." Having been born to the stage, like other great early-Victorian performers Kemble thought the stage beneath her. When she performed, she wanted people to come for Shakespeare's sake, not for hers. Though she benefited from the star system, she hated it. She retired from the stage as soon as she could on moral and temperamental grounds. "The greatest pride of all," James remarked about her, "is to be proud of nothing, the pride not of pretension but of renunciation; and this was of course her particular kind. . . . Nature had so formed her that she was ever more aware of the one fault something beautiful might have than of all the beauties that made it what it was."[18]

She had been a familiar but glamorous presence to him since his childhood, when he saw her name on the billboards and theatrical advertisements of his early Broadway wanderings. One childhood incident remained vividly in his memory: Driving in a carriage with his parents, someone had pointed out a woman on horseback and said, " 'Why, it's Fanny Kemble!' . . . On my inquiring who was the bearer of this name, which fell upon my ear for the first time, I was informed that she was a celebrated actress . . . a brilliant reader of Shakespeare." Some years later, he was taken to hear her read. Sitting at his desk, almost forty years afterward, hesitantly attempting to add a portrait of Mrs. Kemble to his essay-memorials for Turgenev and Lowell, he vividly recalled "even from such a distance of time every detail of the picture and every tone of her voice." In America during the Civil War, either in Boston or New York, he had twice heard her read full plays, which she repeatedly did for charitable causes, though she had retired. "She had a sort of American patriotism, a strange and conditioned sentiment of . . . love for the United States which was a totally different matter from a liking, and which, from 1861 to 1865, made her throb with American passions." Before the war, she would never read in the South because she hated the "peculiar institution." She did not want to be paid for her performances from dollars proceeding from slavery. Her taste was as elevated as her morals. One evening, at his initiative, he took her to a performance of an old chestnut, *The Hunchback,* whose lead female role she had created more than fifty years earlier. "It was a vulgar and detestable rendering. . . . It brought back across the gulf of years her different youth and all the ghosts of the dead, the first interpreters—her father, Charles Kemble . . . Sheridan Knowles himself. . . . They seemed, in the cold, half-empty house . . . to interpose a mute reproach—a reproach that looked intensely enough out of her eyes when at last, under her breath, she turned to her embarrassed neighbor with a tragic, an unforgettable 'How could you bring me to see this thing?' "[19]

Her death, fortunately, came rapidly, painlessly, a properly managed addendum to her eighty-three years of age. In recent years, she had frequently said of people "who met her . . . 'No wonder they were surprised and bewildered, poor things—they supposed I was dead!' " James watched her gradual decline with melancholy anticipation, especially dramatized by the metaphor of Mrs. Kemble as an "extinct volcano." He reported to Sarah Wister that "she 'minds little things,' but she always seems at home with the great even if they take the form of troubles as . . . great things seem always & everywhere, to do. Besides

I think she was distinctly assured, & relieved of a question, by your sister's instantaneous action in 'settling' immediately . . . that the problem of the future home should be solved by her coming to live" with her "at the new & commodious vicarage." She "accepted this like a child." On his last visit with her in Switzerland, he saw the pain in her eyes when she could only look at from a distance, but not get close to, the mountain heights that had been her physical pleasure for decades. Wistfully, "with absolutely tearful eyes," she sat "for hours on the balconies of high-perched hotels . . . gazing away at her paradise lost. She yielded the ground only inch by inch." He admired her "contempt for conditions and circumstances. . . . She was, in the ancient sense of the word, indomitably, incorruptibly superb." Still, he remembered "the melancholy of her silence during a long and lovely summer drive, after the turn of the tide, from one of the places just mentioned to the other; it was so little what she wanted to be doing."[20] He had a momentary, anxious foresight of his own impending limitations.

At her graveside at Kensal Green, with mounds of flowers piled slightly too high for his taste, among "a small knot of old friends . . . in the centre of a rabble of pushing, staring" strangers, he felt an evening chill settle into the balmy morning air. The burial rites themselves seemed, as they always did to him, an "inacceptably horrible, a hideous old imposition of the church." Without Fanny Kemble, the world appeared a more vulgar, more empty place, as if, in his imagination, she had been the high priestess of a religion of personality and art that inevitably had to take notice of and feel her absence. Her grave itself seemed an empty thing, a place for memories. For James, death had no future. The dead were never to be relocated let alone revivified, except within the limits of personal memory. In preparation for writing a memorial essay about her, he reread her letters to him, and he felt the shock of what a loss her extinction had been. He had available lifelong strategies for dealing with such shocks, including acts of "piety of affection. . . . I think none of her friends," he told Sarah Wister, whom he had feared would not like his essay and whose appreciative response made him feel immediately and immensely relieved, "can have had more affection for her—and I had ended (there was something strange & a little awful in it—I never grew quite used to it) by feeling that I *knew* her. Stranger, still, to me is it to sit at my window looking out at this Lucerne lake that she haunted so long and knew so intimately— to sit here with all its splendours in my eyes and that splendour only indifferently surviving *her*! I seem to myself almost to be taking something *from* her—& as if her disinherited spirit were exiled & wronged—

at the same time that one also feels as if her being, saturated with what it had loved here, had passed into all the immensity of beauty and colour and light."[21]

But he had no doubt that it had passed both into physical and spiritual insubstantiality. "What a gulf is death!" And the ultimate abyss of separation would be the gulf that his own death would create. Somewhat surprised at what she surmised of his beliefs about death from his letter describing her mother's funeral, Sarah Wister quietly forced an elaboration. In return, *he* was surprised. He thought he had not committed himself "to any positive declaration of belief on the question of 'extinction.' . . . Yet I confess I used the only word that expresses my own sense of what the great silence means—and of the impenetrable mystery. That I should have used it of such a spirit as your mother's, only proves, I fear, how inveterate in me is the habit of that particular vision. But I cherish the knowledge that in others— many others—abides the *other* vision. But it's *all* mere wrath & yearning in the darkness! I *saw* your mother go—saw it with the tenderest & most leavetaking eyes: & the *reconstruction* of the soul is to me the most difficult of all imaginations. Yet—I must add—she is a part of the universe to me at this hour! So much, at any rate, in simple explanation of my rather chance expression. I wanted only to express the intensity— to *our* eyes—of cessation!"[22] He did not want to oppose or distress anyone's religious solace. But he could not believe in the existence of a state or a place into which his imagination could not go. He could not give credence to what for him had neither vividness, nor intensity, nor experiential reality. He did not believe that he would ever see Fanny Kemble again.

(3)

In March 1889, Aunt Kate died. Her death was a death complicated by distance and by the unexpected oddness of her will, as if somehow she needed to respect one of the family traditions in regard to inheritance. He had last seen her in August 1883 at her vacation hotel in Pennsylvania, where he had gone overnight from New York for a last farewell before sailing. She was the only survivor of his parents' generation to whom he felt a close tie. Of all his siblings, he had the least complicated relationship with her. Still, to her James nephews and niece, her advancing age, her signs of illness, and then the sense of impending death brought tremors of pain and anxiety. Except for one another, she was all that they had left of their parents' world and their childhoods. When, after Alice's departure for England in 1884, Aunt Kate resumed living with her New York cousin, her family had a sense of her being settled for life. In October 1888, Cousin Helen died, leaving Catherine Walsh a life tenancy in her West Forty-fourth Street home. Having always thought she would not be able to afford to stay in the house, she decided reluctantly to make the effort, though her nephews and niece had the impression that she had barely enough money on which to get by. Years before, Alice had seriously considered turning over much of her legacy to her aunt. When the news reached Henry, in an "interesting, moving & agitating letter," that she was not likely to enjoy her New York residence for long, he felt the shock of an unexpected, impending death. His "beloved old Aunt" had apparently suffered a series of strokes. Her speech had been affected, her mental faculties diminished, though she provided the comfort of "as usual lying with folded hands fostering her own aches and pains." By the beginning of 1889, she had become a physical and mental invalid, her state "infinitely touching: & [so too] the idea of her talking helplessly about her helplessness." At Leamington, he had a long talk with Alice, "which relieved somewhat a good deal of emotion & distress that she feels about being so far away from her & so cut off from her natural part of befriending her now. I feel the same pain—& I would go out to her if I were free. But I am, in my way, as helpless as Alice. . . . It would be madness for me to cross the ocean & leave Alice, in her state, alone in this country."[23]

From a distance, he tried to imagine his aunt's situation, grateful to William, who made visits to New York to do what he could. Henry and Alice felt both guilt and relief. "We worry & we wonder, & we wish we could *do* something—but of course it is all vain. Strange & painful it must be to . . . see the dear old aunt of our lifetime laid so low & relegated to such superfluity. Above all it must be 'wearing' & exhausting to have to try to communicate with her . . . to *be* with her at all." They were, essentially, happy not to be there, though "death at a distance from the scene," Alice wrote to William, "is much more shocking. . . . This experience has given me a renewed sense of sorrow & regret that you & Harry were not spectators of the last hours of dear Mother & Father." Catherine Walsh's life seemed to Alice a precursor of the failure that her own life had been, "a person so apparently meant for independence & a 'position' to have been so unable to have worked her way to them & instead to have voluntarily relegated herself to the contrary. But the truth was, as her life showed, that she had but one *motif,* the intense longing to absorb herself in a few individuals, how she missed this & how much the individuals resisted her, was, thank Heaven! but faintly suspected by her. My failing her, after Mother &

Father's death, must have seemed to her a great & ungrateful betrayal; my inability to explain myself & hers to understand, in any way, the situation made it all the sadder & more ugly." The day after her death, Henry sent William's telegram to Leamington. The drama had "all come & gone with a kind of savage speed. I wish I could have seen her more lately—have taken a kind of farewell of her. But amen, amen." He imagined as best he could the details of the funeral, a generational burying. He felt he was actually "present at it . . . in imagination."[24]

What he had not imagined was the oddity of his aunt's will. She had had a great deal more money than her nephews and niece had surmised. She left hardly any of it to them. Absolutely "staggered at finding" that her aunt had had "a good deal more money than she herself," Alice felt insulted, even humiliated, at being left only a life interest in some silver and in a shawl, which deprived her of the opportunity even of deciding to whom those items should go afterward. Worse in Alice's eyes, she did not leave even "some small personal possession to Harry who is always giving & never receiving." Except for ten thousand dollars to William, which seemed meager in the light of the size of her estate, Catherine Walsh passed over the James family almost entirely, leaving everything else to "the Stamford Walshes." "[I] had expected A.K. would leave you," Henry told William, "in view of your 3 children & their absence of moneyed relations . . . about $20,000." Disappointed that she had not done so, it seemed to Henry "a sort of slap in the face at all the past." It was additionally awful for him when he had to arrange for the invalided Alice to sign some legal papers in regard to the will. "I had a dreadful day," he told William, "when I had to take the American consul down to Leamington to witness her signature to two law papers . . . a day when she was in such a condition that after he had waited so long I was afraid he would have to go back to London without doing anything. She was lifted up on bed, on his putting his head through the door, was able simply to give him a gasp of assent, in the midst of a convulsion!"[25]

Alice took it especially hard. Her own health seemed, by mid-1889, very fragile, and there was no other way she could take it. At some level, Aunt Kate had sent them all a message—if not a calculated insult, then at least some arrow of recrimination—an expression of her disapproval of what she had felt to be their failure to love her enough. The message had been most pointedly directed at her niece. Less tolerant, less evasively conciliatory than her brothers, Alice detected a strong element of meanness in the spirit of Aunt Kate's legacy. When she complained bitterly to William, as a fellow sufferer, he attempted to solace her with the arguments of rationality and realism. Hurt, furious, she responded with vigorous excoriation. She had expected supportive agreement rather than what seemed to her unsympathetic explanations. Henry tried to mediate and conciliate. "She honestly felt, on receipt of *your* letter," he wrote to William, "that she had been still more snubbed. . . . Your mistake was, I take it, that you write to her too much as a well woman. . . . She is as little well as it is *possible* to be." With blundering sincerity, assuming that since much of her sickness had an emotional dimension she might try to overcome her physical symptoms by mental effort, William had exhorted her to rise, so to speak, into health. To Alice, his prescription seemed painfully misplaced. Henry thought that William had spoken inappropriately. "I may as well say, frankly," he wrote to him, "that I myself thought it was not fortunate under the circumstances, & tolerably irritated in tone— possessed as I am necessarily with the sense that the extremity of her condition makes it of *prime* importance to allow her a large margin of sensibility." Still, eager to ameliorate the tension, he encouraged, as an opportunity for reconciliation, William's plan to come to Europe that summer for a professional convention. "You might even say you are coming out *because you want to see her.*"[26] Ironically, William intended to use part of his legacy from Aunt Kate to pay for the trip.

In May 1891, Alice became severely ill again. Worried that if he visited, his presence might prove more harmful than helpful, William wondered if it would be better for him not to come at all. "You must not let this episode," Henry urged, "exercise the *smallest* weight in the question of your coming out. . . . You must not let it interfere on *any* ground—& least of all on the idea of Alice's not wanting to see you. . . . I can imagine nothing worse for her than to learn . . . afterwards, that you had given it up from any motive connected with your relation with her. This would distress her more than anything else could do."[27] He came in the middle of July, without announcement, as a surprise to Alice, the excitement of which she felt as happiness more than as shock. They embraced with a revival of their passion of long ago, with a sense of how immediately their deep consanguinity could set aside the five years of separation and the physical and emotional distances between them. For Harry, this long summer moment was precious, the first living word from the world of his childhood American home since he had sailed away in August 1883.

Thick-chested, mostly bald, dark-bearded and sharp-eyed, well-dressed and carefully groomed, the middle-aged Harry seemed to William "nice and simple and amiable as he can be. He has covered himself, like some marine crustacean, with all sorts of material growths, rich sea-weeds and rigid barnacles and things, and lives hidden in the midst of his strange heavy alien manners and customs; but these are all but 'protective resemblances,' under which the same dear old, good, innocent and at bottom very powerless-feeling Harry remains, caring for little but his writing, and full of dutifulness and affection for all gentle things." If William had any sense of the rich confusion and psychological excitement of his brother's inner world, he kept it to himself. The founder of American psychology, unwilling—perhaps emotionally unable—to indulge in any perceptive psychological probing about his brother, preferred to see only the gentleness. Like Henry senior, he found it comfortable to impose on the reality of family relationships and individual personality the protective myths of harmony derived from Swedenborgian idealism. "Beneath all the accretions of years and the world," William wrote to his wife, asserting the myth of the family empire, "he is still the same dear innocent old Harry of our youth. . . . He's really, I won't say a yankee, but a native of the James family, and has no other country."[28] But his brother's deracination was both more simple and more complex. Having spent much of life and energy in flight from his family, Henry had demonstrated the key family fact— that there was no such unitary entity, at least in the sense of engagement and domination that William's phrase implies. It was a wish, not a fact, one that Henry's life and values contradicted. Henry did have another country, which William thought less valuable than the putative family dominions, for which Henry had given up the American soil on which William was making his stand. For Henry, the country for which he had left America was not England but art.

When William went back to America in late August 1889, Henry and Alice resumed their mutual supportiveness. Fortunately, Katherine Loring was able to spend more time in England. In the summer of 1890, when Alice, cadaverously thin, had painful stomach attacks, Katherine and Henry moved her from Leamington to South Kensington, first to a flat, then to a small house. Alice was by now a pain-wracked cripple in search of an opportunity to die. Often she joked mordantly about it. "I am working away as hard as I can to get dead as soon as possible, so as to release Katherine; but this play of Harry's makes a sad complication, as I don't want to immerse him in a deathbed scene on his 'first night,' too much of an aesthetic incongruity! The trouble seems to be there isn't anything to die of." In May 1891, she found her long-sought emotional and physical salvation, a lump in one of her breasts that an eminent specialist diagnosed as a cancerous tumor. She exalted in the prospect of peace. But not in the reality of pain. Hypnotism helped, alternating with morphia. It "soothes her nerves," Harry wote to William. He soon resented the occasional slight movements toward easement that only prolonged "her weary existence. . . . Then come the bad, the very bad times—when she sinks very low—& so it goes. So it will doubtless go for some time longer. She is a mass of malady, suffering *and* life. However, she is very far down—& there are days when the end seems in sight. I am only haunted by the fear of some breakdown or recall of Katherine before the end arrives—but she *won't* collapse & she *can't* . . . go." Visiting in London, Dr. Baldwin— finally, a physician she liked and respected—attended to her for a while. But it was only a matter of caretaking. He soon diagnosed the likelihood of a secondary tumor, probably in her lungs. In September 1891, William came again for a short visit, this time to say good-bye. Alice insisted on talking mostly about the excitement of the London premiere of *The American*. Henry stayed as close to her as he could, grateful for her stoicism and for Katherine's presence. He deeply admired Alice's courage, her mental lucidity, her conversational wit, and her extraordinary "moral command of the situation."[29]

Everyone wished for her death, she most of all. He sat by her bedside, to the extent that she would let him, more frequently at the beginning of 1892, witnessing her "recurring pain & distintegration" during one of the loveliest London winters he could remember, "fogless, rainless, mostly very windless, luminous & charming. . . . The days lengthen, the light *suggests,* the parks smell of spring." Though everyone was weary of her painful life, still "she lives and lives and lives through all her infinite protean dying." Occasionally, she had moments of conversational energy about people and about Henry's plays. She seemed to him then to flash momentarily into brilliance. At the end of February 1892, she took a critical turn, brought on by a bad cold caught from her nurse. Her suffering was immense, "her weakness so great that it is difficult to see what she lives on." Her lungs and chest ached; she coughed deeply and painfully; she could not keep food down. Her heart functioned badly. The lump on her breast was noticeably larger, "a tragic vessel, or receptacle," Henry wrote to William, "of recurrent, renewable, inexhaustible *forms* of disease." Without the morphia and hypnotism she would suffer even more. After missing a day at her bedside, he was summoned by Katherine to witness a blessed change, "a supreme deathlike emaciation" that had come on the night before and now made her "too weak to be actively nervous." She whispered to him to cable to William, "Tenderest love to all. Farewell. Am going soon."[30]

Well prepared, she had other instructions at hand, particularly her testamentary wishes and her burial arrangements. Her body was to be cremated at Woking and taken back to Cambridge to be laid beside

Father and Mother. Henry rejoiced that she was not to be buried "far off from the others, in this damp, black, alien English earth." Of the total estate of a little more than $80,000, Henry, William, and Katherine were each to get $20,000, Bob, $10,000, in consideration of his family having already received some gifts and the likelihood that his rich father-in-law would take care of his two children. Henry's share of the Syracuse rental income, which had been a lifetime-use gift and not part of Alice's estate, reverted to its owner. To him, the will seemed "singularly wise & enlightened." He immediately heard, though, from Bob, who was furious. What had been done to Wilky was now being done to him. As if the family curse were inescapable, "Bob's note," Henry wrote to William, "touches me with an unspeakable horror of the sickening time I went through . . . in regard to the 'discrimination' of *his* will. Alice's decision was the result of the most correct & troubled & conscientious consideration & balancing." But he would oppose neither reason nor fairness to the fact of his brother's pain. "If in short he *feels* unfairly treated, that, I think, represents on his part a reality, & I have written to him that if this *is* his view of the case I shall be quite ready to give him $5,000 of my share, &, I think, substantial justice will be done. . . . You have 4 children—& Bob has only two. I have none—& the above mentioned rectification is designated by every finger of circumstance as coming most fitted from me."[31]

Death finally came "at exactly four o'clock on Sunday afternoon," March 6, 1892, marked in her brother's mind by it being "the same hour of the same day as mother." Early Saturday morning, the pain had disappeared. Her face looked deathly, pure, and quiet. He saw that "the end *might* come at any moment." As she remained conscious during most of the day, he went home to rest for a few hours. In the evening, she expressed her exasperation at still being alive, her impatience to be dead. She then fell into a gentle sleep. When he returned, her breathing had become loud, deep, heavy. The deathbed watch began. From nine o'clock that night to four o'clock the next afternoon, he and Katherine and the nurse sat by her side. Her heavy, labored "almost automatic breathing" continued for seven hours, "infinitely pathetic and, to me, most unspeakable. . . ." There was no appearance in her face of pain, "only more and more utterly the look of death." In midafternoon her breathing suddenly rose into a high, frightening, smothered "whistle in the lungs," which continued for an hour. Then it became almost normal breathing again—quiet, gentle, natural. Soon he missed the sound of her breathing at all. Then it returned, and returned again as deep respiratory sighs exhaled only once a minute for about eight minutes. "Her face . . . seemed in a strange, dim, touching way to become clearer. I went to the window to let in a little more of the afternoon light upon it . . . and when I came back to the bed she had drawn the last breath that was not succeeded by another." Her face looked to him "most beautiful and noble."[32] He felt inexpressibly lonely.

(4)

In a world of deaths, he had been reaching out for new life, partly in the theatre. Since 1891, he had made many efforts and had had no successes. On January 5, 1895, he had his one opportunity to transform his sense of the chances slipping irrevocably away into a redemptive and enriching triumph. This was the night on which the citadel was to be taken, the walls of the theatre to fall. Gripped by anxiety, he plotted with Gosse that during the premiere of *Guy Domville*—a title he hated but to which he had agreed in order to support the vanity of the actor-producer playing the lead role—"he should hide in the bar of a little public-house down an alley close to the theatre." Gosse would "slip forth at the end of the second act and report 'how it was going.' " "Lonely and terrified," eager to have over the hours until the premiere, he felt himself, on the day of the performance, "under chloroform. . . . This is a time when a man wants a religion," he wrote to William, attempting to balance terror with humor. "I'm counting on some Psychical intervention from you—this is really the time to show your stuff."[33]

The St. James's Theatre would be filled with cultural and social celebrities, many of them his friends. It would be lit brilliantly with newly installed electric lights, a brightness that he desperately hoped his play would match. At five in the afternoon, he took another compulsive look at his watch. There were still three and a half hours before "my poor little play will be thrown into the arena—like a little white Christmas Virgin to the lions and tigers."[34] The playwright anticipated that he might finally be ravished and devoured. Changing his mind about hiding in a pub, he fulfilled his "luminous idea" of going to see another play by attending the premiere of Oscar Wilde's *An Ideal Husband*. The audience responded to Wilde's play with a laughter and delight that anxiously highlighted for him the difference between his own drama and the cleverness of Wilde's play that he both envied and despised. Leaving the Haymarket Theatre, he walked back across St. James's Square to a reckoning for which he had been preparing since childhood.

Four years earlier, immediately after the Southport premiere of *The American* in January 1891, he had asked Stevenson, who was bewildered by James's theatrical efforts, not to be "hard on" him. "Simplifying and chastening necessity has laid its brutal hand on me and I have had to try and make somehow or other the money I don't make by literature."[35] It was at best a partial truth, the force of the economic argument soon further undermined by his bequest from Alice and the return of his Syracuse rental income. The argument represented an emotional truth more than a financial reality, a pervasive sense of insecurity rather than the fact of insufficiency itself. His decision to write as many short stories as possible while pursuing theatrical success kept his income reasonably stable, though noticeably lower than what it had been during the 1880s. The failure to earn other than a pittance from the run of *The American* and the subsequent frustrations could not have supported the financial justification for keeping at it rather than writing even more short stories and returning to writing novels. He was motivated partly by obsessive stubbornness, partly by visions of piles of gold so high that they would reclaim the lost family fortune and permit him the same leisure to pursue his art that his father had had to pursue his religious obsessions.

He often pretended there was an aesthetic "kingdom to conquer" in the theatre. But the kingdom contained mostly "ignorant brutes of managers and dense *cabotines* of actors." Still, "I feel as if I had at last *found* my form—my real one—that for which pale fiction is an ineffectual substitute." Yet at the same time he readily granted that he wanted only two or three years of successful playwriting, "time to dig out eight or ten rounded masterpieces and make withal enough money to enable me to retire in peace and plenty for the unmolested business of a *little* supreme writing, as distinguished from gouging—which is the Form above mentioned." The London premiere of *The American* in September 1891 made it clear that this play was not the key that would open the theatrical treasure-house. Still, when the play closed in early December 1891, he was proud of what he had accomplished. "I am sorry you didn't see the thing in the last month of its existence," he wrote to William, "it was so improved—really twice as good. . . . I have lost no grain of courage—& I have gained a tone of resolution & insight. Therefore you have only to wait for me. The great hitch is that the process is costly—plays are terribly expensive *till* they pay. But one plays for the highest stakes." Undaunted, he wrote two more plays, *The Reprobate* and probably *The Album,* "to bolster up," he condescendingly remarked, "poor Edward Compton."[36] Compton turned down both plays.

Absolutely certain that to write successful plays he must write down to his audience, he thought it necessary to descend as far down to his conception of the public as he possibly could. When he published the two plays Compton had rejected, two of his newspaper reviewers expressed their wish that the author "would write some farces to please himself, and not to please the stage." William Archer made the point even more explicitly. "Mr. James has never taken up a natural and unconstrained attitude toward the stage. . . . If he will only . . . write solely for the ideal audience within his own breast, he will certainly produce works of art, and not improbably successful plays." Since money was his dominating objective, James thought it absurd even to consider attempting to write independent of commercial concerns, to aspire to the level of theatrical art other than in the technical sense. In the end, his theatre audiences concluded that he could not even manage successful dramatic effects; his obsession with mechanical structure prevented him from attaining anything theatrically lively. As a playwright, he treaded water for more than three years. As a writer of fiction, he restricted himself to short stories. They did not absorb long periods of time, and editors mostly desired short fiction, a result of the gradual transformation of the nature of magazines and of the relationship between magazines and their readers from the high-Victorian concentration on serial fiction to the shorter economic and literary attention span of late-Victorian readers. Each time he returned to the short story, he felt the relief of a private challenge, the pleasure of exerting his old artistry.[37] In 1891, he published his powerfully homoerotic "The Pupil"; a tightly charged story of sexual conflict among a daughter, her father, and her father's fiancée called "The Marriages"; and "Brooksmith," a subtle indictment of the British class structure. Of the ten stories he published in 1892, six deal with questions of art and the artist. All express the anxieties he felt in regard to the problems of his own career, especially "Nona Vincent," which explicitly embodies the fantasies of a Jamesian playwright tussling with fears of failure and luxuriating in fantasies of success.

While the fictional "Nona Vincent" played on as a fantasy, James and Compton tried to resuscitate *The American*. Disappointed by the London response, Compton gave up his Opera Comique lease at the end of 1891. Returning to provincial tours, he maintained *The American* in his repertoire. James still hoped to provide him with "something that, of a Saturday night, in crowded provincial cities, will help to make all our fortunes—& I mean to tackle the question in right earnest." At least for now, "the poor dear old American is sitting up a little in his coffin." "Full of plans & purposes for our great stroke," he wrote to

Compton from Italy in the summer of 1892, he expected "the next three or four months to be very fruitful." He was pleased that "the poor dear *American* still fights for his life. I hope he *does* something, & I welcome every symptom that managers don't too strongly object to him." On his return from Italy, he offered Compton "the 'scenario' of a three-act play. . . . If the result appears not exactly the right thing for the very particular (alas!) conditions, I think I shall be able to go, bang-off, to another theme. I have two or three in my head. We can try till we hit it!" When Compton proposed what he thought a more effective fourth act for *The American,* James jumped at the possibility. "I am fairly cracking with curiosity to know what your 'magnificent idea' for Act 4th may be. . . . I feel, indeed, if it hadn't been for the grave initial mistake & misfortune of keeping so much of the substance of the *novel* . . . I should have had a greatly freer hand, from an early stage of the experiment, in the work of redemption."[38]

At the same time, he was also trying to maintain John Augustin Daly's interest in "Mrs. Jasper" by writing a new third act. Ada Rehan, a talented Irish-American actress whom he had met in 1891 and whom he had in mind for the starring role, had recommended the play to the American manager and producer. Daly planned to open a new theatre in London in 1893. Having attended the London premiere of *The American,* he seemed to like the new play, enough at least to agree to produce it, though he requested extensive revision. Probably he found attractive the prospect of opening his theatre with a play by the famous novelist. Excited by what seemed to him almost the certainty of a handsome London production, James worked at revising the third act, telling Compton that it was "heroic practice. . . . But it is simply *hellishly* difficult, & I have minutes of black darkness & stoppage out of which I brilliantly emerge." The effort soon seemed, "happily, quite flooded with light." The same radiance he hoped would now shine on the new fourth act of *The American.* "I shall write bang-off a wholly new thing— incorporating *none* of the old matter. . . . That is I shall write a . . . new act of the best comedy I can—& then accommodate what is possible of the play to *it.*" By early November 1891, with most of the new act done, he went through his usual emotional acrobatics. "I am so nervous about the new 4th—so afraid to think it, too cockily & confidently, as good as it very possibly (& even *probably*) is!! . . . I *must* rush down to you with it." Compton, of course, had suggestions for revision. But at least, James rejoiced, the Comptons did not reject it out of hand. They liked it enough to want to work with it. "I clap my hands that Oliver asks for *more*—instead of less!" Biting his lips, he did his best. "Here are the *last* touches, I think, that flesh & blood can yield. I hope they will do. . . . For anything more I must wait till I *see & hear*." He was eager to read the new act to the company, as if only his presence would make it all clear and right. He thought he might join them in Bath in mid-November. "I will come on *Wednesday* to Bristol—if it is a real or urgent need. I will come to Oxford next week (by day,) if *that* will further the cause."[39]

Eager to be accommodating, he wanted both Compton and Daly to know that he was committed to joint ventures. "I don't in the least pretend that any scenario I can send you of any play that is still to be grappled with in the effort to *do* it . . . is . . . my *last word*. Perish the thought—it isn't the way I work. The play, the subject, is a living thing, growing, moving, altering its proportions & relations as one handles it." It baffled him when others could not see the potential in his scenarios. On the one hand, he submitted himself to the authority of theatre professionals, relinquishing the full artistic control that he was used to in writing fiction. On the other, he did not seem to be able finally, fully enough, to carry the day either with scenarios or with fully written scripts. The specter of delay always seemed to hover, embitteringly, over his theatrical efforts. For producers like Compton and Daly, it made sense to encourage him but not to make commitments. "There is some inspiration in attempting to do something which may still see the light *within* 1893," he wrote to Compton, "no matter how late. . . . But I confess there be none (for *me*) in *any* hope further deferred. I am, in general, condemned to drink the cup of delay to the bitterest dregs, & it simply takes all incentive out of me."[40] *The American* remained, despite the new fourth act, an undistinguished light comedy performed for the remainder of its short life every Friday in the obscurity of provincial England. Compton turned down every new script or scenario James sent him.

As he worked at his own theatrical illusions, he had before him the constant irritant of Wilde having a series of successful plays, as if by some mysterious process the Irish playwright had discovered the elusive formula for success. Wilde was an envied and distasteful alter ego. James could not resist passing along, with a combination of wit and maliciousness, "an answer made by the irrepressible Whistler to a lady who asked him (a propos his late idiotic public squabble with Oscar Wilde,) why he couldn't 'let sleeping Oscars lie.'—'Ah, he won't sleep and he *will* lie!' " The fall of the dark curtain on Wilde's career in April 1895 seemed even more horrible to James in contrast to the brightness of his theatrical successes: *Lady Windermere's Fan* in 1892, whose premiere James attended at the same theatre in which his own *Guy Domville* was to open and with the same lead actors; *Salomé* and *A Woman of No*

Importance in 1893, which he thought "a piece of helpless puerility"; *An Ideal Husband* in 1895, which he went to see on the night of the premiere of *Guy Domville;* and *The Importance of Being Earnest,* which opened at the St. James's Theatre immediately after *Guy Domville* closed. He understood that "everything Oscar does is a deliberate trap for the literalist," including "the usual trick of saying the unusual—complimenting himself and his play." He detested Wilde's combination of elegant vulgarity and theatrical cleverness. He had no doubt that *Lady Windermere's Fan* would have a long run, though it seemed "infantine" in "both subject and form," a drama "of a candid and primitive simplicity" made entertaining by drollery and verbal wit. It gave audiences the opportunity to feel decadent, "privileged and modern. . . . I was at the premiere on Saturday last," he wrote to Henrietta Reubell, "& saw the unspeakable one make his speech to the audience, with a metallic blue carnation in his buttonhole & a cigarette in his fingers. The speech, which, alas, was stupid, was only to say that he judged the audience felt the play to be nearly as charming as he did. I expected something more."[41] When *Guy Domville* failed, he suffered the humiliation of being squeezed into theatrical nonexistence between two of Wilde's light but formidable triumphs.

When John Hare complimented but did not pursue the manuscript of "Mrs. Jasper," James pursued Ada Rehan. She soon secured Daly's agreement to produce the play, in 1893, at his new Leicester Square Theatre. At first, Daly had been unenthusiastic about the script. When James sent him a revised version in October 1892, Daly overcame his hesitancy, though all the weaknesses of the play were still there. He still wanted additional revisions, which James made. On his return from New York, Daly inaugurated his new theatre with Tennyson's *The Foresters.* "I come next," James confidently expected.[42] When, in October 1893, Daly, who had already commissioned stage designs, asked for a change of title, James felt uneasy enough to offer him about seventy-five alternatives. Daly chose "Disengaged." The new title was prescient. From the beginning, Daly had difficulties, most of which had nothing to do with his original decision to take on "Mrs. Jasper." His theatre was now having difficulty drawing audiences, because of its unusual location and because Tennyson's play had nothing but Tennyson's name to recommend it as drama. What had seemed to Daly a sensible business calculation two years before may now have seemed no longer worth the risk. If Tennyson's name did not produce box-office results, why then should James's? Certainly he could not have had much commitment to the play itself, given his initial hesitancy and his many requests for revisions.

Early in December 1893, James learned that there had been one, perhaps two, cast readings of the play, which had produced the complaint that "the play lacked story." He had assumed, based on his experience with Compton, that he would be invited as an essential participant both to explain and protect his play. Apparently, though, it was Daly's practice that an author could attend but not participate in rehearsals. Daly did not like what was the absence of action in the play. On December 6, James attended a cast reading for the first time. He was angry at his previous exclusion. When the reading seemed to him superficial and insultingly rapid, he stormed out. "I was not given a simple second's opportunity of having the least contact or words with any member of the company: who began and stammeringly read their parts the instant I came in, and vanished the instant the third act ended." Rehan, to whom he could not bring himself to say a word, looked "white, haggard, ill-looking almost in *anguish*." Humiliated, angry, in "a state of nervous exasperation," he felt he had been set up. Daly "is an utter cad," he wrote to William, "& Ada Rehan is the same. They simply kicked me between them (& all in *one* rehearsal) out of the theatre. How can one rehearse with people who are dying to get rid of you—& what sort of collaboration is that? I simply walked off—to their great joy—with my MS. in my pocket."[43] That night he wrote to Daly, withdrawing the play.

Daly responded that he had provided many instances of good faith, including the cast reading at issue, but that since "it was you who offered me the play in the first instance and it is now you who request its return . . . I am satisfied to accept your word as compliment to my judgment now as then." Responding in detail, with an inevitable rehearsal and rewriting of the history of their relationship, James still maintained that for some reason Daly had gone to considerable trouble and expense simply in order to tell him in a very discourteous way that he did not want to produce the play. What bothered him most was the discourtesy, "the want of ceremony, under the circumstances, with which you addressed yourself to the business of getting rid of me." His skin was thin, his sense of politeness verging on the irritable, "punctilious, ceremonious, and precise," Gosse later remarked. "It is not to be denied that he was apt to be hasty in taking offence, and not very ready to overlook an impertinence." He soon accused "that hopeless cad of a Daly" of purposely provoking him, with Ada Rehan an irresponsible and base collaborator. "The whole manoeuvre and whole situation," he told William, "were as plain as day." Why, if Daly had been toying with delaying the production or even not going forward, he would not have preferred to speak privately to James about his financial problems rather than waste time and energy on three cast readings, James does not seem to have considered, though by late January he began to think that Daly's financial situation must have been the motive. Daly's season, he now told William, had proved "so utterly disastrous . . . that he had but one idea—to *get out* of his contract to produce a new & untried piece on which he should have to pay royalties—with the old things of his repertory, costing him nothing, still to fall back on. . . . Unable to *throw up* a play he had accepted as vigorously & rigorously as he had accepted mine," he treated "me with an incivility which would lay upon *me* the initiative."[44] For the rest of his life, Daly was always that "cad" and "Mrs. Jasper," a fine play basely deprived of its opportunity to triumph.

Whatever his lines of emotional defense, it was an unhappy time. "I tell you nothing about myself," he admitted to Grace Norton, because "I *have* no self—I don't know what has become of it." It seemed partly to have been projected onto some theatrical stage of triumph and rewards that existed mostly in his desires. In late 1892, he responded to Violet Paget's bewildered criticism of his theatrical adaptation of *The American*: "I have plenty of 'Becauses.' . . . Yes, the public is vulgar & vile, yes, a first flag is a mere getting one's feet into the stirrup; yes, one must be in the saddle, in order to go. . . . But wait—ah, wait!—*this* is nothing. Wait till I begin to *ride*." Now, having been shoved half off the horse, his mood took a darker turn, both about his playwriting and about his career as a writer of fiction. He expressed some of his grimness in a powerful short story, "The Middle Years," later to be his title for the final, unfinished volume of his autobiography. A middle-aged, artistically successful but not very popular writer, having recently been seriously ill, feels that his career and probably his life are coming to an end. Dencombe wants another chance at art, which can only come through another chance at life, through recuperation and health. "It had taken too much of his life to produce too little of his art. The art had come, but it had come after everything else. . . . 'Ah for another go!—ah for a better chance!' . . . [He] was a passionate corrector, a fingerer of style. . . . He had wasted inestimable years. He had followed literature from the first, but he had taken a lifetime to get along side of her. Only to-day, at last, had he begun to *see*. . . . 'I want an extension. . . . I want to what they call *live*.' . . . We work in the dark—we do what we can—we give what we have. Our doubt is our passion and our passion is our task. The rest is the madness of art." At the end of the story, Dencombe dies. It was "the virtual end of his first and only chance."[45]

(5)

James's last chance for theatrical success developed out of an idea that came to him in the summer of 1892 about a young Venetian nobleman "who had become a monk." He had been "taken almost forcibly out of his convent and brought back into the world in order to keep the family from becoming extinct. . . . It was absolutely *necessary* for him to marry." The subject touched on personal considerations in regard to his own celibacy and his renunciation of the possibility that he might contribute to carrying on the James family name. From the start, though he determined that he must "adapt this somehow or other to today," it proved such an uncontemporary subject that he could bring it only as far forward as the eighteenth century. He would also have to make the essentially Catholic subject compatible with the interests and prejudices of an English audience. Even more peculiarly, he conceived it as a play for the Compton Comedy Company when it was hardly to be a comedy, when Compton had already turned down a series of his scripts and scenarios, and when Compton had frequently pointed out to him that provincial audiences insisted on happy endings. From Paris, in late March 1893, he sent Compton word of his "fever of composition" and his plan to keep the first act until he had "finished the 2nd, & then take, or send, the two to you, to keep you in heart till you should receive the 3rd. . . . I am trying to do something good enough to be well worth waiting for." Compton's patience for waiting was almost infinite, James's haste, almost irrelevant. Probably Compton had learned to discount most of James's rhetoric. "Act 2 will go straight & swift," he was assured. "And after that Act 3d will go 'of itself.' Courage."[46]

By mid-April, he was able to send, from Paris, a typescript of the first act. He assured Compton about the Catholic element. "You will now appreciate to the full what I meant by my notification to you that it was of the essence that it should be enacted among Catholics! But I hope you will also be struck with the fact that any disadvantage from this is quite conjured away. The 2nd act will be a very lively *contrast* to the 1st: G.D. drinking dregs of *life* etc. . . . The *essence* is all there. . . . The 2d act is to be lovely. . . . I may as well say I *so* like it myself." Though he urged Compton to be "absolutely frank & candid about your impression of this," he was not prepared for Compton's absolute rejection of any possibility that he could produce this play. The news bitterly disappointed him. "I had had as much confidence in my subject as you are so good as to say you had in *me*! The one shade of doubt I felt was in the Catholicity—but I had ended with thinking that that— relegated to the last century & tinted with distance & an old-world effect, would practically *not* count as a stumbling-block, but rather, on the contrary, as a novelty and a prettiness. And I thought my story *simple* and broadly interesting and just picturesque *enough*—I mean romantic enough—and not so picturesque or so romantic as to be strange; & genially human & touching in the right way—& in fact addressed to the simple-minded British public *most* directly and diplomatically. Above all I thought it *dramatic!*"[47]

He went back to the disaster-drawing-board in the hope that some revision might change Compton's feelings. It did not. Without a happy ending, Compton wanted nothing to do with the play. James tried to explain to Compton why the underlying idea of the play forbade a marriage for Domville. "The idea . . . is that Domville throwing up his priesthood to take possession of his place in the world [finds] that he comes into the world only to make himself happy at the *expense* of others . . . and in the face of this reality—ugly and cruel—turns back again to his old ideal, renounces his personal worldly chance, sacrifices himself and makes the others happy. . . . The 'ending' that you express a dread of *is* the only ending I have ever dreamed of giving the play." His own theatrical ending threatened, though, to be as bleak as Domville's. Like Domville, he too had renounced marriage in the interest of an ideal. But, unlike Domville, he had not inherited a fortune, and he was not quite ready yet to forsake his attempt at worldly success and return to his less-compromised monastery. He did have occasional moments of sequestered happiness writing short stories, dipping his pen "into the *other* ink—the sacred fluid of fiction. Among the delays, the disappointments . . . of the horrid theatric trade, nothing is so soothing as to remember that literature sits patient at my door, and that I have only to lift the latch to let in the exquisite little form that is, after all, nearest to my heart and with which I am so far from having done. I let it in and the old brave hours come back."[48]

But still he would not give up the theatre obsession, though when Compton recommended that he try another subject and that the effort be a communal one in which Compton be engaged from the moment of conception, he hesitated. "I don't *know*, with certainty, that I can do anything of the sort. It is a manner of working . . . so foreign to my natural manner & my acquired habits that I shall have to make a great effort to enter into it. . . . It takes some great inspiration, in the way of prospective rewards—of interpretation, profit, etc, to help one to change." He felt confident that "the way to write comedy is not to take a serious subject and try to make it droll—but to take a droll subject and try to *keep* it droll." Having thought that he had done precisely that with most of the plays he had written so far, he was puzzled at why they had not been successes. Within days, he had prepared a scenario of the first act of a new three-act comedy for Compton, based on his short story "The Chaperon," which he had been encouraged to adapt for the theatre by the playwright Arthur Pinero, the premiere of whose *Second Mrs. Tanqueray* he had attended in late May 1893 at the St. James's Theatre. When Compton did not feel enthusiastic, James kept trying. The same pattern repeated itself through summer and fall 1893. As quickly as he sent scenarios to Compton, Compton had objections that James could not overcome, though he would start with optimism before crashing into baffled frustration. Still, he reminded himself, as he wrote in the glowing firelight at his De Vere Gardens apartment the day after Christmas, 1893, there were moments when he thought he could still do it, that he had in his mind and even on the paper in front of him "the stuff of a play, of the particular limited style and category that can only be dreamed for E. C."[49]

He was delighted when, in late spring 1893, the actor-manager George Alexander expressed strong interested in *Guy Domville,* with the notion that the part of the Venetian ex-monk might provide him with an attractive starring role. A vain, hyperbolic actor with great skill and energy within a narrow range, Alexander was a handsome matinee idol in his mid-thirties. He had toured with Irving in America, had begun a successful career as a theatre manager in 1890, had produced and acted in *Lady Windermere's Fan* in 1892, and now eagerly sought to line up new plays in which to perform. From Ramsgate, where he had gone to escape the London heat, James sent him the finished first and "*elaborately full* and detailed" scenarios of the second and third acts. When Alexander, "with instantaneous *rapture*," accepted the play "for imminent production," James was sufficiently self-protective to appreciate the irony of the actor describing *Guy Domville* "as 'the most beautiful poetical play' produced in this country *since* (hold your breath and wait—) 'since *Olivia,*' " a third-rate dramatization of Oliver Goldsmith's *The Vicar of Wakefield,* which James thought abysmal. He knew with whom he was dealing. Acting as his own agent, he managed the business negotiation sensibly, both author and producer aware that terms would be of significance only if the play were a success. With Alexander occupied for the length of the run of *Mrs. Tanqueray* and already committed to an unwritten play, *The Masqueraders*—by the successful Arthur Henry Jones, whose most recent drama James thought "the clumsiest trash"—he eagerly hoped for a quick end to the run of Pinero's play and for Jones's not to materialize in time for it be put on directly afterward. When he was disappointed in both hopes, he could do nothing but wait.[50]

When he stormed out of Daly's cast reading of *Disengaged* in December 1893, he was still waiting for a production of *Guy Domville,* which he had delivered to Alexander in August. He would give himself, he promised William, "one year more. . . . I *have* come to *hate* the whole theatrical subject." One year and no more. Finally, in March 1894, *Mrs. Tanqueray's* run came to an end. Unfortunately, Jones had his play ready. The best James could do was hope that it would fail. "My date depends," he told William in late October, "wholly on the amount of life that thing (the *Masqueraders*) yet has in it. It may have— will probably have, 3 months." Fortunately, it did not survive beyond September. When Alexander came down with the flu, James impatiently waited for rehearsals. Unlike Daly, Alexander was happy to have James read his play to the cast. But since, as soon as Alexander had recovered, James came down with a sore throat, Alexander did the reading in early December. The next week, full-cast rehearsals began "with great violence & continue hard for the month. The play is small & simple—only 3 acts—but pretty . . . a little romantic story" that "will not, at any rate, be a disgraceful work. It will be quite exquisitely mounted, dressed &c & as well acted as London can act. My only anxiety is as to how Alexander will carry the weight of his own part— which is a very beautiful & interesting one. So awfully fearfully much depends on him."[51]

Immersed in his anxiety, he scheduled and ran his life by the clock of the rehearsals, almost every one of which he attended. "Beyond all belief to you," he told William, "wd. be the *time* that the effort toward perfection, & the adjustment to the hard conditions, in a dramatic production, keeps continuing in an *endless* ordeal, to demand, day after day." He felt undermined by nervousness and exhaustion. "Forgive me and pity me," he begged a friend. "I may be meant for the Drama— God knows!—but I certainly wasn't meant for the Theatre." When the St. James's Theatre closed the day before Christmas until the opening of *Domville,* scheduled for January 5, 1895, the company intensified its rehearsal schedule to two a day. James, pleased with what he saw on stage, had regular advice, encouragement, and comfort for the performers, particularly for Marion Terry, playing the female lead. Her performance seemed to him "perfectly beautiful & *right.*" All in all, "the thing 'pans out' very reassuringly & all the omens & particulars as good as I could possibly desire," he wrote to his Cambridge family. He would cable William the morning after the premiere "if the news is worth cabling." The prize glittered closely before him, almost in hand. He knew what he would do with his profits. "I mean to *invest* all the money I make by my play," he told William, "if I make any. If the play fails I shall require the *balance* of the 86 dollars, 78 cents" owed him from the latest payment of the Syracuse rents. "They will be needed. If it is an unmistakable success I will add to my telegram the word *Invest*— which will mean please send the sum in question" to their Boston banker as a prelude to future sums.[52]

"Miserably nervous" as the night of the premiere approached, he seemed to Gosse "positively storm-ridden with emotion." With the doubling of rehearsals, he felt he was going through a "demoralizing & exhausting & incongruous ordeal." He did not seem to believe he could do otherwise, as if the play would be inferior without his twice-daily anguish. After so many minor changes, "the poor little play itself" seemed "aching in every fibre from its wounds." Though the production and the acting seemed as good as it could be, he worried about Alexander's heavy-handedness. "More than ever, this evening, I wish I could be distinguished!" he wrote to a friend. One good omen was that subscription services had "taken in advance £1,600 worth of seats." When he went to the empty theatre early in the evening, he felt anesthetized, yet sensate enough to feel his numbness. His hands shook. "I am your plucky, but, all the same, lonely and terrified Henry," he wrote to William. When the bright new electric lights of the St. James's Theatre came up, he disappeared across the square toward the Haymarket to see Wilde's *An Ideal Husband*. As the sold-out St. James's Theatre filled—the orchestra resplendent with celebrities, some of whom were his friends, including Sargent, Burne-Jones, Leighton, Du Maurier, Mary Ward, Elizabeth Robins, and, of course, Gosse; the galleries with veteran theatregoers and Alexander's following—he watched the curtain rise in another theatre. When he left the Haymarket, he stopped in St. James's Square, paralyzed with terror. The evident success of Wilde's play, the applause and cheers of the audience, probably meant that his own had been a failure. For a moment, he was "afraid to go on and learn more."[53]

Coming through the stage door into the theatre, he thought he heard ecstatic applause, happy confusion. Alexander, on stage, partly bowing, partly backing off, beckoned him forward. He almost floated onto the stage. The bright lights, as he turned to the audience, blanked out everything in front of him but the noise. The sounds that he could hardly distinguish soon became audible. To his shock, they were derisive jeers, "a storm of hoots and . . . catcalls from the gallery, answered by loud and sustained applause from the stalls, the whole producing an effect of hell broke loose, in the midst of which the author, as white as chalk, bowed and spread forth deprecating hands.'' Some of the audience attempted louder applause. They were answered by another volley of howling catcalls. Stunned, with no idea why he and his play were the focus of such a conflict, he got off the stage as quickly as he could. To Gosse's horrified sympathy, James seemed to be on the stage forever. He "finally vanished."[54]

The postmortems were bitterly depressing. Perhaps there had been a cabal against Alexander by some of his enemies. The second act had been a theatrical disaster. Apparently, the audience in the galleries had become irritably restless. The main character seemed too indecisive, too unmanly, too morbidly sensitive. Why should someone who had inherited a fortune and with whom a beautiful, refined woman was in love even consider returning to a monastery? When it began to become likely that the play would not have a happy ending, some members of the audience answered disappointment with disparagement. By the middle of the third act, Alexander had lost confidence. The feel of the theatre was cold, the audience disaffiliated, on the verge of open hostility. When the curtain came down, the gallery began to express its contempt. When those who liked the play, or at least respected James and theatre etiquette, began to insist on applause, the gallery countered with louder jeers. When Alexander tried to mollify the audience with a brief speech of apology, he made enemies of both factions. When James came onto the stage, the audience transferred much of its hostility from actor to author.

Bewildered, he felt that his worst nightmare had come true. He had no doubt that the play was wounded, "probably to death." Though it was to continue for thirty-one performances, with sympathetic though not laudatory reviews—three of the most sensible by a trio of young writer-reviewers who had attended the premiere, H. G. Wells, George Bernard Shaw, and Arnold Bennett—and though James had at least the minor satisfaction of making eleven hundred dollars for the short run, he was bitterly disappointed. How much more he would have made if the play had run four times as long! They were "the horridest four weeks of my life." The public had been barbarous, an epitome of philistinism, *Guy Domville* an "unmitigated disaster." Eager to have the whole experience "ancient history" as quickly as possible, he felt that the play had been too original, too sophisticated, too delicate for the public. His friends rallied round, with letters of affection and support, from America in one direction, from Venice in the other. When no telegram arrived with the injunction "*invest,*" William wrote lovingly, "I only hope . . . that you won't take it tragically . . . if it be a case of bad failure, and conceive yourself to be humiliated in the eyes of public and friends." Protecting himself as best he could, he told the sympathetic Daniel Curtis, "The theatre is an abyss of vulgarity & of brutish platitude; from which one ought doubtless to welcome any accident that detaches one. Please believe that I *am* detached." He felt, for the moment, purged of the poison he had swallowed. "Deep and dark is the abyss of the theatre," he wailed to a new young friend. As he walked home on the night of the disaster, miserably unhappy, he vowed "never again to have anything to do with a business which lets one into such traps, abysses and heart-break. . . . I have practically renounced my deluded dreams."[55] Willfully, with the same strength and stubbornness that had nurtured his career as a playwright, though with less self-deception, he now exerted himself to climb out of the dark abyss.

(6)

It was a difficult climb. The death of his theatre career had been preceded one year before by a death so sudden, so shocking, that he had had to bring to bear every strategy he had learned to deal with absolute ends. He had also had to face the possibility that with greater self-awareness and wisdom the catastrophe might have been avoided. On Thursday, January 25, 1894, he held in his hand at De Vere Gardens a telegram from Constance Fenimore Woolson's sister in New York with the shocking news that Fenimore had died the previous day in Venice. The news had been cabled across the Atlantic to Clara Benedict, who immediately cabled her sister's most intimate friend in Europe. Would he please go to Venice to attend to funeral arrangements? Suddenly, it was "all ghastly amazement and distress." He had had no idea there was any danger. "I had not even heard a word of her being ill. Mrs. Benedict's cable was a bolt out of the blue." What to do? One of his servants had suddenly become "dangerously ill." He needed to make sure his house was in order and make travel arrangements, which would take at least another day. A second telegram from Benedict arrived within hours with the news that Grace Carter, Fenimore's cousin, who had been in Munich, had left for Venice. She would take care of what had to be done immediately. He cabled Carter, asking for details, advice, plans. Two more cables arrived that day, both from William Baldwin in Florence, providing some details, particularly that Fenimore had had influenza. Baldwin also informed him that Carter had arrived in Venice, that she had arranged for burial to take place at the Protestant Cemetery in Rome, which Fenimore had thought among the most beautiful places in the world, and that Carter had cabled Baldwin that "he need not come" to Venice.[56] Baldwin advised James to stay put pending further news. Desperate for guidance, he telegraphed Carter again, with prepayment for an answer, in regard to whether or not he was needed immediately or whether he had two days or so to get himself prepared for the trip. Nothing had prepared him for the news.

Bewildered, he hesitated in the London bleakness, eager to have the moment of delay that Baldwin's telegrams implied he could take. If he left immediately, he would at best arrive on Tuesday to be "confronted with mere accomplished facts." He spent a restless, anguished morning on Friday. When a tentative reprieve came with further unspecified "news" that might make his Saturday departure "unnecessary," he spent part of the day, "in the midst of much bewilderment & uncertainty," writing long, pained, plaintive letters to Baldwin and Carter. What, he wanted to know, had happened? "What sudden disaster overtook her—pneumonia supervening on influenza?" His obsession with details, his need to visualize, tormented him. "I am so utterly in the dark about everything that I am reduced to mere conjecture & supposition as to what has taken place & as *how* Miss Woolson died. It is all—I mean my fear that she was alone, *unfriended* at the last—too miserable to talk about."[57] When he still had not heard from Grace Carter by Saturday afternoon, he went to Cook's travel agency and arranged to depart the next morning, directly to Rome, with the possibility that he might be there in time for the funeral.

When he returned, he found on his table at De Vere Gardens, delivered by one of his English-Venetian friends visiting in London, a note with a clipping from a Venetian newspaper that stated unequivocally that Fenimore had killed herself. She had thrown herself from her third-story window. The London evening newspapers printed the same story. Collapsing "before the horror and pity of it," he sent a telegram to Grace Carter not to expect him at the funeral. He could not go. "The dreadful *image*" of her fall, of the impact of her weight against the pavement, of her bloody, partly crushed body, vividly occupied the eye of his imagination and his pain. Fenimore "was so valued and close a friend of mine and had been so for so many years that I felt an intense nearness of participation in every circumstance of her tragic end and in every detail of the sequel. But it is just this nearness of emotion that has made . . . the immediate horrified rush to personally *meet* these things impossible to me. I can't *think* of Venice for the present." But he could not stop thinking about it. That night, he received a telegram from John Hay that relieved his depression momentarily. It solaced him that Hay, one of Fenimore's oldest friends, whom he had not known was in Rome, was helping with the funeral arrangements. He wired Hay to lay flowers on the grave on his behalf. He felt "too utterly sickened to move." At his desk, writing letters, he did his best to bring the dreadful image under control, to find some words and thoughts that would help him understand "this brutal summarized tragedy."[58]

Flowers were piled high on the funeral mound under a bright Roman sky. Robert Jenkins, the rector of St. Paul's American Church in Rome, had obtained the measurements of the coffin "for the proper building of the vault in the grave" and "secured a lot" on the back rise of the cemetery, framed by high, dark-green cypresses. The lot was close to where William Story's wife had recently been buried and not far from Keats's grave. "We buried poor C.W.," Hay wrote to Henry Adams, "in the Protestant Cemetery, laying her down in her first and last resting place—a thoroughly good, and most unhappy woman. . . . She did much good, and no harm in her life, and had not as much happiness as a convict." All Wednesday afternoon, in wintry London, James wondered whether the Italian heavens had been cerulean enough to meet his and Fenimore's long-held Roman expectations. He prayed that "it might be one of the kind [skies], the exquisite ones, that Rome can show."[59]

Accepting the general claim that her death had been a suicide, he wanted to know what had driven her to kill herself. Perhaps, he unhappily sensed, he might have contributed to a disappointment whose heaviness she found insupportable. She had returned to Venice in late winter 1893. England had proved too damp, too cold, her hope for longer moments with Henry unsatisfied. She had been working hard, driven by her sense of financial necessity. From Egypt in spring 1890, she had exhorted herself, "If I am to get my finances into shape, I *must* give myself to steady work, in the most quiet & unexciting place I can find." Cheltenham was that with a vengeance. Except for the weather, she seems to have found it suitable for a while. "I hope Mr. James has given a good account of me," she wrote to Katherine Loring. "If he mentions me as 'worthy,' let me know in private, that I may think of a revenge. Curiously enough, he considers it a complimentary adjective!" Soon after Alice's death in 1892, Venice beckoned. Perhaps Woolson had the notion that now that Henry could leave England more readily she might see him as much in Italy (and under better circumstances) as in England. He expected, he told her and others, to spend much of every spring there. Her health preoccupied her, her winter depressions, her isolating deafness. Yearning for home, she gradually gave up her initial thought that before going to Italy she would visit America to enjoy the warmth of Florida and the nostalgia of her family home in Cooperstown, New York. She went instead directly to Venice from London, where she and James saw one another for the last time in January 1893. In February, she became badly, painfully ill. "The English doctor here . . . thought the whole affair was neuralgia. 'Neurotic' was his word; that is, a malady of the nerves of the head. I did not, in my heart, agree with him. And I think it is *now* pretty well decided that it has been a slow gathering in the inner ear, first on the right side; & now on the left." The pain was intense. Behind schedule with a serial she had contracted for with *Harper's,* she felt too painfully imbalanced to write. "The loss of time preys upon me most of all. I try not to think of it. I read & read. And when I no longer do that, I even play solitaire! If you . . . could have peeped in half an hour ago, and seen me seated on the rug . . . while I, with tear-stained face, was drearily playing solitaire on an atlas propped on my knees, you would have laughed, I am sure. I never play games, you know; so when I play solitaire, it is desperation indeed."[60] After a month, she was mostly better.

Relieved, Henry, in London, was delighted when, in May 1893, she wrote to him that she had an attractive apartment possibility that would enable her to be more comfortable than at her present rooms in Casa Biondetti. He urged Ariana Curtis not to let her lose the chance, and by September had high hopes himself for spending part of the winter and spring in Italy. "I shall do my best to prove to Miss Woolson that Venice is better than Cooperstown." By early November, she had settled in Casa Semitecolo, but not as comfortably as they had both hoped. She worried about money. Since furnishing the apartment had been expensive, she would have to economize narrowly. She felt ill and old. "For a long time," she wrote to her nephew near the end of the year, "my daily prayer has been that I may not live to be old; I mean really old." The casa was not warm enough. Christmas was cold and lonely. For companionship, she bought a small dog, which she named Tita. In London, dreaming of a Venetian spring, which he had promised her he would have, Henry worried about her. "If she only didn't think it her bounden duty to 'make plans' she might be happy yet. Speriamo that she will be—& at last will find the right house." She worked hard at her novel, finishing and sending it to New York, probably in early January 1894. Such an effort usually "takes such entire possession of me that when, at last, a book is done, I am pretty nearly done myself." At the beginning of the New Year, she apparently felt depressed again. "This deadly enemy of mine creeps in, and once in, he is master. I think it is constitutional, and I know it is inherited. . . . My grandfather gave up to it, and was a dreary useless man; my father battled against it all his life, and again and again worried me about it; but I was young then, and only half believed in it. Now, he is gone, and it has come to me. I try to conquer it and sometimes I succeed, sometimes I don't."[61]

James had no doubt now that this time she had not succeeded. Despite family efforts to explain it as an accident, he believed that she had killed herself. Whether she might have had an inner-ear infection that affected her balance may have occurred to him. If it did, he dismissed it. Perhaps Grace Carter had made it clear that a jump rather than a fall would have been necessary for her to clear the opening of the window from which she had plunged. "Unquestionably," he thought, "she had become actively insane under the influence of her illness and her fever." But the pressure of her death focused his mind. The influenza had only "aggravated a state of melancholy already existing—and then in a moment *determined* the delirious, irresponsible act. . . . I seem to see, now, in the light of the event, how far that depression of spirits to which she was at all times so tragically liable had progressed in her mind, and what a morbid obsession it had become. Other signs and symptoms came to me which I didn't fully read at the time. She was intensely unhappy, by her natural disposition (her deafness greatly increased it,) and unhappy in a way that no one, I think, however much fighting, as it were, on her side—I mean even in the closest sympathy with her—could effectually or permanently combat. But she had got much worse this winter—I now feel sure— and quite in spite of any external cause."[62]

He could not keep completely at a distance the possibility that he might have been a contributor to her problems. Could he have done something more? If her depression had external coordinates, might he have been one of them? He touched the edges of these questions, and searched immediately for a description of Fenimore and her life that would relieve him of such fearful possibilities. What pained him most was his awareness that she had suffered and died alone. "It is too horrible for thought!" He needed to exorcise himself of his imaginative recreation of that vivid moment of horror. "The haunting obsession of the fact, the act, is a thing to try with all one's might to get rid of."[63] The preoccupation with her having died alone implied an awareness that the one presence that she might have most desired was his own.

Beyond that, he needed a larger rationalization both for the fact and for his not having contributed to preventing it. Her suicide itself, he reasoned, could not have been a calculated act. It was the sudden dominance of a depression that had "always haunted her." He had "two or three years ago . . . made up his mind that she was not positively and wholly *sane*." In fact, he had, he now argued, been one of the two or three people whose friendship and whose conscious considerations had helped her live for as long as she had. "Half of my friendship for her was a deep solicitude, a deep compassion, a vigilant precaution, so far as it was possible, about all this." He did not comment on what the other half had been. As with Minny Temple, he needed to think of Fenimore as someone who was so unfit for the rigors of the world that her survival for so long had been surprising, and whose death provided the only happy ending to a long-doomed drama. "So joyously, almost, does one assent to the liberation from life of a person for whom life primarily meant almost unqualified suffering." The problem was endemic, deeply a part of her unchangeable personality. "Save her deafness, she had no definite or unusual thing . . . to minister to her usual depression; she was free, independent, successful—very successful indeed as a writer—and *liked*. . . . But it was all reduced to ashes by the fact that a beneficent providence had elaborately constructed her to suffer."[64]

With the first touch of spring, he went to Italy. Worn out with the London winter, with his painful playwriting fiascos, with the shock of so many deaths, he dreamed about Italian warmth and softness "for at least so long as the London season rages. If, as you pass along Victoria Road, you ever look up at my match factory, don't give my love to it." He was more tired of London than he had ever been. Certainly Fenimore's ghost did not keep him away; perhaps it beckoned him, promising harmlessness, indicating resolutions. As with all such pain, he contained it. The horror of other people's deaths he quickly absorbed into the advantage of his own continued life and work. Having agreed to meet Fenimore's sister Clara Benedict and her daughter, who were coming on the "flourishing new steamer-line from New York & Boston," he left for Genoa in the middle of March 1894. He had not thought they would actually come. "Too dismal an errand, it seems to me. . . . I mean their going to Venice too painful."[65] To his surprise, they had decided to face the ordeal of disposing of Fenimore's sequestered possessions. The apartment was legally locked until the arrival of the next of kin. Reluctantly, he agreed to help. Among other reasons, he wanted to retrieve his many letters to her. Perhaps an engagement with the remnants of Fenimore's life would provide further cathartic distancing and calm, though he carried with him from London to Venice an awareness of some degree of responsibility, of some element of guilt.

After a week in Genoa, he went, with the Benedicts, first to Florence, where he had a ghostly moment seeing for the first time Lizzie

Boott replicated "in majestic and perennial bronze," Duveneck's fune-real memorial to his wife. He climbed sadly up to Bellosguardo. "The whole place is now such a perfect cemetery of ghosts that there is little joy left in it for me." Not even the most beautiful view in the world lightened his spirits. "Villa Brichieri seemed to stare down" at him "with unspeakably mournful eyes of windows." Though he did not want the four months he hoped to spend in Italy to be devoted to acts of mourning, the losses had their inescapable presence. In Florence, Baldwin provided hospitality and companionship. In Venice, Katherine Bronson and the Curtises embraced him. After an absence of so many years, he returned to Rome, where one of his perennial sites of pilgrim-age was to be Woolson's grave. But his immediate, pressing destination as he descended from Genoa—where he had spent part of the week enjoying the hospitality of a London acquaintance, Margaret Brooke, the Ranee of Sarawak—was Venice. "The poor clinging helpless Bene-dicts" needed his assistance. Comparatively inefficient, they exhausted themselves with looking into every aspect of Fenimore's death. He shared the information, and some of the pain. From Genoa he had arranged to stay at Casa Biondetti, in the same rooms that had been Fenimore's until she had moved to Casa Semitecolo. He detested Vene-tian hotels, he explained, "even for a day," though this arrangement had the peculiar feature, on which he made no comment, of his sleeping in the same bed in which Fenimore had slept. With a more intense version of the same intimacy, the Benedicts, to James's surprise, stayed at Fenimore's "sad death-house" in the Casa Semitecolo. The discom-forts of the place helped support his argument, half accepted by the Benedicts, that she had had "some cerebral accident" the previous sum-mer. "The sight of the *scene* of her horrible act is . . . sufficient to establish her utter madness at the time. A place more mad for *her* couldn't be imagined."[66]

For the next "dreary, dreary month," in a Venice heavy with rain, with a roaring fireplace their only bulwark against the dampness, he spent a part of each day with the Benedicts in Fenimore's apartment. The locks had been opened; the rightful heirs and executors had gone through the door to immerse themselves in the accumulations of her wandering life. Some of it needed to be discarded, some the Benedicts wanted to ship to New York. He was startled at how much there was: crowded boxes, trunks, and shelves; letters, books, clothes, an apartment filled with the furnishings of a life he had known so well yet which he had never been quite so close to before. Retrieving his letters, he probably burned them immediately. He marveled that the Benedicts did not collapse with nervous exhaustion. "They took . . . the whole

situation in their own way & not as many people would have done—
I mean those whose foremost wish would have been [never] more to
behold again any of the mere *things* that surrounded Miss Woolson in
her last unhappy days. . . . They did it, moreover, with remarkable
courage and perfection—and it proved a terribly big task." His excellent
Italian helped expedite formal requirements, the bureaucratic details.
One of the most painful tasks fell to him, perhaps because it was beyond
the Benedicts emotionally. He took piles of her dresses—she seemed to
have an almost limitless number of them, all funereal black—onto a
gondola and had them and himself rowed out into the middle of the
lagoon. For some bizarre reason, he thought that he could best get rid
of them by drowning them. "He threw them in the water and they
came up like balloons all around him, and the more he tried to throw
them down, they got all this air, the more they came up and he was
surrounded by these horrible black balloons." Again and again, "he
tried to beat these horrible black things down and up they came again
and he was surrounded by them."[67] He seemed engulfed by these dark
simulacra, by the nightmarish representations of Fenimore that rose one
after another, irrepressibly, making their claim of attachment, as if they
belonged to him forever.

Twelve

PASSIONATE FRIENDSHIPS

1894–1900

(1)

Lingering in Italy for the sake of the sunshine and because there was little in London to which he wished to return, James tried to work on a story, "The Coxon Fund," the central character inspired by a recent biography of Coleridge. "Ah, how the gods are on one's side the moment one enters the enchanted realm! Ah, consoling, clarifying air of *work*—inestimable sacred hours!"[1] But exhortations and affirmations came more readily than the work itself. Writing, in April 1894, in his notebook at Casa Biondetti, he dated an entry 1869, as if he hoped that by an unconscious act of the pen he could turn the clock back twenty-five years.

An infestation of American tourists he greeted with irritable impatience, aghast at what seemed the permanent transformation of the Italy he had known into an "intolerably, almost inconceivably" crowded polyglot world with its own international season. "America in general & Boston in particular have been poured forth upon it." Even in June, when the weather became warm, he met almost as many Americans in Florence and Rome as he had in Venice. Startled to find the rooms below his at Casa Biondetti rented by two women he knew from Boston and five of his Walsh relatives staying at the hotel across the street, it seemed as if "all Boston has been in Venice." The Curtises also "resented the rising, the submerging human tide," from which "the accent of Massachusetts rings up & down the Grand Canal & the bark of Chicago disturbs the siesta." If the Curtises, who lived with the privileges "of the big marble Barbaro all to [them]selves, with space & drafts & gondoliers & gardeners & cooks," resented the crowds, then how could *he* not, since he had so much less protection from them? Except for their companionable son Ralph, whose personal charm and sweetness did not outweigh the moral vacuity of his making "a profession of merely knowing everybody & doing nothing," the hospitable Curtises seemed stale and irritable. Rome and Florence seemed "social traps," the human entanglements compounded by rapid expansion, vulgar reconstruction, and new architectural hideousness. In Rome, though, the unusually cool weather in early June 1894 stimulated warm memories. "Delightfully empty & delightfully cool," the city "breathed almost all its old enchantment on me—& I can scarcely tear myself away. I almost don't mind the 'alterations' & am conscious of nothing but the sweetness." He dined with the Storys "& found poor old W. W. greatly simplified & silent . . . cheerfully childlike & bland." In Florence, he came down with influenza "which Baldwin broke . . . up with a magic hand." Back in Venice, he delighted at least in the refreshment of "the liquid sea—so sweet is it to come back here to its purifying plash, after the dust of the Caesars & the Medicis."[2]

But Italy rapidly was becoming less Italian. "One asks one's self what is at last left of its sweet essence to come to, or for?" As he prepared to depart, he did not think he would come again, or at least for quite some time. "I shall . . . say farewell to Venice, alas, forever. That's the sad part of it," he told William, "that all this closes the gates of Italy for the future; for every year it grows worse. . . . I too must have my Chocorua—must discover some twopenny cottage in some intensely out-of-the-way part of England, & rush down there when I want to get away from London—for these 3 months have been simple hell!" Depressed at how little he had written, he concluded that it had been the "most disastrous three months' attempt" he had "ever made to come 'abroad' for privacy & quiet." Both in London and in Italy, the curse of life, he felt, was "knowing so many *unoccupied* people—people who have nothing to do but conspire with a hideous amiability & an infamous good conscience against one's own concentration." He was, though, to come to Italy again a number of times. The tug of memory and nostalgia remained strong. In early July 1894, anticipating the loss he would feel when he had left, he finally went north to the cities and the breezes of the Como area, through what seemed to him an inordinate amount of dust, heat, rain, and dirt. From Lecco, he came across the lake "by boat & a really very pretty little narrow-gauge railway" to Lugano, "which is lovely, empty & very hot. The heat however isn't intolerable, the hotel is excellent & has 2 big gardens, with *real* shade, & . . . nightingales . . . & my window looks out on all kinds of sublimities & bluenesses." He missed Venice and Italy enough to prophesy, despite his earlier expressions of finality, that he would have to return every year. From Lugano, he went for a week to Stresa, on Lake Maggiore, and then over the Simplon Pass, "amid plashing waters & forests of the pink alpine rose." In late July, at De Vere Gardens, amid dry hot weather, with London smoke and cinders in his nostrils, he wrote to his friends at the Barbaro: "How I shall dream of you all winter—till I see you again."[3]

He took brief respite from the London August at St. Ives in Cornwall, near the Leslie Stephens. On the way, he stayed for three days at Torquay, with which he "fell quite in love." He was the guest of an urbane, ex-lawyer turned novelist, William Edward Norris, with whom he began a friendship. At St. Ives, the gray Cornish seascapes put him longingly in mind of Adriatic azure. Walking on the rocks with the Stephen children, he saw the lighthouse that young Virginia Stephen years later recorded as the symbol of the transience of her childhood and her childhood family in *To the Lighthouse*. He took long walks on the purple and orange moors with the taciturn Stephen, "the silent Stephen, the almost speechless Leslie," one of his oldest English friends whose silences seemed an English virtue that put Italian cacophony to shame. Over the years, his affection for the Stephen family had grown, for the beautiful Stella Duckworth, for the handsome son and the interesting daughters, for Stephen's stoical forbearance under the burden of family tragedy and his decline into deafness and infirmity. The family seemed to "struggle with every human ailment, accident & embarrassment. Leslie is nominally 'better,' but practically, I fear, it doesn't put money in his purse. Their children fail of examinations & get stabbed half to death at school—but Mrs. Leslie smiles & soars courageously triumphant over all."[4]

If he had dreams of Fenimore, he soon transformed them into fiction, both his refuge from life and itself his life. During a September 1894 visit to Oxford to see "the irrepressible Bourgets," where he stayed at the same address, perhaps in the same rooms, in which Fenimore had stayed in 1892, he conceived the idea for a story, "The Altar of the Dead," that indirectly dramatized her death and his own silences. He wanted to "cuddle closer" to his own "little vulgar, personal, special empirical industry," to find solace and pleasure in the transformation of experience into the experience of art. "*Only* live," he had urged the mournful Clara Benedict in March 1894, "and think of living, from hour to hour and day to day: it is perfect wisdom and takes us through troubles that no other way can take us through." Since he now more intensely than ever felt that some part of him had died, the way he could best and most fully live was to write about that loss of self. "Art

. . . makes life, makes interest," he was later to write.[5] When he was at work, he felt most fully alive.

George Stransom, the main character of "The Altar of the Dead," creates an altar in a church to memorialize his dead friends, particularly Mary Antrim, who had died while they were engaged and before they could marry. He has had one love, Mary, and one intimate friend, Acton Hague, who had betrayed him. Gradually becoming aware that an attractive woman of indeterminate age uses his altar for her own remembrances, he learns that she has only one person whose death has been important to her, Acton Hague, and that she was his badly treated, discarded lover. He will not add to the altar, as she desires him to, an additional candle in memory of Hague. Since he will not forgive Hague having betrayed him, the relationship and her worship at the altar cease. Soon seriously ill, he becomes obsessed with "just one more" candle, though it is unclear for whom it would be. When, partly recovered, he visits his altar, he realizes, when the lights flare and he sees her in the church, that he is willing, for her sake, to place there a candle for Hague, though he barely manages to tell her this. At the same time, she tells him that she no longer needs him to do that, that she can return to the altar without it. It is a moment of forgiveness, self-sacrifice, and love. With his head on her shoulder, he dies. The "one more" candle now will be for him, and she will have a second person memorialized at the altar.

Though he feared that its central metaphor was too slight to sustain the story, "The Altar of the Dead" brought to consciousness his long-sustained preoccupation with loss and survival, particularly with the ironies of lives unfulfilled. Minny Temple and Mary James are ghostly presences in the story's background. Minny Temple was in the foreground the next month when he jotted into his notebook an idea about a young woman who has everything but is dying of a fatal illness, the germ of *The Wings of the Dove*. The connecting preoccupation was his sense of the diminishment of his own life. His consciousness of his latest loss filled the foreground of "Altar of the Dead." A story about a neglected woman betrayed by the man she loves, it suggests James's feelings of guilt about Woolson. He had preferred to evade full awareness of the intensity of her love for him. His friendship had fallen far short of empathetic compassion. If the altar of the dead is the altar of art, the worship of those bright candles is a worship that can only be made at great sacrifice of life, of aspects of the self and of experience. At moments, as an artist, even when writing about loss, he felt vividly alive. At other times, he worried that he had not grasped experience fully enough.

(2)

He also felt lonely. It was a condition to which he had long ago partly reconciled himself. But the reconciliation was of the head rather than the heart. In leaving America permanently, he had consciously left behind the family and friends of his childhood and youth. He had needed, he felt, to go to Europe to live in order to function effectively as an artist. Having done that, he could not avoid as a central subject of his art the condition of the American in Europe, which meant that the authorial consciousness permeating whatever he wrote would resonate with an awareness of loss, deracination, and separation. No matter how much social life he might have, that was not the same as having intimate friends, let alone the intimacy of the family into which he had been born or the family he might have created had he married. The more socially rich the web of his fictions, the more dramatically central the absence of emotional intimacy.

But he now felt more than ever his internal alienation, his inner distancing. From early youth, when he had dedicated himself to being an observer, he had accepted that much of his work and life would be lonely. "The port from which I set out was, I think, that of the *essential loneliness of my life*—and it seems also . . . to which my course again finally directs itself! That loneliness . . . what is it still but the deepest thing about one? Deeper about *me,* at any rate, than anything else: deeper than my 'genius,' deeper than my 'discipline,' deeper than my pride, deeper, above all, than the deep countermining of art."[6] Even if he had remained at home, he would undoubtedly have had to some degree the sense of alienation that he felt in England. But he also would have had the opportunity for continuous relationships that might have made his loneliness less burdensome. He had chosen to restrict much of his *doing* to *writing,* the work of the imagination essentially a solitary occupation for which he found relief in social activities, in a multitude of teas, dinners, country visits, theatre excursions, companionable walks, and innumerable letters. By early 1895, these diversions had failed him other than as semimechanical devices of amusement, though some of his social friendships were warmly affectionate; they were his poor but only way of loving. He felt the poverty. He also was in the process of deciding that not only had London social life become a drain but that London had become counterproductive. It seemed to him more and more difficult to work there.

The intimate relationship that he would have had most available to

him if he had stayed in America was with William. In separating himself
from his family, he had purposely separated himself from his older
brother. Henry responded to William's aggressive energy with retreat,
a strategy of accommodation which was only rarely interrupted by
episodes of defiance. One of his lines of retreat was Europe. The living
connection was maintained by a massive transatlantic correspondence;
it was the one connection left to him in which intimacy still had force.
In 1895, William sent via Sally Norton, Grace's sister, bundles of photographs, including "distant Chocorua & the Irving St. house in the
snow," and precious family letters that called up the pleasures and pains
of the distant past. "I love them—such old faint memories—faint, yet
intense. . . . They are full of memories—of a whole extinct yet still
ghostly experience—& the pleasure of handling them is all neuralgic,
as it were, with a kind of anguish. Father's & Mother's lives seem in
them so sweetly & sacredly submissive to the burden of *us*."[7] With
Alice's death, William and William's family were the only family he
had, or at least the only family that meant much to him. Bob hardly
counted: His alcoholism, his separation from his wife, his alienation
from his children, his Swedenborgianism and socialism, his manic dis-
equilibrium, made him impossible. Mostly alone in Concord, Massachusetts, Bob lived a version of Henry senior's religious obsessiveness
without his father's discipline and strength of character. In contrast,
William, like Henry, had transformed his religious heritage into a brilliant secular career. By 1890, it had reached its first climactic point with
the publication of his textbook on the underlying principles of the new
science of psychology.

As William's career soared, Henry's stalled. When William's health
became a worry, and then, in 1898, a threat not only to his work but
to his life, Henry was anxious, supportive, and deeply frightened that
his brother might die; he transformed his feelings into optimistic exhortations. In the back of both their minds hovered the specter of what
seemed the James family nemesis of shortened lives, of emotional and
physical breakdowns. Immediately after his visit to see Alice in September 1891, William had returned to Cambridge and his heavy teaching
duties. Henry went to Italy in spring 1892, first to Siena for a month,
where he had the Bourgets as companions, then to Venice, where
Isabella Gardner, renting the Palazzo Barbaro, thrilled him with the
attraction of having his bed set up in the immense, colorfully decorated
library, where he felt comfortable despite the scorching heat. He then
went to Switzerland to stay ten days with the William Jameses, who
had come to Europe for a sabbatical year.

The brothers saw very little of one another that year. William remained mostly on the Continent. Henry was preoccupied with London obligations, particularly his "dreary theatricalities," including "the composition of unacted, 'unproduced' plays," which continued "to be a most impoverishing pastime." Henry intended to visit William in Florence in the late winter or early spring 1893. His brother and his wife made themselves comfortable with the English and American Florentine communities, especially the Baldwins and another American winter resident, Mark Twain, "a fine, soft-fibred little fellow with the perversest twang and drawl, but very human and good." William amused himself with Violet Paget, who had recently caricatured Henry in a short story. Henry affected not to have read the story. "If I should know I should have to take upon myself the burden of 'caring' . . . and oh, I don't *care* to care." But he did care enough to disguise his distaste and his sense of having been betrayed in the form of advice to William about a woman who "is as dangerous and uncanny as she is intelligent. . . . There is a great second-rate element in her first-rateness." Friendship with Violet Paget was dangerous. "She's a tiger-cat!"[8]

William mischievously made Henry's pain somewhat worse. He not only read the story and told his brother that he found it clever rather than malicious but told Paget that, since he found the story boorish, he would have nothing more to do with her. When she tearfully apologized, William forgave her. "Your note wipes away the affront as far as I am concerned, only you must never," he lectured her, "*never, NEVER do such a thing again in any future book! It is too serious a matter.*" He reported fully to Henry the details of their exchanges. To Henry, Paget's tearful apologies were facile, and William's aggressive enlargement of something that Henry preferred to take no notice of was painfully, boorishly inconsiderate. William probably found Paget's caricature of Henry's style more clever than malicious. He also shared its underlying premise. Henry's anger at William surfaced early in the spring in his criticism of William's decision to leave Florence before the arrival of the warm weather, when he himself had hoped to visit him there. In mid-February 1893, he had expected to "go to Italy, for all the blessed spring, next week." When William went north, Henry, baffled, rejected, angry, stayed in London, and then went, instead, to Paris, which was "wonderfully mild and bright—blond and fair . . . the spectacle beguiling."[9]

In Paris, where he had spent most of spring 1893, he saw, for the first time since he had last been in America, Wilky's widow and children and Bob's wife and children. He felt dutifully loyal, even affectionate. From Paris, he went to Lausanne for a month. "[William's] limited time in Europe has fast ebbed without my seeing him," he wrote to Sarah

Wister, "& seeing his wife & children to speak of—I have joined them for the 3 or 4 weeks of this splendour of early summer that they have just come up from their Florentine winter to meet. . . . His wife is all you remember her—fine and sweet & serene. . . ." They stayed at separate hotels on the lake, five miles apart, "but constant boats, & the loveliest of roads, communicate. . . . I spent yesterday afternoon with them walking home in the declining day all along the charming lakeside." When together, the brothers were lovingly effusive and proud of one another. William was the more impulsive, the more unpredictable of the two, and always tempted by the advantages of disengagement. The previous summer, when they had been together in Switzerland for ten days, he had suddenly gone off on a walking tour, without Henry. The next spring, in Venice, when Henry received one of four copies of Alice's "magnificent diary" that Katherine Loring had had privately printed, differences of temperament became dramatically clear. Since he "used to say everything to Alice," he felt "terribly scared and disconcerted" that, if published, the diary would embarrass him and other people. He urged that William cooperate in keeping the diary private until he could "*edit* the volume with a few eliminations of text and dissimulations of names." After editing, the family would "give it to the world" and "carefully burn with fire our own four copies." As a testament to Alice's life and personality, he found it deeply moving, brilliantly written. She was, he exclaimed, "really an Irishwoman!" which, in this case, he meant as a compliment to her political passion, her imaginative empathy, and her literary skill.[10] William shared Henry's admiration without, apparently, his fear of disclosure.

When William returned home in September 1894, he left behind a brother whom, since Henry now had "real practical relations and a place in the old world," he did not believe would ever return to America again. At the same time, William confided to a European friend that "one should not be a cosmopolitan, one's soul becomes 'disintegrated.' . . . Parts of it remain in different places, and the whole of it is nowhere. One's native land seems foreign. It is not wholly a good thing." Though he was writing about his own difficulty in readjusting to America after having been away for a year, the subtext was about Henry, who commiserated with William's sense of alienation. It reminded Henry of his own experience, more than twenty years before, when he had "returned from Europe . . . in May 1870—& determined . . . on my future life. I felt then, as I felt after subsequent returns, that the only way to live in America was to turn one's back on Europe; that the attempt to *mix* them is a terribly comfortless business. . . . I have been supremely fortunate in being able to do what I wanted—i.e. make my election for the old world; & the only way to make use of my fortune is to accept it frankly & consistently."[11]

Though he did, indeed, have "a place in the old world," he also had a heightened sense of the price that he had to pay. During the late 1890s, he increasingly felt the emotional inadequacy of his situation. The sexual puzzle remained, held in check by his consciousness that sexuality had forms of expression other than explicit sexual relationships. He had access to that sexuality only in the imaginative application of it toward a variety of situations, in the mysterious erotic intersection in literature between feelings and language, in the absolute fact of his body and his own awareness of it. To the extent that he was fastidious, he was equally realistic and sensual, responsive to the tactile world. Still, whatever the private nature of his physical self-awareness, he had denied himself what would have been at best the mixed advantages of marriage. If he had done this for his art, he also had done it because he could not strongly enough imagine himself in a sexual relationship with a woman. His real objects of desire were ones that he had strong reasons to deeroticize as much as possible. He had had considerable success in doing so. The success contributed to his loneliness.

(3)

To his surprise, he found himself one morning in mid-January 1892 at a church in a London suburb performing the "queer office" of giving away at the altar Wolcott Balestier's sister to twenty-seven-year-old Rudyard Kipling. With only four people present, it seemed "a dreary little wedding." For James, his presence betokened his loyalty to his dead friend. He admired Kipling, whom he had met in 1890, one year after the promising Indian-born writer had come to England. Kipling was welcomed and embraced by Gosse, James, and others after his years as a journalist in India, a year of travel in America and the Pacific, and the success of his early short stories. Why Kipling was marrying Caroline Balestier, whom James thought "a hard, devoted, capable, charmless little person," he could not fathom. He had difficulty imagining why Kipling would want to marry at all, let alone Caroline, an odd choice "for the most complete man of genius (as distinguished from 'fine' intelligence,) that I have ever known." He had immediately found Kipling engaging, even prodigious, an "infant monster" of great but narrow talent whose immense success he hardly envied and for whom he had generously written an introduction to a volume of stories published in 1891. The tales seemed to him to have a welcome freshness and boldness, particularly of subject matter, though he liked the man more than the work.[12]

Within three weeks of their marriage, the Kiplings left for New York, with California, the South Seas, even Japan as possibilities. James went to Liverpool to see them off on the *Teutonic*. The good-bye seemed as gray as the dreary wedding, as bleak as any happiness or stability he could forecast for the couple. By the end of the year, the Kiplings had settled in Brattleboro, Vermont, the Balestiers' hometown. The buoyant Rudyard wished "to goodness" that James "could come over and be driven over stone walls in an ox cart. That is life." To James, it was like an invitation to the frigid moon. Kipling's attachment to rural, wintry New England seemed a perversity of temperament that could best be understood as "the strangest of all wife-beatings—I mean beatings *by* the wife." To James, Kipling seemed to have exhausted the India he had absorbed when he was "very young" and to have little possibility of making literary use of London or civilized social life at all. When the Kiplings returned for a visit in spring 1894, James, from Venice, urged Gosse to send him his impressions of their "psychology & sociology." That summer, in London, he enjoyed Kipling's company regularly. In 1896, the Kiplings returned to England permanently, soon to reside in Sussex. "He has come back from America to abide; & laden, as I surmise, with lucre. . . . He is the most curious—to me—of all literary phenomena; so exclusively a genius, as essentially one as a typewriter is a typewriter. I mean as inapt for anything out of his particular line as this machine to boil a potato. Fortunately his particular line is immense. He is very simple, very married, very babyfied, & very happy. Also one irresistibly likes him." Unlike Gosse, who was, Kipling remarked to James, "born a 'laidy' but it slipped in the mould," Kipling had neither the manners nor the temperament of the civilized aesthete, of the married or unmarried English bachelor attracted to the special pleasures of the company of men.[13] Strikingly different from James in temperament and interests, he offered the opportunity for affectionate friendliness but not for intimate friendship.

In contrast, a young English friend, Arthur Benson, was a literary bachelor who shared James's homoerotic temperament. The son of the archbishop of Canterbury, Benson was almost twenty years younger than James. He had met James in the mid-1880s, at about the time he became a master at Eton College. An avid writer and editor of literary history, with impeccable academic and social connections, and soon with sufficient wealth to become an independent man of letters, Benson had a sensitive, depressive personality and an introspective fascination with his own moods and observations. A lifelong bachelor, Benson hovered in the shadowland between homoerotic desires and celibacy. He had become a good friend of James's and of Gosse's by the early 1890s. Another new friend, Edward Warren, was a successful architect from a distinguished upper-class Oxford family, whom James met in the early 1890s. James took delight in having a friend who fulfilled his idealization of the manly Englishman. When James stayed at Whitby in summer 1893, Warren was his guest. He afterward joined James frequently for many "good days and wanderings together" on London streets. When, to James's pleasure, Warren became engaged in spring 1894 to Margaret Cecil Morrell, James was delighted "to strew flowers" in their path at their wedding. It seemed a perfect social and matrimonial union of the best values of the English upper class. Though he did not mind losing Warren to marriage, writing to him on his honeymoon he coyly imagined himself into the bridal bed. "I wish someone would marry *me* & take me [to Spain]! I shall never go otherwise." When the Warrens asked him to be godfather to their first child, he happily consented "to hold at the baptismal font your tiny compendium of all promises and perfections. It is a terrific responsibility—but it's inspiring; & with all else that I shall promise for her, I promise not to drop her in. The splash she will doubtless make in life shall not at any rate begin so early. . . . It is charming of you to show this generous confidence in a lean—that is a fat—bachelor." After a bad night of heat and headache, he asked that someone else hold the baby, but he still cherished his responsibility and kept a lifelong attachment to the Warrens and their children.[14]

Among his English contemporaries, he had many acquaintances but few close friends. Some of the latter were women with whom he had a special compatibility of temperament and social chattiness, particularly Lucy Clifford, or a shared loyalty, as with Ariana Curtis. Many of these relationships were sustained mostly by letters, reinforced by occasional days or weeks of proximity in London or in Italy. Easy with his affections, his often courtly, effusive letters provided an intimacy of sorts from a distance. He now hardly saw his old friends the Clarks. Increasingly burdened by their advanced years, they lived mostly in Scotland, which James had not visited for a long time. He still visited country houses, but infrequently, having decided that even the "gilded halls" of the fabulously wealthy Roseberys were not for him, though "Rosebery . . . is almost the cleverest being I have ever known." Few of his English friends were people with whom he could discuss his writing. Even the much-loved Du Maurier always seemed to him a literary primitive, his "artistic side his least interesting—he, in fact, *hadn't* any such side!" In the mid-1890s, Du Maurier rapidly went "to pieces in health & spirits. Not even the success of *Trilby* in 1894 had the "power to cheer or please him." At Du Maurier's graveside in Hampstead in October 1896, James sadly contemplated "the end of a long relation—in which all sorts of pleasant hours & contacts & walks & talks, a series of delightful & intimate years, are buried." By 1895, Gosse had become his closest friend. "Not the least of [his] merits," James told Stevenson's widow, "is his being the person with whom I can most freely & thoroughly communicate. . . . I am not sure that life is all balm & butter for him; but he has great courage, great spirits—as well as bad ones—& remains, more than many, in the dim & darkening social sense, that rare & precious resource, an intelligence."[15]

Having come to London, among other reasons, for a community of writers, he found that he did not have one there. To some extent, he had envied the community of Parisian writers he had met in 1875. With the death of Flaubert they had lost their center, and with the passage of time they had resumed separately pursuing their lives and their crafts. The two writers of the old group with whom he still had contact were Zola and Daudet. For Zola, he felt admiration and "tenderness," a writer with "not a pennyworth of distinction; but a shopfull of *stuff.*" When he lunched with him in London in October 1893, he found him "very sane and common and inexperienced. Nothing, literally nothing has ever happened to him but to write the Rougon-Macquart." Soon Zola was to do public things that raised James's admiration for him, beginning with a political speech in 1896, preceding the Dreyfus affair by two years, which prompted James to remark that "Zola seems to be more & more becoming." But they had never been and were never to be more than acquaintances. He wished that that were the case with Daudet, to whom he felt an obligation, mostly because of Daudet's serious illness, which produced incontinence and partial paralysis. He felt exploited when the "whole Alphonse Daudet family" came to London in May 1895. They depended heavily on him for arrangements and for social life. He did his best, "with a great hatred of the responsibility," which included hosting a dinner at the Reform Club for which he scraped together as many of his French-speaking friends as he could."[16] When in Paris, he made his literary visits, but they were increasingly few. The Bourgets were often away, traveling in the Orient and in America. Jusserand, leaving the London embassy in 1890, had been assigned to other posts, eventually to become, in 1902, French ambassador in Washington. His warmest, most intimate friend in Paris was an American, Henrietta Reubell, who was as frequently in London as he was in Paris. They provided for each other an affectionate continuity of familiar companionship: they were two aging, elegant gossips who had years and friends to review together, her long-handled eyeglass raised and their wreaths of cigarette smoke circling in her high-roofed salon, dominated by the comfortable, red plush sofa.

Every now and then, the thought of visiting America came to mind. But he had good practical reasons to suppress it, among them that his American friends seemed to come regularly to visit him. Some of them came with letters of introduction and adulatory gazes. The clever "Mrs. Jack" came regularly, emblematic of "the insane movement for movement, the ruin of thought, of life, the negation of work, of literature, the swelling, roaring crowds, the 'where are you going?,' the age of Mrs. Jack, the figure of Mrs. Jack, the American, the nightmare—the individual consciousness—the mad, ghastly climax or denouement. . . . The Americans looming up—dim, vast, portentous—in their millions—like gathering waves—the barbarians of the Roman Empire." That was the dark side—the imaginative extension of the reality into materials for fiction. The daylight experience had its satisfactions. "The mere distant dim image of Mrs. Jack 'going it' on the graves of the Caesars & the lifts of the Grand Hotel makes me huddle closer to my fireside & groan over what *might* have been. She may capture the Pope, but I think she is too amiable to become *really* fashionable. I see her succeeding better at Grand Hotels than at grand manners. She tries too hard & listens too sympathetically—bless her innocent (after all) heart."[17] On the whole, he was pleased at the convenience of Americans coming to him and thought them, particularly the younger ones, smarter, more imaginative, and more energetic than the English.

The most demanding American friends tended to be wealthy, well-connected women traveling without husbands, like Mrs. Jack, who seemed not a woman but "a locomotive—with a Pullman car attached. I travelled . . . my little hour in the Pullman car—that is I took her to a couple of exhibitions &c." When Mary Cadwalader Jones, the sister-in-law of a young American writer from a wealthy, socially elevated New York family, "descended upon" him in 1895, he "collapsed . . . to the extent of accompanying her . . . with her unimaginable accent & her landscape-gardening daughter" to the theatre "to see the infernal Sarah [Bernhardt]. . . . I thought the whole thing unspeakably idiotic & Sarah, for a long time, has bored me to death. On the other hand we take the Duse, here, very seriously. She is very interesting & touching, but I'm sick to death of the theatre." Mary Cadwalader and then her sister-in-law were to become his good friends, their Americanness part of the attraction. John Hay, like Henry Adams, appeared regularly in London between 1890 and 1895, a sad figure to James, hypochondriacal, unsettled, his visit in 1891 "blighted, on his arrival, by the influenza

fiend!" He "brought a lady to call on me, in my own rather stay-at-
home situation, the loveliest of Washingtonians, Mrs. Don. Cameron,"
the woman with whom Adams was in love, "the sweetest apparition
that ever illumined the lowly den of a seedy bachelor." Hay seemed
"swallowed up," to James's vision, "by the muchness of his wife &
progeny."

The two other members of James's Washington triumvirate were
more of a mystery, Adams a visible one, Clarence King increasingly
out of sight. News of the adventuresome King's nervous breakdown
came exclusively through Hay, who knew even less than he thought
about the secretive King's double life in New York, which included a
black mistress and family in Brooklyn. "How strange and sad an end
to all those miscellaneous activities & abilities," he wrote to John Hay.
"In truth I never thought there was no madness at all in his society—
and feel indeed as if there may be some sanity in his madness. But it's
miserable to think one may never again see him as he delightfully was.
He was, in his way, a fascination." When, in 1891, Hay sent James
copies of Adams' letters from the South Seas, James had a glimpse into
the seemingly cool patrician's inner life. "What a power of baring one's
self—hitherto unsuspected in H.A." Astounded that Adams and La
Farge were traveling together, he marveled how either of them could
"have failed to murder the other in Polynesia. Fortunately each lives to
prove the other's self-control." When the restless Adams invited James
to go to Japan with him, James declined. He had work to do, a living
to earn. India, Japan, the South Pacific, seemed to him superfluous,
experiences without a moral core, useless to him as a writer of fiction.
Still traveling in 1895, Adams went to the Caribbean. "Perhaps when
Jamaica fails," James told a mutual friend, "he will come back to old
England."[18] In the next years, Adams spent more and more time abroad.

Three American friends, whose interest for him lay in their connection with his childhood and youth, he hardly saw at all. But when he
did, the occasions had emotional power. Theodora Sedgwick came to
London in the summer of 1894. "I like Theodora very much—find her
very pleasant," he told William. She evoked strong memories of his
Cambridge days. When he was staying at Torquay the next summer,
John La Farge came, visiting with him for two days on his return from
Paris to New York. He had also visited James in late 1891—"one of
the most extraordinary and agreeable of men, a remarkable combination
of France and America." Now he seemed as he had always seemed,
thin, eccentric, distinguished-looking, an artist in every feature, just as
he had been in Newport all those years ago "but much more human &
considerate . . . though with my sense of his gifts & glories much

obscured by his extraordinary confused vagueness. . . . I gather that his big exhibition of South Sea water colours at the Champ de Mars had been a perfect failure. . . . But he was strikingly unexasperated about this." For James, La Farge remained a puzzle, but a welcome one. Grace Norton came to England for a long visit in the spring of 1891, the only time they were to see one another during a period of more than twenty years. He visited her regularly at her London suburban cottage near Hampton Court and put himself at her disposal in London as much as he could. To Alice James, Grace had seemed a prudish New England spinster. To Henry, she was the beloved friend of his youth. She was inseparable from his own sense of himself and what he had become, particularly those days when the Nortons had been his sustaining friends in Cambridge, in Italy, and in England. When Francis Child, whom he and William had known at Harvard and who had been a friend of Henry senior's, died in 1896, he shared with Grace, as he could share with almost no one else, a series of emotional associations. "I enter particularly into your sense of losing in him the last living evidence, as it were, of your youth. But you exaggerate—you still have *me*. And *I* remember it, my dear Grace, with delightful intensity. . . . I pass & repass Queen's Gate Terrace on purpose to be reminded of the spring of 1869; & of a most inspiring & exciting letter about it . . . that I got from you just before I came out to Europe in the Feb'y. of that winter. . . . The great loss I find in growing older is that people—persons—are no longer such mysteries, such impressions & such events."[19] With Grace Norton he achieved a continuity of limited confidences and shared memories that brought him as close as he was capable of coming to intimacy with a woman. Unlike Fenimore, she seems not to have felt or, if she did, to have deeply repressed any more demanding desires. They found a comfortable way to be spinsters together.

(4)

Something extraordinary began happening to James in the mid-1890s, and more frequently in the next decade. He fell in love a number of times. He established intimate relationships, beyond his usual friendships, that for the first time provided him with the feeling of being in love. If it was a feeling more than an articulated awareness, it was a powerful feeling. He had a need for intimacy. He wanted to be flexible, to be open to emotional interaction, to "only live" in the sense of being true to his own desires and needs, difficult as they were to identify. In each case, he fell in love with a younger man. In each case, the expression of love took somewhat different form, related to the special qualities and situation of the object of desire. Each time he fell in love, he placed the emphasis on friendship, not on physical consummation, which remained as dangerous, as threatening, as morally and culturally difficult for him as it had always been. He and his brothers, he told his sister-in-law, advising her about his niece's education, had been brought up with a heavy prescription "of the moral and spiritual. . . . *We* (father's children,) were sacrificed to that too exclusive preoccupation: & you see in Wm & me, & above all in Bob, the *purest* consequence! Take heed in time. With her so definite Puritan heritage Peggy can afford to be raised on almost solely *cultivated* 'social' & aesthetic lines. The Devil (of the moral & spiritual) can . . . be trusted to look out for himself."[20]

The devil of conventional inhibitions showed its presence in his effort, during the 1880s, to keep under restraint his interest in John Addington Symonds, which had expressed itself in "The Author of Beltraffio" and in his encouraging Gosse to fill him in on what he had missed in regard to Symonds. Gosse may never have shared with James the confession that he had made to Symonds of his lifelong struggle with his own desire for young men. "I know of all you speak of," he had written to Symonds in 1890, "the solitude, the rebellion, the despair. . . . I entirely & deeply sympathize with you. Years ago I wanted to write to you about all this, and withdrew through cowardice. I have had a very fortunate life, but there has been this obstinate twist in it! I have reached a quieter time—some beginnings of that Sophoclean period, when the wild beast dies. He is not dead, but tamer; I understand him & the tricks of his claws." James knew many of the details of Symonds' life through Gosse. The Curtises were often Symonds' host at the Palazzo Barbaro. Woolson, in 1883, had lived in the apartment above Symonds. Horatio Brown, an English writer whom James knew, was Symonds' closest friend in Venice. In late 1892, James had the ironic experience of having dinner in London at the Stephens' with "the morally-alienated wife of the erratic John Addington." At the beginning of 1893, Gosse passed along to James one of the fifty privately printed and circulated copies of Symonds' essay "A Problem in Modern Ethics," which, like "A Problem in Greek Ethics" of almost ten years earlier, argued for the moral acceptability and aesthetic attractiveness of homosexuality. "J.A.S. is truly . . . a candid and consistent creature, & the exhibition is infinitely remarkable. It's, on the whole, I think, a queer place to plant the standard of duty, but he does it with extraordinary gallantry. . . . I think we ought to wish him more *humour*—it is really *the* saving salt. But the great reformers never have it—& he is the Gladstone of the affair."[21]

Wilde's situation in 1895 and 1896 illustrated the dangers of homosexual desires. James's distaste for what he believed to be the Irishman's vulgarity gave way to horror at what seemed Wilde's unwarrantedly severe punishment for the wrong weaknesses. "His fall is hideously tragic," he wrote to William, "& the squalid violence of it gives him an interest (of misery) that he never had for me—in any degree—before. Strange to say I think he may have a 'future'—of a sort—by reaction—when he comes out of prison—if he survives the horrible sentence of hard labour that he will probably get. His trial begins today—however—& it is too soon to say. But there are depths in London, & a certain general shudder as to what, with regard to some other people, may possibly come to light." Symonds had removed himself from possible prosecution by living in Venice. When his anxious friends implored him to withdraw his pamphlets even from private circulation, he consented. James admired him in a way that he could never admire Wilde, who was both a competitor and a dangerous exhibitionist. When Symonds died in April 1893 of his tuberculosis, James genuinely grieved at "the so brutal & tragic extinction . . . of poor forevermore silent J.A.S. . . . I too can't help feeling the news as a pang," he told Gosse, "& with a personal emotion. It always seemed as if I *might* know him—& of few men whom I didn't know has the image so much come home to me." Symonds seemed to him almost an alter ego, an education in degrees of self-exploration and self-revelation. "Poor much-living, much-doing, passionately outgiving man. . . . Do let me know of any *circumstance* about Symonds—or about his death. . . . He must have been very interesting—& you must read me some of his letters."[22]

Symonds indirectly helped James focus on his own feelings, which contributed to his increased openness in the late 1890s. But it was not a public openness, and it had its private ambivalences and disguises. He would find it impossible to write of these things, he told Ariana Curtis, who urged him in 1895 to do a review-essay of Brown's two-volume biography of Symonds. He had already eagerly read both volumes "with singular interest. . . . There ought to be a 1st rate article—a really vivid one—about him—he is a subject that wd. so lend itself. But who's to write it? *I* can't; though I shld. like to." Though Brown's volumes were discreet, the obstacle for James was Symonds' homosexuality, expressed in the two *Problem* essays. "The difficulty indeed would be (to my sense) insurmountable. . . . There *were* in him—things I utterly don't understand; and a need of taking the public into his *intimis-*

sima confidence which seems to me to have been almost insane."[23] James was certainly being sincere about both his objections.

Two young Americans whom he embraced as private intimates were Jonathan Sturges and Morton Fullerton. He had probably met Sturges, a twenty-five-year-old journalist and short story writer severely crippled with polio since childhood, in 1889 when he agreed to write a brief prefatory essay for a volume of Maupassant's short stories that Sturges had translated. With a handsome face providing the precarious balance to a short, crippled body, Sturges had graduated from Princeton, briefly studied law at Columbia, spent a short time in Germany as a student, and, in 1889, permanently expatriated himself to London where his social and intellectual energy made him acquainted with circles that James knew well. "Brother Jonathan has his share of the national genius," he told Gosse. In late 1890, he invited Gosse to dinner expressly to introduce him to Sturges, about whom he had already begun to feel avuncular and whom he soon had a desire to look after—as if he could be both nurse and older brother, like Whitman looking after wounded young men. By 1893, the relationship had become a warmly loving one. Perhaps James saw in Sturges something of the crippled young man he had thought himself to be. Sturges moved with and beyond James into the world of Wilde, with whom he soon became friendly, and Wilde's London homosexual circle. Not even James's love for Sturges permitted him to accede to Sturges' request that he sign a petition in late 1896 urging a pardon for Wilde. "James says that the petition would not have the slightest effect on the *authorities* here," Sturges reported to Wilde's supporters, "in whose nostrils the very name of Zola and even of Bourget is a stench, and that the document would only exist as a manifesto of personal loyalty to Oscar by his friends, of whom he was never one."[24]

Sturges visited Henrietta Reubell in Paris in October 1893, preceded by a tender but frank letter from James who told his old Parisian friend that Sturges is "a very nice little chap—ingenious, straightforward—a gentleman; and his poor little blighted physique . . . has (to me at least,) much less painfulness than such blightednesses usually have." He urged her to welcome Sturges in her "saloon for gifted infants." In Paris, the young man visited Whistler, in whose garden he met Howells, briefly in Europe on one of the few visits he had made in the last twenty years, this time primarily to visit his son, a student at the Académie des beaux-arts. To Sturges, Howells looked sad. Two years later, when James asked what had given him that impression, "Sturges remarked, 'Oh—somewhere—I forget, when I was with him—he laid his hand on my shoulder and said *à propos* of some remark of mine: 'Oh, you are young,

you are young—be glad of it: be glad of it and *live*. Live all you can;
it's a mistake not to. . . . This place makes it all come over me. . . . I
haven't done so—and now I'm old. It's too late. It has gone past me—
I've lost it. You have time. You are young. Live!' "[25] James responded
strongly to Sturges' anecdote about Howells, from whom he felt "*remote*," his sense of connection attenuated by the distance between them,
by their infrequent opportunities to meet, and by the difficulty of two
busy writers maintaining the intensity of their earlier relationship. Even
when Howells was in Europe they seemed to have trouble aligning
their schedules so that they could meet. Howells' loyalty and affection,
though, had not flagged, even during the period of James's theatrical
humiliations. James's affection for Howells remained strong. Pained at
what Howells had missed, he had a strong sense that he himself had
not had some important human experiences implied, if not inherent, in
Howells' exhortation. Sturges fulfilled one of his dormant needs, and
in the next half dozen years he warmly enfolded him as a companion
and a charge, someone to whom he could give loving attention.

When they were separated, James missed him greatly. In winter
1895, after "some grave crisis of the heart" in Paris, Sturges had a
breakdown while staying with James in Torquay. "So I brought him
back to town. . . . His doctor clapped him, on his arrival, straight into
a private hospital where he is (very successfully & comfortably) having
his illness now—some form of gastritis, aggravated . . . by nervous
prostration. . . . He is a very attaching & touching little mortal, & I am
kind to him." A year later, Sturges was ill again, "flat on his back in
his private hospital. He is, however, I think, pulling round," he wrote
to Henrietta, "but has been gravely & miserably ill." The attachment
for James became a welcomed dependency. When Sturges stayed with
him, which he soon began to do for long periods, James found him not
only charming but also almost necessary company. His "very interesting young friend" fascinated him. Even when he had too many visitors,
Sturges was welcome. Among other long visits, he stayed with James
for three months in 1899 and six weeks the next year. "He is only a
little body-blighted brilliant intelligence," James told Grace Norton, "a
little frustrated universal curiosity—& a little pathetic Jack-the-giant-
killer soul." When Sturges had a severe breakdown in 1898, James was
deeply pained to see the aspiring but increasingly invalided younger
writer caught between America and Europe, spoiled for America, unlikely ever to achieve anything significant in Europe. Sturges's crippled
form was a mirror of the strange twists of his life and mind, including
the impossibility for him of a marriage, perhaps even of heterosexual
experience at all. After his thwarted affair in Paris, "the poor youth

woke up—with violent suddenness—from the fond dream of believing he could be, for a woman—& for 'love'—as other men are. He *had*, strangely believed it . . . a rude & cruel shock to him—& at the basis of his illness. So at least I fancy the matter."[26]

In early 1890, James met another attractive young man, Morton Fullerton, perhaps through a letter of introduction from Charles Eliot Norton. A child of American puritan idealism and a Congregational minister, Fullerton grew up in Waltham, Massachusetts, with an adoring mother who loved him intensely with a sensual effusiveness that provided him with his ideal of feminine attractiveness. His father's New England limitations provided the countermodel for the males he most admired. At Phillips Academy and then Harvard, where he graduated with highest honors, his interests were literary and sexual, including "two or three early love episodes." He briefly tried journalism in Boston. Then he managed to be appointed to the staff of the London *Times*. After two years in the London office, he was transferred to the powerful *Times* bureau in Paris. He would live much of the next fifteen years in France, a journalist with literary aspirations never fully realized, a young man with a keen eye for people and a reputation for amorous adventure and sexual flexibility. Well-dressed, charming, he cultivated a thick brown mustache that anchored his slim figure, his hair combed straight back, his medium height raised by his serious, eager, handsome face. When he met James in 1890, the attraction was immediate and mutual. James's response was quickly intimate. "Do come on *Thursday* at 2, as the nearer day. And don't, oh don't, my dear boy, insert the hard wedge of 'Mr'—as if for splitting friendship in twain."[27] The choice of metaphor was characteristic of the mystery of James's sexual self-consciousness; it seemed either impossibly innocent or embarrassingly explicit.

How fully aware James was of Fullerton's love affairs of the next half dozen years is unclear. Probably he introduced Fullerton to Mrs. Margaret Brooke, the forty-one-year-old wife of the dour, elderly James Brooke, the Rajah of Sarawak. She had left her husband, whom she respected but did not love, in India and settled in England, where she enjoyed her wealth, the fashionableness of her title, and the literary and social world that she cultivated. A square-faced, strikingly full-figured woman, the Ranee had had seven children with Brooke (three of whom had died of cholera), a number of nervous breakdowns, and a life in India to which she refused to return other than on visits. With a susceptibility to take pleasure where she could find it, she found Fullerton an attractive experiment in love. Fullerton, excited by the difference in age, apparently found her glamorous, well-connected, and physically attractive. While James carried on his frustrating affair with the theatre, Brooke and Fullerton carried on their intense relationship, sometimes with James setting the stage, as he did when he brought them together to applaud and celebrate what he hoped would be his successes. "The Ranee of Sarawak—most benignant of sovereigns—is to come (D. V.) & see me played next week," he wrote to Fullerton in 1891, "either at Stratford-on-Avon . . . or at Leamington. . . . I shall be present both times. . . . If she adopts that night, I shall timidly say to you: 'Is it humanly possible you shld. come too—be, at the Regent Hotel, Leamington, the guest of H. J?' "[28] With Fullerton, James showed some taste for playing the role of facilitator-voyeur as a way of further-ing his own intimacy with his young friend. Between 1890 and 1892, before Fullerton was transferred to Paris, they frequently took lunches and dinners together as well as day excursions in London.

If James knew of Fullerton's involvement in homosexual affairs with the Wilde circle, he mostly ignored them. However, it apparently did not come as a total shock to him to learn years later that Fullerton was having affairs with two men at the same time as his affair with Brooke, one of them a well-known homosexual, the talented sculptor Ronald Sutherland, who had the title of Lord Gower. Fullerton brought James and Gower together at least once at a small lunch that James hosted at a Parisian restaurant in April 1893. Though continuing an affair of several years with his Parisian neighbor, Henrietta Mirecourt, in 1903, apparently convinced of his invincibility, Fullerton married Victoria Camille Chabert, a marriage that lasted one year. Fullerton was able to obtain a divorce on the grounds that his wife's criticism of his sexual conduct in a letter to a third party had injured his reputation. He also directed his enormous sexual energy at James with half con-cealed overtures and hints of tantalizing secrets that he might share. "You write me," James complained, "in mysterious images of wit and grace which tell me nothing whatever about yourself, your life, your occupations or impressions, and you won't say those things are none of my business (even though they may not be,) simply because—you won't." James sensed that there was a great deal more to know. "Even in the face of your mysterious threat to tell me 'too much' about your current life, I persist in my invitation," he assured Fullerton. "I brace myself & await the startling disclosures."[29]

During the next years his young friend was one of the objects of his Paris visits. In Paris they saw one another almost every day. James did what he could to foster Fullerton's career, recommending him to Macmillan as a writer of great talent. Fullerton was now "my dear boy," "my dearest boy," "mon cher enfant." When they were apart,

Fullerton was much missed. "I am worse without you (than I was with you) . . . and only care . . . for sympathy and affection, and for . . . words of magnanimous gentleness." The next year, he remembered fondly their "Parisian café-haunting talks." When he saw "the fierce pathetic Ranee (at Wimbledon)," he did not forget to tell Fullerton that he had seen her. Probably he was aware that the affair had ended. During the painful moments of his theatrical failures, Fullerton held his hand both from a distance and in person. When Fullerton was criticized by his editor for "a flowery style," James explained and proclaimed that journalism would not permit any authentic expressiveness. "Take warning by *me*. I have tried—& I am, unmistakably, lost. Journalism will have absolutely none of me. The Harpers 10 months ago asked me . . . for some 'London letters' for their 'Weekly' & I accepted, for the money. . . . They have just written to me, dismissing me as you scarce would an incompetent housemaid. And yet I tried to be so Base!—Yes, yes . . . be of a platitude—*nothing* else will serve. Be as empty as a vacuum & as general as an omnibus." When Fullerton had further failures, James attempted to comfort him with litanies of his own and the advice of experience. "I'm a wretched man of business, a wretched moneymaker, a wretched adviser—I am in these relations simply grotesque. I have been all my life a silent, fatalistic, fantastic victim. Yet even with this discredited character . . . I venture to speak like a creature responsive & responsible. *Do nothing at all*—attempt nothing—& give no sign of any sort (save utter silence)."[30]

Except to him. He wanted more communication, greater intimacy of the only sort with which at the moment he felt comfortable. But, during the next decade, Fullerton often answered the intensity of James's feelings with long silences. James exaggerated, but only slightly, when at the beginning of the new century he told Fullerton that "my life is arranged—if arranged it can be called—on the lines of constantly missing you. Think thus what you *might* be (though so good is what you *are*) to [me]." When Fullerton was absorbed in the dramatic political events in France in 1898–1899, James cared immensely about both affairs, and responded to Fullerton's detailed account that "everything in it moves me and ploughs me up—& only one thing with a mere unprofitable pang: viz. your saying, inhuman youth, that you didn't know I could be following your affair or drinking in your accents, as if, insatiate archer, I wasn't living on you from day to day & making you my meat & my drink." He desperately wanted Fullerton to visit him. "Don't exaggerate or morbidise the *difficulty* of being with me for a few days. . . . I am intensely, absurdly convenient. . . . You shall be surrounded here with . . . rest & consideration. You talk of the *real thing.* But that is the real thing. *I* am the real thing. I send you a photograph. . . . What talk with you I want! I embrace you meanwhile with great tenderness." He did not hesitate to confess his loneliness. "Can't you now, oh *can't* you, make your presence here for a fortnight a solid, secure fact?"³¹

Fullerton remained elusive, distant, complicated, avidly sought after and occasionally grasped, though more in the imaginative wish than in the physical presence. Apparently, he never made the effort to translate James's homoerotic intensity into a homosexual affair of the sort that he had had with Gower, perhaps because he had refocused his own sexuality exclusively toward women, perhaps because he believed that James would not have responded favorably. From James's point of view, it was Fullerton who was not responding fully enough. "I want in fact more of you," James confessed and complained. "You are dazzling . . . you are beautiful; you are more than tactful, you are tenderly, magically *tactile*. But you're not kind. There it is. You *are* not kind." "I'm alone," he wrote to Fullerton at the beginning of the new century, "I'm alone & I think of you. I can't say fairer. . . . I'd meet you at Dover—I'd do anything for you."³²

(5)

Depressing as his theatre failures had been, James recovered quickly, at least to the extent of returning almost immediately to writing fiction. "I take up my own old pen again—the pen of all my old unforgettable efforts and sacred struggles," as if while writing for the theatre he had held a stranger's pen in his hand. He kept the deep wounds as concealed as possible. Visiting him soon after the *Guy Domville* disaster, Gosse was taken aback at how cheerful he seemed; it was simply the cultivated social side of the coin of misery. Astoundingly, he did not give up completely on the theatre. In April 1895 he spent an evening with Ellen Terry in her private box while *Richard III* was being performed on stage, discussing a scenario for a one-act play that, immediately after the *Domville* premiere, she had invited him to write. With *The Importance of Being Earnest* "a great success & with [Wilde's] two roaring successes running now at once," Henry wrote to William, Wilde "must be raking in the profits."

He needed profits of his own. His income from writing during the past four years had fallen considerably, averaging less than twenty-five hundred dollars a year, most of it from short stories and articles. Unfortunately, he could no longer feel as assured of an unqualified editorial welcome for his short pieces as he once had. He was shocked in 1891 when the editor of *The Century* turned down "The Pupil." Later, in 1896, he was forced to withdraw an article on Dumas when "the ignoble prudish *Century* . . . made a wry face over" it, implying that it was "indecent." But he still had outlets, and short fiction paid well. The talented editor of *Yellow Book,* Henry Harland, a young American novelist, cultivated James, "the supreme prince of short story writers." So too did others—among them Horace Scudder, the new editor of the *Atlantic*—who, even if they did not take Harland's high aesthetic line, had an almost insatiable need for short fiction by well-known writers. To James's annoyance, some of the American editors seemed to want him to write "another 'Daisy Miller.' "[33]

Fortunately, after Alice's death in 1892, he began to receive the income from his Syracuse property and also the money she had bequeathed him to supplement his earned income. He frequently queried William about his quarterly checks. Though London seemed expensive to him, by historical and comparative standards it was not. In fact, he had little difficulty keeping his income and his expenses in reasonable balance, despite making almost nothing from royalties on the novels and volumes of stories he had published over the last twenty years. "[I] have just received," he told Fullerton in October 1896, Macmillan's "annual account of what accrues to me, for 1895–96, from the sale of the *16* books of mine (some of them 3 vol. novels,) in their hands. . . . Payable 3 months hence, so that I have that luxurious interval to gloat over the prospect, are £.7.0.5. . . . The representation of my sales brings the blush to my cheek: the highest number of copies of any book *20*! They have—publishers *always* have—the last word. . . . A little asethetic book never does much. It does a little—that's all." Perhaps because of the theatrical failures, he was now better able to separate his fantasy of gold from his aspirations as an artist, though he always had residual hopes. But he learned the lesson fully enough after the failure of *Domville* to return to writing fiction with as much of a touch of bitterness as a touch of hope that he would ever earn much from writing. Still licking his wounds, he proposed to himself, in July 1895, an idea for a short story, later to be titled, ironically, "The Next Time." It was to be about "the poor man of letters who squanders his life in trying for a vulgar success which his talent is too fine to achieve." He did not hesitate to identify to himself the situation as his own. "It is the old story of my letters to the 'N.Y.T[ribune]' where I had to write to Whitelaw Reid that they 'were the worst I could do for the money.' "[34] He made the confession more indirectly for public observation, giving the title *Embarrassments* to the volume of stories in which "The Next

Time" appeared. As if the public were determined that James should keep his explanations mostly to himself, Heinemann printed and sold a modest number.

Unlike his alter ego in "The Next Time," he had determined that *his* next time, in this new, less monetary sense, was now. He felt young enough as an artist, strong enough, stubborn enough, to have a second chance, the fate of the main character of his story "The Middle Years" a countermodel for the opportunity he wanted to seize. Unlike Dencombe, he was not dying of illness, nor of the theatre, nor of absolute neglect. He could not only "plead the cause of a certain splendid 'last manner,' the very citadel, as it would prove, of his reputation, the stronghold into which his real treasure would be gathered"; he actually could now have, he felt, the opportunity to do better what he had not done well enough before. He felt an increase in energy and commitment. "I am happy to say I have got back to work & peace & quiet," he told William in February 1895. Rather than even think of going abroad, he would look for some country retreat for the spring and summer where he could write without the interruptions of travel and social demands. "I am full of engagements to produce (2 one-volume novels, this year for Heinemann,) & I feel as if my time had never, never been so precious, & am certain that my work will never have been so good." His head suddenly full of ideas for stories and novels, from November 1894 to October 1895 he sketched in his notebook the core of most of what he was to write during the next half dozen years. "I have my head, thank God, full of visions," he wrote in his notebook. "One has never too many—one has never enough. Ah, just to let one's self go—at last: to surrender one's self to what through all the long years one has . . . hoped for and waited for . . . to be able to work *more*. . . . That is all I ask. . . . I bow down to Fate, equally in submission and gratitude. . . . But the form of the gratitude, to be real and adequate, must be large and confident action—splendid and supreme creation."[35]

But, he realized, it would be creation for a smaller audience than he once had hoped for. The "surrender" that energized him was to a vision of the novel that permitted only a select readership. He had, of course, little to lose. Cultural changes in the reading public and changes in the economics of publishing had already made mass readership an impossibility for him. From James's viewpoint, he had been like the writer of "The Next Time," who "tries and tries and he does what he thinks his coarsest and crudest. It's all of no use—it's always 'too subtle,' always too fine—never, never, vulgar enough." But even from the viewpoint of some of the educated public, the fault lay in the writer, not in his audience. A friend of Perry's expressed a widely held view of his readers. "How long is it since you have read any of H.J.'s writings? He seems to me now almost as if he were an antediluvian. My interest in his work began to wane with his 'Portrait of a Lady,' which was, I thought, almost an *awkward* book. It seems to me that he touched his highest point . . . in 'The American.' " The downhill slope was to some extent the descent of generational change—the impression that he belonged to a different, more Victorian world. Ironically, this world was one in which he himself often felt he had been a stranger patiently waiting and preparing for his time. But it was also due to the difference between the young man who had sat during the latter part of the Civil War in his room in Cambridge writing stories in what seemed to his contemporaries a direct style and the older writer who was about to extend into greater complexities the subtleties of his style of the 1880s. For James, clarity now seemed defined only by the fullest expressiveness. He still needed to earn much of his living by his pen, but he had now been forced into, and could also better afford, a more unambivalent vision. "I am sitting close—for immortality," he confided to Fullerton. "One has to buy that with the blood of one's heart."[36]

Two stories and one sketch written during these years illustrate the complications and ironies of the blood of this writer's heart. Having conceived in October 1895 an idea for a story about the relationship between writers and their own works and between writers and their readers, in November 1895 he wrote "The Figure in the Carpet," for publication in a new magazine, *Cosmopolis*. A modernistic gloss on the question of obscurity and hermeneutics in literature, the story builds an open-ended series of ironies on the untrustworthy claim by a famous writer that no one has understood his works, that everyone has missed the key or clue, the special pattern in the literary carpet that he has woven. James mocks both readers who look for secret meanings and authors who pretend that there are secret meanings. The story is an ironic expression of some of the frustration he felt being viewed as a writer of "difficult" works when he himself believed his novels were absolutely lucid.

To demonstrate that lucidity, he was not above writing a potboiler, which would have for him the supreme clarity of providing, as did life, the possibility of multiple interpretations based partly on the degree to which the reader finds the teller of the story credible and reliable. In mid-January 1895, Arthur Benson's father, the ghost-story loving archbishop of Canterbury, provided him with a plot about "servants, wicked and depraved," who "corrupt and deprave" two children. "The servants *die*. . . . they invite and solicit . . . so that the children may destroy themselves, lose themselves by responding, by getting into their power. . . . The story to be told—tolerably obviously—by some outside spectator, observer." In late autumn 1896, he wrote "The Turn of the Screw," relieved to have it ready by December for January to April 1898 publication in *Collier's Weekly,* and to have his desk clear for other, more important work. "I had to correct the proofs of my ghost story last night," he told Gosse, "and when I had finished them I was so frightened that I was afraid to go upstairs to bed!" When he received letters of praise and inquiry from psychologists, including Frederic Myers, William's colleague in the Society for Psychical Research, he responded that he simply did not "*understand*" the requests for an explanation of the psychical elements in the story. It "is a very mechanical matter, I honestly think—an inferior, a merely *pictorial,* subject and rather a shameless potboiler." To an American doctor, he confessed that he feared "that my conscious intention strikes you as having been larger than I deserve it should be thought. It is the intention so primarily, with me, always, of the artist, the *painter,* that *that* is what I most, myself, feel in it—and the lesson, the idea—ever—conveyed is only the one that deeply lurks in any vision prompted by life."[37]

The dark vision of "The Turn of the Screw," a variation on his early story, "The Romance of Certain Old Clothes," is powerfully autobiographical, the indirection of James's artistry at its most effective. More so than ever before, during these years of depression and revival after his theatre failures, aspects of his own childhood came rushing out of his deepest memories and feelings. The brother and sister of "The Turn of the Screw" work variations on the three sibling combinations of his childhood, Alice and William, Alice and Henry, and Henry and William, the last the most telling for the underlying force of the story.

In a sketch for a tale that he never wrote, James made the sibling theme even more direct. On a cold night in February 1895, he went to a dinner at Ockham, the home of Lord and Lady Lovelace, "who, by agreement," wanting his opinion, showed him "some of their extremely interesting Byron papers; especially some of those bearing on the absolutely indubitable history of his relation to Mrs. Leigh . . . the sole *real* love, as he emphatically declares, of his life. . . . As I rolled along there came to me . . . the idea of the possible little drama residing in the existence of a peculiar intense and interesting affection between a brother and a sister. . . . Two lives, two beings, and *one* experience: that is, I think, what I mean. . . . A kind of resigned, inevitable, disenchanted, double suicide. . . . They may be twins, but I don't think it's necessary. They needn't *even* be brother and sister; they may be 2 brothers or even 2 sisters. . . . I remember now—it comes back to me—what little image led to the fancy: the idea of some unspeakable intensity of feeling, of tenderness, of sacred compunction, as it were, in relation to the *past,* the parents, the beloved mother, the beloved father." When, years later, he read, at Lady Lovelace's request, Byron's letters, to provide an opinion about whether or not the letters demonstrated that Byron had had an affair with his sister, he apparently concluded, to Lady Lovelace's great satisfaction, that they did not. Though their sexual content turned the stomach of the man who had also been asked to read them along with James, James "never turned a hair. His only word for some special vileness was 'singular'—'most curious'—'nauseating, perhaps, but how quite inexpressibly significant.' "38

In "The Turn of the Screw," Miles, the brother, embodies both William's predilection for boys that curse and swear and Henry's for boys that love one another, and, in the explicit gender division in the story, Henry is sister to William's Miles. Like *The Awkward Age* and *What Maisie Knew,* the plots for which were already in his mind and notebook, "The Turn of the Screw" dramatizes James's sense of the vulnerability of children to adult impressions, exposures, and manipulations, with, in the deep background, the powerful influence of the adults of James's own childhood exerting their pressure. Catalyzed by the dark framework and the pressures of the ghost story, "The Turn of the Screw" is a nightmare variation on James's own sense of his helplessness as a child; on the sibling drama in the James household; on the role of Aunt Kate, a kind of governess; and on the powerful effect of Mary and Henry senior on the sensibilities of their children. The insidious sexual element in the story—which combines Henry senior's fear of corruption and his role as a corrupting force, Miles's homoerotic sexual adventures, for which he has been expelled from school, and death by shock, like the death of Morgan Moreen in "The Pupil"—resonates as an artistic rendering of homosexual panic.

By the end of 1895, having filled his notebook with ideas for stories, he found three of them so rich with possibilities and necessities that he expanded them into novels, all with female central characters. "A social and psychological" tale, *The Spoils of Poynton* is his most sardonic comment on English culture. At Christmas, 1893, he had been told about a conflict between a mother, her son, and her daughter-in-law, in which the mother had been "*deposed,* by the ugly English custom [of the male heir having absolute rights to the family estate at the death of his father], turned out of the big house on the son's marriage and relegated." He thought it would make an effective short story. Having promised, in spring 1895, three stories to the *Atlantic,* he gave the subject further thought, including "the horrible, the atrocious conflagration—which . . . may serve as my working hypothesis for a denouement." Having in mind his years of profitless writing for the theatre, he felt, partly as rationalization, partly as the inevitable emphasis of his concentration on dialogue, that he now should apply the standard of dramatic structure to his fiction, that just as drama for the stage demanded tightly unified action and dialogue in a structure whose totality was directed at succinctness—the exact fashioning of the means to the ends—so too fiction would be at its best when it embodied such economy. "When I ask myself what there may have been to show for my long tribulation, my wasted years and patiences and pains, of theatrical experiment, the answer . . . comes up as just possibly *this:* what I have gathered from it will perhaps have been exactly some such mystery of fundamental statement—of the art and secret of it, of expression, of the sacred mystery or structure. Oh yes—the weary, woeful time has done something for me, has had in the depths of all its wasted piety and passion, an intense little lesson and direction."[39]

It was an emotionally helpful revisionist myth, a way of allowing himself to turn painful failure into useful exhortation. It was also an intensification of practices and guidelines that had expressed themselves in his fiction before he had begun his assault on the theatre. His articulation of the dramatic principle, of what he grandiloquently called the principle of "the divine scenario," was, in fact, the development and the intensification of practices that had been inherent in his fiction since the beginning. He did not, apparently, ask himself whether his fiction after 1895 would have been noticeably different if he had not made his effort to write for the commercial theatre. His need was to find some subjectively constructive way to deal with what had been a disaster. What better way than to convince himself that out of that disaster he had elicited a triumph, that the years had not been wasted, that they had not been years of stagnation or even retrogression but a necessary part of his development as a writer of fiction?

As his short novel grew, through the summer and fall of 1895, he exhorted himself to be economical. "I must cipher out here, to the last fraction, my last chapters and pages. As usual I am crowded. . . . I mustn't interrupt it too much with elucidations or it will be interminable. IT MUST BE AS STRAIGHT AS A PLAY—that is the only way to do. Ah, 'mon bon,' make *this, here,* justify, crown, in its little degree, the long years and pains, the acquired mastery of scenic presentation."[40] When it was at its most useful, he could, but only parenthetically, admit to himself that he had paid a high price for this added awareness, this "little degree," of the importance of "scenic presentation." In early

April 1896, somewhat ill but pleased with his application, he finished the first novel he had written since *The Tragic Muse,* to be published in the *Atlantic* from April to October 1896 under the awkward, short-lived title *The House Beautiful.*

Renamed *The Spoils of Poynton,* the novel offers no healing process other than the all-consuming fire. Mrs. Gereth, recently widowed, reluctantly accepts that she must leave Poynton and its treasures, by which she has defined her life and which are a surrogate for herself, her sensibility, and her aesthetic taste. Appalled that her amiable, handsome, philistine son has proposed marriage to an insensitively philistine daughter of the nouveau riche, she encourages a romance between her son and her aesthetically sensitive young friend, Fleda Vetch. Told mostly from Fleda's point of view, the novel dramatizes the conflict within Fleda when, almost immediately, she falls in love with Owen Gareth, who soon falls in love with her and out of love with Mona Brigstock, his fiancée. Loyal to both mother and son, Fleda disappoints them both, sending Owen back to Mona until he is really free, until Mona has set him loose. This is what Fleda's sense of honor, of propriety, demands. She cannot seize the moment. She cannot let "herself go," as Mrs. Gereth has urged. Her personality has been formed in a world of impoverished expressiveness, of cowardice about living intensely, of narrow principles about honor and propriety. Her self-regard demands a touch of puritan renunciation. Suddenly, the two women have lost. Fleda has lost Owen, Mrs. Gereth has lost Poynton *and* the treasures. When Poynton burns to the ground, there is speculation that Mrs. Gereth has set the fire herself. The novel centers on Fleda's limitations and strengths, and on Mrs. Gereth's high aesthetic values, which triumph against a world in which the cards of inheritance, culture, education, and law are stacked against them.

While working on *Spoils,* he also began work on *What Maisie Knew,* the story that he had described in his notebook in December 1895 as about "the child whose parents divorce and make such an extraordinary link between a succession of people." He intended it to be a concisely dramatic story of about ten thousand words—concerning a "little girl, whose parents are divorced, and then each marry again, then die, leaving her divided." It would be narrated through "the consciousness, the dim, sweet, sacred, wondering, clinging perception of the child." Like *Spoils,* it grew into a short novel, serialized from January to August 1897 and then published by Heinemann as one of the two novels promised to him. By late September 1896, the form of the story was clear in his mind. In October, he wrote a detailed scenario, emphasizing that he needed to keep in mind as his model the acts of a drama, though, when his pen slipped, he referred to "the scenic philosophy and method" as "vindictive" rather than "vindicating." As he always had done, he planned carefully the action and his characters' movements in relation to theme and dramatic effect. He called it, among other things, sticking to the "*march of an action.*" It was an expression of his determination not to lose his way, as he had in the bloated center of *The Bostonians,* and to guard against his tendency to expand beyond the length to which he had initially committed himself. With *Maisie,* as with *Spoils,* he simply recast his commitment from short story into short novel when the materials proved too rich, too exciting, too desirably expandable, to be contained. But he still needed to struggle to keep it within the bounds of a short novel, even with his heightened consciousness about dramatic form. "I must now," he reminded himself in December 1896, "have a splendid recourse to it to see me out of the wood, at all, of this interminable little *Maisie; 10,000 more words* of which I have still to do. They can be magnificent in movement if I resolutely and triumphantly take this course with them, and *only if I do so.*"[41]

Compared with what he had been paid during the 1880s for serial publication and advances against royalties, he received very little for these novels. The advances were for no more than £150, though he insisted, mostly successfully, on keeping his fees for serialization as high as his fees for short stories, for which he still could demand what he had always received. Despite his exaggerated, overly rhetorical claim to Fullerton that he was "a wretched man of business," he worked (without an agent since Balestier's death) his publishers effectively, pushing Heinemann and Macmillan with the same energy as he had always done. Since now the sums at issue were noticeably smaller, he needed to write as many short things as possible. Anything at greater length than short novels would not pay sufficiently to warrant the greater investment of time and energy. For the moment, the shorter length fitted both his economic and his aesthetic needs. His most profitable publications during these years were serializations of *Spoils* and "The Turn of the Screw," nine London letters he wrote for *Harper's Weekly,* and ten American letters, essentially reviews of American books, published in a new London magazine called *Literature.*

While he worked on *Spoils,* he also wrote another short novel, *The Other House.* It showed "symptoms of being the most successful thing I have put forth for a long time. If that's what the idiots want, I can give them their bellyfull."[42] But he could not. Instead, he created *What Maisie Knew,* a brilliant *tour de force,* one of his most lucid and at the same time aesthetically and morally complicated novels. A sexual maelstrom of coupling and competitiveness swirls around little Maisie. For

Mrs. Wix, her governess, the representative of middle-class conventionality, the crucial concern is does Maisie have, or will she develop, a moral sense? Throughout the novel, Maisie's consciousness is the center of experience and perception, aided by the Jamesian narrator's dexterity in using the indirect narrative to mediate between the young girl's mind and the external world. The central drama in the story is the gradual growth of Maisie's consciousness as she struggles against the rejections and the confusions of the adult world. In the end, like the serpent in the garden, Mrs. Wix becomes the instrument of Maisie's self-awareness. At last, poor Maisie develops a moral sense. Heretofore she had consulted only her needs, and created adaptive strategies to get people to love her. Her basic acts of self-preservation had been instinctive, amoral. What did Maisie know? She knew a great deal. Little by little she knew everything about the sexual relationships and activities swirling around her. But she did not know that they were immoral. She knew them and judged them only insofar as they affected her primary needs. Finally, she returns to England with Mrs. Wix, having done the best, and about to do the best, she can with her freedom, a freedom based on knowledge. She has grown up, into a world of moral complexity, self-consciousness, limitation, and restraint, but also a world of choice, and possibly of sufficient freedom from fear to act on impulses of love and on changing self-definitions. The novel is a telling fictional embodiment of James's sense of his own development. Like Maisie, he knew, gradually, everything. In his depiction, through Maisie, of the stages and the mysteries of growing up and of the pain of the final conflict between deep, intuitive needs and the challenge of socialization, James dramatized his own lifelong problems of growth, choice, and personal freedom.

(6)

He now needed to find an alternative to London. The thought that had been on his mind for at least half a dozen years had, by 1895, become almost an imperative, a desperate necessity. Venice was too far away, too impractical, though he had flirted a number of times with the notion of a small apartment with a view of the Grand Canal. But Italy "is more & more simply the vomitorium of America: so behold me practically & irredeemably British. . . . Some green corner of Britain—where I can ride a bicycle—will probably be my portion." But what corner? After a cold, depressing winter, with ugly politics dominating conversation, he looked for someplace that would free him from the "seething hell" of July in London. The Conservatives were suddenly out again, the Liberals in, the interminable Irish Question as bitterly corrosive of the quality of English life as the bleak economy and the miserable weather. He felt "simply beaten & broken by these horrid conditions." Going to the "fatally delusive 'abroad' " made no sense. He had too much work to do to risk the loss of time. "My work, for the last week, has gone to pieces," he complained to William, "& that simply kills me. But I shall revive—& live in the desert forevermore."[43] But it had to be a desert with water nearby. As always, the ocean appealed to him. In late July 1895, he went to Torquay, to the same hotel where he had been comfortable in September and October the previous year, hoping to get a great deal of work done.

He was not disappointed. "Peace wraps me round," he blissfully wrote to Henrietta Reubell. The "English Riviera" was perfect for the moment. With the small hotel absolutely to himself, he luxuriated in the quiet privacy of its secluded location, with a comfortable, large sitting room and a magnificent view from his "balcony overhanging a garden which overhangs the blue Torbay . . . with a sea of cobalt & milk . . . & lovely afternoon light." He almost immediately began to write, with a happy sense of "picking up the scattered fragments" of his mind and work. Each morning, he worked at *The Spoils of Poynton,* at a table set up in front of his balcony window. In the afternoons he bicycled for miles. Soon the resistance of the hilly landscape undercut his pleasure in the exercise: he wanted comfortable excursions, not hard physical activity. Despite the limitation, he found cycling a blessing, an activity that, at its best, gave him an enjoyable mobility, the pleasures of outdoor viewing, and much-needed exercise. But "the perpetual & precipitous hills" were a mark against Torquay. "I find the upgoing not very congenial to my weakish heart nor the downgoing to my weakish nerves. It is the only fault of the place—& is the fault of all Devonshire." In the evenings, he often saw Norris for small chats and long silences. He knew hardly anyone else in Torquay, though the Bourgets came for a month's stay. Both Minnie and Paul were more relaxed and companionable and Bourget as brilliant a conversationalist as ever. Soon Sturges visited, "gravely ill." When James went up to town briefly in August, he had already decided to spend September and October in Torquay, and to keep his eye open for a house for which he might take a long-term lease, with the notion of spending half the year on the coast, the other half in London. He could easily afford, he felt, fifty or sixty pounds a year for the right cottage. "My abroad has become my at home," he told William. "I am, thank God, losing every last ray of the disposition to travel. I am extremely & finally weary of over-much London—& absolutely determined, in order to save what remains to me of life," to stay away half of each year.[44] To do the immense amount of work he had it in mind to do, he needed to stay at home, if he could only make the right home arrangements.

Home, at De Vere Gardens, had the additional anxiety and occasional discomfort of his servants, the Smiths, becoming increasingly unreliable, mostly because of regular bouts of drunkenness. His liquor and their wages disappeared rapidly into the maw of alcoholism. He was both class-consciously snobbish and personally sympathetic. "It's the universal consequence here that they decay (the domestic in 'easy' places—& with bachelors,) & d—k." But they had been with him now for more than ten years. He felt some loyalty and a great deal of responsibility. Both by temperament and conviction, it seemed best to him to let events take their course, with the likely result that the collapse of their relationship would come later rather than sooner. During his months at Torquay in 1895, he had his De Vere Gardens apartment modernized. Just as he had no intention of firing the Smiths, he had no intention of giving up his Kensington flat. "I am just having the electric light & other dreadful rewirings perpetrated," he complained, "& I feel as if I should have to sit & scribble a long time—the rest of my days—to meet the bills." But when he returned to town on November 1 he loved the improvements, the new paint and wallpaper, and especially the instantaneous light. It was, he told William, as he sat writing in its midnight brightness, "one of the consolations & cleanlinesses of existence."[45]

Before he knew it, the annual question of where to spend the summer, so resonant of his childhood, was forced on him again. As much as he had enjoyed the previous two summers in Torquay, the difficult hills and the distance from London gave him pause. It seemed too far by half for the occasional brief visits he needed to make to town even during the summer months. Rome flickered in his fantasy for a short moment. He had received a query from Story's children about writing a biography of their father. But visiting Rome seemed as impossible as the proposal. In early 1896, during "a wild, moist, grey winter," Torquay still seemed begrudgingly probable. To his delight, the turbulent weather moderated into one of the mildest winters in many years. Also, something else came into view, much closer to London. The previous summer, in late August, the Warrens had urged him, before returning to Torquay, to visit them at Rye, in East Sussex, where they were vacationing. He had never been to that southeastern stretch of the Channel coast other than to the Kentish portion from Dover to Folkestone. Though it sounded attractive, the invitation came too late. He was already back at Torquay. "I hope," he wrote to them, that "this amiable October, after our adorable September, hangs over Rye with as pearly a light as over this warm little town, where the sea is still sweetly blue & the sound of its waves on the beach under my windows still deliciously drawling." In early 1876, at his London home, Warren, whose enthusiasm for Rye was infectious, showed James a small water-color drawing of the street-front portion of the garden house of one of Rye's picturesque old homes. He also recommended a small cottage called Point Hill, owned by his friend Reginald Blomfield, a distinguished architect. Despite never having been to Rye, James thought that he would "probably take for 6 months a tiny cottage that I wot of down in Sussex." At least he was inclined to make use of Warren's good offices and have a look at Point Hill, though, he explained to William in late February, his summer "place is still to find. . . . I am going down next month to look at something—which sounds very promising."[46]

When, in early March, he visited Rye for the first time, he was enchanted by the loveliness of Point Hill. It faced southeast, high above the town, with its magnificent view from its long terrace of the river and town below, of the Romney Marsh stretching away into distant greens and grays, and even of some glitters of the sea two miles away. A quiet medieval town, with scattered monuments of its early glory as a major port from which the sea had withdrawn, Rye rested securely on its own hill. From Point Hill it was a fifteen-minute walk into the valley, where the business streets of Rye ran westward from the main gate. From there, James could walk up to the higher streets. Rye offered views within views, pleasant walks, and the absolutely flat marsh, excellent for bicycling. Though the run-down cottage had little to distinguish it other than the terrace, he immediately felt that this was a place where he could work well, where he could happily spend half the year. He could have it from May 1, though he would have to vacate on July 30. Engaged in redesign of his property at Playden, Blomfield planned to be on-site for extensive renovations during the latter part of the summer. Still, James found Rye and Point Hill too attractive not to proceed. Perhaps he could find something else nearby to move to in August, though at worst he could return to Torquay. Point Hill "is a sweet little picturesque, inexpensive & salubrious bungalow . . . perched on a high little hill with the sleepy red roofed, mediaevally solid little old-world Rye (one of the 'cinque ports') just beneath it. . . . It is just what I want. . . . I count upon private & profitable work there. I take the Smiths of course & the dog & the canary bird; & I hope to be able to buy a bicycle before I go."[47] He could hardly wait to get out of London.

Point Hill turned out to be, for James, an absolute paradise. Setting himself up on the terrace, "steeped in work," he wrote a substantial part of *What Maisie Knew*, probably did revisions of *The Spoils of Poynton*, and wrote "In the Cage," perhaps to some extent a metaphor for what he had escaped. As he soon happily confessed, he practically lived his entire domestic life on the terrace, which he called his "opera box," except, he told Edward Warren, to whom he felt inexpressibly grateful, for walks into town and long bicycle rides "to Brede, to Northiam, Brookland, New Romney, Lydd etc. . . . I love [Point Hill] tenderly & enjoy it every hour. It turns its back too squarely on the sunset . . . but I don't think it has another fault. The little terrace is as amiable as a *person*—as *some* persons. In short I cherish the whole thing." If only he could lease it or buy it. Other cottages would not do. "It is—here, to my sense—Point Hill or nothing! In other words it is nothing—as *proprietorship*—for this little place is (I take it,) far too close in the actual proprietor's clutch. But if he will continue to *let* it—one can live." For the time being, he could not convince Blomfield to alter his plans. Oddly, when he went up to town briefly in late May, where he saw Wilky's widow and her children and Mary, Bob's wife, whom he liked, Blomfield stayed at Point Hill with the Smiths. Returning to Rye as quickly as he could, he had a few visitors of his own, particularly Oliver Wendell Holmes, now a judge on the Massachusetts Supreme Court, who spent the day with such pleasure to both of them that James reserved for him the Sunday of his brief London visit in July. "I only wish I could clutch [Point Hill] as a permanent resource," he wrote to William. "But it is unclutchable: though the price cld. be managed if the *owner* could. Meanwhile however it is delightfully quiet & quaint & simple & salubrious, & the bliss of the rural solitude & peace & beauty are a boon to my spirit."[48]

James's spirits declined when he faced the fact that he would not be able to stay beyond the end of July. Though he searched for a suitable alternative, "to look is not to find; especially as I have been spoiled by . . . a delicious high-uplifted terrace & garden . . . a terrace on which I eat & sleep & live—& a view of all the kingdoms of the earth." Since almost nothing was available, he settled for the Vicarage, a large, dull, house whose only attraction for him was a view directly eastward over the marsh, "a sad drop—though the best one that is feasible here. There is nothing else." At least, "on one side, away from the steep little street . . . one's window in the rear has a garden & a great country view." He moved into the "musty little bourgeois parsonage . . . with cursing & gnashing of teeth," but with the expectation that he might have Point Hill again in September. Within a week of the move a painful, "write"-

hand trauma, a "combination of rheumatism & fatigue, rendered [his right] hand & arm a torture." Through much of August, it rained heavily. From the Vicarage, in the "wet & windy weather . . . the marsh looks wild, & Rye feels small." Unfortunately, the extensive renovations at Point Hill extended themselves through September. Though the summer had become a bit dreary, Rye itself continued to please him. It seemed cozy, domestic. "A little red-roofed & clustered old-world town like this is in a manner a small & homely *family,*" he wrote to Grace Norton, with unintended resonances of his Cambridge family and his home of long ago.[49]

Though he had hoped to go back to Point Hill in October, not even that worked out. "I have found, down here, exactly the small country hole (humble house) I have been looking for—for odd crawls & quiet plunges: only, alas, I can't have it!" Though he complained that he had completed "but 2 shortish novels—of the pot-boiling order, essentially, alas—things done as they were asked for, & for which more serious work has had to be interrupted," he granted that it had been a very successful summer of "monotonous unity." He did not, he told the Curtises, even regret the loss of Italy. "If I had a *home* there—in the Terra d' Lavoro!" that might be a different matter. "But what should I do with my bicycle?" At the end of October 1896, he returned to London refreshed but aware that he would soon have to face the problem of where to go the next summer. For the moment, there seemed no prospect in Rye. At best, Point Hill might be available again for part of the season. He also had to deal with his "lame rheumatic wrist," which pained him sporadically when he wrote. "More than a year ago my [right] hand, for purposes not only of correspondence, but of everything, went utterly to smash, and in so doing, shut me up, practically, and apparently for ever, in a prison of silence and discourtesy." When William advised him to try a typewriter, he hesitated, hoping that he could solve the problem by writing fewer letters, reserving his wrist strength for his fiction. Finally employing a secretary, William MacAlpine, to take dictation, he practiced the new skill during the spring of 1897 with some delight. "Don't pity me for my lame wrist," he wrote to Ariana Curtis. It is "a blessing in disguise; inasmuch as it has made me renounce forever the manual act, which I hate with all the hatred of a natural ineptitude, and have renounced for ever, to devote myself in every particular to dictation. The latter does not hamper me at all: in letters quite the reverse, and in commerce with the Muse so little that I foresee the day when it will be a pure luxury." At first, he experimented with two procedures. Sometimes MacAlpine, an expert stenographer, made longhand copies of the dictation; other times Mac-

Alpine typed his words as he spoke them directly onto the new Reming-ton machine he had bought. He soon preferred the latter. "I have now definitely relegated [my lame right hand] to the shelf, or at least to the hospital—that is, to permanent, bandaged, baffled, rheumatic, incom-petent obscurity."[50] He was almost exhilarated by being able now to concentrate fully and entirely on his imaginative concepts and his articu-lated words.

He had Italy in mind for the spring and early summer of 1897. But he hesitated, as if the attractions of Venice darkened under the shadow of its association with Fenimore's death. His elaborate reservations gathered finally into his realization that he could not go, among other reasons because he had too much work to do. He now hoped to "take again . . . the country cottage" that he had "had last summer." When, to his disappointment, Point Hill was not available at all, he went for part of the summer to Bournemouth, where he secluded himself at a hotel to work on a new novel, *The Awkward Age*. Then he went to Suffolk, to the small seacoast village of Dunwich, near Saxmundham, to which he was enticed by his Emmet cousins, Minny Temple's sister Elly, a widow who had recently married an Englishman, and her three daughters. Except for a short visit to Norris at Torquay, he stayed until early September. His "prime motive" in going to Suffolk was, he told Edward Warren, "to be near some American cousins," though Warren could not have had any notion of what they meant to him in their connection to Minny Temple. He liked the young girls, despite their flat American accents, especially Bay Emmet, who seemed to him to be a talented painter. "I attack [their ugly speech], however, boldly, and as much as I can. It will be hopeless, I fear, ever—or at least for a long time—to interfuse Bay and Leslie with a few consonants. . . . However, they *want* to improve, and are full of life and humour and sentiment and intelligence." The heather and gorse bloomed colorfully, "a glory of purple & gold." Bicycling and walking, he commented on but hardly minded the bad roads or even what seemed to him his crude, primitive accommodations. London had become more unattractive, even more so that summer because of the anniversary celebration of Victoria's sixtieth year on the throne. "I hate more, each month, the stream of travel & the gregarious human hordes. London has been awful—a city of barricades." When Warren joined him for some un-comfortable cycling on the bad roads, one of their topics of conversation was their shared affection for Rye. He felt happy to be out of London, where the hugely overdone celebration of Victoria's jubilee, a "Victo-rian Saturnalia," seemed a noisy "bear-garden of Jubilee bedevilments. Nothing but scaffolds in every street & tickets darkening the air."[51]

He received an unexpected visit in August 1897 from Bob, whom he apparently had little wish to see. He limited their meeting to some hours in Liverpool, though he had not seen him for fourteen years and felt that he "should perhaps never see him again." They talked companionably, Henry purposely avoiding difficult subjects. "He, on his side, didn't let loose the dogs of war; and we parted after much pleasant, but studiously superficial talk." Again, completely unexpectedly, Bob showed up in late December 1897, this time for a visit of two weeks, melancholy but "very tranquil," offering, "mixed with other elements, elements of somewhat darksome entertainment." He "is a very unhappy, difficult, complicated & complicating person for whom all our sympathy & attention & almost all our time, are none too much." Fortunately, he "departed as capriciously as he arrived." Still, strong memories were touched. He had received in May a letter from William's wife, which contained an account of the great success of William's speech at the Boston Commons at the dedication of Augustus Saint-Gaudens' memorial sculpture to Robert Shaw and the 54th Massachusetts. The audience had listened to the words of one of the two James sons who had not fought in the war "with rapt attention from the first word to the last. The cheering was *tremendous* and long continued. Speaking of it to me afterwards William said 'Did you notice that applause, it looks as if I were popular.' He will never know how many people here care for him." When, in early June 1897, Henry received a copy of *Harper's Weekly,* with a reproduction of Saint-Gaudens' bas-relief, he felt deeply moved by its beauty and nobility. He suddenly felt, "for an hour," as if he were once again, "in the depths" of his own being, breathing the atmosphere of the days of the Civil War. "But the strange thing is that however much, in memory and imagination, it may live for one again, with all its dim figures and ghosts and reverberations, it appears to belong yet to some far away *other* world and state of being." The war had been transformed into art. "How I rejoice that something really fine is to stand there forever for [Shaw]—and for all the rest of them."[52] His "all the rest of them" seemed almost to exclude the unspecified Wilky and the unwanted Bob.

(7)

Suddenly an opportunity arose that sent him reeling with hopeful anticipation. He felt as if he had been hit a sharp, nerve-concentrating "blow in the stomach." At the middle of September 1897, he was sufficiently bored with the limited resources of Dunwich to be happy to have returned to London. He learned, on the day of his return, that the attractive house to which was attached the gazebo—the front of which he had seen in a watercolor painting even before ever having been in Rye—was being offered for long-term lease. On his many walks through the winding Rye streets in summer 1896, he had admired Lamb House, a three-story square redbrick building built in 1723 at the top of West Street, with the unusual garden house fixed into the right angle that the property made with the turn of the street. From the cobblestone pavement in this old, attractive residential area of Rye, the house had a quiet, prepossessing dignity. Its unpretentious Georgian stolidity was similar to some of the best houses of Boston and Cambridge. He and Warren had mentioned the attractiveness of Lamb House in their many conversations about Rye. It seemed to him as if "telepathy" had marked "the case for its own," a " 'psychical' wonder" in which the strength of his prescient desire seemed about to create a reality.[53]

Actually, he had done more than just fantasize about Lamb House. He had coveted it enough to leave his name and address with a local merchant in the event, by some extraordinary chance, the house, occupied by a retired banker—the elderly Francis Bellingham, who had served three times as mayor of Rye—should become available. Bellingham conveniently died in 1897. His adventuresome son and heir, preferring Klondike gold to Rye cobblestones, made it known in Rye that he wanted to dispose of the house on a long-term lease. With a letter in hand from his Rye contact containing this precious information, James immediately wrote asking Warren to accompany him the next week to Rye to examine the house. No sooner had he posted the letter than he received a telegram from Rye urging him to make haste if he wanted a chance at Lamb House. An exchange of telegrams on September 15 revealed that he needed to deal directly with "the late owner's son," Arthur Bellingham, to whom he wrote on the same day. As soon as he had put the letter in the post, he received another telegram, urging that he come down immediately.[54] The next morning, having brought his bicycle for a weekend stay at the George Inn on the High Street, he met the new owner. For the first time, he walked through the high paneled doorway, with its carved bracket and large brass knocker, into the house that he was eager to possess.

As soon as he walked in, he felt "*doomed*" to take the house, a fate that he felt had the inevitability, almost of an uncanny sort, that had brought him to precisely the right place at precisely the right time. "It is exactly what I want and secretly and hopelessly coveted (since knowing it) without dreaming it would ever fall."[55] Beyond the modest street front, the house opened to him with an unexpected spaciousness and comfort. To the left of a wide hallway there were two handsome rooms, an oak-paneled parlor and a dining room. Beyond these was an unexpectedly large, handsome, green-swarded garden facing the garden house. To the right of the hallway, there was a small room and then a sizable kitchen. Directly ahead, an elegant staircase with twisted white painted balusters rose to a landing that turned the staircase back toward the front of the house. Upstairs there were four spacious rooms on the first floor, the one immediately to the right known as the Green Room because of the color of its paneling, the one beyond, the King George Room. George I, when he had been caught in Rye by an unexpected snowstorm in winter 1726, had spent four nights at Lamb House as the guest of James Lamb, the mayor of Rye. The interior of the house seemed prettier, more elegant than he had anticipated, with Dutch-tiled corner fireplaces, handsome paneling, and bright light. From the windows of the Green Room, he could see above the red tiled roofs of Rye and across green fields, on which sheep grazed, the outline of the town of Winchelsea perched on its own high hill.

Bellingham agreed to give James right of first refusal until late in the day on Wednesday, the twenty-second. "All my good impression of it is confirmed," he immediately wrote to Warren, "& all my inclination is to take it up." The reliable Warren, whom he wanted to ask, "on the spot, & in its presence, two or three questions," met him at Charing Cross on the morning of the twenty-second for the eleven o'clock train to Rye. Warren's experienced professional eye and examination told James that the house seemed in excellent condition, with very little needed other than "to tidy it up and furnish it." Bellingham's asking price of seventy pounds a year in quarterly payments for a twenty-one-year lease seemed remarkably cheap. With Warren's approval, James, without hesitation, said yes to the house and the terms. The house came with a gardener, George Gammon, whom James met and liked. Bellingham offered him the resident dog, whom James quietly declined. He had a dog of his own. But he had never before had a house of his own. "The merit of it is that it's such a place as I may . . . retire to with a certain shrunken decency and wither away—in a fairly cleanly and pleasantly melancholy manner—toward the tomb. It is really good enough to be a kind of little becoming, high-doored, brass-knockered *facade* to one's life."[56]

With the lease signed, he contemplated his good fortune. With Warren's generous help and the assistance of Alfred Parsons, a landscape designer, he immediately set Gammon to work improving the garden. Small changes were made within the house, including a better waste-disposal system. "I never formally consented," he told Warren in late

November 1897, "to your conception of the higher ash-bin—meaning by 'higher,' nobler in every respect: which I do with all my heart and with all my nose. So, if you *could* go tomorrow—!" Warren went regularly, taking charge of all the work. James frequently joined him there. At Christmas, he wrote affectionately to Katherine Loring about her "old Kensington home. There it stands, where I from time to time go out of the way to take a look at it. . . . It is as if it were all yesterday— and yet, too, in a strange, far past." If only Alice were alive to share his excitement, including the prospect of rummaging through Kensington shops for old furniture. "The only fun, of course, is in getting things cheap; and occasionally one strikes the most thrilling veins on that side of the line. I am doing, at any rate, a room for you, and a room for Louisa, and I very much hope you will come and inhabit them." He particularly missed Alice. "I wish I could show it to you," he wrote to Henrietta Reubell, "the little old oak-panelled drawingroom & the charming old red-walled garden with all the pears & plums & figs I can desire growing on the pink South surfaces, & all the old (& new) flowers everywhere."[57] He felt he could live there, perhaps almost year-round, for the rest of his life.

Beginning in the summer of 1898, he spent much of the next two years at Lamb House, probably his happiest time there, in the first flush of possession. The economics of it became even more favorable when he found a sublease tenant for De Vere Gardens and, soon afterward, sold the remainder of his Kensington lease. Whatever else was wrong, Lamb House was right. He had two rooms for guests. Some guests, like Jonathan Sturges, he enticed for long periods. Some he had difficulty enticing at all, like Morton Fullerton, and another young man, with whom he soon fell deeply in love, Hendrik Andersen. His most deeply cherished friend beginning at the turn of the century, Howard Sturgis, the youngest son of his friend from the 1880s, the American banker Russell Sturgis, became an occasional visitor. So too did three other young men, all friends of the new century and his own flowering awareness of his capacity for love, two of them writers, Gaillard Lapsley and Hugh Walpole, the other a man with nothing to distinguish him but his handsome amiability, Jocelyn Persse. Indirectly, in his imagination, Constance Woolson came. "How *she* (in spite of Venetian lures & spells of illusions) would have liked *this* particular little corner of England," he wrote to Grace Carter, "& perhaps might have found peace in it."[58] William and his family were soon to visit, though William's professional triumphs and the pleasures of personal reunion were severely undercut by his becoming seriously ill. But Lamb House could be a convalescent home as well as a healthful paradise.

On many nights, as he wrote long letters in the lamplight, he watched the moon shining over his garden and happily sensed his little dog breathing softly at his side. As many mornings as possible, he wrote in the garden house, during the winters in the Green Room, with the view of Winchelsea in the distance. Afternoons, he often walked or cycled. He cherished his privacy and his work. He did not make enough money from writing. He worried about William's health and soon, his own. He found the world an increasingly brutal, violent place. He often felt lonely. For a time, Lamb House and his work sustained him. In the "divine" weather of the first September of the new century, he felt the hush of a moment of peace. "There are grapes on the branch, & celery in the beds, & tomatoes on the tree. . . . All the little land is lovely roundabout. It's really an attaching, really in its quiet way, a quite adorable corner of the wicked earth. And the earth is *so* wicked just now. Only Lamb House is mild; only Lamb House is sane; only Lamb House is true."[59]

Thirteen

THE NEW CENTURY

1900–1904

(1)

Staring into the mirror at Lamb House, he was impressed but startled by the newly clean-shaven face that stared back at him, a new face for a new century and for his fifty-eighth year. From one angle of vision he looked stolid, from another corpulent. He tried to adjust the mirror. "I should warn you," he wrote to a friend, "I have cut off every hair of my beard & am a sight to behold—most uncanny & questionable." If he looked, to himself, "uncanny," it was the shock of repressed self-recognition, as if the unshaven child and youth he had been was now reborn as a man of late middle age. He had had "the beard & moustache," he recalled, for "about 37 years," since his twenty-first birthday. By shaving, he had wiped out something of the intervening years. It was an effort to be young again and to be someone he had never been. If, to the rest of the world, the difference was startling, it was the difference of a birth into modernity, the visible expression of putting the Victorian world behind him. With the dark beard gone, his full lips emerged, his gray-blue eyes sharper against his pink cheeks, the upper angles of his large face and forehead sloping brightly into his baldness. He gave the appearance of a man happily poised between sensuality and celibacy. Someone of comparatively nondescript looks seemed to have transformed himself into a distinguished handsomeness, a distinctive combination of "unction . . . gravity . . . [and] vehemence," with "a theatrical look which struck the eye." His manner, reflected in the mobility of his features, was "now restrained with a deep reserve, now suddenly expanding, so as to leave the auditor breathless, into a flood of exuberance." His beard "had suddenly begun," he had told William,

"to come out quite white." "It made me *feel,* as well as look so old."
He did not like looking the way he sometimes felt. "Now, I feel *forty*
and clean and light."[1]

During the first summer of the new century, he sat for his portrait
to his young cousin, Bay Emmet. He was pleased but bemused by this
first representation of his beardless self, "wholly another person from
the old, of all the years." The portrait seemed "rather strong & sound,"
though, when he saw it completed, he thought he looked a little too
much "the smooth and anxious clerical gentleman in the spotted necktie." The portrait was less the issue than the feelings that the bland
representation disguised. He hated the notion of coming "face to face,
at my age, with every successive lost opportunity (wait till you've
reached it!) and with the steady swift movement of the ebb of the great
tide—the great tide of which one will never see the turn. The grey years
gather, the arid spaces lengthen, damn them—or at any rate don't
shorten; what doesn't come doesn't, and what goes *does.*"[2]

His own transformation seemed less successful in the face of a visit
in July 1900 from Charles Norton, sixteen years older than himself. He
had not seen him for almost twenty years. "I found him utterly unchanged and remarkably young," he wrote to Howells, the country
scenes in whose latest novel made James "homesick for New England
smells and sounds. . . .. But I found myself, *with* him, Methusalesque
and alien!" Norton's visit brought back sharp memories of his childhood, nostalgia for his youth and for the country from which he had
separated himself. "The dead awoke for me in his presence, & the
silent spoke, & innumerable ghosts walked." Why Norton seemed so
"*extraordinarily* little altered or aged," he could not fathom. "His speech,
his ideas, his very terminology seemed to belong to some alien epoch
of my youth—& I to have travelled thousands of miles from the order
& air in which they had their home. It was an odd, quaint, really in fact
strange, but not at all a tragic or awkward or unpleasant effect," though
it emphasized that for himself time had moved quickly.[3] As urbane and
kind as ever, Norton reminded James of his past. A benign variation
of this theme preoccupied him in the short novel that he completed in
summer 1900, *The Sacred Fount,* and in a new novel, *The Sense of the
Past,* "an international tale of terror," a few chapters of which he struggled with before giving it up in mid-August to concentrate on a longer
but more manageable subject.

Politics had always been on his mind, despite his efforts to insulate
himself, to muffle his anxiety when issues and conditions threatened
his values, especially his sense of the importance of Anglo-American
hegemony and of world peace. The British political scene that he had

observed closely since the late 1870s seemed to him nasty, brutish, and clumsy, the apparently insoluble Irish Question and the decline of the empire compounded by the incompetence and corruption of a succession of governments. "The crudity of the struggle for place is . . . mainly what strikes one. It isn't pretty."[4] The country seemed no better at the politics of empire than at the open-mindedness of art. Still, he had no doubt that Anglo-American culture deserved his allegiance, and there were no feasible, let alone attractive, alternatives. A deeply conservative liberal, he envisioned progress as the defeat of the dark forces within, as the triumph of the virtues that the society needed to practice as well as to articulate. The notion of war thoroughly nauseated him. He could think of nothing more wasteful, more brutal, more detestable, more personally soul shaking than people killing one another in an organized way.

The Irish Question, which undermined British-American relations, had become less threatening by the mid-1890s. He hoped that it would go away. Britain did not seem inclined to fight. When the Conservative government unexpectedly fell in summer 1895, it still seemed to him that the country was "becoming more rather than less anti-radical; & on the whole in a good sense. . . . Home-rule will not come to pass—& it looks as if it will perish in the most convenient way—by the internecine brawls of the Irish themselves." The problem of Ireland could be left to the Irish to solve. In late 1896, President Grover Cleveland's bellicose rejection of British claims in a boundary dispute involving British Guiana and Venezuela, which invigorated long-simmering American Anglophobia, startled and then frightened him. American jingoistic newspapers proclaimed the dominance of the Monroe Doctrine. "The absolute war-hunger as against this country—is a thing to darken one's meditations," he wrote to William, who shared his views. "It stupefies me—seems to me horribly inferior & vulgar—& I shall never go with it. I had rather my bones were ground into British powder! . . . It is too hateful." For a moment it seemed as if his worst nightmare might be realized. He urged his American friends to keep calm and sane "in the midst of this ugly rumpus. . . . If only *enough* people will do it on both sides of the sea all will still be well."[5] Fortunately, the Anglo-American clash of interests and styles was soon reconciled.

For James, America's claims had an unfortunate imperial resonance "such as no nation should dream of making without the army of Germany & the navy of England, rolled into one, to back it." Though he took great interest in having a ringside seat at the demise of one empire, he had no desire to observe the rise of another. Suddenly there existed an American navy capable of international militancy, as the small republic into which he had been born changed radically by the century's end. In spring 1898, after the sinking of the *Maine* in Havana Harbor and Admiral Dewey's destruction of the Spanish fleet, America suddenly became an imperial power with a vehemence, a vulgarity, and a moral coarseness that shocked him, as it did William, who publicly opposed the Spanish-American War. "Your letter on Roosevelt & the Philippines," Henry wrote to him, "commands all my admiration & sympathy. I agree with you no end—we have ceased to be, among the big nations, the one great thing that made up for our so many crudities & made us above all superior & unique—the only one with clean hands & no record of across-the-seas murder & theft. . . . One would like to be a Swiss or a Montenegrin now." As the drums rolled and the flags waved, literature "goes more than ever to the wall. . . . I am all on the side, now, of the small countries. They are the only honest ones left."[6]

Among his British friends, he "put up a brazen front" and to some extent justified the American attacks and the occupation of Cuba. To his fellow American, Henrietta Reubell, anxiously watching the events from Paris, he confided that though "the misrule, the cruelty of Spain *is* hideous . . . it's none of our business. . . . Cuba will be an immeasurable curse to us. But I can't talk of it—the frivolity & irresponsibility of Congress makes me too deadly sick." He actually for a moment imagined the Spanish fleet bombarding Boston Harbor. Though geography made such an attack unrealistic, his anxiety was real. "I'm mainly glad," he wrote to William, that "Harvard College isn't—near Irving St—the thing nearest Boston Bay." He had no doubt that the European powers would have gone to war more quickly than had America under the same provocation. "But I think it not good enough for *us!*"[7] The American fall from moral superiority into imperial cruelty belied his idealization of his native country, which had its foundation in the moral idealism of the New England in which he had come of age and in the republicanism of the world into which he had been born.

The European scene seemed equally if not more frightening. "We live in a sorry world—& to me there are many nightmares," he told Ariana Curtis in spring 1898. The Crimean War, the Franco-Prussian War, the complications of the Eastern Question, the Turkish presence in the Balkans, the tensions between France, Russia, Germany, and Britain in regard to spheres of influence, had provided strong reminders during the mostly peaceful years of Victoria's long reign of the possibilities for European carnage. When, in autumn 1896, turmoil engulfed the Balkans, James deplored the European response, "the hideous cowardice & baseness of Europe in the face of the Turkish massacres." Such potential for militant savagery and supine self-interest struck him with terror—"more disillusioning to me on the question of the 'progress of the race' than anything that has happened since I was born." The European powers seemed incapable of either disinterested moral acts or enlightened self-interest. "England is only *ashamed* of herself—but it doesn't go any further than that. It's a magnificent chance for her to shame the *others*— but she is too dropsical & bloated to take it. I wish to the 'most high God' she & the U.S. wd. do something *together*. *There* wd. be something for the civilization of the future worth talking about."[8] But England did nothing except regard Queen Victoria's grandson Kaiser Wilhelm with suspicion and protect its own interests.

Violence erupted when the Dutch colonists rebelled against British attempts to maintain dominance in South Africa. Suddenly, for the first time in James's adult life, England was at war. For him, the only thing worse than Britain being at war was the possibility that the war might be lost. At Rye, in 1899, he saw the reserves being called out, the troop trains departing. As the autumn rushed on, bringing "exquisite, delicate effects of bared & rich-skied rural beauty," his impatience and suspense deepened "over this nightmare of an ill-prepared war tent . . . sweeping off to Africa *all* the military resources, to almost the last man, that the country, the war-office, can muster. There is not a scrap of margin for anything *else* to happen! But probably nothing *will*—& the German Emperor & Empress arrive to-day on a visit to grandmamma." In the New Year, he transformed his opposition to the war into support, unable to resist, despite his general pacifism, loyalty to the national spirit of the country that he had adopted as his home. "Now I am primitively, preposterously, profoundly at one—in feeling—with the community in which I more or less incongruously live. It's impossible to be here & not be."[9] He had no doubt that the war was being badly misconducted. More than anything, he wanted it over.

The first winter of the new century was filled with gloom and anxiety. To his surprise, he had for a time the strange sense of reliving the emotions of the great war of his youth. "It brings me back across the years all sorts of far-away (& so unutterly, so dimly & direfully *melancholy*) echoes & memories—illusions almost—of our own war; of the general sense, the suspense & anxiety, stricken bereavement, woe & uncertainty, of that—& more still of the special sense of young men, sons & brothers of one's friends, many magnificent, engorged in their flower. Such grey battalions of ghosts!" At Lamb House during the winter and spring of 1900, as the Boer War raged bitterly, he felt depressed and isolated. In town, the excited hubbub and social activity made him anxious. He could not decide which was worse. "As the days get longer, I bicycle again, & that helps me to live." As the war gradually came to an end, British dominance was eerily punctuated by Victoria's death in January 1901. From the crowded balcony of a wealthy American friend, George Vanderbilt, he watched the funeral procession from behind the high plumes and hats of the ladies in front of him. Kaiser Wilhelm, whom "we seem to have suddenly acquired [as] a sort of unsuspected cousin," looked especially "wonderful and sturdy in the cortege." Apparently the queen had died in his arms, with the Prince of Wales, now Edward VII, holding her hand. Kaiser Wilhelm "and the King are now more than ever close and intimate friends. May it make for peace!"[10] He felt immense relief when the war essentially ended the next year.

But how nightmarish a place Europe was he saw with sharpest definition in the events in France that came to be called the Dreyfus affair. France's internal ugliness became a nightmare that awakened all Europe in 1898. Émile Zola published a pamphlet denouncing the French authorities who had colluded with a high-ranking army officer to convict an innocent French army captain of Jewish background of passing military secrets to the Germans. French royalism, Catholicism, and anti-Semitism exploded into hostility against all those whose French blood was not "pure." Abhorring fanaticism of any kind, anti-Semitism seemed to James even more abhorrent than other prejudices, partly because it had the potential to threaten, if not destroy, the European cultural comity. He immediately wrote a letter to Zola strongly expressing his admiration and support. Avidly devouring the newspaper, he was in imagination every morning in Paris "by the side of the big brave Zola. . . . I find [him] really a hero." His "J'accuse" seemed "one of the most courageous things ever done & an immense honour to our too-puling corporation. But his compatriots—!" Among them was Bourget, whose anti-Semitic anti-Dreyfus sentiments James tactfully but unhesitatingly told him he strongly disapproved of. "The whole Paris business sickens & appalls me," he wrote to Edward Warren in late February 1898, "& I worked off a part of my feeling yesterday by writing to Zola. He won't, I think, however, go to prison. He will appeal, & there will be delays, & things will happen—elections . . . & other things. As it was, I think—I fully believe—his sentence, on Wednesday, saved his life. If he had got less, or attenuation, he wd. have been *torn limb from limb* by the howling mob in the street. *That's* why I wrote to him."

France seemed to have fallen from its republican ideals and aspirations into medieval prejudice and anti-Semitic bloodlust. "I sit in the garden and read L'Affaire Dreyfus. What a bottomless & sinister *affaire* & in what a strange mill it is grinding the poor dear French. . . . I eat and drink, I sleep and dream Dreyfus." At the end of the year, he commented to Bourget on the difference between the French and the English represented by the respectful attendance of the Prince of Wales at Ferdinand Rothschild's "severely simple Jewish obsequies." James had valued the hospitality and friendship of numbers of Rothschilds, and met and respected many of the members of Anglo-Jewish society whose Jewishness he considered completely compatible with their high culture and position. "No one here," he told Bourget, "grudges the Synagogue a single of its amusements—great as is the place which it and they occupy." He lived, he felt, "in the great shadow of Dreyfus. . . . The wretched Alfred is, to one's haunting imagination, *condemned*—a victim inexorably appointed; for even if he be acquitted . . . he will be assassinated the next moment."[11]

By autumn 1899, a resolution seemed imminent, including the terrifying possibility of a military and royalist coup détat. "Half my time is spent in devouring the papers for their interest & the other half in hating them for the horrible way in which they envenimise all dangers & reverberate all lies." The French army, he anticipated, "*will* presumably have its new Caesar-by-acclamation in the person of the younger of the 2 Bonaparte Princes. . . . I thank my stars that the military justice is not the regime it's my fate to live under." Eagerly soliciting Fullerton for whatever inside information or on-the-scene point of view he could provide, he bewailed "poor old fate-ridden France—so hideously condemned to be incomparably interesting. She can't get out of it, 'squirm' as she will, & if she doesn't take care she'll be so again before 6 months, more than ever." In 1899, he found himself an ambivalent guest at the spacious villa that the Bourgets had purchased at Hyères on the Riviera. They housed him in a separate small pavilion which he almost succeeded in burning down. The odd, symbolic conflagration at Hyères probably resulted from his smoking carelessly. "I set fire to my room-curtains . . . smoke & scufflings. . . . However, [the Bourgets] are a long story," he wrote to Grace Norton. It all showed "in the lurid light of Dreyfus." As he awaited the news from Paris, he felt smothered by "palpitations & anxiety. . . . The worst will have been known—or rather *done:* (& something tells me they *will* do the worst,) by the time this reaches you. And that way madness lies—!"[12]

(2)

No sooner had he moved into Lamb House in the summer of 1898 and arranged for the rental of De Vere Gardens than he decided that at long last he would visit Italy again. He had not been abroad for over five years. He felt the right combination of economic stability and restlessness. If he did not go now, he might never have another chance. He "wanted insurmountably, at last, to see . . . the loved Italy" again. At the beginning of 1899, he planned to leave no later than mid-February. But he came down with "an agonizing form of influenza," with which he crawled into bed for ten days.[13]

In expectation of departing in the morning, he sat up very late in his Green Room study writing letters on Sunday night, the twenty-seventh of February, 1899. At two o'clock in the morning, he became aware of the smell of burning wood. Suddenly, he saw "smoke issuing from the crevices of the floor." Immediately arousing Smith, together they "pried & chopped up some planks—near the fireplace—to find the place on fire underneath & behind the hearth." Probably the chimney had been smoldering for weeks, perhaps months, "one of the lurking tricks & traps that old houses may play you, when . . . an old hearth (on re-arranging the rest of a whole chimney) has not been stirred on acct. of its pretty & pleasant last-century type. . . . Beneath it were infamous old floor beams . . . on which the hot stove *sat*—& which had not combusted before only by reason of generations of parsimonious firelessness. The whole place had got ignited." Fortunately, the local fire brigade, which came immediately, was able to put out the fire with small damage to the house, hacking upward through the dining room wall. But they stayed till almost morning. Exhausted, he tumbled into bed around five o'clock. If he had gone to bed early, he consoled himself, the damage would have been much greater. If the fire had occurred just one day later, his servants, especially the heavy-drinking Smiths, might not have awakened in time to save themselves, let alone the house. "It was a great escape & a great warning—an escape above all through the blessing of my late vigil. . . . As it was, it was a scare & a mortal bore—but above all an admonition—& cheaply got."[14]

Two days later, in response to an urgent telegram—"I AM NOW HELPLESS IN FACE OF RECONSTRUCTIONS . . . WILL BLESS YOU MIGHTILY IF YOU COME DEPARTURE OF COURSE PUT OFF"—Edward Warren, with his usual generosity, had taken the reconstruction in hand. Within days, James felt in good spirits. "It is all," he told Gosse, "to be made again better & saner & safer than it *ever* was!" He happily postponed his departure. The attractions of Lamb House appealed to his desire for sedentary domesticity. He feared the drain of traveling and visiting. "Abroad it's all a battle," he complained, "from the waylaying Emmets in Paris, and the waylaying Bourgets at Costebelle," the latter a visit "promised year after year these 4 or 5 last & never yet performed." But he still hoped to be in Venice by the end of March. He made his unnecessary excuses to Warren. "I must at last depart—there's a very serious obligation on me, long shirked, in Rome, & it's getting late."[15]

The middle two weeks of March 1899 he spent in Paris, often entertaining two of his young Emmet cousins. Paris seemed its usual sybaritically pagan self, especially highlighted by the extravaganza of the Great Exhibition, which struck him "as a monstrous massive flower of national decadence, the biggest temple ever built to material joys & the lust of the eyes. . . . It's a strange great phenomenon—with a deal of beauty still in its great expensive symmetries and perfections—& such a beauty of light." The city, though, seemed empty of familiar faces. "My old circle here has faded away into the twilight." Toward the end of the month, he went southward to Hyères, where he spent sixteen days with the "profusely kind and considerate" Bourgets at their palatial twenty-five-acre estate whose vastness made Lamb House seem minuscule, though the local villas themselves he thought tasteless. The landscape, however, was superb. "It is so long since I had seen the foreign & the Southern that it all rather rolls over me here like a wave—the harmony & loveliness & nobleness of this wondrous French riviera, the light, the grace & style & general composition." At Costebelle, he acted the good guest, except for setting fire to his pavilion curtains. The acrid air of France's Dreyfus madness made him homesick for what seemed to him English moral sanity.[16]

In Genoa, he worried about how he might protect his privacy for the next weeks. There were visits that had to be made, including a day trip to Bogliasco, where he had tea with the Ranee, and then dinner with her next day, during which her ex-lover, Morton Fullerton, was doubtless a topic of conversation. He had found waiting for him in Genoa a note from a Mrs. Edith Wharton—a friend of the Bourgets and an aspiring young American writer whose name he had heard a number of times from mutual acquaintances—"announcing to me that she is sending me a fruit of her literary toil and that she further expects to be at 'Claridge's'—London—the sojourn of kings—in May." Francis Marion Crawford beckoned from a villa at Sorrento he had built with the huge proceeds from his novels. James had promised the Swedish psychiatrist Axel Munthe that he would visit him at Capri. Mrs. Humphry Ward expected him to stay at the villa she and her husband had taken at Castel Gandolfo in the Alban Hills near Lake Nemi, a short distance from Rome. Most of all, he wanted to see Venice again and to visit Fenimore's grave in Rome. He had also promised Story's children that he would discuss with them their desire that he write a biography of their father. The schedule seemed threateningly heavy. "It's really to escape them *all*," particularly the social obligations of Rome, "that I am cultivating the cunning of the Choctaw & if need be the rudeness of the Apache. Five years ago they were the ruination of Italy to me, & the reason why I have suffered these 5 years of privation to roll by."[17] But he could hardly delude himself into even hoping that he would be able to work.

He was happy to be in Italy again. The mild, chattering Genoese ambiance came into his hotel room "with such sunny warmth of Italian air and shuffle of Italian feet and revival of Italian memories . . . the little old throbs and thrills of the great old superstition." He stayed for three weeks in Venice at the Palazzo Barbaro with the Curtises. They indulged his fantasy of sleeping in the vast library "*upstairs,* for the rare romance of it, & the looking out, of my famished eyes, on the Canal Grand. I should be in a sort of splendid 'isolation' up there, 'mornings,' working." Surrounded by white mosquito netting, he slept in royal dignity and virginal seclusion in a bed set up for him in the center of the eloquent room. Visiting the decrepit Katherine Bronson for three days at Asolo, he was distressed at her semi-imprisonment by her two nurses and her houseful of exploitative servants. She was, though, better than he had "feared to find her—but with a good deal of rheumatism, an enormous appetite . . . the strangest mixture of folly of purchase & discomfort about necessaries. . . . It's the queerest saddest situation." Evenings at Asolo he spent mostly with the philandering Pen Browning, whom he had met accidentally at the railroad station in Venice and who proudly showed the owner of minuscular Lamb House "all his wondrous property including the boa-constrictor, the new mountain," and his villa.[18]

Fortunately, Rome, in early May 1899, did not prove as socially demanding as he had feared, though he spent more hours than he wanted with the Storys' son Waldo, also a sculptor. James was unable to reject his insistent plea that James write a biography of his father. The money attracted James, and he found himself disarmed by the inherent understanding that he would do it at a time of his own choosing. Despite the modern desecrations, Rome itself seemed quietly attractive, his days "singularly prosperous & pleasant." One of the unexpected pleasures of Rome was in his meeting a young Norwegian-born American sculptor, Hendrik Andersen, whom he found as alluringly attractive as his work. In a side trip from Rome, he visited for almost a week the Humphry Wards, who had taken a "vast, rambling, bare, shabby & uncomfortable" apartment in a villa near Lake Nemi in order for Mary Ward to work up the background for a novel set in Italy. The tactful, good-natured visitor did not comment on what seemed to him a ludicrous fictional strategy. Instead, he enjoyed the beautiful vistas, the stunning views of lake and *campagna,* "with Rocca d'Papa & Monte Cavo perched opposite," the delightful walks, despite the cool weather and the rain, "in our garden, among ilexes & old statues, wondrous perspectives & cedarn alleys, the huge ruins & porticoes of a villa of Domitian."[19] It was Italy at its most romantically picturesque.

So too were Sorrento and Capri. Toward the middle of June 1899, as he was about to leave Rome for Florence, the persistent Crawford sent "his *mother-in-law* & his daughter, to bodily snatch me hence. . . . I struggled—but I have succumbed." As usual, "people, peoples, alas, are in spite of every precaution the eternal enemy." The popular novelist's luxurious villa raised his envy, made him irritable, provoked his impatience to get away—"Crawford . . . a prodigy of talent & of wealth. He is humiliating," he told William. From a lifetime spent writing detestable potboilers, Crawford had become rich. From a lifetime of dedication to his own art, James could hardly afford to stay abroad any longer, though he managed successfully to restrain his anger and resentment. At the Protestant Cemetery, "the sweetest spot on earth," he visited Fenimore's grave. The simple plaque and the high deep green cypresses were as much a memorial as the monumental statue a few yards away that Story had created to commemorate his wife's grave site. "It represents the angel of Grief," James was to quote from one of Story's letters in the biography he was not to write and publish until 1903, "in utter abandonment, throwing herself with drooping wings and hidden face over a funeral altar. It represents what I feel."[20]

James's own feelings were, for the time being, unarticulated, except that he had to visit Florence and that he wanted one last week in Venice, which he feared he would have to forgo, the heat already having become oppressive. His week in and around Florence in late June was, though, "tolerably torrid," his time with Florentine acquaintances, including Munthe, whom he had already visited at Capri, pleasurable. Homesick and eager to return to Lamb House, to his delight he still found that he could manage almost two final weeks in Venice. At the beginning of July, crossing the Alps, traveling "in tunnels & perspirations," he rested briefly in Paris, "yearning rather intensely, after so very many weeks, to return & repossess" Lamb House. "Italy has been again a thoroughly delightful experience, but my capacity for the wastefulness . . . of travel shrinks year by year, & after a few weeks I long again for my small regularities & privacies." By the second week of July 1899, the "weary homeward pilgrim" had returned to Lamb House, "all impatient to re-enter the modest hermitage he left nearly 4 months ago & which he really hopes never again to quit for scenes so expensively alien."[21]

Happy as he was to be home, he brought with him a heavy burden of anxiety. In early June 1899, he had felt "agitated to the depths" at the news that William had a serious cardiac illness, ascribed to the strain that he had put on his heart during a difficult climb in the Adirondacks in summer 1898. A year later, William realized that it was more than a temporary muscular condition. An undisciplined workaholic, under heavy pressure to earn money to support his family, William labored at constant lecturing in addition to his Harvard responsibilities. He wanted to give up his endless round of well-paying but exhausting lectures at disparate colleges and universities even as distant as California—invitations for which came in at the rate of almost one a day—and his wildly applauded performances on the Chautauqua circuit. He wanted entirely to retire from teaching, which he disliked, as soon as possible. Constantly on edge, he lived with the tension of a restless, anxious personality and with the pressures of insistent self-exhortation. Experiments with his own health included visits to psychics. William "deals in ghosts," Henry amiably remarked to a childhood friend, "but is blessedly not *one*." More questionably, he prescribed medicines for himself. At the end of each school semester, he applied self-administered electric shocks to stimulate his nervous system. Most of all, he hiked and climbed for stimulation and narcotic exhaustion as frequently as he could get away to the mountains. "There was," a friend remarked, "in spite of his playfulness, a deep sadness about [William] James. You felt that he had just stepped out of this sadness in order to meet you, and was to go back into it the moment you left him."[22]

Europe beckoned; he had accepted in 1896 an invitation from the University of Edinburgh to deliver the prestigious Gifford Lectures. This was a startlingly remunerative honor, "the ridiculous figure," William wrote to his brother, "of 'about 700£' for . . . 10 lectures . . . or $350 per lecture. I never knew before how much my time was worth an hour!" From England, Henry expressed his elation at the success of William's 1896 Lowell Lectures, though he confessed he felt the pang of his own "disinheritedness," his distance from the American scene and his American family. "You, William, don't even allude to the possibility of your coming out for your Edinburgh degree. . . . If you see your way to it it will be a sight to behold you."[23] The commitment to give the lectures at some unspecified date in the near future did not make Europe as imminent as the hope, in early 1899, that a European cure would work once again. William thought he might find relief from frequent heart palpitations, shortness of breath, and sharp chest pains at a traditional European spa like Nauheim, where medical experts provided variations on the water cure. He hoped to repeat what he and Henry had experienced as young men: the European cure in which the James family had so deeply believed.

From Rome, in spring 1899, Henry assured William and himself that it was only a question "of care & taking account." The De Vere Gardens apartment, which would be empty beginning in July, and the infinitely restful Lamb House, would be perfect for that. He and his wife Alice would be welcome guests whenever they were not at Nauheim, De Vere Gardens "yearning for you & aching for you. You've only to consider it a convenient, commodious, excellent resting-place & refuge for the interval before Edinburgh & . . . for all intervals after." William immediately provided reassurances. This heart condition "doesn't menace either longevity or life—it only checks me in too-rapid mountain climbing." Such reassurances were not convincing. "I think of you day & night," Henry wrote to him at Nauheim, to which he and Alice had gone directly, sailing from New York in July 1899. William optimistically expected, Henry reported to Grace Norton, an "apparently guaranteed" cure, though with "imperative periodical re-turn." He himself suspected that William's heart condition must "make a marked difference in all his adjustments of life," though "I must see him before I know." When he did see William in October 1899, for the first time in seven years, he was hardly reassured. The London specialist whom William now saw regularly "takes a very interested & hopeful view of him." But it was clear that the Nauheim regime and doctors had been an utter failure. Dr. Baldwin had come up from Italy to see William at Nauheim; he had unhesitantly told him that his life was in danger. Henry's own healthy heart more than shrank, his life suddenly in turmoil. "I always regarded him as the pillar of my family-life (so far as I have—or *have* had—one), & to see him down while I am up bewilders & disorients me. But *speriamo* ["let us hope"]."[24]

Hope did not come easily, but Henry's resilience, stubbornness, and will to be cheerful and productive, had enough force to sustain him through this crisis. Despite the turmoil, Henry found himself both counting his blessings and continuing with his work. One of the blessings was William's wife, whom Henry now came to adore as an embodiment of female beneficence and loyalty almost equal to that of his own mother. Another was William's twelve-year-old daughter, Peggy, enrolled in a London school, and now, with her parents and by herself, a frequent visitor at Lamb House. "As she grows older, [she] *may* be the consolation of my declining years. But she will have to hurry!"

Eagerly, solicitously, he hovered over his brother during October 1899 at Lamb House. He could do and think of nothing else.[25] When William went up to London for the last two months of the year, Henry breathed a sigh of relief, both because William's health seemed stable for the moment and because he had his privacy again. Lamb House was blessedly, tremulously quiet for the last months of the old century.

It was also now completely his in another sense. In late July 1899, he had been offered its outright ownership. "Arthur Bellingham, my landlord, has suddenly died, in S. Africa," he wrote to William at Nauheim, "& his widow inheriting this house has, without delay— from S. Africa, where she is & belongs—offered to *sell* it to me." He was ecstatic. At last he could have a property of his own. Concerned about the money, he readily allayed his anxiety with the notion of borrowing a portion of it from the British firm he had banked with since 1872. If he were to obtain a tenant for De Vere Gardens for the new year, he would need to borrow only a small amount. When he expressed to William his "tears of joy at the thought of acquiring this blessed little house so promptly & so cheaply" and confidingly, fraternally, asked his opinion, William, to his shock, responded with irritable words of caution and conveyed Baldwin's judgment that the house could not possibly be worth the two thousand pounds Bellingham's widow was asking. Why did Henry need to own a house at all? Wasn't the expense an unwarranted risk? Furious, Henry angrily told William that that aspect of it was none of his business, that he expected William's support in his pursuing something that his "whole being cries out aloud for," and that he had assurances based on knowledge far superior to Baldwin's that the purchase price was not only reasonable but cheap. At fifty-six years of age, with a long life of work and accomplishment behind him, was it too much to ask that he be allowed to curl up "in a poor little $10,000 shelter" when the Crawfords, Bourgets, Wards, and Howellses of this world live in splendid villas? It was enough to make him feel "the bitterness of humiliation."[26]

What he had wanted was William's loving support. Miserably unhappy at Nauheim, William had little sympathetic energy to spare. Henry stood firm against his older brother's criticism, after a brief moment of self-doubt, with reason, facts, and a passionate statement of his own deep desire to have the house. Everything, he believed, validated his position. "I am not yet wholly senile," he told William. He then laid out a convincing brief for the value of the purchase. "The house was bought some 15 years ago for £1200 . . . just before Rye had begun to be a great golfing-place. . . . Since that time everything has gone up. . . . A few years after buying the house my late landlord bought the studio which abuts on the garden & more or less commands it. This is a little *old* Wesleyan chapel. . . . I don't know how much more he paid for it. . . . I assure you that no one here thinks the proposal excessive." Guided by his wife, William had already relented and partly apologized. Henry declined his brother's repentant, and his sister-in-law's eager, offer to lend him whatever additional money he needed. He now saw that he would not have to borrow a penny to make the purchase. "I have no payments whatever to make till February 3rd 1900, & then only of a sum of money which I have already & have had for some time . . . besides another balance at the Rye bank, & which, 6 months hence, will be but a fraction of my cash funds." The eight hundred pounds he had with his banker were "the *only* purchase payment" he would have to make. "The other £1200 are in a mortgage on the house at 4 percent, in most respectable hands here, & which is eminently content to remain, as I shall let it. I can easily . . . pay it off in a year." When he rented the De Vere Gardens flat to the Stopford Brookses, he found that the rent amounted to almost half the purchase money of the house. Kipling wrote from his own recent purchase, The Elms, at Rottingdean, near Brighton, to congratulate him. "Lawful matrimony (in real estate) is ever the most honourable. . . . She will be expensive but at least she won't rebuke you for extravagance incurred on her account." His nerves calmed, amity between the brothers reestablished, by the middle of August 1899 he had bought Lamb House. When William arrived in October to see the house for the first time, "the whole," for Henry, was "infinitely settled & sweet."[27]

William's health was not. For two difficult years, he oscillated between Rye, Nauheim, southern France, and Italy in occasionally sensible, sometimes frenetic efforts to find the right doctor, the right medicine, the right climate. In late January 1900, having again postponed the Edinburgh lectures, he went to southern France to stay at a villa near Hyères that had been lent to him. "Thankful for small mercies," Henry accompanied brother and sister-in-law as far as Dover, slightly uplifted by what seemed a small improvement in William's health in the weeks before departure. He believed the improvement was a result of his having created at Lamb House "an atmosphere of optimism & an illusion of ease." William "is my only thought & almost my only news," he wrote to America. In Paris, William later confessed, he "made an ass" of himself, "letting that spider of hell the 'healer' touch me. . . . Altogether it has been a nasty job, and I shall never dabble in their like again." From southern France, Henry heard that "the air & sun & change are already immensely sustaining him." Eager to be hopeful, in early February he passed on to a friend the report that

William was, "thank heaven, already definitely better for climate & out-of-door life." Later the same day, he received dismally pessimistic news from William. He wrote back that "my heart is heavy with your mention of your ten poor days." He was certain that his brother would never be himself again.[28]

William, soon back at Nauheim, had a nervous collapse in the spring, with "fever and bleeding." Unexpectedly, a heart specialist in Geneva opined that, despite his worsening symptoms, he was actually getting better. In May, Henry, in London, had met Mark Twain, who had just returned from Sweden, looking "rosy as a baby," and who reported, Henry thought, that Lord Kelvin had said that "it was all 'Albumen' and he was putting W. on it, I didn't know Lord Kelvin was a 'Doctor' and don't understand 'why *Sweden?*'" He had misheard the entire comment, including the names, which had had nothing to do with William. While Alice and Peggy stayed at Lamb House for six weeks in the summer of 1990, Baldwin joined William at Nauheim in the dual role of doctor and patient. "Poor Baldwin—poor Baldwin! I can't say more," Henry wailed, "it's all so wild & *mixed.*"[29]

In the summer at Nauheim, and in the fall and winter of 1900–1901 in Rome, under the supervision of Baldwin, himself ill with a series of manic episodes and nervous breakdowns, William had a treatment of "Robert-Hawley animal extract" injections, Baldwin's "famous remedy," which filled the patient with hope. "The statistics are marvellous in all kinds of degenerative troubles, and there is no *bad* result. . . . If it were only possible to have begun 3 weeks ago, I dare say I should greet you," he told Henry, "an unrecognizable youth." Frightened, irritable, always willing to experiment, William tried whatever came to hand. When Alice left Rye in September 1900 to join her husband, Henry was "alone for almost the first time" in what seemed years. But, though his "existence for a good many months, has been, in all ways, rather a deluge of family history," he had "sat firm here, letting the waves break & managing to accomplish, in spite of them, some of the essentials of work."[30] It had been an extraordinary year for both brothers. Despite living the life of an invalid in Nauheim and in Rome, with baths, injections, and electric treatments, William managed to write his Gifford Lectures for Edinburgh. Despite incessant guests and perturbing worries, Henry managed to conceive and write an extensive outline for a new novel, *The Ambassadors.*

From Rome, at the beginning of 1901, while Henry worked on his new novel, William kept him informed of his progress. Changes were more an expression of his moods than of his physical condition. Ever the medical and pyschological optimist, he assured him that, despite his exhaustion, the treatment was going well. Henry rejoiced at the "comfortable beginning of Baldwin's injections. . . . It makes all the difference in the world in my feelings about your 'exile' that it is subject to his ministrations. May his reason be spared him at least to see you through!" As he worked on the Gifford Lectures, which examined varieties of religious experience and whose case histories resonated with the emotional eccentricities of Henry senior, William confided his worst fears only to his notebook. "I find myself in a cold, pinched, quaking state when I think on the probability of dying soon with all my music in me. My eyes are dry and hollow, my facial muscles won't contract, my throat quivers, my heart flutters, my breast and body feel stale and caked." At the same time, Henry assiduously worked at *The Ambassadors,* his own confrontation with loss and with the fear of death. He felt, at the middle of March 1901, "very intensely and inexorably" bound to his "belated book."[31]

At Easter 1901, William and Alice came to England to stay at Lamb House, and then to travel at last to Edinburgh for the Gifford Lectures. Greeted at Edinburgh as an intellectual hero, William basked in the publicity and the adulation. The lectures were a smashing success. He felt, at long last, liberated. His health seemed immediately better. Having resigned his professorship at Harvard, he hoped to have the opportunity to write two or three more books. If William took care of his health, Henry believed, that would be possible. In late summer 1901, William's wife returned to America. In early July, Henry finished *The Ambassadors* and began *The Wings of the Dove,* the idea for which had been on his mind for eight years. At home at Cambridge, William immediately resumed the animal extract injections, which he credited with working miracles. "I am going on splendidly," he wrote to his brother, and have "days with feelings just like my old ones of pride and power and adaptation to the world's demands." At Lamb House, Henry felt both relieved and lonely. He missed his brother and sister-in-law, and his niece, who had spent much of the summer with him "in idyllic intimacy and tranquillity." They were all gone. He had a poignant sense "of the beautiful vanished days."[32]

(3)

When James had left Rome in June 1899, the most precious possession that he carried away was a small bust that he had purchased, "out of the frenzy of my poverty," from the twenty-seven-year-old Norwegian-born American sculptor from Newport, Hendrik Andersen. A child of immigrant poverty and of an alcoholic, unreliable father, Andersen worshiped his hardworking mother, the financial and emotional center of the family. "No matter how old I get or how far advanced I become," he had pledged to his mother on his twenty-first birthday, "my mother will always be the first in my remembrance." After his mother, his closest relationship was with his brother Andreas, a struggling painter. Following four years of study in Boston and Paris, and sponsored by wealthy Bostonian patrons, Hendrik Andersen, in 1897, had settled in Rome. With a strong sense of vague religiosity, originating in his parents' Lutheran piety, he cast his artistic ambitions in terms of a religious, God-ordained mission. Both naively idealistic and ingenuously self-promoting, the strikingly good-looking Andersen had been taken up by Lord Ronald Gower, who promoted him and his work. In 1897, in Rome, they were constant companions. When Lord Ronald returned to England, Andersen "missed him very much indeed." In London, in the spring of 1897, on his way to America for a visit, Andersen stayed with the poet Arthur Symons, who had posed for him in Rome and with whom he had become warmly friendly. Gower lavishly entertained him at the Royal Society and at his comfortable home "full of valuable and beautiful works." The homosexual Lord Ronald had had both realized affairs, including one with Morton Fullerton, and warm friendships of the sort he now had with the innocent, emotionally engaged young sculptor. "I have met many of his friends and am invited everywhere to dine and lunch," Andersen boasted to his family in Newport. He visited Sargent, Burne-Jones, and Watt at their studios. In Rome, Saint-Gaudens came to his studio, "and said very nice things."[33]

Slim, fair, boyishly beautiful, the handsome young man immediately attracted James's attention and support. The moment James climbed the stairs into Andersen's sun-filled studio in Rome he began a memorable relationship that was to clutch at his heart for the next five years. Inviting Andersen to lunch, he extended their companionship through dinner. Though he had never felt that he could afford to be a patron of the arts, before leaving Rome he insisted on purchasing, for fifty pounds, Andersen's portrait bust of a young boy, Count Alberto Bevilacqua, which looked somewhat like Andersen himself. A few weeks before, at Castel Gandolfo, staying with the Wards, James had been fascinated by "a beautiful youth" who, for a few coins, guided them through the ruins of the Temple of Diana on the shore of the lake. In the golden early evening, in a scene that became fixed in Mary Ward's memory, this "young Hermes," whose name was Aristodemo, seemed to absorb all James's attention. " 'Aristodemo!' he murmured, smiling, and more to himself than me, his voice caressing the word. 'What a name! What a place!' "[34] Perhaps the bust of Bevilacqua reminded him of emotions associated with this and similar experiences, but, whatever its evocative powers, it was the one work by Andersen that James ever genuinely liked, mostly because of its emotional association with their first meeting. Obsessed with gigantic nude figures and with what James soon thought of as overly blunt, megalomaniacal, and commercially impractical statues, Andersen had an immense, Michelangelesque ambition. At first, it seemed to James idealistically, engagingly benign, a young man's temporary impracticality. Later, he saw it as his friend's fatal flaw as an artist.

Within two weeks of his return from Italy in July 1899, "the beautiful bust" had arrived at Lamb House, where he placed it in a position of prominence on the corner mantelpiece in the dining room. "I shall have him constantly before me, as a loved companion and friend. He is so living, so human so sympathetic and sociable and curious, that I foresee it will be a lifelong attachment." The fifty-pound bank draft was immediately on its way to Rome. "Little Bevilacqua . . . is meanwhile, dearer and dearer." He soon had, he told his distant friend, "struck up a tremendous intimacy with dear little Conte Alberto, and we literally can't live without each other. He is the first object that greets my eyes in the morning, and the last at night."[35] Andersen's work stood in for Andersen himself, the part for the whole, a combination of phallic synecdoche and marital displacement. It was to be, mostly, an epistolary relationship. James assumed that that was the way, for him, such relationships had to be, though if Andersen had been willing to accept his invitations to visit more frequently in England and even to stay indefinitely at Lamb House, the relationship might have taken on some of the domesticity for which James occasionally longed. Andersen's passion mostly went into his obsession with his gigantic statues and his preoccupation with his mother.

Some of his passion, in a quiet way, came to James. Soon after the delivery of Bevilacqua, the sculptor himself, on his way to America in summer 1899, arrived at Lamb House to stay briefly with James "who is kindness itself and whom I care very much for. . . . He has such a pretty little red brick cottage, very old but beautifully arranged. . . . I have one of the most beautiful rooms I ever slept in, with rich old oak walls in panels polished so that they look like strong iron and in every way I am in a little paradise here." During the all-too-brief visit, they took long walks and bicycle rides together. James expected to renovate his small Watchbell Street studio so that Andersen would be able to work there when he returned. "We shall be good for each other; and the studio good for both of us." At the railroad station, he felt "absurdly sorry to lose" his young friend. "I have *missed* you out of all proportion to the three meagre little days . . . we had together." Probably he had sent him off with whatever introductions he thought might be helpful, including one to Isabella Gardner. In New York, preoccupied with his family and his mostly unsuccessful efforts to get commissions, Andersen began work on a statue of Lincoln, for which he had great hopes. His father's alcoholism and his mother's martyrdom weighed heavily on him, his refuge a disembodied aesthetic idealism in which the nobleness of art substituted for ordinary feeling. "Keep to high ideals and work them out day and night," he told his youngest brother. "Get above every sentimental passion, and far above every physical passion!—and aim to make the mind noble." At Lamb House, James suffered through William's difficult visit and kept assiduously at work. Jonathan Sturges visited. Morton Fullerton was much on his mind. From Boston, Andersen reported on his progress, to which James responded with supportive, optimistic exhortations. "Gird your strong loins, nurse your brave visions, bear with your stupid sitters, gouge in your master-thumb. . . . I continue to have long talks with little Bevilacqua about you, and we help each other to bear up."[36]

From Lamb House, James kept his eye on Andersen's frustrations in New York and Boston. "I gather that your installation and start in New York are a grimishly uphill matter and I think of you with infinite sympathy and understanding." He urged Andersen to do what was necessary to find patrons. "I don't, I can't for the life of me see how such extraordinarily individual and distinguished portrait busts as you have the secret of shouldn't be ferociously wanted as soon as people *have begun to become aware of them. Make them* aware, and then wait. You won't have to wait too long." Unfortunately, it soon became clear that Andersen could not earn a living in America. "I think of you," James wrote to him, "with hope in the big, kind, ugly country—so monstrous and yet so responsive—with hope and with confidence, as well as with compassion."[37] Probably while Hendrik was in New York, his brother Andreas painted a portrait of the two Andersen brothers. Unfortunately, James never saw the double portrait. In Andreas' homoerotic painting, Hendrik, nude, slender, blond, with deep red lips, reclines in bed, partly covered with a sheet that rises noticeably over his genitals. With his right hand he strokes a white and black cat. Andreas, dark haired, also nude, equally handsome, sits at the edge of the bed, beginning to dress himself.

When Hendrik sailed for Rome via England late the next autumn, James rejoiced at the opportunity of Andersen being with him again in

Rye. It was "news of joy. . . . It will be delightful to see you and I shall pat you lustily on the back." The best guest room in the house awaited him. "I keep your place for you hard—or rather soft." On December 1, 1900, Andersen was "safe and sound with dear Henry James," he wrote to his "own loving mama. . . . I am very fond of him and we get on beautifully together. He is very sensitive and has such a good heart. . . . He works so hard, and when I look at his fine strong head, I can see how much bigger and greater he is than his works." The face had recently been shaved—partly to look younger, perhaps with Andersen's visit in mind—a change for which James had prepared him with a "poor little kodak-thing of my brother and me" that he had sent to Andersen in New York. "He is thin and changed and I am fat and shaved." Just as James began to look at Hendrik's statues, or at least photographs of them, with some dismay, Andersen looked at James himself with more pleasure than he read James's fiction. "I never feel the flesh and blood in any of his characters," he confided four years later to his sister-in-law. "To me they are sexless, glimmering, with a complete commonplace of intellectual social etiquette," without "vital force."[38] Andersen's criticism loosely echoed James's comments over the years on Andersen's statues. The sexuality in James's fiction seemed beyond Andersen's perception. Andersen's nude, immense, essentially faceless statues seemed to James impotent, anti-erotic posturing. The friendship was based on something other than an appreciation of one another's works. On James's part, there was, for a brief time, a strongly articulated love for a young man whose beauty and youth seemed breathtaking.

Andersen, though, mostly stayed away. In Rome, he allowed himself to believe that he was creating masterpieces, whatever the opinion of patrons and fellow artists. James felt himself essentially committed to England and work. He wrote his much-missed friend long, comforting, exhortative, occasionally avuncular letters, some of them with extravagant expressions of love and the frequent imagery of physical embrace that had begun now to be his characteristic eroticism, as if a kiss and a hug represented as full an expression of love as any other physical act. "I feel, my dear boy, my arm around you. I feel the pulsation, thereby, as it were, of your excellent future and your admirable endowment." To Andersen's frustrations and depressions he ministered with the wisdom learned from his own experience. "The only thing that makes life tolerable [is] to forget everything in some sort of creation. That's what *you* can do—none better. It's probably what you *are*, doing. *Dio vuole!*"

For the next two years, James regularly wrote long, amorous letters to Andersen. Sometimes the tone was flirtatious good cheer. The message, though, always implied Symonds' idealized connection of love between men with dedication to the pure life of the mind and of art, "the pure and independent passions of the mind and of the imagination." In early 1901, William and Alice saw the young man in Rome. William was particularly taken by his "strangely fascinating" statues, "ideally significant of human nature before its eating of the fruit of the fatal tree," the paradox of a self-conscious nudity that seemed to deny sexuality. "We have both, you see, you and I," Henry wrote to Andersen, "such endowed brothers, that we can boast of them." As soon as William left for Nauheim in July 1901, James urged Andersen to come to Rye, particularly to rest after a difficult winter of illness and frustration with his work. At Lamb House, "a small but secure apartment opens, from to-night, to its utmost width to you, and holds itself open till you come. Isn't it possible for you to come" and remain until you are "wholly rested and consoled and cheered." Let me feel that [my friendship] "reaches you and that it sustains and penetrates." To his delight, Andersen came in September, mostly to try to get commissions in London. "I am very fond of him and it will be a good change for me," he wrote to his mother. By comparison, James was ecstatic. "Your letter has been a joy. . . . Think of me as impatiently and tenderly yours." The difference highlighted the disparity in passion and commitment. To James's disappointment, Andersen stayed only a week. "I miss you—keep on doing so—out of all proportion to the too few hours you were here—and even go so far as to ask myself whether visits so damnably short haven't more in them to groan, than to thank for. . . . Addio, caro. . . . I can't bear not to know your nightmares. I hold you close. . . ."[39]

Hendrik was devastatingly shattered in January 1902 when the recently married Andreas unexpectedly died. James responded with his characteristically loving, supportive compassion, his desire to comfort and even heal with the touch of his hands, the warmth of his embrace, the articulation of his empathy. "Your news fills me with horror and pity, and how can I express the tenderness with which it makes me think of you and the aching wish to be near you and put my arms round you? My heart fairly bleeds and breaks at the vision of you *alone* . . . with the haunting, blighting, unbearable sorrow. The sense that I can't *help* you, see you, talk to you, touch you, hold you close and long, or do anything to make you rest on me, and feel my participation—this torments me, dearest boy, makes me ache for you. . . . I wish I could go to Rome and put my hands on you (oh how lovingly I should lay them!)." Come to England, he urged, "so that I might take consoling, soothing, infinitely close and tender and affectionately-healing *possession* of you." I would "put my arm round you and *make* you lean on me as on a brother and a lover. . . . I will *nurse* you through your dark passage." Henry had already begun nursing William. His pain at Hendrik's loss resonated with his love for William. When Henry suddenly collapsed at the end of January with a painful bowel infection, he needed nursing of his own. He had a few weeks of thinking himself close enough to death's door for Andreas' death and Hendrik's misery to resonate with his own accumulation of the deaths of people who had been precious to him. "I've gone through Death, and Death, enough in my long life," he wrote to Hendrik at the end of February, "to know how all that we *are,* all that we *have,* all that is best of us within, our genius, our imagination, our passion, our whole personal being, become then but aides and channels and open gates to suffering, to being flooded. But, it is better so. Let yourself go and *live,* even as a lacerated, mutilated lover, with your grief, your loss, your sore, unforgettable consciousness. *Possess* them and let them possess you, and life, so, will still hold you in her arms, and press you to her breast, and keep you, like the great merciless but still *most* enfolding and never disowning mighty Mother, on and on for things to come."[40]

Andersen, though, hardly came to England, and James went not at all to Italy during these years. When he indirectly asked Andersen to live with him, the invitation probably did not presume an overtly sexual relationship. Emotional companionship and convivial embraces may have been what his imagination evoked. In effect, he got neither. Andersen had other preoccupations, familial and professional. He soon brought his mother, as well as his younger brother, his sister, and Andreas' widow, to Rome to live with him. As to his lost brother, "Andreas is not dead," he wrote to his sister-in-law. "He has only gone before us. There is no death. It is only a sleep that comes over us." On his way to America in late summer 1902, he did not, to James's disappointment, visit him in England. James registered pain but no offense. If only he could come to Italy, they would have time together. "The dream . . . is always there, and you are always *in* the dream, and the fact of your being so counts immensely in making me work and strive and pray, and say to you Hold on tight and have patience with me and I will repay you tenfold."[41]

But disinterest and illness kept Andersen away, particularly a long hospital treatment for Ménière's disease in Turin, where he claimed to have astounded the doctors with his invulnerability to pain. In Rome, he had his studio and the American artists' community. He met Edith Wharton, who was spending the winter of 1903 in Italy and whom he knew of from Newport—the woman, he told his sister-in-law, who "lived down Ledge Road" and who "has written some interesting books. . . . She seems fond of meeting titled people and has a very cunning little dog and I don't think her literary success is turning her head." When Andersen did visit Lamb House again, briefly, in October 1903, James was delighted, though Andersen's schedule necessitated that he come at a time when James had other visitors also. It was a less intimate occasion than James had hoped for. "I meanwhile pat you affectionately on the back, across Alps and Apennines. I draw you close, I hold you long." Just as Fullerton remained elusive, so too did Andersen. The elusiveness partly was inherent in the lack of full sexual self-definition in the relationship. With Fullerton, more explicit sexual considerations might have been possible at the beginning, if they had been possible for James. With Andersen, they were probably out of the question from the beginning. The young sculptor believed that "the meeting of physical bodies is nothing and never can be. It is the meeting of mental forces that count, and that force has *always been first.*"[42] Whether or not the claim rationalized a frightened evasion of the intense homoeroticism that Andreas' double portrait embodied, it probably did mean that he was, always, a safe match for James's own evasions.

So too was Gaillard Lapsley, another American with whom James became warmly friendly from their first meeting in 1897, when Lapsley was twenty-six. The relationship never took on the intensity of his friendships with Fullerton and Andersen. "I like & am easy with all young creatures who like *me,*" James wrote to Grace Norton. He felt innocently fraternal and avuncular. Equally safe was Percy Lubbock, and later Hugh Walpole, partly because James had with these young men the tacit understanding that anything beyond warm embraces would be distasteful to him, and also because they and James never defined themselves as homosexuals. They all apparently expressed their homoeroticism emotionally rather than physically. A pupil of Arthur Benson's at Eton, Lubbock, a handsome young man "of long limb & candid countenance," probably met James in 1900 when Lubbock, at the age of twenty-one, seemed a prodigy of literary sensitivity and literary ambition. He immediately fell in love with James. "I am touched by what you tell me," James told a mutual friend, "of the young Percy & quite *envy* him." He wished, though, he were "a worthier object" of Percy's love. James met Lapsley through Isabella Gardner in London in the winter of 1897–1898. A Harvard graduate, with an advanced degree in medieval history, Lapsley became, for a brief time, a frequent dinner and theatre companion. When he returned to America to take up a position at the University of California in Berkeley and then to live briefly in Philadelphia, James missed his "beautiful & gentle,

though somewhat inadequately robust & reckless . . . young friend,"
who had visited a number of times at Lamb House before the end of
the century. "I miss you, in truth, at all times," James wrote to him in
California in 1902, "and when you tell me that you too are solitary,
am disposed to urge it upon you to chuck up your strange and perverted
career [at Berkeley] and come over here and share *my* isolation." Finally,
in 1904, with the prospect of a lectureship at Trinity College, Cambridge, Lapsley determined on his own expatriation. "This is brave
& beautiful news," James responded, "& I have nothing for it but
jubilation. . . . It is the very best thing you can possibly do, & . . . the
prospect of having you here seems to reveal to me how all the while I
have been quite mournfully &, as it were, lawfully, logically . . . missing you."[43]

James had no sense that he had ever stepped over the clearly demar-
cated physical boundary into unlawfulness. But he knew that the
boundary existed. He looked at it quite deliberately, and allowed himself the feelings and the language of transgression in these relationships,
but not more. As James remarked from Rome in 1899 to Howard
Sturgis, there is nothing "so indelicate as a bed!"[44] Closer to him in age
than his other new male friends, Sturgis, almost forty-five years old
when they revivified their relationship in 1899, soon became his closest,
most emotionally sympathetic companion. He provided a connection
between a past that they both shared and a turn away from it into freer,
more openly expressed relationships. A sturdy, prematurely gray man,
with wavy hair, a wide, dark mustache, and bright eyes below dark
full eyebrows, Sturgis had a less restrictive sense than James of the
indelicacy of beds. Though a New Englander, he had been less molded
by the Puritan tradition.

James had seen him as an adolescent in his father's London and
country homes, the spoiled child of a possessive mother whose relationship with her favorite son was claustrophobically intimate. After
schooling at Eton and Cambridge, where he revealed admirable acting
skills in female roles, he lived at home. His closest relationship, other
than with his parents, had been with his Eton tutor, with whom he
maintained a lifelong mutual devotion and with whom he spent long
periods of time. With his father's death in 1887, he inherited a fortune
and a mother who was more than lover or wife. With his mother's
death in 1888, he found himself, as Edith Wharton, who met him in
Newport in 1889, later remarked, "a middle-aged man, as lost and
helpless as a child." Literary in his tastes and sensibilities, an entertaining
mimic and conversationalist, Sturgis published two novels in the 1890s,
one of which, *Tim: A Story of Eton*, embodies a homoerotic fantasy—

in the tradition of Tennyson's *In Memoriam*—about which it is difficult
to tell whether the homoerotic elements are the result of innocent,
unconscious confusions or are self-consciously subversive. Sturgis was
not in the least embarrassed by his cross-gender eccentricities, including
his preference for warm shawls and knitting needles. The latter were
constantly in his hands at Queen's Acre, the "commodious Victorian
house" at Windsor that he purchased in the 1890s and that became the
hospitable center for family visitors and for his growing circle of male
friends—which soon included Lapsley, Lubbock, Benson, and then
Walpole, as well as James—and whose primary co-occupant was his
lifelong companion, William Haynes, familiarly known as the Babe.
"Our dear Howard is like a cake," Lubbock later quoted James as
remarking, "a richly sugared cake—always on the table. We sit round
him in a circle and help ourselves."[45]

To whatever degree the bed and the cake went together for Sturgis
and Haynes and for any of the visitors to the lively household at
Qu'Acre, James had no difficulty with these relationships. Sturgis' homosexuality was unthreateningly benign. It was eccentric rather than
flamboyant. James enjoyed the warmth, the emotional closeness, the
constantly familial holding of hands. "I can never pray for myself, but
I can, in a manner, for my friends," he had confided to Fullerton. He
often prayed that Sturgis would be less "oppressed with company—
with the multitudinous penalty of your hospitality & other graces,"
particularly the depredations of a vast number of American relatives
who came frequently and stayed for long periods. "There's nothing so
tragic in life as to be generous & to have let it be discovered," James
wrote to him. "It's not for our vices we pay, but for our Virtues."
Sometimes quite lonely at Lamb House, he urged Sturgis to escape his
visitors by coming to stay with him. "The potted chicken shall be
sacrificed to you; the house swept & garnished; the retinue freshly
drilled." It was a long-deferred friendship for which they were both
ready.

After Sturgis made his first visit early in 1900, James, exchanging
presents afterward, pronounced it "our so happy little congress of two."
In the Green Room, he had read to him each evening from his work-
in-progress, *The Ambassadors*. Sturgis was at work on a new novel, the
details of which he shared with his host, who urged him on. James
began frequent visits to Qu'Acre, which he had visited as early as 1897,
at least to the extent that work and his Lamb House routines permitted.
"Dearest Howard" seemed more and more "a fairy prince," a friend as
intelligent, as conversational, as emotionally responsive as he had ever
had. And also as sustaining and supportive. "You are indeed as a missing

mother to me, & I, babi-like, (though indeed as if you hadn't Babe enough & to spare!) gurgle back my gratitude." James was serious as well as affectionately flirtatious, when, in 1903, he both memorialized a visit by Sturgis to Lamb House and urged a further visit with a vision of a domesticity that might have been. "Yes—I *could* have lived with you. That is you might with me!"[46]

He also somewhat carelessly, that same year, gave well-meaning but insensitive criticism of Sturgis' new novel, *Belchamber,* particularly the passivity of the autobiographical main character. Part of the novel Sturgis had read to him. He now read all of it in manuscript. "You *keep up* the whole thing bravely—& I recognize the great difficulty involved in giving conceivability to your young man's marriage." But he should "not be *all* passivity & nullity." Deeply wounded, Sturgis declared that he would not publish the novel. James apparently failed to realize, or realize in time, that Sturgis' failure in depicting the marriage echoed the author's traumatic memories of his mother and his rejection of heterosexual relationships. Shocked, even horrified, he soothingly begged Sturgis to reconsider. "It all holds the attention from beginning to end, and has never a dull nor ineffectual page nor moment. So the public will declare. . . . If you *think* of anything so insane," he argued, "you will break my heart and bring my grey hairs, the few left me, in sorrow and shame to the grave. . . . If it springs from anything I have said to you I must have expressed myself with strange and deplorable clumsiness." Sturgis' sensitivity to criticism matched his own. Neither James nor Sturgis referred to the autobiographical sore points that James's criticism had raked. To James's great relief, Sturgis published the novel. Though Sturgis continued to write, he apparently never attempted to publish any other fiction thereafter.[47]

While Sturgis worked on *Belchamber,* James wrote his most powerful short story on the subject of sexual and marital inaction, confused sexual identity, and evasive personal self-deception—"The Beast in the Jungle." Perhaps he had seen in Gosse's letter to Symonds or perhaps Gosse had mentioned to him his reference to his struggles with "the wild beast" of homosexual desire that "is not dead, but tamer; I understand him & the tricks of his claws." Whatever James understood about his own desires, he expressed them indirectly with dramatic power in the story of "a man haunted," as he put it in his notebook in August 1901, "by the fear, more and more, throughout his life, that *something will happen to him.*"[48] The sense of special destiny that determines much of John Marcher's life turns out in the end to be his emotional inability to love, which suggests sexual impotence. Deeply repressed feelings lie in wait to takes revenge against him, to spring out as a hallucinatory embodiment of his inner emptiness, his massive unfeeling egoism, and his lifelong repression of his own sexuality. It springs out into consciousness and takes its revenge when he knows what it is he has done, what he has missed, what he has been incapable of. The beast that he has repressed has the same claws as the homoerotic desires against which Gosse struggled.

Because he has a deeply vested interest in maintaining self-deception or even ignorance about his sexual identity, Marcher never permits himself to be self-questioning about sexuality, relationships, marriage. He allows himself to be totally oblivious to what it is that is absent from his sense of himself and his life. Unlike James, he apparently never even considers what it is he has forgone, as if a repression so powerful is at work that not the slightest tremor of sexuality or self-awareness can surface. At May Bartram's funeral, he begins to feel the presence of "the beast," the loosening of repression, the coming to consciousness of what he has always repressed. Soon after, visiting her grave and seeing the ravaged face of a nearby mourner, he has a sudden insight into the depth of love and pain that face expresses. He has allowed himself at last to become aware of what it is that has prevented him from loving May Bartram.[49] Suddenly, horrifyingly, he is aware that he has missed love and passion—represented in heterosexual terms by the opportunity that was given him from the beginning to respond to May's love for him and to feel deeply thereafter whatever love and time offered him—even, at her death, the opportunity to have had his face and heart ravaged by deep feeling. What he has missed, most fully and devastatingly, is himself.

For Marcher, there is no second chance, no renewal—an embodiment of James's nightmare vision of never having lived, of having missed the depths and the passions of life, of having denied love and sexuality. His experience with Constance Fenimore Woolson tremulously informs the surface pattern of the story and the depiction of May Bartram. James did indeed ponder what he had missed. Marcher, who is not an artist, cannot claim the relevance of an incompatibility between art and marriage—that rationalization must have seemed slim, both consciously and unconsciously, even to James. It was not devotion to art alone that kept him from loving women. It was also a deep fear of the experience itself, primarily based on his indirectly articulated panic about what the experience would entail for him. At some level, the story suggests, he sensed that such an effort would be a misplaced failure. For Marcher, awareness, let alone contemplation of the alternative, is frighteningly traumatic. Not once ever desiring her or any other woman, he has missed the opportunity to love May Bartram because of his incapacity to function heterosexually. His most effective defense against the potentially frightening, perhaps disabling, confrontation with homoerotic desire has been the renunciation of physical sexual relationships entirely.

In various forms, many of them disguises, such a retreat from overt sexuality had been central to James's life and work, one of the hidden sources of dramatic power and obsession. He could not get it out of his mind or his stories. In his relationships with Morton Fullerton and Hendrik Andersen, he had, for the first time, articulated his obsession. At the beginning of the new century, Henry Adams, having in hand a copy of the *The Sacred Fount,* finally found what he believed to be his crucial point of identity with his old, somewhat puzzling friend. "Harry and I had the same disease, the obsession of the *idée fixe.* . . . It is insanity, and I think that Harry must soon take a vacation, with most of the rest of us, in a cheery asylum."[50] But he was on the loose and working harder than ever. It was also going extraordinarily well. There was seemingly no end to his artistic cunning, his obsessive imaginative inventiveness, in dramatizing the interconnections between his life and his art.

(4)

Sometimes looking out through the bow windows at the occasional traffic on West Street, sometimes staring down at the manuscript or the letters on his table, he sat in the "little ancient garden house" that he had "converted into an excellent work-room or 'study.' " His secretary was away in London for a few days. The usually "regular Remington-ticker" was quiet, dictation postponed for the moment. "The doors and windows" are "open to the garden & the birds twitter & the insects hum & the butterflies." Workmen were repairing the greenhouse. Drawing his breath in, he found pleasant "the queer musty odor" of the large fig tree that provided a Mediterranean screen for the window near where he sat.[51]

From his desk in the garden house he had a clear view of the advantages and the disadvantages of life at Rye. It was not always summer at Lamb House. Sometimes he was bored, particularly in the cold months, which seemed to him increasingly dreary after the rosy bloom of his first two winters. He was often lonely. With De Vere Gardens rented and then the lease sold, he had no London winter quarters, though, at about the time of the purchase of Lamb House, he had put his name down at the Reform Club for "one of the valued *bedrooms.*" Neither of his two other clubs, the Athenaeum and the Savile, offered permanent rooms, just as Rye did not offer year-round company. During the summer months, he had Fanny and George Prothero nearby—the latter a distinguished historian and editor of the *Quarterly Review*—new friends whom he grew to like and rely on socially. Up the hill at Playden, the beautiful Lady Maude Warrender, a talented amateur singer and avid hostess, whom he found amusing, held court. H. G. Wells, whom he had recently met and whom he admired more for his energy and ideological "cheek" than for his literary skills, built a house in 1900 at nearby Sandgate. Spade House was close enough to seem accessible but far enough away to make visits impractical, though an exchange of hospitality in June 1901 had Wells bringing the novelist George Gissing to stay overnight at Lamb House. Kipling at Rottingdean was close but not close enough—"poor great little Rudyard," who seemed to James a combination of talent and brutality. A visit to Kipling demanded either that Kipling send his car to transport James, which he did on a few occasions, or that James go all the way to London in order to get a train to Rottingdean. It was not very practical.[52]

When Stephen Crane, a twenty-eight-year-old American journalist and novelist, constantly in need of money, and whom James had met in London in 1898, rented Brede House, eight miles from Rye, James had another potential literary friend in the neighborhood. He bicycled over for conversation, for a Christmas party with amateur theatricals, and for a large tea party on the immense Brede House terrace. The view of valley and hills from the terrace was splendid, a view and a residence, whatever its disrepair and discomfort, for which Crane never paid its owner any of the rent. The cavernous, impractical disarray of Brede House matched the chaos of Crane's menagerie, which included his companion, a former prostitute from Florida, frequent visitors, the adopted children of a friend, constant poverty and hackwork, a usually bare pantry, and Crane's mostly disregarded, rapidly progressing, fatal tuberculosis. James, who liked Crane, thought his situation sadly, tragically impossible, and the sheer anarchic muddle of his environment distasteful. In a desperate effort to save Crane's life, Cora Crane raised money to take him to a German health resort, to which James unhesitatingly contributed fifty pounds, "which was really, out of pity for *him,* more substantial than I could afford." He later refused to send anything more, having come to the conclusion that Cora was fraudulently using the money for her own purposes. When, in June 1900, he bicycled over to Brede with some friends to show them the austere, handsome exterior of the house, "the melancholy of it," he wrote to Cora in

Germany, "was quite heart-breaking." Later the same day, the news of Crane's death reached him in Rye. "What a brutal, needless extinction— what an unmitigated unredeemed catastrophe! I think of him with such a sense of possibilities and powers."[53]

For a short while, there were two other literary friends nearby; twenty-seven-year-old Ford Madox Hueffer—later, during the next war, to change his last name to Ford—an easygoing poet and aspiring novelist; and Joseph Conrad, the forty-three-year-old Polish-born English novelist. Conrad had started vocational life as a sailor, had learned English working on English merchant ships, and had begun to publish, in the mid-1890s, a series of novels that James read and deeply admired. When, in 1902, Gosse rallied support for a Royal Society of Literature grant for the constantly impoverished Conrad, James testified both privately and publicly to his esteem. "I lose not an hour in responding to your request about Conrad," he wrote to Gosse, "whom I had not in the least known to be in the state you mention. It horrifies me more than I can say." His formal letter to the society epitomizes the effective foundation recommendation. "His production . . . has all been fine, rare & valid. . . . His successive books have been real literature, of a distinguished sort. . . . *The Nigger* . . . is in my opinion the very finest & strongest picture of the sea & sea-life that our language possesses— the master-piece in a whole great class; & *Lord Jim* runs it very close. When I think moreover that such completeness, such intensity of expression has been arrived at by a man not born to our speech . . . I greatly hope that the Royal Literary Fund may be able to do something for him." Conrad no doubt owed to James and Gosse the three-hundred-pound grant that he received the next month. Years later, James was to write to Conrad praise from his heart to Conrad's private ear. "I read you as I listen to rare music—with deepest depths of surrender, and out of those depths I emerge slowly and reluctantly again, to acknowledge that I return to life. . . . You stir me . . . to amazement and you touch me to tears."[54]

He had a substantial friendship with neither Conrad nor Hueffer. Conrad, who admired James, sent him a copy of *An Outcast of the Islands* in 1896. Reciprocating with *The Spoils of Poynton,* James entertained Conrad for lunch at De Vere Gardens early the next year. Despite his respect for Conrad, he apparently had no sense of the possibility of anything more than a professional friendship. Ford Madox Hueffer, a great admirer of James's fiction, was the grandson of the Pre-Raphaelite painter Ford Madox Brown, whose biography he had just written. Hueffer introduced himself to James in Rye in 1896, hoping that James would review the book favorably. The next year, eager for company,

James extended an open-ended invitation to Hueffer to visit at the newly leased Lamb House. Hueffer, in 1898, sublet his farmhouse, on the northern part of the Romney Marsh in Kent, to Conrad, whom he had just met, and who had agreed to collaborate with Hueffer on a novel. Hueffer stayed nearby. In 1901, he moved to Winchelsea, a short walk from Rye. There he negotiated the difficulties of his collaboration with Conrad, which James thought absurd, and of his complicated personal life, which included a love affair with his sister-in-law.

In Rye, James was a treasured resource, with whom Hueffer had occasional afternoon walks, often along the Winchelsea road and up the steep hill to the medieval town with its channel vista. James's essay, "Winchelsea, Rye, and 'Denis Duval,' " written before Hueffer's arrival and published in *Scribner's* in 1901, captures James's love of both towns and some of the spirit of the walks they were to have. They also had some winter evenings over a blazing fire. James found Hueffer amiable, likable, worshipful, sometimes foolish, occasionally intrusive—at worst, acceptable company—at best, a pleasure to talk to. On one occasion, James mistakenly assumed that Hueffer was soliciting a loan and offered to lend him money. Conrad, collaborating with Hueffer, came regularly to Winchelsea. At Christmas, 1899, he and James were guests in the bohemian chaos of the Christmas revels at Brede House. They had some time together, apparently, though not much. Conrad was unavailable for spontaneous walks and chatter. Hueffer, who was, had his limitations, and the writers who lived in the Romney Marsh area in the ten years around the turn of the century neither formed a regular social community nor, for various reasons, provided James with opportunities for sustained companionship.[55]

When, late in 1900, he learned that he could have a bedroom at the Reform Club much sooner than he had expected, he was delighted. He needed to have a London alternative. No matter how many visitors came to Lamb House during the summer months, the winters were mostly desolate. Annie Fields and her companion, Sarah Orne Jewett, whose *The Country of the Pointed Firs* he thought "really exquisite," came in the summer of 1898, happily evoking for him memories of "my far-away youth . . . where she was so pretty & I was so aspiring." Apparently, those years were much on his mind, even in resonantly comic ways. He was startled when his terrier, one in a series of dogs with which he had bad luck and sadly buried in his garden, seemed to have an "extraordinary facial resemblance to the late James T. Fields," the Boston publisher and editor of the *Atlantic*. "It's one of the funniest likenesses I ever saw (and most startling); and yet I can't write to Mrs. Fields of my daily joy in it. . . . I've wintered as well as summered" at Lamb House, he told Mrs. Fields, "& wintered perhaps enough." Homesick for London and abysmally lonely, he vowed that he would never again spend a winter in Sussex. "Nose to nose with the dark, wet country winter . . . I pine for the sound of the buses & the colour of the jars, at night, in the chemist's windows. . . . My hibernating here (a second time,) has been a somewhat unconsidered accident." Sometimes the advantage that isolation provided for work was irresistible, and bearable. In the cold January of 1900, "mere diluvian sleet and slush rule the day," he wrote to William, "a muddle of snow & rain & biting wind, & a fall of sudden snow tonight, over all. But the green room holds its own . . . & fosters my genius each a.m." When working well, he readily admitted that "the lack of human intercourse is rather excessive," but "I don't in the least mind it—& *do* [like] . . . the freedom & quiet & the favourable way my little work ticks on." When he felt lonely, "the long stretch of short days & measureless rains" seemed unbearable. "Then you see why 'man made the town'—& pavements & gaslamps & shop-windows & clubs."[56] In the summer, usually, there were too many guests, a procession of London and American visitors. Some of them he quartered at the nearby Mermaid Inn, others he had to deal with in his own house, often with a strain that he felt, in its way, as difficult as winter isolation.

He liked being master of a house, but he did not like the responsibility and the work. It irked, bored, and tired him. Fortunately, in an economy in which they cost, by modern standards, next to nothing, he was able to afford servants to do much of the work, as distinct from the worrying, of which he did a great deal. He employed a general housemaid, a gardener, a houseboy, and the Smiths, with whom his long-standing, precarious relationship ended, finally, in September 1901. Lamb House suddenly became "a scene of woe." With three guests in the house, the Smiths, having been abysmally drunk for days, collapsed into paralyzed incoherence. James called the local doctor. Medication made no difference. He soon got Smith out of the house. Mrs. Smith's sister came to take her away. He was shocked to learn that the Smiths had spent on drink every penny they had earned and that there were outstanding liquor debts, which he soon paid along with generous severance money. "The romance of sixteen years is closed, and I sit tonight amid the ruins it has left behind. . . . They were, at the end, simply two saturated and demoralized victims, with not a word to say for themselves and going in silence to their doom; but great is the miracle of their having been, all the while, the admirable servants they were and whom I shall ever unutterably mourn and miss." He felt even more lonely and unprotected. "I miss Mrs. Smith's cuisine and Smith's hourly ministrations." For a while he could get no work done and felt as if he almost wanted "to close the house and bolt altogether." His cries, he recognized, were "a puerile wail."[57] But he felt betrayed and adrift. The domestic order that he had counted on had become a chaos.

With his new base at the Reform Club, he had London regularly available to him at a very economical price. He needed, he felt, to avoid winters in Rye. With the servant problem soon under control, with a new, excellent cook, magisterially referred to as Mrs. Paddington, and the increasingly reliable, useful houseboy, Burgess Noakes, he could alternate between Rye and London. "I've at last got reconstituted," he wrote to Ariana Curtis late in 1901, "with 3 women & a houseboy— & feel under petticoat sway as never before." When, after a long absence, he had returned to town in March 1900, he had found London "most pleasant & refreshing; & every one, old friends, acquaintances, &c, such as I have seen, have greeted me almost as if I had returned from African or Asian exile. Every one has been absurdly kind & welcoming." What had seemed stale to him in 1898 now seemed "most renewedly amusing & exciting." By early December 1900, he had his Reform Club perch, "a town-cradle for my declining years," where he installed bed, window blinds, and curtains. He stored his London clothes there. Service was fully provided by an excellent butler in a room longer than wide, with a fireplace and space for a typist, in easy walk of everything, near Charing Cross Station and trains to Rye, looking "full (due) South—high, high up." From his room, he saw "nothing, across the charming Carlton House Terrace 'gardens' but embassies & lordly houses." In the mornings, just as at Lamb House, from about ten or ten-thirty, to about one or one-thirty in the afternoon, he dictated to his secretary. At first MacAlpine filled this position, though he soon arranged an amicable parting. "It's simply that he's too damned *expensive,* & always has been—& too place-taking in my life & economy. I can get a highly competent little woman for half. . . . It's simply that I don't want to put so much more money into dictating than I *need.*"[58] With MacAlpine, he had felt a social obligation to take at least lunch and walks together in Rye. In town, he could hire a woman who would make less money and fewer demands. Soon he hired an attractive, undemanding young lady, Mary Weld, who, beginning in early 1901, took his dictation in London and in Rye.

In town, he could see Lucy Clifford regularly as well as a new friend, Jessie Allen, whom he had met in 1899 at the Palazzo Barbaro. A friend of the Curtises, she was a witty, generous, well-connected widow with little money of her own but with contacts that kept her constantly at the homes of the great. She had taken such a fancy to him that their relationship became a warm continuum of gift exchanges—though mostly from her to him—and happy conversations. Many of his literary and social friends from the 1880s were gone. "I have lost sight of many people & greatly simplified my London contacts, but there are always people enough & the simplification blesses. Besides, half my friends are dead, & the other half, including myself, soon will be—so nothing much matters." The ever-faithful Gosse was his regular companion. Sargent, like others he would have been happy to see, had disappeared, in his case only into the social stratosphere inhabited by the most successful living portrait painter. He moves, James reported to the curious Henrietta Reubell, "in an orbit so much larger & higher than mine that I only see him as you see a far sail, at sea, passing on the horizon—a big shining ship that leaves your own slow steamer behind. He sails over the rim & the great curve of the globe—straight for the Golden Isles."[59]

He himself sailed, between 1901 and 1904, despite the trepidations of time, lovers, servants, the problems of rural isolation, and the anxieties of William's illness, into his own Golden Isles. It was a period of sustained creativity in which he brought to bear the self-focusing intensity of the artistic and experiential lessons of a lifetime. His eye was still on his financial needs, which at some moments he evaluated realistically, and at others distorted with the semipanic of someone who had expected to have much more and feared he would have much less. He felt a sustained bitterness at what seemed to him, comparatively, the paltriness of his earnings. Serial publication, from which much of his income had come, was now more difficult to effect. Fortunately, in late 1897, the ever-reliable Howells had arranged publication of *The Awkward Age* in *Harper's Weekly* for the unexpectedly high sum of three thousand dollars, "exactly what would have been the form of *my* golden dream," James told him. For the moment, he felt validated, revivified. "I [had] felt myself," he told Howells, "somehow perishing in my pride or rotting ungathered, like an old maid against the wall and on her lonely bench."[60] The money helped pay for Lamb House. He also, at last, had an agent again, the excellent James Pinker, who began to organize his copyrights and sell his fiction in a professional manner, as he was also doing for Conrad, Crane, Wells, and others. Pinker was the first literary agent who emphasized the connection between the British and American markets. Under Pinker's guidance, Methuen, which paid more generously than his previous publishers, became his main, though not his only, British publisher. James felt that at least he was in good hands. With Pinker's help, against the obstacles of an increasingly indifferent reading public, his income from writing for the next eight years averaged about five thousand dollars a year, which he supplemented with about three thousand dollars a year from the Syracuse property. Though less in demand, at least he was being more effectively sold.

Often he felt as if he were being sold out, not by Pinker or Howells, but by a world that devalued what he did. He managed frequently enough to put that aside, particularly during his sustained burst of creative energy between 1901 and 1904. He had enough ironic good humor to "greatly applaud the tact" with which one of his best readers, Howard Sturgis, told him "that scarce a human being will understand a word, or an intention, or an artistic element or glimmer of any sort, of *The Awkward Age*. . . . But it's an old, old story—& if I 'minded' now as much as I once did, I should be well beneath the sod." He knew what he did not want to write, the kind of bluntly undershaped, psychologically unmodulated novel like Hardy's "great success," *Jude the Obscure,* which he thought "ineffably dreary & stupid." He had enough money for his needs. His expenses were quite manageable. He had the security of Lamb House, the availability of London. He had friends whom he kept at a distance that allowed him to maintain, more or less, his emotional equilibrium and his work patterns. He had a new excellent typist to whom he could dictate. His creative voice was now liberated from the limitations of his tired hand and his semilegible handwriting. His own voice, in the garden room and in his high perch at the Reform Club, modulated, with rhythmic energy, into fictional representations that epitomized a lifetime of reaching for such fulfillments. "He dictated beautifully," Mary Weld recalled. "He had a melodious voice and in some way he seemed to be able to tell if I was falling behind. Typewriting for him was exactly like accompanying a singer on the piano."[61] When he dictated, apparently his stammer disappeared.

"The joy of production, with me, almost limits itself to feeling the silver cord positively not snap," he wrote to Mary Ward in October 1900. He had just put together a new book of short stories, which he somehow managed to keep writing at the same time that he worked on longer fictions. He "began a new book the instant the old one was finished." That was "his only chance," he told Arthur Benson, "because he worked so slowly, and excised so much." In November 1900, he corrected the proofs of *The Sacred Fount,* destined to have even fewer readers than *The Awkward Age*. Originally a short story, the subject of which was "a small fantasticality," it had irrepressibly expanded into a complicated experiment in dialogue and point of view whose richnesses remained, for most readers, obscured by its demands for an attention and concentration that few novelists had ever dared request. "My hand-to-mouth economy condemned me," he confessed, "to put it through in order not to have wasted the time already spent. So, only, it was that I hatingly finished it; trying only to make it—the one thing it *could* be—a *consistent* joke. Alas, for a joke it appears to have been, round about me here, taken rather seriously." He had begun two other novels, one of which, *The Sense of the Past,* a response to Howells' request for an international ghost story, he soon put aside. He was more interested in the ghosts of his own present. The novel that he had first formulated in response to Jonathan Sturges' account of Howells' Paris comments, about never having lived fully enough, provided the ideational germ for the novel that now preoccupied him, *The Ambassadors.* Pinker had arranged its serialization "from next autumn on. . . . The date gives me time, but the curse . . . is that if one catches hold of a subject good enough to—well, to be good enough, it is also good enough to be damnably difficult. That side of my job fills all my consciousness now."

By March 1901, he felt "intensely and inexorably" bound to the new novel. "I can't get away from [it] for a day." He kept at it through the spring and early summer of 1901, his spirits buoyed by his sense of achievement. "Oh, sacred days that are still somehow *there*—that it would be the golden gift and miracle, to-day, still to find *not* wasted." Sending, in early July, the final sections to Pinker for transmission to the *North American Review,* he held back three and a half chapters of the manuscript, which had exceeded the length agreed upon.[62] At the same time that he sent off the manuscript of *The Ambassadors,* he asked Pinker to negotiate with Scribner's a postponement of its immediate due date until the end of 1901 a novel whose origin had been one of his notebook entries in 1894 and to which he now gave the title *The Wings of the Dove. The Ambassadors* had taken him six months longer to complete than he had expected.

By mid-July 1901, he was "well launched" into the new book, his only interruption the fulfillment of a deeply felt obligation to visit the Godkins near Epping, where the seriously ill Godkin had recently settled. Later in the year, he stayed a week at Torquay with Godkin—"old & very ill . . . & whom it has been a question of seeing now or probably never." *Wings* had now been promised for January 1. He expected, he told Kipling, to "be occupied grinding my teeth and breaking my heart" until Christmas. By mid-January 1902, he had not finished—"In a desperate state of arrears . . . & so abashed & disgraced that I can do nothing else till the incubus in question is floored." He stayed on in Rye, desperate both to have it done and to have the relief of London. By the end of the month, he still had not finished. To get away from Rye for the worst of the winter, he went to London at the end of January, where he came down with a painful bowel infection that sent him back almost immediately to the spaciousness and comparative comfort of Lamb House. The newspapers were wrong, he soon wrote to a friend, in reporting that he was so ill that he had to postpone indefinitely the completion of his novel.[63]

Just as the newspapers lied, publishers were unreliable. He finished *Wings* early in the spring, for autumn publication. But *The Ambassadors* still had not begun its "vulgarist Harper-'serialization.' " It was to be delayed until 1903. *Wings* appeared in August 1902, though without the benefit of serial publication at all. Pinker had had no success in placing it with a magazine. "I pray night and day for its comparative prosperity, but no [magazine] publisher, alas . . . have told me that it has 'taken their fancy.' So I'm preparing for the worst," he told Howells. The worst came. Howells' optimism that an apartment building in Manhattan having recently been named "The Henry James" portended a revival of its namesake's popularity seemed to James a bitter irony. Howells had clipped out the advertisement and sent it to James. "No power on earth can ever do that," he responded. My books "are *behind,* irremovably behind, the public, and fixed there for my lifetime at least; and as the public hasn't eyes in the back of its head, and scarcely even in the front, no consequences can ensue." What he could and did do was hardly to lift his head from his writing desk. From late autumn 1902 to early 1903, working at it part-time, he fulfilled his long-standing promise to write a biography of Story—a book that he padded with long selections from Story's letters—sorry that he had ever agreed to do it. The problem was that there was no subject. In review, Story seemed insubstantial. James's only subject was the resonances of his own youth and the evocation of the Rome he had lived in as a young man. "One has to put as much as one can of one's self in it to make up for all there is that is absent."[64] The subject of the American artist in Europe, of losses and gains, was much on his mind while writing Story's biography. In late summer 1902, he began a new novel, *The Golden Bowl,* the idea for which he had sketched out in his notebook more than ten years before. By late February 1903, he had finished *William Wetmore Story and His Friends.* By the beginning of 1904, he had finished *The Golden Bowl.*

In the composition of *The Ambassadors, Wings of the Dove,* and *The Golden Bowl,* his lifelong preoccupations as a novelist were part of the rhythm of his voice as he dictated. These were to be the last completed novels he would write. The three novels embody a culmination of his concern with the international theme. Now raised to a level of intense complication and subtlety, the theme is transformed from the satirical comedy of misperception into a drama of the search for self-knowledge. In *The Ambassadors,* the novel he thought the most formally perfect of all his works, the main character, Lambert Strether, an American, "*is* the subject, the subject itself."[65] Having been dispatched to France in order to find out why young Chad Newsome declines to return to America, Strether—from whose point of view the reader sees the world of the novel—gradually realizes that he himself gives more value to experience than to theory, to pleasure than to principle, to humane considerations than to moral codes. He has had to come to Europe to discover that he is a Jamesian pragmatist. Like James, Strether, who is about the same age as his creator, has the ambivalent satisfaction of being an observer observing himself making observations rather than a participant. He embodies James's heightened sense, at the beginning of the twentieth century, of looking over his own shoulder at where he has come from and where he is now. For Strether, a depleted version of what James might have been if he had remained mostly at home, European residence is impossible. For James, it had become the only possibility. With his own eyes partly raised toward the possibility of a visit to America, James sends Strether back to Massachusetts to deal, as best he can, in terms of what he has learned and what has changed him, with what has remained the same.

In mid-December 1902, he wrote to Grace Norton that "you your-self, dear Grace, are a presence so terrifically arranged as an absence."[66] James had arranged many of the presences that meant most to him as absences. In *Wings of the Dove,* the central symbolic presence of the novel is Milly Theale, an imaginative transformation of James's memory of Minny Temple and an allegorical representation of a version of "the American Girl." She is the significant absence around whose symbolic nonpresence the two main characters position themselves in an effort to determine who they are and what they are capable of doing to resolve their crucial needs. Beautiful, determined, and energetic, the abandoned daughter of a manipulative, mercenary father, Kate Croy is the culmina-tion of James's long series of flawed heroines who must deal with the exigencies of the marriage market. The brilliant first scene of the novel, between father and daughter, propels into some degree of sympathetic credibility Kate's actions and attitudes thereafter. Unwilling to marry Merton Densher—a working journalist for whom Morton Fullerton claimed to be the model—unless they can obtain enough money to live well, she conspires with Densher to encourage the wealthy, fatally ill Milly Theale to fall in love with him, which Milly does. Though aware that Densher has an agreement with Kate, she bequeaths him a large sum of money. After Milly's death, the two Europeans must face the consequences of their success, a consequence complicated by Densher's having, to some extent, fallen in love with Milly. Having had reservations about the conspiracy, Densher had, before he would proceed to encourage Milly, gently compelled Kate to consummate their love. Now he asks her to consent to his declining the inheritance. He had been open enough to fall in love with Milly, even if the realization of his love arises only after her death, and admirable enough never directly to lie to her. Now he insists that he and Kate do not need the money. The transforming experience has made him sufficiently strong to know that she must either make the choice that will allow them to marry or end the relationship. Her sexual attractiveness will not keep them together. Neither will their love for one another.

Unless Kate chooses to cooperate with him in not accepting the bequest, he knows that he and Kate are morally incompatible. They will be emotionally distressed and morally corroded if they do not renounce the money that they will have gotten by deception and through a gift of love. Kate accuses Densher of being in love with Milly's memory. "Her memory's your love. You *want* no other." But, he insists, if she will decline, he will do nothing more happily than marry her. " 'As we were?' 'As we were.' But she turned to the door, and her headshake was now the end. 'We shall never be again as we were!' " Kate is right. The experience has changed the personal reality. James, the novelist of process, has achieved his most effective affirmation of the determining force of the flow of experience, of mind, of awareness itself, as the value that transcends all values.

His effort to depict consciousness, he believed, also demanded a style that embodied the rhythm of the way the mind moves, a constant interaction between the external consciousness of the authorial voice and the point of view of the individual character through whose eyes and mind experience is being dramatized. "I would have written, if I could," he told Fullerton with stoic exasperation, "like Anthony Hope and Marion Crawford." But he could not. Unlike the successful popular writers who were his contemporaries, he was always concerned with the "bottomless questions of How and Why and Whence and *What*— in connection with the mystery of one's craft. . . . After all, it is the *doing* that best meets and answers them." Aware that he often did not meet his own high standards, he patiently told Mary Ward that "I think I see the faults of my too voluminous fiction exhaustively myself; indeed when once my thing is done I see nothing *but* the faults." Rereading *The Ambassadors* in 1903, it seemed to him to have "a kind of staleness & mistimedness in it." He had, he confessed, "felt a good deal of despair after 'The Ambassadors' were launched, & said to myself 'what can be

expected for a novel with a hero of 55, & properly no heroine at all?' "
Still, "I have slowly felt a little better, & the book is, intrinsically, I
daresay, the best I have written." As to *Wings of the Dove,* it had two
or three major faults, one of which is that "the centre . . . isn't in the
middle, or the middle, rather, isn't in the centre, but ever so much too
near the end, so that what was to come after it is truncated." As
he worked on *The Golden Bowl,* he worried about the "the opposite
disproportion—the body too big for its head." But dictation, he believed, actually worked against the problems of misproportion and
expansiveness, helping him to rewrite, to improve, to be more concise,
"to do over and over, for which it is extremely adapted, and which is
the only way I can do at all. It soon enough, accordingly, becomes
intellectually, absolutely identical with the act of writing . . . so that the
difference is only material and illusory—only the difference, that is,
that I walk up and down: which is much to the good." No matter what
he did, though, sometimes he found "it all a *too* damnably difficult
art—& have so to pretend that it isn't! However, we pretend life isn't,
either."[67]

In *The Golden Bowl,* James provided his most sustained dramatization of what he thought of as "everything"—his shorthand way of
referring to consciousness, to its permutations and growth, and to the
human and moral awareness that inevitably follows out of its fullest
expression. He had no doubt that consciousness most fully expresses
itself in relationships between people and between people and their
culture. His own consciousness as narrator permeates the novel whose
four main characters represent aspects of James's experience. Amerigo,
the resonantly named Italian prince, settled in London, marries one of
the two American girls of the novel, Maggie Verver, and has an adulterous affair with the other, Charlotte Stant, the wife of Maggie's father,
Adam Verver. The latter, who has spent his recent years in Europe
collecting treasures for the museum he has founded in American City,
epitomizes an American businesses redeemed by art. The story moves
in and through the mediated consciousnesses of three of the four characters. Adam Verver remains unrevealed. When Maggie discovers the
adulterous relationship, she carefully, with stubborn, even ruthless,
awareness of her selfhood and her strength, determines the only satisfactory resolution. In order to separate the lovers and fully regain her
husband, she must separate from her father and stepmother. Adam and
Charlotte return to America. Amerigo and Maggie remain in London.
The price of consciousness, of awareness, and of the judgments and
actions that experience demand, is a high one. In this particular contingent world, much as in James's own experience, daughters must be

separated from fathers, the young James from his family and from America. Early on, when given the opportunity by Mrs. Francis Bellingham to see the beautiful bowl, with "the tone of old gold," that King George I had given to his hosts at Lamb House, James had his title and the symbolic representation of the deception.[68] But he had from much farther back the psychological and artistic components of *The Golden Bowl,* whose nuances in regard to consciousness and perception had been in formation in his consciousness from his first visit to Europe as an infant. For James, the nuances of *The Golden Bowl* were more than part of "everything." They created and defined the level of consciousness at work. They were beyond any morality but that of art.

(5)

After almost twenty years of absence, America was increasingly on his mind as the new century began. When he had a letter from a childhood friend, Edward Emerson, memories of Newport made him quiver with tender recollection of two worlds he had left behind, his country and his youth. "I don't know that I could really quite *bear* to see again, with aged eyes, La Farge's beautiful picture of Paradise Rocks—so many dead things would, with the vision, come again too touchingly to life. I've only to close those eyes, however, to call it all up." His reawakened memories went back even farther, to "the Washington Squareish region trodden by the steps of my childhood, and I wonder," he wrote to a new friend, Mary Cadwalader Jones, Edith Wharton's former sister-in-law, "if you ever kick the October leaves as you walk in Fifth Avenue, as I can to this hour feel myself, hear myself, positively *smell* myself doing. But perhaps there are no leaves and no trees now in Fifth Avenue—nothing but patriotic arches, Astor hotels and Vanderbilt palaces." He felt the October leaves gathering about him at Lamb House, the impending short twilights. When, in late 1900, he heard from Annie Fields of a London newspaper rumor that he was considering returning to live in America, he assured her that it was "wantonly woven of air; without a germ of justification at its root. . . . It's embarrassing, ungracious, rude almost, to be saying it, but I am *not* returning to my native land to live or ceasing to live in this snug corner of this one. . . . Such is the shy, the stammering truth."[69] He wanted to revisit, not repatriate.

When Howard Sturgis visited America in autumn 1900, James wrote that "my own imagination recoils before such terrors—so that I always take a certain amount of convincing as to others. How you toss off these great things! I wish you could teach me your way. I *must* go once again, but am afraid to go alone & in fact don't know how." The notion that he *must* go had become set in his mind, at least as an injunction of the imagination, by late 1900. But there were obstacles. He feared the discomfort of the sea voyage itself. Having been sedentary for so long, he did not look forward to making the tedious arrangements, nor did he relish the temporary absence from domestic pleasures and familiar routines. If he went, he needed to do so in a pause between books and also to have some writing arrangement that would make the trip pay, or at least pay his expenses. He had a strong recommendation from an American acquaintance that he give readings in America "for the money and the boom."[70] He initially dismissed the idea; it may have revived a distasteful recollection of Wilde's American tour in 1883. But it may also have, more beneficently, brought to mind Thackeray, whom he had met in his childhood home in New York in 1852, and Dickens, whose 1867 readings in Boston he had tried to attend. If he could manage the finances, he might be able to overcome the other obstacles to something he felt ambivalent about but still more and more interested in doing.

He most of all feared that he would return to a country so vastly changed that he might feel more than ever the permanent exile rather than the visiting son. "*All* reports of the land of my birth . . . are, to me, bewildering now, and I know not what to think of anything," he wrote to Oliver Wendell Holmes. Beyond all the obstacles, as he worked on his recent novels he felt increasingly drawn westward for what he expected would be one last time. "I have never been more curious" about America, "nor interested in it," he wrote to Grace Norton. "The idea of *seeing* American life again & tasting the American air, that luxury & amusement [is] a very difficult one to organize. But if I *could!*—if I *can!*" If he went, he wanted to see more than he had ever seen before, more than the restricted travels of his American years. He would want not only to revisit the scenes of his childhood and youth but, for the first time, to see the South and the West, the palm trees of Florida, the shores of California. He wanted personal expansion, a final travel experience that he could write about. Paradoxically, it would be both a journey backward and forward to the patrimony he had voluntary given up and to the larger America that he had never made his own. At times, he doubted that he had the energy for such a voyage. "You strike me," he wrote to a young friend, as "always in the thick of the fray, and I look at you through a hole in the curtain of a broken-down ambulance pulled off into a distant field." He felt his age. His sixtieth birthday was rapidly approaching. Physically, he was fine, except for being enough overweight, so that with comic exaggeration, he thought of himself as "painfully fat." Occasional attacks of the "gout-fiend" forced him off his feet. But the attacks were manageable. He need not stay home because of his health.[71]

If he went, he would have to protect his time from the press of too many social obligations—"Boston, New York, Washington, all making the most insidious signs to me." Rye solitude made that threat less forceful than it otherwise might have been. He told Sarah Wister that he echoed "without the least reserve" her declaration that he "ought to come home again. . . . My native land, in my old age, has become, becomes more and more, romantic to me altogether: *this* one, on the other hand has, hugely and ingeniously ceased to be. But the case is, somehow, absurdly, indescribably difficult." As much as he was at home in England, he was still a stranger. He missed living in a place that was genuinely home, particularly as his old age approached. But he was, he felt, " 'too late' . . . too late for myself. It would be grotesque to treat the molehill of a 'run' like the mountain of a repatriation (for that I am utterly too late—on all sorts of material grounds as well as others)." He was especially aware, as he wrote his biography of Story, of the price that he had paid for his expatriation. His own situation was the subtext between the lines. "Somehow, in the long-run, Story *paid*— paid for having sought his development" in Europe. "It was as if the circumstances on which, to do this, he had turned his back had found an indirect way to be avenged for the discrimination. Inevitably, indeed, we are not able to say what a lifetime of Boston would have made, in him, or would have marred; we can only be sure we should in that case have had to deal with quite a different group of results." His imagination began to play with the alternative of what he himself might have been if he had never left. "You have written not Story's life," Adams wrote to him, "but your own and mine,—pure autobiography. . . . Improvised Europeans, we were, and—Lord God!—how thin!"[72]

As to his own visit, "I don't, constitutionally, *run;* I creep and crawl and falter and fumble—and in short the question lives in a cloud of complications." The complications gradually resolved themselves. Money had been much on his mind. The trip would be costly, and earnings from recent books hardly permitted him to feel financially expansive. The three hundred pounds he had received for each as an advance against royalties for *The Ambassadors* and *The Golden Bowl* sufficiently exceeded earnings from sales to make him feel both resentful and anxious. When Pinker thought he had "a good opportunity" for American serial publication of *The Golden Bowl,* James "feverishly" divided it into twelve sections. "Then they cruelly cabled 'Declined,' " he told Howells, "& the Golden Dream was as broken outside, as the Golden Bowl within." He wanted additional income to offset the cost of the trip. "I am scared, rather—well in advance," he confessed to William, "by the vision of American expenses." Every book he now published lost money for its publisher. From the generous Macmillan in June 1903, he accepted a proposal to write a book on London. It was to be illustrated by a young American artist Joseph Pennell for a series on European cities, which ironically had as one of its best-selling volumes Marion Crawford's *Ava Roma*. James asked for and received an advance of a thousand pounds. He made it clear, though, that he would not do the book until after returning from America and completing an account of his American impressions for both serial and book publication. He was, he told Macmillan, "thinking, rather definitely, of going to America for 6 or 8 months (some time in 1904)."[73] In early 1904, he delivered the completed manuscript of *The Golden Bowl* to Pinker, for American publication by Scribner's in November 1904, when he expected to be in America, and British publication in early 1905.

William immediately expressed reservations about the wisdom of his brother's tentative plans and stressed the difficulties he would confront returning to what he warned would seem an alien culture. Henry responded with defensive self-justification, as if he were still demonstrating his good sense to his parents, emphasizing that his "primary idea in the matter is absolutely economic." He would have the subject for a new, well-paying book. His presence on the scene would facilitate making "old contracts pay better." Most of all, if he did not go now he would perhaps never go at all. Like the four dogs he had buried "in the little cemetery in the angle" of his garden, he would, if he did not go, be burying himself in the form of a premature acceptance of "incipient senile decay." America was his birthplace. He wanted to revisit before he was so old that he lost "*the impulse* to return." The voyage, he felt, would be revivifying, a travel experience that would at least partly compensate for the more wide-ranging travel that he had never done. He had had, he felt, to give up, "one by one," his visions of exotic places—Spain, Greece, Italy and Egypt—to which both Hay and Adams had invited him. He had always had, he believed, to stay at his desk, grinding away at the wheel of financial necessity. In fact, he recognized, he had hardly traveled at all. He was the most parochial of cosmopolitans. If William's argument or his own timidity resulted in his forgoing this voyage, it would have "all the air of giving up, chucking away without a struggle, the one chance that remains to me in life of anything that can be called a *movement:* my one little ewe-lamb of possible exotic experience."[74]

He had made up his mind that this was a spiritual and professional journey that he could not afford *not* to make. The obstacles were real, and represented by the maze of practical details that had to be attended to. On a dark mid-November afternoon in 1903, courteously seeing off aboard her transatlantic ship Tom Perry's sister (John La Farge's wife), he had an emotional moment of tempting efficiency. "I said to myself 'Now or never is my chance; stay and sail—borrow clothes, borrow a toothbrush, borrow a bunk, borrow $100: you will never be so near it again. The worst is over—the arranging; it's all arranged *for* you, with two kind ladies thrown in.' " If only he had a thick enough overcoat! If only there had been an extra bunk! He "turned and fled."[75] Still, he told Clara and Clare Benedict, Fenimore's sister and niece, who were annual European regulars at Bayreuth, "I want to go as much as ever." He soon made a tentative arrangement to sail with them to New York in August 1904.

He also put his house in order, as best he could. In early February 1902, he had published a memorial essay for Katherine Bronson, who had died in Venice the previous year. In November 1903, he visited "the infinitely touching and backward-reaching Leslie Stephen" on his deathbed, surrounded by "beautiful ghosts, beautiful living images," including his daughters, Vanessa and Virginia. "He is so gentle and friendly to me that he almost makes me cry." He was also leaving behind living friends, one of whom, Jocelyn Persse, a thirty-year-old, handsome, undemanding, well-to-do and well-connected Irishman, with a shock of blond hair and an "enchanted physique," he had met in mid-1903. Without any talent or intellectual interests of his own, the fashionable Persse was the nephew of Lady Gregory, the cofounder of the Abbey Theatre in Dublin, who had been born a Persse and whom James had known in London since the early 1890s. "I . . . envy you . . . the magnificent *ease* with which you circulate & revolve," James told his new friend, "spinning round like a brightly-painted top that emits, as it goes, only the most musical hum." James admired his youth, his beauty, his amiable self-confidence in the London social world, "the mysterious genial power that guides & sustains you through the multitude of your contacts & the mazes of your dance." They quickly became close companions, with an exchange of photographs and the promise of intimacy. "There is, for me, something admirable & absolute between us. . . . But these things are beyond words—words almost vulgarize them. Yet the last ones of your note infinitely move me & I am, my dear Jocelyn, yours ever so tenderly."[76]

He had at last met Edith Wharton, who had been pursuing an introduction since 1885 (they had twice been guests at large dinner parties without their being introduced or his even noticing her). She finally became part of his consciousness in December 1903 when they met in London. Their hesitant relationship was to become unequivocal during his American visit. The next May, the Whartons visited him in Rye, motoring down from London, impressing him with their automobile and their mobility. In early August 1904, despite his conviction that he was "destitute of the English mania for *letting* . . . & for persuading servants to be let," he succeeded in renting Lamb House for six months to an acceptable tenant at five pounds a week. He was pleased that the house and the servants, even his "precious" dachshund puppy, Max, his fifth effort at having a reliable, undemanding household companion, were in good hands. When he learned that Howard Sturgis was also sailing to America, he excitedly hoped they might be shipboard companions. Since only the most expensive berths were available, Sturgis declined the extravagance. James consoled himself with the likelihood of seeing him in America, particularly at the Whartons' Lenox home, where "Mrs. Wharton has held you out to me as a bait . . . and I have opened my mouth wide."[77]

His late August departure rapidly approaching, he felt "pressed & positively ridden & haunted with things to be done & work, above all, to be finished before I sail. . . . The heat & the crowd & the treacherous depths of the whirlpool" [of London] made him ill. To the Benedicts in Bayreuth, he confirmed, early in July, the irrevocability of his commitment with the news that he had ordered new clothes, bought a steamer trunk, and paid the remainder of his boat fare. From late July, in a miserably torrid summer, he would be at the Reform Club, "watch in hand, timing your approach, reading the weather-prophecies and trying to make a clink in my pocket of my few remaining shillings." He had hoped that Andersen would visit Lamb House before he sailed. Instead, he was to discover, he would have the opportunity to see his young friend in America, at Newport. By late July, he was, he told Ariana Curtis, "pretending hard now, not to be afraid." He had a whole ghostly world of American friends and family, some of whom he had not seen for decades, whose embrace he both yearned for and feared. "I spend the most of September with Wm & Alice at Chocorua. . . . But California is my desired goal." Though he still had "350 things to do" before embarking, he could almost taste his impending victory over his fears, his resistances, the sheer number of details he had had to confront. Friends came to say good-bye. He wrote farewell notes to those already behind him, anticipatory notes to those to come. The weather became a little cooler. On August 24, 1904, at sixty-one years of age, with Constance Woolson's sister and niece, he sailed from

Southampton on the German liner *Kaiser Wilhelm II,* which expected to make the summer crossing to New York in a record five days. Now "bald and grizzled, this perfect American," a description of an American traveler in Europe in one of his early stories, was returning to the New World.[78]

Fourteen

"CLOSING THE GATES"

1904–1910

(1)

Sailing into New York Harbor on August 30, 1904, he saw for the first time technology triumphant. The Republic he had sailed away from twenty-one years before had been transformed into a great modern state; the modest city into which he had been born had become "the most extravagant of cities, rejoicing, as with the voice of the morning, in its might, its fortune, its unsurpassable conditions," from "the throb of ferries and tugs, to the plash of waves and the play of winds and the glint of lights and the shrill of whistles and the quality and authority of breeze-borne cries."[1] The sunlight and the seagulls seemed to be exploding with extravagant energy. Ahead of him, as the massive *Kaiser Wilhelm II,* with three thousand passengers, swung toward its Hoboken pier, the "multitudinous sky-scrapers" dominated the Manhattan sky-line, "like extravagant pins in a cushion already overplanted." The now-obscured Gothic steeple of Trinity Church on lower Broadway had been the tallest pinnacle of the New York skyline of his childhood. When he had departed in August 1883, the towers of the Brooklyn Bridge had been the highest man-made structures in the New World. Now people rode in elevators to building heights that dwarfed even the great technological achievement of twenty years before. It was both frightening and exciting. A new world, for better and worse, had been built on the same ground where the old had been.

Within three hours of docking, he had crossed the Hudson in search of the Manhattan he had known, the familiar scenes of his childhood. Most of them were gone, including the house in which he had been born, or substantially altered except to the quick-rushing, superimposed images of memory. For the moment, the late afternoon glow of Manhattan views provided a warmth of reflections and impressions, mostly sentimental. After an afternoon walking from Washington Square to Union Square and Gramercy Park, he recrossed the Hudson to spend the last night in August at the beachside home of George Harvey, president of Harper & Bros. His firm had contracted to publish some of James's essays on America in *Harper's Weekly* and thereafter a full volume of them. Harvey's private secretary had met him at the Hoboken pier. So too had his nephew Henry James III. Having accepted Harvey's invitation, he left Harry junior to struggle at the dock with his luggage, which was to be sent on to Boston. Newspapers had noted his arrival. Denying requests for interviews, he managed to evade reporters, with the exception, two weeks later, of an interviewer for the *New York Herald*. Exhausted as much as excited, he now rested in what seemed to him the delicious air and light of the New Jersey coast. "Poor dear old Mark Twain" was a fellow guest, stretching his feet on "the deep piazza."[2] Thirty-six hours later, escorted by Harvey's secretary to the train station in New York, he traveled northward to Boston and then to New Hampshire to see William, whom he had not seen since they had parted three years before, and to see his brother's much-vaunted Chocorua paradise for the first time.

In the embrace of William and his family, "full of the stir of very old, & very young, chords of memory," he responded to the astounding New England autumn as if it were a long-lost paradise, an "Arcadian elegance & amiability to which my remembrance hadn't done fair justice. . . . There is a September exquisiteness that I quite drink in." William enjoyed his brother's alert sensibility. "It is a pleasure to be with anyone who takes in things through his eyes," he remarked. "Most people don't." Henry had timed his arrival at Chocorua to experience a full American autumn; one of the great losses of expatriation had been that season of glowing colors that he remembered always as *the* happiest American time. In "this great region of forest & mountain & lake & crystal brook . . . the New England September is glorious & golden," even "beyond what I remembered . . . & there has been a real spell of sweetness on the whole experience." At moments, as he walked over hills and through woods, the countryside seemed lonely, offering solitude as much as beauty. At least "you can read anything you like into it," he wrote to Mary Ward, which "is remarkably convenient." The newspaperwoman from the *New York Herald* disturbed the solitude. "In defiance of all my machinations & escapes from the whole crew since my arrival [she] pushed her way on here today & there is nothing for it (I am told) short of stony cruelty, but for me to see her an hour hence."[3]

He managed the guest and the interview as gracefully as the heavy mailbag filled with letters conveying greetings and invitations, "the enchanted wood of hospitality that appears to frame all my horizon." Annie Fields and Sarah Orne Jewett urged a Boston visit. Sarah Wister from Philadelphia assumed that he would appear there sometime soon, though he shared with her his increasingly anxious sense of the likely clash between his ambitious travel schedule and his limited time. Edith Wharton had already successfully cajoled him to commit himself to stay for a few days in October at The Mount, her new home in Lenox, aware that he would be at least as eager to see Howard Sturgis as to see her. "I am bearing up a little bewilderedly," he told "dearest Howard," in anticipation of their meeting, "but on the whole beautifully, & even to the pitch of extreme enjoyment. This place is both funny & lovely." For a long moment, England seemed far away. "What a chasm of immeasurable width yawns behind one's steps after one has got here; so that it wd. really seem easy to neglect & forget the old world one has quitted—forget it (or at least desperately break with it) for the time, & only to come back to it, after all, ah, with such a rush." He had no intention of not returning. But, in this early happy glow of New England autumn, he determined that June, not earlier as he had thought, would be his departure month. He felt "in substantial touch & fact restored, for the time to the land of my birth!"[4]

But he had also begun to feel anxious, even slightly frightened, in the presence of what he had determined he must experience: the potentially bewildering size and openness of the country, "where one's exposure to unknown correspondents seems to be on the scale of everything else," and those few small places that carried all the lifelong force of emotion. Cambridge was the place where all the significant "motionless ghosts" were assembled. One of the revenants, nearby at Concord, was his brother Bob, to whom he wrote within a few days of his arrival, adding his voice to William's invitation to Bob to join them at Chocorua. "It will minister greatly to the richness of the family life, and the sense of reunion offered to my long-starved spirit, to have you here. The Dead we cannot have, but I feel as if they would be, will be, a little less dead if we three living can only for a week or two close in together here." When Bob declined, Henry promised to make his "pilgrimage" to Concord "for its old ghosts & as a note in the American 'modernity' too."[5] But what he had most essentially, most deeply and emotionally, come for, was his long-desired, long-destined meeting with his beloved ghosts in Cambridge, with Alice and his parents on that high cemetery ridge with Boston in the distance. He had for a long time imagined the scene, the place, even the season and the time of day.

He had various reunions to experience and lesser visits, important as they were, to make in September and October, with Bob in Concord, with Charles Eliot Norton in his study at Shady Hill, with Grace Norton in Cambridge, with Isabella Gardner in Brookline, with Howard Sturgis at Cotuit, with the Whartons in Lenox, and with his Temple cousins in Connecticut. Some of the visits had a mildly elegiac note. At Shady Hill, he walked up onto the porch that he had sat on almost forty years before to find Norton "very ancient & mellow now." His eldest daughter is "much the prettiest. . . . They are known in College as Paradiso, Purgatorio & Inferno. (The 3d. is very plain)." On his first day in Boston, his nephew took him on a tour of the expanded Harvard, where he had the startling sight of an elderly John Chipman Gray, bent over a book, "reading in the great new [Law] Library." Perhaps Minny Temple came sharply to mind. He remembered his "melancholy little years (oh, so heart breaking)" at Dane Hall. At Harvard Yard, he was appalled at the absence of fences, no visual and physical demarcation between college and town, between old and new, his European sense of space demanding definition and refinement. How could one have art, life, and culture without the boundaries that expressive form and discriminating shape demanded? While it was still early autumn, he went with William to Fresh Pond, where he used to walk on Sunday afternoons with Howells. All had changed, except his delight at being with William, who chatted interestingly as they walked home from the tram in the twilight. He admired the memorable "liquidity" of William's "extraordinary play of mind . . . how he gave light and life" to the world about which he spoke.[6]

From Boston, in mid-October 1904, he took the train to Lenox and a carriage the additional two miles to the Whartons' recently built "delicate French Chateau."[7] Acquaintances, they now became friends. Edith was the bookish daughter of an old, wealthy, intellectually dull New York family that had found itself the fortunate possessor of some of Manhattan's most valuable property. In 1885, at twenty-three years of age, shy, nervous, plain-looking Edith Jones had married Edward "Teddy" Wharton, a handsome, mentally plain Bostonian of high social standing, little money, and no ambition to do anything but lead a leisured life. Her imaginative world had been richly peopled by literary reading, a refuge from loneliness and philistinism. Too plain-looking to shine in New York social life, too shy to perform in the Boston social milieu, she carried with her a suppressed but restless sense of alienation and desperation. With a large Newport mansion and a small but handsome Park Avenue brownstone, the newly married Whartons alternated between Newport, New York, and European travel. Deeply depressed by her marriage, which apparently had neither sexual nor emotional nor intellectual rapport, and by her alienation from the worlds into which she had been born and into which she had married, she had a series of nervous breakdowns between 1894 and 1898.

Treated in Philadelphia by Dr. Weir Mitchell, who had treated Alice James twenty-four years before, she recovered her emotional stability, perhaps because she had begun to write seriously. Published in 1897, her first book, *The Decoration of Houses,* was a study of domestic architecture, with which she was helped by an old friend, Walter Berry. Berry's failure years before to propose marriage to her had been a grave disappointment. Her efforts to meet James in 1885 and in 1890 had produced contact but not a meeting. In early 1895, through Minnie Bourget, she had sent him her best wishes for *Guy Domville.* In 1899, she sent James her first volume of short stories, *The Greater Inclination;* in 1900, through Mary Jones, her first novel and another volume of stories; in 1902, her newest novel, *The Valley of Decision.* James finally responded, first with a copy of *The Wings of the Dove,* then with a number of friendly, somewhat magisterial letters that offered qualified praise and the strong advice that she write about and set her fiction in contemporary New York. "The *American Subject*" should be hers. "DO NEW YORK!" he urged. "Profit, be warned, by my awful example of exile & ignorance."[8] He had little sense that one of their shared experiences, since she too had spent many years in Europe, was an affinity for expatriation, an alienation from the American scene—in James already fully expressed, in Wharton mostly incipient, still held back by her American commitments, including Teddy's desire to live in America. Her last, final expression of her temporary repatriation was the imitation French château, The Mount, which she had just had built, lovingly supervising every detail.

They finally met in London in late December 1903. "Mr James came up from Rye," Wharton wrote to a friend, "& spent the day with us. He looks, without his beard, like a blend of Coquelin & Lord Rosebery, but . . . talks, thank heaven, more lucidly than he writes." For James, Wharton was to be a talented, artistically amateurish, psychologically thin novelist whose frenetic life and wealthy milieu seemed incompatible with the literary life. Her great popular successes exemplified the difference between a talented popular novelist and a serious artist like himself. For Wharton, James was always to be a great but semicomprehensible novelist whose novels became more arcane in his later years. While she had liked *The Portrait of a Lady,* the later novels seemed to her unreadable. With his penchant for evasive tactfulness, James always could find something good to say about her latest work.

His complimentary fulsomeness was sometimes a strategy for making criticism more acceptable, for influencing future writing. He had the dubious talent of being able to praise without genuinely liking or even respecting the work in question except insofar as he valued good relations with the author. Sometimes, indeed, she did not need redeeming. Before he left England in August 1904, he had liked some of her recent short stories enough to tell her that "they confirmed me so in my strong sense of your wise & witty art & your real practice of the Mystery."[9]

With her desire to please the older, recognizably great man, Wharton had the social grace and literary wit always to keep her responses to his fiction within the impersonal framework of historical generalities. Except for *Wings* and *The Golden Bowl,* James's fiction was mostly finished before they met. What was new was their genuine interest in one another. Hers was greater, an expression of her desire to have the company of the man many prestigious literary people thought the greatest American writer of his generation. For Wharton, he had an avuncular glow of authority and affection, providing in a limited way the male companionship that she had always wanted and rarely had. For James, Wharton had the attraction of her comparative youth, her talent, her shyness, her wealth, and her witty sociability. Despite their distance from one another's work, it became a sustaining friendship for both of them.

Arriving at The Mount, he was disappointed to learn that Sturgis had canceled his visit because of a death in his Massachusetts family. "I can only howl at losing you," he responded. They had been happily together at Cotuit, on the coast near Boston, for three days in late September before James went to Salisbury, Connecticut, to stay briefly with his Emmet cousins. With a letter of "tender supplication," he and Wharton successfully turned Sturgis' regrets into a postponement until the next week. "Don't fear or doubt this place: it is most soothing, beneficent & harmonious, & we love you, desire you & feel with you, ever so softly & surroundingly. The whole thing here is really too exquisite to miss—& I will keep my arm, all the while, round you . . . even as a brother & a guide. I trust you to understand the nature of this fond pressure." He also exerted epistolary pressure on Jocelyn Persse. His letters to Persse were a form of lovemaking. How wonderful it would be, he wrote to Persse from The Mount, if, as he was driven "through mountain, valley & woodland, & by the blue expanse of recurrent lakes that are both vast & sweet—motor-rides that have converted me to the awful machine . . . I had you beside me to grip, once in a while, at some of the leaps & bounds of the occasionally too primaeval road. But I grip you across the wide sea." He was already, he admitted to Gosse, "transcendently homesick." But he had been sedentary for so long that, despite his terror at the thought of so much traveling, he began to feel like a man of action. "I am getting to brave it, & to like it, as the sense of adventure, of holiday & romance, & above all of the great so visible & observable world that stretches before one more & more."[10]

Instead of staying two or three days, he stayed ten, partly because delaying departure enabled Sturgis to join them, but also because he was having such a good time. His expectation, formed more than two years before when Mary Jones had described to him the splendors of Wharton's "Lenox house," that it "must be a love," was completely fulfilled. He liked the house and its furnishings. The air was like champagne, the weather perfect. "This exquisite Indian summer day sleeps upon these really admirable Massachusetts mountains." Quickly getting over his initial distaste for the automobile, he felt the sheer pleasure of airy mobility and the luxury of a chauffeur-driven car that had the miraculous power to whip them up hills and over the beautiful autumn Berkshire countryside. With thin, airless tires and an open seating compartment, they all wore riding coats and goggles, each drive an adventure on primitive roads that went on and on. "The mountain-and-valley, lake and river beauty extends so far . . . that even the longest spins do not take one out of it."[11] With a house full of invisible servants, an immense stone terrace looking eastward, comfortable fires in the evening, Sturgis' and the Whartons' company, he had a delightful time. Teddy's inarticulate but amiable mentality was limited mostly to sporting events. James enjoyed Edith's good taste and low-key wit, her energy and unpredictable movements. He did not mind too much that everyone in the Wharton neighborhood seemed millionaires. As an example of one aspect of American life, it was better than he had expected.

By late November 1904, in Cambridge again, it was time for him to fulfill the mission for which he had come. The trees were bare, the dusk had begun to fall early, "the western sky more and more turning to that terrible, deadly, pure polar pink that shows behind American winter woods." From William's dark brown solitary house on Irving Street, he walked alone to Cambridge Cemetery. As he stood on the ridge looking at the three graves, night began to fall. "The moon was there, early, white and young, and seemed reflected in the white face of the great empty Stadium, forming one of the boundaries of Soldier's Field, that looked over at me, stared over at me, through the clear twilight, from across the Charles." For the first time, he saw Alice's grave, with William's inscription that mournfully celebrated the resolution of all her pain into this place of peace. To her immediate left, with a space that left room for his own, was his mother's grave and then his father's. Suddenly, "it was the moment; it was the hour, it was the blessed flood of emotion that broke out . . . and carried me away. I seemed then to know why I had done this; I seemed to know why I had *come*. . . . Everything was there . . . the recognition, stillness, the strangeness, the pity and the sanctity and the terror, the breath-catching passion and the divine relief of tears." He cried the tears of a long-delayed fulfillment, the absolute "penetrating *rightness*" of his being there at that moment, "as if one sank down on one's knees in a kind of anguish of gratitude before something for which one had waited with a long, deep *ache*."[12]

He had hoped to spend November 1904 in domestic comfort in Cambridge and much of December in a socially amiable New York. From The Mount, he had returned to Cambridge, enjoying William and Alice's hospitality, and their children, whom he liked. He then spent four days in mid-November at Newport, which he found "quite exquisite, like a large softly-lighted pearl (and with the light partly of far-away associations)," staying with old friends, the Masons. To his delight, Scribner's put into his hands an advance copy of *The Golden Bowl* so handsomely produced that almost for the first time ever he was proud of the physical appearance of one of his books. When Sturgis praised the novel, James admitted that each time a book of his was published he feared "ignoble failure." As he had as a young man, he found the Cambridge "suburban & car-haunting relation to Boston intolerable." Still, Boston itself "doesn't speak to me, never has, in irresistible accents, or affect me with the sweet touch of an affinity. My want of affinity with it in fact is so almost indecent that I have to resort to concealment & dissimulation." Sturgis, who came over from his family hosts at Wellesley to visit at Irving Street, listened to his complaints, mostly about his rarely successful efforts to keep his mornings free for writing. More serious were his abysmal difficulties with his teeth. What had seemed at first some necessary minor dental work had turned into a prolonged, stultifying episode with a Boston dentist, lasting over a month, from November 10 to December 20, blighting "my days, my nights & my nerves breaking quite into my work." It seemed an "interminable nightmare," taking up afternoons and many evenings, interrupting his normal eating patterns—one of the results, a chronic sore throat, and another, attacks of gout. "At the last my Dentist-Demon couldn't *touch* me without torture, and yet I had to be handled by him for hours together." He managed to joke that the work was "a monument of Classical art." But it was mostly "a bottomless gulf of physical agony & financial ruin: the 'bill' as for a great surgical operation."[13]

When he finally got to New York early in December 1904, he had to limit his visit to a few days in order to return to his dental chair. Not that he especially wanted to stay longer. "New York affects me rather fearfully, just on this first blush," he wrote to Hendrik Andersen, whose sister and mother he had visited in Boston, "and I am full of all sorts of homesicknesses and bewilderments. Nevertheless I am interested too: everyone is extraordinarily kind and friendly." As always, he missed Hendrik. "I hold you, dear boy, in my innermost love and count on your feeling me—in every throb of your soul and sense." He had moments of "painful loneliness," particularly for friends in England and for Lamb House. Later in December, with the dental misery over, he returned to New York, which "bristles and blazes," sorry to have left "the blessed shelter of Irving Street; whose every thing is on such high & sustaining lines of felicity & value!" Still, he told Edward Warren, the guardian of the Lamb House hearth, "I find my native land (so far as I've seen it) full of the quality (& still more of the promise, as I sense further) of a bewildering interest." The weather had turned sharply cold, the early harbinger of what was to be the bitterest winter in years. "The awful blasts blowing through the dark canyons formed by the skyscrapers" terrified him. Perhaps he could postpone his necessary weeks in New York for a warmer time. His notion now was "to work southward," particularly to Florida, where Bob's wife and daughter were spending the winter. "I think of the South ever so yearningly," he wrote to his niece. "To get into a comfortable train & simply get there—& then get out in the tropics: that for me is a dazzling vision."[14]

He stayed in New York part of the time with the Whartons but mostly with Mary Jones, in whose handsome home on East Eleventh Street he awoke on New Year's morning 1905. He was "bearing up, but . . . half killed (with kindness)," contemplating the acceleration of his schedule, aware that he would pay for lingering so long in New England. "New York bristles with Babylonian picturesqueness & grovels at the same time with a horror that is only New Yorkese. Through it all it somehow, too, gets you to like it, or forgive it." From East Eleventh Street, he went to the Whartons on Park Avenue. "We were more compressed than at Lenox," he wrote to Sturgis, "& Teddy more sandwiched between, & we gave a little more in each other's nerves, I think, & there was less of the sweet Lenox looseness. Still, she was charmingly kind." On January 9, he traveled to Philadelphia, greeted by Sarah Wister and her son Owen, to give the first of his lectures,

"The Lesson of Balzac," to an audience, more fashionable than literary, of more than five hundred people at the Contemporary Club. "Don't come to my horrid little mercenary lecture if you can possibly help it," he had urged Mrs. Wister, but if you do, "brace yourself." Most important, "*em*brace me!" Despite his lifelong fear of public speaking, the difficulty of sustaining his long sentences through his stammer, and his distinctive, unusual accent, he felt his performance "a complete success, a brilliant one, an easy one," he told William. Filled with good feeling about the kindness and dignity of the Philadelphia people, "the gentlest and most sympathetic in the world," he was also relieved that, on the basis of this experience, he could expect to carry off the rest of his mostly midwestern lectures. His heavy American traveling expenses weighed on his mind. Despite staying with people, the costs were high, his sense of his resources distorted. Quite pleased with himself, from Philadelphia he went on to Washington to experience the long-committed hospitality of Henry Adams, with whom, Adams jokingly remarked, James and La Farge have "engaged rooms," and to see, for the first time since 1883, the provincial city that had now become a world capital.[15]

(2)

Walking up the driveway of the White House in mid-January 1905 to attend an elite dinner as a guest of Theodore Roosevelt and John Hay, he appreciated the architecture of the White House more than he admired its tenant. James had last seen Hay in September 1897 at Surrenden Dering, a spacious country home in Kent that the Camerons had rented to offer live-in hospitality to their American friends, particularly Adams and Hay. As American ambassador to Britain, Hay had made it his summer embassy. Cameron himself mostly stayed away. Lizzie Cameron and Adams seemed as unfruitfully committed to one another as ever. In mid-August 1897, Hay, receiving a telegram from McKinley offering him the office of secretary of state, after some hesitation accepted. In September 1897, with admiration and compassion, James, at Surrenden Dering, said good-bye to his old friend, whom he had hoped to have in England for a longer time.[16] After President McKinley's assassination in September 1901, he was succeeded by Roosevelt, his vice president. Roosevelt had finally arrived at the position he had spent much of his life aspiring to. In James's eyes, Roosevelt made the most of it, elevating himself to the position of "Theodore Rex." He initiated garish pomp and circumstance at the White House, including for the first time putting every staff member in uniform. The new presidency seemed immeasurably distant from the Republic of James's childhood and the simplicity of Lincoln's White House, where Hay, whom Roosevelt had pressured to stay on as secretary of state, had served as one of Lincoln's only two private secretaries. Across Lafayette Square, Adams, who attended neither the large diplomatic reception nor the smaller dinner afterward, sardonically commented, as he had been doing for some time, on the fall of a dignified republic into imperial vulgarity.

To James, sitting for hours one person to the right of "the extraordinary & rather personally-fascinating President," the conqueror of Cuba was personally likable and culturally ugly. The clever, nonstop talker with the aggressively jutting chin advocated patriotism and manliness. "I had a great deal of his extraordinary talk and indescribable, overwhelming, but really very attaching personality," James wrote to Jessie Allen. He is an "extraordinary creature for native intensity, veracity and *bonhomie*," with a raw energetic charm that sometimes captivated, as it did Edith Wharton, and sometimes repelled, as it did Adams. He seemed "a wonderful little machine. . . . It functions astoundingly, and is quite exciting to see. But it's really *like* something behind a great plate-glass window 'on' Broadway," a department-store display, an American spectacle.[17] James's more complicated response was embedded partly in his fear of an imperial presidency, his detestation of American aggression in the Spanish-American War, his distrust of Roosevelt's impetuosity, and particularly his sense that the homophobic Roosevelt reduced all the rich complications of personality, intellect, and culture to simplistic slogans and primitive resolutions.

Roosevelt's anxiety about James was equally self-defining. In 1894, Roosevelt had written in "What Americanism Means" of that "miserable little snob" whose Anglophilia he detested, "the undersized man of letters who flees his country because he, with his delicate, effeminate sensitiveness, finds the conditions of life on this side of the water crude and raw; in other words, because he finds that he cannot play a man's part among men." In 1898, James had retaliated, reviewing Roosevelt's *American Ideals and Other Essays*. Roosevelt's interesting exposition "of experience and participation," James wrote, is undermined "by the puerility of [the author's] simplifications." For James, almost "the worst feature" of that "hideous American episode," McKinley's assassination, was that he did not "either like or trust the new President, a dangerous and ominous Jingo—of whom the most hopeful thing to say is that he may be rationalized by this sudden real responsibility."[18] If he had had any inclination to take personal offense, it would have been at Roosevelt's attack in expressively sexual terms on the kind of sensibility with which James was quietly associated. At dinner, the two men chatted as if they had never done anything but compliment one another.

Washington itself he found "delightfully amiable," even more the self-conscious city of conversation and hospitality than it had been twenty years before. It now had a new and more prominent role in world affairs, which James's friends helped define. James was delighted to see Jusserand again, now French ambassador to Washington, "all pleasant welcome & hospitality." Senator Henry Cabot Lodge, who took him to visit the Senate, and his wife, with whom he was becoming pleasantly friendly, and whose handsome son, Bay Lodge, he grew fond of, entertained him. So did the Hays, each lunch, each dinner, rippling with additional guests in "this so oddly-ambiguous little Washington," whose charm overcame its nullity. He made a pilgrimage to Washington Cemetery in the rain to visit Clover Adams' grave and La Farge's statue of a veiled figure that memorialized Adams' grief. From Adams' extraordinary house on H Street, James went back to Philadelphia for five "hyperborean days" with Sarah Wister. He read his essay on Balzac again, this time at Bryn Mawr College to an audience of about seven hundred. He was surprised and delighted at how easily he was earning his bread and butter. Staying at people's homes was more difficult. Much as he liked "poor dear queer flat comfortable Philadelphia," he was happy to leave the tensions of Butler Place, where Sarah Wister got on his nerves, and to head southward. The "Florida names & places" that Wister recommended seemed "to exhale warm air & to dangle patches of blue sea."[19]

After two dreary days in what seemed to him a culturally desolate Richmond, he arrived in early February 1905, with a howling snowstorm pushing at his back, at what turned out to be the most extraordinary house he had stayed in or visited so far, George Vanderbilt's immense imitation French château, Biltmore—a wintry ice palace, isolated in the high snowbound foothills of the Blue Ridge Mountains in Asheville, North Carolina. Everything was so cold to sight and touch that he felt his eyes would freeze, the flesh of his hands stick to surfaces. This was not what the South was supposed to be like. With a sudden severe gout attack, he went to bed soon after he arrived, his left foot immersed in a hot medicinal solution, the rest of him chattering with cold and loneliness. His room, which not even roaring fires could keep warm, overlooked "an ice-bound stable-yard." The "blessed new remedy *Aspirin*," which he had recently discovered, helped with the pain. He was the only guest. Apparently, everyone else had sent their regrets. Vanderbilt seemed a hopelessly amiable dullard, slowly awakening from his Biltmore delusion into the reality of the impossibility of the location for the social life, at least during the winter, that its immensity implied—"a thing of the high Rothschild manner." The "strange, colossal heartbreaking house," with "spaces too vast for a gouty patient to hobble about," felt "more or less [like] a cave of the winds." Imagine, he wrote to the curious Sturgis, "three or four Rothschild houses" rolled "into one, a principality of mountain, lake & forest, 200,000 acres, surround *that* with vast states of niggery desolation, & make it impossible, through distance & time, to get almost any one to stay with you, & you have the bloated Biltmore."[20]

After his requisite week, he wearily fled, still hobbling, from its "polar rigour" and misconceived giganticism. Taking the overnight train to Charleston, where Owen Wister awaited him for a two-day visit, he suddenly had his first long-anticipated taste of mild weather. "I *yearn* for your sunshine—I languish for your balm," he wrote to Bob's wife, Mary James in St. Augustine, with the details of his arrival time. Meanwhile, Charleston, which seemed "charming—blighted though it be," had much to offer: its historical monuments; the visible social life of a southern city, where the blacks seemed to him more vigorous and more interesting than the whites; and the special associations of his Civil War youth that he brought to his first sight of the American flag flapping in the breeze above the walls of Fort Sumter. The Civil War ruins interested him more than anything else. As they stood at the battery, looking out at the fort, Wister remarked that the sight of it made his "heart harden again to steel." To James, it all looked different from how he had so often imagined it. Apparently the one ruin he had no desire to see was Fort Wagner. As he looked out at the harbor in the mild afternoon light, "the whole picture . . . exhaled an innocence. . . . The Forts, faintly blue on the twinkling sea, looked like vague marine flowers. . . . The antique folly" seemed "conjured away."[21]

On a rainy Sunday morning, he left Charleston by train, having in mind, as he almost always did now, a self-conscious record of his impressions for the book that he hoped shortly to begin about his American experiences. "The restless analyst," which he named himself, replaced "the sentimental traveller" of his early European days. Whereas Europe had displayed picturesque historicism, America now presented social issues. Also, his own interests had changed. The issues arising out of his visual and social observations, the daily pregnant significance of what he saw and heard, preoccupied him: the comfortable cavernous American hotels, the apparent inaptitude of blacks for personal service, the efficiency of luggage transportation, the lone child with the run of the breakfast table, the independence of American women as travelers, the effect of the vast distances and cultural thinness on manners and emotional states, his constant awareness of innumerable disproportions and alien manners, the sheer wearisomeness of travel in a country in which so many people seemed, effortlessly, to be on the move. To some extent, as he wrote to Howells, he was "simply clutching the sides of the car of the balloon for dear life, and feeling, with the vast movements of the monster, that this was all that could be asked of me." At the same time, tenaciously, he held both to his schedule and his work, less fragile than his friends had feared. If he never became, as Norton hoped he would, "acclimated to our democratic social vulgar atmosphere," and never completely lost "the terror" that he had declared had possessed him during the first months of his visit, he was not as helpless as Norton had imagined. Norton's concern for his old friend, though, went beyond the immediate. "His essential solitariness & the blankness of the years before him, have invested him with a garment of pathos."[22] But the anxiety was misplaced in regard to his immediate toughness and his commitment to get the most from his effort.

From rainy Charleston James descended into the mildness of Savannah and then, the next night, to Jacksonville. "The air was divinely soft—it was such a Southern night as I had dreamed of." Florida did not disappoint him, his first (and last) venture into a semitropical world with which his European travel had never provided him. After dinner, on the hotel porch in Jacksonville, Florida, as he smoked his occasional cigarette, there emerged for him "the finer vibration of a sense of the real thing"—the dusky evening, the dusty air, the tropical vegetation. For ten days in mid-February 1905, first in Palm Beach, where he saw the "hotel-spirit" of his wandering childhood broadened into its largest expression, then in disappointing St. Augustine, with its "poor little scraps of Florida's antiquity, so meagre & vague," he luxuriated in his escape from "the grim white north." In St. Augustine, he joined Mary and her daughter, both of whom he liked, especially his attractive niece. As he had with Peggy at Rye, he found "the relation of Uncle & Niece full of satisfaction, of all pleasant possibilities. She is intelligent & charming. One can really talk with her." Florida seemed to him mostly delightful, mysterious, warm, dark, inscrutably American, "the softest lap the whole South had to offer," a new world of exotic sensuality, like the Nile and Egypt without Cleopatra and the Sphinx. Most of all, "the [Florida] softness was divine—like something mixed, in a huge silver crucible, as an elixir, and then liquidly scattered." He had had "a revelation of the possible blandness & munificence of nature in these latitudes (I had never had it anywhere else). . . . But "the true revelation

. . . is that of the huge American people taking its ease in its huge American hotels . . . with a wondrous liberality . . . decent, gregarious & moneyed," though "unacquainted with the rudiments of tone, or indeed with any human utterance."[23]

He gave a little howl of distress as he trained northward. The winter chill froze his spirit. Since he had ahead of him some visits to his "Dentist of Damnation," he would have preferred to be completely numb. As he arrived in New York, the heaviest blizzard since 1888 covered the city with three feet of snow. At Irving Street, at the beginning of March, he prepared himself for his longest, most demanding excursion, first to the Midwest for a series of lectures, then to California. Fortunately, he had taken the advice "on the subject of preparing a lecture" that Howells had given him when visiting Lamb House in June 1904. "That advice has been blest to me," he wrote to Howells, now wintering in Italy, "for it is helping to see me through. Without it, I really think I should have had a collapse." He was about to *"re-spout"* it in Indianapolis, St. Louis, and Chicago, for "a positively quite maximum fee" of five hundred dollars a lecture. Early in March 1905, he left for almost three weeks in the Midwest. As he traveled across the snow-covered landscape, Roosevelt celebrated the inaugural of his first full term, and William prepared to sail eastward to Mediterranean sunshine. In St. Louis, Henry read his Balzac lecture to the Contemporary Club; in Chicago, to the Century and the Fortnightly; in his one day in South Bend, in the morning at Notre Dame and in the afternoon at the Convent School; in Indianapolis, to three separate organizations. Responding as much to the sight of a literary celebrity as to the interest of his words, the large audiences provided respectful acclamation. His appearances were prominently reported in local newspapers. Though he thought his lecture "too special and literary" for these disparate groups, he felt that he was "truly earning" his bread, even at the cost of his own infinite boredom with his one prepared script. Amid Chicago's dark wintry hugeness, exhausted from the lecturing, he yearned for Lamb House almost with "nostalgic *rage.*"[24]

But he also had a rage to see California. From Chicago, he traveled three days and nights, "an endless dreary weary run," despite the comfortable train, "through desperate 'alkali' deserts of Kansas, New Mexico & Arizona," both fascinated and horrified by the endlessness of the landscape. "This country is too *huge,* simply, for any human convenience, & so unalterably empty that I defy any civilization, any mere money-grabbing democracy, to make on it any impression of the name. It has made worthy none yet, save that of the 3 or 4 long transcontinental railways." In Los Angeles, "at the end of the awful dusty grind," he stepped into the balmy late March air and into the exotic vistas that warmed his body and filled his eyes, "this extraordinary California . . . this great blooming *garden-realm,* enclosed between the grand mountains & the Pacific." From his hotel in downtown Los Angeles, he went almost immediately to see the ocean, "the great green Pacific." On either side of the route from Los Angeles to Santa Monica were "golden orange groves." The hillsides, covered with what seemed purple irises, the "great violet mountains" in the distance, then the coral and jade intensity of his first sight of the ocean, stunned him with their beauty. It was as if, suddenly, he had come to a coastline whose aesthetic intensity awaited a culture to complement it, a magnificent Riviera without people or history.[25]

Southern California "has completely bowled me over," he wrote to his sister-in-law. "No one had given me the least inkling that I should find [it] so sympathetic." Within a few days, he went to Coronado Beach, in San Diego, to stay at the highly recommended Hotel del Coronado for a restful, restorative week after his exhausting midwestern schedule. "The days" were "of heavenly beauty, and the flowers, the wild flowers just now in particular, which fairly *rage,* with radiance, over the land, are worthy of some purer planet than this. I live on oranges and olives, fresh from the tree, and I lie awake nights to listen, on purpose, to the languid lisp of the Pacific, which my windows overhang." During the day, sitting by the "green Pacific" whose "soft breath . . . cools and studies and inspires," he felt more imaginatively alive than he had since leaving England, overflowing with memories of all his American years before he had expatriated himself, with the sense that nothing of the distant or the recent past had been lost. "Everything sinks in . . . everything abides and fertilizes and renews its golden promise."[26]

Aware now that he had scheduled too little time for the California visit, that two full months rather than less than one would have been more sensible, he felt annoyed at his need to rush and condense. He consoled himself with the notion that he could not have known, that such a misjudgment had been inevitable. Returning to Los Angeles, he read his lecture, which had become loathsome to him through repetition, to a huge audience at a woman's club. At least "I make them pay me through the nose." He consoled himself with thoughts of his July departure for England. In better spirits, at the beginning of the second week in April 1905 he took the train northward, "spent and sore with the process" of seeing his "native country," to "Monterey & Frisco (for 4 days only)." He had, he wrote to Lapsley, "promised to go to Berkeley (for 2 hours,) to inhale the fragrance of your memory there." In

San Francisco, he lectured to the Bohemian Club, met Enrico Caruso, spent a tedious afternoon with Stevenson's widow, and thought the scenery more interesting than the local culture. He went farther northward, to Portland and Seattle, where he visited with Bob's son Edward, who later reported that his uncle "was bored by the west, by the 'slobber of noises,' which we call our language, by the stream of vacant stupid faces on the streets and everywhere the 'big ogre of business.' "[27] From Seattle, he took a sleeper to St. Paul, where he spent a night, then to Chicago, which he immediately left, awakening the next day in the Albany of his childhood. He was relieved to be in Greenwich Village the next morning, in cosseted luxury at Mary Jones's. Almost immediately, he lectured in New York, then in Washington at the end of April, and at Smith College in Massachusetts at the beginning of May. After a brief visit to Boston and Cambridge, once again he was in New York at the end of the first week in May, this time to stay for three weeks. He was at last face to face with his long-delayed necessity of gathering New York impressions.

New York's past was partly his own. From New York's present and future he felt mostly excluded. When he went to see his birthhouse, he found a New York University building on its site. The family home on Fourteenth Street had recently been torn down. A nearby church, a monument to eternity, whose erection he had watched as a child, had disappeared. Change happened so rapidly, so persistently, that not only had much of the New York into which he had been born been essentially obliterated but the New York that was being built when he was a child had not even outlasted the years he had been away. The city did not allow the opportunity for people to accumulate shared communal memories symbolized by enduring structures. The new buildings seemed almost always worse than those they replaced. Skyscrapers dwarfed the desirable human scale and demanded dependence on elevators, crowded cages that seemed to James to diminish the most luxurious privilege of all, privacy. Buildings should never exceed, he believed, the height of what the eye can take in without raising one's head. In elevators, he felt squeezed; by skyscrapers he felt dwarfed. At the corner of Fifth Avenue and Forty-second Street, where until recently had stood a huge reservoir, he took aesthetic comfort in the humanistic proportions of the new library whose construction he paused to watch. Another exception to dehumanized gargantuanism was the new parkside building of the Metropolitan Museum, the second new one since he had been taken as a child to the original gallery on Fourteenth Street. The constant destruction seemed to him, as did so much of New York, driven by the city's commitment to money and power, and by real estate, as the generating machine of American materialism.

When he had first arrived in late August 1904, he had seen, near the New Jersey dock, a large group of laborers, who he soon realized were Italian immigrants. In September, having lost his way on a long walk in the woods near Chocorua, he had met, at the parting of two roads, a dark-eyed young man whom he had asked for directions. The man had stared back at him blankly. Since the man looked Latin, he had assumed he was French Canadian. But he had not responded to the question put to him in French, then in Italian. "What *are* you then?" James had asked. Somehow the young man now understood. " 'I'm an Armenian,' he had replied, as if it were the most natural thing for a wage-earning youth in the heart of New England to be." In Boston and New York, he silently asked, looking at the ethnic faces, "*whom did they look like the sons of?*" What would happen to the American physiognomy in the inevitable intermarriages between the old and the new? In Boston, the answer mostly reduced itself to Italian or Irish. In New York, the melting pot had a thicker stock, fuller, more varied, the process of transmutation so slow as to seem intractable. What was happening to the America he had known? At Ellis Island, he spent some hours watching "the ceaseless process of the recruiting of our race, of the replenishing of our huge national *pot au feu*." The visual splendors of the bay were nothing to the startling impact of actually seeing a portion of the million "immigrants annually knocking at our official door." "The question that hangs so forever before one here [is] that of what effect of the great infusion (call it that) is going to be."[28] He had no doubt that the immigrants would become the defining measure and characterizing force of the American future.

With New York handsomely available to him in the bright, mild spring weeks of May 1905, he went out in every direction. He admired the handsome new rows of apartment buildings and the dignity of Grant's Tomb on the Upper West Side, noticing that so mobile was everything American that even Columbia College had moved. After wandering through Central Park, he was struck by the "golden elegance" of Saint-Gaudens' statue of Sherman being led by "winged-victory." He enjoyed the comfort of some of the nearby clubs at which he was a welcome guest, and the infinite variety of New York street and social life that had a distinctiveness of energetic vulgarity. It seemed a city "where the very restaurants may on occasion, under restless analysis, flash back the likeness of Venetian palaces flaring with the old carnival." Behind the carnivalesque masks he saw his own real face

imaging, and his own restless mind analyzing, the ambivalence he felt
in confrontation with the ultimate variety, the stranger's face, the non-
English-speaking people who seemed to dominate the city. In early
June, with an expert guide from the community, he went to the Lower
East Side, to the dense commingling of southern Italian and Slavic
European Jewish immigrants, particularly to visit the energetic Yiddish-
speaking world, to see for himself the extent and the character of "the
Hebrew conquest of New York."[29]

The numbers, the sounds, the busy streets, rose in the twilight to
his vantage point, a multitudinous swarming of the assertive, prolific
Orthodox assured in their God-ordained certainty that all the important
things of the world belonged to them, emblemized by "the intensity of
the Jewish aspect . . . that makes the individual Jew more of a concen-
trated person, savingly possessed of everything that is in him than any
other human, noted at random." He had the highest regard for the
vitality that such intensity implied. His hesitation was about how its
values would affect other values that he cherished, particularly privacy,
separateness, individual dignity, and the standards of decorum that he
had been born into and had assumed would always define the American
experience. Looking at the tumultuous, overfilled tenement streets, the
fire escapes like external staircases, he was for the moment frightened
by the sheer, unconscious, unintended, but devastatingly effective impact this foreign culture would have on traditional arrangements. He
had at the same time intimations of hope, the optimism that such
intensity would produce enough wealth to overcome poverty, to transform the slums into a "New Jerusalem."

Worried that the American gift to the immigrant would be the
"freedom to grow up to be blighted," perhaps "the only freedom in
store for the smaller fry of future generations," he gazed into his crystal
ball with a keen sense of what some of the crucial issues would be for
the pluralistic society taking shape before his eyes. Though the immediate social issues distressed him, as a writer, the crucial issue framed itself
for him in terms of the fate and the future of the English language. The
words of Shakespeare, Milton, and Dickens, he feared, were likely, like
himself, to become strangers in the country that their language had
created. Just as surely as restless New York had obliterated the house
in which he had been born, an ever-changing America would obliterate
the culture in which its origins had been forged. Without a shared
history and language, the Anglo-American alliance would be threatened. The immigrants eventually would bring other loyalties, other
national affiliations, into American politics and policy. And what new
language would come out of the polyglot transformations of this lin-

guistically plural, multicultural Babylon? He strained to hear the "Accent of the Future." The language of America "may be destined to become the most beautiful on the globe and the very music of humanity . . . but whatever we shall know it for, certainly, we shall not know it for English—in any sense for which there is an existing literary measure."[30] What he most feared was that this new society would have no place for him. He had spent a lifetime creating works of literary art in a language that might be as irrelevant, impenetrable, and foreign in the American future as he felt himself to be on the Lower East Side.

As the weather became warmer, he looked eagerly to the date of his departure, scheduled with inadvertent irony for the Fourth of July. He still had some lectures to give in late May at Harvard, then in June in Baltimore and at Bryn Mawr, where for the commencement address he would read a new essay that was prompted by his long-standing concern with what seemed to him the relationship between the ugliness of American pronunciation and the national character. It was an idealized disquisition on mellifluous pronunciation as a moral quality. Witty and quaint, the lecture had as its subtext his anxiety about a readership in America for his own works. At Atlantic City, he enjoyed the relief of the ocean breezes. He had gotten some writing done, including his New England chapters, which the *North American Review* published in three sections from April to June 1905. But since he had not written nearly as much as he had hoped, he would have to do most of the book after his return. Pinker arrived from London, among other things to begin negotiating with Scribner's a project that he and James had discussed in England, a sizable edition of the fiction by which he wanted to be represented, with substantial revisions of the older pieces to bring them up to his present standard. The idea had originated with Scribner's in April 1900, and been put on indefinite hold. In New York, in mid-June, he embraced Hendrik Andersen, another expatriate making one of his more frequent returns, to whom America seemed "the same busy, rushing, colossal place, almost over-powering!" and James "a howling success" who was "very much lionized." Having promised to visit Howells, James went up to York Harbor, Maine, to stay for a few days with the friend who had "dreaded for him his coming" to America and who suspected that it had been even worse than he had feared. Actually, it had been much better than Howells ever knew. James's mood at Kittery reflected his impatience to return home after such a long visit, especially when the "hottest weather of the summer," which he hated and for which Howells felt somehow responsible, bathed him in an irritable "sea of perspiration."[31]

From Kittery he went to Newport, via Boston, where he had a last visit with Annie Fields, feeling "decidedly spent, and at the end of my tether," particularly with people and hospitality. "I am 'feeling my age' and fearing the cord will, nervously, snap." Newport refreshed him, as it always had. So too did Andersen, who joined him there, where they spent much of three days together. "I took James about," Hendrik wrote to his mother, "and we had some pleasant talks and he spoke of Newport of fifty years ago and his father's house and of many of the old families here." One evening after dinner, James read his Bryn Mawr lecture on American speech to an audience of five people. "Well," Andersen remarked," all those things will come in good time, I suppose." From Newport, where Andersen saw him off at the station, he went to The Mount for a promised second visit. Teddy Wharton was away fishing in Canada. Walter Berry was also a guest. Though Wharton had hoped that he would bring Howells with him, James's supposition that "he wouldn't prove induceable . . . he somehow never is," proved correct. He had been looking forward to a revival of his happy autumn days in the Berkshires, particularly the automobile drives "of the Pagellino vintage." Their diminutive for the Whartons' new car was one of many sobriquets he was to invent over the years, this one an expression of their mutual fascination with George Sand's erotic life.[32]

Noticeably oppressed by the heat, his "already broad" bodily surface seemed to Wharton "to expand to meet it. . . . Electric fans, iced drinks, and cold baths" gave "no relief." Imagining that the hot weather would damage his health, particularly his heart, he found relief only in "incessant motoring" and with the nocturnal coolness. The Whartons' powerful car aggressively absorbed the mountain miles and churned up steady breezes so refreshing that, despite the dust, he was happy to be on the move as much and as fast as possible. One day they drove forty miles to Ashfield to visit Norton at his summer home, where James seemed to his critical host "a most pathetic figure in his solitude." Norton could not imagine that James had no regrets about being childless. "Children by all means to those who want them, is always my feeling," James had told Grace Norton. "I don't want them myself, but I *should,* myself, like a grandchild." One night, on the cool terrace at The Mount, he surprised his hostess and Walter Berry by reading aloud in a deeply rich, flexible voice Emily Brontë's "Remembrance." His normally slow, hesitant speech, a strategy for suppressing his stammer, became, as if by magic, unhesitatingly clear and steady. Another day, when someone spoke of Whitman, Wharton put into James's hand a copy of *Leaves of Grass*. "All that evening we sat rapt while he wandered from 'The Song of Myself' to 'When lilacs last in the door-yard bloomed.' " When he read "Lovely and soothing Death," "his voice filled the room like an organ adagio." He then crooned, "Out of the Cradle" "in a mood of subdued ecstasy." Wharton was delighted to discover that he thought Whitman, as she did, "the greatest of American poets." She was unaware of his hostile review of *Drum-Taps* years before and of the long process of sexual self-acceptance that had allowed him to become a lover of Whitman. "He read from his soul, and no one who never heard him read poetry knows what that soul was."[33]

Distressed that he was suffering so severely from the heat, Wharton asked Berry, whom James liked, to suggest to him that she telephone to arrange passage on a steamer leaving from Boston in two days rather than his passage a week later. "*Two days*—how could I lightly suggest anything so impractical? And what about his heavy luggage, which was at his brother William's in New Hamshire? And his wash, which had been sent to the laundry only the afternoon before? Between the electric fan clutched in his hand, and the pile of sucked oranges at his elbow, he cowered there, a mountain of misery, repeating in a sort of low despairing chant: 'Good God, what a woman—what a woman! Her imagination boggles at nothing! She does not even scruple to project me in naked flight across the Atlantic.'"[34] James stayed on at The Mount, and in America, despite the heat, a few days more.

From Cambridge, at the beginning of July 1905, he prepared for his departure; there were sad family farewells, but also impatience to be off at last. He was happy to learn that Berry, whom he had urged the month before to take the *Saxonia* from Boston, and his friend Elizabeth Robins would sail with him. He confessed to his sister-in-law that "so much travelling and lecturing and seeing and doing have been a great deal of a strain and a tension; the final result of which, these last days . . . is something of a collapse." He longed "for the peace of home & a return to normal conditions. . . . I have felt, all these last weeks, that the strain is getting rather the better of me. But my natural habitat & a return to regularity & *privacy* (in particular!) will cure all that!" His mind, though, for a moment, was focused on what he was leaving behind. Before sailing, he learned of John Hay's death and wrote immediately to Clara Hay "to hold out my hand, in all deep tenderness, as a very old friend—full, to keenest pain, of the memory of his kindness, his sympathy & generosity to me for long years." The irretrievable losses were accumulating. He did not think that he himself would ever return to America. At sixty-two years of age, he felt that his traveling days were behind him. He had dealt, as best he could, with the question of expatriation. Though America was and would always be his land of self-formation and self-definition, his home was England. He had hoped that he had closed the gates on his American experience. Why, Howells asked, thinking about "the folly of nationalities and the stupid hypocrisy of patriotism," should not James or even he himself "live forever out of America without self-reproach? The worst is perhaps that he will grow lonelier with age. But one grows lonely with age, anywhere!"[35]

(3)

Back from his "long American carnival" by mid-July 1905, he got to work as quickly as he could on *The American Scene*, the title he had settled on since his preference, *The Return of the Native*, had been pre-empted. He felt in good health, energetic but burdened with work. One great advantage of being home was that he could more regularly practice "Fletcherizing," the doctrine espoused by an American nutritionist that chewing all one's food into liquid pulp was necessary for sound digestive and bodily health. By early 1904, he had become an enthusiastic convert. "It's the greatest thing that ever was," he told a friend. "Grapple it to your soul with hoops of steel." Fletcherizing "*has renewed my elderly life,*" working "off all my ailments of dire and lifelong indigestion, gout and rheumatism." For long periods, he sat at his meals, slowly masticating every fiber into mush, even when dining out. Dining out less, though, was an advantage both to his digestion and his work. " 'No, I *don't* go out to supper'—it's a proceeding . . . that I have utterly foresworn and unspeakably abhor. . . . I swore my mighty oath. 'No more, no more!' "

At home, domestic arrangements needed readjustment and replenishing, his tenant having driven away some of his servants. Lamb House, as always, seemed a wonderful refuge but also a tedious responsibility. Mounds of correspondence, often fifteen letters high, appalled him; there was "a mountain of arrears," as well as new business. "I squeak . . . from under it like a ridiculous mouse." Mary Weld was no longer available to take dictation. He made do, for a time, with unimpressive substitutes. Fortunately, his hand had recovered sufficiently from its carpal tunnel syndrome for him to write, if necessary, many of his own letters. The most precious of these were to Sturgis, to Persse, to Fullerton in Paris, and to Andersen, who went directly back to Rome in the autumn. He sent them with caressing warmth and his usual expressive mea culpas for his difficulty in finding time for correspondence. Within weeks of returning, he also began revising *The American* and *Roderick Hudson,* the two novels chosen to initiate the selected edition of his works. It was to be called the New York Edition in explicit homage to his "native city." Scribner's had agreed to publish it in a deluxe edition. When a well-wisher explicitly questioned his judgment in having decided to revise his earlier work, he confidently appealed to his "own lucid literary sense." If he were not to "revise closely," then, he argued, he would have to reprint everything he had ever written. "Trust me—I shall be justified."[36] Mulling over how many volumes it would contain and his principle of selectivity, he hoped that its imposing monumentality and physical beauty would speak forcefully to the reading audience of the claim that he believed his fiction legitimately had on its attention. The pain of being the most famous unread writer in the world he transformed into desperate revisionary energy, into an opportunity to make a better, more attractive, more widely available text out of the text of his entire lifetime as a writer.

Having failed in his expectation that he would write much of *The American Scene* in America, he feared that if he did not get his impressions down on paper as quickly as possible they would fade away. Already having been paid an advance of fourteen hundred dollars from *Harper's Magazine* for four of the essays, he needed to get those done as well as those he had committed to the *North American Review*. Two more were to be placed with *The Fortnightly Review*. Having already earned over four thousand dollars from his lectures, he had the prospect of earning more than nine thousand dollars in 1905, more than he had ever earned before and a sum the like of which he had not even approached except in the banner year of 1888. By late November 1905, his American impressions seemed to be "taking, irresistibly and inevitably, the form of two moderately long books," which, for the moment, he thought of as a first and a second series, totally independent of one another. "Purely book-making and universally (otherwise) dumb," by the end of the year he had completed his essays on New England, New York, Washington, D.C., and Philadelphia, reserving the South, the Midwest, and California for a second volume.[37]

Having just had hot-water heating and radiators installed, he could now work comfortably during the winter even in the garden house. But the new indoor warmth did not warm him to the task of the second volume, which, as he completed the first and began to write the essays on his visits to Charleston and to Florida, slipped away from him. As he confronted "the immense incoherence of American things," he found the problems of formal organization difficult, even wearisome. "I am gouging it out as I can," he told Paul Bourget. As he began to work, during spring 1906, more and more on the revisions for the edition, he put off the second volume for a time. By the next spring, "a projected sequel [had] proved so difficult" that he had "given it up altogether." Whether he articulated it to himself or not, the midwestern and far western travels had had for him little autobiographical force. On the East Coast, he had been visiting the world that had made him what he had become, a world where impressions were richest and most personally significant and where, in his eyes, the complicated urban scenes most fully touched on the problems of the American future. For him, California was a travel essay; Boston and New York were autobiography, both personal and national. One of his responses to America he dramatized three years later in "The Jolly Corner," a psychological ghost story set in New York City, at the climax of which the main character sees the figure of a man who looks just like himself. When, from in front of his face, the man removes his hand, from which he has lost two fingers, he sees a horribly disfigured face, a projection of what he would have become if he had never left America.[38]

In his initial discussions with Pinker on the New York Edition, he had insisted that the volumes were to be handsome, which, though apparently he did not make the connection, also meant expensive. He had also made up his mind that it would not "include absolutely *every-thing*. . . . I want to quietly disown a few things by not thus supremely adopting them." As he worked out the pattern for the edition, he came to a total of twenty-three volumes, with the possibility of "a supplementary volume or two" if he should later feel he had missed something essential, and of additional volumes for his new novels. When Scribner's expressed dismay at the possibility of his exceeding the twenty-three volumes, he stoically embraced the limitation. To the dismay of Howells, who thought it "the greatest blunder and the greatest pity," he omitted *The Bostonians,* partly because it pained him to reread it. Also, he felt revising it would be a massive undertaking that he would rather indefinitely postpone. It would take "a great deal of artful re-doing."[39] *Washington Square,* which he found impossible to reread, he set aside with less sense of loss. *Watch and Ward* and *Confidence* were among the novels he quietly disowned. He excluded a number of stories only because of space.

The edition was an immense challenge; he insisted that his earlier novels had to be substantially rewritten, and he had committed himself to writing a preface of about five thousand words for most of the volumes—"My convictions, meditations, fantastications (whatever they may be abusively called), on the great craft & mystery." He attempted to explain the circumstances in which each novel had been written and to provide a theoretical, an imaginative, and a metaphorical exegesis both on the challenges of writing the particular work at issue and on the general guidelines that help define fiction as an art. What he had most in mind was "a sort of plea for Criticism, for Discrimination, for Appreciation on other than infantile lines."[40] Summarizing a lifetime of thought and practice, he stressed the uniqueness of each work and the crucial considerations of narrative integrity and artistic vision that, for him, governed the creation of each novel and short story. Most of all, he provided a partly remembered, partly created record of his sense of what the experience of writing that particular work had been. As to the revisions, they reflected his absolute belief that his style in the present was the evolutionary result of a lifetime of effort and experiment. The Henry James that he wanted posterity to read was the Henry James of the first years of the twentieth century.

He had engaged a young American photographer-friend, Alvin Coburn, to do the illustrations for the London book he was to write for Macmillan. After some initial hesitation, he had decided that each volume of the New York Edition would have a photographic frontispiece, which he hoped would communicate something of the mood of the work it represented. James chose Coburn for this also. Coburn had written to him in New York in January 1905 asking permission to photograph him, which he did in April. James liked and respected the talented photographer. When Coburn visited and photographed him in Rye in June 1906, Coburn soon became the solution to the problem of illustrations for the edition. With James's support, and with detailed suggestions and instructions, Coburn was dispatched to Paris and Venice, among other places, for subjects. When Coburn returned at the end of 1906, James loved the photographs. Together they took purposeful London walks in the summer and autumn of 1907, and James made some long notebook entries of his impressions of the sites, the scenes, and the light for the London book. But, in April 1908, he abjectly apologized to Macmillan, who had finally made an inquiry about his progress. "How can I tell you coherently, or inspire you with any patience to hear, what a long train of fatality and difficulty and practical deterrence" had prevented him from honoring his promise? First there had been the novels of 1901–1904. Then the American trip and the writing of *The American Scene.* And then his promise (vague as it was) in New York, probably to Harper & Bros., to write two novels for serialization, both of which he had put off indefinitely. Most of all, though, the edition was at fault—"an elaborately revised and retouched and embellished and copiously prefaced and introduced Collective, and selective, Edition of my productions, in 24 volumes—which I have been putting through, and which has proved a task of the most arduous sort, such as I can't but be glad of, but such as I at the same time wouldn't have had the courage to undertake had I measured all the job was to cost me."[41]

The edition became an oppressive burden that preoccupied him for three full years. If he got pleasure out of writing the prefaces, he also soon felt the weight of how many he had to do. The autobiographical and theoretical aspects of these essays sustained him more than anything else. He compared his constricting burden of paperwork to "an enormous feather-bed" that was smothering him. It closed around him like a "steel trap." By summer 1907, he thought he was "at last out of the wood," though he still felt "like the thing they call here a Revising Barrister—pleading at the bar my poor case . . . decking out my volumes with long (—perhaps too long) Prefaces." If the first volume did not appear in the autumn, he would feel as if he had "ploughed through the desert of proofreading in vain." In October, his wood was still a "*selva oscura* . . . now exceptionally dark & thick . . . a perfect tangle of occupation." The first volumes appeared in December 1907, the last not until July 1909. By April 1908, he was deathly sick of the whole business. "I am ridden—and have been for months and months—by the fearful nightmare . . . pursued . . . as by a pack of hell-hounds; the hell-hounds being the volumes already out, revised, rewritten, copiously prefaced and seen through the Press, and crowding close on my heels while I pant and strain over the preparation of the awful bloated remainder. It has really been a colossal task, and has made me inhuman and remorseless toward everything else, all the more that the end is not yet." He felt ill, experiencing heart palpitations—sudden rushes of accelerated throbbing. By December 1908, the edition seemed finally off his hands. After all his tedious labor, he looked forward to rewards, including royalties and an increased readership. He had, he felt, paid a heavy price for the edition—in time, and effort, and life—much beyond what he had anticipated. He prayed that "it *may* make a little money" immediately, "the consummation sordidly aimed at."[42] He received shocking news from Pinker in October 1908. After the expense of permission fees from the original publishers and the small sales, he was due only $211.

The hopes that he had as late as the end of 1908 were smashed decisively in the next two years. What had gone wrong? Had Pinker and Scribner's misadvised him? Had they been unrealistically oversanguine themselves? Had their business judgment been overwhelmed by the impressive monumentality of the venture? Perhaps they had not given thought to whether it would pay monetarily for the author or, if they had, had assumed that the author cared more about presence than about money. In fact, he cared about both. But he had allowed himself to create something akin to the gigantic and uncommercial statues that he constantly urged Andersen to stop making. "The long, unbroken tension of your Scheme" is devastating, he told Andersen, "the scheme of piling up into the air this fantastic number of figures on which you are *realizing nothing* (neither money nor judgement, the practical judgement, practical attitude towards them, of the purchasing, paying, supporting, rewarding world) on which you are not even realizing that benefit of *friction with the market*. . . . Stop your multiplication of unsaleable nakedness for a while and hurl yourself, by every cunning art you can command, into the production of the interesting, the charming, the vendible, the *placeable* small thing." By early 1909, James wailed that the edition had for three years taken "*all* my time, making every other remunerative labour impossible, & . . . it has been, in other words . . . the most expensive job of my life."[43] Its publication had a funereal monumentality. He was never to complete another novel.

(4)

Warm friendships brought relief from the burden of the New York Edition. Jonathan Sturges, "poor unspeakable little demon," spent an occasional week with him at Lamb House. James visited him at Eastbourne where Sturges spent long periods under nursing care. He was ill and intermittently alcoholic. James rarely saw Fullerton and Andersen but their correspondence was warm. Fullerton was still mysteriously vague about his private life, Andersen monomaniacally obsessed with his work. In Rye, the Protheros continued to be happy company. To James's surprise, Tom Perry, the "Sargy" of his youth, from whom he had been emotionally distant for twenty-five years, suddenly became a friend again. A prolific but uninteresting professional writer, Perry had been living in Paris and Giverny. He and his wife Lilla, whose talent as a painter had blossomed into achievement, had become friends of Monet. James had known and liked Lilla Cabot even before she married Perry. Putting behind him any misgivings, James invited Perry to visit at Lamb House. With the proximity of Paris-Rye-Dover, "we are practically quite neighbours." By mail, he eagerly welcomed him to London—"Don't get run over—the motor-buses are very dangerous—& 'report yourself' as Wm. C. Leverett used to say (What did he-ever mean?)"—to the Athenaeum, for an honorary month—"where the high intellectual tone is supposed to make up" for the miserable food. He invited Perry to Lamb House for a week's visit in mid-November 1906. Except for premature aging, Perry seemed to James hardly changed, "very genial and amusing," no different in mind and personality than when they had been young together. In the mornings, as always, James worked. In afternoons and evenings, the two had long walks and conversations. When Perry left, James felt a sense of personal loss. "Your visit did me great good," he wrote to him, "& renewed (in spite of failing breath) the sources of my youth for me."[44]

Edith Wharton returned to Europe in March 1906, having in mind a long stay in Paris that would include excursions to England for motor trips and visits with James and Sturgis. "*I'll* meet you," James told her, "at Dover on [April] 25th, or anywhere in the world—*this* world— you suggest, and motor with you as long as the machine consents to resist my weight." When the new automobile with which Teddy Wharton met them at Dover had mechanical problems, the excursion was postponed. James later spent three mostly rainy days driving with "the rich, rushing, ravening Whartons," parting with them at Malvern, where he amused and frustrated his hosts by his maladroit, overconfident, and long-winded directions. They joined him a few days later in London before returning to France. Soon he heard with envy about their new "Vehicle of Passion" and their visit to George Sand's home at Nohant. Both automobile and Nohant were immediate evocative referents, for both James and Wharton, to sensual liberation and the erotic imagination. The next spring, James agreed to join them in Paris for ten days of a visit of several weeks at their luxurious apartment on the Rue de Varenne on the Left Bank. "I know I shall (inevitably) be involved [in Paris] in the movement, the general rhythmic rush of my host & hostess—the latter especially—to say nothing (alas!) of that of their automobile; & they probably have plans." He hoped to spend time with his nephew William, who was studying art. He looked forward to seeing the mysterious Fullerton. Perry would claim some of his time. He hoped Howard Sturgis would join him there, to share his curiosity about their "always more or less palatial friends," the Whartons. If not, "I shall doubtless have plenty to tell you about that when we do meet. Trust me at least to cull for you every sweet flower of incoherency that blooms in the table-talk—or stable-talk—of my host!"[45]

Having been at his desk with almost no break since returning from America, he was eager for a vacation. He could work on revisions and proofs in Paris, even, he hoped, while traveling. Edith promised luxury in Paris and adventure on the road. Arriving at the end of the first week of March 1907, to his disappointment, having coming down with flu, he needed immediate bed rest for a week. As soon as he could get out of bed, it was all "very interesting & social & Parisian & funny & indescribable," Edith "a great & graceful lioness. . . . I have come in for many odd bones & other leavings of the Christians (if Christians they can be called) who have been offered to her maw in this extraordinary circus. In fact I have an indigestion of Chères Mesdames & other like phenomena." The next week his "exquisitely kind" hosts whirled him off "on india rubber wings . . . to the Pyrenean frontiers," a three-week, high-speed excursion via Nohant, through Burgundy and Provence, to Lourdes and Pau and into the foothills of the Pyrenees, "with servants sent on ahead by train everywhere" to have their hotel rooms ready. "The whole thing [was] an expensive fairy-tale" that he thoroughly enjoyed except for the wry realization that being associated with the rich was costly. Though he paid only for his deluxe hotels, his expenses seemed high to him. He never would otherwise have stayed at such expensive places. Fortunately, his spirits were also high. "The magical monster the touring Panhard" gave them wings that effortlessly flew them through "this incomparable France" in a "chariot of fire." It "has been almost the time of my life . . . the old travelling-carriage way glorified & raised to the 100th power . . . a wondrous, miraculous motor-tour."[46]

In Paris at the middle of April 1907, he readily succumbed to "this fine gilded captivity—my friends having utterly refused to let me desert them for an hotel." The gilt had been "laid on so thick that my limbs are charged & stiff & bloated with it, & the very movement of escape difficult." He could only leave 58 Rue de Varenne by leaving Paris, which he had no intention of doing until at least May 1. "I haven't been here for years," he wrote to Sturgis, whom he expected to meet in Italy, "& shall probably never once again be here (or 'come abroad' once again, like you) for the rest of my natural life. *Ergo* I am taking what there is of it for me—I can't afford, as it were, not to." He admitted to being homesick for Lamb House "even in the midst of this gilded bondage" (he began to imagine how costly it would be to give each of the seven servants the requisite tip on departure) in the "singularly well-appointed privacy in this fine old Rive Gauche quarter, away from the horrible boulevards & hotels & cosmopolite crowd." When Lapsley joined him as a guest at Rue de Varenne, the three of them went to Port Royal, where they probably all shared the conservative Edith's opinion that "nothing could be more revolting than the destructive rage of the Revolution." "The Teddies are divinely good," he told Lapsley.[47]

The person he most eagerly returned to from the Pyrenees was Morton Fullerton, whom he was reunited with soon after arriving in March. Although he had written "I can't keep my hands off you" to Fullerton in December 1905, his efforts at such embraces existed only metaphorically. After a number of missed attempts, soon after his arrival in Paris he had introduced Fullerton to the Whartons, who were happy to have him frequently at Rue de Varenne. Curious about him, Edith wrote to Sarah Norton that "he is very intelligent, but slightly mysterious, I think." From Carcassonne, on his way back from the Pyrenees, James signaled Fullerton that he was "facing again toward Paris & W.M.F.—with a lively yearning & after immense impressions." As soon as he arrived, he had an afternoon with him, and then, arranging another, wrote that "Mrs. W. is planning to put her hand on you— though tomorrow . . . appears uncertain & probably compromised, alas. However, that's not our affair in the sense I understand our affair." Their affair could best be attended to in Rye. "You must absolutely & utterly come soon & spend five or six days with me at L.H."[48]

James's stay in Paris (for ten weeks rather than the two he had planned) had deepened his friendship with Edith Wharton. They now had an almost familial relationship. For Edith, her long-standing desire to become James's friend had been fully realized. She felt the two and a half months of his company to be "unfailingly delightful, wise & kind." James transcended her sense of the limitations of his work and filled for her an avuncular, if not paternal, role formerly held by a man who often was not there, Walter Berry. "The more one knows [James]," Wharton wrote to Charles Norton, "the more one wonders & admires the mixture of wisdom & tolerance, of sensitiveness & sympathy, that makes his heart even more interesting to contemplate than his mind." For James, the visit seemed the happiest time he had ever had in Paris, his hostess "sympathetic, admirable, amazingly intelligent." Now he had Italy ahead of him, and particularly Andersen, whom he longed to see. When, the previous fall, Andersen had had some hope of coming to England, James's heart had leaped at the possibility. He even considered offering to pay his round-trip ticket. But Andersen had felt compelled to keep working on his "vast stripped stark sublime family on whose myriads of penises and bottoms and other private ornaments how can you ever financially realize in America? Forgive this anxious cry from your tenderest H.J." Having sensibly declined Andersen's invitation to stay at his apartment, which he did not want to encumber with his "large and heavy presence," he had Andersen reserve a room in the Hotel de Russie in the Piazza del Popolo, a few minutes from Andersen's place. He promised that he would spend so much time on Andersen's terrace and share so many meals with him that it would seem as if he were living there.[49]

Once again he was in Italy, in Rome by May 20, 1907, hoping that he had missed the worst of the tourist hordes and the Roman social season. The weather was delightful, not too warm, and "the nights

delicious for coolness after the good Roman sort." Despite "the abate-
ments and changes and modernisms and vulgarities," he still felt the
happy associations of the Rome that he had known for forty years. But
"the crowd and the struggle and the frustration . . . are quite dreadful—
and I really quite revel in the thought that I shall never come to Italy *at
all* again—in *all* probability." Worst of all, the tourist hordes were
mostly American. "It makes me, alas, glad that I'm 97 years old & can
thereby remember the comparatively unprofaned years, also that I am
preparing to exchange this frantic scene for a world in which there will
be, I trust, no Southern Route." Sensing that this time his prediction
of finality was to prove correct, he stayed on in Rome and Italy longer
than he had intended. As the guest of an engaging couple, the Filippis,
he made a number of motor excursions southward, one to Fiumicino,
where they "crossed the Tiber on a medieval raft & then had tea—out
of a Piccadilly tea-basket," another to Subiaco, where he had never
been, the third a wildly exciting, sensually gratifying two-day excursion
to Naples, "going by the mountains . . . & returning by the sea . . .
quite an ineffable experience" that brought home to him "with an
intimacy & a penetration unprecedented how incomparably the old
coquine of an Italy is the most beautiful country in the world." Notwithstanding awful roads, terrible Italian drivers, and a nearly fatal driving
accident, he felt in a scenic and automobile ecstasy.[50]

At the Protestant Cemetery, in "the exquisite summer luxuriance,"
he visited Constance Woolson's grave "below the great grey wall, the
cypresses and the time-silvered pyramid." It seemed almost the most
beautiful place in Italy, "tremendously, inexhaustibly touching," he
wrote to Fenimore's niece. "Its effect never fails to overwhelm." Much
of every afternoon in Rome he went to Andersen's studio, where he sat
for his bust, thinking to do Andersen a favor; he mostly suppressed
his reservations about his friend's giant statues and unhealthy work
compulsions. "I am getting on well with James," Andersen wrote to
his sister-in-law, "but Jameses mean nothing to me, all I pray for is
physical strength to give to my work—for I have so much to do." The
green bronze bust, which began to bore them both, did not turn out
well. Andersen objected to James's constant avuncular pronouncements
and directions. "He has a keen way of modifying and analyzing real
matters and expression into a pulp of dullness, and that is about what I
have," in revenge, "turned his head into." When James deserted him
for his Naples excursion with the Filippis, it seemed to Andersen that
James was always "trying to avoid dull people and yet throwing himself
gently into their arms, caring for their wounds, and becoming Major
General of the great swelling crowd of dull dead people." For James,

the afternoons and evenings at Andersen's apartment had a romantic glow—"the cool arched workshop and the slowly breathing bust, the subtle Ettore and t'other models chat, and the wild sessions at Aragno's, and above all that wondrous terrace-dinner of my last night . . . unforgettably sweet in the cool high Roman evening." When Andersen's sister later sent him photographs she had taken, James did not like them. But it was only the fault, he admitted, of his "own deadly and unmanageable mug. Your mug, dearest Hendrik, is much sweeter and shines as silver beside heavy pewter." When he finally left, Andersen was not sorry to see him go. James seemed to him to have gotten "a bit tiresome with his cocksure penetration," a phrase that James would have taken to be as innocent as Andersen probably meant it to be. "I see clearer where the gates open and shut and how narrow the roads are that lead up to his shrines," Andersen remarked, "And all this is for the best."[51]

From Rome, in the middle of June 1907, James went first to Cernitoio, outside Florence, to stay at the villa of old American friends, the wealthy, well-connected Edward Boits. Howard Sturgis was staying there for the summer with the Babe and his sister-in-law, recovering from a nervous breakdown that seemed to James "irritatingly gratuitous and trivially tragic." James thought it the result of an overly nervous, generous personality having spent itself on being excessively hospitable at Qu'Acre to long-term visitors. To fulfill his "solemn promise" to the Curtises, James went on to Venice. To his delight, the city of his dreams proved as extraordinarily beautiful as it had always been. He was the only guest at the Barbaro. "The full-blown summer" seemed "divine, even if pretty torrid," the city "more characteristically exquisite and loveable" than he had "*ever* known it. I have this vast cool upper floor—all scirocco draughts and easy undressedness quite to myself; I go out with Ariana at 5, in the cool (comparative), and then again by moonlight. . . . Every note strikes true from the cool dim dawn, when the canal is a great curly floor of dark grim marble, to the still cooler blue night when I go forth with my Lady to be cradled by the plash outside the Giudecca." It was, though, "new heartbreak . . . just only to feel this enchantress (I allude now to the terrible old Venice herself!) weave her spell just again supremely to lose her. One dreams again so of some clutched perch of one's own here. But it's the most drivelling of dreams." Despite cars at Mestre and the raging *vaporetto*, Venice, unlike vulgarized Rome and Florence, had never seemed to him "more loveable." It was the only place in Italy that "I feel—ever *shall* feel again—the *ache* of desire to go back to."[52]

Another erotic drama was soon under way. Perhaps it had been contemplated in Paris in spring 1907. In the fall, James hoped to be the forty-two-year-old Fullerton's host at Lamb House. He urged Fullerton to come, if only for three days, on his way to America. "My difficulty is that I love you too fantastically much. . . . You touch and penetrate me to the quick, and I can only stretch out my hand to draw you closer." He was disappointed. Fullerton had other loves, two of whom he left behind in Paris, two of whom he sailed toward in October 1907. He went first to Bryn Mawr, where he proposed and then became formally engaged to a young cousin who had grown up in the Fullerton household under the impression that she and Morton were siblings. She was now blissfully happy, even for an engagement that she knew would be a long one. With James's urging, Fullerton then went to The Mount. James had skeptically prophesied to Wharton, "You won't see Fullerton." After a few days of drives and talks, an unexpected intensity of mutual awareness developed. When Fullerton left, Wharton began to keep a private diary addressed to him, though for her eyes only. On his way back to Paris in November, Fullerton finally stayed over at Lamb House "for just one night," the only visit he had paid James "in all these years."⁵³ Within days, by letter from Paris, Fullerton finally confided to James selected details of his bisexual history. His former mistress, for revenge and blackmail, had stolen a stack of his letters that explicitly highlighted his many love affairs. Fullerton perhaps hoped for James's financial support as well as advice.

Though sympathetic, James also felt deeply betrayed. "I think of the whole long mistaken perversity of your averted *reality* so to speak, as a miserable *personal* waste, that of something—ah, so tender!—in *me* that was only quite yearningly ready for you, and something all possible, and all deeply and admirably appealing in yourself, of which I never got the benefit." If he could not have been one of his lovers, why could he not at least have been his fraternal confidant, an indirect participant? As for his former mistress, if she attempted to use the letters she would seem to everyone "a mad, vindictive and obscene old woman." No one cared anymore except, in his own way, James. "I am with you, in the intensity of my imagination and affection, at each moment of the day—and I immensely cultivate the feeling that you know I am." As for Fullerton himself, after buying back the letters as cheaply as possible, he should throw himself, for relief and happiness, on his genius and his art, "on the blest *alternative life*—which embraces all these things and is what I mean by the life of art. She has seen *me* through everything."⁵⁴

Instead, early the next year, Fullerton threw himself on Wharton. It was the first of his affairs that James had the opportunity to participate in. Accelerating their European plans by almost two months, the Whartons came to Paris in December 1907, to the Rue de Varenne apartment that they had taken for another year. By February 1908, Wharton and Fullerton had become intimate friends. Teddy Wharton, who had been depressed for much of the past year, sailed in March back to America for medical diagnosis. He is "worryingly, nervously, a bit ominously ill," James told Lapsley, "& the best 'advice' is that he may be cerebrally compromised." Sometime in spring 1908, perhaps in March or April, Wharton and Fullerton became lovers. "I am mad about you Dear Heart," she soon told him. Though James had told his "dear Edith" that he would "never, never, cross the Channel again," she persuaded him to come to Paris for the last two weeks of April. The lovers met him at Amiens. In Paris he sat, at Wharton's urging, for a portrait by Jacques Émile Blanche. With Wharton, he lunched with Henry Adams and then with Adams and Howells. Adams, to whom he served as a reminder "that people as old as I still seem to exist," soon sent to "Mon Cher Jacques" a copy of his privately printed *Education,* the volume "a mere shield of protection in the grave. I advise you to take your own life in the same way, in order to prevent biographers from taking it in theirs."[55] With Wharton and Fullerton, James had dinners, excursions, readings.

James returned early in May 1908 to England, never to visit France again. Wharton made numbers of visits in the next year to England. By early autumn 1908, she had confided to James about the affair. He was fascinated, engaged, supportive of both of them. With James offering to stand surety for half of a two-hundred-pound advance, on his and Wharton's covert urging Macmillan contracted with Fullerton to write a book on Paris for his great cities series. The money was to be used to purchase back the stolen letters, a process that dragged on for almost two years. Though the book was never written, Macmillan never asked James or Wharton to make good on the promissory note. In November, Wharton stayed at Lamb House. She and James explored the countryside, visited Sturgis, saw Walter Berry off to Egypt, and stopped at Box Hill to visit the elderly George Meredith. He seemed to Wharton to be "radiating light & life from every feature & every tone of his voice." She watched James and Meredith conversing, "James's heavy Roman head, so realistically and vigorously his own" as he listened to Meredith "eloquently discoursing . . . their old deep regard for each other burning steadily through the surface eloquence and the surface attentiveness. . . . I felt I was in great company."[56]

He had Fullerton and Wharton's company again in spring 1909. Her whirlwind visit of the previous fall was repeated, though this time with her lover. "*What* an incoherent life! It makes me crouch more dodderingly than ever over my hearthstone," James had confided to

Sturgis the previous year. But the entertainments at Qu'Acre all sounded "glorious & god-like. . . . I rejoice in it save for squirming a little over the sight of what the mighty machinery of Quacre is able to do for our friend—after the lean yield of my tenth of an acre & no cow! But the great thing about me is that I can still grin even in humiliation!" In April 1909, Wharton completed a six-week visit in England. James mock-heroically complained about his "angel of desolation," the "general eagle-power & eagle-flight, of her devouring & desolating, ravaging, burning & destroying energy. . . . Howard Sturgis, chauffeur Cook & I bore the brunt." The impending collapse of her marriage and her heightened erotic awareness left her with even greater frenetic energy than usual, which both frightened and attracted James. Early in June, she returned to England, this time with Fullerton. How much, James told her, he yearned for "the real & intimate . . . details."[57] At Charing Cross Hotel, where they had taken a suite, James joined them for a long dinner of flowing champagne and exuberant conversation. The three of them dined, so to speak, in the anteroom of the lovers' passion. Late in the evening, soon after James said good-night, Wharton and Fullerton went upstairs to their suite to spend a passionate night together. As James left, he knew that he had come as close as he ever would to holding Fullerton in his own arms.

That autumn, he came as close as he ever would to Jocelyn Persse. The handsome young Irishman, a "Celtic man of imagination like myself," James had affectionately joked soon after they had met in 1903, had become an important part of his imaginative and emotional life. As he always did with a new relationship, James initiated an exchange of photographs almost immediately. He could not get over his young friend's handsomeness. "I want to hold on to *you*," he told him. They shared long London walks, brief Rye visits, and evenings at dinner and the theatre. "There is, for me, something admirable & absolute between us." Without artistic or intellectual interests, Persse could not be a part of those aspects of James's life. When James sent Persse a copy of *The Ambassadors,* he genially warned him that it would be a struggle to read. If he did, James urged him "to try to like the poor old hero, in whom you will perhaps find a vague resemblance (though not facial!)" to the author. He preferred to have Persse to himself. The presence of other people spoiled the joy for him. He longed for "faraway quiet out-of-the-crowd evening[s]" with him. "I think our happy occasions together have most price when we are alone." When Persse was in Greece in winter 1904, James impatiently "haunted" his Park Place home, eagerly anticipating his return. "God grant accordingly that I be here when you turn up with the rich glow of travel in your manly cheek & the oaths of all the Mediterranean peoples on your mustachioed lips: (as I hope, at least, I shld. like so to hear you rip them out). But I yearn, dear Jocelyn, for all your sensations & notations, & think with joy of your coming to me for a couple of days near at hand a little later on, shaking the dews of Parnassus from your hair." A letter from Persse was the first he opened, "no matter what others arrive with it."[58]

When they were both again in England in summer 1905, James, at work on *The American Scene,* welcomed him to Lamb House. "I rejoice greatly in your breezy, healthy . . . adventures, & envy you, as always, your exquisite possession of the Art of Life,—which beats any Art of mine hollow." During the next years, they were regular London companions. James had no doubt of Persse's affection for him. The young man was an increasingly powerful stimulant to his imaginative life. "Please don't deflower our pure young virginal evening together by seeing the 'Perfect Lovers' *before*" they could see it together, James urged, his playfully erotic language typical of their exchanges. Persse became his most constant companion, a fulfillment of his long-held image of "the most expressibly beautiful creature" [he] had ever looked upon." When Persse was away, James missed him terribly. "I greet you, I miss you, I love you," he wrote to him in late 1906. "The least sign or word from you, or intimated wish makes me vibrate with response & readiness—so attached am I to your ineffaceable image." In Italy for the winter of 1907–1908, Persse was, for James, a constant aching absence. "Come back," he urged him, "as gorged & replete [with impressions] as possible—you will fit the tighter into my embrace!" Though distant, they were never apart. "Irresistible to me always any tug on your part at the fine & firm silver cord that stretches between us—as I think I never fail to show you: at any twitch of it by your hand, the machine within me, enters into vibration & I respond ever so eagerly & amply!"[59]

From Paris in spring 1907, James tugged on the silver cord. How he wished Persse could be there with him. Back from one of his many visits to Ireland, Persse joined James at Lamb House just before Christmas. When, in early spring 1908, James attended the premiere in Edinburgh of an extension of the one-act play, *Summersoft,* that he had written years before, into a three-act play now called *The High Bid,* he was thrilled that Persse timed his rapid journey back from Rome so that he could be there. He happily paid all of Persse's expenses. His theatre ambitions, which had never completely died, had been reawakened by the solicitations of Johnston Forbes-Robertson, a well-connected, successful theatrical manager and actor and his actress wife. The pain of "the dark abyss" had receded as the years had passed, not as fully buried "beneath fifty years of dead nightmares" as he had claimed. Again, he attended rehearsals regularly. For a moment, he *again* had a vision of theatrical gold, of security and luxury in his old age. "It is a homely fact," he disingenuously told Macmillan, "that nothing can possibly conduce more to my having a real free and deliberate and leisurely hand for 'London,'" which he still had on indefinite hold, "than a definitely good and sustained success or two at the box-office! I haven't published a Novel, alas, since just before I went to America!"[60] Though the play was a modest critical success and nothing more, he was pleased to have Persse with him in Edinburgh.

They spent some happy days together in July 1909, James glowing with "the felt beauty of our intercourse. We shall never fall below it— it is the dearest thing possible. . . . I am ever so tenderly faithful to you & addicted to the intimate visions & thoughts of you." So filled was he with the happiness of their intimacy that he wrote to Persse, who had left for Ireland, to "thank you & generally yearn over you—in addition to greatly loving you! . . . Life consists for me here of being pretty successfully quiet & of missing you acutely—whenever I think of you— which therefore is all the time." He was an expressive, generous lover, perhaps because the drama was substantially in the words and in the heart. In November 1909, they had their tenderest, happiest moments together, probably never to be repeated or equaled. They could not have known that during the weekend they spent together at Ockham, the home of Lady Lovelace, where James once again looked at and evaluated the family's Byron papers. The titillating Byron correspondence provided an additional erotic resonance. For the next few years, James remarked the anniversary of these two happy days. One year later, under vastly changed circumstances, he wrote to his young friend, with stubborn but plaintive optimism, that "we shall make it live again. Before long will come round the anniversary of our rather odd & melancholy, but also exquisite, Sunday at Ockham—Nov. 27th–29th, 1909—in those fantastic contiguous apartments. When I think of such scenes & occasions from *this* point of view I grind my teeth for homesickness, I reach out to you with a sort of tender frenzy."[61]

(5)

In early January 1910, he seemed perfectly fine, other than "very big and fat and uncanny and 'brainy' when I last saw myself." His scare about his heart the previous winter had been diagnosed by an eminent London specialist, Sir James Mackenzie, as an "irregular action of the heart . . . 'of the common or garden sort, such as *everyone* has after sixty and such as he himself has had for fifteen years.' " As to his Fletcherizing, which he thought might be the cause of his palpitations, Mackenzie assured him that it was harmless and, indeed, beneficial. What he needed, Mackenzie advised, was to take regular exercise and to lose a great deal of weight. He needed more recreation, more automobile and other excursions, more London sociability and less Rye winter isolation, into which his interminable work on the New York Edition had regularly tempted him. "Go neither to bed nor to Nauheim," Mackenzie warned. "He is the absolute reverse of an alarmist," Henry wrote to William, "and thinks the tendency to flurry and worry over so-called heart-conditions greatly overdone." He made it clear to his patient that he could find no physiological basis for his symptoms. Referring to "The Turn of the Screw," he asked James how he created terror in his fiction. James replied that he attempted to make his readers' imaginations "run riot and depict all sorts of horrors." "It is the same with you, it is the mystery that is making you ill. You think you have got angina pectoris and you are very frightened lest you should die suddenly."[62]

The crisis of the "queer *heart-condition* that had for a long time given [him] obscure intimations" was over. He granted that it had been of "a superficial sort." Like the "obscure hurt" of his youth, obscurity spoke for essentially emotional pains. He did, though, have good reasons for feeling depressed. By early 1909, he had become heartsick over the New York Edition. Also, when he looked into the mirror he saw an old, fat, unattractive man. Despite all his efforts, some successful, to love and be loved, he felt deeply lonely, with a strong sense of internal isolation. When he had been young, he had had the physical energy, the emotional strength, and the artistic dedication to make loneliness bearable. It was the necessary price, he had felt, for his vocational commitment. He had less strength now, and less commitment. He had not composed a novel since he had finished *The Golden Bowl,* the longest period in his writing life during which he had not written a full-length fiction. He thought he would again. He had *The Sense of the Past* to complete. But if, outwardly, he still had hope that he would be a novelist again, he might have had some glimmer, some anxious inward concern, that his novel-writing days were over. So too he felt were his traveling days, even to the Continent, let alone to America. "I shall never alight" in America again, he told Perry, "save as upborne on the wings of some miracle that isn't in the least likely to occur."[63]

But he could feel hopeful, after his consulation with Mackenzie, that at least *he* was not about to die of a heart attack. His condition had "proceeded from causes which are essentially controllable & susceptible of modification & even removal—& this course has been more or less successfully taken with them." The "more or less" was an honest qualification. "I've walked & walked more, and eaten less & less and felt my clothes grow looser & looser & all to my distinct benefit." Still worried about his heart, he admitted plaintively that he "felt *compromised,* in reach & range, as not before."[64] His own fear of heart failure was in part a reflection of his fear for William's life. William had a medically indisputable heart condition, with severe angina and noticeable difficulty in breathing, soon to be made palpably visible by an X ray that showed the heart and aorta malignantly enlarged. Henry feared William's dying. He feared his own death. Despite differences of opinion of various kinds, despite an ocean between them, despite occasional surges of rivalry, the brothers could hardly conceive of a world without one another.

Their consanguinity and their rivalries remained strong. When the National Institute of Arts and Letters had been founded in 1898, with Howells as president, Henry and William had been immediately elected members. When, in 1904, the institute members had created a smaller semi-autonomous organization called the American Academy of Arts and Letters, the first seven of whose fifty members were to be drawn from and elected by the much larger number of institute members, neither Henry nor William were among the first seven to be elected. Howells, who was elevated, along with La Farge, Twain, Saint-Gaudens, Hay, and Edward MacDowell, switched his presidency from the institute to the academy. Thereafter, the members of the academy were to hold elections until their fifty members had been chosen. On the second round of elections, the initial seven members elected eight colleagues, among them Henry Adams, Henry James, Charles Norton, and Theodore Roosevelt, the latter as the author of a history of the American West. Shortly after returning from Europe in June 1905, William learned of his own election on the fourth round of balloting. It can be assumed that Henry voted for him, though Henry's attitude toward the academy was, at best, tolerantly indifferent. He expressed his strongest feeling about the organization in his somewhat ironic, somewhat serious notion that they perhaps ought to wear uniforms. But, if they did, who would design them, and wouldn't they most likely be ugly? "Well, I am crowned," he told Adams, his fellow electee, enjoying the royalist metaphor, "and I don't know that that makes much difference; but, still more, I am *amused,* and that very certainly does."[65]

William responded with a declination. Since the academy had no duties, he thought it his duty as a philosopher committed to pragmatism and humility not to accept. Also, "I am the more encouraged to this course by the fact that my younger and shallower and vainer brother is already in the academy, and that if I were there too, the other families represented might think the James influence too rank and strong." With his usual tart irony, William may have meant that philosophy should not take second place to literature, that the Academy of Arts and Letters should have been an Academy of Philosophy, Arts, and Letters. Though he had been readily elected to the institute, he may have felt that the institute and especially the academy represented the politics of the arts community rather than the seriousness of his own interdisciplinary intellectual achievements. His *Principles of Psychology* was not the kind of book institute members normally read. Perhaps Henry never learned of the specific language of his brother's declination. Howells did, and partly agreed. "I long to have the Academy do something. It is beautiful but not beautiful enough to be its own·excuse for being."[66] For good measure and consistency, William, at the same time, resigned from the institute. The honor did not impress him—the company mixed, the politics evident.

He was also weary. The parting of the brothers, in August 1905, had been in a low key; William and his family had been suffering from a prolonged summer flu. They had little doubt that they would see one another soon in Europe, though no date had been set and William had a commitment to lecture at Stanford for spring term 1906. He shared his fear with Henry that the lectures would further undermine his health. "I think I lecture much better than I ever did; but I seem to be pretty unfit for all unwanted forms of exertion." Arriving at Palo Alto in January 1906, he felt that if he could "only get through the next four months and pocket the 5000," he would "be the happiest man alive." In early April, at a little past five in the morning, the ground opened beneath his feet. Henry soon learned of the San Francisco earthquake. He thought it likely that his brother and sister-in-law were injured or even dead. To William, the earthquake was both an exhilaration and a relief. As the house pitched, the walls cracked, and the fireplace collapsed, he felt electrically alive, excited to be at the scene of a great event. The next day, he went from Stanford to San Francisco to see the damage. To his relief, his lectures, and the entire school term, were canceled, and he was still to be paid his five thousand dollars! "He is jubilant," his wife remarked, "at getting through his lectures!" In London, Henry fearfully waited for news, anguishing over the possibilities. After "a horrible week," a telegram came: "BOTH UNINJURED." When no further news arrived, he had "obsessions & visions of miseries, squalors, exposures, without name." "*Frantically*" sending cables, he got no answer. At the very end of the month, a telegram announcing a long letter came from his nephew in Cambridge. His brother and sister-in-law were perfectly fine. They had not suffered at all. "But it is all darkness to me—& I had passed till last night, 12 days of almost unrelieved tension. Now that it's comparatively over I feel quite weak!" Another cable came, announcing that they had returned to Cambridge. He now had room for further sympathies. "I am haunted with the sense of the myriad miseries, tragedies, obscure abysses of ruin of the individual San Franciscans."[67]

William, who brought the standards of the pragmatist more than those of the psychologist to his reading of fiction, had little tolerance for Henry's recent novels. Like Adams, he thought them the product of a madhouse obsessiveness. "You know," he wrote to Henry, "how opposed your whole 'third manner' of execution is to the literary ideals which animate my crude . . . breast, mine being to say a thing in one sentence as straight and explicit as it can be made, and then drop it forever; yours being to avoid naming it straight, but by dint of breathing and sighing all round and round it, to arouse in the reader who may have had a similar perception already . . . the illusion of a solid object, made . . . wholly out of impalpable materials, air, and the prismatic interferences of light, ingeniously focused by mirrors upon empty space. But you *do* it, that's the queerness. . . . But it's the rummest method for one to employ systematically as you do nowadays; and you employ it at your peril. In this crowded and hurried reading age, pages that require such close attention remain unread and neglected."[68]

In 1902, returning from Europe, William had granted that he and Henry were "so utterly different in all our observances and springs of action, that we can't rightly judge one another." *The Wings of the Dove,* he had told him, was " 'in its way' . . . most beautiful," with "unique and inimitable touches." But "it's a 'rum' way; and the worst of it is that I don't know whether it's fatal and inevitable with you, or deliberate and possible to put off and on. At any rate it is your own, and no one else can drive you out or supplant you, so pray send along everything else you do, whether in this line or not, and it will add great solace to our lives." Happily accepting the praise, Henry hoped he would not lose William as a reader. "At any rate my stuff, such as it is, is inevitable for me." But William would not accept no for an answer. Why could not Henry be more like William? "Your methods and my ideal seem the reverse, the one of the other." *The Golden Bowl* seemed to him perversely brilliant. "But why won't you, just to please Brother, sit down and write a new book, with no twilight or mustiness in the plot, with great vigor and decisiveness in the action, no fencing in the dialogue, no psychological commentaries, and absolute straightness in the style? Publish it in my name, I will acknowledge it, and give you half the proceeds. . . . Seriously, I wish you *would,* for you *can*." *Can* was not, for Henry, the issue. If William did not like *The Golden Bowl,* the failure was the reader's, not the author's. The very things that made writing novels interesting for him and that other writers were not doing were the very aspects of his fiction that William wanted him to eliminate. With his characteristic mixture of irony, humor, and sincerity, he offered to write just such a novel for William's gratification. But "I shall be greatly humiliated if you *do* like it, and thereby lump it . . . with things, of the current age, that I have heard you express admiration for and that I would sooner descend to a dishonoured grave than have written." The brothers were on more harmonious ground with *The American Scene,* which William thought "*supremely great.*" The compliment gave Henry much pleasure. He responded with high praise for his brother's most recent book, *Pragmatism.* He soon made the general claim that he had been pragmatizing all his life without knowing it—that that was what, as an artist, he did.[69]

In the summer and autumn of 1906, William's heart gave him "trouble again." The worst symptoms of "seven or eight years ago have broken loose." His heart beat rapidly, his head ached. He found it difficult to sleep. Various therapies, from spiritualism to homeopathy, did not help. After completing more lectures in the fall of 1906, he finally insisted that Harvard accept his resignation, rejoicing at the notion of being "free forever." Nevertheless, unable to resist the opportunity and the flattery, he accepted an invitation to lecture at Oxford in spring 1908, though lecturing was "profoundly odious." He also had in mind returning to Nauheim for treatment. When Henry returned from his two weeks in Paris in early May 1908, William and Alice were in England. William was determined to have an active, happy summer at Oxford, in London, and at Lamb House. On an effort of sheer will, he carried off his lecture and social obligations, in excellent spirits for a sick man. With Henry, he saw Kipling, Chesterton, who lived next door in Rye, and H. G. Wells, with whom both brothers had been having for some years a mutually congratulatory correspondence. London seemed to William to have "grown chaotic & blackguardly all motor buses and straw hats and cheap-jacks." But he found rural England, when he toured the Cotswolds and the Lake District, beautiful. Lamb House was as attractive and restful as ever, and Henry, "stolid and grave, the natural result of years, but he seems to have lost none of his early pleasure in the possession of this house" (Rye itself seemed increasingly the victim of "the invader, the despoiler, the profaner, the summer tenant, & the autumn bore"). For Henry, the pleasure he took in William's visit was undercut by worry. In this "summer of rare loveliness . . . I take great pleasure in giving my rather 'neurasthenic' & fatigued brother a long, healing, soothing bath of [the sunlight in my] green garden." In early October, though, William did what he wanted most to do—"take passage for home."[70] There was a hovering sense of finality in the farewells.

He also kept his eye on the painful collapse of the Wharton marriage and Edith's misery. In the lovely summer of 1909, he managed a number of country drives with "the Angel of Devastation"—twice to visit Kipling, once with William and once with Edith, and then two days as the guest of some youthful admirers at Cambridge, one of whom was the handsome poet Rupert Brooke. He felt "rather like an unnatural intellectual Pasha visiting his Circassian Harem!"[71]

On the first day of 1910, at Lamb House, Henry was happy to have put a difficult year behind him. There had been some pleasures, and the relief of finally completing the edition. From America, he had had bad news about William's health. With Mackenzie's help, he had taken the toxin out of his *own* heart scare. But he felt that he would never be quite the same as before. With the edition finished, he wanted to return to writing a full-length novel. He now had an excellent typist to whom he could dictate. Hired in 1907, Theodora Bosanquet was moderate in manner, literate, intelligent, and inexpensive. But he had no clear idea of what work he would do.

As the days grew shorter in autumn 1909, he felt isolated at Lamb House. The long-dead Wilky was on his mind. "Poor Wilkie haunts my retrospective memories," he wrote to Bob, "as *such* a pathetic defeated ghost that I can almost wail over him—& the memory of our childish years together (for he was with me, & you had Alice, & William in isolated eldest superiority!) grows more vivid as I grow older—& so, I find, does one live over things." One day, probably in the autumn, he made "a gigantic bonfire," on which he burned almost all the letters he had ever received. With his mind much on his "latter end," it seemed time to clear things out. He did not want to leave "personal and private documents at the mercy of any accidents."[72] Suddenly, in late January 1910, at almost sixty-seven years of age, the ultimate accident occured. He became seriously, debilitatingly ill.

Fifteen

THE IMPERIAL EAGLE
1910-1916

(1)

Insisting that he would soon be well, he kept on his feet, he wrote letters, he hoped to have a better year than the last. It had seemed "12 months of uninterrupted dreary rain." Sitting late into the night writing letters, as "the old chimes of Rye [rang] in the New Year under a cold moonlight sky," he felt, at sixty-seven, an old man who had survived much. To his notebook, he expressed his enduring optimism as an artist. He would live to create more. "I seem to emerge from these recent bad days—the fruit of blind accident."[1] But the long-anticipated accident had a will of its own. Food seemed detestable—the sight of it, revolting. His hands shook so much that he could not write anything legible at all. With weak limbs, rapid weight loss, short breathing, nervous palpitations in chest and arms, he finally, late in January, crawled into bed.

When his local physician, Dr. Ernest Skinner, could find nothing organically wrong, James felt perplexed and frightened. But he telegrammed in response to a foreboding on the part of Wharton and Fullerton to assure them that there was no ground for fear. The painfully anxious Wharton had gotten Theodora Bosanquet to question Skinner about his condition. Absolute rest and quietness had been prescribed. It appeared to the doctor that his patient was deeply depressed. The fault, James was certain, lay with that damn Fletcherism, which had ruined his stomach and brought on, he told Henrietta Reubell, "a fiendishly bad & vicious gastric & digestive crisis." The rest of his physical miseries followed from that. With a nurse immediately installed in the house, he had small feedings every few hours. Within the week, he felt that he was on the mend, that he had "got the better of the cursed state." A few days later, he had a setback. To his shock, instead of getting steadily better, he began to alternate a day or two of improvement with a day or two of relapse. By the beginning of February, he was sitting up in bed for four hours a day, "mostly . . . without the prospect," he hoped, "of tumbling back into the sheets of platitude." Within days, he had "a sharp but brief relapse—a tumble back into bed again & the regime of a small lowly sip or swallow." Writing a few letters, he struggled to control the pencil. Ink was too difficult to manage. He felt painfully lonely, "without Babes or Kith or Kin of any kind," he told Howard Sturgis, "& no company but doctor & nurse & thoughts—*these* such bad company." The past was much on his mind, the future frightened him, though he had the courage to write optimistically to Wharton, who had immediately offered him any support she could, including money. He urged her not to have "lurid fears" about him. "I shall be at work again by . . . the 1st of next month, & *never* has the fire of genius burned more luridly or impatiently within me." Money was not a problem. "I have my modest 'independent income' . . . my father's patrimony . . . *and* this house."[2]

At the beginning of February, he felt well enough for Skinner to take him out on some drives. Desperate for air and company, he sat in the car while the doctor called on patients. But he ached with loneliness. Regular letters from Sturgis had "about them every attribute of the angels' save that of fewness & far-betweenness. . . . I thank you almost with tears for your adorability—& want you to know that I am really picking up." He had more letters of sympathy than he could answer, and he was not up to dictation, though he soon managed brief letters to Fullerton, Andersen, and Persse. When a gift of fruit from Edith arrived—"grapes of Paradise . . . in a bloom of purple & a burst of sweetness"—he literally cried. When Henry cabled and then wrote to William with full details early in February, he attempted to describe his "queer and indescribable history." It was Fletcherism that had weakened and "lowered" him. In panic, he had then had to struggle "in the wilderness." What he feared most was prolonged illness like his sister Alice's, and mental incapacity. Without the sustaining satisfaction of work, his life would be unbearable, as his father's had been after Mary James had died. Both Henry and William may have had in mind Henry senior's last days, when, having had enough of life, he had starved himself to death. His son, who wanted to live, tried to struggle out of the immediate wilderness of what William soon openly called "a nervous breakdown . . . due to intense monotonous application to writing and proof-reading, most of it in solitude at Rye, for over 2 years.

Coinciding with the crisis that everyone seems to have to go thru in growing old." To Henry, it seemed as if emotional and physical death had gripped him, as if the James family curse, whether paralysis of the heart or the limbs or the feelings, had said that it was now his turn. "I am in a bad moment," he wailed at the beginning of March, "& feel beaten & demoralized. I *may* come up a little again—but the devil is that when I do it doesn't last. Still, I mustn't *really* despair! Only I'm *done!—or all but!*"[3]

From Cambridge, Henry's position looked plaintively miserable. Experienced in such illnesses, William had no reason to be optimistic that recovery would be rapid. If good professional care was important, so too was the attentive consolation that only a member of the family could provide. The notion of Henry utterly alone, in that sense, seemed unbearable to William and Alice. Having in mind the likelihood of coming to Europe soon to consult a well-known heart specialist in Paris and to try Nauheim again, they wondered whether they should come immediately or wait until summer. To Henry's delight and relief, his own namesake, his nephew Harry, sailed from New York a little after the middle of February 1910 to see if he could be of help and to report back to his parents. "That alone lifts up my heart," his uncle responded, "for I have felt a very lonesome and stranded old idiot."

At Lamb House, he felt in dismal enforced exile from anything lively or interesting. At the beginning of March, he had another, but this time more dismal, relapse. "I have been having a very bad and black and interminable time and am keeping, for these days again, very guardedly in bed," he told Gosse. He admitted to Edith that he had gotten "at last rather demoralized—in the sense of feeling blighted beyond my power to throw it off." He was still "having a difficult & dreary time." Food seemed "detestable—loathsome!—& at the worst, nutrition, almost impossible. It is a black sick state. & I struggle along between exhausted doctors & nurses." Worst of all, the relapses began to seem interminable. "I'm *down,*" he told Sturgis, "& I've been again much down of late. My little flickers & flares go out—& the reactions seem rather grim. I've been having, again, my 50th relapse—though at times it all seems one large & continuous lapse without any 're,' in which I helplessly welter." In despair that he would ever be fully well again, he considered suicide. Fortunately, young Harry arrived, William's thirty-year-old eldest son, a graduate of Harvard Law School, for whom his uncle had great affection and whose work in Washington permitted him this time to travel for family responsibilities. When his nephew appeared at Lamb House, Henry collapsed into trembling sobs, tearfully confessing his worst fears, clinging "to him almost with the frenzy of despair," finding him "indeed an immense alleviation & support."[4] Harry wrote to his parents, recommending that they come as soon as possible.

On his nephew's supportive arm, James went up to London in mid-March 1910 for a medical consultation with a renowned expert from Oxford—apparently even more exalted than Mackenzie—Dr. William Osler, who had examined William years before. After putting Henry through the most thorough physical examination he had ever had, Osler declared him "splendid for his age," an ambiguous declaration that avoided the nature of his illness. Still, he felt cheered, reassured, sustained, even inspired. If there was nothing wrong with him physically, then he would be entirely well soon. He was "another creature from the one who even on Wednesday last lay in bed in a blue funk & a cold sweat," fearful that he would be there forever and, at the same time, fearful of "getting up & travelling & throwing himself on the terrible London."[5] London, in fact, perked him up. But he had to go back to Rye, he felt. Harry was about to return to America; he could not stay much longer in a hotel; his Reform Club room was inadequate for his recuperative needs. Five days later, with Osler's prescription for prolonged rest, he was back at Lamb House, with Osler's "explicit instructions" to Skinner for a " 'rigid' rest cure"—fresh air, windows wide open, constant massage, feeding, and "packing" under the ministrations of a nurse he had hired in London. If that did not work, he had recommended a more extended hydropathy and massage rest cure in an institution.

But "don't dream that I am not fighting," James wrote to Fullerton, "with all the intensity of my volition & intelligence to get well. I *am* so fighting, & with faith & with art (oh 'art!') & I shall prevail. I want too much to be with *you* again." But his hands still trembled. Food still seemed unattractive. He disliked the massage and the hydrotherapy so much that he insisted that it stop. It would make him worse. "I assured the Doctor and the 'specialist' Nurse that if I was *touched* again for maddening massage & water-cure 'packing' I would throw myself out of the window . . . & that stopped *that,* with prompt alleviation." But for the next three weeks, he happily responded to the fresh air and the "resolute & successful feeding," though the regimen of six punctual feedings a day irked him, "with Nurse standing over me like Queen Eleanor over the Fair Rosamund with the cup of cold poison."[6]

When, at the end of the first week in April, William came through the door with Alice, he felt that the worst was over, their presence "an unspeakable blessing." He had sent the nurse away, since he had no use for her speciality and now would be ministered to by people he wanted

near him. He felt at last that he was on "the right & straight path."
Though he continued for a few days more with his feeding schedule,
he decided that it had been more harmful than beneficial, that he became
even more nervously agitated by its constant imminence and by his
need to adjust everything else he might do to its regularity. William
agreed. Skinner did not seem to mind the change of regimen at all.
After a few days, Henry seemed to William to be "slowly recovering
from his malady." Suddenly, he was free to take walks and drives
without the restrictions of sickroom discipline. When Wharton sent her
car and chauffeur from Paris, he gratefully insisted that he must pay
"their Garage & bed & board expenses." After a few days of drives,
though, he confessed that he was "not up to them." Motoring exhausted, dizzied, and confused him. "I am afraid it will be a long time
before I am in any condition for this particular pleasure." He was
heartbroken, depressed. Why could he not get steadily better? He now
readily admitted that his "worst trouble" was a "*nervous* one," which
he thought of as a vicious circle, with Fletcherism still the initiating
cause of the "prostrating trepidations & agitations, which acting on my
poor stomach, deprives me of power to feed, my original source of
illness, which misfortune & aggravation in turn reacts on my nerves
for the worst." The one comfort of his situation was "the presence—
so beneficent—of my companions; without whom I should, frankly,
go under." They were not only companions but "caretakers. . . . I
utterly cling to them."[7]

He admitted unequivocally that he was "wholly unfit to be alone,"
that their company kept him just barely on the bearable side of collapse.
Though William felt the chill of April in Rye, where "the days pass
slowly," still, "Henry needs our company, and we are glad to stay."
He has, he wrote to Bob, "a mild form of melancholia, or rather what
the Rye doctor calls an hysteric imitation of that disease . . . from which
he is emerging gradually."[8] William's own health, though, was pressing
on his and Alice's minds, even if not on Henry's. Constantly fighting
for sleep and for breath, his painful angina and dyspnea were worse
than ever. When, early in May, Henry seemed noticeably better, William finally left for his medical appointment in Paris, where he tried,
unsuccessfully, a new electric treatment. He called on Edith Wharton,
dined with Henry Adams, and had lunch with William Baldwin. Baldwin's animal extract therapy was mostly now a bitter memory. Exhausted, William finally went to Nauheim.

Unhappily torn between two allegiances, Alice, at William's urging,
stayed with Henry. "My poor mother was at Rye," their son later
recollected, "distracted and half mad with anxiety and doubts—acting

nurse to Uncle Henry who clung to her . . . wondering whether W.J. really wanted to be alone for a while, and all the time frantic to get to Nauheim to look after him." In Paris, Adams asked William for news of Henry. "I lose a friend," Adams told him, "every day, except when I lose two, and in the last month or so, I've lost so many that I have no longer a vehicle of communication with anything but the next world. It is grotesque." At Nauheim, William got visible evidence of his long-standing pain and imminent mortality—an X ray and early form of cardiogram that showed an enlarged aorta and a heart substantially weakened so as not to be able to pump sufficient blood. He felt comforted, he wrote to his brother, to have "a definite diagnosis of aortic enlargement to explain my symptoms by, and banish the reproach of mere nervousness." If "the baths here can't cure the condition," they can at least " 'adapt' the heart to meet it better."[9]

To Henry, Alice's presence made all the difference. Like his mother, she seemed a maternal angel created by nature to minister to lesser creatures. Under her sheltering wing, he went with her in mid-May to stay in Epping Forest for two weeks with his lavishly hospitable friends the Charles Hunters, under "vehement kind urging & medical persuasion" to try the benefit of change and more company. He had been urged to break the spell of his "long imprisonment at Lamb House. . . . My enemy now is *all* my liability to nervous distress & trepidation, but the time has blessedly come when (as I feel better—almost normally,) *movement* in my legs, is good for it & tends to dissipate it. It is almost as if I could *walk* myself well." The change helped a little. While he struggled through the visit, Alice's mind was mostly on her husband. William, at Nauheim, consolingly rationalized that at least Epping provided Alice with "some reward" after her dull, demanding six weeks at Lamb House. From Epping, Henry wrote to Edith that "adventures of any kind terrify me, & the future looks uncertain. . . . There is a plan of our joining William at Nauheim, but that undertaking fairly appalls me." After Nauheim, William wanted to go to Switzerland. "So everything," Henry told Edith, "is mixed & dark!"[10]

He went anyway, to a Germany that, unlike William, he generally detested. At Nauheim, he made an even bolder, more desperate decision, the "monstrous truth" of which he came to fully accept as the inevitable result of his situation. If it was "depressing, almost degrading, to speak" of his dependency—his clinging to his brother and sister-in-law "even as a frightened cry-baby to his nurse & protector"—then he at least would have the courage to accept the consequences of his dependency. He would go where he had never expected to go again. "I have taken my passage with them to America by the Canadian Pacific steamer line . . . on August 12th—to spend the winter in America. I must break with everything—utterly—of the last couple of years in England."[11] He wanted a break from Lamb House winter isolation, which he now strongly associated with his becoming ill.

At Nauheim, he began to feel better. "The black devils of Nervousness" took a brief holiday. But he never felt completely free of them, even as his physical strength returned sufficiently for him to take long walks. The warm and toneless Nauheim summer air oppressively weighed on him. At unpredictable intervals, his general nervousness exploded into intense episodes of trembling, incoherent anxiety, "acuter visitations. . . . The blackness of darkness & the cruellest melancholia— are my chronic enemy & curse." If he dared to imagine himself better, the illness, mockingly, took its revenge. William was visibly not only no better but noticeably worse. Henry had bad nights, often relieved by sleeping powder, but he felt physically strong enough for daytime activities, despite his nervousness. William, though, had nothing but bad nights *and* days, frequent angina attacks, painful shortness of breath, and constant sleeplessness. As Henry's health improved, he began to see his brother's situation more clearly. He still expected that William would be all right, despite Nauheim clearly having done him no good. In retrospect, it seemed a "dreadful mistake."[12] With their August 12 sailing date in mind, William wanted one last visit to Switzerland, one final happy moment of walking in the mountains.

Late in June 1910, they went to Zurich, then Lucerne, and finally Geneva. Switzerland turned out to be a "nightmare." At William's insistence, they attempted to climb a small peak, "a dire ordeal" that drove the long-suffering Alice to despair as she looked after her fatally ill husband and her depressed brother-in-law. In the high air, Henry was often nauseous, William even more heartrendingly short of breath. The weather was bad, either rainy or hot, until they arrived in Geneva. As Alice and Henry were ferrying across the lake on a steam launch, she gently told him the painful news that Robertson James had quietly died in his sleep of heart failure. It had been two days before his body had been discovered. "Poor dear Bob's so *lonely* passing away" deeply touched and saddened him. "It half breaks my heart," he wrote to his niece, "that I couldn't have seen *him* as you describe him as you last saw him—cleared of all the darkness & pain of his stormy life." A life that had long ago gone astray had finally ended. In early June, Bob had remarked that "the James brothers are beginning to crumble fast and are a good deal more than half way on a return to the paradise in which they grew up." He felt that William had traveled in the wrong direction. As to Henry, he had never been interested in "father's ideas" anyway.

Henry was "devoutly grateful" that Bob had not suffered in his dying, "a painless, peaceful, enviable end to a stormy & unhappy career." With William's sufferings before their eyes, they decided to wait for a better time to break the news. When a telegram that had gone astray came into his hands, William felt only relief that his brother's unhappy life had finally ended. In Concord, Bob was buried in Sleepy Hollow Cemetery. William's sons were notified too late for them to be in time for the funeral. Bob's wife and son were, as they had been for a long time, great distances away. The only family member by his graveside was his daughter.[13]

Slowly coming out of his "long & wretched ordeal," Henry was relieved to be back in London before the middle of July 1910. "I am emerging, rising to the surface again, in spite of everything," he wrote to a friend. He was still sick, on occasional bad days, "with unspeakable nervous agitation & depression." William, though, who had gotten progressively weaker and worse, felt, justifiably, "completely discouraged about himself." He wanted nothing more now than to go home, to live if he could but to die if he must. He was hardly able to breathe. In his own odd way, Henry, too, wanted to go to America, though he could not quite tell why. He desired a change. America had the remnants of his family. And he had persuaded himself that William would be better there. That William would actually die was inconceivable. Also, the notion of separating from his brother and sister-in-law still seemed unbearable. But, beyond that, he still had what he called an "uncanny" desire to go. With sufficient strength to see people, Henry stayed on his feet as much as he could. Soon after arriving in London, he went with Gosse to call on Howells, who was visiting. To Howells, James looked "better than he felt." After a short visit with Jocelyn Persse, he hoped that he would "somehow once more" hold him in his arms. Mackenzie, who clearly could do nothing for William, had prescribed bromide as a sedative for Henry's nerves and stomach, which was helping. So too were frequent visits to the reassuring Mackenzie, who listened one day with great interest to William's account of a discussion that the two brothers had had about suicide. William "told Henry that if he felt life was no longer bearable, he was justified in putting an end to it, & they discussed the question as to how this should be done, & they decided in favor of chloroform or opium."[14]

At the end of the third week in July, he awakened in his Reform Club room with a feeling of "great relief." Perhaps the bromide had taken full effect. Perhaps he had accepted that he was going to live, that there would be life for him after his illness and even after William. When they went down to Rye to stay till their August departure, he noticed that as his brother got worse, he got better. "In spite of everything. . . . Heaven preserve me," he wrote in his diary. Worrying about whether William would have enough strength to travel, sadly, he began to close Lamb House—"that nest of associations of illness"— discharging the servants, except Noakes, who was to travel with him, and saying a "temporary farewell" to the house and its good and bad memories.[15] Edith and Walter Berry came from France and drove him to Qu'Acre, where he stayed one night. Sturgis and the others did their best to raise his spirits. Though somewhat more vocally stammering and ponderous, somewhat more slow afoot, noticeably older, he was still essentially himself—witty, interestingly convoluted, affectionate, and very much the dignified artist in his afflicted old age.

Rest in Rye helped William. Unexpectedly, in London, five days before departure, he seemed noticeably better, still "gravely ill" but "gaining strength, sleeping without narcotics, eating better and beginning to take gentle exercise." Alice was elated. Henry reported himself "better, ever so much—on the way, with a little more patience—to be well—with a big W." With departure imminent, he realized now that he hated to go and would come back as soon as he could. But liking to go or not had become utterly irrelevant. He could do nothing else. Inexplicably, on an absolutely smooth, fast, bright six-day voyage from Liverpool, William got much worse. Henry and Alice felt their high hopes smashed, the voyage "tormented & distressed." In a heavy rain, they stayed overnight in Quebec and then, in one "long fatiguing & dreary day," descended to Chocorua, the destination that William had insisted on and that had determined their northern crossing. They had "a heartbreaking unforgettable week" ahead of them. Racked with pain, absolutely exhausted, William gave up. He wanted only to die. "But so we go on from hour to hour & from day to day."

The two local doctors did their best. Still unable to breathe, William's suffering "would be too pitiful & terrible to witness didn't the doctors keep him now constantly" sedated. When a specialist from Boston provided the hope that he had "a fighting chance," Henry's heart sank. They seemed funereal words. Sitting by his bedside, watching William suffer, he wanted him to die more than he wanted him to live. It was as if he felt all the pain himself. The exhausted Alice seemed "spent & broken down with *her* long & unspeakably devoted strain." As Henry sat by the bedside, William's unconscious presence filled the house in the hot late August weather. The next day, the weather became blessedly cooler. He confessed, writing to Grace Norton at midday on the twenty-sixth, that "at the prospect of losing my wonderful beloved brother out of the world in which, from as far back as in dimmest childhood, I have so yearningly always counted on him, I feel nothing but the abject weakness of terror and grief." Later, in the afternoon, he added a postscript. "I open my letter of three hours since to add that William passed unconsciously away an hour ago—without apparent pain or struggle. Think of us, dear Grace—think of us!"[16]

Only practical details and mourning remained. The body was brought down for a service at the Harvard College Chapel and then burial. William was followed to the grave by his daughter and sons and wife and his only living sibling, to the high ridge of the cemetery in Cambridge, next to his mother and father and Alice. There was room next to him for his own Alice and for Henry. His survivors returned, then, to Chocorua, for the relief of the cool weather, with the conviction that William would have wanted them to begin their mourning there. On the day of his death, Alice had written her first letter as a widow. "I did mean, God knows, to make my life serve his. To stand between him and all harmful things." At Chocorua, they comforted one another. "I cling to my sister-in-law & her children for the present, & they to me—we hang, we almost huddle, so closely together." William's presence hovered amid the "melancholy American beauty of mountain & lake & forest." Indoors, Henry enjoyed "the smell and sound of wood fires crackling consolingly." For exercise, he walked for miles in the golden weather. "Not bad," he remarked to Grace Norton, "for one coming back to life from pretty—from very—far off."[17]

For a time, he did not want to leave. "I cling to this quasi-dismal scene of our sorrow, for the strange sad sweetness that pervades it—& as if communing with my beloved Brother's beautiful & noble ghost who abides here as through his making of the poor pleasant place, such as it is, from far back, & through his having liked & lived among the hillsides & woods & waters for 23 summers." For the moment, he could sense William's spirit in the early autumn air. He had been, for Henry, his "ideal Elder Brother. . . . I still, through all the years, saw in him, even as a small timorous boy yet, my protector, my backer, my authority and my pride." He would never receive praise or criticism from William again. He would never receive another of those inimitably engaging, intellectually vivid letters. It was a loss so large that it was a loss of self. "His extinction," he told Tom Perry, "changes the face of life for me." There were no other of his parents' children alive. "I am alone now, of my father's once rather numerous house." He decided to remain with William's family at Irving Street until the New Year. Then he would make further plans, perhaps to stay until the spring. When he left America, he knew that this time, for a certainty, he would never return.[18]

(2)

When he returned to England in July 1911 after "a whole year's absence," he hoped that he had "closed the gates" on the most terrible period in his life. He also had the reluctant sense that life was closing its gates on him. But it was doing so in a gentler, more gradual way than it had done on William. When he and his brother's family left Chocorua for Cambridge in late September 1910, he had felt that he had recovered almost completely from the nervous breakdown that had made his life a misery for more than six months. He had brought some general depression from his illness into the darkness of William's death, into the autumn and winter of mourning. But his moods did not have the incapacitating effect of the breakdown of the previous winter. His episodes of nerves tended to be briefer, and less wrenching. Three times in November and December, and then once more in early 1911, he had therapeutic conversations with a psychiatrist, Dr. James Jackson Putnam, his brother's intimate friend, Putnam was a disciple of Freud. Henry reported, in early 1912, that he was "enormously better." He thanked Putnam for tiding him "over three or four bad places during those worst months."[19]

He had other help also, particularly from William's family, and American friends. At Chocorua and into the autumn, he had had mounds of consolatory letters. One postal delivery brought thirty from England alone. At Irving Street, he and Alice listened for William's voice, strained for the possibility of William's presence, even to the extent of participating in a séance. Though they quickly decided that it was ludicrous, even fraudulent, they both felt that such efforts were compatible with William's own beliefs and experiments. Henry had in mind that by staying at Irving Street he increased the chances for such communication. He did it mostly for Alice, who hoped somehow to be in touch with her husband again. In Cambridge, Grace Norton lived within a short walk. He saw her almost every day, happy for a renewal of the intimacy that letters had carried for so long. "How strange & sad," he had written to her from Chocorua, "the way of the bringing about of even the best things *can* be!" They were together again as mourners, two elderly people with almost a lifetime of shared memories of loss. "The soreness of one wound meanwhile aches, as you say, through everything—the same wound that will never have ached itself out for *you* (any more than it has done so for me, in its degree, for that matter,) in all the long years since Jane [Norton] died." He also had

Lilla and Tom Perry, in Boston and in Hancock, New Hampshire, where he went in late September. By then he was eager to have a break from Chocorua, which had begun to become emotionally oppressive. Though his telegram to them went awry, they did not let on that his arrival was a surprise. Their shared memories touched on his and William's childhood. After a day of rain, he had a lovely walk with Sargy and a drive with Lilla in the mountains. Back at Chocorua, via Boston and Cambridge—where he spent "exactly *4 times* as much" on taxi fares as he would have paid in London or Paris—he found "a White Mountain of letters—the highest of all the range."[20] But the weather was beautiful, the autumnal "pyrotechnical display" a feast for the eyes.

Cambridge bored him, New York attracted him. In mid-October 1910, from his "far-overlooking" twelfth-floor room at the Hotel Belmont on the corner of Park Avenue and Forty-second Street, he delighted in the view and in the cool breezes that relieved an unusually warm Indian summer. For a moment, he was again at the center of the Wharton drama. "I came on to New York . . . only a few days after the silver steam-whistle of the Devastating Angel reached my ear," he wrote to Howard Sturgis. "Being devastated (in another way, for a change, from the one in which I *had* been) has done me perceptible good." Fullerton had just arrived. Teddy Wharton was about to leave on a world tour to recuperate from his ongoing nervous instability. He "departed all tragically, as if the great Chicago express were the bloody tumbril of the scaffold." As soon as he had left, Fullerton and Walter Berry joined Edith and Henry for dinner at the Belmont. Edith left for Europe the next day. James lunched with Berry, and dined with Fullerton. New York seemed convivial, delightful, even more so when he moved from the Belmont to Mary Jones's, his "admirable kind old friend." She was like "a nursing sister to me—sifting & sampling this formidable city for me with an art & a hospitality all her own." Feeling a definite improvement in his health, he thought that he would return to New York in January and then perhaps go south. At moments, he felt desperately homesick, which he partly relieved by long reminiscing conversations with Noakes, "my small British Burgess . . . who is sturdily & faithfully useful & devoted; though, in general, in this country, one is divided between the impossibility of doing without some species of valet or doing *with* one. . . . I want you to feel," he longingly wrote to Jocelyn Persse, recalling their happy time at Ockham just one year before, "with what a rush, a passionate, yearning rush, I shall return."[21]

At Cambridge, in November 1910, he became depressed again, so miserable that he began his helpful visits to Dr. Putnam. In the next months, his dental miseries also were renewed, "a period of wretched tension & fatigue through Dental . . . storm & stress & strain & sorrow" that went on through February 1911. He felt chained to a "bed of steel," his face disfigured, his mouth sore. Fortunately, the dental miseries were finite, though at times it seemed to him that he was attached to an irremovable black chain of depression. Each time he felt better, he hoped that the heavy weight might have been discharged forever. Each time he felt it again, his disappointment dragged him further down. In November, he resumed taking the bromide sedative. By the New Year, his spirits had risen, though even his pronouncements about his improvement had a frenetic, desperate tone. "I am, I *am,* I *am,* enormously better these last two or three months in particular," he wrote to Edward Warren, "& should be still more so if I hadn't so very, very far to come back from. All the same, I am *coming.*"[22]

In January 1911, he happily went to New York, thinking it would be good for him. He stayed for more than five weeks, part of the time with Edwin Godkin's son, part of the time with Mary Jones. He also went to consult with a highly recommended New York psychiatrist, Dr. Joseph Collins, who treated him then and in his next visit to New York with almost daily "baths, massage and electrocutions," and also prescribed an abdominal support, which he began to wear in early February. In the end, "he did nothing for me at all," he claimed. Putnam's talk therapy had been much more effective. But New York itself helped, "the big Bablyon with its great spaces for circulation, for movement, and for variety." A friend arranged for a guest membership at the elite Century Association. He saw some plays, and lunched and dined with friends. New York "relieved & beguiled" him. Attending a meeting of the American Academy, he found it "simply sickening." But, for him, it was the better kind of illness. Alvin Langdon Coburn, whom he had not seen for years, came to see him. At the end of January, he again had trouble eating. Collapsing into bed, he sent for the doctor, to whom he felt grateful for "help, encouragement, support," and for the pronouncement that he was "sound and well!" It was as if he had short-circuited the possibility of a major illness. Returning to Cambridge, he attended to his teeth again, his "abyss of *dentistry,* the most painful of all my dental life, which has . . . ravaged my days & my nerves." But he felt well enough for walks and visits, for an afternoon with Annie Fields, for social visits with the Perrys, for evenings and the opera with Isabella Gardner, for Cambridge teas with famous names and vague faces from the past. In late February, he took a long walk with his nephew. "Lovely winter day with such hints of spring, such a sunset and such melancholy, tragic hauntings and recalls of the old far-off years."[23]

Going home was much on his mind. As spring approached, even in "grim and prim Boston" he sniffed the aromas of his Lamb House garden. But he had no intention, no matter how homesick, of rushing his return. He had indicated to Alice and her children that he would stay until summer. With bitter memories, the prospect of even the tag end of winter alone in Rye frightened him. He booked passage to sail on "the swift Mauretania" on the fourteenth of June. He also wrote to the secretary of the Reform Club to hold for him a viewing place for the coronation procession on June 22 of King George V and Queen Mary. But after four delightful weeks in New York in March and April, he had another relapse, which made a later departure more desirable. Staying with the inexhaustibly hospitable Mary Jones, he had found New York more interesting and pleasant than he had ever imagined it could be. It seemed "a very extraordinary and terrific yet amiable place, as to which my sentiment is a compound of an hourly impression of its violent impossibility and of a sneaking kindness for its pride and power (it's so clearly destined to be the great agglomeration of the world!) born of early associations and familiarities." Almost every morning he went to the Neurological Institute on East Sixty-seventh Street for treatment by Dr. Collins. But, on April 19, he became miserably depressed again. He did not want to eat. Having thought that he had put his illness behind him, it now seemed to him that his ordeal was to be endless. "I blush to the depths of my being to be still regaling & afflicting you with such dreary refrains," he wrote to Howard.[24] His nephew Harry immediately came down from Cambridge, and, the next day, he went back with him to the comparative seclusion of Irving Street. In a few days, the episode had passed.

When the president of Harvard, Charles Eliot, offered him an honorary degree, he committed himself to attend the June 28 commencement and changed his departure date to early August. Perhaps he felt William would have wanted him to accept it. Certainly Alice and her children urged him to stay. He would also have more time to recuperate. As the weather became milder, he felt immeasurably better. From one day to the next, his mood would change from complaint to optimism and back. But the constant was that he got "more ill with homesickness even as [he got] less so from [his] crisis of a year ago." Though he complained to Ariana Curtis about living in a suburb "& having neither a carriage nor a motor-car nor a gondola," he began, in the mild weather, to get around more. In Boston, having spent much time

with Isabella Gardner, he grieved at her precipitous physical decline—
"ominously ill" suddenly with fainting attacks and heart palpitations.
"I went in to see her yesterday, & . . . found her reclining on a sort of
pretty dreary sofa or loggia in the open air, under an awning, with
nothing but the ugly, scrubby ragged Fenway view to look at, & a sad
appearance of forlorn *loneliness*. . . . Even the 'palace' looks thankless
& but half pleasing to me now." In late May, he spent two weeks in
Connecticut, handsomely hosted by assorted people who drove him
to Hartford, Farmington, and New Haven, where he had "very happy
impressions of Yale," and then to Salisbury to stay with his Temple
cousins, Minny Temple's sister Elly and her daughters. Though the
weather was unseasonably hot, "the summer . . . too much of a summer,"
he enjoyed walks and long drives along the "splendid river" through the
handsome Connecticut scenery, the "deep warm heart of 'New England'
at its best." Rural Connecticut seemed unexpectedly romantic, "full of
. . . dispeopled & disformed vastnesses, wondrous mighty trees . . . &
general Arcadian emptiness & grace."[25]

As the weather continued compellingly dry and hot, he became a
little edgy, then almost desperate. Much of June he spent cooled by the
brisk sea breezes at Nahant, "a charming headland far out into a deep
blue sea," an hour ferry ride from Boston, with an elderly, kind, very
deaf old friend, who had been married to Henry Cabot Lodge's sister.
It had "beautiful gardens (wondrous flowers) & lawns & trees . . . great
breezy verandahs of the good old American sort of which I am fond."
He received news of Jonathan Sturges' death, "poor dauntless but at
last tragically vanquished little desolate Jonathan." His comfort was
undermined by the sickeningly hot weather at the Harvard commencement late in the month. Distressed by the heat, the crowd, "& the
general stress & strain," he got away from the ceremony as quickly as
he could. Feeling fragile, fearing he would be ill again, he returned to
Nahant, exerting himself to stay well for his departure. He had his
first sight of an airplane in late June, an "Atwood Wright machine.
Extraordinary thrilling beauty." In the oppressive heat, he did not feel
well enough or eager enough to go out of his way to see Andersen,
who had come from Rome to visit his family.[26]

Edith Wharton met him in July 1911 at Springfield with the chauffeur and car to take him to The Mount. The oppressive heat continued.
But, as long as they were driving in "the blest Car," he was happy—
"the beauty of the Country admirable," the pleasure of Edith's company, and of Gilliard Lapsley's, who soon joined them, sustaining. He
felt less lonely, less an exile. When he was being driven rapidly in a
motorcar, he felt as if he were "fleeing before fate," as if he could

outspeed illness, old age, and death. When Teddy arrived the next week, the heat became "a great sad tension." He wanted rain, revivifying rain. It seemed as if it had not rained in the entire year that he had been in America. Teddy seemed "impossibly & excitedly futile & foolish—& I left her to him," he wrote to Lapsley, "with a pang." He felt his own "yearning to depart" as "an unutterable ache." From Nahant, late in July, he went to "hot stale" Cambridge and sadly said good-bye to Grace Norton. It seemed to him probably "for the last time." Alice came down from Chocorua to be with him "at the last." In New York, he stayed again in "beautiful cool rooms" at the Belmont. His nephew and namesake kept with him until the last moment before the *Mauretania* sailed out of the harbor.[27]

(3)

One day at Irving Street in "that terrible winter of 1910," when he had been reminiscing about William and himself as children, Alice had spontaneously said, "Oh Henry, why don't you *write* these things?" With his final return to England in August 1911, he saw ahead of him the challenging mission to write what he had begun to call the "Family Bible," an account of the world into which he and William had been born and in which they had spent their formative years. With ample selections from William's letters, it would serve as a memorial to his much-loved brother. He left Cambridge with the general understanding that he would write a tribute to William and that his nephew Henry would edit and publish a selection of his father's letters. In England, in August and September, he hoped to begin. But, appallingly, the weather was even hotter than it had been in America. After several rainless months of dry torrid heat, on his arrival the temperature had reached 97 degrees. The parched earth was like a remorseless Sahara. Having fantasied about the beauty of wet umbrellas, he felt betrayed, as if he had been transferred "from one sizzling gridiron to another." Fleeing a Sussex "sky of brass" and "earth of cinders," he went to the Charles Hunters in Epping for three weeks, then to London briefly, where he had an afternoon with Howells, then to Scotland for a week. He took long walks, though he felt pain in his chest if he tried to walk quickly. It was "red-hot in all sorts of ways"—English life was distempered with "the base alloy of heat and drought & civil strife— of general strikes & labour-riots & threatened social & economic convulsion, to which are added looming wars or hideous rumours of such. . . . The thermometer soars like an airman & the perspiration streams from my brow."[28] Exhausted, worrying about a railroad and coal strike, he found it difficult to work.

After a few late-September–early-October weeks at Lamb House, he went to London for the winter. Living in Rye seemed "impossible to health and well-being."[29] Memories of illness distressed him. The shortening days filled him with lonely dread. He wanted people, streets, lights, the diversions of cosmopolitan activity. Though less physically comfortable at the Reform Club than at Lamb House, at least there he did not quiver with dark tremors of anticipatory winter depression. Rather than visit London from Lamb House, he would visit Lamb House from London. In the autumn and winter, he saw friends regularly, dined out, enjoyed social teas, and went to the theatre. Rhoda Broughton, Margaret Brooke, Mary Ward, Ethel Sands, Lucy Clifford, Jessie Allen, Mary Hunter, Ottoline Morrell, among others, provided female company. The Warrens and the Protheros were as affectionate as ever. He dined with the Macmillans. The Gosses at Hanover Terrace encouraged and welcomed his every visit, and made it a point to have him as their guest each year for either Christmas or New Year's Eve dinner.

With Jocelyn Persse, he went to see a new production of Wilde's *Lady Windermere's Fan*. Though still passionate about Persse, his feelings had been transformed by time and illness into solicitude, the affection of a self-involved, aging uncle for whom a passionate relationship was not an economical use of his limited energy. Andersen in Rome seemed at best a warm memory, at worst a baffling, frustrating, infuriating worry, an artist so mistaken in his basic sense of artistic reality that his grand scheme for a "World City," to be designed by innumerable architects and peopled with his own megalomaniacal sculptures, seemed to James an indication of madness and certain artistic self-destruction. Fullerton had mostly disappeared, though his appearances had less importance for James, as they did for Wharton. He had proved a fickle lover and an unreliable companion. By 1911, as she hesitantly began divorce proceedings, Fullerton was increasingly absent. To Henry's and Edith's relief, Walter Berry took Fullerton's place, apparently in every way but sexually. They planned an autumn 1911 tour of Italy together, on which they invited James to join them. He immediately declined. His traveling days were over.

But he managed the short trip to Qu'Acre easily, where Howard embraced him with tremulous affection. Howard's own health had noticeably declined through a series of illnesses. The Qu'Acre warmth immediately absorbed him. Sturgis' hospitality was still a center of attraction for Percy Lubbock and Gaillard Lapsley, both of whom James felt happily reunited with in London and at Windsor. In early December 1911, when Wharton came from Paris with car and chauffeur, a week of visits to Epping and to Qu'Acre and London dinners had enough whirl in it to be happy, enough brevity to be manageable. Early in the New Year, James had three sittings with Sargent for a charcoal portrait that Wharton had commissioned. When Sargent decided he did not like it, he tore it up and began again. When Wharton found the final version unattractive, she offered it to the sitter, who himself had liked it a great deal. Perhaps she had had such a gift in mind from the beginning. In London, in the fall and winter, he began to see more of Hugh Walpole, the young literary journalist and novelist he had met in 1909. Determined to be a disciple, Walpole had become a worshiping acolyte, eager to have as much of his master's company as possible, to elevate him into the supreme deity of high art.

In the year or so before his departure for America, James's affection for Walpole had combined with his loneliness into effusive expressions of tenderness. They resumed contact in the fall of 1911. The last of James's young men, the handsome, hardworking, ambitious Walpole, sexually energetic and emotionally bisexual, was enough in love with James to take great pleasure in his increasing affection. Maintaining the center of their relationship not in literature but in life, James took little to no pleasure in Walpole's almost annual novels. Eager for company, he found Walpole endearing, an entertaining gossip and storyteller, always affectionate, always needy and eager to please. Walpole's youthful energy and loyalty provided some of the rewards of a lover and of a son. James enjoyed pampering him with affection and presents. Walpole later claimed that he sexually propositioned James, and James responded, "I can't! I can't!" When Lapsley told him that Arthur Benson was giving a course of lectures on John Addington Symonds, "with the disagreeable side left out," he responded with a joking fictional dialogue, "Symonds Without the Key": " 'How charming that sounds,' " but " 'don't you think we ought to have [the key]?' 'No— & it's forbidden to bring it *with* you.' 'Mayn't we even leave it at the door with one's umbrella?' 'Well—if you leave it in the lavatory.' 'But don't you think it might so be lost?' 'It's for you to judge. But such a key *should* be lost. Yes—I remain outside.' 'Outside the lavatory?' 'Outside the subject.' " After his illness of 1910, what had been unlikely before had become an impossibility.[30]

Desperate to resume writing, he enlisted Theodora Bosanquet in finding a flat in London that he could use as a writing studio. Reform Club rules forbade his having a female typist in his room. Herself a Londoner, probably happy to have less of Rye, she located next to her own flat in "deepest Chelsea" two "small sequestered rooms" absolutely perfect for his needs.[31] Having returned to a motorized London, he could now each morning take a taxi, the cheapness and the speed of which he marveled at, from Pall Mall to Lawrence Street in ten minutes. With a fireplace and a bath, to which he added a comfortable chair and carpet, the studio became a private place where he could work without interruptions. In November 1911, he began the autobiographical volume that Alice had encouraged him to write, dictating each weekday morning to Bosanquet. The project seemed more vivid, more challenging, more pertinent than any ideas for fiction that came to mind. It offered him an alternative at a time when he felt hesitant about his powers as a novelist, fearful that his illness had drained him of some of the imaginative energy he would need for fiction. Worst of all, he feared imminent illness again, with the sense that what had happened before might repeat itself. He could ease himself back into writing by beginning with family documents, with the letters that he, Alice, William, and Harry had spent time in Cambridge reading and arranging, particularly his father's and brother's, some of which he had brought with him, many of which he had arranged to be sent. If he were interrupted by momentary bafflement or even by prolonged illness, he imagined that it would be easier to resume an autobiography where he had left off than it would a novel.

Also, he needed money. He had, he felt, more likelihood of publisher and profits from an autobiographical volume than from fiction. His assumption was sensibly dictated by his awareness that, though widely acknowledged to be among the greatest of living authors, he was also among the most unread. His fame determined that there would be more of an audience to read *about* him than to read him. With an autobiography, he could purvey both, a book that would have readers because it would be about himself and other famous people with the additional advantage to him, and perhaps to others, that he would also be its author. His preoccupation with the New York Edition, his incapacitating illness of 1910, the recuperative anguish of his year in America, had reduced his literary income in his worst year, 1908, to less than one thousand dollars. Forbes-Robertson's production in 1908 of *The High Bid* had earned him very little. In winter 1909, he had hoped that the Incorporated Stage Society, a nonprofit theatrical consortium interested in staging worthy plays, would produce *The Saloon,* his own dramatization of his story "Owen Wingrave." When it declined the play, he exchanged a number of letters with the society's spokesman, George Bernard Shaw, some of whose plays James had seen and mostly disliked. The two writers good-humoredly exchanged their fundamentally different assumptions about literature and life. James was interested in ideas in the service of art, Shaw in art in the service of ideas, preferably political ones. In early 1911, he had nervously observed, from the American distance, the manipulations of his text and the performance of *The Saloon* in London under the direction of Gertrude Kingston, an actress interested in psychic phenomena. James correctly assumed that it had been "damnably acted," though he still had allowed himself the delusion that it would not have gone astray if he had been there at rehearsals to set it right.[32]

James was blissfully unaware of an unsuccessful effort by his friends to affirm his fame in the spring of 1911, the result of which would have confirmed his disgust with literary prizes and his distaste for a vulgar public. While in New York, a flurry of letters between Wharton, who originated the idea, Gosse, and Howells initiated his nomination for the Nobel Prize. Gosse managed the campaign in Britain, Howells in America, both with vigor, enlisting individual letters and the imprimaturs of their respective literary societies, including the American Academy. Howells' buoyant, anxiously frenetic pessimism proved appropriate. "It is such a good cause I feel it *must* fail," he wrote to Gosse. By May, the secretary of the Swedish Academy of Literature had responded that, unfortunately, it was too late for that year.[33] There were to be no other years. Unwilling to encourage translations of his difficult fiction, this most cosmopolitan of writers had few non-English readers. In 1911, the minor Belgian playwright Maurice Maeterlinck, whom James had met in London in 1909, won the prize. James represented a national literature that still seemed to the Swedish Academy on the distant, blurred edge of civilization.

Though he welcomed New Year's Day, 1912, with the sound of the church bells of Rye, he essentially settled in London for the winter. Paradoxically, "the biggest agglomeration of paving-stones & chimney-pots in the world" provided "aid & comfort." Having in mind a flat at which he could have his servants and where he could live comfortably, he had begun, in November 1911, to do some casual searching. Nothing, though, had turned up that suited him. Comfortable enough at his economical Reform Club room, he could afford to wait. The gray and quiet of the Christmas holiday season in town brought back pleasurable reminders of how much he had once loved that nurturing silence. His illness of two years before sometimes seemed like only a memory. At other times, he had the sudden, brief anxiety that a moment of depression might deepen. But mostly he felt recovered, though at the price of a certain noticeable reduction in energy and ambition. During and after his illness of 1910, he had seemed like "a portentous invalid." Now "I feel on the whole as if there were a good deal of me left still."[34]

Always self-dramatizing, he directed what energies he had into his daily imaginative ventures into autobiography. *A Small Boy And Others* was a re-creation of his childhood resonant with the adult mediation between past and present. "I have got back to work—which is *the* inestimable balm: I have a couple of small & sequestered rooms in the depths of Chelsea, of which labyrinth no one has the clue, where I go every a.m. very promptly & remain till toward 2, wrestling more or less successfully (really *more* I think now,) with the Muse of literary composition."[35] It soon became clear to Henry that his ostensible memorial to William needed an entire prefatory volume, the central focus of which had to be his own consciousness, and the world of his childhood from his adult perspective. Each moment of the reconstituted past was given its place in the development of his artistic sensibility. His artful autobiography was both a recuperative act—recapturing and restoring his creative powers, a statement of triumph over the illness that had sapped his energy—and a mythic embodiment of his view of himself and his family. Inevitably, all other actors in the drama, no matter how lovingly evoked, were secondary. In this version of the family romance, through the power of artistic shaping and consciousness, he made himself both bearer and firstborn, father and brother, the giver and maker of life to them all. After years of illness and fading powers, he had found a way to have one last sustained expression and triumph of himself as an artist.

With life-enhancing work to do, he easily overcame a short relapse into depression in London in February 1912 by retreating to bed at Lamb House. He blamed the episode on too many social engagements. He would swear off "for evermore, literally—no more social engagements—they have, after long years and much dilapidation, become impossible." Such episodes terrified him. He brooded about their causes and what he could do to master them, a preoccupation that increased rather than diminished his anxiety. In May 1912, on Gosse's invitation, he gave a lecture on "The Novel in [Browning's] 'The Ring and the Book' " to the Royal Society of Literature, part of the celebration of the centenary of Browning's birth. His lecturing experience in America had been sufficiently gratifying to encourage him to feel that he could perform well in public. "Browning's great generous wings," he told his audience, many of whom, Howard Sturgis told him, could not hear because he spoke too quietly, "are over us still and even now, more than ever now; and . . . shake down on us his blessing." He would not have been inaudible, he claimed, if "the thundering" Arthur Pinero hadn't gone on so long and loudly immediately before him, though he also blamed it on his own "morbid modesty."[36] In June, he was not so modest that he declined to go to Oxford to receive an honorary degree from Magdalen College.

When the weather became hot in mid-July, he went to Lamb House. He felt tired, mostly from having broken his pledge to himself to be positively unsociable. There were some people and invitations to which he did not want to say no. Whatever the wear and tear, without company he felt lonely. Without social life, he had no company. He now regularly had gout attacks. Walking quickly distressed his chest—what he called "pectoral" attacks. "Slow and sustained walking," he felt, benefited him. When Wharton arrived from Paris a little after the middle of July, he motored with her on brief excursions. These were additionally pleasurable because the weather was so unexpectedly torrid. The last excursion was a visit to Nancy and Waldorf Astor's Cliveden, where, on August 1, he had a severe angina attack, and then another that evening after walking upstairs to his room. Wharton's chauffeur immediately returned him to Lamb House, where he went to bed, wanting only "to keep quite superstitiously *still* . . . between the sheets of recuperation." When Wharton left England in mid-August 1912, he breathed a sigh of relief that the greatest "whirligig . . . known to us, or to the Annals of Man, is revolving at maximum pace to Auvergne. . . . Long life to her—even at the cost of a shorter . . . to others."[37] Regular doses of nitroglycerin, as needed, kept the angina pain manageable.

He stubbornly kept at work, rarely so discomfited or depressed that he could not write. There were, fortunately, good days as well as bad through the summer of 1912. When Sturgis urged him to move from Rye to the hospitable and, if necessary, hospital-like Qu'Acre for an indefinite residence, he gratefully declined. In September, he found a large five-bedroom, affordable flat that he liked, the fifth-floor apartment at 21 Carlyle Mansions, Cheyne Walk, in Chelsea. It had large, wide-windowed front rooms looking southward over the embankment to the bustling life of the river and to Battersea Park in the near distance. With a sterling letter from the impeccably positioned Gosse, who wrote on House of Lords stationery, he had the hostile satisfaction of convincing the initially dubious "City and West End Properties Limited" that he was respectable enough for them to trust with a lease, his occupancy to begin at the end of the year. Gosse's letter "brought the silly landlords fluttering like pheasants" at his feet. "I swore," Gosse told him, "looking (or writing) very much down the bridge of my nose, that no other man quite so eligible and respectable exists. But a haunting fear comes over me. Was I telling the truth? *Are* you respectable?"[38]

At Carlyle Mansions, he had room for his three servants to have separate bedrooms as well as for a guest, who might, he feared, have to be a nurse. Soon after he first saw the flat, he became painfully ill with "a most violent and vicious" attack of shingles, "herpes zonalis," a disease of which he had never before even heard, an inflammation of the nervous system by the reactivated long-dormant virus from childhood chicken pox. As the autobiography was taking shape, the childhood virus had become reactivated. After a short, painful incubation period, he became unspeakably miserable for four months. First, he had the anguish of the difficulty of diagnosis—Skinner was initially baffled. Within a week, "vivid red welts—sores—blisters" determined the diagnosis of "unmistakable shingles." Initially, he hoped for rapid recovery: often the illness lasted no more than two or three weeks; in rare cases, it continued for three months. He soon classified himself as a medical curiosity, "a record case of the horrible thing, for persistent duration."[39] He managed only a few hours out of bed for occasional visitors. When his daylight hours were better, his nights were miserable. Feeling victimized, his exasperation and resentment pushed his patience almost beyond endurance as the untreatable disease continued to torment him. Local palliatives barely relieved the topical irritations. Sharp pain from inflamed nerves remorselessly continued. Worst of all, brief days of semirelief were followed by relapses that reminded him of the pattern of his nervous breakdown.

When a new palliative prescribed in late November 1912 by an eminent specialist failed to help, his anger about doctors exploded. "*The great Authority*" had left him "more crucified & more helpless" than he found him. Having at last begun to write again, he felt especially frustrated and resentful that he could hardly write at all. "It is a peculiarly devilish and excruciating ailment," he wrote to Andersen, "meaning, at its worst (and only at its worst do I seem to be knowing it) perpetual and dreadful pain, and above all, dismal and incurable persistence." He recognized, of course, that it was not incurable. In time it would go away. But, still, it had the "power to hang on and begin again and keep grinding at you until your heart almost breaks." He felt almost ashamed of having lived in a world in which such a disease "*could* rage and of having brushed carelessly and detachedly by its victims."[40] He was, he told Perry, having a "devil of a time." By mid-December, though, his darkness had become a "dreary dimness." He could look ahead to Scribner's and Macmillan bringing out *A Small Boy* in spring 1913. At least he had finished that. With materials at hand

and some sections under way, he wanted to get on with the second volume. If only he could have more days on which he felt well enough to work.

Though still sick, he agreed desperately with his doctor's recommendation that he would benefit from a change of scene, from a move as soon as possible from Lamb House winter darkness to London lights. Whatever the connection between mind and body, he felt he could do no worse than he had been doing where he was. Even if he had "to be dragged howling" from his bed and "goaded on in [his] bedclothes," he would do it, for "the celebrated 'change' dear to all physicians is a recognised specific in this case when every other tattered trick has at last failed." By mid-December, he was in a London hotel, his spirits raised, his physical pain diminished. On New Year's Eve, 1913, exhausted and in great pain, he settled, with a resident nurse, into his Carlyle Mansions flat, for the time being in "a wilderness of heaped-up impediments, with no forks, knifes, spoons or tableclothes unpacked." As soon as he could, he had a telephone installed. He loved it. "I hope you don't mind being rung up," he told everyone else who had one. "I myself rest upon the telephone as upon my nurse's lap in infancy." Though he quickly felt better, no sooner did the shingles disappear than he had a long period of severe stomach discomfort and pain. When that subsided, the angina reasserted itself with a vengeance. Calling it "chronic pectoral pain," he apparently convinced himself that it did not come "directly . . . from heart-trouble," that it was a non-life-threatening illness that mimicked angina.[41]

At times, he seemed to accept that the health of his heart was at issue. He was regularly using nitroglycerin, thinking of himself as an ambulatory invalid who, on his better days, with careful restraint, could both work and socialize moderately. At first, he took fresh air from a bath chair pushed along the embankment. By March 1913, he told the ailing Sturgis that "the worst is over & my nurse, thank God, is gone." As the winter misery declined, he felt better enough to lunch and dine regularly with friends, including Sargent's sister Emily, his neighbor at Carlyle Mansions. His usual London friends and visitors came and went. By late winter, he was at work on the second volume of his autobiography. "On good days," he told Macmillan, "I really feel as if I had at last struggled quite *through*." "He is looking much better," Gosse reported to Thomas Hardy, "but the *angina pectoris* is there, unrelenting, and he goes nowhere without the strange exploding specific they now give at the moment of paroxysm." When Alvin Coburn, in London again, expressed surprise about his limited schedule, he replied, "Of course I am ill—I am ill all the time; having . . . a grave chronic ailment which I have constantly to take into account. . . . Please understand that I am always and inveterately handicapped." Still, he enjoyed seeing Coburn and enlisted his help in preparing the photographs for the autobiography. In mid-July 1913, he moved to Lamb House for four months, from which, in early November, he mailed to Macmillan the finished manuscript of *Notes of a Son and Brother*. "I am no more fit," he wrote to Andersen, who expressed hope that he might see him on the Continent, "for journeys and transmigrations then for *tours de force* or other acrobatic feats in the market-place. My travel-power of every sort is dead and buried and I don't even weep on its tomb."[42]

No sooner had he risen to his feet in spring 1913 than he had the pleasure of sitting for a large-scale oil portrait by Sargent, for which he began in May the first of ten convivial sittings, to commemorate his seventieth birthday. Since Sargent encouraged him to bring friends with whom to chat during the sittings, he delighted in selecting the people for the honor of watching the great man at work. The birth date itself on April 15 was "a grim anniversary, a day almost as terrible as it has been beautiful." He did not like being seventy, especially at the cost of the burden he bore in illness and enervation, in the bitter memories of recent years and in the anticipation of worse. He avoided being seen or recorded wearing his reading glasses in public. Having had lifelong problems with his teeth, he soon consented to his London dentist's opinion that having all his teeth replaced by dentures might alleviate his angina. If the reasoning was obscure, the remedy at least would liberate him from having to be concerned about his teeth at all. It was "a desperate experiment for mitigation, if possible, of my too utterly distressful ailment of chronic angina, at times scarcely to be borne."[43] Having suffered so much from his teeth, he had no fondness for them. It all seemed to him consistent with his precipitous physical decline that had begun in early 1910.

The portrait itself was another matter, one that he initially agreed to reluctantly but that soon became a source of pleasure and pride. He feared that he would not like the image of him that Sargent would convey on canvas. He retained an enduring sense that the person whom others saw was not himself but an inferior version of the more attractive reality. He also felt uncomfortable that the portrait was one of a number of expensive efforts under way by his friends and supporters to memorialize his "extraordinary, prodigious, portentous, quite public Birthday." On the day itself he received a graceful, laudatory letter announcing the gifts, written by Percy Lubbock, and signed by 250 friends and supporters, among them almost the entire British literary world. In a delicately phrased letter of response, to which he appended every name and which he had printed as private gifts to all these friends, he thanked them for, among other things, the two gifts to which they had subscribed, a modern reproduction of a seventeeth-century golden bowl and the portrait by Sargent.

In the case of the bowl, he did not feel patronized by the gift. The cost was modest, the expense spread out among a large number of people. He felt differently about the portrait. Its value would be inestimable, not because of the subject but because of the fame of the artist. He would only accept the honor of sitting for the portrait on condition that it be offered to the National Portrait Gallery. Since he did not want the artist's labors to be a gift, he insisted that Sargent be paid. He had no objection to the painter giving his fee to a young sculptor, Derwent Wood, in payment for his creation of a bust of James. The young artist took a series of starkly candid working photographs. In no uncertain terms, James refused ownership of the portrait. His pride already had been challenged by a well-intentioned effort of Wharton's, assisted by Walter Berry, to provide him with a handsome gift of money composed of gifts from all his American friends and supporters.

With good reason to believe that he needed money more than he needed beautiful things, Wharton blundered into a project that might have damaged their relationship. Since he had lost almost no occasion over many years to complain to her about his poverty, to highlight the gap between the comparatively impoverished hospitality he could offer at Lamb House and what was offered him at Qu'Acre and in Paris, Wharton had good reason to think that he genuinely needed money for ongoing expenses, especially since his income had been further reduced by his illnesses. "Haunted by the spectre of impoverishment," he gave her and others the impression that "he was on the brink of ruin." Whereas she had purchased automobiles with royalties from her bestsellers, he had, he remarked, with a mixture of condescension and self-pity, been able to buy from royalties only the wheelbarrow used to bring visitors' luggage from the railroad station to Lamb House. In 1912, she had arranged to have Scribner's offer him an advance of eight thousand dollars for a novel (half of which he received on signing the contract) that Wharton herself would secretly pay from her Scribner's royalty account. Though suspicious, he had assumed that the idea and the money were Scribner's. When, in March 1913, he learned from his nephew about the "dreadful" American subscription project, he acted immediately to stop it, expressing his "indignant, and wholly prohibitive, protest." As a gesture of fraternal reassurance, he soon wrote to tell Edith that he had taken the liberty of adding her and Berry's name to the British testimonial. "It was simply not to be borne that you were out."[44]

Sargent's brilliant portrait of James is the nuanced counterpoint to La Farge's portrait of the young writer at seventeen years of age. Nature, time, and art had transformed the profile of the artist from the immature young man, for whom all experience existed in the unknown future, into the full-faced portrait of an old man whose promise is now absorbed into what has already been done. It is a social, accepting portrait, with a monumental element expressed in the bulk of his great full figure, of his sturdy expansive head, and in the flesh of his face that manages at the same time to be both childlike and worn. But it is also a sad, elegiac representation of James as social creature and James as isolated artist, the distinctiveness of this artist and the universality of experience revealed in his eyes and burnished in the rich, dominant browns. James loved the painting. Everything about it seemed wonderful, awesome. He felt "almost ashamed to admire it too much—& yet can't help being proud of my so limited connection with it." "There is a plaid waistcoat in it," Gosse wrote to Hardy, "heaving like a sea in storm, which is said to be prodigious."[45] Much in the portrait was stillness, quietness, and dignity—the depiction of a Victorian revenant. When the painting went on exhibit at Sargent's studio, James took every one of his visitors to see it.

Despite his invalidism, he found that with prudence, he could maintain the small social engagements that meant so much to him. He escorted people to see his portrait. He allowed himself to be whisked up by solicitous friends with automobiles for country drives. In September 1913, when Wharton returned to France, he told Howard Sturgis without complaint that "I am a snail of snails . . . & she is still, she is even in *some* ways more & more, an eagle." But on Christmas Day, 1913, the snail dined with Emily Sargent—"a family Xmas party"—then went to Hanover Terrace to have his Christmas dinner with the Gosses. He told Gosse to assure Max Beerbohm that he had read Beerbohm's latest book, which contained a parody of James, with "wonder and delight."[46] On New Year's Eve, 1914, he dined with the Gosses "*en famille.*" In the week between Christmas and the New Year, he twice had guests for lunch and made five brief social calls to, among others, Jessie Allen, Emily Sargent, and Rhoda Broughton, whose sharp, witty cynicism he more and more enjoyed. Despite his angina, he took a two-hour walk. If he walked slowly, he found that he could walk happily. If he kept on his feet, he felt sufficiently alive and independent. Except for occasionally severe, immobilizing attacks of angina or depression, he essentially kept to this schedule during the next two years.

(4)

Day after day in August 1914 he gazed eastward from Rye to the farthest edge of the horizon to where the waters of the English Channel disappeared. His imagination conjured unhappy Belgium into view. He could not believe that Europe was at war, that Austria and Germany were barbarically slashing away at the European comity that had lasted, more or less, almost a hundred years. "I didn't think to live to know this day, & it seems for the time to take all the meaning out of all the years of comparative decency which now tell us that their sense was but to lead up to it. Woe to art & beauty & the ingenious mind!"[47] It was as if Europe had indulged for a century in a dream of peace whose underlying reality was brutal aggression—the trumpets and flags that he had taken to be the banners of civilization were indeed now revealed to have been the announcements and instruments of brutal aggression. If the civilization that he had idealized was capable of such horrific viciousness, how then could it have been, even when it had seemed so fine, anything more than what it now revealed itself to be at its worst?

With heavy cannon fire resounding across the channel, with neutral Belgium burning only fifty miles away, he not only felt that he had been deceived and betrayed but that he had been a willing accomplice in his own betrayal. Despite his awareness of European prejudices, of widespread ethnic and national hatreds, of corrupt cynical governments, of ruthless economic competitiveness, and of general disregard for the sanctity of individual life, he had allowed himself the illusion that rational self-interest and high culture would prevail. In an essay in dialogue that he had published twenty-five years before, one of the civilized voices expressed dark foreboding about "the European family . . . a perfect menagerie of pet aversions." But "the world has become a big hotel, the Grand Hotel of the Nations," in which rational civility and enlightened self-interest must triumph."[48]

In the year leading up to August 1914, his mind had been focused on his youth. *Notes of a Son and Brother* turned out to be as much about the centrality of the Civil War experience to his and his family's life as about anything else. While writing, he had both relived and refashioned the complications of what he now called his "obscure hurt." The autobiography became a mythic representation of what, as an old man, he felt best dramatized his growth and development as an artist in a time of national turmoil. Whatever guilt he felt at not having been a participant he absorbed into a larger story, both a memorial to those who had fought and a testimony to the engagement of his own consciousness. Invoking a ghostly world from the past, he felt almost a ghost himself. Every member of the family that had shared the war years with him was dead. Remembering the horrors of war, he sensitized himself even more acutely to the horrors that were about to occur. As he read a stack of Wilky's letters, he felt his nerves tingle, "so trying so upsetting" did he "find it to plunge into this far-away and yet so intimate ghostly past where everything and everyone lives again but to become lost over again, and what seems most to come forth are the old pains and sufferings and mistakes." Nonetheless, rewriting his youth provided relief from the pain of the present. "How strangely one's *associations* with the far-off times & things get themselves twisted & turned." In November 1913, he sent off to Macmillan the completed manuscript of *Notes,* which he thought "much better" than *A Small Boy.* For months he had been reading Tolstoy's *War and Peace,* as if to bring into focus in his consciousness the three great wars of modern times—the Napoleonic Wars, the American Civil War, and the impending Great War, the tremors of which he seems to have intuited in his own reading and writing.[49]

Three witnesses to the world into which he had been born wrote to him about the autobiographical volumes—Howells, Perry, and Adams. Now a widower, Howells seemed to be living the life of a restless wanderer, more interested in constant change than in a single place of residence. To James, it seemed sad, pathetic, bizarre. While Howells flirted with the thought of settling in London, James was ecstatic about the possibility of having his old friend as a neighbor and companion. Immediately before sailing for Boston in August 1913, Howells visited Lamb House; they would never see one another again. They corresponded almost to the end, exchanging gossip and harsh opinions about the National Institute and American Academy, exchanging kind words and encouragement. Always committed to happy endings, Howells complimented him on "those two blithe books." But James expected not Howells but Perry to be his closest, most fully engaged reader. "I felt again & again that you would be the only person alive who would understand what I meant *there,* & though that others might think that they did it wouldn't be so true of any of them as of you." The English reaction to the book was on the whole acclamatory, congratulatory; the American response, hesitant, uneasy, distressed. He took as typical Grace Norton's carping, misconceived corrections. She even wanted "to know whether 'really & truly' " Minny Temple didn't " 'commit suicide'—dear M.T. every flicker of whose progressive extinction is laid bare & who at the last clung to life, & longed still to live on, with an intensity that was the essence of her tragedy." Perry gave him "intelligent sympathy." The cynical, caustic Adams gave him little sympathy. After reading the autobiography, Adams wrote to James a black, melancholy version of his calmer comment to Cameron that "James thinks it all real . . . and actually still lives in that dreamy, stuffy Newport and Cambridge, with papa James and Charles Norton—and me! Yet, why!" James wrote back, "I still find my consciousness interesting. . . . I still, in presence of life . . . have reactions—as many as possible. . . . It's, I suppose, because I'm that queer monster the artist, an obstinate finality, an inexhaustible sensibility."[50]

In May 1914, in a bizarre prelude to the violence to come, a militant suffragette broke the glass protecting his portrait by Sargent. Drawing out a meat cleaver concealed under her coat, she made three long slashes in the painting. She had no idea who Henry James was. Her act was not intended as a statement about the depiction of women in his fiction. To draw as much newspaper attention to her cause as possible, she had attacked a prominently displayed, widely discussed painting, a political act of violence that seemed to him both self-defeating and barbarically insane. "That those ladies really outrage humanity, & the public patience has to me," he wrote to Howells, "a very imbecile side." The more politically radical Howells commented ironically, "What a cruel shame to spoil one of the most beautiful portraits in the world! I think it must have been the work of some capitalist in disguise." James felt that his own body had been slashed. "I naturally feel very scalped and disfigured." Sargent and others, though, assured him that the wounds were curable.[51]

A year later, to his shock, he painfully found himself the subject of a parodic cannonade from someone he had no reason to think would extend to him anything but affection and respect. Over the years, his relationship with H. G. Wells had been congenial. The two were immensely different as writers, though James emphasized that the strength of the novel as a literary form was that it could happily contain such differences. To James, Wells lacked art and artfulness. His great strength was raw literary energy. To Wells, James had art without the ideas that art existed to serve. Like Shaw, Wells' primary interest was in a social and political message. Though their relationship had been ostensibly entirely warm, Wells apparently began to feel irked by James's criticism, no matter what the extent and nature of the praise. He probably sensed the fact that James was harsher about him to others than he was in speaking to him directly. "Strange to me," James had remarked to Mary Ward, "the coexistence of so much talent with so little art, so much life with . . . so little living!" It was hard for James to accept that a great talent would not deeply care about writing well. In America, after William's death, he expressed concisely, to Grace Norton, his judgment about Wells as a writer, remarking that he had just received a condolence letter from him "of a really beautiful brief eloquence—& he is not often beautiful."[52]

In spring 1914, James published, in *The Times Literary Supplement,* a broad, ineffective article surveying "The Younger Generation." He undoubtedly irked the already irritated Wells with what seemed narrow favoritism, general misjudgments, and magisterial dismissiveness, disguised as tolerance, of writers for whom he did not care. Wells impulsively struck back with a sharp parody of James in a chapter of a new book called *Boon,* a copy of which was hand-delivered to James in July 1915. Gently, effectively, James defended himself against an attack that seemed far out of proportion to his offense. Somewhat ruefully, but with honest regret in regard to the personal attack, Wells apologized. "I had rather be called a journalist than an artist, that is the essence of it, and there was no other antagonist possible than yourself. But since it was printed I have regretted a hundred times that I did not express our profound and incurable difference and contrast with a better grace." James assured him that he had not taken it personally, that he still admired what he had always admired about Wells. What he did imply, though, is that what he most feared, as he had all his life, was the victory of journalism over art, of Wells over James. For "it is art that *makes* life, makes interest, makes importance . . . and I know of no substitute whatever for the force and beauty of its process."[53]

Art, though, had been attacked most forcefully not by Wells but by the war. From Rye, in August 1914, he looked across the channel "at the fields of unthinkable blood" with a sense of dull misery. "The German crucifixion and whole treatment of the utterly harmless and innocent Belgium is an atrocity that cries aloud for some future penalty from the gods . . . that I am convinced will be extracted to the last squirm of the criminal." Britain, he was convinced, had done the right thing, the only moral thing, in not having "*merely* surrendered [Belgium] to butchery and atrocity," and in having remained committed to France. Not to have done so would have been "ignoble self-abasement." As much as he was outraged, he was frightened, his imagination vividly dwelling on "the enormous bloody blackness" and on the fate of numbers of friends who were caught on the Continent at the outbreak of war. Mary Jones and her daughter were in Paris, Sargent in the Tyrol, Persse in Austria. To his relief, Ariana Curtis managed to make her way from Venice to England. Unfortunately, Wharton, with Walter Berry, had recently left on a motor excursion to Spain. Previous to, and entirely separate from, the war she had rented the Humphry Wards' country house, Stocks, which James knew well, and where her household staff now awaited her arrival. Happily, his niece and nephew were with him through the summer at Rye. He hated to be alone, especially in such circumstances. "The plunge of civilization," he wailed to Sturgis the day after war had broken out, "into this abyss of blood & darkness by the wanton fiat of those 2 infamous autocrats is a thing that so gives away the whole long age during which we had supposed the world to be with whatever abatement gradually bettering, that to have to take it all now for what the treacherous years were all the while really making for *meaning* is too tragic for my words." Why, he asked himself, had he "lived on to see such a triumph of evil?"[54]

He made an effort to write. Having begun the third volume of his autobiography, to be called *The Middle Years,* he did not have the energy and concentration to carry it forward. Having accepted an advance against royalties of four thousand dollars from Scribner's for a new novel on the scale of *The Golden Bowl,* he returned to the American scene, with Newport as his setting. His characters were familiar variants on the dramatization of self-consciousness around themes of money, inheritance, love, and betrayal. He managed only a sizable fragment of what he called *The Ivory Tower.* Returning to a long fragment of what he had named *The Sense of the Past* when he had put it aside almost fifteen years before, he was able in his two or three hours of work each morning only to push it "uphill at the rate of about an inch a day." Whatever he tried, it "was very slow, very difficult, very delayed." Though he needed work to help him "escape turning too abjectly sick" in spirit, the war contributed to making it almost impossible in any sustained way.

Also, by late summer 1914, it made Rye impossible. He made a quick visit to London to see Wharton, where he stayed for a few nights at the London house she had rented as part of her arrangement with the Wards. He then went to Dorset to visit Adams, who had taken a house there. The two old friends stayed up late into the night talking about the war. On a late September evening, he watched, with an aching heart, large numbers of refugees, shell-shocked and destitute, stream through his small town, "our first small contingent . . . of the never-enough-to-be-pitied Belgian refugees; the sight of whom, in their misery, seen through the multitudinous welcome and the September dusk, brought home the image of the ravaged and tortured country." As unprepared Britain roused itself into full-scale conscription, even Rye became a training and staging crowd for soldiers, whom he watched with pride, foreboding, and restlessness. By the end of September, cutting short his summer, he returned to London. In Rye, he felt too isolated, too lonely. "I can't stand, amid all this awful tension, & not less this horrible immeasurable interest, the . . . 'out of it' life of the country any longer—I must be where I can hear & see & have informational contact: I eat my heart out alone."[55]

In London he had the solace of friends, of the possibility of distractions, of the circulation of rumors, people, activity. He felt some self-loathing at "so having lived on & on (with opportunities not to,) into anything so hideous & horrible," which "seemed to be a 'give-away' of all the long past of one's life, & of our age, which had been so perfidiously & treacherously leading up to it." As almost every young man he knew became a participant in the conflict, he worried for the safety of his friends. Persse went to training camp. "Try to think of something 'rich & strange,' " he urged him, "either in the way of tobacco, underclothing or literature. I will send you any underclothing but female—which I am told the Germans are often found uncannily wearing! I draw the line at *that*—even to make you even with them."[56] Denied active service because of poor eyesight, the restless Walpole went off as a reporter to Central Europe and then to Russia, hoping to participate as a partisan. Rumors circulated in London that he had left to escape the draft, which James defended him against. From Moscow, Walpole wrote sad lonely love letters. In Paris, Henrietta Reubell contributed to the war effort. Returning to France, Wharton engaged herself energetically in two all-consuming charitable war-support projects. The Angel of Devastation became a competent, committed Angel of Mercy. Able to get close to the front, she wrote graphic letters to James that stirred his heart and his tears. By late autumn, Burgess Noakes had departed for the front, temporarily replaced by a servant lent by Wharton. He soon returned, wounded, with a permanent limp.

When one of his undergraduate hosts in Cambridge in 1908, the young poet Rupert Brooke, died in the Mediterranean the next year, James felt an ache as painful as his angina. "I confess that I have no philosophy, nor piety, nor patience, no art of reflection, nor theory of compensation to meet things so hideous, so cruel, and so [mad], they are just unspeakably horrible and irremediable to me and I stare at them with angry and with almost blighted eyes." It was one of many deaths of people he knew whom he had expected would have the same chance to grow old as he had had. "It's the destruction of our splendid young manhood, the wasted seed of the future, that I most deplore & find heart-breaking." Perhaps he remembered his handsome cousin, Gus Barker, whom he had gazed at all those years ago in Newport posing nude at William Hunt's studio and who had been killed in the Civil

War. He took some solace now in being old, when he could no longer envy the young.[57]

But he did find a way to tend the young, to have the satisfaction of being active in the war effort in a way that was consistent with his health and his personality. Two charities engaged him—raising money for the destitute Belgian refugees and the American Volunteer Motor-Ambulance Corps, of which he became honorary president. Regularly visiting "our Chelsea Belgian circle for Refugees," a place "of reunion and conversation," he was able to offer verbal solace to the French-speaking Belgians and expressive sympathy to the Flemish-speaking Belgians, a virtual nation of strangers in a strange land to whom his heart went out in identifying sympathy. "Twice a week is held a sort of musical teaparty for them, at which we furnish the tea & cake—& they mostly the music. . . . They strike me as, in the cruelty of their desolation, of a natural courage & dignity that can't be sufficiently praised. And the *scale* of their tragedy is enormous & one doesn't see the end of [it] & I feel a little less finished & useless & doddering when I go on certain days & try to pull the conversational cart up hill for them." One of the more powerful self-defining fantasies of his life at last found fulfilling expression in December 1914, when he began to spend afternoons "at a great hospital full of the wounded—whom I have discovered in myself an unsuspected appetite for 'visiting.' " He had begun at St. Bartholomew's by visiting the Belgian wounded, but "then sloped off on the British as so much more interesting & full of savour—the best of them admirable, delightful."[58] They seemed to find his conversation, his attentiveness, his small gifts and efforts to help them with services and money, attractive. Suddenly, he felt extraordinarily useful, gratified, his extended grasp returned by young hands, his attentive touch on the brow of the youthful wounded a mercy that reaffirmed the presence of the "angelic Harry," that gave substance to that fantasy of himself that he had presented in his autobiography. Like Walt Whitman, he had become a nurse to the wounded flower of the nation. Having over the decades become a lover of Whitman, he now had a chance to do what Whitman had done. At last he did his Civil War service.

New Year's Day, 1915, broke on a fractured world. Physically, he felt better, as if the turmoil of wartime London and the larger international fractures made his own aches less substantial. Though angina attacks came with their usual regularity, the nitro alleviated the pain quickly. In mid-January 1915, invited by his friend Violet Asquith, he had enough energy to spend the weekend at Walmer Castle in Kent with her father the prime minister—"the good kindly friendly easy

Asquith"—one of whose other guests was "the great Winston," the first lord of the admiralty, who apparently had so much energy that he loudly outtalked the three or four other guests, including James. He soon claimed that he had "become a perfect Buddha of immobility," but in fact he managed during the first half of the year to be as active as he had ever been in recent years. In fact, in the late winter and early spring, he even managed to do some writing. He joked with the Perrys that he had "mastered more or less the trick of pretending to 'write' again, heaven help me, and don't at all despair of something's coming of it." Looking backward, he wrote a memorial essay on James and Annie Fields, which *The Cornhill* and the *Atlantic* published, and a brief article on Godkin and the origin of *The Nation*. With his aching eyes firmly on the present situation, he wrote a brief essay, "The Long Wards," evoking his hospital experiences for a volume called *The Book of the Homeless* that Wharton edited to raise money for refugees. Without having planned to do so, he even occasionally dedicated Lamb House to the war effort, at one point allowing it to be used to house refugees, and a number of times lending it to war-involved acquaintances as a place for rest and restoration. With his "inexhaustible sensibility," he did not want to leave London, the place where he could have and feel the full force of the sensations of this extraordinary time. That "things are horrible at present only seems to make them the more true." Though he felt within himself and all around him the protective surface that allowed him to live amidst such misery, "that surface is itself but a form of intensity, the need of a working as distinguished from a collapsing faith or passion."[59]

One day in April 1915, he went into Harrods to make a small purchase. It astounded him to see "people buying Easter eggs, of the most fantastic embellishment by the thousand, to all appearance—though perhaps of course for the trenches, where their shells will be of such use. Forgive the desperate refuge of the gibe." That they were Easter eggs meant nothing to him. His own passion was for a different register. Though the war's destructiveness repelled him, he felt pride and pleasure in the solidarity and self-sacrifice that, on the whole, it had elicited from the nation whose guest he had been for forty years. "There is a tremendous interest & upliftedness through it all too—& I am really divided between wishing I had gone before it & feeling a certain joy in not having missed some aspects & revelations of it."[60] With none of the ambivalence that he had felt, for personal reasons, about the American Civil War, he found that this war had an element of nobility that not even the ugly realities could completely discharge. Every cultural and political value in which he believed was under merciless attack by a barbaric enemy. To say that Britain itself was less than perfect only reaffirmed the laws of society, history, and nature. That it was as good as it was seemed to him the appropriate observation.

But why, he asked, was his own country not more engaged, more committed, more forthcoming in expressing solidarity with the Allies and affirming the Anglo-American values that German barbarism had so viciously assaulted? An intimate of the American ambassador and a regular visitor to the embassy, he kept his ear close to the ground of American politics and possibilities. In June 1914, at lunch at the embassy, he met Franklin Roosevelt, the assistant secretary of the navy in the new democratic administration. Unexpectedly, he soon had reason to praise the otherwise roundly despised cousin of Franklin's, Theodore, now a prematurely aged former president whose bellicose patriotism overlapped with James's own Anglophilia. Teddy Roosevelt thunderously preached American participation against Germany, especially as, in the next year, German submarines on the high seas continuously violated American neutrality. At first, James thought American nonparticipation would be an advantage, viewing America as an untainted moral arbiter for which the combatants might have good use in the future. "The outsideness of the U.S. will become after a bit, I feel sure, an enormous asset for us," he told Ariana Curtis. "Stand all of you to your guns," he urged Perry in America, and "think and believe how you can really and measurably and morally help us!"[61] By *us* he of course meant more than Americans residing in Europe.

By the beginning of 1915, six months of American neutrality had disappointed him. Even if neutrality might be of some help to Britain, the quality of American neutrality seemed unattractive, insufficiently moral, forceful, and engaged, as if the New World would prefer to leave the Old to its own miseries. President Wilson at first irritated then infuriated him—"our so very high & dry President" seemed more committed to protecting American business and monetary interests than to acting on moral values. His silent comparison was with Lincoln, the other wartime president of his life. The German purpose for years, he wrote in anguish to the Perrys, had been "to try & clumsily brew trouble between the '2 great branches' of the English-speaking race." German hands are now clasped "in glee just in proportion as Mr. Wilson's so spare & bare & lean & mean words of restriction & of dismal detachment (they sound *so* thin & poor in the thickness of our battle smoke & beside the audible beating of our hearts!) come forth as the best the U.S. (*as* the U.S.) have to offer us!" He hoped that Germany would act so aggressively against American shipping that America would have no choice but to join the Allies. In early June, he told

Lapsley that the official American attitude was jarring his nerves, assaulting his self-respect. Whatever understandable grounds there might be for not wanting to become a party to the international bloodletting, America did not have to be so amiably accommodating to Germany. She almost seemed to be "*fraternizing* with the common foe." Wilson's pleas for neutrality now struck him, in London, as irresponsible, self-serving cowardice. James felt as if he were being deprived of the moral America of which he had once been so proud.[62] By refusing to become a combatant in a war against evil, America was demonstrating that it had risen to the hateful maturity of the very European nations whose immorality had been the cause of the war. Angry that America would not do more, he looked to what he himself could do to help the cause in which he so deeply believed.

Early in June 1915, he made up his mind to apply for British citizenship. The possibility had been in his mind since the beginning of the war. He had lived in Britain for almost forty years. The America that had been his home and his nationality had long ago disappeared. Though, in every sense, America had formed and shaped him, now he could express both his disappointment with the country of his birth and his symbolic identification with the country whose guest he had been for so long by making the boldest, most public statement within his power. If America was not yet ready to help Britain, *he* was. His decision was triggered by his discovery that as a noncitizen, categorized as a "friendly alien," he could not travel to Rye without getting a certificate of permission from the government. He pronounced it an unbearable inconvenience. Actually, it distressed him much more as a symbol than as a practical matter. With the well-placed Gosse's advice and help, he initiated an application for naturalization, expedited rapidly by his obtaining as his four witnesses to his character and to competency in the English language—which the application ironically required— Prime Minister Asquith himself, who was amused and delighted; Edmund Gosse; George Prothero; and James Pinker. "You give us the most intimate thing you possess," Gosse responded to the news. "It is most moving, and most cheering, a grand geste indeed. . . . How I rejoice to think of you as about to be *of* us in this anxious time, as you have been *with* us without fail ever since the troubles began!" The gates of naturalization were opened in record time. As he went through, he felt, he told Gosse, "a deep & abiding peace."[63]

When the London *Times* and other newspapers printed, on the completion of the process in mid-July, his statement of his reasons for becoming a British subject, Kipling, the poet of imperialism, with whom he had not been in touch for years, expressed his appreciation for the act in language that James in other circumstances might have had some ambivalence about. "You don't know what it means or what it will go on to mean not to the Empire alone but to all the world of civilization that you've thrown in your lot with them." All lovers of literature "in this country will welcome the decision of this writer of genius, whose works are an abiding possession of all English-speaking people," the London *Times* remarked. In America, some of the response was ambivalent, most of it a mixture of disappointment and hostility. Immediately, the major American newspapers headlined the act of national apostasy. Its political ramifications were soon absorbed into the varied American editorial views on the war. The *New York Herald* added to its long, mostly biographical story that in addition to his long life in England and his sympathy for the Allies he had "changed his nationality [because of his] great disappointment over America's attitude regarding German atrocities." The sophisticated urban newspapers disguised regret with analysis, leavening the underlying feeling of rejection and national betrayal with rational, even sympathetic, explanations. Pro-British newspapers served their common cause by quoting extensively from British newspaper comment on how gratifying it was to have James's support in their dark hour and in their righteous cause.[64] Americans who supported Wilsonian neutrality, especially the large pro-German voice, naturally deplored James's decision on political grounds.

But whatever the political pressures, beneath almost all American comment was a sense of loss, which in its crude but widespread expression took the form of hearty, sometimes nasty statements of pleasure at being rid of bad baggage. "We think it alright for foreigners to like this country better than their own," *The New York Times* commented, "but when an American shows a similar preference for some part of Europe, we do not often refrain from saying that there is something distinctly and seriously wrong with him—that his desertion is a good riddance." To his American friends and his Cambridge family, James offered explanation and asked for understanding. "I think it quite natural," he responded to Lilla Perry, "you should regret my not having been able to stick to my American citizenship; you can't regret it more than I do, but that 'able' contains the whole essence of the matter. I hold that one should always so stick—save in the presence of facts . . . that altogether transform the case. The immediate presence of the Enemy transforms it from head to foot when one's own nationality does nothing for one that keeps pace with the transformation." He did not have to justify himself to the sensible, ever-loyal Howells, whose fury at Wilson's neutrality did not overcome his hostility to British royalism, but who seriously joked that he would be glad to exchange citizenship with "some Frenchman." He was sorry to lose James as an American, "but he had a full right to do what he has done." With an extraordinary sophistication of its own, *The New York Times* provided the most thoughtful, generous gloss on the complications of James's life as an American writer. "Henry James has long been most at home in England. Most of his friends live there. As to his desire . . . to throw his 'moral weight and personal allegiance' . . . in the scale of the contending nations,' his brother William might have smiled a little, but we shall not smile. The war is too grave a matter to stir much smiling, even if it is responsible in part for the loss of James's American citizenship, long lightly held. It is easy enough to be severe or sarcastic at this defection and to insist that an American should remain an American. But, after all, the United States wants no citizens by compulsion. And as a literary absentee Mr. James has a long line of predecessors, Byron and Landor, Turgenieff, Heine, Wagner, Nietzsche rise at once in the memory. To the literary man choice of his scene is to be granted."[65]

(5)

The final, involuntary scene began to gather its determinants. In late spring and summer 1915, as the warm weather came on, he had numbers of episodes of hostility to food and severe depression. He interpreted sharp angina attacks, for which he took nitroglycerin, as functions of his stomach, not his heart. If not eating would not cure him, it might end the need for a cure at all. Somehow he thought he would regain his stomach and his health by starving himself. "I *am* laid up once in a while for 24 hours or so with a wretched recurrent kick of my horrid illness of 1910–12" he told Howard Sturgis, "but less & less often, happily—though the possibility is always there." Unwilling to leave London, he decided against Lamb House for the summer. He preferred the heat to the isolation. Besides, even traveling to Rye seemed formidable. In late August, he became severely ill—"a bad sick week"—and he also had difficulty breathing.[66] At the beginning of September, he tried to resume his usual social activities. But he had a relapse that frightened him enough to call a doctor, who stopped by almost every day now, mainly for reassurance. Though he was able to go out, he felt weak and drained. After a miserable night, he exhorted himself to take his usual walks. He struggled into some mobility. But it was very limited. Mostly, now, friends came to see him.

With the wounded Noakes back from the war, with the invaluable

Bosanquet to assist him, he mustered his willpower to go down to Rye for a week in October. He thought it would do him good. Also, he wanted to oversee the packing of his books and bookcases for removal to his Chelsea apartment to make it more "homelike." But difficulty in breathing at night made sleep uncomfortable and elusive. He called in his old friend Dr. Skinner, who lectured him on his misconception about his stomach. In London, Dr. Des Voeux and Dr. Mackenzie, taking up Skinner's message, together at last convinced him that it undoubtedly was not his stomach but his heart. Des Voeux immediately put him on digitalis. To his "belovedest Hugh," he confessed that he had "been having a regular hell of a summer and autumn . . . during the first weeks of which I lost valuable time by attributing my condition . . . to mistaken causes." Whether he had been mistaken or not, he had a clear view of his situation. "The past year has made me feel twenty years older, and, frankly, as if my knell had rung."[67] When he sat up his last autumnal night at Lamb House before departing, perhaps writing letters, as he had for so many years, into the earliest morning hours, he heard some of the same nocturnal sounds that had accompanied him in so many of the quiet hours of his life—the audible silence of his small Sussex world. He was never to see Lamb House again.

By late October 1915, he had lost the energy to make entries in his diary except those of regular visits from the doctor. He was not an easy victim, a ready collaborator with illness, his naturally strong constitution providing the regular illusion of revival—better days to alternate with bad ones. In early November, he felt enough better to do some walking and to have visitors, though little of both. "My doctor pronounces me very successfully better than for some time back, but I have a complication or two that holds on still." He tried to write letters, but the difficulty mostly balked him. "My poor old state has made writing very difficult." Since Des Voeux and Mackenzie had convinced him that his heart condition had gone beyond angina, he was now willing to call it "an aggravated condition of heart." He consoled himself a little by feeling lucky in his doctors. "I get [from them], and evidently shall get, a good deal of relief," he wrote to Peggy on the first of December. He ended the letter, though he had dictated it to Bosanquet, with farewell to his life as a writer—"the pen drops from my hand." The next morning, when he tried to get out of bed, he fell on the floor. His left leg had collapsed under him. As he fell, he thought, "So it has come at last—the Distinguished Thing." When he tried to ring the bell next to his bed, his hand got entangled in some electric lamp wiring. Unable to ring, he called out for help. When Burgess and another servant ran into the room, they found him on the floor. With difficulty, they raised him to his bed. Miss Bosanquet came from Lawrence Street immediately. James was completely conscious, his eyes wide open, his manner calm. He had had a stroke, he told her, "in the most approved fashion."[68] His left side was paralyzed.

Fully alert, he dictated a telegram to his nephew Henry in New York. His sister-in-law, who had been visiting her son, immediately booked passage for the wintry voyage to London. Both Harry and Peggy would follow as soon as their schedules permitted. Alice was loyally determined that her husband's brother would have at least one James hand to hold as he died. In London, Miss Bosanquet called and wrote nearby friends, including Edith Wharton in Paris. She provided regular bulletins. To Edith, the immediate concern was would she serve him best by coming directly to his bedside or would she damagingly frighten him about the seriousness of his condition by making the journey from Paris in the midst of a devastating war. She indecisively waited in Paris, always thereafter to regret having lost this last chance.

The next day he had a second stroke. Mackenzie was very alarmed as his patient faded into unconsciousness. Then unexpectedly, within days, he was alert again. James assured them that he did not quite feel paralyzed, that there must be a better word for his condition. He asked for a thesaurus to help him find it. He also asked that his friends not be unduly alarmed. Sargent, who lived nearby, told the devastated Gosse that he "has had two slight strokes within the last forty eight hours. He is paralyzed on the left side—his brain is clear, and his speech." Other nearby friends came to help, or at least to get information. On the suggestion of the doctors and nurse, they were asked not to telephone, "for the bell disturbs him." An informal news network developed. At any change in his condition, one of the servants or Miss Bosanquet called Lucy Clifford, Percy Lubbock, or Fanny Prothero, who then called those whom they knew would be grateful to have any news. From Paris, Elizabeth Cameron wrote to Adams in America that "it is slight so far and it affects only his left side. If Edith . . . is allowed by the doctors she will go to England but I am sure it will be forbidden as I was when you were ill." Adams responded mordantly that "all my contemporaries have got paralysis." When Edith sent a loving note, Henry listened thankfully and asked Theodora to give her his love. "Our world will have a large hole in it—if he goes," Lucy Clifford achingly remarked, "one that will never be filled!" When the news reached him, Howells painfully exclaimed, "He is the last that is left of my earthly world."[69]

Pulling back from unconsciousness at the end of the first week of December 1915, he suddenly expressed the desire to work again. He wanted to write. His attendants were alarmed. It seemed inconceivable except as a conception of delirium. Besides, he was weak, he had hardly slept, he had not the energy to talk much. He seemed dislocated, as if he were someplace else, though where exactly he could not make clear to anyone. He was not in London. Why would they not tell him where he was? He wanted detailed descriptions of the landscape and the weather. He seemed much worse. When he developed a fever, the doctors diagnosed embolic pneumonia. For a while he was unconscious and delirious. Tell Gosse, he said, responding to a note from his old friend, "that his powers of recuperation were infinite!"[70] Reluctantly, Bosanquet brought the Remington into his bedroom. Perhaps the clicking sounds of the keys would comfort and reassure him. On December 8, he dictated a paragraph about his impending death, evaluating its prospect as a subject for new interest, for new writing. That it was a new subject did not seem to make it interesting enough. Five years before, he had expressed himself on the subject of an afterlife in a brief essay, "Is There Life After Death?" His answer was that he did not know, that he thought it unlikely, but that it was a valuable idea because it created life, it made for interest. Still, even if it was not interesting now to be dying, "I feel sure I shall discover plenty of fresh worlds to conquer, even if I am to be cheated of the amusement of them."

Three days later he had entered another imaginative world, one connected to the beginning of his life as a writer, to the Napoleonic world that had been a lifelong metaphor for the power of art, for the empire of his own creation. He began to dictate notes for a new novel, "fragments of the book he imagines himself to be writing."[71] As if he were now writing a novel of which his own altered consciousness was the dramatic center, he dictated a vision of himself as Napoleon and his own family as the imperial Bonapartes. His first infant and childhood sights of Napoleonic Paris glimmered in the background of his imaginative conquest. His lifelong interest in Napoleon, about whom he had always read with fascination, provided him with a unitary image of great art and great triumph. The guns of the two wars of his lifetime now merged into the guns of the Napoleonic Wars, whose vast campaigns he had most recently been experiencing in Tolstoy's novel. The grand images of terror and of accomplishment that had stalked the halls of the Louvre in his powerful dream resonated with the Louvre as Napoleon's palace and as the museum to which he had brought all the artistic treasures from his European conquests. Searching for an image of the imperial family, whose highest power was the ruler who glorified art, he brought together both his beginning and his end. William and Alice he grasped with his regent hand, addressing his "dear and most esteemed brother and sister." To them, to whom he had granted countries, he now gave the responsibility of supervising the detailed plans he had created for "the decoration of certain apartments, here, of the Louvre and Tuileries, which you will find addressed in detail to artists and workmen who take them in hand." The family into which he had been born was to have a brilliant destiny, its achievements immortalized. He counted on them for that. He would be unforgivingly harsh if they failed. He was himself the "imperial eagle." His mind was let loose from conventions and restraints, from the qualifying metaphor into pure symbolic representation.

Taking down the dictation, Theodora felt it to be almost more than she could bear. "It is a heart-breaking thing to do, though, there is the extraordinary fact that his mind *does* retain the power to frame perfectly characteristic sentences." After the twelfth, he did no more dictation. When Alice arrived on December 14, he rallied briefly. Des Voeux thought that he might pull through, though the paralysis would be permanent. Happy to see Alice, he smiled at her in recognition. Frequently conscious, he was able to speak intelligibly. Soon his sister-in-law took over supervision of his narrowed world, which now excluded Miss Bosanquet. With a sense of family possessiveness and propriety, Alice wanted nothing to do with Theodora and especially Edith, of whom she disapproved. The self-sacrificing Theodora, who now found herself shut out, still felt "unspeakably glad that Mrs. James has come." He ate very little. The constant pain in his chest and lungs was relieved by morphine. When he was unconscious or asleep, the nurse allowed intimate friends to come in for a last look. Theodora had a glimpse of him looking "desperately ill—his face all drawn and wasted and unshaved, head falling right over to the paralyzed side, and his body barely covered by a brownish Jaeger blanket—his feet sticking out beyond it at the bottom." To Bob's widow, Alice wrote that there is no hope of "much recovery . . . with the left side paralyzed, but his mind is clear—save when now and then he wanders—and his speech unimpaired. . . . I realize how you will feel the going of the last of the brothers."[72]

Toward the end of the month, the doctors discovered pleurisy in his right lung—his breathing was even more labored than before. Still, he had a remarkable reserve of strength. At moments, suddenly, for very brief periods, he would seem almost as if he were recovering, with a clear mind and normal speech, except that he was convinced that he was someplace else. At Christmas, his mental powers began to fade noticeably, separate from the effect of the sleeping powders and the regular morphine injections. As the New Year approached, he wrenched the hearts of his attendants with the dramatic paradox of his being more physically strong than he had been for a month but less mentally himself. He insisted on being taken out of bed. He wanted to go to the front room, to gaze southward over the river, where there was sunlight and a view. A number of times he was put in a chair and carried to the window, where he sat for hours and hours.

On New Year's Day, 1916, the revolving world stopped for a moment to pay homage in the form of an announcement that he had received the Order of Merit. His friends, particularly Gosse, had made sure that it would occur, and occur quickly. When told the news, he seemed pleased. When the insignia was brought to his bedside, having hardly said a word, he asked his servant, as everyone left the room, "to turn off the light so as to spare my blushes." One of the congratulatory letters came from Thomas Hardy on behalf of The Society of Authors. The letters appeared to mean nothing to him. For almost two months, he seemed to his sister-in-law "like a tired child but tranquil, comfortable, enjoying his food and the sitting on a big lounge in the window whence he can look out at the river, with the ever-creeping barges and the low-lying clouds."

Recognizing his family and friends, he apparently had little or nothing to say to them or to anyone else. Harry and Peggy had arrived. To Burgess, he sometimes gently murmured "Burgess James," as if he had decreed him a member of the family. It seemed to him, literally, as he looked at the barges on the Thames, that he was aboard a ship. Harry assured Tom Perry that at least they did not have to feel the pain of his being aware of his condition, for "he suffers no pain and no more mental distress than is inseparable from a state of drowsy muddle. . . . His fragmentary speech abounds in amplified courteousnesses—sometimes more ample than ever—and in broken but solicitous enquiries about the welfare of anyone who appears beside him. He also wanders a great deal in the past, and seems often to think that my father is here, tho' not in the same room." One day in February, he said to Peggy that he hoped her father would be in soon—"he is the one person in all Rome I want to see. . . . I should so like to have William with me." Gosse wanted to visit for one last time. Alice delayed answering him for a month. "I waited first in the hope that Henry was really gaining and that I might ask you to come and see him. But he is never coming back to us. He does not suffer and the mental confusion which distressed him at first no longer weighs on him. He thinks he is in foreign cities, among old friends, and that his brother William, the only one he asks for, will be coming in ere long. Such serenity of spirit shines through the wrecked brain that his presence is still a comfort to us."[73]

Late in the month, he felt he was about to die. Frightened, he stayed up all night and then asked Alice to stay with him. The change was noticeable, massively transformative. The next day, he became unconscious. Apparently he made efforts to speak, but nothing could be heard. He stopped eating. On February 28, 1916, as his breath came in short gasps, he seemed to the doctor to be dying. Early in the evening, he sighed noticeably. As the last of three sighs faintly expired, he was dead. The fires of the crematorium at Golders Green soon transformed his corpse into ashes that were placed in a small urn. A few days later, there was a public service a few hundred yards away from where he had died, in Chelsea Old Church. Alice readily agreed to the request that a plaque be erected in his memory. But though she found it easy to think of "Henry in the Heavenly Country toward which he has journeyed, never more faithfully than during these weeks of bewildered helplessness," she did not find it easy to think that England would be his final resting place. She made other plans for her beloved brother-in-law, perhaps at his request.[74] Neither British law nor wartime prohibitions interested or deterred her. Without declaring her precious cargo, she soon boarded a transatlantic liner, determined to submit herself and the last member of her generation of the family she had married into to whatever perils the journey held, and to the fulfillment of her insistence that Henry would have wanted to be reunited with William and Alice, with his beloved mother and his extraordinary father. His last crossing was a winter voyage. His ashes were carried by his sister-in-law to the cemetery in Cambridge, with the view of Boston in the distance, to be buried and blended in the American earth from which he had come.

Notes

Primary Names

AB	Anna Balestier	ER	Elizabeth Robins
AC	Ariana Curtis	ET	Edmund Tweedy
ACB	Arthur Christopher Benson	EVW	Edgar Van Winkle
AF	Annie Fields	EW	Edward Warren
AHJ	Alice Howe James (MrsWJ)	FB	Francis Boott
AJ	Alice James	FK	Frances Anne Kemble (Fanny)
AK	Catherine Walsh (Aunt Kate)	FLB	Florence Bell
ALC	Alvin Langdon Coburn	FM	Francis Mathews
BE	Betham-Edwards	FPC	Frances Power Cobbe
CB	Charles Brookfield	FRM	Fanny Rollins Morse
CC	Cora Crane	FS	Fanny Stevenson
CEN	Charles Eliot Norton	GC	Grace Carter
CFW	Constance Fenimore Woolson	GDM	George du Maurier
CHA	Clover Hooper Adams (MrsHA)	GL	Gaillard Lapsley
		GN	Grace Norton
CLB	Clare Benedict	GW	J. J. Garth Wilkinson
CMG	Charles Milnes Gaskell	GWJ	Garth Wilkinson James (Wilky)
COM	Edward Compton	HA	Henry Adams
DC	Daniel Curtis	HB	Henry Brewster
EB	Elizabeth Boott	HCA	Hendrik Christian Andersen
EC	Elizabeth Cranch (Mrs. C. P. Cranch)	HDK	Helena de Kay
		HGW	Herbert George Wells
ECA	Elizabeth Cameron	HJ	Henry James
EDE	Edward Emerson	HJSR	Henry James, Sr.
EDW	Edith Wharton	HJ3	Henry James III (Harry)
EE	Ellen Emerson	HR	Henrietta Reubell
EG	Edmund Gosse	HS	Howard Sturgis
EGB	Elizabeth Gibbens	HW	Horace Walpole
EL	Elizabeth Lewis	IG	Isabella Gardner
ELG	Edwin Lawrence Godkin	JA	Jessie Allen

JAD	John Augustin Daly	OW	Owen Wister
JC	John Clark	OWH	Oliver Wendell Holmes
JH	John Hay	PB	Paul Bourget
JJP	James Jackson Putnam	RB	Rhoda Broughton
JLF	John La Farge	RJ	Robertson James (Bob)
JM	James Mackenzie	RK	Rudyard Kipling
JO	James Osgood	RLS	Robert Louis Stevenson
JP	Jocelyn Persse	RUJ	Robert Underwood Johnson
JPI	James Pinker	RWE	Ralph Waldo Emerson
JRL	James Russell Lowell	SBW	Sarah Butler Wister
JS	Jonathan Sturges	SC	Scribner's
JSS	John Singer Sargent	SGW	Samuel Gray Ward
JTF	James Thomas Fields	SM	Samuel Mather
KDB	Katherine De Kay Bronson	SN	Sara Norton
KPL	Katherine P. Loring	SSD	Sarah Sedgwick Darwin
LCL	Lucy Clifford	TA	Thomas Aldrich
LCP	Lilla Cabot Perry	TB	Theodora Bosanquet
LH	Louise Hooper	TBS	T. Bailey Saunders
MAC	Frederick Macmillan	TC	Theodore Child
MB	Minnie Bourget	TH	Thomas Hardy
MCJ	Mary Cadwalader Jones	TSP	Thomas Sergeant Perry
MF	Morton Fullerton	VC	Virginia Compton
MJ	Mary James (MrsHJSR)	VH	Violet Hunt
MJV	Mary James Vaux	VP	Violet Paget
MMJ	Mary Margaret James	WB	Wolcott Balestier
MRJ	Mary Robertson James (MrsRJ)	WDH	William Dean Howells
MT	Minny Temple	WEH	William E. Henley
MW	Mary Ward (Mrs. Humphry Ward)	WEN	William Edward Norris
		WJ	William James
MWA	Margaret Warren	WR	Whitelaw Reid
OA	Olivia Andersen	WWB	William Wilberforce Baldwin

Libraries

BL	British Library
BR	John Hay Library, Brown University
CL	Colby College Library
DA	Dartmouth College Library
DK	Duke University Library
HO	Houghton Library, Harvard University
HU	Huntington Library
LC	Library of Congress
TX	Harry Ransom Humanities Center, University of Texas
VX	Mr. and Mrs. Henry Vaux
VB	Barrett Collection, University of Virginia

Titles

AI	Edmund Gosse, *Aspects and Impressions*, 1922.
AJD	*The Diary of Alice James*, ed. Leon Edel, 1964.
AL	Gay Wilson Allen, *William James: A Biography*, 1967.
AMS	Henry James, *The American Scene*, 1907.
AN	Michael Anesko, *"Friction with the Market": Henry James and the Profession of Authorship*, 1986.

BJ   Daniel W. Bjork, *William James: The Center of His Vision*, 1988.
DJ   *The Death and Letters of Alice James*, ed. Ruth Yeazell, 1981.
ED   *Henry James Letters*, ed. Leon Edel, 4 vols., 1974–1984.
EDEL   Leon Edel, *The Life of Henry James*, 2 vols., 1977.
EDWL   *The Letters of Edith Wharton*, ed. R.W.B. Lewis and Nancy Lewis, 1988.
EGL   Evan Charteris, *The Life and Letters of Edmund Gosse*, 1931.
EHJ   Austin Warren, *The Elder Henry James*, 1934.
ELL   Richard Ellmann, *Oscar Wilde*, 1988.
GALE   Robert Gale, *A Henry James Encyclopedia*, 1989.
GLA   Edith Wharton, *A Backward Glance*, 1933.
GR   Bernice Groskopf, " 'I'll Be a Farmer': Letters of William James," *Virginia Quarterly Review* 66, no. 4 (1990): 587–600.
GROS   Phyllis Grosskurth, *The Woeful Victorian: A Biography of John Addington Symonds*, 1964.
HAB   Alfred Habegger, *Henry James and the "Woman Business,"* 1989.
HAL   *The Letters of Henry Adams*, ed. Ernest Samuels, 6 vols., 1982–1988.
HAR   Virginia Harlow, *Thomas Sergeant Perry: A Biography*, 1950.
HAS   Jorg Hasler, *Switzerland in the Life and Works of Henry James*, 1966.
HF   Howard M. Feinstein, *Becoming William James*, 1984.
HORN   Philip Horne, *Henry James and Revision*, 1990.
HY   Montgomery Hyde, *Henry James at Home*, 1969.
LB   *The Letters of Henry James*, ed. Percy Lubbock, 2 vols., 1920.
LE   R.W.B. Lewis, *The Jameses: A Family Narrative*, 1991.
LEW   R.W.B. Lewis, *Edith Wharton: A Biography*, 1975.
LR   *The Literary Remains of Henry James*, ed. William James, 1884.
MA   Jane Maher, *Biography of Broken Fortunes*, 1986.
MAT   F. O. Matthiessen, *The James Family*, 1948.
MO   *Selected Letters of Henry James to Edmund Gosse, 1882–1915*, ed. Rayburn S. Moore, 1988.
MON   George Monteiro, *Henry James and John Hay: The Record of a Friendship*, 1965.
MY   *The Middle Years*, in *Henry James: Autobiography*, ed. Frederick W. Dupee, 1983.
NBK   *The Complete Notebooks of Henry James*, ed. Leon Edel and Lyall H. Powers, 1987.
NOR   *Letters of Charles Eliot Norton*, ed. Sara Norton & M. A. De Wolfe Howe, 2 vols., 1913.
NSB   *Notes of a Son and Brother*, in *Henry James: Autobiography*, ed. Frederick W. Dupee, 1983.
OT   Patricia O'Toole, *The Five of Hearts*, 1990.
PER   Ralph Barton Perry, *The Thought and Character of William James*, 2 vols., 1935.
PL   *The Complete Plays of Henry James*, ed. Leon Edel, 1990.
POW   *Henry James and Edith Wharton: Letters: 1900–1915*, ed. Lyall H. Powers, 1990.
SAM   Ernest Samuels, *Henry Adams*, 1989.
SB   *A Small Boy and Others*, in *Henry James: Autobiography*, ed. Frederick W. Dupee, 1983.
SEY   Miranda Seymour, *A Ring of Conspirators*, 1988.
SL1   *The Selected Letters of Henry James*, ed. Leon Edel, 1955.
SL2   *Henry James: Selected Letters*, ed. Leon Edel, 1987.
ST   Jean Strouse, *Alice James: A Biography*, 1980.
TEH   Arline Boucher Tehan, *Henry Adams in Love*, 1983.
THE   *The Letters of Mrs. Henry Adams*, ed. Ward Thoron, 1936.
TO   Cheryl B. Torsney, *Constance Fenimore Woolson: The Grief of Artistry*, 1989.

WARD Mary Ward, *A Writer's Recollections*, 2 vols., 1918.
WDHL *William Dean Howells: Selected Letters*, ed. David J. Nordloh and Christoph K. Lohmann, 6 vols., 1981.
WJL *The Letters of William James*, ed. Henry James (III), 2 vols., 1920.
WWS Henry James, *William Wetmore Story and His Friends*, 2 vols., 1903.

PRIMARY TEXTS

For James's novels, I have generally followed the editorial principles embodied in the Library of America editions of the novels and in *The Complete Tales of Henry James*, ed. Leon Edel, 1964; both these editions are especially appropriate for a biographical narrative: the first English or American edition, depending on local considerations, is the text of record. The New York Edition speaks only to the considerations of the edition itself and to what was on James's mind in 1905–1907.

CHAPTER ONE. REMEMBERED SCENES, 1843–1855

1. *NSB*, 439–40; *NBK*, "The Turning Point of My Life," 437–38.
2. "From Venice to Strasburg," *The Nation*, 3/6/1873; republished as "Venice: An Early Impression" in *Italian Hours*, 1909.
3. HJ/JA, 6/24/1907. *ED4*, 451–52; *NBK*, 582–84.
4. *LE*, 3–5.
5. *LR*, 148.
6. Computing modern equivalents of the value of money from previous historical periods is extremely difficult. Economic historians disagree about a feasible formula. When I have been forced into positing equivalents, I have generally multiplied by ten, particularly in regard to the purchasing power of dollars and of British pounds during the second half of the nineteenth century. But the availability of human services at paltry sums, by today's standards, needs to be taken into account.
7. *NSB*, 397.
8. *NSB*, 397.
9. *LR*, 181–86.
10. Jeanette James/Marcia Ames James, 9/30/1827? HO; Augustus James/Rev. WJ, 5/1/1828. *ST*, 8–9.
11. Eventually, Nott was able to repay his debt to James when a complicated scheme for raising money through a series of marginally legal and mostly corrupt state-supported lotteries produced close to $300,000 for the college and made Nott and others personally wealthy; *HF*, 48–50; *EHJ*, 17–18.
12. *NSB*, 348–51; HJ/Isaac Jackson, 1/30/1830. *EHJ*, 18–19; *HF*, 51–53; Eliphalet Nott/Archibald McIntyre, nd. Harold Larabee, "The Flight of HJ the First," *The New England Quarterly*, 12/1937, *HF*, 57.
13. *NSB*, 396–98.
14. Caroline Dall, 1/13/1865. Dall Papers. Quoted *HAB*, 206–7.
15. HJSR/RWE, nd/1842. *PER1*, 43; *NSB*, 345–46; RWE/HJSR, 10/11/1843. *PER1*, 52–53.
16. HJSR/SGW, 1/31/1854. HO.
17. *SB*, 32–33.
18. MJ/MrsGW, 11/29/1846. HO.
19. *HAB*, 27–62; HJSR/"My dear Friend," 4/8/1855. VB.
20. *AL*, 13; HJSR/SGW, 1/31/1854. HO; MJ/MrsGW, 11/29/1846. HO.
21. *NSB*, 342–44.
22. *SB*, 58, 16–17.

23. *SB*, 32.
24. HJSR/ET, nd/1853. *ST*, 33–34.
25. *SB*, 38.
26. *SB*, 15, 38.
27. *SB*, 51, 30–31.
28. *SB*, 188–89.
29. HJSR/SGW, 3/9/1854. HO; NSB, 330–341; SB, 132–34.
30. *NSB*, 277–80.
31. *SB*, 113–14, 115–20.
32. *SB*, 121–30.
33. *SB*, 36.
34. *SB*, 68–69.
35. *SB*, 89, 92.
36. *SB*, 68–69, 148–50.
37. *WWS*1, 259–60.
38. HJSR/RWE, 8/31/1849. *PER*1, 57–59; HJSR/SGW, 3/16/1855. HO; HJSR/GW, 9/6/1852. *PER*1, 22–24; HJSR/ET, 2/24/1852. *PER*1, 74–75; HJSR/RWE, 10/30/1851. *PER*1, 71–72.
39. RWE/HJ, 6/25/1855. *PER*1, 82; HJSR/SGW, 6/26/1855. HO.

CHAPTER TWO.   BELONGING, 1855–1860

1. *SB*, 169–71.
2. *SB*, 157–61, 197–98.
3. *SB*, 167–71; *PER*1, 83–86.
4. *SB*, 174–75.
5. *WWS*2, 29–31.
6. MJ/Catherine Barber (MrsWJ), 8/25/1856. HO; WJ/EVW, 8/2/1856. GR, 588–89; SB, 192–97.
7. *SB*, 205–17.
8. HJSR/EC, nd/1857, 9/14/1857. VX; WJ/EVW, 1/1858. GR, 591.
9. Charles P. Kindleberger, *Manias, Panics, and Crashes*, 1989, 156; HJSR/WJ (of Albany), 10/28/1857. HO.
10. HJSR/EC, 3/21/1858. VX; WJ/EVW, nd/1858. GR, 592; SB, 234–35.
11. *SB*, 196–97.
12. HJ/EVW, nd/1856. *ED*1, 5.
13. *SB*, 10.
14. *SB*, 105–6.
15. HJSR/Fanny MacDaniel, 5/13/1858, 6/10/1858, 8/15/1858. HO; *PER*1, 122–23; HJSR/EC, 5/1/1858. VX; WJ/EVW, 5/1858. GR, 596.
16. *NSB*, 277–80.
17. WJ/EVW, 8/1858. GR, 596.
18. HJSR/EC, 10/18/1858. VX.
19. *NSB*, 302–4; *LB*1, 6.
20. *NSB*, 287–92.
21. HJSR/EC, 10/18/1858. VX.
22. *NSB*, 302–4; *AL*, 54–55; HJSR/Francis G. Shaw, 7/22/1859. *MA*, 8.
23. HJSR/SGW, 9/18/1859. *AL*, 55; WJ/EVW, 9/10/1859. GR, 598; HJ/TSP, 10/8/1859. *ED*1, 6.
24. HJSR/ET, 7/24/1860. *ST*, 58–59; HJ/TSP, 1/26/1860. *ED*1, 11–14; *NSB*, 239–44.
25. HJSR/MrsWJ, 10/15/1857. *ST*, 56–57.
26. *NSB*, 242–45.

27. *NSB*, 242–45; HJSR/EC, 3/25/1860. VX; GWJ/TSP, 5/28/1860. DK; HJSR/ Caroline Sturgis Tappen, 3/1860. *NSB*, 374; HJ/TSP, 6/13/1860. DK.
28. HJSR/ET, 7/1860. *BJ*, 33; *The Memoirs of Julian Hawthorne*, ed. Edith G. Hawthorne, nd, 120–21; *NSB*, 253–62; WJ/HJSR, nd/1860. *SB*, 245.
29. *NSB*, 267–69; HJSR/ET, 7/18/1860. *BJ*, 28–29; GWJ/TSP, 8/5/1860. DK; WJ/ parents, 8/19/1860. *MA*, 4; *NSB*, 254–65; HJSR/ET, 7/24/1860. *ST*, 58–59; HJ/ TSP, 7/18/1860. *ED1*, 22–26.
30. WJ/EVW, 12/18/1859. *GR*, 599; WJ/TSP, nd/1858. *MA*, 7.
31. HJ/TSP, 9/3/1860. *ED1*, 35–36; *NSB*, 270–74.

CHAPTER THREE.   "GARLANDS AND LIGHTS," 1860–1867

1. *WWS2*, 29–31; RJ/EE, nd. VX; RJ recollections. VX; See David Donald, *Charles Sumner and the Coming of the Civil War*, 1960.
2. HJSR/SGW, 9/18/1859. *AL*, 55; RJ/EE, nd. VX; RJ recollections. VX.
3. HJ/TSP, 9/26/1860. *ED1*, 37–38; *NSB*, 275, 293–95, 284–86.
4. *NSB*, 284–86; *LB1*, 8–9.
5. *NSB*, 282–84.
6. EDE, *The Early Years of the Saturday Club*, 1918, 328; *LB1*, 9.
7. *NSB*, 292; *LB1*, 8–9.
8. *NSB*, 368–70; HJSR/RWE, 3/26/1861. *WJL1*, 91–92; *MA*, 19–20.
9. *NSB*, 365–67.
10. *HAR*, 18; Kitty Barber James/Julius Seelye, nd. *ST*, 69; LCP/Van Wyck Brooks, nd. *ST*, 44.
11. *LB1*, 9; *ST*, 44–45; HJSR/WJ (brother), 12/21/nd. HO.
12. HJSR/WJ (brother), 12/21/nd. HO; *NSB*, 308.
13. *NSB*, 414; *EDEL1*, 142.
14. RB/WWS, 12/17/1861. *WWS2*, 105; HJSR/?, nd. frag. VX.
15. *EDEL1*, 149–51; *NSB*, 414–16.
16. HJSR/Howard James, 4/12/1862. HO.
17. *NSB*, 411–14.
18. *MA*, 25; *NSB*, 411–14, 417–18.
19. "JRL," *Atlantic Monthly*, 1/1892; *NSB*, 438–39.
20. *NSB*, 456–57; *MA*, 38.
21. HJSR/Elizabeth Peabody, 7/22/1863. *ST*, 75–76; *NSB*, 383–84; HJSR/EC, 9/23/ 1863. VX.
22. HJSR/RJ, 8/29/1864. VX; Charles Sumner/WWS, 1/1/1864. *WWS2*, 158–59; *NSB*, 475–76.
23. *NSB*, 423–24; *SB*, 423–24, 453–54.
24. WJ/MJ, 11/2/1863. HO.
25. *NSB*, 478, 480.
26. HJ/TSP, 11/1/1863. *ED1*, 43–47.
27. *NSB*, 475–76, 492–94.
28. HJ/TSP, 3/25/1864. *ED1*, 49–50.
29. CEN/G. W. Curtis, 10/16/1863. *NOR1*, 266; *SB*, 476–77.
30. *NSB*, 488.
31. "The Founding of the 'Nation,' " *The Nation*, 7/8/1915.
32. "James Anthony Froude," *The Nation*, 10/31/1867.
33. AF, *Memories of a Hostess*, 1922, 72; "Mr. and Mrs. JTF," *Atlantic Monthly*, 7/1915; *NSB*, 492–94.
34. HJ/F. P. Church, 10/23/1867. *ED1*, 73–74; MJ/GWJ, 1/28/1868. VX.
35. *SL1*, 198; *WDHL1*, 271.

36. *NSB*, 391–92, 494–95; *ST*, 97; MJ/GWJ, 3/27/1866, 9/3/1866, 10/28/1866. VX; HJSR/GWJ, 10/30/1866. VX; MJ/RJ, 6/28/1867. VX.
37. *WDHL1*, 271, 273; HJ/AJ, 2/3/1867. *ED1*, 69–70; MJ/AJ, 12/1866. HO.
38. *WDHL1*, 283.
39. AJ/WJ, 8/6/1867. ST, 113, 115; WDH, *Literary Friends and Acquaintances*, ed. David F. Hiatt and Edwin H. Cady, 1968, 226.
40. MT/HDK, 1/1/1863, 8/30/1862, 5/12/1863. *HAB*, 130–131, 135.
41. *NSB*, 483–87; WWS/daughter, summer 1865. *WWS2*, 181–83.
42. *WWS2*, 177–80; MJ/AJ, 1/1867. HO.
43. AJ/WJ, 8/6/1867. *ST*, 113, 115; MJ/GWJ, 3/13/1866. VX.
44. MT/HDK, 4/3/1863. *HAB*, 169–70.
45. MT/HDK, 4/3/1863. *HAB*, 138.
46. "Modern Women," *The Nation*, 11/22/1868.

CHAPTER FOUR. "AN ABSOLUTE REMEDY," 1867–1870

1. HJ/WJ, 11/22/1867. *ED1*, 79–82; MJ/RJ, 11/28/1867. VX.
2. *NSB*, 388–90.
3. HJ/TSP, 3/27/1868. *ED1*, 80–84; HJ/TSP, 9/20/1867. *ED1*, 75–78.
4. HJ/WJ, 11/22/1867. *ED1*, 79–82; HJ/TSP, 3/27/1868. *ED1*, 80–84; HJ/WJ, 4/22/1867. *ST*, 97; WJ/AJ, 5/14/1868. *ST*, 112; WJ/parents, 10/5/1868. *ST*, 112.
5. HJ/TSP, 3/27/1866. *ED1*, 80–84; review of "Modern Women," *The Nation*, 10/22/1868.
6. HJSR/GWJ, 1/22/1867. VX; MJ/WJ, 6/10/1867. HO.
7. MJ/GWJ, 1/26/1868. VX.
8. HJSR/RJ, 4/28/1865. VX; *WJL1*, 61; WJ/HJ, 7/1865. *BJ*, 53.
9. MJ/AJ, 4/1867. HO; WJ/Tom Ward, 9/12/1867. *HF*, 207; MJ/WJ, 1/21/1867. *HF*, 207.
10. *WJL1*, 27; *HF*, 204–5.
11. MJ/WJ, 12/21/1867. HO; GWJ/HJSR, 4/7/1866. *MA*, 84; MJ/GWJ, 3/27/1866. VX; *MA*, 77–108; HJSR/RJ, 9/13/1864. VX; MJ/GWJ, 5/14/1866. VX; GWJ/WJ, 9/29/1866. *MA*, 91; MJ/GWJ, 3/18/1867. *MA*, 94.
12. MJ/GWJ, 9/3/1866. VX; MJ/RJ, 6/1867. HO; GWJ/parents, 12/31/1868. *MA*, 105–6.
13. MJ/WJ, 11/21/1867. HO; MJ/WJ, 12/21/1867. HO.
14. *ST*, 118.
15. MJ/RJ, 6/29/1867. VX; MJ/GWJ, 3/18/1867. VX.
16. HJ/WJ, 5/11/1867. *ST*, 111; MJ/WJ, 5/21/1867, 6/10/1867. HO; MJ/AJ, 4/1867. HO; MJ/RJ, 6/26/1867. VX; CEN/HJ3, 9/7/1915. HO; HJ/WJ, 11/22/1867. *ED1*, 79–82.
17. AJ/WJ, 8/6/1867. *ST*, 115; HJSR/Julia A. Kellogg, nd/1864. *HAB*, 205–6; MJ/"My darling boys," 6/5/1867. VX; WJ/HJSR, 9/5/1867. *BJ*, 76; WJ/RJ, 1/27/1868. VX.
18. AJ/WJ, 8/6/1867. *ST*, 113, 115; AJ/WJ, 10/13/1867. HO.
19. HJ/WJ, 3/29/1870. *ED1*, 226; *NSB*, 514.
20. HJ/MJ, 3/9/1869. *MAT*, 253–54.
21. MJ/RJ, 5/3/1868. VX.
22. Kermit Vanderbilt, *Charles Eliot Norton*, 1959, 104; HJ/MJ, 3/9/1869. *MAT*, 254.
23. "An English Easter," *Lippincott's Magazine*, 1/1877; HJ/AJ, 3/10/1869. *ED1*, 89–97.
24. HJ/MJ, 3/20/1869. *ED1*, 102–5.
25. *NSB*, 568–71; HJ/AJ, 3/10/1869. *ED1*, 89–97.
26. HJ/WJ, 3/19/1869. *ED1*, 98–100; HJ/MJ, 3/20/1869. *ED1*, 102–5.

27. HJ/AJ, 3/10/1869. *ED1*, 92; *MY*, 572.
28. HJ/AJ, 3/10/1869. *ED1*, 93; HJ/WJ, 5/13/1869. HO.
29. HJSR/HJ, nd/1869. *NSB*, 384–95; HJ/WJ, 4/26/1869. *ED1*, 109.
30. HJ/GN, 4/6/1869. *ED1*, 106–8; HJ/WJ, 4/8/1869. HO; HJ/MJ, 3/20/1869. *ED1*, 102–5; HJ/AJ, 3/10/1869. *ED1*, 90–97; HJ/WJ, 4/8/1869. HO.
31. HJ/WJ, 4/26/1869. *ED1*, 108–114.
32. HJ/GN, 4/6/1869. *ED1*, 106–8.
33. Review of Eliot, "Felix Holt," *The Nation*, 8/16/1866; review of "The Novels of George Eliot," *Atlantic Monthly*, 10/1866; review of Eliot, "The Spanish Gypsy," *The Nation*, 7/2/1868; MT/HJ, 11/17/1869, HO; *NSB*, 15.
34. HJ/AJ, 5/5/1869. HO; HJ/HJSR, 5/10/1869. *ED1*, 116–17; MT/HJ, 8/15/1869, 11/7/1869, HO.
35. HJ/HJSR, 5/10/1869. *ED1*, 114–15; HJ/WJ, 5/13/1869. HO.
36. HJ/WJ, 5/30/1869. HO.
37. MJ/HJ, 7/24/1869. HO.
38. HJ/JLF, 6/20/1869. *ED1*, 121; HJ/MJ, 6/28/1869. *ED1*, 122–26.
39. HJ/MJ, 6/28/1869. *ED1*, 122–26; MJ/HJ, 8/8/1869, 7/24/1869. HO; HJ/WJ, 7/12/1869. HO.
40. MJ/HJ, 8/8/1869. HO; HJ/WJ, 7/12/1869, 8/12/1869. HO.
41. HJ/AJ, 8/31/1869. *ED1*, 126–33.
42. MJ/HJ, 9/6/1869. HO; HJ/WJ, 9/25/1869. *ED1*, 143–44.
43. HJ/JLF, 9/21/1869. *ED1*, 133–35; HJ/WJ, 9/25/1869. *ED1*, 136–44.
44. HJ/WJ, 9/25/1869. *ED1*, 137, 142; HJ/AJ, 10/6/1869. *ED1*, 145; HJ/HJSR, 10/26/1869. *ED1*, 154.
45. HJ/MJ, 10/13/1869. *ED1*, 149; HJ/AJ, 10/6/1869. *ED1*, 145–49.
46. HJ/MH, 10/13/1869. *ED1*, 151–53; HJ/HJSR, 10/26/1869. *ED1*, 155.
47. HJ/WJ, 10/7/1869. HO.
48. HJ/WJ, 10/16/1869. *SL2*, 44–47; HJ/WJ, 10/7/1869. HO.
49. HJ/WJ, 10/26/1869. *ED1*, 158; HJ/WJ, 10/30/1869. *ED1*, 159.
50. HJ/AJ, 11/7/1869. *ED1*, 164; HJ/AJ, 11/7/1869. *ED1*, 164; HJ/WJ, 10/30/1869. *ED1*, 160.
51. HJ/MJ, 11/21/1869. *ED1*, 173–74; HJ/MJ, 11/21/1869. *ED1*, 174–75; HJ/WJ, 12/27/1869. *ED1*, 181–82.
52. HJ/AJ, 11/7/1869. *ED1*, 162–69; AJ/HJ, 11/1/1869. HO.
53. WJ/RJ, 12/26/1869, 1/2/1870. VX; HJ/WJ, 11/30/1869. HO; MJ/AJ, 1/14/1870. HO.
54. HJ/WJ, 12/27/1869. *ED1*, 182; HJ/WJ, 1/1/1870. *ED1*, 184; HJ/HJSR, 1/17/1870. *ED1*, 190–91.
55. MT/HJ, 6/3/1869. HO.
56. HJ/WJ, 3/29/1870. *ED1*, 224; WJ/RJ, 11/14/1869. VX.
57. HJ/WJ, 9/25/1869. *ED1*, 144; MT/HJ, 8/15/1869, 8/22/1869, 11/17/1869. HO.
58. HJ/WJ, 3/8/1870. *ED1*, 208; HJ/MJ, 3/26/1870. *ED1*, 218.

CHAPTER FIVE. "CATS AND MONKEYS," 1870–1875

1. HJ/GN, 4/1/1870. *ED1*, 231.
2. HJ/WJ, 3/29/1870. *ED1*, 223; HJ/MJ, 3/26/1870. *ED1*, 219.
3. HJ/MJ, 3/26/1870. *ED1*, 221.
4. HJ/WJ, 3/29/1870. *ED1*, 224.
5. HJ/WJ, 2/29/1870. *ED1*, 227; WJ, diary. *BJ*, 88–89.
6. HJ/WJ, 2/29/1870. *ED1*, 226; HJ/WJ, 3/29/1870. *ED1*, 228.
7. HJ/WJ, 3/29/1870. *ED1*, 228.

8. HJ/WJ, 3/29/1870. *ED*1, 228; WJ/RJ, 5/23/1870. VX.

9. HJ/GN, 4/28/1870. *ED*1, 233.

10. HJ/GN, 5/20/1870. *ED*1, 238–41; HJSR/Jane Norton, 5/28/1871. HO; WJ/RJ, 5/23/1870. VX.

11. HJ/GN, 9/26/1870. *ED*1, 243; WJ/RJ, 5/23/1870. VX.

12. "Saratoga," *The Nation*, 8/11/1870.

13. WJ/RJ, 7/25/1870. VX.

14. *NSB*, 495.

15. HJ/GN, 9/26/1870. *ED*1, 242–44.

16. HJ/EB, 1/24/1872. *ED*1, 269.

17. HJ/GN, 9/27/1870. *ED*1, 245–47; HJ/CEN, 1/16/1871. *ED*1, 252.

18. "Lothair," *Atlantic Monthly*, 9/1870; HJ/CEN, 1/16/1871. *ED*1, 252; HJ/GN, 11/27/1871. *ED*1, 264.

19. WJ/RJ, 7/25/1870. VX; HJ/JTF, 9/24/1870. *ED*1, 241–42.

20. HJ/JTF, 11/15/1870. *ED*1, 248; HJ/GN, 8/9/1871. *ED*1, 262.

21. HJSR/Julia A. Kellogg, 9/9/1871. *HAB*, 221.

22. HJ/CEN, 8/8/1871. *ED*1, 262.

23. HJ/GN, 11/27/1871. *ED*1, 266; *AN*, 167–97; HJ/GN, 1/16/1871. *ED*1, 257–58; HJ/CEN, 2/2/1872. *ED*1, 273–74.

24. HJ/EB, 1/24/1872. *ED*1, 270.

25. AK/MJ, 6/1/1872. *ST*, 147.

26. HJ/HJSR, 5/29/1872. *ED*1, 287; HJ/CEN, 6/1/1872. *ED*1, 289; HJ/parents, 6/4/1872. *ED*1, 290–93; HJ/parents, 6/11/1872. *ST*, 147.

27. HJSR/AJ, 5/21/1872. *ST*, 150; HJSR/AJ, 8/20/1872. *ST*, 156; HJ/AJ, 8/1872. *NSB*, 407–8; MJ/AJ & HJ, 7/26/1872. HO.

28. MJ/AJ, 7/18/1872. HO; HJ/WJ, 7/24/1872. HO; HJ/EB, 7/2/1872. HO; HJ/parents, 7/13/1872. *ST*, 149.

29. HJ/WJ, 7/24/1872. HO; HJ/GN, 8/8/1872. *ED*1, 293–94; HJ/parents, 8/11/1872. *ST*, 154–55; HJ/EB, 8/13/1872. HO; HJSR/AJ, 8/20/1872. *ST*, 156; "From Venice to Strasburg," *The Nation*, 3/6/1873; HJ/parents, 9/9/1872. *ED*1, 295–97.

30. HJ/parents, 9/15/1872. *SL*2, 94–96; HJ/WJ, 9/22/1872. *ED*1, 299–300; HJ/WJ, 7/24/1872. HO; HJ/parents, 10/10/1872. *ED*1, 304–306.

31. HJ/WJ, 1/8/1873. *ED*1, 324; MJ/AJ & HJ, 7/26/1872. HO.

32. WJ/HJ, 10/10/1872. *ST*, 152; HJ/WJ, 9/22/1872. *ED*1, 300–301.

33. HJ/HJSR, 11/1872. *ED*1, 307; MJ/RJ, 3/10/1872. VX; HJ/CEN, 5/6/1872. *ED*1, 276.

34. HJ/WJ, 11/31/1872. *ED*1, 312–13; HJ/WJ, 11/31/1872. *ED*1, 313; HJ/HJSR, 11/1872. *ED*1, 308–9; HJ/WJ, 11/31/1872. *ED*1, 313; HJ/CEN, 11/19/1872. *ED*1, 310.

35. HJ/WJ, 11/31/1872. *ED*1, 312; HJ/WJ, 11/31/1872. *ED*1, 314; HJ/HJSR, 12/25/1872. *ED*1, 315; HJ/MJ, 12/19/1872. *ED*1, 317.

36. HJ/parents, 5/4/1873. *ED*1, 375; HJ/WJ, 5/19/1873. *ED*1, 385; *The Nation*, 1/2/1873; MJ/HJ, 4/27/1873. HO.

37. MJ/HJ, 4/1873. HO; "The Madonna of the Future," *Atlantic Monthly*, 3/1873.

38. HJ/HJSR, 2/1/1873. *ED*1, 333–34; MJ/HJ, 2/28/1873. HO.

39. HJ/AJ, 2/10/1873. *ED*1, 337; MJ/HJ, 1/21/1873. HO; MJ/HJ, 3/21/1873. HO; WJ/RJ, 4/20/1873. VX; HJ/WJ, 1/8/1873. *ED*1, 325.

40. HJ/HJSR, 1/19/1873. *ED*1, 328; HJ/HJSR, 3/4/1873. *ED*1, 347; HJ/CEN, 3/31/1873. *ED*1, 362; HJ/WJ, 4/9/1873. *ED*1, 364; HJ/MJ, 1/26/1873. *ED*1, 332; HJ/CEN, 3/13/1873. *ED*1, 353; *SAM*, 101.

41. MJ/HJ, 1/21/1873. HO; HJ/HJSR, 3/4/1873. *ED*1, 347; HJ/MJ, 1/26/1873. *ED*1, 331.

42. WJ/RJ, 4/27/1873. HO; HJ/WJ, 7/6/1873. HO; AK/HJ, 5/1/1873. HO.

43. HJ/HJSR, 2/1/1873. *ED*1, 335–36; HJ/HJSR, 3/4/1873. *ED*1, 346.

44. HJ/HJSR, 3/4/1873. *ED1*, 346–48; HJ/AJ, 4/25/1873. *ED1*, 372; HJ/HJSR, 3/28/1873. *ED1*, 360; HJ/WJ, 4/9/1873. *ED1*, 368.
45. HJ/WJ, 4/9/1873. *ED1*, 365–66; HJ/parents, 5/4/1873. *ED1*, 376; HJ/WDH, 6/22/1873. *ED1*, 396.
46. HJ/AK, 8/1/1873. HO; HJ/EB, 8/15/1873. HO; HJ/WJ, 8/5/1873. HO; HJSR/HJ, 8/8/1873. *ST*, 49.
47. HJ/WDH, 9/9/1873. *ED1*, 402–3.
48. HJ/HJSR, 11/2/1873. *ED1*, 408; WJ/RJ, 9/27/1873. VX; MJ/HJ, 3/17/1873. 9/12/1873. HO.
49. HJ/WJ, 6/18/1873. *ED1*, 393–94; WJ/RJ, 10/10/1873. VX; MJ/HJ, 12/8/1873. HO.
50. HJ/WDH, 1/9/1874. *ED1*, 423–25; HJ/GN, 1/14/1874. *ED1*, 426–27; HJ/parents, 2/5/1874. *ED1*, 429–30; HJ/parents, 2/27/1874. *ED1*, 431–32.
51. HJ/RJ, 12/8/1873. VX; MJ/HJ, 5/18/1874. HO.
52. HJ/GN, 1/14/1874. *ED1*, 428–29.
53. HJ/EB, 4/7/1874. HO.
54. HJ/WDH, 5/3/1874. *ED1*, 443–44.
55. HJ/MJ, 5/17/1874. *ED1*, 448.
56. HJ/MJ, 7/28/1874. *ED1*, 458–59; HJ/EB, 7/29/1874. HO; MJ/HJ, 7/6/1874. HO; HJ/EB, 7/29/1874. HO; MJ/RJ, 9/27/1874. HO.
57. WJ/RJ, 9/20/1874. VX; WJ/RJ, 7/4/1874. VX.
58. HJ/MJ, 3/24/1873. *ED1*, 357–58; *AN*, 31–33.
59. HJ/WDH, 1/13/1875. *ED1*, 469; HJ/EB, 1/27/1875. *ED1*, 472; HJ/WDH, 1/13/1875. *ED1*, 469; HJ/SBW, 1/23/1874. *ED1*, 470; HJ/EB, 3/8/1875. *ED1*, 474; HJ/WDH, 3/26/1875. *ED1*, 475; HJ/FB, 4/12/1875. HO; WJ/RJ, 2/20/1875. VX.
60. HJ/JH, 7/21/1875. *ED1*, 476–77; JH/WR, 7/24/1875, WR/JH, 7/27/1875. Royal Cortissoz, *The Life of Whitelaw Reid*, 1921, 62.
61. HJ/parents, 11/9/1875. *ED2*, 5; HJ/family, 11/1/1875. *ED1*, 484.

CHAPTER SIX. "PERMANENT HEADQUARTERS," 1875–1878

1. "Mr. Henry Irving's Macbeth," *The Nation*, 11/25/1875; "The London Theatres," *The Galaxy*, 5/1877; HJ/parents, 11/9/1875. *ED1*, 5; HJ/HJSR, 11/11/1876. *ED2*, 72; HJ/HJSR, 11/18/1875. *ED2*, 6–7.
2. HJ/WR, 11/22/1875. *ED2*, 8.
3. HJ/WJ, 4/25/1876. *ED2*, 41; HJ/HJSR, 4/11/1876. *ED2*, 39; WR/HJ, 3/27/1876. BR; HJ/WR, 4/11/1876. BR.
4. HJ/MJ, 1/24/1876. *ED2*, 18–19.
5. HJ/WJ, 4/25/1876. *ED2*, 41; HJ/WJ, 3/14/1876. *ED2*, 34; "Honofe de Balzac," *The Galaxy*, 11/1875.
6. HJ/Francis P. Church, 12/1/1875. *ED2*, 8–9; HJ/WJ, 12/3/1875. *ED2*, 13.
7. HJ/MJ, 5/8/1876. *ED2*, 45.
8. HJ/WJ, 7/4/1876. HO.
9. HJ/WDH, 10/24/1876. *ED2*, 70; HJ/WDH, 3/30/1877. *ED2*, 105.
10. HJ/EB, 12/31/1875. HO; "The Minor French Novelists," *The Galaxy*, 2/1876; *NBK*, 217; HJ/EB 12/31/1875. HO.
11. HJ/EB, 11/11/1876. HO; HJ/WJ, 7/4/1876. HO; *NBK*, 216.
12. HJ/WJ, 4/25/1875. *ED2*, 41–42.
13. HJ/EB, 12/31/1875. HO; "The Minor French Novelists," *The Galaxy*, 2/1876; "Flaubert," *The Nation*, 6/4/1874; "Flowers of Evil," *The Nation*, 7/27/1876.
14. HJ/TSP, 1/11/1876. *HAR*, 290–91; HJ/HJSR, 12/20/1875. *ED2*, 14–15.
15. *NBK*, 216; HJ/WDH, 2/3/1876. *ED2*, 23.
16. HJ/TSP, 5/2/1876. *ED2*, 44.

17. HJ/TSP, 2/28/1887. *HAR*, 295; review of Edmond de Goncourt, *The Nation*, 5/10/1877; "Nana," *Parisian*, 2/26/1880; HJ/TC, 2/17/1880. *ED2*. 274.

18. HJ/WJ, 7/6/1873. HO; HJ/WJ, 8/17/1873. HO; HJ/TSP, 12/13/1876. *HAR*, 293–94; Turgenev/HJ, 8/7/1874. Jean Seznec, "Lettres de Tourgueneff à Henry James," *Comparative Literature* I, no. 3 (Summer 1949).

19. Review of Turgenev, "Frühlingsfluthen; Ein König Lear des Dorfes," *North American Review*, 4/1874.

20. HJ/AK, 12/3/1875. *ED2*, 10; HJ/MJ, 5/8/1876. *ED2*, 45; HJ/HJSR, 4/11/1876. *ED2*, 37; HJ/HJSR, 12/20/1875. *ED2*, 16.

21. HJ/EB, 12/31/1875. HO; HJ/TSP, 1/11/1876. *HAR*, 290–91; HJ/WDH, 2/3/1876. *ED2*, 23; HJ/HJSR, 4/11/1876. *ED2*, 37.

22. HJ/WJ, 4/25/1876. *ED2*, 42; HJ/AJ, 5/24/1876. *ED2*, 49–50.

23. HJ/AJ, 5/24/1876. *ED2*, 50; HJ/EB, 4/3/1876, 6/1/1876. HO; HJ/TSP, 6/4/1876. *HAR*, 292–93; HJ/WDH, 5/28/1876. *ED2*, 53; HJ/WJ, 7/4/1876. HO; HJ/AJ, 11/2/1877. *ED2*, 142; AJ/Anne Ashburner Richards, 4/12/1876. *ST*, 88; HJ/EB, 7/1876. HO.

24. HJ/EB, 7/29/1876, 8/19/1876. HO.

25. HJ/EB, 8/19/1876. HO; HJ/MJ, 8/24/1876. *ED2*, 61–62; *NBK*, 217.

26. HJ/HJSR, 9/16/1876. *ED2*, 64–66; "From Normandy to the Pyrénées," *The Galaxy*, 1/1877.

27. WDH/JH, 12/18/1875. *WDHL2*, 112; WR/HJ, 8/10/1876. BR; HJ/WR, 8/30/1876. *ED2*, 64; HJ/HJSR, 9/16/1876. *ED2*, 66; HJ/WR, 12/21/1876. BR.

28. HJ/Arthur Sedgwick, 9/29/1876. *ED2*, 68; HJ/WJ, 10/23/1876. HO; *NBK*, 215–16.

29. HJ/EB, 10/10/1876. HO; HJ/WJ, 10/13/1876. HO.

30. HJ/WDH, 10/24/1876. *ED2*, 70–72; HJ/WJ, 10/23/1876. HO; *NBK*, 217; HJ/EB, 11/11/1876. HO; HJ/HJSR, 11/11/1876. *ED2*, 73.

31. "Paris Revisited," *The Galaxy*, 1/1878; HJ/Mrs. John Rollin Tilton, 4/3/1878. *ED2*, 163; HJ/AJ, 12/13/1876. *ED2*, 82; HJ/WJ, 1/12/1877. *ED2*, 90; HJ/EB, 12/26/1876. HO; "An English Easter," *Lippincott's Magazine*, 7/1877.

32. HJ/EB, 12/26/1876. HO; "An English Easter," 7/1877; *NBK*, 218; HJ/MJ, 12/24/1876. *ED2*, 86.

33. HJ/WJ, 2/28/1877. *ED2*, 101; HJ/WJ, 2/28/1877. *ED2*, 101.

34. HJ/family, 11/1/1875. *ED1*, 486; HJ/HJSR, 2/13/1877. *ED2*, 99; HJ/HJSR & AJ, 5/20/1877. *ED2*, 113.

35. HJ/EB/ 2/11/1877. HO; HJ/WJ, 2/9/1877. HO; HJ/HJSR, 2/13/1877. *ED2*, 98–99; HJ/AJ, 3/2/1877. *ED2*, 103–4; HJ/WJ, 2/28/1877. *ED2*, 102.

36. HJ/HA, 5/5/1877. *ED2*, 109; HJ/MJ, 1/31/1877. *ED2*, 95.

37. HJ/WJ, 2/28/1877. HO; HJ/HJSR & AJ, 5/20/1877. *ED2*, 113; HJ/GN, 1/4/1878. HO.

38. HJ/EB, 2/11/1877. HO; HJ/WJ, 2/28/1877. *ED2*, 100.

39. "An English Easter," 7/1877.

40. HJ/WJ, 1/28/1877. *ED2*, 117; "Two Excursions," *The Galaxy*, 9/1877; "London at Midsummer," *Lippincott's Magazine*, 11/1877; HJ/GN, 12/15/1877. *ED2*, 145; HJ/HA, 7/15/1877. *ED2*, 125–27; HJ/EB, 8/5/1877. HO; HJ/EB, 8/22/1877. HO; "In Warwickshire," *The Galaxy*, 11/1877; HJ/WJ, 7/10/1877. *ED2*, 122; JRL/HJ, 9/24/1878. HO.

41. HJ/HA, 7/15/1877. *ED2*, 127; HJ/HA, 5/5/1877. *ED2*, 111.

42. HJ/WDH, 12/18/1876. *ED2*, 84; HJ/WDH, 2/2/1877. *ED2*, 96.

43. HJ/WDH, 2/2/1877. *ED2*, 96–97.

44. "George Sand," *The Galaxy*, 7/1877; HJ/EB, 5/26/1877. HO.

45. HJ/TSP, 4/18/1877. *ED2*, 108; HJ/WDH, 3/30/1877. *ED2*, 105–6.

46. HJ/MAC, 8/7/1877, *ED2*, 131–32. HJ/MAC, 8/27/1877. BL; *A Bibliography of Henry James*, ed. Leon Edel & Dan H. Laurence, 1982, 34.

47. MJ/RJ, nd/1875? VX; MJ/RJ, 2/12/1878. VX; HJ/WJ, 1/28/1878. ED2, 150–51.
48. HJ/MJ, 8/6/1877. ED2, 128–29; HJ/EB, 8/22/1877, 9/7/1877. HO.
49. HJ/HJSR, 9/19/1877. ED2, 139–40; "Paris Revisited," The Galaxy, 1/1878.
50. HJ/WJ, 5/1/1878. ED2, 171–72; NBK, 227–28.
51. HJ/EB, 9/28/1877. HO; "Rheims and Laon: A Little Tour," Atlantic Monthly, 1/
    1878; "Italy Revisited," Atlantic Monthly, 4–5/1878.
52. HJ/GN, 12/15/1877. ED2, 144; HJ/EB, 11/2/1877. ED2, 142.
53. "Italy Revisited," Atlantic Monthly, 4–5/1878; HJ/EB, 12/17/1877. HO; HJ/TSP,
    12/15/1877. HAR, 297–98.
54. HJ/HR, 3/26/1878. HO.
55. HJ/MJ, 2/17/1878. ED2, 155–56.
56. HJ/AJ, 2/17/1878. ED2, 157; HJ/HJSR, 3/28/1878. ED2, 161; "The Picture Sea-
    son in London," The Galaxy, 8/1877; HJ/HJSR, 4/19/1878. ED2, 167.
57. HJ/AJ, 12/29/1877. HO; HJ/HJSR, 5/29/1878. ED2, 175–76.
58. HJ/WJ, 5/1/1878. ED2, 178; HJ/TSP, 9/13/1878. HAR, 229–301.

CHAPTER SEVEN.   "THE SENTIMENTAL TRAVELLER," 1878–1881

 1. MY, 578–84.
 2. MJ/RJ, nd/1878. VX; WDH/JRL, 6/22/1879. WDHL2, 230–31; AK/MRJ, 9/26/
    1878. VX.
 3. HJ/MAC, 5/1878. BL; see "Appendix B," in AN, 176–87.
 4. HJ/EB, 11/24/1878. HO.
 5. HJ/WJ, 6/15/1879. HO.
 6. AK/RJ, 1/16/1879. VX; HJ/EB, 5/4/1879. HO; HJ/HJSR, 10/24/1878. ED2,
    187–88; HJ/MJ, 5/31/1879. ED2, 237; HJ/WJ, 7/23/1878. ED2, 178–79.
 7. MJ/RJ, nd/1878. VX; HJ/MJ, 5/14/1879. ED2, 232; HJ/WJ, 7/23/1878. ED2,
    179.
 8. HJ/WJ, 11/14/1878. ED2, 193–94; HJ/MJ, 1/18/1879. ED2, 213; HJ/WJ, 5/1/
    1878. ED2, 170; HJ/MJ, 1/18/1879. ED2, 212; HJ/GN, 1/4/1879. ED2, 209–10;
    HJ/John Barrow, 1/19/1880. VB.
 9. HJ/WEH, 2/5/1879, 4/9/1879. VX.
10. HJ/EB, 10/30/1878. ED2, 190; MY, 590–93.
11. HJ/GN, 6/8/1879. ED2, 240.
12. HJ/WJ, 4/4/1879. ED2, 217; HJ/MJ, 1/18/1879. ED2, 212; HJ/WJ, 3/4/1879.
    ED2, 218.
13. HJ/TC, 3/8/1879. VB; "The New Year in England," The Nation, 1/23/1879; HJ/
    Mrs. Hertz, 4/11/1880. VX; HJ/WJ, 1/28/1878. ED2, 153.
14. HJ/EB, 11/24/1878. HO; HJ/TC, 3/8/1879. VB.
15. HJ/MAC, nd/1878. BL; AN, 63–64.
16. HJ/CEN, 11/17/1878. ED2, 198.
17. MJ/HJ, 3/9/1878. HO.
18. AJ/SSD, 9/20/1877. ST, 178; HJ/EB, 11/24/1878. HO; HJ/WJ, 5/1/1878. ED2,
    170.
19. HJ/EB, 6/28/1879. ED2, 246; HJ/WJ, 6/15/1879. HO.
20. MJ/RJ, 5/23/1878. VX; HJ/EB, 6/15/1878. HO; AK/MRJ, 8/1/1878. VX.
21. HJ/EB, 5/22/1878. HO; HJ/AJ, 6/5/1878. ST, 183; MJ/RJ, 5/23/1878. VX; HJSR/
    RJ, nd/1878? VX; HJSR/RJ, 9/14/1878. VX; AJD, 230; GWJ/WJ, 5/16/1878. ST,
    182; WJ/RJ, 7/9/1878. VX.
22. HJ/WJ, 5/29/1878. ED2, 174; HJ/FB, 3/26/1878. HO; Agnes Irwin/TSP, nd/
    1877. HAR, 58–59.
23. HJSR/MRJ, 3/16/1881? VX.
24. HJ/WJ, 3/4/1879. ED2, 216; HJ/AJ, 3/26/1879. ED2, 225; HJ/WDH, 4/7/1879.

ED2, 227; HJ/MJ, 4/8/1879. *ED2*, 229; HJ/TSP, 5/16/1879. *HAR*, 301–2; HJ/MJ, 5/14/1879. *ED2*, 231; HJ/WJ, 12/16/1879. HO.

25. HJ/GN, 9/18/1878. HO; HJ/MAC, 9/26/1878. BL; HJ/WEH, 2/5/1879. VX; HJ/WDH, 5/30/1877. *ED2*, 106; HJ/AJ, 9/15/1879. *ED2*, 184–85; HJ/EB, 9/13/1878. HO.
26. HJ/HJSR, 5/29/1878. *ED2*, 176–77.
27. HJ/MJ, 1/18/1879. *ED2*, 211–12; HJ/MJ, 5/31/1879. *ED2*, 236–37; *MY*, 585–90.
28. HJ/WJ, 8/30/1879. HO; HJ/TSP, 9/14/1879. *ED2*, 255; HJ/MAC, 9/29/1879. BL; HJ/Mrs. Still, 9/24/1879. CL; HJ/IG, 1/29/1880. *ED2*, 265; HJ/GN, 10/17/1879. HO; HJ/HJSR, 10/11/1879. *ED2*, 258; HJ/WJ, 10/10/1879. HO; HJ/TSP, 11/2/1879. *HAR*, 304–5.
29. HJ/MAC, 7/14/1879, 7/15/1879, 7/19/1879, 7/21/1879. BL.
30. HJ/HJSR, 10/11/1879. *ED2*, 259–60.
31. HJ/CEN, 5/31/1880. *ED2*, 279; HJ/EB, 11/20/1879, 12/7/1879. HO; HJ/W. H. Huntington, 11/22/1879. VB; HJ/HJSR, 1/11/1880. *ED2*, 264; HJ/RJ, 1/11/1880. VX.
32. HJ/EB, 2/22/1880. HO; *SAM*, 159; HJ/GN, 9/18/1878. HO; HJ/EB, 2/22/1880. HO; HJ/IG, 1/29/1880. *ED2*, 265; HJ/WDH, 1/31/1880. *ED2*, 267.
33. HJ/HJSR, 2/15/1880. *ED2*, 270–72; MJ/RJ, nd/1880. VX.
34. MJ/RJ, nd/1880. VX; HJ/GN, 1/17/1880. HO; HJ/EB, 2/22/1880. HO; HJ/TSP, 4/18/1880. *HAR*, 306–7.
35. HJ/WDH, 1/31/1880. *ED2*, 268.
36. HJ/CEN, 3/31/1880. *ED2*, 280; HJ/WJ, 11/10/1879. HO; HJ/AK, 5/3/1880. HO.
37. HJ/AJ, 4/25/1880. *ED2*, 288; *TO*, 16–17; HJ/AK, 5/3/1880. HO.
38. HJ/GN, 4/9/1880. *ED2*, 283.
39. HJ/GN, 4/9/1880. *ED2*, 282–83.
40. HJ/GN, 4/9/1880. *ED2*, 284; HJ/WDH, 4/18/1880. *ED2*, 285; HJ/WDH, 4/18/1880. *ED2*, 284–85.
41. *NBK*, 219; HJ/WJ, 5/9/1880. HO; HJ/GN, 11/11/1880. HO.
42. *WJL1*, 209; WJ/parents & AJ, 7/13/1880. VX; HJ/WJ, 5/9/1880. HO; HJ/HJSR, 6/20/1880. *ED2*, 209; HJ/MJ, 7/4/1880. *ED2*, 292.
43. HJ/WJ, 6/15/1879. HO; HJ/WJ, 7/23/1878. *ED2*, 180; HJ/MJ, 7/4/1880. *ED2*, 292.
44. HJ/TSP, 7/26/1880. *HAR*, 307–8; WJ/parents & AJ, 7/13/1880. VX; WJ/AHJ, 7/31/1880. *BJ*, 130.
45. HJ/GN, 1/17/1880. HO; MJ/RJ, 8/4/1880. VX; HJ/MJ, 7/4/1880. *ED2*, 293, 295; MJ/RJ, 8/4/1880. VX.
46. HJ/GN, 8/18/1880. HO; HJ/AJ, 1/30/1881. *ED2*, 337.
47. HJ/MJ, 10/31/1881. *ED2*, 310; HJ/GN, 11/11/1880, 12/28/1880. *ED2*, 314, 323.
48. HJ/MJ, 11/28/1880. *ED2*, 317–18; HJ/MAC, 12/28/1880. BL; HJ/MJ, 1/10/1881. *ED2*, 329.
49. HJ/WJ, 11/27/1880. *ED2*, 316; HJ/TSP, 1/24/1881. *ED2*, 334.
50. HJ/TSP, 2/16/1881. *ED2*, 341–42; *NBK*, 220; HJ/WJ, 3/21/1881. HO; HJ/FK, 3/24/1881. *ED2*, 352; HJ/GN, 6/12/1881. *ED2*, 355.

CHAPTER EIGHT. "NEVER TO RETURN," 1881–1883

1. "Venice," *The Century Magazine,* 11/1882; HJ/GN, 6/12/1881. *ED2*, 354; *NBK*, 221.
2. *NBK*, 221–22; HJ/GN, 6/12/1881. *ED2*, 355.
3. "Casa Alvisi," *The Cornhill Magazine,* 2/1902; "Venice," 11/1882.
4. "Venice," 11/1882.

5. HJ/KDB, 1/19/1881. *ED2*, 350; *NBK*, 222–23; HJ/WJ, 3/21/1881. HO; HJSR/
   RJ, 9/14/1877–80. VX; MJ/MRJ, 4/24/1881. VX; MJ/MRJ, 5/1881. VX; HJ/GN,
   7/20/1881. HO; HJ/HJSR, 6/5/1881. *ST*, 198.
6. HJSR/AHJ, 7/1880. *ST*, 219; AJ/SSD, 8/9/1879. DJ, 82; AJ/FRM, 10/7/1879. *DJ*,
   84
7. WJ/FRM, 12/1879. *WJL1*, 196; HJ/parents, 8/28/1881. *ST*, 199; AHJ/WJ, nd/
   1882. *LE*, 365; HJ/MJ, 7/18/1881. *ST*, 198.
8. HJ/HR, 9/28/1881. HO; *NBK*, 223–24; HJ/MJ, 7/18/1881. *ST*, 198; AK/MRJ,
   11/14/1881. VX.
9. *NBK*, 226; HJ/HR, 9/28/1881. HO.
10. HJ/MAC, 10/14/1881. BL; *AN*, 176, 188; HJ/WDH, 7/18/1881. *ED2*, 356.
11. HJ/MAC, 10/20/1881. BL.
12. AK/MRJ, 11/14/1881. VX; HJ/CHA, 11/26/1881. *ED2*, 361; *NBK*, 229.
13. HJ/CHA, 11/6/1881. *ED2*, 362.
14. *NBK*, 213–14, 225.
15. *NBK*, 224–25.
16. See William Veeder, "The Portrait of a Lack," in *New Essays on "The Portrait of a
   Lady,"* ed. Joel Porte, Cambridge, 1990, 113–16, for an excellent discussion of
   correspondence between Gilbert Osmond and WJ.
17. HJ/GN, 11/1881. HO; AK/MRJ, 1/6/1882. VX.
18. HJ/JC, 1/8/1882. *ED2*, 367; HJ/GN, 12/13/1881. *ED2*, 365; HJ/MAC, 12/27/
   1881. BL.
19. *NBK*, 224; HJ/MAC, 12/27/1881, 12/30/1881. BL; HJ/JC, 1/23/1882. VB; HJ/
   JC, 1/8/1882. *ED2*, 367.
20. *THE*, 321; HA/CMG, 1/29/1882. *HAL1*, 248; HJ/TSP, 1/23/1882. *HAR*, 311;
   HJ/JC, 1/23/1882. VB.
21. *ELL*, 167–79; *THE*, 328, 333; HJ/IG, 1/23/1882. *ED2*, 372; HJ/JO, 4/19/1883.
   ED2, 414.
22. *SAM*, 159, 176; HA/CMG, 1/29/1882. *HAL2*, 448; *THE*, 321; FK/HJ, 1/23/
   1882. HO.
23. RJ/MRJ, 1/31/1882. *MA*, 140; HJ/RJ, 1/27/1882. VX; RJ/HJ, 1/28/1882. *MA*,
   140; HJ/MJ, 1/29/1882. *ED2*, 375; *NBK*, 228–29; *THE*, 336.
24. HJ/FM, 2/13/1882. *ED2*, 379; *NBK*, 229.
25. RJ/MRJ, 1/31/1882. *MA*, 140; *NBK*, 229; RJ/MRJ, 2/1882. MA, 141–42; MJ/
   RJ, 11/1/nd. VX.
26. AK/MRJ, 2/9/1882, 2/26/1882. VX; RJ/MRJ, 2/1882. *MA*, 141–42; *NBK*, 229.
27. AK/MRJ, 2/9/1882. VX; HJ/TSP, 2/3/1882. *HAR*, 311–12; HJ/FM, 2/13/1882.
   ED2, 379; AK/MRJ, 2/9/1882, 2/26/1882. VX; HJ/FK, 4/5/1882. *ED2*, 381.
28. HJ/TSP, 2/3/1882. *HAR*, 311–12; HJ/Francis Child, 2/1881. *ST*, 203; AK/EC,
   3/22/1882. *ST*, 203.
29. WDH/HJ, 3/18/1882, 10/4/1882. *WDHL3*, 13, 34; HJ/TSP, 2/16/1881. *ED2*,
   341.
30. HJ/HR, 3/4/1882. HO; HJ/CB, 11/22/1882. *ED2*, 389; *NBK*, 232; HJ/WDH, 1/
   31/1880. *ED2*, 268.
31. CFW/HJ, 2/12/1882. *ED3*, 536.
32. *NBK*, 230; HJSR/HJ, 5/9/1882. *PER1*, 111–13; AK/MRJ, 5/13/1882. VX; *THE*,
   384; HJ/GN, 5/25/1882. *ED2*, 382; HJ/MRJ, 5/25/1882. VX.
33. HJ/EG, 7/27/1882? HU; HJ/EB, 8/2/1882. HO; HJ/GN, 8/2/1882. HO; HJ/IG,
   6/5/1882. *LB1*, 93; HJ/JO, 8/2/1882. VX; HJ/CB, 11/22/1882. *ED2*, 389–90;
   PL, 119.
34. *NBK*, 232–33.
35. HJ/GN, 8/2/1882. HO; WJ/Josiah Royce, 6/13/1882. *BJ*, 134; *WJL1*, 209.
36. HJ/EB, 10/7/1882. HO.
37. HJ/WJ, 10/15/1882. HO; HJ/IG, 11/12/1882. *ED2*, 386–87.

38. HJ/IG, 11/12/1882. *ED2*, 387; HJ/WDH, 11/27/1882. *ED2*, 392; JH/HA, 10/22/1882. *OT*, 114; HJ/JC, 11/13/1882. VB.
39. HJ/HR, 12/15/1882. HO; WJ/AHJ, 9/14/1882. 9/25/1882. *BJ*, 135, 296; AK/HJ, 12/2/1882. VX; AHJ/WJ, 11/20/1882. *BJ*, 143; HJ/EL, 12/10/1882. *ED2*, 393.
40. HJ/MAC, 12/26/1882. BL; AJ/HJ, 12/19/1882. *DJ*, 87; HJ/WJ, 12/26/1882. *ED2*, 293–94.
41. AK/HJ, 12/2/1882. HO; AHJ/WJ, 11/30/1882. *BJ*, 143.
42. AK/HJ, 12/2/1882. HO; KPL/RJ, 12/11/1882. VX; AK/MRJ, 12/14/1882. VX; AHJ/WJ, 12/17/1882. HO; AHJ/WJ, 12/25/1882. *MA*, 146–47; AHJ/WJ, 12/18/1882. *BJ*, 144.
43. WJ/AJ, 12/20/1882. *ST*, 212; KPL/HJ3, 9/1/1920. *ST*, 209; WJ/AHJ, 12/19/1882. *BJ*, 145; HJ/WJ, 1/1/1883. *ED2*, 398; WJ/HJSR, 12/14/1882. *WJL1*, 218–22; WJ/AHJ, 12/20/1882. *BJ*, 145–46.
44. HJ/MAC, 12/26/1882. BL; HJSR/WJ, 11/7/1882. *MA*, 144; GWJ/RJ, 12/26/1882. VX; AHJ/WJ, 12/22/1882. *MA*, 148–49.
45. GWJ/RJ, 12/26/1882. VX.
46. GWJ/RJ, 12/26/1882. VX.
47. AHJ/WJ, 12/27/1882. *HAB*, 200; AHJ/WJ, 12/22/1882. *MA*, 148–49; HJ/WJ, 1/11/1883. HO; HJ/MAC, 1/27/1883. BL; GWJ/HJ & AJ, 2/6/1883. ST, 214–25; HJ/WJ, 1/23/1883. HO.
48. HJ/WJ, 1/23/1883. HO; WJ/AHJ, 1/22/1883. *NBK*, 18.
49. HJ/WJ, 2/5/1883. HO; WJ/HJ, 2/22/1883. *HAB*, 200; HJ/WJ 1/11/1883. *ED2*, 404–6.
50. HJ/FK, 2/1/1883. *ST*, 215; HJ/MAC, 1/27/1883. BL.
51. HJ/HR, 6/27/1883. HO; HJ/MAC, 3/29/1883. BL; HJ/GN, 4/15/1883, 4/26/1883. HO; HJ/GDM, 4/17/1883. *ED2*, 409; *THE*, 443.
52. HJ/JO, 4/8/1883. LC.
53. HJ/JO, 4/8/1883. LC; HJ/MAC, 4/19/1883. BL.
54. HJ/TSP, 5/22/1883. CL; HJ/GN, 5/29/1883. HO; HJ/FB, 7/26/1883. HO; HJ/MAC, 6/11/1883. BL; HJ/AF, 6/15/1883. HU.
55. HJ/GN, 8/8/1883, 8/18/1883. HO; HJ/TSP, 8/10/1883. *HAR*, 313–14; *TEH*, 71.

CHAPTER NINE. "THE GREAT MONEY-QUESTION," 1883–1888

1. HJ/GN, 11/14/1884. HO.
2. HJ/HR, 10/13/1883. HO; HJ/GN, 11/14/1883. HO; HJ/EB, 12/11/1883. *ED3*, 17.
3. HJ/GN, 11/3/1884. *ED3*, 54; HJ/SBW, 2/27/1887. *ED3*, 171–72; HJ/GN, 11/14/1883. HO.
4. HJ/R. W. Gilder, 2/1/1884. *ED3*, 23; HJ/MAC, 11/30/1887. BL; HJ/MAC, 1/29/1884. *ED3*, 22.
5. WJ/AJ, 10/2/1883. *MA*, 162; HJ/RJ, 12/2/1883. VX; HJ/WJ, 11/24/1883. *ED3*, 16.
6. HJ/WDH, 2/21/1884. *ED3*, 28; HJ/GN, 1/19/1884. *ED3*, 20–21.
7. HJ/AJ, 2/29/1884. *ED3*, 34.
8. HJ/WJ, 3/3/1884, 2/20/1884. HO; HJ/MW, 2/21/1884. VX; HJ/GN, 2/23/1884. *ED3*, 33.
9. NBK, 22; HJ/TSP, 3/6/1884. *HAR*, 315–16.
10. HJ/GN, 3/29/1884. HO; HJ/WJ, 3/3/1884. HO.
11. HJ/EB, 6/2/1884. *ED3*, 43; HJ/GN, 3/29/1884. HO.
12. HJ/EG, 2/2/1896. *MO*, 138; HJ/GN, 5/6/1884. HO; HJ/EG, 6/5/1884. *MO*, 31; HJ/EB, 6/2/1884. *ED3*, 42.

13. HJ/AHJ, 2/1884. HO; AK/MRJ, 2/2/1884. VX; AJ/SSD, 5/5/1884. *ST,* 228, 212; AK/MRJ, 2/2/1884. VX; AJ/FRM, nd/1884. *ST,* 228.
14. HJ/GN, 11/3/1884. *ED3,* 52; HJ/AK, 11/11/1884. HO; HJ/GN, 11/14/1884. HO.
15. HJ/EB, 3/23/1885. HO.
16. *NBK,* 30.
17. HJ/EB, 4/24/1885. HO.
18. HJ/OW, 12/18/1887. VX; HJ/WJ, 8/30/1879. HO; HJ/TSP, 9/14/1879. *ED2,* 255; HJ/RLS, 12/5/1884. *ED3,* 58; HJ/WJ, 5/9/1885. HO.
19. "The Art of Fiction," *Longman's Magazine,* 9/1884.
20. Review of "RLS, *Letters,*" *North American Review,* 1/1900.
21. HJ/RLS, 4/28/1890. *ED3,* 278.
22. AK/MRJ, 6/5/1885. VX; HJ/AK, 5/12/1885, 5/18/1885. HO.
23. HJ/MW, 7/3/1885. VX; *WARD2,* 17–18; HJ/EB, 8/3/1885. HO; AK/MRJ, 8/20/1884. VX; CEN/Eliot Norton, 6/11/1907. *NOR2,* 379; AHJ/Katherine Prince, 10/3/1884. *HAB,* 200–1; HJ/WJ, 12/4/1884. HO.
24. HJ/WJ, 1/2/1885. *ED3,* 62; HJ/WJ, 2/25/1885. *ED3,* 72; ELG/HJ, 2/17/1885. HO.
25. HJ/WJ, 6/13/1886. *ED3,* 121; *NBK,* 19–20; HJ/TSP, 3/6/1884. *HAR,* 315–16.
26. HJ/WJ, 5/26/1884. HO; HJ/GN, 1/19/1884. *ED3,* 21; HJ/GN, 8/2/1884. HO; HJ/MAC, 8/26/1884. BL; HJ/WJ, 10/5/1884. HO; *NBK,* 31, 19.
27. HJ/JO, 4/18/1885. *ED3,* 78; *AN,* 80.
28. HJ/FB, 5/9/1885. HO; HJ/AK, 5/12/1885. HO; WJ/HJ, 5/21/1885. HO; *AN,* 104–5; HJ/Benjamin H. Ticknor, 6/26/1885. *AN,* 106; HJ/WJ, 8/21/1885. HO.
29. HJ/WJ, 10/9/1885. *ED3,* 102; AJ/WJ, 5/19/1886. *ST,* 262; HJ/WJ, 8/21/1885. HO.
30. HJ/MAC, 9/15/1885. LC; HJ/MAC, 11/4/1885. BL; HJ/VP, 7/31/1884. CL.
31. HJ/TSP, 3/6/1884. *HAR,* 315–16; HJ/TA, 2/13/1884. *ED3,* 25; HJ/WDH, 2/21/1884. *ED3,* 27.
32. *NBK,* 27.
33. *NBK,* 31; HJ/RLS, 9/10/1885. *ED3,* 100; HJ/TSP, 12/12/1884. *ED3,* 61.
34. HJ/JC, 3/1884. VB.
35. HJ/MAC, 6/24/1886, 6/26/1886, 9/20/1886, 9/22/1886, 10/22/1886. BL; HJ/WDH, 1/2/1888. *ED3,* 209.
36. *NBK,* 29–30.
37. *NBK,* 23–24.
38. HJ/WJ, 10/29/1888. *ED3,* 244.
39. "An Animated Conversation," *Scribner's Magazine,* 3/1889; HJ/EG, 6/29/1888. *MO,* 58–59.
40. HJ/RUJ, 10/1/1888. VX.
41. HJ/RLS, 4/29/1889. *ED3,* 256; HJ/WJ, 3/29/1887. *LB1,* 53; HJ/GN, 5/6/1884, 5/9/1884. HO.
42. HJ/TSP, 1/14/1886. *HAR,* 321–22; HJ/WJ, 4/7/1886. HO; HJ/GN, 2/7/1886. HO.
43. HJ/WJ, 4/7/1886. HO; HJ/AC, 12/18/1889. HU; HJ/TSP, 1/14/1886. *HAR,* 321–22; HJ/GN, 7/16/1886. HO.
44. HJ/SBW, 3/9/1890. VX; HJ/GN, 4/29/1889. HO; HJ/CEN, 3/25/1889. *ED3,* 253; HJ/WJ, 12/9/1890. HO.
45. HJ/WJ, 3/9/1886. *ED3,* 114; HJ/EB, 1/7/1886. *ED3,* 107; HJ/GN, 2/7/1886, 7/16/1886. HO; HJ/AK, 4/13/1886. HO.
46. HJ/HR, 12/21/1885, 5/19/1886. HO; HJ/AK, 4/13/1886. HO; HJ/GN, 7/16/1886. HO.
47. HJ/GN, 1/4/1888. *ED3,* 214.
48. HJ/GN, 1/4/1888. *ED3,* 212; HJ/WJ, 2/20/1888. HO.

49. HJ/HR, 11/12/1886. HO; HJ/EB, 6/2/1884. *ED3*, 43; HJ/Mrs. Robb, 3/10/1886. VX.
50. HJ/GN, 8/23/1885. *ED3*, 98–99; HJ/CEN, 12/6/1886. *ED3*, 146.
51. HJ/EG, 4/8/1885. *MO*, 126.
52. HJ/WJ, 2/28/1877. *ED2*, 101.
53. HJ/TSP, 8/10/1883. *HAR*, 313–14; HJ/J. A. Symonds, 2/22/1884. *ED3*, 29–30.
54. "From Venice to Strasburg," *The Nation*, 3/6/1873; *GROS*, 241–42; *NBK*, 25–26.
55. "The Author of Beltraffio," *The English Illustrated Magazine*, 6–7/1884; HJ/EG, 6/9/1884. *MO*, 32.
56. "The Pupil," *Longman's Magazine*, 4–5/1891.

CHAPTER TEN. "MISS GRIEF," 1886–1889

1. HJ/FK, 5/20/1887. *ED3*, 184; HJ/GN, 7/23/1887. *ED3*, 196.
2. HJ/WJ, 4/7/1886. HO; HJ/HR, 11/12/1886, 3/11/1886. HO; HJ/EB, 3/17/1886. HO.
3. AJ/WJ, 9/18/1886. *ST*, 237; HJ/AK, 6/13/1886, 9/27/1886. HO.
4. HJ/WJ, 7/24/1885. *ED3*, 94; HJ/WJ, 2/18/1887. HO; WJ/HJ, 9/17/1886. *BJ*, 193; WJ/AJ, 7/6/1891. *ST*, 303–4.
5. HJ/WJ, 9/10/1886. *ED3*, 133–34; AJ/WJ, 4/24/1887. *DJ*, 129; GDM/HJ, 11/1/1886. HO.
6. HJ/EB, 8/12/1886. HO; HJ/GN, 8/2/1884. HO.
7. HJ/ELG, 2/6/1886. *ED3*, 111.
8. HJ/EG, 7/18/1884. *MO*, 33; HJ/GN, 8/24/1884. HO; HJ/TSP, 9/26/1884. *HAR*, 317–18; HJ/AC, 12/18/1888? DA; HJ/WJ & AHJ, 12/29/1893. *ED3*, 450.
9. HJ/EB, 1/23/1885, 2/1885. HO; HJ/HR, 7/5/1885. *ED3*, 93; HJ/RB, nd. VB.
10. HJ/WJ, 10/1/1887. *ED3*, 200; HJ/HR, 11/18/1885, 5/19/1886, 12/19/1887, 2/22/1888. HO; HJ/WJ, 9/10/1886. *ED3*, 132; HJ/EB, 10/18/1887. HO.
11. HJ/HR, 11/12/1886. HO; HJ/VP, 12/1/1886. CL; HJ/CEN, 12/6/1886. *ED3*, 145; HJ/GN, 12/7/1886. HO.
12. HJ/WDH, 2/21/1884. *ED3*, 28.
13. HJ/FB, 5/25/1886. *ED3*, 119–20; HJ/EB, 10/18/1887. HO.
14. CFW/Belle Carter, nd. *TO*, 25.
15. HJ/FB, 11/26/1886. *ED3*, 138; HJ/JH, 12/24/1886. *ED3*, 153.
16. HJ/GN, 12/7/1886. HO; HJ/AK, 2/26/1887. HO.
17. HJ/GN, 1/25/1887. *ED3*, 158–59.
18. HJ/KDB, 1/15/1887, 1/26/1887. *ED3*, 154–55, 160; HJ/WJ, 2/18/1887. HO.
19. HJ/KDB, 2/5/1887. *ED3*, 163–64; HJ/WJ, 2/18/1887. HO; HJ/AK, 2/26/1887. HO.
20. HJ/TSP, 9/26/1884. *HAR*, 317–18; HJ/EG, 4/24/1887. *MO*, 46; HJ/VP, 7/31/1884, 6/8/1885, 12/1/1886. CL.
21. HJ/GN, 2/27/1887. *ED3*, 166; *NBK*, 33–34.
22. HJ/SBW, 2/27/1887. *ED3*, 168–69; HJ/GN, 2/27/1887. *ED3*, 166–67; HJ/GDM, 3/2/1887. *ED3*, 174; HJ/JRL, 3/1/1887. *ED3*, 173.
23. HJ/FB, 3/15/1887. *ED3*, 175; HJ/WJ, 4/7/1887. *ED3*, 178; HJ/MrsEG, 4/14/1887. HU; HJ/WWB, 3/23/1887. *ED3*, 176–77; HJ/Angelina Milman, 2/27/nd. VB; HJ/RLS, 11/6/1885. *ED3*, 103; AI, 27.
24. HJ/MrsEG, 4/14/1887. *MO*, 45; HJ/WJ, 4/7/1887. *ED3*, 178; HJ/AC, 4/24/1887. DA; HJ/FK, 5/20/1887. *ED3*, 184; HJ/RUJ, 6/13/1887. *ED3*, 187; HJ/EG, 4/24/1887. *ED3*, 46.
25. HJ/Emma Wilkinson Pertz, 4–5/1887. *ED3*, 179; HJ/AC, 5/15/1888, 4/84/1887. DA.

26. HJ/TA, 6/12/1887. *ED3*, 185; HJ/AK, 6/16/1887. *ED3*, 188; HJ/FB, 3/15/1887. *ED3*, 175; HJ/GN, 7/23/1887. *ED3*, 196.
27. HJ/AC, 4/24/1887. DA; *NBK*, 36–40; HJ/SBW, 10/7/1887. VX; HJ/AC, 4/23/ 1887. DA.
28. HJ/VP, 5/23/1887. CL; HJ/AC, 7/9/1884. DA; HJ/SBW, 2/27/1887. *ED3*, 171; HJ/SBW, 10/7/1887. VX; HJ/AC, 5/15/1888. DA.
29. HJ/AK, 7/26/1887. HO; HJ/SBW, 10/17/1887. VX; HJ/HR, 9/27/1887. HO; HJ/ GN, 7/23/1887. *ED3*, 197.
30. HJ/SBW, 10/17/1887. VX; HJ/AK, 9/30/1888. HO; HJ/WJ, 10/1/1887. *ED3*, 201; HJ/GN, 7/23/1887. *ED3*, 190; HJ/TA, 5/3/1888. *ED3*, 223.
31. AJ/AK, 11/15/1887. *ST*, 220; AJ/WJ & AHJ, 11/20/1887. *ST*, 255; HJ/EB, 1/ 29/1888. HO; CFW/KPL, 10/9/1887. *ST*, 259.
32. HJ/EB, 1/29/1888. HO; HJ/AC, 5/15/1888, 12/18/1887. DA; HJ/HR, 12/21/ 1887, 4/21/1888. HO; HJ/JC, 12/18/1887. VB.
33. HJ/AC, 5/15/1888. DA; AK/FM, 6/24/1888. *ST*, 270; HJ/HR, 5/24/1888. HO; HJ/FB, 5/15/1888. *ED3*, 233; HJ/FB, 4/3/1888, 5/15/1888. *ED3*, 232–33; HJ/HR, 4/1/1888. *ED3*, 230–31.
34. HJ/GN, 9/30/1888. HO; HJ/RLS, 9/30/1888. *ED3*, 240; HJ/HR, 8/29/1888, 5/24/ 1888, 9/29/1888. HO; HJ/Angelina Milman, nd. VB.
35. HJ/AK, 9/30/1888. HO; HJ/GN, 9/30/1888. HO; HJ/MAC, 10/13/1888. BL; HJ/ WJ, 10/29/1888. *ED3*, 242; HJ/HR, 10/29/1888. HO.
36. HJ/RUJ, 11/1/1888. VX; HJ/AC, 10/30/1888. DA.
37. HJ/RB, 11/6/1888. *ED3*, 248; HJ/HR, 11/19/1888. HO; AJ/AK, 12/9/1888. *ST*, 259; CFW/SM, 12/10/1888. *TO*, 16.
38. HJ/WJ, 1/19/1889, 2/14/1889. HO; HJ/GN, 9/22/1889. *ED3*, 262; HJ/CEN, 3/ 25/1889. *ED3*, 251–52.
39. HJ/FB, 10/29/1888. *ED3*, 247.
40. HJ/MAC, 7/5/1888, 5/24/1888, 7/11/1888. BL.
41. HJ/WJ, 2/20/1888. HO; HJ/MAC, 3/24/1890, 3/26/1890, 3/28/1890. *ED3*, 274–75.
42. *NBK*, 53–54.
43. HJ/EG, 10/15/1912, 10/17/1912. *MO*, 278–82; *NBK*, 44–46.
44. HJ/MAC, 3/24/1890. *ED3*, 274; *NBK*, 47.
45. *NBK*, 46.
46. HJ/HR, 3/23/1889. HO.
47. HJ/COM, 12/10/1888. TX.
48. HJ/Lawrence Barrett, 8/11/1884. *PL*, 44; HJ/COM, 12/10/1888. TX.
49. *AI*, 30–31; NBK, 52–53.
50. *NBK*, 52–53.
51. *NBK*, 54; HJ/AJ, 6/6/1890. *ED3*, 285–86.
52. HJ/HR, 5/15/1890, 8/9/1890, HO; HJ/WJ, 6/23/1890. HO; HJ/AC, 7/7/1890. DA; HJ/MAC, 7/20/1890. BL.
53. HJ/AC, 12/18/1890. HU; HJ/WJ, 12/9/1890. HO.
54. HJ/FLB, 12/7/1890, 12/11/1890. *PL*, 257–58; HJ/WJ, 12/9/1890. HO.
55. HJ/WJ, 12/9/1890. HO; HJ/FLB, 12/29/1890. *ED3*, 310; HJ/AC, 12/18/1890. HU.
56. HJ/WJ, 12/9/1890. HO; HJ/GN, 12/30/1890. HO.
57. HJ/AC, 12/18/1890. HU; HJ/EG, 1/3/1891. *MO*, 73; *AJD*, 161; HJ/WJ, 1/3/1891. *ED3*, 318.
58. HJ/AJ, 1/4/1891. *ED3*, 320.
59. HJ/EG, 1/4/1891. *MO*, 73; HJ/AJ, 1/4/1891. *ED3*, 320.
60. HJ/William Archer, 12/31/1890. BL; *AJD*, 162; HJ/AJ & KPL, 1/4/1891. *ED3*, 321.
61. HJ/AC, 1/10/1891. DA; WB/WDH, 1/1891. *EDEL2*, 23.

62. HJ/AC, 1/10/1891. DA; HJ/VC, 1/11/1891. TX; HJ/HR, 1/16/1891. HO.
63. HJ/VC, 2/2/1891. TX; HJ/AC, 1/10/1891, 2/13/1891, 3/15/1891. DA; *Theatricals: Two Comedies*, 1894.
64. HJ/HR, 5/6/1891, 9/9/1891. HO; *NBK*, 57–58.
65. HJ/AC, 10/4/1891. DA; *NBK*, 61.
66. HJ/WJ, 11/15/1891, 12/13/1891. HO; HJ/HR, 12/31/1891. HO.

CHAPTER ELEVEN. "THE DARK ABYSS," 1888–1895

1. HJ/FK, 5/20/1887. *ED3*, 185; HJ/Constance Leslie, 3/18/1888. *ED3*, 224; *WWS1*, 227–28.
2. HJ/GN, 2/27/1887. *ED3*, 167; HJ/AC, 3/20/1889. DA.
3. *NBK*, 60–61; *Atlantic Monthly*, 4/1892; HJ/MJ, 1/31/1877. *ED2*, 94; *MY*, 594; HJ/AC, 10/30/1888. DA.
4. HJ/KDB, 1/12/1890. *ED3*, 268–69; "The Novel in 'The Ring and the Book,' " *The Quarterly Review*, 7/1912; HJ/FB, 1/11/1890. *ED3*, 268.
5. HJ/TSP, 11/25/1883. *ED3*, 14; HJ/Mrs. Cyril Flower, 4/21/1888. VB.
6. HJ/CEN, 12/6/1886. *ED3*, 146; HJ/AJ, 1/30/1881. *ED3*, 336; HJ/TC, 2/16/1885. VB.
7. "The Life of George Eliot," *Atlantic Monthly*, 5/1885.
8. HJ/CLB, 11/22/1901. *ED4*, 180–81; HJ/MF, 3/10/1901. HO; HJ/OWH, 2/20/1901. *ED4*, 184–85.
9. HJ/GN, 9/30/1888. HO; HJ/WJ, 9/21/1889. HO; HJ/LCP, 3/9/1890. CL; HJ/JRL, 7/20/1891. *ED3*, 346–47; HJ/SBW, 3/9/1890. VX; HJ/Julia Jackson Stephen, 8/13/1891. *ED3*, 352.
10. "JRL," *Atlantic Monthly*, 2/1892; HJ/SBW, 3/24/1892. VX; HJ/AF, 1/26/1892. *ED3*, 371; HJ/WJ, 9/18/1893. HO.
11. HJ/WDH, 5/17/1890. *ED3*, 284; HJ/AJ, 6/6/1890. *ED3*, 286; HJ/EG, 8/24/1891. MO, 81; WB/HJ, 12/1890. HO.
12. HJ/WJ, 12/13/1891. HO; HJ/JC, 12/13/1891. VB; HJ/GN, 12/13/1891. HO; HJ/HR, 12/13/1891. HO.
13. EG/George Douglas, 12/27/1912. *EGL*, 345; HJ/EG, 3/17/1891. MO, 86; EG, "WB," *The Century Magazine*, 4/1892; HJ, "WB," *Cosmopolitan*, 5/1892; HJ/WJ, 12/13/1891. HO; HJ/Mary Sands, 12/12/1891. *ED3*, 366.
14. HJ/EG, 12/27/1894. *ED3*, 502; HJ/RLS, 3/21/1890. *ED3*, 272; RLS/HJ, 3/21/1890. *ED3*, 272; RLS/HJ, 8/1890. *Henry James and Robert Louis Stevenson: A Record of Friendship*, ed. Janet Adam Smith, 1948, 191; HJ/RLS, 1/12/1891. *ED3*, 324; HJ/RLS, 4/29/1889. *ED3*, 255.
15. HJ/RLS, 4/28/1890. *ED3*, 278; HJ/RLS, 1/12/1891. *ED3*, 325.
16. HJ/RLS, 2/18/1891. *ED3*, 337; HJ/WJ, 12/22/1894. HO; HJ/FS, 12/26/1894. *ED3*, 499.
17. "Frances Anne Kemble," *Temple Bar*, 4/1893.
18. HJ/FPC, 3/3/1893. HU; "Frances Anne Kemble," 4/1893; HJ/SBW, 1/20/1893. *ED3*, 400.
19. "Frances Anne Kemble," 4/1893.
20. HJ/SBW, 3/9/1890. VX; HJ/GN, 11/24/1892. HO; HJ/SBW, 3/24/1892. VX; "Kemble," 4/1893.
21. HJ/SBW, 1/20/1893. *ED3*, 400; HJ/SBW, 5/9/1893. VX; HJ/WJ, 1/20/1893. *ED3*, 401–2; "Frances Anne Kemble," 4/1893.
22. HJ/SBW, 3/13/1893, 11/11/1893. VX; HJ/FPC, 2/27/1893. HU.
23. AK/MRJ, 10/23/1888. VX; AJ/WJ, 1/29–31/1891. *DJ*, 158; WJ/HJ, 2/1/1889. HO; HJ/WJ, 1/19/1889. HO.
24. HJ/WJ, 2/14/1889, 3/8/1889. HO; AJ/WJ, 3/22/1889. *DJ*, 162.

25. AJ/WJ, 4/7/1889. *DJ*, 168; HJ/WJ, 5/25/1889. HO.

26. HJ/WJ, 6/13/1889. HO.

27. HJ/WJ, 6/13/1889. HO.

28. WJ/AHJ, 7/29/1889. *WJL1*, 288; HJ/AHJ, 7/29/1889. *ST*, 286.

29. HJ/AHJ, 11/26/1890. *DJ*, 185; HJ/WJ, 12/13/1891, 3/2/1892. HO.

30. HJ/WJ, 2/6/1892, 3/2/1892. HO; HJ/GN, 2/6/1892. HO; HJ/WJ, 2/15/1892. *ST*, 310–11; HJ/WJ, 3/5/1892. *ED3*, 375–76.

31. HJ/RJ & MRJ, 3/8/1892. VX; HJ/WJ, 3/8/1892. *ED3*, 378; HJ/WJ, 3/19/1892, 4/1/1892. HO.

32. HJ/WJ, 3/8/1892. *ED3*, 376–78.

33. HJ/WJ, 11/15/1891, 12/13/1891. HO; HJ/HR, 12/31/1891. HO; *AI*, 33–34; HJ/EG, 1/3/1895. *ED3*, 504; HJ/WJ, 1/5/1895.*ED3*, 507.

34. HJ/MB, 1/5/1895. *ED3*, 506.

35. HJ/RLS, 1/12/1891. *ED3*, 326.

36. HJ/RLS, 1/18/1891. *ED3*, 336–37; HJ/WJ, 12/13/1891. HO; HJ/EG, nd/1894. HU.

37. PL, 346; NBK, 61.

38. HJ/VC, 5/22/1892. TX; HJ/COM, 7/17/1892, 9/11/1892, 9/15/1892. TX.

39. HJ/COM, 10/10/1892, 10/12/1892, 10/1892, 10/31/1892, 11/21/1892. TX; HJ/VC, 11/17/1892. TX.

40. HJ/VC, nd/1893. TX.

41. HJ/HR, 6/5/1893. HO; HJ/EG, 1/24/1890. *MO*, 68; HJ/FLB, 1/23/1892. *ED3*, 372–73; HJ/HR, 2/25/1892. HO.

42. HJ/Ada Rehan, 1/6/1892. *ED3*, 368; HJ/JAD, 9/1/1892. *ED3*, 395–96; HJ/Isaac Austen Henderson, 7/22/1893. *ED3*, 425.

43. HJ/ER, 12/6/1893. *ED3*, 443–44; HJ/WJ, 1/24/1894. HO.

44. HJ/JAD, 12/7/1893. *ED3*, 444–45; JAD/HJ, 12/8/1893. *ED3*, 445; HJ/JAD, 12/11/1893. *ED3*, 446–47; *AI*,30–31; HJ/WJ, 12/29/1893. *ED3*, 451; HJ/WJ, 1/24/1894. HO.

45. HJ/GN, 11/24/1892. HO; HJ/VP, 10/20/1892. VB; "The Middle Years," *Scribner's Magazine*, 5/1893.

46. *NBK*, 71; HJ/COM, 3/25/1893, 3/27/1893. TX.

47. HJ/COM, 4/8/1893, 4/16/1893, 4/29/1893. TX.

48. HJ/COM, 5/2/1893. *ED3*, 411; *NBK*, 76–77.

49. HJ/COM, 5/6/1893, 5/14/1893, 6/1/1893, 5/1893, 6/8/1893. TX; *NBK*, 80–82.

50. HJ/WJ, 1/12/1891. *ED3*, 332.

51. HJ/WJ, 1/1894. HO; HJ/WJ, 12/29/1893. *ED3*, 452; HJ/WJ, 10/27/1894. HO.

52. HJ/WJ, 12/8/1894, 12/22/1894. HO; HJ/EL, 12/15/1894. *ED3*, 496; HJ/Marion Terry, 12/29/1894. CL.

53. *AI*, 33–34; HJ/EG, 12/22/1894. *MO*, 122; HJ/MB, 1/5/1895. *ED3*, 506; HJ/WJ & AHJ, 1/5/1895. *ED3*, 507; HJ/WJ & AHJ, 2/2/1895. *ED3*, 514.

54. *AI*, 33–34.

55. HJ/MF, 1/25/1895. HO; HJ/VC, 3/15/1895. *ED3*, 521; HJ/WJ, 2/2/1895. *ED3*, 514–18; *PL*, 482–83; HJ/DC, 1/14/1895. DA; HJ/MF, 1/9/1895. *ED3*, 510.

56. HJ/WWB, 1/26/1894. *ED3*, 457; HJ/GC, 1/26/1894. VB; HJ/Angelina Milman, nd/1894. VB.

57. HJ/WWB, 1/26/1894. *ED3*, 457; HJ/Angelina Milman, nd/1894. VB; HJ/GC, 1/26/1894. VB.

58. HJ/JH, 1/28/1894. *ED3*, 459–60; HJ/GC, 2/2/1894. VB.

59. HJ/EG, 1/30/1894. *MO*, 97; Robert Nevin/GC, 1/28/1894. VB; JH/HA, 2/5/1894. William Roscoe Thayer, *Life and Letters of John Hay*, 1915, II, 107; HJ/GC, 2/2/1894. VB; HJ/KDB, 2/2/1894. *ED3*, 466.

60. *TO*, 18–19, 155; CFW/KPL, 9/19/1890. *ST*,260.

61. HJ/AC, 5/4/1893, 9/19/1893, 12/27/1893. DA; *TO*, 19, 16; CFW/SM, 11/20/

1893. *TO*,16–17; CFW/Katherine Mather, nd. *TO*,16; CFW/C. Steadman, 7/23/ 1876. *TO*,16; CFW/A. C. Washburn, nd. *TO*,16.
62. HJ/GC, 2/2/1894. VB.
63. HJ/WWB, 2/2/1894. *ED3*, 464.
64. HJ/WJ, 3/24/1894. *ED3*, 470; HJ/JH, 1/28/1894. *ED3*, 460; HJ/WWB, 2/2/1894. *ED3*, 464; HJ/KDB, 2/2/1894. *ED3*, 467.
65. HJ/W. B. Squire, Easter Sunday, 1894. BL; HJ/HB, 6/22/1894. HO; HJ/GC, 2/ 2/1894. VB.
66. HJ/FB, 12/15/1894. *ED3*, 493–94; HJ/KDB, 3/20/1894. *ED3*, 467–68.
67. HJ/GC, 5/11/1894. VB; Alide Cagidimetrio, "Sceltadi Città: Venezia, Black Balloons and White Doves," in *Henry James e Venezia,* ed. Sergio Perosa, 1987, 54–55.

CHAPTER TWELVE. PASSIONATE FRIENDSHIPS, 1894–1900

1. NBK, 91–93.
2. HJ/WJ & AHJ, 6/29/1894. HO; HJ/MF, 6/30/1894. HO; HJ/AC, 8/19/1894. DA; HJ/HB, 6/22/1894. HO; HJ/HB, 6/24/1894. VX.
3. HJ/MF, 6/30/1894. HO; HJ/WJ & AHJ, 6/29/1894. HO; HJ/EG, 6/25/1894. *MO*,112–13; HJ/AC, 6/3/1894, 7/22/1894. DA; HJ/HR, 6/22/1894. HO.
4. HJ/EG, 8/22/1894. *MO*,116; HJ/AC, 8/19/1894. DA; HJ/GN, 11/24/1892. HO; HJ/JC, 7/1/1891. VB.
5. HJ/HB, 4/23/1894. VB; HJ/CLB, 3/1/1894. *HAS*, 136; HJ/HGW, 7/10/1915. *ED4*, 770.
6. HJ/MF, 10/2/1900. *ED4*, 170.
7. HJ/WJ, 7/3/1895. HO.
8. HJ/WJ, 11/15/1893. HO; *AL*,352; HJ/MF, 1/16/1893. *ED3*, 399; HJ/WJ, 1/20/ 1893. *ED3*, 402.
9. *AL*,356; HJ/RLS, 2/17/1893. *ED3*, 407; HJ/WJ & AHJ, 3/21/1893. *ED3*, 408.
10. HJ/SBW, 5/9/1893. VX; HJ/HR, 5/4/1893. HO; HJ/WJ & AHJ, 3/21/1893. *ED3*, 409; HJ/WJ & AHJ, 5/28/1894. *ED3*, 482.
11. *AL*,364–65; HJ/WJ, 10/19/1893. HO.
12. HJ/MF, 1/18/1892. *ED3*, 371; HJ/AC, 1/27/1892. DA; HJ/WJ, 2/6/1892. HO; HJ/RLS, 1/12/1891. *ED3*, 327; "Introduction," *Mine Own People,* 1891.
13. HJ/WJ, 2/6/1892. HO; RK/HJ, 12/9/1892. HO; HJ/RLS, 6/6/1893. *ED3*, 414; HJ/RLS, 6/8/1893. *ED3*, 414; HJ/AC, 7/14/1893. *ED3*, 421; HJ/EG, 4/15/1894. *MO*,109; HJ/FS, 5/30/1897. BL; RK/HJ, 1/7/1894. HO.
14. HJ/WJ, nd/1893, 9/18/1893. HO; HJ/EW, nd/1894, 12/25/1893, 9/8/1894, 11/8/ 1894, 1/5/1895. HU; HJ/MWA, 4/16/1894, 8/6/1895, 8/22/1895. HU.
15. HJ/GN, 4/19/1890, 10/17/1896. HO; HJ/EW, 10/6/1896. HU; HJ/FS, 5/30/1897. BL; HJ/WJ, 7/22/1895. HO; HJ/AC, 9/23/1895. DA; HJ/EG, 8/9/1895. *MO*,129.
16. HJ/MF, 2/29/1896. HO; HJ/RLS, 10/21/1893. *ED3*, 439; HJ/EG, 7/25/1896. *MO*,144; HJ/WJ, 4/26/1895. HO; HJ/HR, 6/20/1895. HO.
17. HJ/HR, 10/14/1890. HO; *NBK*,126; HJ/AC, 2/12/1895. DA.
18. HJ/HR, 6/20/1895, 11/10/1895. HO; HJ/JC, 7/1/1895, 2/14/nd. VB; HJ/JH, 6/ 1891. *ED3*, 343; HJ/JC, 12/13/1891. *ED3*, 367–68.
19. HJ/WJ, 7/25/1895, 7/22/1895. HO; HJ/JC, 12/13/1891. *ED3*, 367; AJ/AHJ, 1/9/ 1890. *DJ*,262–63; HJ/GN, 10/16/1896. HO.
20. HJ/WJ, 4/16/1900. HO.
21. *GROS*, 280–81; HJ/GN, 11/24/1892. HO; HJ/EG, 1/7/1893. *MO*, 90.
22. HJ/WJ, 4/26/1895. HO; HJ/EG, 4/21/1893. *MO*, 94.
23. HJ/DC, 1/14/1895. DA; HJ/AC, 2/12/1895. DA; HJ/AC, 3/1/1895. *SL2*, 286–87.
24. HJ/EG, 10/30/1890. *MO*, 72; *ELL*, 493.
25. HJ/HR, 10/19/1893. HO; HJ/JS, 10/19/1893. *ED3*, 435; *NBK*, 140–42.

26. HJ/JS, 11/5/1896. *ED4*, 40; Henry Blake/Louisa Washburn, 8/10/1894. HU; HJ/HR, 11/10/1895, 12/31/1897, 10/19/1898. HO; HJ/MF, 10/1897. HO; HJ/EW, 10/1898. HU; HJ/AC, 10/30/1898. DA; HJ/GN, 9/7/1899. HO.
27. *LEW*, 199; HJ/MF, 3/11/1890. *ED3*, 269.
28. *LEW*, 188; HJ/MF, 1/7/1891. HO.
29. HJ/MF, 2/4/1893, 2/12/1891. HO.
30. HJ/MAC, 3/4/1891. BL; HJ/MF, 1/18/1892. *ED3*, 371; HJ/MF, 1/16/1893. *ED3*, 399; HJ/MF, Easter Sunday/1894, 6/30/1894, nd/1897, 10/2/1895. HO.
31. HJ/MF, 3/22/1900, 9/16/1899, 11/5/1899. HO.
32. HJ/MF, 9/26/1900. *SL2*, 325; HJ/MF, 9/21/1900. HO.
33. *NBK*, 109, 99; HJ/WJ, 2/23/1895. HO; HJ/MF, 2/10/1896. HO; GALE, 292.
34. HJ/WJ, 7/3/1895, 2/21/1896. HO; HJ/MF, 10/2/1895. HO; *NBK*, 123–25.
35. HJ/WJ, 2/23/1895. HO; *NBK*, 114.
36. *NBK* 109–10; Hercules Fay/TSP, nd/1895. *HAR*, 163; HJ/MF, 2/10/1896. HO.
37. *NBK*, 109; HJ/Louis Waldstein, 10/21/1898. *ED4*, 84; *AI*, 38; HJ/Frederic Myers, 12/19/1897. *ED4*, 88.
38. *NBK*, 110–12, 310; Janet Adam Smith, *John Buchan: A Biography*, 1965, 174–75, 472.
39. *NBK*, 79, 122, 127.
40. *NBK*, 131–36, 158–60.
41. *NBK*, 144–45, 147–55, 161–67; HJ/MW, 3/16/1897. VB.
42. HJ/WJ, 5/29/1896, 10/30/1896. HO; HJ/EG, 10/6/1896. *MO*, 149.
43. HJ/MF, 12/23/1894. HO; HJ/AC, 7/3/1895. DA; HJ/WJ, 7/3/1895. HO.
44. HJ/HR, 7/21/1895. HO; HJ/WJ, 7/22/1895, 8/20/1895. HO; *NBK*, 407.
45. HJ/WJ, 8/20/1895, 2/21/1896. HO; HJ/AC, 9/23/1896. DA.
46. HJ/GC, 1/8/1896. VB; HJ/MWA, 9/4/1895, 10/13/1895. HU; HJ/MJV, 2/12/1896. VX; HJ/WJ, 2/21/1896. HO.
47. HJ/WJ, 4/7/1896. HO.
48. HJ/EW, 5/1896. HU; HJ/WJ, 5/29/1896. HO; HJ/WJ & AHJ, 9/4/1896. *ED4*, 26.
49. HJ/HR, 7/6/1896. HO; HJ/MW, 7/14/1896. VB; HJ/EW, 7/1896. HU; HJ/MF, 7/31/1896. HO; HJ/EG, 8/28/1896. *MO*, 145; HJ/MWA, 9/11/1896. HU; HJ/GN, 9/12/1895. HO.
50. HJ/MW, 9/17/1896. VB; HJ/AC, 9/25/1896. DA; HJ/MF, 12/2/1896. HO; HJ/SBW, 6/8/1897. VX; HJ/WJ, 10/30/1896. HO; HJ/AC, 4/20/1897. DA; HJ/MF, 2/28/1897. *ED4*, 41.
51. HJ/GC, 12/28/1896. VB; HJ/MF, 12/19/1896. HO; HJ/EW, 9/1/1897. HU; HJ/WJ, 9/1/1897. HO; HJ/HR, 7/2/1896. HO; *HY*, 77; HJ/FS, 5/30/1897. BL.
52. HJ/MRJ, 8/28/1897. *MA*, 184; HJ/KPL, 12/27/1897. VB; HJ/HR, 12/31/1897. HO; AHJ/HJ, 5/31/1897. *BJ*, 203; HJ/FRM, 6/7/1897. *ED4*, 46–47.
53. HJ/EW, 9/15/1897. HU.
54. HJ/EW, 9/15/1897. HU.
55. HJ/ACB, 9/25/1897. *ED4*, 57.
56. HJ/EW, 9/20/1897. HU; HJ/KPL, 12/27/1897. VB; HJ/ACB, 10/1/1897. *ED4*, 59.
57. HJ/EW, 11/29/1897. HU; HJ/KPL, HJ/KPL, 12/27/1897. VB; HJ/HR, 12/31/1897. HO.
58. HJ/GC, 6/7/1890. VB.
59. HJ/GC, 6/7/1900. VB; HJ/MF, 9/21/1900. HO.

CHAPTER THIRTEEN. THE NEW CENTURY, 1900–1904

1. HJ/HS, nd/1900. HO; HJ/GN, 7/8/1900. HO; *AI*, 41–42.
2. HJ/WJ, 5/12/1900. *ED4*, 139; HJ/GN, 8/5/1900. HO; HJ/Ellen "Bay" Emmet, 10/20/1901. *ED4*, 164; HJ/MF, 10/2/1900. *ED4*, 169.
3. HJ/WDH, 6/29/1900. *ED4*, 152; HJ/GN, 7/8/1900. HO.

4. HJ/AC, 7/3/1895. DA.
5. HJ/WJ, 7/3/1895, 12/18/1895. HO; HJ/AC, 12/19/1895. DA; HJ/GC, 1/8/1896. VB.
6. HJ/HR, 12/18/1898. HO; HJ/WJ & AHJ, 6/3/1899. HO; HJ/AC, 10/13/1899. DA.
7. HJ/HR, 4/17/1898. HO; HJ/WJ, 4/22/1898. HO; HJ/AC, 5/11/1898. DA.
8. HJ/AC, 5/11/1898. DA; HJ/WJ, 9/17/1896. HO.
9. HJ/DC, 11/6/1899. DA; HJ/AC, 11/20/1899. DA; HJ/MF, 1/27/1900. HO.
10. HJ/SBW, 1/29/1900. VX; HJ/AC, 2/10/1900. DA; HJ/AC, 2/3/1901. *SL2*, 328–29.
11. HJ/HB, 2/22/1898. VB; HJ/EW, 2/25/1898. HU; HJ/MW, 9/22/1898. VB; HJ/ECA, 10/15/1898. *ED4*, 83; HJ/PB, 12/23/1898. *ED4*, 90; HJ/EG, 8/19/1899. *MO*, 167.
12. HJ/AC, 10/30/1898. DA; HJ/MF, 9/16/1899. HO; HJ/GN, 9/7/1899. HO.
13. HJ/MJV, 2/25/1899. VX; HJ/Mrs. Trower, 2/2/1899. VB; HJ/EW, 2/17/1899. HU.
14. HJ/WJ, 3/2/1899. HO.
15. HJ/EW, 2/27/1899, nd/1899, 3/1899. HU; HJ/EG, 2/28/1899. *MO*, 165; HJ/WJ, 3/2/1899. HO.
16. HJ/EW, nd/1899, 3/29/1899. HU; HJ/AC & DC, 3/16/1899. DA; HJ/WJ, 4/2/1899. *ED4*, 101.
17. HJ/AC & DC, 3/16/1899. DA.
18. HJ/MB, 4/8/1899. *ED4*, 104–5; HJ/AC, 4/1899, 5/10/1899. HU.
19. HJ/DC, 5/1899. DA; HJ/EW, nd/1899. HU.
20. HJ/EW, nd/1899. HU; HJ/WJ & AHJ, 6/3/1899. HO; HJ/AC, 6/15/1899. DA; *WWS2*, 324.
21. HJ/EW, 6/22/1899, 7/4/1899. HU; HJ/HS, 6/1899. HO; HJ/WJ & AHJ, 6/3/1899. HO.
22. HJ/WJ, 4/10/1898. *BJ*, 203–4; HJ/AHJ, 4/19/1898. *BJ*, 204; AHJ/HJ, 2/4/1898. *BJ*, 204; RJ/AHJ, 2/24/1898. *MA*, 194–97; RJ, autobiographical fragment. VX; HJ/EDE, 12/24/1898. VX; John Jay Chapman, *Memories & Milestones*, 1915, 26.
23. WJ/HJ, 2/21/1898. *BJ*, 204; HJ/WJ, 5/29/1896. HO.
24. HJ/WJ & AHJ, 6/3/1899. HO; WJ/HJ, 6/21/1899 *BJ*, 231; HJ/WJ, 9/6/1899. HO; HJ/GN, 9/7/1899. HO; HJ/MF, 11/5/1899. HO; HJ/HR, 10/25/1899. HO.
25. HJ/HR, 10/25/1899. HO; HJ/MF, 11/5/1899. HO.
26. HJ/WJ, 7/21/1899. HO; HJ/WJ & AHJ, 8/9/1899. *ED4*, 115.
27. HJ/WJ, 8/4/1899, 8/5/1899, 8/9/1899, 11/12/1899. HO; RK/HJ, 9/19/1899. HO.
28. HJ/Sarah Orne Jewett, 12/24/1899. HU; HJ/MF, 1/27/1900. HO; HJ/WJ, 11/28/1899. VX; WJ/HJ, 5/7/1900. *BJ*, 234; HJ/WJ, 2/10/1900. HO; HJ/GN, 2/12/1900. HO.
29. HJ/WJ, 5/30/1900, 7/18/1900. HO; HJ/WJ, 5/12/1900. *ED4*, 138; WJ/HJ, 5/14/1900. *BJ*, 233; HJ/AHJ, 5/22/1900. *ED4*, 142.
30. WJ/AHJ, 9/8/1900. *BJ*, 236–37; HJ/MF, 9/21/1900. HO; HJ/MW, 10/14/1900. VB.
31. HJ/WJ, 11/17/1900. HO; WJ, notebook, nd. *BJ*, 241; HJ/MW, 3/15/1901. *ED4*, 185–86.
32. HJ/MF, 8/9/1901. *ED4*, 196–97; WJ/HJ, 12/7/1901. *BJ*, 239; HJ/AHJ, 9/26/1901. *ED4*, 204–7.
33. HJ/EG, 8/19/1899. *MO*, 166; HCA, diary. LC; HCA/family, winter 1897, 5/1897. LC; HCA/Andreas Andersen, autumn 1897. LC.
34. HJ/HCA, 3/9/1900. VB; *WARD2*, 199–200.
35. HJ/HCA, 7/19/1899. *ED4*, 108–9; HJ/HCA, 7/27/1899. *ED4*, 113.
36. HCA/parents, 8/6/1899. LC; HJ/HCA, 8/9/1899. VB; HJ/HCA, 9/7/1899. *ED4*, 188–89; HJ/HCA, 10/23/1899. VB.
37. HJ/HCA, 12/22/1899, 3/20/1900. VB.

38. HJ/HCA, 9/7/1900, 10 or 11/1900, 11/3/1900, 12/22/1899. VB; HCA/mother, 12/1/1900. LC; HCA/OA, 10/16/1904, LC.
39. HJ/HCA, 3/20/1900, 3/9/1900, 1/12/1901, 7/1/1901, 9/17/1901, 10/5/1901. VB; HCA/HJ, 7/22/1901. LC; HJ/HCA, 9/13/1901. *ED4*, 201. WJ/HCA, 1/10/1901. LC.
40. HJ/HCA, 2/9/1902. *ED4*, 225–27; HJ/HCA, 2/28/1902. *ED4*, 227–28.
41. HCA/OA, 2/6/1902. LC; HJ/HCA, 8/3/1902, 11/15/1902. VB.
42. HCA/OA, 3/1/1903, 12/2/1904. LC; HJ/HCA, 12/3/1903, 8/23/1903, 9/3/1903, 9/22/1903. VB.
43. HJ/GN, 7/8/1900. HO; HJ/HS, 7/1901, 2/4/1904. HO; HJ/HS, 2/4/1904. HO; HJ/GL, 10/14/1897, 12/25/1897, 3/2/1898, 3/29/1898, 4/5/1898, 5/6/1898, 6/17/1898, 7/6/1899, 7/9/1899, 7/20/1904. HO; HJ/GL, 9/15/1902. *ED4*, 240–41.
44. HJ/HS, 5/19/1899. HO.
45. *GLA*, 227; Frederick Kirchoff, "An End to Novel Writing: Howard Overing Sturgis," *English Literature in Transition* 33 (1990), 425–41; *SEY*, 228; *GALE*, 636.
46. HJ/MF, 3/23/1897. HO; HJ/HS, nd/1899, 2/25/1900, 2/2/1900, 3/4/1900, 4/26/1900, 4/10/1900, 4/26/1900, 1/9/1901, 11/12/1903. HO.
47. HJ/HS, 11/18/1903. HO; HJ/HS, 12/7/1903. *ED4*, 296; HJ/HS, 11/23/1904, 12/2/1904. *ED4*, 294–95.
48. *GROS*, 280–81; *NBK*, 198–99.
49. See Eve Kosofsky Sedgwick, "The Beast in the Closet: James and the Writing of Homosexual Panic," *Sex, Politics, and Science in the Nineteenth-Century Novel*, ed. Ruth Bernard Yeazell, 1986, 148–86.
50. HA/ECA, 5/6/1901. *HAL6*, 248.
51. HJ/GN, 9/7/1899. HO.
52. HJ/HS, 12/2/1901. HO; HJ/EG, 2/28/1899. *MO*, 165.
53. HJ/CC, 6/5/1900. *ED4*, 144; HJ/JPI, 8/29/1900. *ED4*, 163; HJ/CC, 6/7/1900. *ED4*, 145.
54. HJ/EG, 6/26/1902. *MO*, 198–99; HJ/JC, 11/1/1906. *ED4*, 418–19.
55. See *SEY*, 131–66.
56. HJ/MW, 9/22/1898. VB; HJ/WDH, 1/25/1902. *ED4*, 222–25; HJ/AF, 10/24/1900. HU; HJ/Frances Sitwell, 1/27/1900. VB; HJ/MF, 1/27/1900. HO; HJ/WJ, 2/2/1900, 2/10/1900. HO; HJ/GL, 4/1/1900. HO.
57. HJ/AHJ, 9/26/1901. *ED4*, 204–7.
58. HJ/AC, 11/4/1901. DA; HJ/WJ, 3/25/1900, 11/17/1900, 12/9/1900. HO; HJ/HS, 12/2/1901. HO; HJ/EW, nd/1901. HU.
59. HJ/GN, 1/22/1902. HO; HJ/HR, 12/22/1903. HO.
60. HJ/WDH, 11/27/1897. *ED4*, 60.
61. HJ/HS, 5/19/1899. HO; HJ/HR, 12/18/1898. HO; *HY*, 152.
62. HJ/MW, 10/14/1900. VB; *HY*, 152; HJ/HS, 11/12/1900. HO; HJ/MW, 3/15/1901. *ED4*, 185–86; HJ/MW, 3/15/1901. *ED4*, 185–86; *NBK*, 194–95; HJ/WDH, 8/10/1900. *ED4*, 198–200.
63. HJ/HS, 12/4/1901. HO; HJ/RK, 10/30/1901. *ED4*, 209–11; HJ/GN, 1/22/1902. HO; HJ/VH, 6/7/1902. VB.
64. HJ/MF, 11/17/1901. *ED4*, 214–15; WDH/TA, 1/19/1902. *WDHL5*, 11; HJ/WDH, 1/25/1902. *ED4*, 222–25; HJ/AC, 12/24/1902. DA.
65. HJ/VH, 1/16/1902. *ED4*, 221–22.
66. HJ/GN, 12/18/1902. *ED4*, 257.
67. HJ/MF, 10/18/1902. *ED4*, 244; HJ/MW, 9/23/1902. *ED4*, 242–43; HJ/MW, 10/27/1903, 12/16/1903. VB; HJ/MCJ, 10/23/1902. *ED4*, 245–47; HJ/MW, 12/16/1903. VB.
68. HJ/Mrs. Francis Bellingham, 12/31/1902. *ED4*, 254.
69. HJ/EDE, 12/24/1898. VX; HJ/MCJ, 10/23/1902. *ED4*, 245–47; HJ/AF, 10/24/1900. HU.

70. HJ/HS, 11/12/1900. HO; *NBK,* 197.
71. HJ/OWH, 2/20/1901. *ED4,* 184–85; HJ/GN, 1/22/1902. HO; HJ/VH, 11/5/1902. VB; HJ/CLB, 11/21/1903. *ED4,* 292; HJ/GN, 12/18/1902. HO; HJ/HGW, 1/24/1904. *ED4,* 304.
72. HJ/GN, 12/18/1902. HO; *WWS2,* 223–26; HA/HJ, 11/1903. *SAM,* 372–73.
73. HJ/SBW, 12/21/1902. *ED4,* 258–61; HJ/WDH, 8/5/1904. HO; HJ/WJ, 5/24/1903. *ED4,* 274; *HY,* 168; HJ/MAC, 6/17/1903, 6/19/1903. BL.
74. HJ/WJ, 5/24/1903. *ED4,* 270–75.
75. HJ/CLB, 11/21/1903. *ED4,* 292.
76. HJ/Anne Thackeray Ritchie, 11/19/1903. *ED4,* 290; HJ/JP, 11/5/1909, 8/10/1904, 10/23/1903. HO.
77. HJ/HR, 12/22/1903. HO; HJ/Louise Horstmann, 8/12/1904. *ED4,* 311–14; HJ/HS, 7/25/1904, 9/5/1904. HO.
78. HJ/HS, 7/25/1904. HO; HJ/CLB, 7/5/1904. *HAS,* 154–55; HJ/HCA, 6/27/1904. VB; HJ/AC, 7/25/1904. DA; HJ/GN, 7/25/1904. HO; "Travelling Companions," *Atlantic Monthly,* 11–12/1870.

CHAPTER FOURTEEN. "CLOSING THE GATES," 1904–1910

1. *AMS,* 74–75.
2. HJ/JP, 9/6/1904. HO; HJ/WJ & AHJ, 8/31/1904. *ED4,* 319.
3. HJ/SBW, 9/8/1904. VX; WJ/Pauline Goldmark, 9/21/1904. *WJL2,* 215; HJ/MW, 9/8/1904. VB; HJ/GN, 9/12/1904. HO; HJ/HS, 9/11/1904. HO.
4. HJ/AF, 9/5/1904. HU; HJ/HS, 9/5/1904. HO; HJ/MW, 9/8/1904. VB; HJ/SBW, 9/8/1904. VX.
5. HJ/HS, 9/11/1904. HO; HJ/SBW, 9/8/1904. VX; HJ/RJ, 9/4/1904. *ED4,* 320; HJ/RJ, 9/14/1904. VX.
6. HJ/EG, 10/27/1904. *MO,* 212; *NBK,* 242–43.
7. HJ/HS, 10/17/1904. *ED4,* 325.
8. HJ/EDW, 8/17/1902. *POW,* 34.
9. EDW/William Brownell, 1/7/1904. *EDWL,* 88; HJ/EDW, 8/17/1904. *POW,* 35.
10. HJ/HS, 10/19/1904. HO; HJ/HS, nd/1904. HO; HJ/EG, 10/27/1904. *MO,* 210.
11. HJ/MCJ, 10/23/1902. *ED4,* 245–47; HJ/EG, 10/27/1904. *MO,* 210; HJ/JA, 10/22/1904. *ED4,* 330.
12. *NBK,* 240.
13. HJ/EDW, 11/18/1904. *ED4,* 334; HJ/HS, 11/17/1904, 12/2/1904. HO; HJ/EDW 11/18/1904. *POW,* 40; HJ/"Dear Sir," 11/15/1904. VB; HJ/RJ, 12/22/1904. VX; HJ/EW, 12/26/1904. HU.
14. HJ/HCA, 12/9/1904. VB; HJ/RJ, 12/22/1904. VX; HJ/EW, 12/26/1904. HU; HJ/MJV, 12/11/1904. VX.
15. HJ/SBW, 1/1/1905. *ED4,* 336; HJ/EW, 12/26/1904. HU; HJ/HS, 2/20/1905. HU; HJ/SBW, 1/12/1905. VX; HJ/WJ, 1/10/1905. *ED4,* 336; HA/LH, 1/8/1905. *HAL6,* 625.
16. HJ/JH, 4/3/1900. *MON,* 123; *OT,* 300–302.
17. HJ/EG, 2/16/1905. *MO,* 213; HJ/JA, 1/16/1905. *ED4,* 339; HJ/MCJ, 1/13/1905. *ED4,* 337; HJ/EDW, 1/16/1905. *ED4,* 341.
18. Edmund Morris, *The Rise of Theodore Roosevelt,* 1979, 467–68; review of Theodore Roosevelt, "American Ideals." *Literature,* 4/23/1898; HJ/JA, 9/19/1901. *ED4,* 202.
19. HJ/SBW, 1/12/1905. VX; HA/LH, 1/1/1905. *HAL6,* 625, 631; HJ/EG, 2/26/1905. *MO,* 213; HJ/EDW, 1/16/1905. *ED4,* 341; HJ/EDW, 2/8/1905. *ED4,* 347; HJ/SBW, 1/1905. VX.
20. HJ/EDW, 18/18/1905. *POW,* 58; HJ/HS, 10/3/1903, 2/20/1905. HO; HJ/EG, 2/16/1905. *MO,* 213; HJ/EDW, 2/8/1905. *POW,* 47–48; HJ/MJV, 2/5/1905. VX.

21. HJ/MJV, 2/5/1905, 2/18/1905. VX; *AMS*, 413–14.
22. HJ/WDH, 1/5/1905. *WDHL*5, 126; CEN/WDH, 1/19/1905. *WDHL*5, 126.
23. *AMS*, 432–35, 451, 461–62; HJ/RJ, 2/19/1905. VX; HJ/HS, 2/20/1905. HO.
24. HJ/HS, 2/20/1905, HO; HJ/MJV, 2/27/1905. VX; HJ/WDH, 3/1/1905. *WDHL*5, 103–4; HJ/WJ, 3/8/1905. *ED*4, 353–54; HJ/EW, 3/19/1905. *ED*4, 355–56.
25. HJ/JP, 3/25/1905. HO.
26. HJ/AHJ, 4/5/1905. *ED*4, 356–57; *NBK*, 237.
27. HJ/AHJ, 4/5/1905. *ED*4, 337, HJ/GL, 4/2/1905. HO; *EDEL*2, 595.
28. *AMS*, 119, 64; *NBK*, 236.
29. *AMS*, 208, 131–39.
30. *AMS*, 138–39.
31. HJ/SBW, 6/15/1905. VX; E. E. Burlingham/JPI, 4/2/1900. *HORN*, 4; HCA/mother & Arthur, 6/19/1905. LC; HJ/TSP, 7/5/1905. *WDHL*5, 126; WDH/Hamlin Garland, 8/20/1905. *WDHL*5, 130.
32. HJ/AF, 2/24/1905. CL; HJ/SBW, 6/15/1905. VX; HJ/HCA, 5/11/1905. VB; HCA/mother & Arthur, 6/22/1905, 6/24/1905. LC; HJ/EDW, 6/7/1905. *POW*, 50–51.
33. CEN/WDH, 10/19/1905. *WDHL*5, 133; HJ/GN, 1/22/1902. HO; *GLA*, 185–94.
34. *GLA*, 189.
35. HJ/MRJ, 7/3/1905. VX; HJ/Clara Stone Hay, 7/2/1905. *MON*, 134; HJ/CEN, 9/10/1905. *WDHL*5, 133.
36. HJ/EW, 9/18/1905. HU; HJ/MW, 9/25/1906. VB; HJ/HCA, 11/25/1906. VB; HJ/VH, 1/26/1906, 7/18/1905. VB; HJ/SC, 7/30/1905. *ED*4, 366–68; HJ/Robert Herrick, 8/7/1905. *ED*4, 371.
37. *AN*, 177; HJ/WJ, 11/23/1905. *ED*4, 381; HJ/VH, 1/23/1906. VB.
38. HJ/PB, 12/21/1905. *ED*4, 388; HJ/MW, 6/22/1907. VB; "The Jolly Corner," *The English Review*, 12/1908.
39. HJ/JPI, 6/6/1905. *HORN*, 5; HJ/SC, 6/12/1906. *HORN*, 13; HJ/SC, 5/9/1906. *ED*4, 403; WDH/HJ, 2/1/1910. *WDHL*5, 12; HJ/WDH, 8/17/1908. *LB*2, 100.
40. HJ/OW, 8/28/1907. VX; HJ/WDH, 8/17/1908. *LB*2, 99.
41. HJ/ALC, 1/27/1905, 9/2/1906, 10/9/1906, 11/26/1906, 11/27/1906, 1/2/1907. VB; *NBK*, 274–78; HJ/MAC, 4/5/1908. BL.
42. *HORN*, 2; HJ/JPI, 11/2/1908. *LB*2, 107; HJ/EDW, 3/7/1908. *POW*, 89; HJ/OW, 8/28/1907. VX; HJ/HS, 10/17/1907. HO; HJ/VH, 4/10/1908. VB; HJ/TSP, 12/13/1908. *HAR*, 327; HJ/MAC, 12/8/1908. BL; HJ/MJV, 5/6/1909. VX; HJ/WEN, 1/30/1908. *HORN*, 3.
43. HJ/HCA, 11/25/1906. VB; HJ/MAC, 3/17/1909. BL.
44. HJ/OW, 8/22/1906. VX; HJ/GL, 10/13/1908. HO; HJ/TSP, 11/14/1906, 11/7/1906, 11/12/1906. HAR, 322–24; HJ/WJ, 11/17/1906. *ED*4, 423; TSP, diary, 11/20/1906. *HAR*, 187; HJ/TSP, 11/27/1906. CL.
45. HJ/EDW, 4/2/1906. *POW*, 62; HJ/GL, 5/6/1906. HO; HJ/EDW, 7/2/1906, 11/17/1906. *POW*, 65–67; HJ/TSP, 2/16/1907. *HAR*, 325–26; HJ/HS, 2/27/1907. HO.
46. HJ/MJV, 3/14/1907. VX; HJ/HS, 3/20/1906. HO; HJ/JA, 3/28/1907. *ED*4, 441; HJ/George & Fanny Prothero, 4/13/1907. *ED*4, 445; HJ/HS, 4/13/1907. HO; HJ/HS, 4/13/1907. *ED*4, 442; EDW/SN, 4/21/1907. *EDWL*, 113.
47. HJ/HS, 4/27/1907, 4/13/1907. HO; HJ/TSP, 4/13/1907. CL; HJ/JP, 5/4/1907. HO; EDW/SN, 4/21/1907. *EDWL*, 113; HJ/GL, 4/19/1907. HO.
48. HJ/MF, 11/17/1905. VB; EDW/SN, 4/21/1907. *EDWL*, 113; HJ/MF, 4/3/1907, 4/19/1907. HO.
49. HJ/HCA, 11/5/1905, 4/19/1907, 10/18/1906. VB; EDW/CEN, 5/15/1907. *EDWL*, 115; HJ/JP, 5/4/1907. HO; HJ/HS, 4/13/1907. HO.
50. HJ/WJJr, 5/30/1907. *ED*4, 449; HJ/OW, 8/28/1907. VX; HJ/EDW, 8/11–12/1907. *POW*, 71.

51. HJ/CLB, 9/13/1907. *ED4*, 460; HCA/OA, 6/1/1907, 6/9/1907. LC; HJ/HCA, 7/18/1907. VB; HCA/OA, 6/10/1907. LC.
52. HJ/HS, 4/27/1907. HO; HJ/JA, 6/24/1907. *ED4*, 451–52; HJ/EDW, 8/11–12/1907. *POW*, 72; HJ/CLB, 9/13/1907. *ED4*, 460–61.
53. HJ/MF, 8/8/1907. *ED4*, 453; HJ/EDW, 10/4/1907. *POW*, 74; HJ/EDW, 10/4/1907. *POW*, 74; EDW/MF, 10/15/1907. *EDWL*, 116; HJ/EDW, 11/24/1907. *POW*, 78.
54. HJ/MF, 11/14/1907, 11/19/1907, 11/29/1907. *ED4*, 473–75, 480.
55. HJ/GL, 5/4/1909. HO; EW/MF, 5/20/1908. *EDWL*, 145; HJ/EDW, 11/24/1907. *POW*, 78; HA/CMG, 5/6/1908. *HAL6*, 135; HA/HJ, 5/6/1908. *HAL6*, 136.
56. EDW/SN, 11/18/1908. *EDWL*, 165; *GLA*, 253–54.
57. HJ/HS, 11/2/1908, 11/21/1908. HO; HJ/GL, 5/4/1909. HO; HJ/EDW, 5/9/1909. *POW*, 113.
58. HJ/JP, 10/23/1903, 10/26/1903, 3/21/1904, nd, 8/10/1904. HO.
59. HJ/JP, 8/14/1905, 11/22/1905, 4/4/1906, 1/22/1907, 5/4/1907, 1/30/1908. HO; HJ/JP, 11/4/1906. *ED4*, 419.
60. HJ/WDH, 3/7/1902. *WDHL5*, 15; HJ/MAC, 4/5/1908. BL.
61. HJ/JP, 7/4/1909, 8/21/1908, 7/16/1909, 7/19/1909, 10/27/1910. HO; *NBK*, 310.
62. HJ/Ellen "Bay" Emmet, 11/3/1908. *ED4*, 500; HJ/WJ, 2/26/1909. *ED4*, 516–18; *ED4*, 518, from JM, *Angina Pectoris*, 1903.
63. HJ/GL, 5/4/1909. HO; HJ/RJ, 10/14/1909. VX; HJ/TSP, 12/22/1909. *LB2*, 146–48.
64. HJ/GL, 5/4/1909. HO; HJ/RJ, 10/14/1909. VX.
65. HJ/HA, 2/1/1905. *ED4*, 343.
66. WJ/RUJ, 7/17/1905. *ED4*, 787–88; WDH/RUJ, 7/6/1905. *WDHL5*, 126–27.
67. WJ/HJ, 10/22/1905. *BJ*, 251; WJ/AHJ, 1/17/1906. *BJ*, 251–52; AHJ/HJ, 4/10/1906. VX; HJ/HS, nd/1906. HO; HJ/GL, 5/1/1906, 5/6/1906. HO.
68. HJ/WJ, 5/4/1907. HO.
69. WJ/Mrs. Henry Whitman, 6/18/1902. *WJL2*, 169; WJ/HJ, 10/25/1902. *MAT*, 338; HJ/WJ, 11/11/1902. *MAT*, 338; HJ/WJ, 11/22/1905. HO; HJ/WJ, 11/23/1905. *ED4*, 382; WJ/HJ, 5/4/1907. HO; HJ/WJ, 10/17/1907. *ED4*, 466.
70. WJ/Charles William Eliot, 9/23/1906. *BJ*, 252–53; WJ/AHJ, 8/23/1906. *BJ*, 253; WJ/HJ, 12/4/1906. *BJ*, 253; WJ/HJ, 11/30/1907. *BJ*, 254; HJ/OW, 8/20/1907. VX; HJ/GL, 8/11/1908. HO; HJ/RJ, 7/18/1908. VX.
71. HJ/GL, 1/1/1910. HO; HJ/AB, 1/1/1910. HO; HJ/JP, 8/21/1908. HO; HJ/GL, 5/4/1909. HO.
72. HJ/RJ, 10/14/1909. VX; HJ/AF, 1/2/1910. *ED4*, 541.

CHAPTER FIFTEEN. THE IMPERIAL EAGLE, 1910–1916

1. HJ/AB, 1/1/1910. HO; HJ/HCA, 1/1/1910. VB; HJ/GL, 11/1/1910. HO; *NBK*, 260–70.
2. HJ/MF, 1/22/1910. TX; HJ/HR, 2/17/1903. HO; HJ/TBS, 1/27/1910. *LB2*, 155; HJ/VH, 2/14/1901. VB; HJ/HS, 2/1/1910, 2/16/1910. HO; HJ/EDW, 2/2/1910. *POW*, 143–44.
3. HJ/HS, 2/6/1901, 3/4/1910. HO; HJ/EDW, 2/8/1910. *POW*, 146–47; HJ/WJ, 2/8/1910. *ED4*, 546–47; WJ/RJ, 5/24/1910. VX.
4. HJ/JA, 2/20/1910. *LB2*, 158; HJ/EG, 3/9/1910. *MO*, 250; HJ/EW, 3/2/1910. HU; HJ/HS, 3/4/1910. HO; JM/Harold Rypins, 1/12/1925. NY State Library, Albany; HJ/EDW, 3/2/1910. *POW*, 150.
5. *ED4*, 550; HJ/EDW, 3/14/1910. *POW*, 153.
6. HJ/MF, 3/21/1901. TX; HJ/EDW, 4/14/1901, 4/16/1910. *POW*, 155–56; HJ/EG, 4/12/1910. *MO*, 251.
7. HJ/EG, 4/12/1910. *MO*, 251; WJ/RJ, 4/15/1910. HO; HJ/EDW, 4/16/1910, 4/25/1910. *POW*, 156–58; HJ/EW, 4/28/1910. HU.

8. HJ/EDW, 6/10/1910. *POW*, 161; WJ/RJ, 4/15/1910, 5/24/1910. VX.
9. HJ3, note, nd/1910. *BJ*, 258; HA/WJ, 5/8/1910. *HAL6*, 335; WJ/AHJ, 5/18/1910, 5/20/1910. *BJ*, 259; WJ/HJ, 5/28/1908. *BJ*, 259–60.
10. HJ/GL, 5/26/1910. HO; HJ/HS, 5/1910. HO; WJ/RJ, 5/24/1910. VX; HJ/EDW, 5/21/1910. *POW*, 160.
11. HJ/EDW, 6/10/1910. *POW*, 161.
12. HJ/HW, 5/13/1910. *ED4*, 551; HJ/EG, 6/13/1910. *MO*, 252; HJ/MJV, 7/25/1910. VX.
13. HJ/MMJ, 7/25/1910, 8/26/1910. 7/9/1910. VX; HJ/EDW, 7/29/1910. *POW*, 165; MMJ/AHJ, 7/9/1910. *MA*, 191–92.
14. HJ/MJV, 7/9/1910. VX; HJ/Clare Frewen, 7/14/1910. VB; HJ/HS, 7/16/1910. HO; AHJ/EGB, 7/15/1910. *BJ*, 260; WJ/Theodore Flournoy, 7/10/1910. *BJ*, 236; HJ/EDW, 7/29/1910. *POW*, 165; WDH/EG, 7/14/1910. BL; HJ/JP, 7/19/1910. HO; JM/Harold Rypins, 1/12/1925. NY State Library, Albany.
15. *NBK*, 318; HJ/HS, 7/16/1910. HO.
16. HJ/MJV, 7/25/1910, 8/26/1910. VX; AHJ/EGB, 8/7/1910. *BJ*, 260; HJ/EW, 8/10/1910. HU; HJ/EG, 9/10/1910. *MO*, 253; HJ/GN, 8/26/1910. *ED4*, 560.
17. AHJ/FRM, 8/26/1910. *BJ*, 261; HJ/EG, 9/10/1910. *MO*, 253; HJ/GN, 9/2/1910. HO.
18. HJ/GL, 9/1/1910, 9/10/1910. HO; HJ/EG, 9/10/1910. *MO*, 253; HJ/TSP, 9/2/1910. *ED4*, 261; HJ/WEN, 12/13/1910. *LB2*, 174.
19. HJ/BE, 8/16/1911. BL; HJ/JJP, 1/4/1912. *ED4*, 594–98.
20. HJ/GN, 9/1/1910, 9/2/1910, 9/3/1910. HO; HJ/LCP, 9/30/1910. CL.
21. HJ/GN, 10/16/1910. HO; HJ/HS, 10/18/1910. HO; HJ/JP, nd/1910, 10/27/1910. HO.
22. HJ/LCP, 2/14/1911. CL; HJ/EW, 1/5/1911. HU.
23. *NBK*, 328–31; HJ/JJP, 1/4/1912. *ED4*, 596; HJ/Thomas Tryan, 1/20/1911. VB; HJ/EDW, 1/9/1911. *POW*, 176; HJ/TSP, nd/1911. CL.
24. HJ/RB, 2/25/1911. *LB2*, 179; HJ/EDW, 1/9/1911. *POW*, 175; HJ/Colonel Newbigging, 4/7/1911. Maggs Catalogue 1096, 1989; HJ/HW, 4/25/1911. *ED4*, 577; HJ/HS, 4/19/1911. HO.
25. HJ/AC, 5/11/1911. DA; HJ/HS, 5/1911. HO; HJ/TBS, 5/27/1911. *LB2*, 187; HJ/TSP, 5/27/1911. *HAR*, 330–31.
26. HJ/Lady MAC, 6/16/1911. VB; HJ/EDW, 6/27/1911. *POW*, 180; HJ/EW, 8/15/1911. HU; HJ/MJV, 6/29/1911. VX; *NBK*, 337; HJ/HCA, 6/21/1911. VB.
27. HJ/TSP, 6/6/1911. *HAR*, 331–32; *NBK*, 338–39; HJ/GL, 7/17/1911. HO.
28. HJ/AHJ, 3/29/1914. *ED4*, 707; HJ/HJ3, 11/15–18/1913. *ED4*, 801–2; HJ/EW, 8/15/1911. HU; HJ/HS, 8/17/1911. HO; HJ/TSP, 9/2/1911. *HAR*, 332–33.
29. *NBK*, 343.
30. HJ/HS, 2/20/1912. *SL2*, 397; HJ/GL, 2/13/1912. HO; *EDEL2*, 334, 694.
31. HJ/TSP, 1/19/1912. *HAR*, 336–37.
32. HJ/Louis Shipman, 2/22/1911. CL.
33. WDH/EG, 3/6/1911, 4/7/1911; BL; WDH/EG, 5/13/1911. BL.
34. HJ/GN, 1/12/1912. HO; HJ/EG, 11/16/1911. *MO*, 258; HJ/AC, 12/10/1911. DA.
35. HJ/LCP, 1/3/1912. *HAR*, 334–36; HJ/TSP, 1/19/1912. *HAR*, 336–37.
36. HJ/VH, 3/7/1912. VB; HJ/HS, 5/9/1912. HO.
37. *NBK*, 364; HJ/HS, 8/5/1912, 8/20/1912. HO.
38. HJ/EG, 10/10/1912. *MO*, 272; EG/HJ, 10/11/1912. HO.
39. HJ/HS, 10/23/1912. HO; *NBK*, 368; HJ/HCA, 11/10/1912. VB.
40. HJ/HS, 12/10/1912. HO; HJ/HCA, 11/10/1912. VB; HJ/TSP, 11/29/1912. CL.
41. HJ/HS, 12/10/1912. HO; HJ/GL, 1/1/1913. HO; HJ/Ottoline Morrell, 7/1/1913. TX; HJ/AHJ, 4/11/1913. *ED4*, 662.
42. HJ/HS, nd/1913. HO; HJ/MAC, 2/8/1913. HO; EG/TH, 6/17/1913. *EGL*, 349;

HJ/ALC, 6/21/1913, 6/23/1913. VB; HJ/HCA, 3/15/1913. VB; HJ/GL, 1/1/1913. HO.

43. HJ/EW, 3/1/1914. HU.

44. *GLA*, 243–44; HJ/WJ3, 3/29/1913. *ED4*, 653; HJ/EDW, 5/2/1913. *POW*, 252.

45. HJ/EW, 8/9/1913. HU; EG/TH, 6/17/1913. *EGL*, 349.

46. HJ/HS, 9/2/1913. HO; HJ/GL, 12/25/1913. HO; EG/Max Beerbohm, 12/25/1913. *EGL*, 350–51.

47. HJ/OW, 8/1/1914. VX.

48. "An Animated Conversation," *Scribner's Magazine*, 3/1889.

49. HJ/Caroline James, 7/31/1913. VX; HJ/TSP, 10/13/1913. *HAR*, 342–43; HJ/MAC, 11/6/1913. BL.

50. HJ/TSP, 2/3/1913, 5/17/1914. CL; WDH/HJ, 6/29/1915. *WDHL6*, 80; HJ/WDH, 2/19/1913. HO; HJ/TSP & LCP, 3/27/1915. CL; HJ/TSP, 4/13/1914. *HAR*, 345–47; HJ/TSP, 1/19/1912. *HAR*, 336–37; HJ/TSP, 2/3/1913. CL; HJ/TSP, 8/13/1913. *HAR*, 339–40; HJ/TSP, 1/11/1914. *HAR*, 343–45; HA/EC, 3/15/1914, 3/8/1914. *HAL6*, 642, 638; HJ/HA, 3/21/1914. *ED4*, 706.

51. HJ/WDH, 5/13/1914. *WDHL6*, 54; WDH/TSP, 5/8/1914. *WDHL6*, 53; HJ/JA, 5/6/1914. *ED4*, 712; HJ/MW, 5/6/1914. VB.

52. HJ/MW, 10/24/1912. VB; HJ/GN, 9/2/1910. HO.

53. HGW/HJ, 7/8/1915. *Henry James & H. G. Wells*, ed. Leon Edel & Gordon N. Ray, 1958, 264; HJ/HGW, 7/10/1915. *ED4*, 770.

54. HJ/AC, 8/15/1914. DA; HJ/OW, 9/4/1914. LC; HJ/HS, 8/4–5/1914. HO; HJ/LCP, 8/2/1914. CL.

55. HJ/HW, 4/10/1915. *ED4*, 751; HJ/GL, 6/3/1914. HO; HJ/OW, 9/25/1914. VX; HJ/JP, 8/11/1914. HO; HJ/EW, 9/18/1914. HU.

56. HJ/HR, 12/18/1914. HO; HJ/JP, 11/15/1914. HO.

57. HJ/Marie Belloc-Lowndes, 4/27/1915. TX; HJ/HR, 12/18/1914. HO.

58. HJ/TSP & LCP, 1/15/1915. *HAR*, 347–49; HJ/HR, 12/18/1914. HO.

59. HJ/GN, 1/1/1915. HO; HJ/EDW, 1/16/1915. *POW*, 321; HJ/HS, 4/4/1915. HO; HJ/TSP & LCP, 3/27/1915. CL; HJ/HCA, 3/16/1915. VB.

60. HJ/HS, 4/1/1915. HO; HJ/AB, 12/27/1914. HO.

61. HJ/AC, 8/23/1914. DA; HJ/TSP, 10/25/1914. CL.

62. HJ/TSP & LCP, 1/15/1915. *HAR*, 347–49; HJ/GL, 6/8/1915. HO; HJ/LCP, 6/17/1914. *ED4*, 758.

63. H. H. Asquith/HJ, 6/29/1915. HO; HJ/EG, 6/18/1915. *MO*, 309.

64. HJ/RK, 7/18/1915. HO; *The New York Times*, 7/28/1915, 7/29/1915, 7/31/1915; *New York Tribune*, 7/29/1915; *The New York Herald*, 7/28/1915.

65. *The New York Times*, 7/31/1915; HJ/LCP, 9/15/1915. CL; WDH/TSP, 7/24/1915. *WDHL6*, 83; WDH/Brander Matthews, 8/7/1915. *WDHL6*, 84; *The New York Times*, 7/29/1915.

66. HJ/HS, 7/8/1915. HO; HJ/BE, 8/25/1915. BL; HJ/EG, 8/25/1915. *MO*, 313–15.

67. TB/EDW, 11/4/1915. *POW*, 367–68; HJ/HW, 11/13/1915. *ED4*, 781.

68. HJ/HW, 11/10/1915. VB; HJ/Rita Jacomb Hood, 11/26/1915. BL; HJ/MMJ, 12/1/1915. *ED4*, 782.

69. JSS/EG, 12/4/1915. LC; EC/HA, 12/1915. *TEH*, 257; HA/EC, 2/6/1916. *HAL6*, 721; TB/EDW, 12/22/1913. *POW*, 383; LCL/?, 12/1915. BL; WDH/HJ3, 12/15/1915. *WDHL6*, 89.

70. TB/EDW, 12/8/1915. *POW*, 372.

71. TB/EDW, 12/12/1915. *POW*, 376.

72. TB/EDW, 12/12/1915. *POW*, 376; AHJ/EG, 12/15/1915. BL; TB/EDW, 12/17/1915. *POW*, 380; LC/?, 12/20/1915. BL; AHJ/MRJ, 12/21/1915. VX.

73. TH/HJ, 1/10/1916. HO; HJ3/TSP, 2/1/1916. *HAR*, 349–50; AHJ/EG, 2/11/1916. LC.

74. AHJ/?, 3/4/1916. HO; TSP/Van Wyck Brooks, nd/1923. *HAR*, 210.

Acknowledgments

For the more than ten thousand unpublished letters by James and by members of his family, I am indebted to the Houghton Library at Harvard University for gracious access to their immense collection of James family papers and to other archives that house smaller but still important manuscript treasures: the Beinecke Library at Yale University, the British Library, the John Hay Library at Brown University, the Special Collections of the Miller Library at Colby College, the Dartmouth College Library, the Duke University Library, the Huntington Library, the Library of Congress, the Harry Ransom Humanities Center at the University of Texas, and the Barrett Collection at the University of Virginia. Mr. and Mrs. Henry Vaux of Berkeley, California, who possess a James cache of which any library would be proud, graciously trusted me with their hospitality and their family treasures. For the published writings, I am grateful to Leon Edel, especially to his work as an editor. His bibliography of James's writings and his editions of James's plays and letters have been a valuable resource. Without the generous cooperation of the executor of the James estate, Alexander R. James, this biography would not have been possible.

A recent flowering of critical and historical books on James and his world have helped me immensely, particularly Howard M. Feinstein, *Becoming William James* (1984); Michael Anesko, *"Friction with the Market": Henry James and the Profession of Authorship* (1986); Daniel W. Bjork, *William James: The Center of His Vision* (1988); Alfred Habegger, *Henry James and the "Woman Business"* (1989); and Philip Horne, *Henry James and Revision* (1990). Robert L. Gale's *A Henry James Encyclopedia* (1989) has been uniquely useful. Two outstanding editions of James's correspondence, Rayburn S. Moore's *Selected Letters of Henry James to Edmund Gosse, 1882–1915* (1988) and Lyall H. Powers' *Henry James and Edith Wharton: Letters: 1900–1915* (1900), have saved me hundreds of hours of the eye-and-back-exhausting need to transcribe James's abominable handwriting. These vital books, along with the excellent Library of America editions of James's criticism and novels, have been my living companions. Their authors, all but one personally unknown to me, have my warmest thanks. So too do those many James scholars to whom a general biography cannot extend individual credit but whose labors have produced textual editions and a body of scholarship, some of it published in the excellent *Henry James Review*, that have made my work as a biographer much easier than it otherwise would have been.

I am grateful for the expertise, encouragement, and support of my excellent editor at William Morrow, Maria Guarnaschelli. At Morrow, Michael Goodman has been the model of a helpful, committed copyeditor. In London, John Curtis of John Curtis Books, Hodder & Stoughton, has provided thoughtful editorial guidance. In New York, Georges Borchardt, assisted by Cindy Klein, has given supportive advice and excellent agenting. As this book's first reader, Rhoda Weyr has helped immeasurably.

Generous institutional support from many sources helped make this book possible: the Huntington Library, San Marino, California, where Martin Ridge, James Thorpe, and Elizabeth Donno have been unfailingly generous and warmly hospitable; the Rockefeller Foundation, through a residency at its study center at Bellagio and the graciousness of the late Roberto Celli, Gianna Bellei Celli, and Susan E. Garfield; the City University of New York, whose research arm has provided a number of travel grants; and Queens College, which provided a Presidential Fellowship through the courtesy of President Shirley Kenny. The National Trust has my appreciation for the excellence of its care of Lamb House, as do its present residents, Ione and William Martin, whose daughter Marina kindly showed me through the house. Jenny Hadfield at Jeake's House made my stay in Rye warmly comfortable. I am also grateful to Jean and Hidalgo Moya for their kind hospitality at Point Hill and to Thomas S. Hayes at the Edith Wharton Restoration in Lenox. For acts of support and assistance I am indebted to Jerome Badanes, Murray Baumgarten, John Bayley, Dennison Beach, Shari Benstock, Katharina Buck, Philip Collins, Philip N. Cronenwitt, Enid Davy, Wally Davy, Rodney Dennis, Daniel Donno, Leon Edel, Edwin Eigner, Ruth Eigner, Laura A. Endicott, Leslie Epstein, Cynthia Farar, K. J. Fielding, George Ford, Lydia Goehr, Harold Goldwhite, Marie Goldwhite, Alfred Habegger, John Hall, Rupert Hart-Davis, Richard Howard, John Jordan, Benjamin Kaplan, Julia Kaplan, Noah Kaplan, Alfred Kazin, Norman Kelvin, David Kleinbard, Barbara Leavy, Peter Leavy, Patience-Anne W. Lenk, R. W. B. Lewis, Steven Marcus, Carol Molesworth, Charles Molesworth, Sylvère Monod, Tim Moreton, Anthony Neville, Patricia Neville, John Reilly, Celia Riddell, James Riddell, Clyde Ryals, Miranda Seymour, Donald Stone, Jean Strouse, John Sutherland, James Thorpe, Sarah Tobias, Charles Tolk, Maureen Waters, Garret Weyr, Joseph Wittreich, Carl Woodring, and Ruth Yeazell.

INDEX